Latin America
and the World Economy
Since 1800

Latin America
and the World Economy
Since 1800

Edited by
John H. Coatsworth
and
Alan M. Taylor

Published by
Harvard University
David Rockefeller Center for Latin American Studies

DISTRIBUTED BY
HARVARD UNIVERSITY PRESS
CAMBRIDGE, MASSACHUSETTS
LONDON, ENGLAND

Library of Congress Cataloging-in-Publication Data

Latin America and the world economy since 1800 / edited by John H.
  Coatsworth and Alan M. Taylor.
      p.   cm.
   Includes bibliographical references and index.
   ISBN 0-674-51280-4 (alk. paper). — ISBN 0-674-51281-2 (alk. paper)
   1. Latin America—Economic conditions—19th century.   2. Latin
America—Economic conditions—1918-   3. Latin America—Foreign
economic relations.   I. Coatsworth, John H., 1940–   .   II. Taylor,
Alan M., 1964–   .   III. David Rockefeller Center for Latin American
Studies.
HC125.L3435   1998
330.98'03—dc21   98-40390
                                                                         CIP

Contents

List of Tables and Figures

14. Graciela Márquez, Tariff Protection in Mexico, 1892–1909: Ad Valorem Tariff Rates and Sources of Variation

15. Daniel Díaz Fuentes, Latin America during the Interwar Period: The Rise and Fall of the Gold Standard in Argentina, Brazil, and Mexico   *443*

Acknowledgments

The editors wish to thank the John D. and Catherine T. MacArthur Foundation for the timely grant that enabled the authors to meet and discuss the papers that became the chapters of this book. The MacArthur Foundation grant also helped defray the costs of publication. The MacArthur Foundation's tradition of support for innovative research is deeply appreciated.

The editors also thank the Rockefeller Foundation for making available its Bellagio Study and Conference Center. The efficiency of the Bellagio Center's able staff, and the extraordinary organization and kindness of the Center's director, Ms. Gianna Celli, contributed notably to the success of the meeting. Thanks are also due to the Mellon Fellowships in Latin American History at Harvard University for travel support for two of the participants.

Special thanks are due to the colleagues whose thoughtful comments on the papers at Bellagio helped to ensure the quality of the revised versions published here: Gustavo Franco, Colin Lewis, Pablo Martín Aceña, Clara Eugenia Nuñez, and Gabriel Tortella. Colin Lewis contributed valuable insights and suggestions to the editors in a separate written report.

The editors planned the publication of this book to coincide with the XII International Economic History Congress, scheduled to take place in Seville, Spain in August 1998. That Congress was canceled due to organizational difficulties, but later was revived and scheduled for the same dates in Madrid. The final versions of these papers were presented and discussed at an all-day panel at the Madrid Congress.

This book is the second in a new series published by the David Rockefeller Center for Latin American Studies and distributed by Harvard University Press. The editors are grateful to the Center for its support, especially to the Center's Publications Committee chaired by Professor Marcelo Suárez-Orozco.

Finally, thanks are due to Jonathan Schrag, who managed the publication process for the Center with considerable skill and good humor; to Kelly McMurray, who designed the cover, which reproduces a portion of the mural at the San Francisco Art Institute by Diego Rivera entitled "The Making of a Fresco Showing the Building of a City"; and to Sarah Kimnach of Editorial Services of New England, Inc., who provided copyediting, management, and other essential services to bring this book to press.

Introduction

John H. Coatsworth
Alan M. Taylor

Latin American Economic History in Transition

The essays collected in this book, and the conferences in Bellagio and Madrid at which the essays were presented and discussed, come at an exciting moment in the study of the economic aspects of Latin American history. Over the past decade, the number of scholars engaged in economic historical research on Latin America using modern, neoclassical economic theory and quantitative methods has increased dramatically. Perhaps this book can serve to mark the moment in time when this field achieved some kind of critical mass. For many years the field attracted little attention. A small number of scholars contributed landmark works, but the dominant methodologies applied to Latin American development in both economics and history departments tended to go their separate ways: historians focused a great deal on social and cultural history, with economic conditions supplying context or backdrop; economists typically focused on development policies applied to current problems with little reference to historical context.

The first generations of economic historians of Latin America worked in a variety of often contradictory intellectual traditions. Much of the empirical work accomplished in the half-century or so before World War II came from Latin American civil servants working in new government agencies that began compiling and publishing historical data in the late nineteenth century.[1] Even before the establishment of official statistical bureaus, however, much important work had already been accomplished by amateur historians and statisticians, who published their own compilations of historical statistics and assembled compendia on the evolution of laws and government policies.[2] In the first decades of this century, a small but increasing number of intellectuals offered critical historical analysis of the evolution of land tenure systems, labor policies, and social structures in the countryside.[3] In the United States before World War II, much of the early work on the economic history of Latin America came from progressive economists and historians, who focused on

U.S. economic relations with Latin America[4] and on the comparative study of exploitative labor systems such as slavery and *encomienda*.[5] Despite these promising beginnings, Myron Burgin, himself the author of a pioneering work in Argentine economic history (1946), was certainly right to observe in a review essay published in 1947 that the field had been largely neglected due to the widespread perception that Latin America constituted "a mere appendage of the industrialized economies."[6]

In the post–World War II era, the economic historiography of Latin America developed even greater diversity of empirical and theoretical focus. Structuralist ideas, promoted by the United Nations Economic Commission for Latin America (ECLA), inspired lively debates and stimulated new analytical and quantitative research, particularly on the impact of external economic relations on the Latin American economies.[7] In several countries, the first serious efforts to construct historical estimates of national income and output going back to 1900 were undertaken by ECLA staff or stimulated by ECLA's examples.[8] ECLA-based economists produced many of the first analytical economic histories of several Latin American countries.[9] Varieties of ECLA-style structuralism, or "dependency-school" analysis, as it came to be called, became so influential that by 1977, Roberto Cortés Conde and Stanley Stein could sum it up by observing that "[w]hat was before 1930 viewed complacently and approvingly as the successful incorporation of Latin America in the expanding world economy is now considered at the root of Latin America's shortcomings in recent decades—what has been described as the 'development of underdevelopment.'"[10]

Simultaneously, however, competing approaches to economic history developed and flourished. Followers of the Anglo-American emphasis on archival research, mostly historians, tended to focus on the history of institutions and policies, but pathbreaking quantitative work in historical demography also began in the 1950s.[11] Economic historians in the United States and Britain as well as in Latin America initially focused on the colonial era and addressed such issues as trends in prices, mining production, and external trade,[12] whether there had been a depression in the seventeenth century,[13] and how rural estates or merchant firms functioned.[14] They did not usually concern themselves with the issues raised by the dependency school nor did most attempt to measure, let alone explain, trends in real wages, productivity, or terms of trade, but they added enormously to knowledge of Latin America's rich and extremely varied economic history before independence in the 1820s.

The field was further enriched in the 1960s and 1970s by a diverse set of writings that ranged in inspiration from the institutional economics of the

Wisconsin school, embodied in William Glade's pathbreaking survey,[15] to varieties of structuralist,[16] dependency,[17] "Annales" school,[18] and Marxist[19] approaches. The first works of economic history influenced by the neoclassical approaches taught in U.S. economics departments also appeared in this era.[20] Scholars working in every one of these traditions pushed against the limits of conventional wisdom and fragmentary data to offer fresh perspectives and much new information, including quantitative data. The transition to the "new" economic history occurred in the 1980s. The utility of the approaches embodied in the new economic history gradually overtook, though never completely supplanted, the traditions with which it competed. Critiques of structuralist and particularly dependency models centered their attacks on the lack of logically consistent theories and the failure to derive and test relevant hypotheses.[21] Debates within these competing paradigms tended to make scholars working in them more receptive to the range of analytical tools offered by the cliometricians. Dialogue across traditions was also facilitated by the growing interest of the new economic history in the crucial role of institutions and, more recently, in the history of welfare.

All these interests are represented in the research papers collected in this volume. These interdisciplinary scholars bring an economist's appreciation for formal theory, testing, and empirical research, and they apply economic tools as they fashion their interpretations. They also bring a historian's insight into processes of historical change in the political and institutional context of economic activity, and they relish the demands of the primary archival and source work that supplies the data and contextual foundations to undergird their analyses. In short, this new scholarship brings Latin America fully into the realm of the new economic history. This school of thought now dominates scholarship in North America and Europe, and the pages of all the leading journals in economic history. While in the past, individual pathbreaking studies applied this approach in the Latin American context, the next generation of scholars have broader aims: to firmly establish the methods of quantitative economic history as the main lens through which many of the key analytical issues in the development of Latin America should be viewed. Their work is rapidly transforming the field of Latin American economic history with research of a new character.

THE NEW ECONOMIC HISTORY OF LATIN AMERICA: A ROAD MAP

The essays brought together in this book illustrate the methodological variety within the field of quantitative economic history. The degree of theoretical formalism and empirical sophistication varies appropriately given the demands of the questions posed and the limits of the data available. The works range from broad, comparative, international work to detailed studies of individual, national, local, or sectoral experiences. Notably, the contributions come from both economists and historians, whose fruitful collaboration this book well illustrates.

What does the present book indicate about the current state of the field and the profitable directions for future research? No single book could hope to present an exhaustive survey of the new economic history of Latin America, although many of the key figures are represented here as contributors. However, it does provide signposts for the future by highlighting fruitful approaches, useful types of data sources, cogent comparative analyses, insightful theory, practical empirics, and compelling counterfactuals. In what follows we highlight some of the lessons from our collection of essays, under various headings. Is this a useful guide? Let us just note that were these headings applied to North American or European economic history, one could list countless studies dating back to the 1960s, and remarkable advances in knowledge under each category. In the case of Latin America, so much more remains to be done that the marginal productivity of research on almost any issue is still extremely high.

Data Collection

The foundation of quantitative history and applied economics is the existence of plentiful, reliable data. In this respect, students of Latin American economic history have been disadvantaged by the relative paucity of work in basic historical statistics. Despite a number of pioneering efforts,[22] primary archival work to discover, evaluate, collate, and process the vast mountains of primary data in the archives and to publish the results has scarcely begun in many countries. This does not mean that doing quantitative economic history is impossible, but it does shift the onus onto today's scholars to incorporate this valuable but often underappreciated form of research into their repertory of skills. Indeed, as primary research has shown repeatedly, multitudes of hitherto ignored records of quantitative data on nearly every aspect of Latin American history from every historical era have never been seen, let alone subjected to rigorous empirical economic analysis. The enormous scope for work here cannot be exaggerated. Latin American economic history is now, at its core, a mass of new and old theories and hypotheses drawn from economics and history in need of validation or rejection, that is, in search of data. Thus, an immediately obvious and rewarding direction for new scholars opens up. In libraries, public and private archives, company records, and government documents, manifold sources of information lie dormant, waiting to be exposed to the penetrating light of analysis.

Several chapters here illustrate the potential return from work devoted to searching out and assembling new data sets to address specific questions. Graciela Márquez supplies original estimates of tariff rates in Porfirian Mexico, and, with information on exchange rate and price changes, estimates changing levels of real protection. Aurora Gómez-Galvarriato's work on pre-Revolutionary Mexico focuses on wage and price trends to bring us a new perspective in the classic tradition of long-term studies of living standards. André Hofman and Nanno Mulder take the techniques of productivity analysis so often applied to developed countries' historical data and show their applicability to postwar Brazil and Mexico.

Other studies, less explicitly oriented toward data collection per se, also illustrate the importance of having the right data set at hand. The data collected by Anne Hanley from the São Paulo Bolsa (stock exchange) and by Leonard Nakamura and Carlos Zarazaga from the Buenos Aires Bolsa permit us to ask new questions about the role of equity finance in Latin American development. Historical banking data, used by Gail Triner for Brazil, and by Gerardo della Paolera and Alan Taylor for Argentina, allow us to examine the evolution of other financial markets.

Comparative analyses stretch data requirements still further and offer challenges to scholars seeking to ensure compatibility and commensurability of data and concepts across locations. Michael Twomey has exhaustively examined the extant data on overseas investment to vastly improve our long-term comparative view of the role of foreign capital in various regions of the globe. Even institutional analysis, if it is to move from *testable* to *tested* hypotheses, must confront data, as is evident in John Coatsworth's attention to long-term series in exploring the region's economic growth over several centuries; Alan Dye's innovative use of contractual records to examine organizational aspects of the Cuban sugar industry; and the pioneering use of data from the Brazilian frontier to examine the violence and the enforcement of property rights by Lee Alston, Gary Libecap, and Bernardo Mueller.

In short, every chapter in this book has, like every paper in the field, built on data as its foundation so as to support empirically an explicit economic analysis of historical events. No work, whether of broad international comparison or narrow local focus, can escape this demand. The breadth of the chapters collected here shows the potential for future work. By considering the same questions for other countries or other time periods, we could generate enough research questions to last many years. How important was the stock market in Mexico pre- and postrevolution? What happened to wages and prices in Brazil in the interwar period? How did banks perform in Chile before 1914? And so on.

Rapid dividends will accrue in cases where data are easily available and where the extant historical literature includes important controversies or conjectures about economic development that command attention, but the targets for research in the near-term are abundant, and we confidently expect researchers to continually surprise us with new data used to make a big impact on previously unresolved issues.

External Conditions: Small Economies, Comparative Methods

Never in Latin America have economic conditions in other countries or world markets been far from concern for students of politics, economics, or history. The openness of the region's markets in the nineteenth century and the marked autarkic turn in the mid-twentieth century have offered a fertile area for proponents of all kinds of economic theories and historical interpretations. Classic liberals of the last century, and neoliberal responses of late, have emphasized the dreadful *relative* economic performance (a comparative criticism) that accompanied the pursuit of isolationist policies like import substitution, especially after the 1960s. Earlier dependency scholars and structuralists justified that turn of events as a response to an alleged unequal system of exchange that favored the industrialized core nations at the expense of the periphery or distorted development in ways that blocked growth and exacerbated inequalities.

Economic historians will play a critical role in understanding the evolution of these views and in judging their ultimate merit in the light of more rigorous analysis of the trajectories of Latin American economic development. Analysis will be vital at the level of macroeconomic phenomena such as depressions and financial crises or long-term growth and productivity, as well as at the level of microeconomic phenomena such as individual market structures, market power, commercial policy, capital flows, and foreign direct investments.

The first critical question is to what degree we can measure the costs and benefits of engagement in the wider global economy by individual Latin American states and economic agents therein. Did the rich economies at the core of the world economy exploit the poorer countries at the periphery? Did market volatility in goods and capital markets impose costs that outweighed any benefits? Did that justify tariffs and quotas? Who gained, and how much, from foreign capital inflows? Did that justify capital controls? Did isolationism impose costs via distortions, and how big were they? As state control grew and increasing barriers to external trade were deliberately erected, who gained and who lost, in the short run and in the long run? All these types of questions require basic economic analysis applied to historical data, with an understanding of the political and institutional context, and an appreciation for potential path dependence in political and economic spheres, so as to judge the optimal (or a feasible counterfactual) response against the actual.

The second critical task here is to set relevant benchmarks for comparison. This applies with special force for the study of Latin American economies, more so than in the study of, say, U.S. economic history. The region's economies were small. They could not plausibly affect the rest of the world's economic conditions, except in a few rare circumstances (Brazil in the coffee market, for example). They were price takers, facing world conditions they could not alter. Each economy thus had to develop its own terms of engagement with these external markets, subject to economic and political costs and benefits that varied considerably. The variety of cross-country economic conditions and policy responses creates a laboratory for the study of how economies react to external economic flows.

Comparisons within the set of small Latin American economies, and between this set and comparable countries in the rest of the world, allow us to apply controls to the analysis of a particular case study. Where, for example, U.S. historians constantly struggle with U.S. exceptionalism, that is, the exceptional weight of the U.S. economy in the world, students of Latin America can more readily conjure up a large number of reference cases for the study of a country, a specific industry, sector, or market. Several chapters illustrate this point well: Twomey's foreign investment analysis is exemplary, as is Hofman and Mulder's productivity study. See also Coatsworth's examination of cross-country patterns of economic growth or della Paolera and Taylor's use of financial and developmental benchmarks to put the Argentine situation in comparative perspective.

Economic Growth and Productivity

If one subject may be considered at the center of the field of economic history, it is the age-old question of what determines the wealth of nations. Why are some rich, some poor? Or, why do some grow quickly, others slowly? This topic reverberates not only for Latin American economic history, but history as a whole. The poverty and underdevelopment of the region have long shaped developments in the social, political, and cultural spheres.

The question is, of course, comparative, so all the preceding concerns apply. Even poverty is a historically and geographically relative concept in many ways. To say that Latin America fell behind requires us to measure and show how it fell behind and relative to which other region. This is, then, first and foremost a data question, before any terms of the debate can be set. Important progress can be made in many ways here by improving our as yet fragmentary knowledge of the evolution of Latin American standards of living. Even basic data such as national income and product are in hopeless shape for many countries before 1900, or even before 1960. Data on income distribution in history are urgently needed. Even some new data on factor prices, such as the real wages of labor, or land prices, or profits to capital, could better illuminate our knowledge of development and its beneficiaries. The chapter by Coatsworth highlights the need for long-term studies to refine our measurements of income and living standards to make meaningful and accurate comparisons.

Going beyond measuring growth to explaining growth will require work to account for inputs of labor, capital (physical and human), raw materials, and land, and some measurement of technology and productivity. The chapters by Twomey, Hofman and Mulder, and Newland show some of the difficulties in measuring basic inputs like capital and labor. Independent study of factor accumulation is also warranted. Why did Latin America follow its particular demographic transition when and where it did? Why did it vary so much by region and country? Studies of fertility and mortality, and, of course, the external labor market, via migration, will make vital contributions to our understanding of the evolution of Latin America's human resources. Breaking these resources down by skill and occupation at the micro level may well be a more distant goal. Capital resources also demand measurement, and an accounting for their accumulation through personal or market channels. Other features also demand attention here. First, we may note the often impersonal transactions of the capital market, ever more apparent in monetizing and increasingly market-oriented developing economies; these historical trends require us to study the evolution of financial intermediation and its role in the mobilization and allocation of capital, including both debt and equity markets. Second, since few developing economies exhibit high savings rates, but most have high investment demands due to capital scarcity, it is likely that they will at some point tap into external, that is, foreign, supplies of savings. International capital flows—their magnitude, volatility, and interactions with local political economy—thus become an important object of study. The chapters by della Paolera and Taylor, Nakamura and Zarazaga, Hanley, and Triner all touch on these concerns.

For many countries and sectors this work is scarcely begun. Primary work such as that of Gómez-Galvarriato on real wages would be valuable for other periods and other countries. Hofman and Mulder show how to get behind aggregate output data to estimate productivity. Such studies only scratch the surface of what future researchers can achieve for the region as a whole at macro- and microeconomic levels with sufficient access to data, adequate research support, and a determination to get at that most essential of economic variables, the level and growth of productivity, the basis of wealth and income.

Market Size, Efficiency, and Integration

Along with productivity, the next core feature of organization dear to economic historians is the institution of the market—its efficiency, its scope, and its implications for activity and development. Since Smith noted how the division of labor was limited by the extent of the market, empiricists have struggled to identify a unified market, test for its efficiency, and study its relation to other markets and its own internal economic and political characteristics. These objectives open up a vast area of Latin American economic history to new scrutiny.

Many questions naturally come to the fore. How integrated were Latin America's internal and external markets in different eras? Did internal barriers to market integration hinder development significantly and radically change the rate of growth or the allocation and specialization of economic activity? When and where did the integration into global markets make its impact felt? And in all cases, how was the functioning of markets affected by policies and regulations, and to what ends?

Several of our chapters either directly or indirectly confront these questions. Newland's study of Argentina documents persistent regional disintegration after independence. Márquez's study of the Mexican tariffs is essentially a study of protectionism and the policy-induced obstacles to external market integration. Triner's chapter on money markets in Brazil poses explicitly the question of financial market integration or lack thereof. The chapter by Nakamura and Zarazaga explicitly focuses on the stock market and its role in Argentine development, and della Paolera and Taylor examine a different part of the financial markets, banks, in search of the effects of global conditions, via the gold standard, on domestic markets. Summerhill's study of railroads measures the impact of the new transportation technology on the physical integration of the country.

All economics, it might be claimed, is a study of markets, but the extent to which market forces can and do operate is at all times subject to question.

Were actors fully informed? Did technology permit markets to work and arbitrage to happen? Did political forces permit market forces to operate freely, partially, or not at all?

Thus, in addition to carefully collecting the data on prices and quantities necessary to gauge the operation of markets, and in addition to evaluating these results in the relevant comparative framework so as to assess the gains or losses, economic historians need to be careful to assess the institutional setting, a subject we shall shortly consider. The rich variety of economic experience in Latin America, from free markets to black markets, from competition to monopoly, and the history of contested ideas and policies regarding the place of the market in society indicate the enormous scope for research in this area to enhance our understanding of the past.

Institutions and Economic Performance

At the broadest level, future scholarship in the field of Latin American history must concern itself with documenting and explaining the path of institutional development, distinguishing between features of that path common to other regions and those unique to the region, or to specific countries or industries.

This task will complement other work in the new economic history tradition. Examining institutional history and its interaction with economic development requires substantial progress in all of the areas mentioned above, and perhaps several other fronts as well. Scholars will be seeking broader models of political economy, examining public choice, lobbying, voting, influence, populism, time consistency, contracts, and numerous other aspects in the tradition of what has come to be called the new institutional history.

By dint of their pervasive effects on the economy, institutions do not submit readily to the kind of analysis that is easily pigeonholed by technique or scope. In this area, scholars will be needed on a broad front. Economic historians of institutional change cannot focus solely on narrow, microeconomic, and domestic developments as they affected Latin American economies. Nor is institutional analysis likely to concern itself exclusively with factors internal to the economies of Latin America; rather, it will also need to focus on the institutional aspects of international economic relations. It will apply a magnifying glass not only to the institutional microstructures of the Latin American economies but also to the macro-level policies and structures that affected economy-wide and external markets.

The chapters in the present book illuminate the wide range of this task. Coatsworth's piece takes a long-term, comparative, and mostly macroeconomic view of economy-wide structures in the region as a whole over several centuries. Dye deconstructs the terms of the contracts between *colonos* (producers) and processors to show how the changes that imposed tight schedules and other obligations on the producers resulted in greater efficiency to the benefit of both parties. Haber makes imaginative use of data on the efficiency of the Brazilian textile industry to measure the impact of changing access to credit. Summerhill's study of Brazilian railroads looks at the effects of government-induced investment in infrastructure. Della Paolera and Taylor study the institution of the gold standard in Argentina as both a macro-phenomenon, with implications for monetary policy, and a micro-phenomenon, through its impact on the financial market via the banking channel. Gómez-Galvarriato's careful study of prices and wages allows her to draw conclusions about the impact of the multiple institutional and policy changes that occurred during the Mexican Revolution.

As in the current economic history of other countries and regions, institutional perspectives will be vital to almost all topics of study. The remarkable feature of the current boom in the field of Latin American economic history is that, unlike the literature on other regions, we now have growth in the traditions of the new economic history and the new institutional history simultaneously. This fruitful development of parallel and mutually informing and reinforcing research approaches will likely continue for many years.

CONCLUSIONS

This book appears at a timely moment for Latin American economic history. The production of new scholarship appears to be at its highest level in many years, both in terms of quantity and quality. Moreover, and perhaps this is not unrelated, today's practitioners are finding their work well received by scholars beyond disciplinary boundaries. At conferences, in journal publications, and in other interactions, a dialogue among economists, historians, and other social scientists interested in the region seems genuinely feasible.

It is hard to say if any one feature of the recent scholarly work could account for these new possibilities, but we see one common thread in much of the new work, sometimes implicit and often explicit, that could increase its accessibility and breadth of appeal to other researchers, namely, the increasing use of comparative perspectives to inform historical economic analysis. This idea motivates the title of our book, *Latin America and the World Economy Since 1800*. We are sensing here perhaps a turning point in the nature of work in economic history at its intersection with area studies or country studies.

Like more traditional scholarship, much of the work in this book is grounded in country- or region-specific data and analysis. Unlike much of the work discussed at the beginning of this introduction, however, today's scholars are drawing on all manner of comparative techniques and using the technical, statistical, and inferential apparatus needed to make sense of Latin America's economic development through a wider-angle lens. Methodologies have been adopted or adapted from research in economic history on other regions, notably the core economies in the modern era, and this parallelism in technique in itself acknowledges an implicit comparative dimension: the application of fundamental or universal economic theory at points widely differing in time and space. For other authors, the empirics themselves afford a chance to place Latin American experience in a world context and to draw useful comparisons and contrasts between the regions, countries, and industries of this peripheral region, and the historical experience of other regions, rich or poor, elsewhere in the world.

So it is probably safe to say that this book will by no means be the last study on Latin America and the world economy. All the big questions are comparative: Why was Latin America underdeveloped (relative to where)? Why did Latin America grow slowly (compared to where)? Why did it go protectionist (more than where)? Which institutions were peculiar (which not uncommon)? Comparative analysis will likely never be exhausted and will surely never become irrelevant.

If we can crudely speak of the historian's urge to focus on and tell the story of the unique, and the economist's urge to classify and develop a universal model, then economic historians with comparative tools can have the best of both worlds. They can exploit statistical inference in large samples to pick out the ordinary and the unusual in their study of a country, region, or industry. They can then invoke economic inference to tell us how those differences mattered quantitatively and qualitatively and thus make controlled conjectures as to what might have been in a counterfactual world, thereby evaluating the impact of policies, market conditions, endowments, and a host of other variables. With just the beginnings of a scholarly assault on the problems in hand, Latin American economic history has a busy future ahead.

NOTES

1. The colonial development of official census taking, especially in the late eighteenth century, combined with the widespread notion that modern governments must collect masses of quantitative data, led most governments in Latin America to create such agencies as soon as they could staff and fund them.

2. For example, Mexico's Dirección General de Estadística was created and began publishing its *Anuarios* in the 1890s. By that date, the private Sociedad Mexicana de Geografía y Estadística, founded in 1839, had already been producing historical data in its *Boletín* for decades.

3. See, for example, Molina Enríquez (1909) and Mariátegui (1928).

4. See the book series entitled *Studies in American Imperialism*, under the general editorship of Harry Elmer Barnes, which included works by Leland Jenks on Cuba (1928), Melvin M. Knight on the Dominican Republic (1928), and Margaret Alexander Marsh on Bolivia (1928). See also J. Fred Rippy (1929, 1944).

5. See, for example, Tannenbaum (1946), Simpson (1929), and Zavala (1935).

6. Burgin (1947), p. 3.

7. See, for example, United Nations Economic Commission for Latin America (1950).

8. For the Argentine estimates of gross product and other series back to 1900, see United Nations Economic Commission for Latin America (1959a, b). For Chile and Colombia, the most important ECLA work concentrated on constructing series for the 1925–1952 period. See United Nations Economic Commission for Latin America (1954, 1957).

9. For example, Furtado (1959, 1967) on Brazil; Ferrer (1963, 1972) on Argentina; Thorp and Bertram (1978) on Peru.

10. Cortés Conde and Stein (1977), p. 5.

11. Borah and Cook (1960), Kubler (1952), Sánchez Albornoz (1974).

12. See Hamilton (1947) and Borah and Cook (1958) on prices; Brading (1971), Fisher (1977), and Bakewell (1971) on mining; and the Chaunus (1959) on trade.

13. Borah (1951) and Bakewell (1971), chap. 1.

14. For exemplary studies of rural estates and merchants, see Barrett (1970) and Socolow (1978), respectively.

15. Glade (1969).

16. Ferrer (1972), Furtado (1976).

17. Cardoso and Falleto (1969, 1979), Frank (1967).

18. Florescano (1969).

19. Semo (1973, 1993), Kay (1973, 1980).

20. For example, Coatsworth (1976), Cortés Conde (1973), Díaz Alejandro (1970), McGreevey (1971), Reynolds (1970), and Solís (1970). The new economic history is sometimes called *cliometrics* or econometric history. Recent developments in the analysis of the role of institutions in economic history are often referred to collectively as the *new institutional history*. This new area of research is sometimes subsumed under the general rubric of the new economic history, but owes much to rational choice developments in other disciplines, especially political science.

21. See the introduction to Haber (1997) for such a critique. The Haber book adds more evidence on the recent growth of new economic history approaches applied to Latin America with its studies of Brazil and Mexico in the "long nineteenth century." As this book suggests, the range of new work now extends over an even wider range of time and space.

22. Colegio de México (1960, n.d.), Mamalakis (1976), Klein and TePaske (1982, 1986).

REFERENCES

Bakewell, Peter J. *Silver Mining and Society in Colonial Mexico: Zacatecas 1546–1700.* Cambridge: Cambridge University Press, 1971.

Barrett, Ward. *The Sugar Hacienda of the Marqueses del Valle.* Minneapolis: University of Minnesota Press, 1970.

Borah, Woodrow W. *New Spain's Century of Depression.* Berkeley: University of California Press, 1951.

Borah, Woodrow W., and Sherburne F. Cook. *Price Trends of Some Basic Commodities in Central Mexico, 1531–1570.* Berkeley: University of California Press, 1958.

Borah, Woodrow W., and Sherburne F. Cook. *The Indian Population of Central Mexico, 1531–1610.* Berkeley: University of California Press, 1960.

Borah, Woodrow W., and Sherburne F. Cook. *The Aboriginal Population of Central Mexico on the Eve of the Spanish Conquest.* Berkeley: University of California Press, 1963.

Brading, David A. *Miners and Merchants in Bourbon Mexico, 1763–1810.* Cambridge: Cambridge University Press, 1971.

Bulmer-Thomas, Victor. *Economic History of Latin America Since Independence.* Cambridge: Cambridge University Press, 1995.

Burgin, Myron. *Economic Aspects of Argentine Federalism, 1820–1852.* Cambridge: Harvard University Press, 1946.

Burgin, Myron. "Research in Latin American Economics and Economic History." *Inter-American Economic Affairs* 1, no. 3 (1947): 3–22.

Cárdenas, Enrique. *La industrialización mexicana durante le gran depresión.* Mexico: El Colegio de México, 1987.

Cardoso, Fernando Henrique, and Enzo Faletto. *Dependencia y desarrollo en América Latina.* Mexico: Siglo XXI, 1969; English-language edition entitled *Dependence and Development in Latin America.* Berkeley: University of California Press, 1979.

Chaunu, Pierre, and Huguette Chaunu. *Séville et l'Atlantique: Structures et conjoncture de L'Atlantique espagnol et hispano-américain (1504–1650).* Paris: S.E.V.P.E.N., 1959.

Coatsworth, John H. *Growth Against Development.* Dekalb, IL: Northern Illinois University Press, 1976.

Colegio de México. *Estadísticas económicas del Porfiriato: Comercio exterior de México, 1877–1911.* Mexico: El Colegio de México, 1960.

Colegio de México. *Estadísticas económicas del Porfiriato: Fuerza de trabajo y actividad por sectores.* Mexico: El Colegio de México, n.d.

Cortés Conde, Roberto. *The First Stages of Modernization in Latin America.* New York: Harper and Row, 1973.

Cortés Conde, Roberto, and Stanley Stein, eds. *Latin America: A Guide to Economic History, 1830–1930.* Berkeley: University of California Press, 1977.

Díaz Alejandro, Carlos. *Essays on the Economic History of the Argentine Economy.* New Haven: Yale University Press, 1970.

Ferrer, Aldo. *La economía argentina: Las etapas de su desarrollo y problemas actuales.* Mexico: Fondo de Cultura Económica, 1963; English-language edition entitled *The Argentine Economy.* Berkeley: University of California Press, 1972.

Fisher, John R. *Silver and Silver Miners in Colonial Peru, 1776–1824.* Monograph Series, no. 7. Liverpool: Center for Latin American Studies, 1977.

Florescano, Enrique. *Precios del maíz y crisis agrícolas en México (1708–1810).* Mexico: El Colegio de México, 1969.

Frank, Andre Gunder. *Capitalism and Underdevelopment in Latin America: Historical Studies of Chile and Brazil.* New York: Monthly Review Press, 1967.

Furtado, Celso. *Formação econômica do Brasil.* Rio de Janeiro: Editora Fondo de Cultura, 1959; English-language edition entitled *The Economic Growth of Brazil.* Berkeley: University of California Press, 1967; English-language edition entitled *The Economic Development of Latin America: Historical Background and Contemporary Problems.* New York: Cambridge University Press, 1976.

Glade, William P. *The Latin American Economies: Their Institutional Evolution.* New York: Van Nostrand, 1969.

Haber, Stephen H., ed. *How Latin America Fell Behind: Essays on the Economic Histories of Mexico and Brazil, 1800–1914.* Stanford: Stanford University Press, 1997.

Hamilton, Earl J. *War and Prices in Spain, 1651–1800.* Cambridge: Harvard University Press, 1947.

Jenks, Leland. *Our Cuban Colony: A Study in Sugar.* New York: Vanguard Press, 1928.

Kay, Cristobal. "Comparative Development of the European Manorial System and the Latin American Hacienda System." *Journal of Peasant Studies* 2 (1973).

Kay, Cristobal. *El sistema señorial europeo y la hacienda latinoamericana: Estudios sobre el desarrollo del capitalismo en la agricultura.* Mexico: Ediciones Era, 1980.

Klein, Herbert S., and John J. TePaske. *The Royal Treasuries of the Spanish Empire in America.* 3 vols. Durham, NC: Duke University Press, 1982.

Klein, Herbert S., and John J. TePaske. *Ingresos y egresos de la Real Hacienda de Nueva España.* 2 vols. Mexico: Instituto Nacional de Antropología e Historia, Colección Fuentes, 1986.

Knight, Melvin M. *The Americans in Santo Domingo.* New York: Vanguard, 1928.

Kubler, George. *The Indian Caste of Peru, 1795–1940: A Population Study Based on Tax Records and Census Reports.* Smithsonian Institution, Institute of Social Anthropology, Publication no. 14. Washington, DC, 1952.

Mamalakis, Marcos. *The Growth and Structure of the Chilean Economy.* New Haven: Yale University Press, 1976.

Mariátegui, José Carlos. *Siete ensayos de interpretación de la realidad peruana.* Lima: Amauta, 1928.

Marsh, Margaret Alexander. *The Bankers in Bolivia: A Study in American Foreign Investment.* New York: Vanguard, 1928.

McGreevey, William. *Economic History of Colombia, 1845–1930.* New York: Cambridge University Press, 1971.

Molina Enríquez, Andrés. *Los grandes problemas nacionales.* Mexico: A. Carranza, 1909.

Murra, John. "The Economic Organization of the Inca State." Ph.D. dissertation, University of Chicago, 1956.

Reynolds, Clark W. *The Mexican Economy: Twentieth-Century Structure and Growth.* New Haven: Yale University Press, 1970.

Rippy, J. Fred. *Rivalry of the United States and Great Britain over Latin America.* Baltimore: Johns Hopkins University Press, 1929.

Rippy, J. Fred. *Latin America and the Industrial Age.* New York: Putnam, 1944.

Sánchez Albornoz, Nicolás. *The Population of Latin America.* Berkeley: University of California Press, 1974.

Semo, Enrique. *Historia del capitalismo en México: Los orígenes, 1521–1763.* Mexico: Ediciones Era, 1973; English-language edition entitled *History of Capitalism in Mexico: Its Origins, 1521–1763.* Austin: University of Texas Press, 1993.

Simpson, Lesley Byrd. *The Encomienda in New Spain: Forced Native Labor in the Spanish Colonies, 1492–1550.* Berkeley: University of California Press, 1929.

Socolow, Susan Migden. *The Merchants of Buenos Aires, 1778–1810: Family and Commerce.* Cambridge: Cambridge University Press, 1978.

Solís, Leopoldo. *La realidad económica mexicana: Retrovisión y perspectivas.* Mexico: Siglo XXI, 1970.

Tannenbaum, Frank. *The Mexican Agrarian Revolution.* New York: Macmillan, 1929.

Tannenbaum, Frank. *Peace by Revolution: An Interpretation of Mexico.* New York: Columbia University Press, 1933.

Tannenbaum, Frank. *Slave and Citizen: The Negro in the Americas.* New York: Vintage, 1946.

Thorp, Rosemary, and Geoffrey Bertram. *Peru, 1890–1977: Growth and Policy in an Open Economy.* New York: Columbia University Press, 1978.

United Nations Economic Commission for Latin America. *The Economic Development of Latin America and Its Principal Problems.* New York: United Nations, 1950.

United Nations Economic Commission for Latin America. *Antecedentes sobre el desarrollo de la economía chilena 1925–52.* Santiago, Chile: Pacífico, 1954.

United Nations Economic Commission for Latin America. *Análisis y proyecciones del desarrollo económico.* Vol. 3, *El desarrollo económico de Colombia.* Mexico: United Nations, 1957

United Nations. Economic Commission for Latin America. *Análisis y proyecciones del desarrollo económico.* Vol. 5, *El desarrollo económico de Argentina.* No. 1, *Los problemas y perspectivas del desarrollo argentino.* Mexico: United Nations, 1959a.

United Nations Economic Commission for Latin America. *Análisis y proyecciones del desarrollo económico.* Vol. 5, *El desarrollo económico de Argentina.* No. 2, *Los sectores de la producción.* 2 vols. Mexico: United Nations, 1959b.

Zavala, Silvio A. *La encomienda indiana.* Madrid: Imprenta Helenica, 1935.

PART I

International Comparisons

The opening chapters of *Latin America in the World Economy* reflect the breadth implied in its title and seek to place the Latin American experience in a broader context. Although comparison is at least implicit in almost all recent contributions to the field, as noted in the introduction, these essays make explicit use of cross-national comparison to address key issues. Such a focus recognizes certain essential qualities of Latin America's historical and geographical placement in the nineteenth and twentieth centuries. After wars of independence, the countries of the region were numerous, mostly small, abundant in resources, and no longer part of a larger political and economic empire. For the most part, at least until well into the twentieth century, external economic conditions had to be taken as given, and worked with as best as possible. Even autarkic policies could not shift budget constraints and world prices very much. The responses of economies and polities in the region, given these kinds of initial conditions, helped form the basis for future development or underdevelopment in the two centuries that followed. Comparativist scholarship on the region aims to exploit the similarities and differences between countries within and beyond the region to try to explain the various paths taken.

Coatsworth's essay is a very broad attack in this tradition (Chapter 1). The various traditional and more recent revisionist explanations for Latin America's slow growth are revisited, and new compilations of long-term data are brought together to advance some basic hypotheses. An accounting of long-term per capita trends in output reveals the poor performance in the region, even as early as the eighteenth century. Scholars of the region, from the dependency school to that of the new economic history, have long agreed that there is a historic Latin American "failure" to be explained.[1] However, almost all such approaches tend to lump all Latin America into one case and to blur distinctions between what were highly diverse economies in the postcolonial period. Analyses have focused mainly on such variables as land tenure, wealth distribution and inequality, and external shocks to explain persistent backwardness. Instead, Coatsworth's essay and quantitative research reconnects us to the vast differences between the Latin American nations in economic performance and thus in the range of explanatory variables that are helpful in understanding it. Moreover, in a link to the recent economic growth literature, it is reasonable to ask why analysis has not focused on more conventional explanatory variables such as trade and openness, taxes, and the like. In these dimensions, Coatsworth's essay suggests that a more careful multicausal approach to explain Latin American economic growth will be needed for these historical epochs, just as for the postwar era that is the focus of modern growth empiricists. Not only that, but such data are available and provide at least *prima facie* evidence that a marriage of institutionalist and cliometric traditions will be needed to tell the full story.

In the same growth tradition, but working on the modern postwar era, Hofman and Mulder (Chapter 3) take a much different route to explore the comparative productivity performance of Brazil and Mexico. This is not surprising, since compared with pre-1900 studies they have a wealth of data with which to explore macro-level trends in productivity for the two countries. Data on outputs and inputs are carefully sifted and adjusted, and total factor productivity calculated, in a systematic way that uses the most modern techniques. This research is important since, although Mexico and Brazil were two of the world's fastest growing economies in the post–World War II era, only productivity estimates, not growth alone, can reveal the true extent and potential for "catching up" in these two developing economies. Sectoral breakdowns reveal marked differences that are unclear at the aggregate level: Although manufacturing had high productivity growth, many other sectors, such as agriculture, were beset by slow productivity advances. A rather pessimistic picture emerges, as in the case of the much-glorified "Asian Miracle" economies—one of overall output growth driven more by factor accumulation (especially physical investment) than by the more efficient deployment of existing factors.[2] With hindsight, this might seem less surprising. If even the hugely successful Asian economies could not pull off amazing productivity advances, it is hard to imagine the more lethargic Latin American economies doing any better. Broader cross-sectional data show that almost half the gap between the Latin American economies and the United States is due to productivity differences, and this gap is rather stable over time. This highlights a major challenge for the economies of the region to overcome in order to achieve long-term convergence.

The essay by Alston, Libecap, and Mueller (Chapter 2) addresses a different set of international micro-level comparisons to uncover the causes of violent conflict and the importance of well-defined property rights in frontier regions. The test cases here are the nineteenth-century U.S. West and contemporary Brazilian frontier zones bordering the rain forest. The U.S. case is famous for legendary conflicts between cattlemen, sheepherders, dirt farmers, and other new settlers and for the rough "justice" that settled them. Brazil faces similar problems of violence among landowners and squatters, with a justice system that is straining to cope. In both cases, the law struggled in upholding the property rights of those originally given rights to settle and work the land, often invoking distributional reasons—favoring poor squatters or tenants against rich and supposedly powerful landowners. Often, explicit law was designed this way to encourage small-scale homesteading versus mass land purchases for speculative purposes by landowners not interested in productive operation. Still, the violence of the nineteenth-century United States was far less than that seen today in Brazil. Why? The authors argue that understanding this difference, and its economic implications, requires an analysis of how policies and institutions function. The key element is the government's willingness and ability to use legal processes to help the underdogs. In the U.S. case, the General Land Office was a small operation that failed to overwhelm the large landowners. But in Brazil today, the land reform agency (INCRA) has more tools and capabilities and has responded, though inconsistently, to assist squatters against landowners. Economic theory, backed by econometric evidence, suggests that in such circumstances squatters will be encouraged to raise the stakes by invading more land, causing more conflict, and provoking more violence, since headlines help to get INCRA to intervene on their behalf.

Landlords are similarly induced to preemptive violence. Alston, Libecap, and Mueller show that this is exactly what is happening and conclude with observations on the importance of designing policies and implementing mechanisms that take into account the predictable rational responses of agents. The comparison with events a century before in the frontier days of the United States adds a helpful historical perspective to this tale. Ironically, the United States—despite its failure to help the poor very much in the homesteading era—achieved far more equitable long-term results in the settler areas than Brazil, as it did in the economy as a whole.

NOTES

1. See, for contrast, Cardoso and Faletto (1979) versus Engerman and Sokoloff (1997).
2. On the "myth of the Asian Miracle" see Krugman (1994), who builds on the work of Young (1995).

REFERENCES

Cardoso, Fernando Henrique, and Enzo Faletto. *Dependence and Development in Latin America.* Berkeley: University of California Press, 1979.

Engerman, Stanley L., and Kenneth L. Sokoloff. "Factor Endowments, Institutions, and Differential Paths of Growth Among New World Economies." In *How Latin America Fell Behind: Essays on the Economic History of Brazil and Mexico, 1800–1914,* edited by Stephen Haber, 262–275. Stanford: Stanford University Press, 1997.

Krugman, Paul. "The Myth of Asia's Miracle." *Foreign Affairs* 73, no. 6 (November/December 1994): 62–79.

Young, Alwyn. "The Tyranny of Numbers: Confronting the Statistical Realities of the East Asian Growth Experience." *Quarterly Journal of Economics* 110, no. 3 (August 1995): 641–680.

1

Economic and Institutional Trajectories in Nineteenth-Century Latin America

John H. Coatsworth
Harvard University

The economic history of modern Latin America addresses two fundamental questions. First, why did the region fail to achieve sustained economic growth before the last quarter of the nineteenth century? Second, why has the region failed to grow fast enough to catch up since then? This chapter addresses only the first of these questions.

Latin America fell into relative backwardness between roughly 1700 and 1900. At the beginning of this period, the economies of the Iberian colonies in the New World were roughly as productive as those of the British. For most of the ensuing 200 years, the Latin American economies stagnated while those of the North Atlantic achieved sustained increases in productivity. As early as 1800, most of the Latin American economies had already fallen well behind the United States. A century later, most had fallen far enough behind to qualify as "less" (or "under-") developed by contemporary standards.

In the twentieth century, the Latin American economies have achieved respectable rates of economic growth, equal on average to that of the United States. Thus, the relative gap between Latin America and the United States has not changed at all in the past 100 years, though the relative positions of individual countries have shifted. To understand how the Latin American economies fell into relative backwardness, therefore, it is crucial to look at the region's pre-1900 economic history.

Latin America stagnated for most of two crucial centuries because economic institutions distorted incentives and high transport costs left most of the region's abundant natural resources beyond the frontier of profitable exploitation. Early in the colonial era, comparatively high *levels* of productivity were achieved in economies that managed, despite these constraints, to specialize in export production. The successful cases were those that combined relatively scarce supplies of free or slave labor with accessible natural resources and a favorable policy environment. In contrast, colonial economies that relied on relatively cheap indigenous or slave labor to produce exportables in less accessible regions with high tax and regulatory burdens tended to have smaller export sectors and to be less productive. Cycles of export growth and decline, linked to market fluctuations or to freshly discovered and subsequently depleted natural resources, produced variations on these patterns well into the twentieth century in some areas.

Once the opportunities created by more (or less) favorable initial conditions were seized and exploited in a given colony, further economic *growth* usually depended on some combination of institutional modernization and transport innovation. Not until the late nineteenth century did liberalism (or, in some cases, modernizing conservative regimes) and railroads remove the two fundamental obstacles to growth in Latin America and push most of the region's economies onto new trajectories—and thus beyond the scope of this chapter.

After reviewing long-term trends in the productivity of the major Latin American economies, this chapter will summarize what is currently known about the causes of the region's dismal pre-1900 economic performance. It will argue that variations in factor proportions, opportunities to engage in external trade, and government tax and regulatory policies help most to explain variations in productivity levels among the stagnant Latin American economies at the outset of the nineteenth century. It also analyzes the contradictory evidence on inequality in this era. The chapter concludes by emphasizing the significance of transport innovation and institutional change in facilitating economic growth in the twentieth century.

COLONIAL AND NINETEENTH-CENTURY TRENDS

As the first permanent English settlers in North America set about chopping down trees to make crude cabins in December of 1620, the Spanish and Portuguese empires in the New World had already passed their first century. It would take the English more than 200 years to catch up to the most prosperous of Spain's possessions. In 1650, Cuba had a gross domestic product (GDP) per capita of roughly $60; the British North American colonies did not reach that level until more than a century later. By 1800, Cuba's GDP per capita was near $90, whereas that of the United States had barely reached $80. The United States did not close the gap with Cuba until the 1830s.[1]

The U.S. performance looks much better in comparison with Spain's mainland colonies. The 13 British colonies probably caught up to Mexico before 1700. Over the eighteenth century, Mexico stagnated as the U.S. economy grew at perhaps a half a percent a year. In 1800, Mexico's per capita GDP of $40 stood at half that of the United States. Brazil, recovering finally from the collapse of its short-lived gold boom (1750–1780), had fallen well behind.

The race ended long before the nineteenth century was over. By 1900, the United States had become a formidable economic power with a GDP per capita, adjusted for purchasing power parity (PPP), nearly four times higher than the mean of Latin America's eight largest economies. Even Argentina, slightly ahead of the United States in 1800 and growing rapidly by the 1870s, had fallen far behind, with a GDP per capita not much more than half that of the United States.

These comparisons are summarized in Table 1.1. Estimates for benchmark dates before 1900 are available only for six of the major economies: Argentina, Brazil, Chile, Cuba, Mexico, and Peru. Twentieth-century figures for Colombia and Venezuela are also included. The table shows GDP per capita, where available, as a percentage of the U.S. level for each of six benchmark dates. The estimates for 1700 and 1800 range from crude guesswork to fairly reliable calculations, but are not adjusted for PPP.[2] They are thus not strictly comparable with the estimates of Maddison and Mulder for later years. The possible effect of a PPP adjustment on the estimates for the two earliest dates is difficult to judge, but would not in any case alter the estimates enough to affect the trends indicated in the table.

The estimates in Table 1.1 show a consistent pattern of failure from as early as 1700 until at least the end of the nineteenth century. Every Latin American country for which we have estimates grew more slowly on average than the United States for the two centuries up to 1900. Most simply stagnated; some, like Mexico, experienced prolonged periods of economic decline.[3] There is no reason to believe that this record would look any less dismal with more data. The twentieth-century pattern, however, is more mixed. While Argentina declined toward the regional mean of about 27% of U.S. GDP per capita in 1994, Brazil and Venezuela rose to meet or surpass it.

The gap between the richest and the poorest of the Latin American economies has not varied much over time, though the position of individual countries has changed. The ratio of the richest to the poorest economy in Table 1.1 stood at nearly 3:1 in 1800 and rose to 5:1 by 1900. The 1800 ratio probably

TABLE 1.1

GDP per Capita as Percentage of the U.S. Level, 1700–1994

Country	1700	1800	1850	1900	1913	1950	1994
Argentina		102		52	55	41	37
Brazil		36	39	10	11	15	22
Chile		46		38	40	33	34
Colombia				18	18	19	24
Cuba	167	112	78		39		
Mexico	89	50	37	35	35	27	23
Peru		41		20	20	24	14
Venezuela				10	10	38	37
Mean	128	66	51	27	28	29	27

Note: The last row reports the arithmetic mean of the countries for which there are data for each year. If each country were assigned a weight equal to its share of population, the mean for each year would be lower, since the high-income cases (Argentina and Cuba, for example) had smaller populations. In 1800, the unweighted mean in the table is 66, but the population-weighted mean of the six reported cases would be 51.

Sources: The Mexican estimate for 1700 is from Coatsworth (1990a, chap. 3). The Cuban figure for 1700 extrapolates between estimates for 1650 and 1750 reported in Fraile Balbín, Salvucci, and Salvucci (1993, part II, chap. 3). The 1800 estimates are discussed in the appendix. The 1850 Cuban estimate is from the Fraile Balbín, Salvucci, and Salvucci essay just cited. The 1850 Mexican estimate is for 1845 and is taken from Coatsworth (1990a, chap. 3). The remaining 1850 figures are based on Maddison (1994, appendix D), as are the figures for Peru in 1913, 1950, and 1994. The remaining figures (except Cuba in 1913) are taken from the essay by Hofman and Mulder in this volume. The Cuban figure for 1913 is based on the ratio of Cuban to Argentine GDP per capita in Bulmer-Thomas (1994, p. 439).

comes close to capturing the extent of the variation across the region on the eve of the independence wars. It may be compared with Maddison's suggestion that a gap of 4:1 separated the richest and poorest of the world's economies in 1820.[4] Thus, the variation in the productivity of Latin America's colonial economies in 1800 was almost as great as for the entire world. For 1900 and 1913, the ratio of 5:1 also appears fairly representative since it includes both wealthy Argentina and backward Brazil and pre-oil Venezuela. The 1994 ratio of less than 2.6:1 is another matter. Although the sample of eight cases does show clearly the tendency toward convergence among the larger economies during the twentieth century, it excludes all of the poorer, smaller economies and thus exaggerates the extent of intraregional convergence since 1900. In 1995, for example, the ratio of PPP-adjusted Argentine to Honduran GNP per capita was 5:1.[5] This suggests that the intraregional productivity gap, like the interregional gap between Latin America and the developed world, did not change much in the twentieth century.

In summary, the available quantitative evidence shows that Latin America became an underdeveloped region between the early eighteenth and the late nineteenth centuries. Although all of the Latin American economies fell further behind in this period, the Argentine performance was consistently better than the rest until the twentieth century, that of Brazil almost as consistently the worst. In the twentieth century, these two economies reversed positions, with Brazil consistently outperforming the rest of the region and Argentina far behind. Cuba, with the highest GDP per capita in relation to the United States in 1700, fell furthest in relative terms over this period, though the lack of GDP estimates for the rest of Latin America (except Mexico) for 1700 makes this conclusion more tentative.

FACTOR ENDOWMENTS

The New World factor endowments encountered by the first European entrepreneurs did not matter much. Most of Latin America's potentially exploitable natural resources lay dormant and remained inaccessible throughout the colonial era. Most of the New World's indigenous population died.

Europeans transformed the natural and human resource base of the entire New World, including vast areas they never conquered or even visited. They did so by bringing in pathogens, people, plants, animals, technologies, and institutions hitherto unknown to the Western Hemisphere. The pathogens destroyed most of the New World's inhabitants by the end of the sixteenth century, so the Europeans repopulated the hemisphere with African slaves. Old World plants and animals displaced indigenous species in many areas and in doing so transformed entire landscapes. European technologies and organizational forms, from transoceanic navigation and deep-shaft mining to metal coinage and commercial credit, transformed production and commerce. The Europeans adopted and adapted Amerindian organization, products, and technologies as well, pushing them toward patterns that facilitated money-making in all its forms.

The Europeans did not distribute themselves evenly over the landscape. "Spanish society in the Indies," James Lockhart reminds us, "was import-export oriented at the very base and in every aspect."[6] So, too, was the great Portuguese adventure in Brazil. Publicly licensed but privately financed, the Iberian entrepreneurs who set out to conquer the New World mainly wanted to get rich. Officials and priests in both empires followed them about, careful not to miss any reasonable opportunity to collect a tax, impose a fee, or save a soul. Any exploitable resource, natural or human, that could profitably be turned into silver or gold attracted both private greed and official attention. But vast areas of these New World empires remained unexploited and ungoverned by Europeans or their descendants until long after independence. The "empty spaces" (that is, empty of Europeans) where little or no money could be made added up to more territory than Spain and Portugal actually managed to control or govern in the three centuries after the conquest.

Location determined which of the New World's people and resources the invaders rushed to exploit. The cost of overland transportation proved to be prohibitive for most commodities, even in the relatively easy terrain of plateaus and pampas. Thus, the Europeans and the slaves they brought in from Africa hardly ever settled far from navigable rivers or the seacoast. Since navigable rivers were few (and the few there were, like the Amazon, did not run past much tradable wealth), they eventually settled mainly on islands in the Caribbean and along coastlines. There they produced a variety of plantation products for European markets, including sugar, cacao, tobacco, rice, cotton, and, later in the nineteenth century, coffee, henequen, and bananas. Not until the advent of the railroad did agricultural production for export shift from seacoasts to the interior of the continent.

When Europeans settled further inland during the colonial era, as in central Mexico and parts of the Andes, it was generally to exploit opportunities to profit from the production of commodities with high value-to-bulk ratios or to supply the producers of these commodities with inputs and consumption goods.[7] High transport costs limited the interior regions of the continent to exporting precious metals, gems (like emeralds and diamonds), and dyestuffs such as cochineal and indigo. Local markets took nearly everything else. Where export production generated market demand for food and other inputs and yielded taxes to support the royal bureaucracy, Europeans specialized in these ancillary activities. In the rest of the Americas, they had to make do with whatever they could extort from indigenous populations whose productivity was too low to generate much surplus.

At the time of the Columbus voyages, as many as 50 million Amerindians lived in the vast territories that became Latin America. By the end of the colonial era, more than half of Latin America's population of perhaps 15 million people consisted of Europeans, Africans, and the descendants of Europeans and Africans. Amerindians and mestizos, most of whom lived in Mexico, constituted less than half of the Latin American population in 1820.[8]

The demographic and economic reorganization of New World spaces caused by Latin America's integration into the two Iberian empires with their links to the developing world market can be glimpsed from the data in Table 1.2 on population densities and productivity in 1800. Argentina, a settlement colony with a huge territory and tiny population, was the most thinly populated. Mexico and Cuba were the most densely populated. In Mexico, as in the Andes, the population figures reflect the partial recovery of the indigenous populations, though at comparatively low levels of per capita GDP. In Cuba, the high population density reflects the importation of large numbers of slaves toward the end of the eighteenth century, spurred by the island's high export-based GDP per capita.

As the table suggests, African slaves did not always end up where the marginal product of their labor was highest. Backward Brazil, with a low per capita GDP, imported nearly a third of all slaves that came to the New World, whereas the more productive Spanish islands like Cuba imported far fewer until the end of the eighteenth century. This difference was due in part to Portuguese commercial access to slave-exporting regions of Africa and Spanish restrictions on imports (including slaves) from outside the empire. Slaves were far more costly in the Spanish colonies than anywhere else until the crown relaxed restrictions on slave imports beginning in the late 1760s.[9] In the seventeenth century, the Portuguese brought slaves to Brazil and set them to work in activities where their productivity was low, because slaves cost so little. When slave prices rose in response to Caribbean demand in the eighteenth century, Brazilian production declined.[10] In Cuba, where slaves cost two to three times as much as in Jamaica, Europeans purchased them only when certain that they would be productive enough to compensate for their high price.[11]

Europeans migrated to the New World in much smaller numbers than the Africans they forced to come. Migration to the Spanish colonies from Spain

TABLE 1.2

Population Densities and GDP, 1800

Colony	Area (1000s sq km)	Population (1000s)	Density (Pop. per 1000 sq km)	Total GDP (1000s)	GDP per Capita
				(current dollars)	
Argentina	2,777	329	118	26,978	82
Brazil	8,457	3,250	384	94,250	29
Chile	757	535	707	19,795	37
Cuba	115	272	2,365	24,480	90
Mexico	1,967	6,000	3,050	240,340	40
Peru	1,280	1,300	1,016	2,900	33

Note: All estimates exclude indigenous population and economic activity beyond the frontiers of Spanish or Portuguese authority.

Sources: Areas correspond to modern political boundaries. Population estimates are from a variety of sources. For Argentina, see Maeder (1969, pp. 22–23). For Brazil, see Graham and Merrick (1979, pp. 26–30), but note that Alden (1987, p. 287) accepts a much lower (though admittedly undercounted) total of only 2.1 million. For Chile, see Mamalakis (1978, vol. 2, p. 9). For Mexico, see Coatsworth (1990a, p. 46). On Peru, see Gootenberg (1991). For GDP estimates, see the appendix to this chapter.

reached a peak at the end of the sixteenth century, but revived somewhat in the eighteenth. Throughout the colonial era, Spain tried to control and limit immigration to the New World and refused permission for the citizens of other countries (except for naturalized Irish Catholics) to settle in its possessions. By the eighteenth century, low wages on the Spanish American mainland and rising slave imports to the islands kept the flow of Europeans low and made Spain's efforts at controlling immigration fairly easy. Portuguese emigration to Brazil followed a somewhat different trajectory. Like Spanish emigration, that of the Portuguese fell during the seventeenth-century depression, but revived more strongly in the eighteenth century due to the pull of high earnings in the gold and diamond booms in the interior.

In the nineteenth century, slaves continued to arrive in large numbers only in Brazil and Cuba. British pressure finally helped to end the slave trade in the 1850s. Meanwhile, European immigration to Latin America slowed after 1800, reversed during the independence wars from 1810 to the 1820s, and in some cases virtually ceased for up to half a century after independence despite the end of Spanish and Portuguese restrictions. The persistence of slavery tended to discourage European migration to Brazil and Cuba. Low wages compounded by political instability and international war kept numbers down everywhere else. When the slave trade ended, Cuba (for sugar) and Peru (for guano mining as well as sugar) imported large numbers of indentured Chinese laborers. Mass European migration did not begin until the 1870s and 1880s and when it did, most of the immigrants went to Argentina and the southern half of Brazil.[12]

Paradoxically, the most productive economies in Latin America at the beginning of the nineteenth century were the two, Cuba and Argentina, where labor was most costly. No free person would go to Argentina without some assurance of gain; the few that went were not disappointed (especially in high-wage Buenos Aires). In Cuba, no one bought slaves at the high prices prevailing for most of the colonial era without some highly productive use to make of them. The high cost of labor in these two colonies resembled the pattern established in British North America. Most of Latin America, however, consisted of far less productive, low-wage territories with limited access to the sea. None of the Iberian colonies or the nation states that succeeded them, not even the most prosperous in 1800 like Cuba and Argentina, managed to achieve rates of growth comparable to the United States until the nineteenth century had nearly ended.

ACCESS TO TRADE

Great debates once raged over the impact of trade on the colonial economies. Recent scholarship has tended to reverse the once widely held notion that external trade is necessarily (or even often) harmful to backward economies. Of course, colonial restrictions on trade, such as the commercial monopolies that prohibited direct trade with foreign countries, did impose costs on colonies throughout the New World, but did so precisely because they reduced the gains such regions would otherwise have enjoyed from external trade.

The Latin American case suggests that the static gains from trade can be large, even in economies that experience little or no sustained economic growth. The cross-section data in Table 1.3 compare the export performance of the six major colonial economies in 1800. Note that the colonies are listed in the table in rank order of GDP per capita. The data demonstrate that the Latin American colonial economies with the largest export sectors tended to have the highest GDP per capita. This is because productivity was higher in export industries than in other sectors of the colonial economies, though the gap between export and domestic-use agriculture and industry must have varied considerably. The colonial economies that managed to specialize more did better.

As in the case of the GDP estimates, some of the figures in this table are subject to larger error margins than would be acceptable in such data today. For most of the years between 1796 and 1812, international warfare disrupted shipping and inflated export prices. Since exports from the Spanish colonies fluctuated considerably from one year to the next, the export figures in the table were constructed to approximate "normal" conditions, either by taking the mean of several years or by using data from a year just prior to the outbreak of warfare.

TABLE 1.3

Export Performance, circa 1800

Colony	Total Exports (current dollars)	Exports per Capita	Exports as % of GDP	GDP per Capita (current dollars)
Cuba	5,000,000	18.35	20.4	90
Argentina	3,300,000	10.03	12.2	82
Mexico	12,640,800	2.11	5.2	40
Chile	874,072	1.63	4.4	37
Peru	2,998,000	2.31	7.0	33
Brazil	15,526,750	4.78	16.4	29

Source: See appendix.

Cuba and Argentina were the most successful exporters in per capita terms by 1800. Argentina also had the largest export sector in relation to GDP, followed by Brazil and Cuba. The mainland economies that produced mainly silver for export (or, in the case of Chile, foodstuffs for export to mining colonies) had much smaller export sectors both in per capita terms and in relation to total output.

Mexico's relative failure as an exporter is perhaps the most surprising. For most of the eighteenth century, Mexico served as the cash cow of the Spanish American empire, regularly exporting huge quantities of silver along with substantial amounts of cochineal and other products. In per capita terms, however, only Chile had a smaller export sector. Although the income generated by the mining industries in Mexico and Peru was substantial, the productivity effect was limited by the relatively small proportion of the labor force employed in mining and the relatively slow growth of silver production even during boom periods.[13]

Throughout the Caribbean, by contrast, exports accounted for a relatively high proportion of GDP.[14] Brazil's export sector was also quite large, despite its regional concentration in the northeast (except during the gold and diamond export booms further south). The most striking aspect of Brazil's performance, however, is the low level of per capita exports and GDP per capita in comparison with Cuba. This may be explained in part, as mentioned above, by lower slave prices that may have encouraged more marginal producers to enter the market. By the early nineteenth century, Brazil's sugar plantations were notoriously inefficient producers in comparison with those in the Caribbean. In addition, Brazilian sugar was excluded from the markets of the European countries with sugar islands of their own.

Perhaps most surprising is the relative success of Argentina. Table 1.3 includes exports from Buenos Aires that were produced within what became the national territory. They consisted chiefly of cattle hides and salted beef, derived mainly from exploiting the wild herds of the pampas. The table also includes an indirect measure of Argentine exports to Bolivia. There are no direct data on these exports. Instead the table assumes that all of Bolivia's privately owned silver exports to Buenos Aires consisted of payments for the cloth, sugar, mules, yerba mate, and other Argentine products imported each year. Some of this private silver actually went to pay for European goods that eventually made their way to Bolivian consumers and should thus be excluded, but these amounts must have been small in comparison with the silver earned by Argentine producers. In addition, Argentines supplied commercial and transport services and paid taxes on European products transshipped to Bolivia.[15]

The patterns revealed in the cross-section data in Table 1.3 persisted into the nineteenth century. Table 1.4 shows exports per capita at intervals over the course of that century. As the data show, nothing much happened to alter relative positions until after 1850, except for the beginnings of Chile's copper boom and a blip from Peru's short-lived guano windfall between 1840 and 1870. Even by the end of the century, Cuba and Argentina still led the region in exports per capita, though Chile had risen fast, with nitrates replacing copper after the War of the Pacific (1879–1883) as the driving force of its export success. The trade data in Table 1.4 offer some support to the notion of path dependence, at least through the nineteenth century. With the notable exception of Chile, the less successful exporters did not improve their relative positions, while the successful exporters continue to lead the region.

In sum, Argentina and Cuba managed to prosper in the colonial era, despite high labor costs, in part because their well-located natural resources allowed them to specialize in export production. The less successful agricultural economies like Brazil managed to substitute cheaper labor for location, pushing export production further from the sea by using low-cost labor to compensate for higher transport costs. The remaining colonies produced small quantities (in relation to GDP) of high-value metals in primitive surroundings, especially in the Andes. Even in ostensibly opulent Mexico, at least 80% of the population in 1800 worked in domestic-use agriculture at low levels of productivity.[16]

INSTITUTIONAL CONSTRAINTS

The Iberian colonial regimes and their successor states imposed a wide array of institutional constraints on productive enterprise in the New World. These constraints distorted incentives by raising the private costs and risks of productive enterprise that could have contributed to economic growth. Three

TABLE 1.4

Exports per Capita, 1800–1913 (in current U.S. dollars)

Country	1800	1850	1870	1890	1913
Argentina	10.0	10.3	16.5	32.4	62.0
Brazil	4.8	5.0	8.6	9.6	14.2
Chile	1.6	7.8	14.2	20.3	44.7
Cuba	18.3	22.2	44.3	55.7	64.7
Mexico	2.1	3.2	2.3	4.4	10.7
Peru	2.3	3.7	10.1	3.3	9.4

Sources: Table 1.2 and Bulmer-Thomas (1994, p. 69).

were particularly harmful: the political risk associated with unpredictable policies and policymakers; the costs due to inefficient property rights and burdensome tax and regulatory systems; and the opportunities lost for lack of public goods, especially investment in human resources and material infrastructure.

Political risk stemmed from the arbitrary character of Iberian regalism and succeeding personalist and military dictatorships, the discretionary authority exercised by colonial and national officials whose private gain often took precedence over the public interest, and the social conflicts that erupted constantly in the slave and caste societies that constituted most of the region. Political risks increased steeply with the outbreak of the independence wars in the Spanish possessions after 1808 and remained high for decades in many of the new nations. Particularly troublesome was the persistence of slavery and of certain caste privileges, which in most cases could neither be maintained nor abolished without turmoil.

The costs and associated risks of engaging in productive economic activity, including commercial and other services, in the Iberian New World were substantially higher than in the British colonies and former colonies. In part, this was due to Iberian legal norms, the lack of well-defined or needed property rights, inefficient and often corrupt judicial systems, and the persistence of archaic forms of property holding, such as entail and the "corporate" (inalienable) property rights of the Church, the *ayuntamientos* (town councils), and indigenous villages. In part, it was also due to the primitive tax systems of the two empires, which relied on burdensome regulations, monopolies, licensing fees, and the like to generate revenues.

The two empires and successor governments provided few public goods. Neither of the colonial powers and few of the successor states managed even to define and provide for the defense of land borders. None exercised a secure monopoly on the legitimate use of violence and all relied on militias and other irregular forces to maintain order. Governments throughout Latin America consistently failed to invest in their human resources and physical infrastructure. Colonial governments left schooling and social services to the Church, delegated road maintenance to merchant guilds, left major ports and fortifications to decay, and paid consistent attention to little beyond collecting taxes. The national governments that followed took decades before they began to perform such basic public functions.

Taken together, these institutional constraints constituted powerful obstacles to economic growth throughout the Iberian New World. Not all of the colonies suffered equally, however. Levels of taxation, for example, varied considerably from one colony to another. Table 1.5 provides rough estimates of

TABLE 1.5

Tax Revenues per Capita and as Percentage of GDP, circa 1800 (in current U.S. dollars)

Colony	GDP/capita	Revenues (1000s)	Revenues/capita	Revenues as % of GDP
Cuba	90	1,500	5.51	6.1
Argentina	82	1,121	3.40	4.2
Mexico	40	31,618	5.27	13.2
Chile	37	2,003	3.74	10.1
Peru	33	2,455	1.89	5.7
Bolivia	[33]	2,644	2.93	(8.9)
Brazil	29	4,200	1.68	4.9

Sources: See appendix and text.

government revenues, revenues per capita, and revenues as a proportion of GDP in the major colonies in 1800. Government revenue estimates for mainland Spanish America are based on data in the Klein and TePaske compilations adjusted to eliminate double counting, funds carried over from previous years, deposits (to be returned later), transfers from other treasuries, and loans.[17] Bolivia is included by assuming its GDP per capita was equal to that of Peru. Comparable data for Cuba, but not for Brazil, are also available. The most commonly cited and earliest figure for Brazil is for 1805 and may understate revenues somewhat. Later figures for Brazil are available only for the years after 1808, when expenditures rose considerably as a result of the transfer of the Portuguese court from Lisbon to Rio de Janeiro. Data for other colonies are not available.

In absolute terms, Mexico with its large population and rich silver mines paid the most in taxes; in 1800 tax revenues amounted to $31 million, far larger than any other colony. In per capita terms, Mexico also paid more than any other colony but Cuba, followed by Chile, Argentina,[18] Bolivia, Peru, and Brazil. Variation in tax levels was considerable; in per capita terms, Mexico paid roughly three times as much as Brazil and Peru.[19]

The data in Table 1.5 show that no linear relationship existed between GDP per capita and tax revenues, either in per capita terms or as a percentage of GDP. Colonies with relatively productive economies could afford to pay a higher proportion of GDP in taxes; in poor colonies, the surplus available for taxation was much smaller. The data show, however, that the most heavily taxed colonies were neither the richest nor the poorest. The two most productive economies bore relatively light burdens. Cuba, with the highest per capita GDP, paid the highest per capita tax revenues, but this represented a smaller proportion of GDP than in much poorer colonies.[20] Argentina, with the second most productive economy of all, was the most lightly taxed of all the colonies in relation to GDP.

Table 1.5 actually understates the variation in tax burdens in the Spanish empire. That is because substantial portions of the taxes paid by the relatively poorer colonies of Bolivia and Mexico were exported each year to subsidize civil administration and defense in the richer colonies of Argentina and Cuba, respectively.

Though relative tax burdens were not well correlated with GDP per capita, it is reasonable to hypothesize that they were correlated with the size of the colonies' export sectors. To test this hypothesis, Table 1.6 reproduces the figures on per capita exports, tax revenues, and GDP. The data in this table show a strong correlation between tax revenues and the size of the export sector, but contrary to what one might expect, the correlation is negative. That is, the tax burden (taxes as a proportion of GDP) rises as the export sector shrinks in both relative and per capita terms. Successful exporters bore a smaller tax burden than colonies with smaller export sectors. This negative correlation is not perfect, but it is strong enough to compel explanation.

It is worth noting that the substantial variations in tax burdens registered in Table 1.6 occurred (except for Brazil) within a single political unit, the Spanish empire, in which tax policy, structure, and administration were theoretically governed by one sovereign authority and one set of rules. Tax rates and incidence, however, varied from one colony to the other. The Cuban treasury, for example, did not collect mining taxes or Indian tribute, major sources of tax revenues on the mainland, because there were no mines or (by the eighteenth century) Indians in Cuba. In Argentina, a portion of the Indian population survived, but mainly outside of Spanish control, so little tribute was collected

TABLE **1.6**

Exports, Revenues, and GDP per Capita, circa 1800 (in current dollars)

Colony	Exports per Capita	Exports as % GDP	Revenues per Capita	Revenues as % GDP	GDP per Capita
Cuba	18.35	20.4	5.51	6.1	90
Argentina	10.03	12.2	3.40	4.2	82
Mexico	2.11	5.2	5.27	13.2	40
Chile	1.63	4.4	3.74	10.1	37
Peru	2.31	7.0	1.89	5.7	33
Brazil	4.78	16.4	1.68	4.9	29

Source: See text.

in that colony either. Mining taxes passed through Buenos Aires from Potosí, but were not collected within the boundaries of modern Argentina. Most of the taxes collected in Mexico and the Andes came from sources other than export production and imports. By contrast, most of the taxes collected in Cuba, and probably Argentina as well, were levied on external trade.

This seemingly paradoxical result is explained by the much smaller foreign trade sectors of the Mexican and Peruvian economies. Had Spain taxed only exports and imports in Mexico or Peru, government revenues would have dropped precipitously. During the era of the Bourbon reforms, the Spanish authorities actually lowered taxes and other charges on silver production to boost output. At the same time, new taxes, fees, monopolies, and regulations to enforce them struck hard at most other nonagricultural activities.[21] In Mexico, exports grew but the economy stagnated. A similar process occurred in the Andes, where economic life was further disrupted by the massive revolts, linked to increases in taxation and other exactions, that erupted in the 1780s.

Taxpayers in Argentina and Cuba paid low to moderate taxes because the colonial government had virtually no sources of revenue that could be taxed outside of the export sector itself. As in Mexico and the Andes, the authorities recognized that higher taxes on exports would simply discourage the production of taxable exports. In all of its colonies, Spain raised import and excise (*alcabala*) tax rates in the late eighteenth century, hitting mainly urban entrepreneurs and consumers. However, without a subject Indian population to pay tribute and a sizable nonexport sector to tax, Spain could not do much more to raise the tax burden in Argentina and Cuba without diminishing the sources of the wealth it sought to tax.

The magnitude of colonial tax burdens probably mattered less than the debilitating regulatory regimes that enforced them. Legal impediments to productive activity and trade tended to vary with the number and weight of the taxes collected. Worse yet, these burdens were heaviest in the poorer colonies with the smallest export sectors. The sociology of this pattern is equally clear. Colonies with large indigenous populations paid more taxes not only because the Indians were subjected to a tax not levied on others (the head tax or *tributo*), but also because large indigenous populations raised the value to creoles and mestizos of the privileges and the protections guaranteed by Spanish colonial rule.

The achievement of independence in most of Latin America in the early 1820s created opportunities for political and institutional modernization. Most of these opportunities were squandered. Though caste systems were attenuated or legally abolished and external trade was freed from colonial fetters, most of

the countries in the region fell into internal civil strife and multiple international wars that lasted for decades. Insecurity tended to swamp the otherwise
positive effects of independence.

The weight of the colonial institutional legacy after independence proved to
be heaviest in those regions where pressures for modernization confronted
entrenched interests attached to caste systems and the regimes of privilege and
regulatory intrusiveness linked to them. In the mainland conquest colonies,
the creole population and even many mestizos had become enmeshed in a web
of corporate and caste privileges that tied them to the colonial regime and thus
facilitated the imposition of the most burdensome fiscal and regulatory systems in the empire. Even the indigenous population, which could be moved to
rebellion by new taxes and intrusive officials, paid the tribute and accepted
Spanish authority in exchange for minimal autonomy and protection of its
inalienable communal land titles. In Mexico, the conservatism of the Church
and the great creole magnates with their provincial allies delayed institutional
modernization for decades after independence. In Peru, protected from
change by geographic fragmentation, by the prolongation of a colonial com-
pact that traded social peace for indigenous autonomy, and by the resistance
of landed elites who controlled provincial governments, liberal modernization
failed to outlast the midcentury guano boom and remained a fragile and mostly foreign aspiration that seldom penetrated the sierra until late in the nineteenth century or even later.

Chile's attachment to managed trade (the basis of its successful wheat
exports to Lima in the eighteenth century) dissolved after independence, and
the discovery of rich copper ores just as prices skyrocketed with the onset of the
industrial revolution promoted economic recovery earlier than in most of the
rest of Latin America. Nothing was accomplished quickly or cheaply, of course,
but institutional modernization faced fewer obstacles there than almost anywhere else but Argentina.

Argentina suffered least. The struggles between Buenos Aires and the interior provinces over constitutional principles, tariffs, and tax revenues took
many years to resolve, but in most of the years between 1808 and 1865 the
country was actually at peace and its exports growing.[22] Moreover, the complex class, ethnic, and institutional issues that so intensified civil strife in
Mexico and the Andes, and later in Cuba and even Brazil, played virtually no
role in Argentina. Export-based economic growth began shortly after independence and took off with the unification of the country after 1865.

Cuba and Brazil enjoyed the benefits of peace during the tumultuous
decade of the independence struggles elsewhere. Cuba, of course, remained a

Spanish colony until 1898, a fate linked in part to the island's dependence on sugar exports produced by slave labor. Although the island's economy expanded in the first half of the nineteenth century, productivity appears to have stagnated, despite impressive efforts by planters and the Spanish government to modernize transportation and sugar milling. By midcentury, the Cuban economy had fallen far behind that of the industrializing United States and fell still further behind as a consequence of the civil strife over slavery and independence that struck the island in the Ten Years' War (1868–1878) and the subsequent renewal of the independence struggle (1895–1898). Brazil's peaceful achievement of independence helped to consolidate the country's commitment to a minimally productive slave-based export agriculture and to the inherited pattern of a simultaneously weak and highly centralized government. State and slavocracy collaborated, but neither had the resources, interest, or will to invest adequately in modernizing the colony's antiquated institutions and infrastructure.

In the second half of the nineteenth century, virtually every Latin American country carried out a series of similar (occasionally identical) reforms that eliminated or substantially reduced the most important of the institutional constraints inherited from the colonial era. In most cases, the process began with the elimination of state monopolies, Church and military *fueros* (exemptions from ordinary civil and criminal jurisdiction) and other privileges, a wide array of domestic taxes and fees, and archaic property rights (entail, ecclesiastical and indigenous mortmain, and slavery), and continued with the privatization of public lands, the enactment of new civil and commercial codes, and efforts to attract foreign capital and labor to the development of railroads and other public works as well as a wide range of productive activities. The timing and sequence of the reforms varied with the political fortunes of contending parties and factions in each country. In those that took longer, economic growth was delayed until later than elsewhere.

INEQUALITY

The distribution of legal and civil rights, assets such as landed wealth, income from wages and property, and human capital such as education or health, affects and is affected by the economic performance of nations. Latin America lagged behind the North Atlantic in equality of rights and in human capital formation throughout much of the modern era. On the other hand, the region does not appear to have become markedly more unequal in the distribution of assets or income than the developed world until the onset of economic growth at the end of the nineteenth century.

The caste and slave systems of the colonial era made inequality in legal and civil rights fundamental to the juridical structure of the two empires. Most individuals of indigenous or African descent were legally defined as inferior to Europeans and to people of mixed ancestry. In Mesoamerica and the Andes, indigenous people alone paid the hated *tributo*. They were excluded by law from high-status occupations and from holding important posts in government or the Church. They were also forbidden to bear arms or ride horses, needed the permission of both political and ecclesiastical authorities to move to another town, had to observe a legislated dress code, and suffered from numerous other restrictions and rules. At the same time, however, Spanish colonial rule provided for the election of indigenous political leaders at open village meetings and left most villages wide latitude to manage their own affairs. Spanish magistrates supervised and sometimes interfered, as did local priests, but in the complex local politics of colonial rule, indigenous leaders, customs, and resources were often decisive. The crown's interest lay in preserving the indigenous population and its economic base for taxation. The crown also sought to prevent indigenous labor and organizations from falling under the sway of colonial elites, the better to keep both groups dependent on Madrid and its agents.

Caste restrictions on physical and occupational mobility were removed by the Spanish Cortes in 1811, partly in response to the independence revolt in Mexico. Most of the new nations adopted constitutions that proclaimed equality of legal rights for citizens, but restricted the franchise in national elections, reimposed the *tributo* under various guises (usually as a head tax on all citizens), and allowed for the continuation of inalienable communal property holding and a large degree of political autonomy for indigenous communities.

Quantitative work on the distribution of wealth and income in colonial and nineteenth-century Latin America is scarce and fragmentary. In the predominantly rural economies of the region, landownership probably constituted the main asset of most wealth holders. Trends in the distribution of landownership can serve to illuminate trends in the distribution of wealth and income as a whole, at least until the urbanization and industrialization of the twentieth century.

Indigenous status allowed Indian villagers in the colonial era to invoke Spanish law and policy to defend communal lands from usurpation by outsiders. Isolation also helped; much of the land occupied by indigenous villages could not have been turned into profitable *haciendas*. Thus, in most of the mainland colonies, widespread indigenous landownership survived three centuries of Spanish rule. In many regions, such as southern Mexico, the Guatemalan highlands, and major portions of the Peruvian altiplano, indigenous communities and entrepreneurs owned most of the exploitable land until long after independence. Even in the areas adjacent to major towns and cities, where land values were highest, Indian landownership persisted. After independence, the economic decline and insecurity that accompanied independence in most countries reduced the profitability of the existing estates. Many were broken up into leaseholds, sold off in parcels to tenants, or simply abandoned. Images of vastly wealthy *patrones* lording it over armies of landless peons bear little resemblance to most of the Mesoamerican or Andean countryside until the onset of economic growth in the second half of the nineteenth century.

The liberal economic reforms that accompanied and sustained economic growth at the end of the nineteenth century facilitated and in some cases provided special incentives to encourage widespread assaults on peasant (and Church) landownership as well as the alienation of vast quantities of public lands to large, politically connected landowners. Liberal regimes everywhere made formerly inalienable village lands subject to private ownership and sale. Railroad construction often precipitated waves of privatization of landholding by linking hitherto isolated tracts of village or public lands to distant markets, thus increasing their potential value to powerful outsiders. Often, small holders sold their lands at attractive prices to outsiders who had better access to information and capital. The concentration of landholding was also facilitated by the region-wide trend toward more stable governments. Economic growth produced increases in revenues. Telegraphs and railroads helped governments to learn of trouble and suppress it more quickly. In many countries, elected local governments were suppressed in favor of appointed governors and mayors; elected local governments did not reappear throughout the region until the last decade of the twentieth century. The legal status of women actually deteriorated in the nineteenth century and did not recover until the second half of the twentieth century. Universal manhood suffrage in national elections did not reach Latin America until well into the twentieth century, beginning in Argentina in 1912 and moving in stages across less homogeneous ethnic terrain until even women, mostly after World War II, received the franchise.

In slave regions of Latin America, the slaves themselves were deprived of the right to their own labor. Their owners appropriated a portion of the returns to labor that would have been paid as wages had they been free. Thus, slave regions probably tended to be more unequal in the distribution of income than nonslave areas, and much more unequal than areas in which rural producers owned their own land. In the subset of countries where slavery predominated, both legal rights and wealth or income tended to be more equally distributed in less productive areas and eras. In boom periods, such as in Cuba in the early nineteenth century, high prices for slave-produced export commodities and relatively inelastic supplies of slave labor led to increases in work intensity and reductions in leisure time and in access to garden plots as well as the adoption of new, more draconian slave codes and assaults on the rights of freedmen intended to push them into plantation employment. Conditions in more backward Brazil in the colonial era seem to have varied considerably but are generally described as less dynamic and less polarized. Landownership, too, was historically more concentrated in Cuba than in backward Brazil.[23]

Between 1803 (Haiti) and 1888 (Brazil), every country and colony in the Western Hemisphere abolished slavery. Postemancipation societies varied dramatically in the extent to which former slaves received full civil rights and access to economic opportunity. In the earliest emancipations in Haiti, the remaining French islands, and the British colonies, emancipation dealt a severe blow to sugar plantation agriculture, which suggests that the distributional effects of ending slavery were relatively high. In Brazil and Cuba, the effects of emancipation on the distribution of wealth or income were probably smaller. These two late emancipators paid a price for their delay in economic growth foregone. In both cases, political regimes linked to slavery collapsed soon after emancipation; had these transitions occurred earlier, the Brazilian and Cuban economies might have begun growing earlier, rather than later than the rest of Latin America.

In Argentina, the concentration of landownership developed in cycles of "conquest"—military campaigns against indigenous nomads that culminated in the early 1880s. After each of the campaigns, large tracts of land became available to reward the participants and their friends or for sale at low prices to wealthy investors. Thus, the process of concentration in Argentina was linked directly to government policy and, unlike elsewhere, largely anticipated the late-nineteenth-century acceleration of economic growth. However, since land was relatively cheap in Argentina in relation to scarce supplies of labor, the early concentration of ownership appears to have had minimal impact on the distribution of wealth. Lyman Johnson found that the distribution of wealth in the province of Buenos Aires in the decades after independence was at least as egalitarian as in the nonslave regions of the United States in the same era.[24] Not until railroads, immigrants, and rapid economic growth spread throughout the pampas in the late nineteenth century did landownership provide the basis for a more unequal social order.

Throughout the Spanish and Portuguese empires, and in the nation states that succeeded them, the accumulation of human capital lagged behind the

North Atlantic. Since the colonial era, Latin America's public and private investment in education, public health, nutrition, and health-related infrastructure (e.g., potable water) has lagged far behind the North Atlantic at comparable levels of GDP per capita. Lack of human capital can retard economic growth, while pronounced inequality in human capital investment sharpens inequality in the distribution of income. Both of these effects appear to have had an impact on the economic performance of the Latin American economies, though possibly more in the twentieth century than earlier. Nearly every Latin American country has made serious efforts to catch up in human capital over the past 100 years, but convergence to the standards of the developed world has lagged because of past neglect, high rates of population growth, and the frequent breakdown of democratic regimes in this century.

The contradictory but positive and cumulative evolution of legal and civil rights in Latin America contrasts with the sharp increases in inequality of wealth and income that occurred as growth began in the late nineteenth century. Kuznets' suggestion that income or wealth inequality increases in the early stages of modernization seems amply confirmed by the history of land tenure patterns in much of Latin America, though Kuznets would also have predicted a countertendency back toward greater equality long before the region attained its current level of per capita GDP. The relative equality that characterized much of colonial and early-nineteenth-century Latin America did not promote rapid economic growth, though it did perhaps help to foster a kind of penny capitalism, that is, widespread participation in commercial activity even among slaves and indigenous groups. At least in the countryside, the distribution of wealth seems not to have been unusually skewed until after economic growth began.

Inequality of rights and civil status, inherited from the colonial era, persisted into the postindependence era, especially in the case of slaves. Though abolition finally brought legal equality, civil rights like the franchise and access to government generally took much longer to attain. Long periods of authoritarian rule in most countries persisted until the 1980s. These difficulties may help to explain the debilitating failure of governments in Latin America to invest adequately in human capital and physical infrastructure.

CONCLUSIONS

For most of two crucial centuries, from the early 1700s to the late 1800s, virtually all of the Latin American economies stagnated. Since sustained growth was occurring at the same time in the United States and parts of western Europe, Latin America fell behind. Physical and institutional barriers blocked growth throughout the region, though some colonies, like Argentina and Cuba, managed to reach comparatively high levels of productivity before stagnation set in.

Beginning in the last quarter of the nineteenth century, railroads, steamships, and eventually motor vehicles (and future *hidrovías*) helped the Latin American economies overcome the physical barriers to improved productivity. The sweeping institutional changes that began at the same time removed old obstacles and created new incentives for productivity advance. These changes moved the Latin American economies onto new trajectories. On average, the Latin American economies in the twentieth century have grown as fast as the economy of the United States, but more slowly than the more dynamic economies of Europe and Asia.[25]

Abrupt increases in inequality, particularly in landownership, appear to have accompanied Latin America's transition to economic growth in the late nineteenth and early twentieth centuries. The region's historic neglect of human capital was reinforced by the relatively low cost of importing technology and technicians (as opposed to producing it or training them) from other countries. Eventually, economic growth allowed for higher wages, physical welfare improved, and schools and clinics were built, but (with the exception of Argentina, Costa Rica, and Uruguay—the most ethnically homogenous of the former Spanish colonies) much more slowly than in other world regions.

Persistent inequality has had a doubly negative effect on economic growth in twentieth-century Latin America. The direct effects include the reduced productivity of perhaps a third of the contemporary Latin American workforce due to malnutrition, illness, and lack of education. The indirect effects include the substantially higher risks of political and social upheaval that have discouraged investment and further dampened growth.

Appendix

Quantitative data on the colonial economies of Spain and Portugal, often fragmentary and unreliable, were collected with greater consistency and care as the eighteenth century advanced. Nonetheless, estimates of aggregate economic performance even for the late colonial economies are inevitably subject to fairly wide margins of error.

Estimates of GDP in the late colonial era are available for Cuba and Mexico and for Peru in the 1820s. Still cruder approximations can be constructed for Argentina, Brazil, and Chile. The figures are reported in Table 1.1. With two exceptions, the population figures and GDP estimates refer to regions that corresponded to the national territories of the independent states established later. The exceptions are Argentina, where the estimate excludes the Chaco, Misiones, and the areas of the pampas and Patagonia outside European control, and Chile, where it omits the population and economic activity beyond the Araucanian frontier in the south.

In the case of Mexico, Cuba, and Peru, the figures in the table correspond to direct estimates of GDP at some point in the late eighteenth or early nineteenth century. Mexico's GDP per capita in 1800 stood at about 40 pesos, according to various estimates, while that of Peru was probably somewhat lower.[26]

Fraile Balbín and the Salvuccis put Cuba's GDP per capita at 66 pesos in 1690, 90 pesos in 1750, and 98 pesos by the mid-nineteenth century. Choosing the lower of the latter two figures for circa 1800 still places Cuba's GDP per capita above the United States in that year. Cuba's ranking here is consistent with that of the other Caribbean export economies. Estimates of GDP per capita for the Caribbean sugar islands of Britain and France are actually higher than for the United States in the late eighteenth century.[27]

The Argentine and Chilean figures are based on more fragmentary evidence. In both cases, the GDP figures in the table are really income estimates based on extrapolations from wage data. In the case of Argentina, Lyman Johnson's Buenos Aires study cites an average monthly wage of 17 pesos or 204 pesos per year for urban unskilled construction laborers in the first decade of the nineteenth century,[28] while various sources put rural wage levels at 6 pesos per month plus food rations, for a total of 76.5 pesos per year.[29] This implies a per capita income of roughly 94 pesos for the province of Buenos Aires; using the same wage rates for the remaining provinces brings down the colonywide per capita income to 82 pesos.[30]

I am not aware of any comparable work on urban wages in late colonial Chile, though fragmentary data suggest urban unskilled wage levels at about two reales (0.25 pesos) or so per day.[31] Using Bairoch's empirical observation that a rough measure of income per capita may be derived by multiplying the urban unskilled daily wage rate by 200 puts Chile at 50 pesos.[32] Using the same ratio for other colonies, however, yields figures substantially above known levels. Bairoch's ratio and the Mexico City wage rate of 0.375 pesos, for example, yield a per capita income of 75 pesos, well above the accepted figure of 40 pesos. Buenos Aires wage data yield an estimate of 142 pesos for Argentina, far above the more cautious estimate in the table.[33] The Chilean figure in the table is reduced by 25% to correct for the upward bias in the Bairoch method.

Finally, the estimate for Brazil in Table 1.1 is based on extrapolating Leff's estimates of nineteenth-century growth rates back to 1800.[34] The result may be too low; applying the ratio of U.S. to Brazilian GDP per capita estimated by Maddison for 1820 would yield an 1800 estimate of $38 in current dollars (versus the $29 accepted here).[35]

The estimates of GDP per capita in Table 1.1 are not intended to do more than establish rough orders of magnitude. All of the estimates in the table are subject to substantial error margins, even the Mexican figure, which is based on considerable research and has survived much scrutiny. Even if the precise numbers are fragile, however, the ranking among the colonies seems relatively robust. Argentina and Cuba probably had the most productive economies, with the remaining mainland colonies well behind.

Bolivia is omitted from Table 1.1 for lack of data, but would probably rank toward the bottom, probably below Peru. The sharp decline in silver output in Potosí in the 1790s coupled with scattered evidence on the decline of manufacturing and persistently low levels of productivity in agriculture suggest that the Bolivian economy lagged behind most others in the colonial era.

The population estimates in Table 1.1 are taken from a variety of sources cited in the table.[36]

The trade data in Table 1.2 are subject to smaller error margins than the GDP estimates. For Argentina, the figure in the table refers to the year 1796 and is based on Cortes Conde and Moutoukias.[37] This was the peak year for exports via Buenos Aires until after independence. Total exports amounted to $5.5 million, but have been reduced to eliminate public exports of silver (net tax revenues) from Bolivia. This adjustment was made by assuming half of all silver exports from Buenos Aires consisted of public revenues that should not count as exports. Also omitted from the estimate in the table are Argentine exports to Bolivia. For Brazil, exports to Portugal are taken from Alden's work.[38] Alden's figure for 1800 is raised 10% to account for smuggling and converted to pesos at $1.363 to the milreis. For Chile, the export figure in the table is the average for 1790–1799 from Carmagnani.[39]

For Cuba, the figure in Table 1.2 may be a bit low. Guerra y Sánchez puts exports in 1794 at "more than five million," while Marrero cites figures for 1805 to 1807 that range from $5.1 to $8.1 million.[40] For Mexico, the figure in the table is the average for exports from Veracruz during the years 1796 to 1805; the figures were collected by *consulado* officials at the time and reproduced in a report by Lerdo de Tejada, first published in 1853.[41] I have added 20% to the Veracruz figures to take account of exports from other ports. For Peru, the export figure takes peak silver production of 637,000 marks in 1799, assumes that half of this total was exported (as was the case in New Spain), and uses the 1791–1794 ratio of silver exports to total exports (85%) to reach the figure in the table.[42]

Notes

1. For the Latin American data, see Table 1.1. The U.S. figures are from Atack and Passell (1994, p. 4).
2. See appendix.
3. Between 1800 and 1860, Mexican GDP per capita declined by nearly 30% (Coatsworth 1990a, chap. 5).
4. Maddison (1994), p. 23.
5. World Bank (1997), Table 1.
6. Lockhart (1991), p. 103.
7. Exceptions there were, such as the missionary efforts of the various regular orders in remote locations, but these were often displaced (sometimes violently) upon the discovery of opportunities for private gain.
8. Plausible estimates have ranged from 8.4 to 112 million. See Newson (1985) for a survey.
9. Slave prices in Cuba for most of the eighteenth century were two to three times as high as in Jamaica and the other English islands. See Eltis (1987), pp. 35, 40.
10. Schwartz (1985), chap. 7.
11. Even after the Spanish crown relaxed restrictions on importing slaves in the late 1760s, unsettled international conditions drove prices back up. This was especially evident in periods of international war. Slave prices skyrocketed during the conflict that accompanied the U.S. War for Independence (1776–1783) and again

during the wars of the French Revolution and Napoleon (1796–1815).

12. Sánchez Albornoz (1989), p. 89. Between 1853 and 1874, 124,000 Chinese coolies entered Cuba, while 87,000 went to Peru between 1859 and 1874.

13. On the output of Mexico's mining industry, which rose at an annual average rate of 0.7% between 1775/79 and 1805/09, see Coatsworth (1990a, chap. 4). The rate of increase in silver production at Potosí slowed considerably after 1791 and fell sharply in the first decade of the nineteenth century, according to Tandeter (1993, p. 116).

14. In addition to Cuba, see Eltis (1995, pp. 328–330) on Barbados. Exports amounted to one-third of Barbados's total product in the mid-1660s.

15. The creation of the viceroyalty and the "free" trade decree that followed in 1778 also affected the interior provinces that supplied Potosí and the rest of Upper Peru with a variety of products, including mules, sugar, wine, and yerba mate. Although it legalized and facilitated this commerce, increasing imports of manufactured goods through Buenos Aires adversely affected some local industries in the northwest. For a recent revisionist view on this question, see Amaral (1990).

16. See Coatsworth (1990a), chap. 5.

17. See Klein and TePaske (1982, 1986). In one case, that of the *caja* of Lima, revenues from the excise tax, or *alcabala*, were reported as coming from *otras tesorerías*, a line item amounting to $1.7 million that probably included surplus tax revenues shipped in from other *cajas*. To avoid underestimating revenue, this sum was included in the Peruvian data, though it introduces a small upward bias in the estimates in Table 1.5.

18. The Argentine figure in the table requires some explanation, since accounting procedures in the Buenos Aires *caja* make it especially difficult to use the Klein and TePaske data. Aside from distinguishing internal and external transfers from actual revenue, the main problem is that the receipts of the Buenos Aires customs house and from the collection of the *alcabala* are lumped together with tax revenues from Potosí in the account labeled *otras tesorerías* (a practice that began in early 1780s). In 1800, the year represented here, the total reported received from *otras tesorerías* exceeded $2.4 million. The figure in the table assumes that approximately $200,000 represented *alcabala* and customs revenues originating in Buenos Aires. Though consistent with earlier years, this figure may be too low. On interpreting the Buenos Aires data, see Amaral (1984, pp. 287–295) and the comments by Javier Esteban Cuenca, John J. TePaske, Herbert S. Klein, J. R. Fisher, and Tulio Halperín-Donghi that follow.

19. An additional case for which such estimates have been constructed is Ecuador. Andrien (1994, p. 178) has estimated that per capita tax burdens in the late eighteenth century ranged from less than half a peso in the relatively backward high-

land district of Cuenca to six pesos per capita in the port of Guayaquil; in Quito, the burden amounted to $1.62. Given their relative populations, the average for the entire colony was probably closer to the Quito figure than to that of Guayaquil.

20. The revenue estimate in the table is the average for 1795–1800 (annual figures are not reported) in Marrero (1985, vol. 4, p. 323).

21. Nonagricultural, because throughout the Spanish colonies and Brazil, taxes on land did not exist or went largely uncollected and the tithe, a tax on agricultural output, went mainly to the Church.

22. Newland (n.d.) estimates that Argentine exports grew at an annual average rate of 5.5% per year (3.0% per capita) between 1811 and 1870.

23. See Schwartz (1985), chaps. 11 and 16.

24. See Johnson (1994), pp. 197–214.

25. See Maddison (1994), Appendix D.

26. For Mexico, see Coatsworth (1990a, chap. 3). For Peru, see Gootenberg's rough calculation for the late 1820s (1985, p. 53n).

27. For Cuba, see Fraile Balbín and the Salvuccis (1993, part II, chap. 3). The productivity advantage of the Caribbean sugar islands had its origins in the seventeenth century and persisted until the abolition of slavery in Haiti in 1803 and in the British empire in 1832. For a recent discussion, see David Eltis, "The Total Product of Barbados," pp. 321–338. U.S. per capita GDP in 1800 was roughly $80. The Spanish American peso and the U.S. dollar exchanged at roughly 1:1 in this era.

28. Johnson (1990), pp. 137–172.

29. See, for example, Brown (1979), pp. 43, 164 and Chiaramonte (1991), pp. 108–112.

30. For the predominantly urban population of Buenos Aires province, this figure multiplies the urban wage rate ($204) times the Buenos Aires urban labor force of 25,600 (assumed to be 64% of the Buenos Aires population of 40,000) and applies the rural wage rate ($76.50) to the rural labor force of 32,168 (64% of the remaining population of 50,262). According to Maeder's account (1969, chap. 1), roughly a third of the total Argentine population (including the province of Buenos Aires) lived in towns and urban areas. Again assuming a labor force participation rate of 64% for both rural and urban populations, the same wage rates yield a per capita income estimate of $81.50. This colonywide estimate excludes the Chaco, Misiones, and the areas of the pampas and Patagonia outside European control. The per capita income of the colony without Buenos Aires province comes to $69.

31. Vicuña MacKenna (1938, vol. 2, 228n) cites a 1792 Santiago construction proposal in which peons' wages are calculated as two reales per day, comparable with

Guadalajara at the same time. The Santiago proposal is likely to have understated wages and other costs.

32. Bairoch (1977); a summary with additional data is in Bairoch (1993, chap. 8).

33. Van Young's study of wages (1987) in late colonial Mexico cites wages for unskilled construction workers in 1794–1804 of two to two and a half reales per day (0.25 to 0.31 pesos) in Guadalajara and three reales (0.375 pesos) per day in Mexico City. Living costs are likely to have been higher in Mexico (though not in Santiago) than in Buenos Aires, but not so much as to eliminate a wage gap of the magnitude suggested by these data.

34. For Brazil, the estimate is based on Leff's "most likely" estimate of Brazilian growth between 1822 and 1913 (1982, vol. 1, appendix). Leff's estimate is converted to current pesos using the Warren-Pearson and Bureau of Labor Statistics Wholesale Price Indexes to deflate from 1950 dollars. It is likely that Brazil's GNP grew slowly if at all between 1800 and 1822. The price indexes are in U.S. Bureau of the Census (1958, pp. 115–117).

35. See Maddison (1994), Table 1-3.

36. For Argentina, see Maeder (1969, pp. 22–23); for Brazil, see Graham and Merrick (1979, pp. 26–30), but note that Alden (1987, p. 287) accepts a much lower (though admittedly undercounted) total of only 2.1 million; for Chile, see Mamalakis (1978, vol. 2, p. 9); for Mexico, see Coatsworth (1990a, p. 46); for Peru, see Gootenberg (1991, pp. 109–157).

37. Cortes Conde (1985), Table 1, p. 359, and Moutoukias (1992).

38. Alden (1997), p. 335.

39. Carmagnani (1973), pp. 59, 76, 96.

40. See Guerra y Sánchez (1964), p. 197; Marrero (1985), p. 72.

41. Lerdo de Tejada (1967, no pagination).

42. See Fisher (1986), pp. 49–55.

REFERENCES

Adelman, Jeremy. "Republic of Capital: Buenos Aires and the Legal Transformation of the Atlantic World." Unpublished book manuscript, 1997.

Alden, Dauril. "Late Colonial Brazil, 1750–1808." In Colonial Brazil, edited by Leslie Bethel, 284–343. Cambridge: Cambridge University Press, 1987.

Amaral, Samuel. "Comercio libre y economías regionales: San Juan y Mendoza, 1780–1820." Jahrbuch fur Geschichte von Staat, Wirtschaft und Gesellschaft Lateinamerikas, 7 (1990): 1–67.

Amaral, Samuel. "Public Expenditure Financing in the Colonial Treasury: An Analysis of the Real Caja de Buenos Aires Accounts, 1789–91." *Hispanic American Historical Review* 64, no. 2. (May 1984): 287–295.

Andrien, Kenneth. "The State and Dependency in Late Colonial and Early Republican Ecuador." In *The Political Economy of Spanish America in the Age of Revolution, 1750–1850,* edited by Kenneth Andrien and Lyman L. Johnson. Albuquerque: University of New Mexico Press, 1994.

Atack, Jeremy, and Peter Passell. *A New Economic View of American History from Colonial Times to 1940.* 2nd ed. New York: W. W. Norton, 1994.

Bairoch, Paul. "Estimations du revenu national dans les sociétés occidentales pré-industrielles et au XIXe siècle." *Revue Économique* 28, no. 2 (1977): 177–208.

Bairoch, Paul. *Economics and World History: Myths and Paradoxes.* New York: Harvester Wheatsheaf, 1993.

Brading, David A. *Miners and Merchants in Bourbon Mexico: 1763–1810.* Cambridge: Cambridge University Press, 1971.

Brown, Jonathan C. *A Socioeconomic History of Argentina, 1776–1860.* Cambridge: Cambridge University Press, 1979.

Bulmer-Thomas, Victor. *The Economic History of Latin America Since Independence.* Cambridge: Cambridge University Press, 1994.

Cardoso, Fernando Henrique, and Enzo Faletto. *Dependency and Development in Latin America.* Berkeley: University of California Press, 1979.

Carmagnani, Marcelo. *Les mécanismes de la vie économique dans une société coloniale: Le Chili (1680–1830).* Paris: S.E.V.P.E.N., 1973.

Chiaramonte, José Carlos. *Mercaderes del Litoral: economía y sociedad en la provincia de Corrientes, primera mitad del siglo xix.* Mexico: Fondo de Cultura Económica, 1991.

Coatsworth, John H. "The Limits of Colonial Absolutism: Mexico in the Eighteenth Century." In *Essays in the Political, Economic and Social History of Colonial Latin America,* edited by Karen Spalding, 25–51. Newark, Delaware: University of Delaware, Latin American Studies Program, Occasional Papers and Monographs no. 3., 1982.

Coatsworth, John H. *Los orígenes del atraso: siete ensayos de historia económica de México en los siglos XVIII y XIX.* Mexico: Alianza Editorial Mexicana, 1990a.

Coatsworth, John H. "Economic History and the History of Prices in Colonial Latin America." In *Essays on the Price History of Eighteenth-Century Latin America,* edited by Lyman L. Johnson and Enrique Tandeter, 21–34. Albuquerque: University of New Mexico Press, 1990b.

Cortes Conde, Roberto. "The Export Economy of Argentina, 1880–1920." In *The Latin American Economies: Growth and the Export Sector 1880–1930,* edited by Roberto

Cortes Conde and Shane J. Hunt, 319–381. New York: Holmes and Meier, 1985.

Eltis, David. *Economic Growth and the Ending of the Transatlantic Slave Trade.* New York: Oxford University Press, 1987.

Eltis, David. "The Total Product of Barbados, 1664–1701." *Journal of Economic History* 55, no. 2 (1995): 321–338.

Engerman, Stanley L., and Kenneth L. Sokoloff. "Factor Endowments, Institutions, and Differential Paths of Growth among New World Economies." In *How Latin America Fell Behind: Essays on the Economic History of Brazil and Mexico, 1800–1914,* edited by Stephen Haber, 260–304. Stanford: Stanford University Press, 1997.

Fisher, John. "Mining and the Peruvian Economy in the Late Colonial Period." In *The Economies of Mexico and Peru During the Late Colonial Period, 1760–1810,* edited by Nils Jacobsen and Hans-Jürgen Puhle, 46–60. Berlin: Colloquium Verlag, 1986.

Fraile Balbín, Pedro, Richard J. Salvucci, and Linda K. Salvucci. "El caso cubano: exportación e independencia." In *La independencia americana: consecuencias económicas,* edited by Leandro Prados de la Escosura and Samuel Amaral, 80–101. Madrid: Alianza Universidad, 1993.

Gootenberg, Paul. "Merchants, Foreigners and the State: The Origins of Trade Policies in Post-Independence Peru." Ph.D. dissertation, The University of Chicago, 1985.

Gootenberg, Paul. "Population and Ethnicity in Early Republican Peru: Some Revisions." *Latin American Research Review* 26, no. 3 (1991): 109–157.

Graham, Douglas H., and Thomas W. Merrick. *Population and Economic Development in Brazil: 1800 to the Present.* Baltimore: Johns Hopkins University Press, 1979.

Guerra y Sánchez, Ramiro. *Manuel de historia de Cuba (económica, social y política).* Havana: Editorial Nacional de Cuba, 1964.

Johnson, Lyman. "The Distribution of Wealth in Nineteenth-Century Buenos Aires Province: The Issue of Social Justice in a Changing Economy." In *The Political Economy of Spanish America in the Age of Revolution, 1750–1850,* edited by Kenneth J. Andrien and Lyman L. Johnson, 197–214. Albuquerque: University of New Mexico Press, 1994.

Johnson, Lyman. "The Price History of Buenos Aires During the Viceregal Period." In *Essays on the Price History of Eighteenth-Century Latin America,* edited by Lyman L. Johnson and Enrique Tandeter, 137–172. Albuquerque: University of New Mexico Press, 1990.

Klein, Herbert S., and John J. TePaske. *The Royal Treasuries of the Spanish Empire in America.* 3 vols. Durham, NC: Duke University Press, 1982.

Klein, Herbert S., and John J. TePaske. *Ingresos y egresos de la Real Hacienda de Nueva España.* 2 vols. Mexico: Instituto Nacional de Antropología e Historia: Colección Fuentes, 1986.

Lang, James. *Portuguese Brazil: The King's Plantation.* New York: Academic Press, 1979.

Larson, Brook. "The Cotton Textile Industry of Cochabamba, 1770–1810: The Opportunities and Limits of Growth." In *The Economies of Mexico and Peru During the Late Colonial Period, 1760–1810,* edited by Nils Jacobsen and Hans-Jürgen Puhle, 150–168. Berlin: Colloquium Verlag, 1986.

Leff, Nathaniel. *Underdevelopment and Development in Brazil.* 2 vols. London: Allen and Unwin, 1982.

Lerdo de Tejada, Miguel. *Comercio exterior de México desde la Conquista hasta hoy.* Mexico: Banco Nacional de Comercio Exterior, 1967.

Lockhart, James. "Trunk Lines and Feeder Lines: The Spanish Reaction to American Resources." In *Transatlantic Encounters: Europeans and Andeans in the Sixteenth Century,* edited by Kenneth J. Andrien and Rolena Adorno, 90–120. Berkeley: University of California Press, 1991.

Maddison, Angus. "Explaining the Economic Performance of Nations, 1820–1989." In *Convergence of Productivity: Cross-National Studies and Historical Evidence,* edited by William Baumol, Richard Nelson, and Edward Wolff, 20–61. Oxford: Oxford University Press, 1994.

Maeder, Ernesto. *Evolución demográfica argentina de 1810 a 1869.* Buenos Aires: Editorial Universitaria de Buenos Aires, 1969.

Mamalakis, Marcos, ed. *Historical Statistics of Chile.* 2 vols. Westport, CT: Greenwood Press, 1978.

Marrero, Levi. *Cuba: economía y sociedad.* Vol. 4, *Azucar, ilustración y conciencia (1763–1868).* Madrid: Playor, 1985.

Maxwell, Kenneth. *Pombal: Paradox of the Enlightenment* . Cambridge: Cambridge University Press, 1995.

Moutoukias, Zacarías. "Crecimiento económico y política imperial: El patriciado colonial de Buenos Aires, 1760–1796." Unpublished paper, 1992.

Newland, Carlos. "Exports and Terms of Trade in Argentina, 1811–1870." Unpublished paper, n.d.

Newson, Linda A. "Indian Population Patterns in Colonial Spanish America." *Latin American Research Review* 20, no. 3 (1985): 41–74.

Sánchez Albornoz, Nicolás. "Population." In *Latin America: Economy and Society, 1870–1930,* edited by Leslie Bethel, 83–148. Cambridge: Cambridge University Press, 1989.

Schwartz, Stuart B. *Sugar Plantations in the Formation of Brazilian Society, 1550–1835.* Cambridge: Cambridge University Press, 1985.

Tandeter, Enrique. *Coercion and Market: Silver Mining in Colonial Potosí, 1692–1826.* Albuquerque: University of New Mexico Press, 1993.

U.S. Bureau of the Census. *Historical Statistics of the United States from Colonial Times to 1957.* Washington, DC: Government Printing Office, 1958.

Van Young, Eric. "The Rich Get Richer and the Poor Get Skewed: Real Wages and Popular Living Standards in Late Colonial Mexico." Unpublished paper, 1987.

Vicuña MacKenna, Benjamín. *Obras completas.* Vol. 11, *Historia de Santiago.* Santiago: Dirección General de Prisiones, 1938.

World Bank. *The State in a Changing World: World Bank Development Report 1997.* Oxford: Oxford University Press, 1997.

2

Property Rights and Land Conflict: A Comparison of Settlement of the U.S. Western and Brazilian Amazon Frontiers

Lee J. Alston
University of Illinois and NBER
Gary D. Libecap
University of Arizona and NBER
Bernardo Mueller
University of Brasilia

Much of economic history has involved migration to and settlement of new lands. An important aspect of this process is the assignment of property rights to land. The nature of this allocation of land, the dominant form of wealth in an agrarian society, critically affects the structure and functioning of the overall economy. If rights to land are secure, investment and trade can occur to promote the expansion of economic activity and wealth. Further, the allocation and enforcement of rights to land set precedents for granting property rights to other assets and establish expectations for the development of private markets in other areas of the economy. Moreover, landownership determines the distribution of wealth and income, and hence the identity of the principal economic and political actors in the society.

In the United States, probably no other factor of production was as important for the early development of a market-based economy than the complete, secure, and rapid assignment of private property rights to land.[1] Beginning with the Land Ordinance of 1785, and increasingly so in the nineteenth century, a major objective of U.S. land policy was to assign title to private claimants as quickly as possible. Given the absence of economies of scale in most of northern agriculture, the ultimate distribution of land in the Midwest was relatively egalitarian.[2] Frontier settlement from the Atlantic seaboard westward proceeded sequentially and relatively peacefully, with little evidence of serious conflicts among migrants over rights to land.[3]

This smooth allocation of land, however, began to break down as the frontier moved to the more arid regions west of the 100th meridian in the early 1880s. In those areas, small farmers, who planned to stake claims to 160 acres as allowed by the Homestead Act of 1862 and similar land laws, found much of the land occupied by ranchers, who informally claimed large areas, often 5,000 acres or more. Until 1891, when the federal government halted cash sales of public domain, ranchers could purchase land at $1.25 per acre, but except for areas that had access to water, the price set by the government exceeded the expected returns. Nevertheless, the land had value to ranchers, as it did to many homesteaders, who could acquire formal title to land by occupation and improvement of the land. The result was that the informal property claims of ranchers conflicted with the formal (legal) claims of homesteaders. Without consistent government enforcement of either the informal rights of ranchers (recognizing the customs of the region) or the formal rights of homesteaders (enforcing allocations under the land laws), limited conflicts between the two ensued.

A similar, although later, frontier settlement process has occurred in the Brazilian Amazon. Individuals have migrated to the region and staked claims to government land (*terra devoluta*) through purchase, government colonization projects, or occupancy and improvement (squatting). In all three cases, title is transferred to private claimants once they have satisfied the requirements of the land laws. For example, squatters can obtain title to up to 100 hectares of government land if they occupy and improve the land for at least a year. Conflict, however, has occurred between large farmers, some with 5,000 hectares or more, and squatters who have invaded their land. Squatters occupy titled land when it appears not to be placed in production. As we describe below, the Brazilian Constitution authorizes such invasions whenever land is not in "beneficial use." Naturally, landowners often attempt to evict squatters. The violence accompanying some of the conflicts over property rights to land in the Amazon have attracted considerable international attention.[4]

The conflicts over frontier land in North and South America are similar in that both involve the settlement of squatters (homesteaders) on large tracts of land claimed by others. In the United States and Brazil, the federal government did not enforce the property rights of the large claimants. In the case of the United States, the large claims were locally based and not recognized by the federal government; in the case of Brazil, the large claims are often titled, but not enforced by the federal government because of a lack of beneficial use.

In this paper, we examine the sources of disputes over land on these two frontiers and analyze why there were comparatively fewer conflicts in the United States. Economists are interested in conflict over property rights for several reasons.[5] One is that secure property rights generally are accepted as essential for promoting investment, raising land values, and encouraging economic growth.[6] Conflict over land weakens or delays the assignment of property rights. A second reason is that conflict leads to dissipation of rents as the conflicting parties devote valuable inputs to offensive and defensive activities.[7] Finally, deaths, as the most extreme manifestation of violent conflict, represent an important loss in welfare. For these reasons it is worthwhile examining the sources of conflict over land on these two historical and contemporary frontiers in North and South America.

AN ANALYTICAL FRAMEWORK FOR UNDERSTANDING LAND CONFLICTS ON FRONTIERS

The specified formal property rights to land include the right to use the land (*usus*), the right to appropriate the returns from use and investment (*usus fructus*), the right to sell or otherwise transfer the land, the right to pass the land to heirs, and the right to transform the land in the process of production (*abusus*).[8] Enforcement involves ensuring that these rights are respected by other claimants.

Specification and enforcement can occur privately and, indeed, often do so in the early stages of frontier settlement when land values are low and competition for control is limited. Under those circumstances private, informal arrangements for defining and enforcing rights cost less than formal specification and enforcement. As land values rise with settlement, competition among claimants with informal rights leads to rent dissipation.[9] When competition reaches some threshold level, governments have lower costs of enforcing property rights and their intervention to enforce existing claims reduces competition for control and rent dissipation.[10]

In this paper, we argue that the basis for violent conflict on both North and South American frontiers was an inconsistency in government enforcement of property rights to land. In the United States, the specification of property rights to land was clear. Both ranchers and homesteaders expected to use, invest in, and sell land. Because ranchers opted not to purchase and thereby receive title to all the land that they claimed, their property rights were informal and had to be enforced privately. As long as no outside parties contested these claims, the government did not interfere. The federal government, however, did not formally recognize the informal claims of ranchers, as it did earlier, for example, for miners with the Mining Law of 1872. The potential for conflict arose when homesteaders, following the provisions of the Homestead Act, attempted to settle on the informal claims of the ranchers.

The General Land Office (GLO) was the government agency charged with the administration of the land laws, and the agency's budget and staffing depended on fulfilling this mission.[11] Because the large claims of ranchers exceeded the provisions of the land laws, the GLO could be expected to intervene to assist homesteaders in staking homestead claims to ranch land. Homesteaders required such assistance because of the superior capability of ranchers and their organized grazing associations to evict individual homesteaders.

The ability of homesteaders to enlist the support of the GLO, however, depended on their organization and relative political influence. The agency neither enforced the local land claims of ranchers nor intervened on the behalf of homesteaders to remove the fences and other means by which ranchers enforced their holdings.[12] The lack of general GLO intervention on behalf of homesteaders, although lamented by them, appears to be a major reason why there was comparatively less violent conflict over lands in the Far West than occurs today in Brazil. Because homesteaders did not expect the GLO to routinely back their claims, even though their claims were legally authorized, homesteaders tended to avoid the lands informally claimed by ranchers. Other than a few sporadic incidences of violence, the western U.S. frontier appears to have been characterized by much less conflict than currently is found in Brazil.

In Brazil, there has been more violence for two related reasons: First, there has been inconsistent political support for land-reform policies, so that neither titleholders nor squatters can be certain that their claims will be backed by the government. This uncertainty encourages conflict. Second, violence is used strategically by squatters as a means of forcing government action on land reform. Expectation of government support in turn encourages invasion by squatters and resistance to rancher eviction.

The specification of rights is quite clear in Brazil. That is, titleholders under statutory law expect to be able to use the land, invest in it, sell or pass it to heirs, and to modify it for production. Enforcement of property rights to land, however, is another matter. Government enforcement of private rights to land is conditional on a constitutional provision that requires land to be kept in production. This populist provision of the constitution is designed to facilitate land reform by distributing *unused* land. In theory, landless peasants should register as beneficiaries of land reform and wait their turn to be settled.

However, in practice, squatters invade private lands to expedite land reform.

Squatters eventually can obtain title through adverse possession if they occupy and develop their holdings for approximately five years. Beneficial use is a vague criterion. A generally understood, but unwritten, violation is that land left in natural forest is not productive. Accordingly, large farms where much of the land remains forested are most likely not to comply with the beneficial use requirement and, hence, to be subject to invasion by squatters. Naturally, conflicts arise. The courts, in applying statutory law to land conflicts, tend to uphold the right of titleholders, but the federal land reform agency, INCRA (the National Institute for Colonization and Agrarian Reform), uses the beneficial use clause as its mandate for expropriation of titled land on behalf of squatters.

Even so, INCRA has not always enforced the land claims of squatters. Squatters must organize and lobby the agency to intervene, but the agency's response depends on competing demands, its budget, and the political influence of the farmer whose land is being invaded. The resulting uncertainty affects both titleholders and squatters and how they respond to the invasion.[13] If the owner is confident that INCRA will intervene, he will seek a formal court injunction as part of a negotiating strategy with INCRA. Alternatively, he may acquiesce to the invasion and negotiate the best possible compensation from INCRA. Similarly, if squatters are confident of INCRA's support, they will occupy the land with less concern about the farmer's reaction.

A symmetric case is when both titleholders and squatters are confident that INCRA will *not* intervene. Large farmers in Brazil have an advantage in the use of force relative to individual squatters. Upon invasion, they can intimidate squatters and demand that they evacuate the site, often with the use of private police (*pistoleiros*). If that action proves ineffective, they can obtain a court order for eviction and enlist the local police to carry out the order. In either case, squatters are likely to leave voluntarily because of the certainty of the use of force if they do not comply.

Uncertainty as to INCRA's response creates confusion for both owners and squatters and creates the environment for violent conflict. Squatters may invade and resist eviction if they mistakenly believe INCRA will support them, and farmers may resort more forcefully to an eviction if they mistakenly believe that INCRA will not intervene. Changing budgets and political conditions affect INCRA's position. Recently, squatters have become more organized to increase their influence on the agency.

Notice that on both frontiers conflicts were between dissimilar claimants—between ranchers and homesteaders and large titleholders and squatters—

rather than among ranchers or among titleholders. Where the land claimants were relatively homogeneous, the net returns to establishing informal mechanisms for defining and enforcing rights were high enough to foster agreement on cooperative action. In the United States, cattlemen's associations were formed to allocate range land. Among homesteaders and other small claimants, claims clubs were organized.[14] In Brazil, large farmers organized to obtain government enforcement of their rights through the Rural Democratic Union (UDR), and squatters organized through the Landless Peasant Movement (MST), to pressure INCRA to move on expropriations.[15]

THE SPECIFICATION AND ENFORCEMENT
OF PROPERTY RIGHTS TO LAND IN THE U.S. WEST

The disposal of the public domain was one of the leading issues confronting the federal government in the nineteenth century. Beginning with the Land Act of 1800, Congress continuously liberalized the means of acquiring land. Over time, Congress reduced both prices and the minimum acreage requirement, culminating in the Homestead Act of 1862, which allowed a settler to acquire a title to 160 acres by continuous residence on the land for five years and a $10 registration fee. It also allowed purchase of the land after six months for a fee of $1.25 per acre. Despite the seeming largesse of the Homestead Act, more land was sold than homesteaded: Of the increase in farmland between 1870 and 1900, homesteading accounted for less than 20%. On reflection this should come as no surprise because much of the land open for homesteads was arid and often not suitable for raising crops on small parcels of 160 acres. In addition, the railroads and states had better land available, although it had to be purchased. Homesteading, where it did occur, was most likely on land that was marginal for farming and was already in use by ranchers.[16]

Following the Civil War, ranchers moved westward onto land in the western plains and then, in the late 1870s and 1880s, beyond the 100th meridian. Although the land was ideally suited for grazing, it was not worth $1.25 per acre and hence was not purchased from the federal government. Moreover, in areas where 25 acres or more were needed to sustain a single cow for a year, viable ranches required holdings much larger than the 160 acres allowed by most of the land laws that were operational in the last half of the nineteenth century. Accordingly, ranchers typically purchased or homesteaded a parcel of land containing water and grazed their livestock on a much larger area, which they claimed informally. The specification of rights was determined through private agreement within cattlemen's associations, where customary use and the prior appropriation of water determined range rights. Even in the early twentieth century many ranchers still respected informal range rights.[17] Further, ranchers fenced large areas of land that they claimed to demarcate their ranches and to control the drift of cattle. Nevertheless, without government-enforced title there was a threat of entry, particularly as homestead settlement moved into the region after 1880.

Ranchers observed the threat and attempted to obtain government enforcement of their property rights. A Public Lands Commission was established by Congress in 1879 to investigate problems with the disposal and use of heterogeneous lands in the West. The Commission gathered testimony regarding range and timber lands at various locations, and a common plea was for more lenient federal laws to reflect variations in land quality and production potential and to provide for the speedy patenting of private land claims. After assembling this testimony, the Commission issued a report to Congress calling for the classification and sale of western lands according to their best use.[18] To reflect arid conditions and the need for larger claims than the 160 acres authorized under existing land laws, the Commission called for 2,560-acre homesteads on range lands.

Congress, however, did not respond to the Commission's recommendations. After 1880, there simply was less federal land available for claiming by all parties, ranchers and homesteaders alike. Recognizing the large land claims of ranchers would have precluded others from obtaining a share of the remaining federal estate under the land laws.[19] Also, the homestead lobby likely was formidable. The size of the homestead lobby can be approximated by the number of new homestead and preemption claims from 1880 through 1900. During that 20-year period, 991,372 original homestead entries were made for 138,584,000 acres, and 185,511 preemption claims were filed for 27,279,000 acres.[20] In the late nineteenth century, the failure of small dry-land homesteads had not yet been experienced. Farms of 160 acres or 320 acres were often presented as viable, especially by railroads and federal agencies promoting settlement.[21] Congress responded by passing the Kinkaid Act (1904), the Enlarged Homestead Act (1909), and the Stock Raising Homestead Act (1916) to allow for small grazing homesteads of up to 640 acres.[22] The combined impact of the three pieces of legislation, along with administrative support to enforce the rights of settlers, was to increase the potential for conflict on the range.

Further, as noted by Libecap, officials in the General Land Office were paid in part on the basis of the number of claims filed.[23] Recognizing the large land claims of ranchers would have reduced the number of land filings through the agency and hence the income of GLO officials at each land office. The influence of homesteaders contributed to provisions placed in the Republican and

Democratic party platforms from 1872 through 1888 calling for federal land to be distributed only to actual settlers as outlined in the Homestead Act.[24] The rhetoric of the political platforms was put into practice in 1891 when Congress stopped the cash sales of the public domain.

Despite this potential for conflict between homesteaders and ranchers, the incidence of violence appears to have been quite small, with most of it concentrated in parts of Wyoming and isolated cases in New Mexico, Colorado, and Montana.[25] We base this assessment on a review of the large secondary literature on western settlement and the *Annual Reports* of the Commissioner of the General Land Office.[26] There is nothing comparable to the scale of violent conflict that exists in the Amazon frontier of Brazil. Although homesteaders complained of informal rancher claims, there was little concerted action by the GLO to support homesteaders. The agency did not receive the commensurate increases in budgets from Congress to engage in such actions.

The GLO was in the Interior Department, and the Commissioner of the General Land Office served at the pleasure of the Secretary of the Interior, who in turn was appointed by the president. Hence, national political conditions, budgets, and staffing affected the agency's actions. Between 1884 and 1890 the federal government disposed of an average of 20 million acres a year.[27] Yet Congress did not fund increases in the GLO's staff. Indeed, the staff had been cut by 25% in 1867.[28] An understaffed GLO benefited ranchers, and these interests appear to have opposed major increases in GLO funding.

Until the early 1880s, the GLO more or less condoned irregularities in western land claims and appears not to have been active in removing the fences constructed by ranchers to mark their holdings. By the 1880s, however, complaints from homesteaders grew. In response to these complaints, Noah McFarland (Commissioner of Public Lands, 1881–1885) sent special GLO agents to determine the extent of illegal enclosures of the public domain by ranchers. In 1884, the GLO reported to Congress on the extent of the problem in *Unauthorized Fencing of Public Lands*.[29] Antifencing legislation was drawn up and passed on February 25, 1885.[30]

This effort was intensified by McFarland's successor, William Sparks. In 1886 Sparks printed the names of those ranchers against whom he recommended proceedings be initiated, and persuaded the War Department to use the cavalry to bring down fences in Wyoming. Sparks also suspended processing of all original entries (new private claims) on western federal lands, except those paid for in cash or military scrip. Growing GLO recognition of the problem of illegal fencing is reflected in the reports of special agents. Libecap's calculations of illegally fenced acreage for the years 1883 to 1887, based on their reports, show that illegal enclosures ranged from approximately 2,000,000 acres in 1883 to over 8,500,000 acres in 1887.[31]

Sparks' efforts antagonized powerful special-interest groups in western states, who sought to remove him from office. Homestead groups supported him, but the political melee continued. Finally, Secretary of the Interior Lamar asked for Commissioner Sparks' resignation in 1887. After his resignation, the GLO relaxed its antifencing enforcement efforts until the presidency of Theodore Roosevelt in 1901. The decline in antifencing efforts, however, did not mean that ranchers could purchase the land that they held to firm their claims to western range land. In 1889, Congress ended all cash sales of federal lands. In 1891, the enactment of the General Revision Act repealed the most lenient land laws for arid regions, the Timber and Culture Act and the Preemption Act, and extended the time period required for homestead occupancy for cash purchases (commutation) from 6 to 14 months. These actions made it more difficult for ranchers to obtain formal property rights to their lands, forcing them to continue to rely on informal enforcement methods such as patrolling by grazing associations and fencing.

Table 2.1 presents data on illegal enclosures for a later period where data are available and when illegal fence removal had increased. Notice that most of the reports of illegal enclosures come from the states of New Mexico, Colorado, Wyoming, and Montana.[32] These are the states where there was considerable unappropriated land (land that often was claimed by ranchers, but unrecognized by the federal government) that was perceived as potentially suitable to

TABLE 2.1

Illegal Enclosures by State and Territory, 1909–1919 (in thousands of acres)

Year	NM	AZ	CO	WY	MT	ID	UT	NV	CA	OR	WA	Total
1909	713	35	130	94	31	—	172	14	2	81	9	1,341
1910	303	21	140	47	280	11	68	93	8	20	37	1,162
1911	1,418	23	63	52	12	3	—	—	49	13	5	1,667
1912	58	12	26	—	14	4	—	7	1	15	54	214
1913	368	18	21	11	17	1	—	—	—	5	—	458
1914	127	38	47	37	12	—	—	7	6	6	—	284
1915	122	3	16	—	5	—	—	1	13	—	—	165
1916	68	1	2	—	16	—	—	—	—	—	—	86
1917	26	—	—	11	1	—	—	—	—	1	1	44
1918	3	—	—	4	—	—	—	—	—	—	—	8
1919	3	3	—	7	1	2	1	—	4	—	—	22

Source: Special agent reports, Record Group 49, Illegal Enclosures, National Archives. Reported in Libecap (1981a), p. 21.

small-scale settlement, as compared with the more arid regions of Arizona, Nevada, and Utah.

We do not have data on actual incidents of conflict over land in the West for direct analysis or for comparison with Brazil. Data on illegal enclosures are an indication of areas of potential conflict between ranchers and homesteaders. These fences represented the efforts of ranchers to enforce their property rights in the absence of government enforcement. Their removal by the GLO allowed homesteaders to occupy the land claimed by ranchers.

As a proxy for analyzing the sources of conflict in the West, we examine the determinants of illegal fencing. We estimate the coefficients of the following regression equation:

$$\text{Illegal Enclosures} = \beta_1 \text{ Homestead Entries} + \beta_2 \text{ Unappropriated Land} + \beta_3 \text{ Time} + e \quad (1)$$

We have data for the eleven western states contained in Table 2.1 for the years 1909 to 1919. The data on illegal enclosures are in thousands of acres, as are the data on officially unappropriated land. Homestead entries are the number of original entries per year. Illegal enclosures are areas recognized by the GLO as illegally fenced by ranchers. We expect that the identification of such areas (and fence removal by government agents) will be a function of the number of homestead entries in a state and the overall amount of federal land available for claiming. We include a time trend in the regression to control for any spurious relationship between illegal enclosures and unappropriated land because both were declining over time. The coefficients are estimated with ordinary least squares, allowing for fixed effects by state. We present the results in Table 2.2.[33]

The results described in Table 2.2 support the notion that potential conflict over federal lands as represented by illegal fencing was most likely to occur in states with more homestead entries and where there was more federal land available for homestead claiming. In addition, it appears that the potential for conflict declined over time. Homesteaders competed with ranchers for the land, and the unappropriated land often was informally claimed by ranchers. Although the federal government created conditions for confused property rights to land and for potential conflict over the land by specifying a small-farm focus in the land laws, the secondary historical literature on western frontier settlement reveals little violent conflict between ranchers and homesteaders in the settlement of most of the arid West. The reason appears to be that the GLO was never funded to intervene in a major way on behalf of homesteaders.

The absence of concerted action by the GLO to assist homesteaders and others who sought access to rancher lands is noted by Louis Pelzer in his clas-

TABLE 2.2

Determinants of Fencing Removal

Regression Coefficients (Dependent Variable = Illegal Enclosures)

Time	Homestead Entries	Unappropriated Land
−4.24	.005	.002
−(2.17)	(2.29)	(1.89)

Notes: *t*-statistics are in parentheses; R^2 = .48. Illegal enclosures come from data contained in the National Archives (see Table 2.1); homestead entries and unappropriated land come from the *Annual Reports* of the Commissioner of the Public Land Office.

sic book *The Cattlemen's Frontier*.[34] Pelzer describes conflicts over the possessory rights of ranchers in Colorado in the mid-1880s. In one case of a fenced track over 40 miles long, travel to a local post office was blocked by erection of a rancher's fence. Pelzer argues that although the General Land Office in 1883 encouraged homesteaders to remove the illegal fences of ranchers, the agency itself would not intervene directly. Even during William Sparks' tenure as Commissioner of the General Land Office, the agency appears to have encouraged homesteaders to rely instead on the courts.[35] Even as late as 1905, Mari Sandoz in *The Cattlemen* describes minimal penalties for illegal fencing of public lands by ranchers.[36] Because homesteaders had a disadvantage relative to ranchers in the use of violence and understood that the GLO could not support them, they avoided infringing on the large claims of ranchers whenever possible. This practice reduced the incidence of violent conflict.

To demonstrate the lack of government assistance to homesteaders in the arid West, we gathered data on funding for expenses for the operation of GLO district land offices and on total homestead acreage claimed from 1870 to 1925.[37] The data are presented in Figure 2.1. Although the total acreage claimed by homesteaders rose, particularly after 1897 as more homesteaders moved to the dry plains, real appropriations for the operation of local GLO offices did not rise appreciably, and indeed began to decline after 1909. The lack of funding and staffing to assist homesteaders in their competition with ranchers was emphasized by Milton Conover in his history of the General Land Office.[38]

One hundred special agents to cover the entire West would not provide sufficient backing for squatters to give them the confidence to invade rancher-claimed lands. Conover stressed the need for more appropriations by pointing to the 1910 report of Commissioner Fred Dennett, who complained that with only $150,000 for special agent service the government could not assist homesteaders.[39] Ironically, however, the absence of government assistance to homesteaders appears to have avoided more violent conflict in the West, particularly

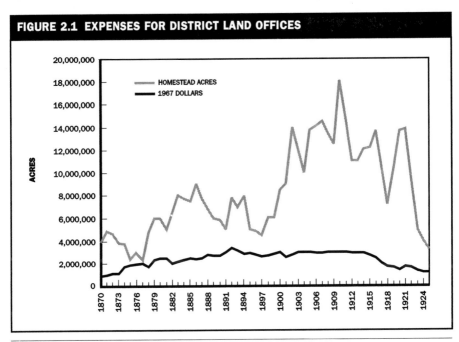

FIGURE 2.1 EXPENSES FOR DISTRICT LAND OFFICES

Source: See text and note 37.

if such support had been highly variable.[40] Indeed, the funding pattern revealed in Figure 2.1 indicates that the federal government was consistent in not raising real appropriations for the GLO.[41]

THE SPECIFICATION AND ENFORCEMENT OF PROPERTY RIGHTS TO LAND IN THE BRAZILIAN AMAZON

Although the Amazon frontier has long attracted settlers and adventurers from other parts of Brazil, the region remained relatively unexploited until the early 1970s. By that time, new road construction, such as the Transamazon, Belém-Brasilia, and Cuiaba-Santarem highways, had linked the area to the rest of Brazil and reduced transportation costs. Further, colonization efforts were instituted by the Brazilian government to accelerate the settlement of the Amazon and to address political pressures for land reform. Ambitious programs were announced that encouraged migration through formal colonization from southern Brazil and informal migration from northeastern Brazil. Currently, the government's goal is to settle 280,000 families over four years.[42] INCRA was created in 1970 to administer colonization and titling of federal lands and to implement federal land-reform programs throughout the country. However, because of the limited scope of formal colonization programs, most small-holder settlement occurred outside colonization areas.

In addition to encouraging small-scale settlement, the federal government, beginning in 1966 under the auspices of SUDAM (Superintendency for the Development of the Amazon), provided tax and credit incentives to private firms for investment in specific areas in the Amazon.[43] Subsidized credit through the Banco do Brasil also was made available. To expand its authority for colonization and development, the federal government in 1971 extended its jurisdiction by fiat over a 100-kilometer strip of land on both sides of federal highways, federal highways under construction, or highways planned in the Amazon through Military Decree Law 1164. This expansion occurred at the expense of the state governments, which lost a considerable portion of the public lands under their jurisdiction.[44]

With these programs and the resultant increase in migration, the population and number of ranches or farms in the Amazon grew sharply in the 1970s. For example, between 1970 and 1985 the population of Pará, the second-largest state in Brazil and a major frontier region, grew from 2.2 million to 4.3 million and the amount of land in farms doubled.[45] The price of land per hectare in Pará in constant 1970 cruzeiros rose from 37.0 in 1960 to 41.4 in 1970 and then jumped to 98.7 in 1975 and 152.6 in 1980.[46]

In this migration, there were two general types of land claimants: those with large farms or ranches and small holders. Farmers and ranchers obtained large holdings through the purchase or granting of state and federal lands for development, much as occurred in North America with the sale of land to developers and grants to railroads. Operation Amazonia, initiated in 1966, provided fiscal incentives for such development, including allowing the investment of 50% of a corporation's tax liability in the Amazon, duty-free import of equipment, and exemption from export duties for regional production.[47] These incentives were managed by SUDAM. Some of the areas designated to be ranches and to receive SUDAM subsidies were huge—24,000 hectares or more. Although state land sales could be made for 3,000 hectares or more only with the approval of the Brazilian Senate, this requirement appears not to have been a binding constraint.[48]

As a result of these policies, many areas of Pará were claimed by large landholders who often had formal title to their claims. These large holdings were referred to as latifundia. Many of these latifundia, however, were not immediately put into what the constitutional provisions would call productive use because of high transportation costs.[49] Ranchers waited, often until 1975 or later, when increased investment by the federal government in roads or the inauguration of other subsidies raised the value of the lands sufficiently to justify clearing and land-specific investment.

The limited use of their lands by many large ranchers is emphasized by Gasques and Yokomizo (1986), who found that from a sample of 29 SUDAM-subsidized cattle ranches between 1974 and 1985, 14 of the projects sold no cattle at all, and only two projects reached more than 50% of their target production. The average size of the ranches in their study was 16,334 hectares.

The other major group of claimants was small holders, who claimed government land (*terras devolutas*) through formal colonization projects administered by INCRA or through squatting on either government or "unused" private land. Squatters (*posseiros*) were quite different from larger land claimants. Typically, they were poor, with little education and low opportunity costs.[50] Under Brazilian law, *posseiros* long have had the right (*direito de posse*) to live on unclaimed public land and to put it into private use. If they use it "effectively" for at least one year and one day, squatters can receive a usufruct right over 100 hectares. The squatter can obtain title after continued occupancy and beneficial use of the land (*cultural efetiva e morada habitual*) for at least five years.

Similarly, as described in Article 191 of the Brazilian Constitution of 1988, squatters can occupy up to 50 hectares of privately owned land that is not in production for their own use. If they develop and occupy their claim for five consecutive years without opposition from the owner, they can obtain title through adverse possession. This legal provision is designed to facilitate land reform in a country where there are very large holdings or latifundia. Naturally, this constitutional provision is a potentially explosive issue. Accordingly, the two types of land claimants on the Amazon frontier are in a position to be in conflict. The property rights of titleholders are well specified, recognized, and enforced under the Brazilian statutory law and courts. However, these rights are abridged by the federal constitution, which adds a beneficial use criterion as a condition for recognition and enforcement against encroachment by squatters.

There is potential for violent conflicts over land because INCRA has been inconsistently funded to support squatters, and this condition has created uncertainty among titleholders and squatters as to the actions of the agency. Second, the strategic use of violence appears to be an effective mechanism by which squatters can force the agency to intervene on their behalf. The courts appear to consistently enforce the statutory rights of titleholders, but INCRA sporadically intervenes to enforce the constitutional rights of small-scale claimants. Nevertheless, conflict has not been ubiquitous in the settlement of the Amazon. For example, of the 105 *municípios* (counties) in Pará, the most populous Amazonian state, only 42 had recorded deaths from land conflict between 1983 and 1994.[51] Moreover, nine *municípios* accounted for 77% of the total 311 deaths over land conflict.

In Table 2.3 we present data from Pará on the number of land conflicts and resulting deaths for the years 1981–1989. The amount of conflict appears to have escalated in the early 1980s, peaked in the mid-1980s, and then declined in the latter part of the decade.

With compliance with the beneficial-use provision of the Brazilian Constitution as a condition for enforcing property rights and INCRA's mandate to support small land claimants, the agency has become involved in expropriating the land of large titleholders if their property appears not to be in production. INCRA may expropriate nonproductive land and transfer it to those who will make it productive. Alternatively, INCRA may purchase the land, but this practice involves reaching agreement with the titleholder on the transfer and on land value, a process that may take a long time. A third option is for INCRA to negotiate compensation for squatters for their improvements and to persuade them to leave the titleholder's property.

An expropriation by INCRA involves several steps. The first is selection of the area to be expropriated (*seleção*), followed by field inspection, survey, and valuation of the land and improvements (*vistoria de campo*). INCRA performs official appraisals (*pericias*) and submits the proposed expropriation to the court (*ajuizamento*) to obtain authorization for title transfer to the agency for subsequent distribution to squatters (*imissão de posse*).

Selection of the land to be expropriated is based on the lobby efforts of squatters and their rural workers' unions, such as the Landless Peasant Movement (MST). Moreover, the MST provides INCRA with information

TABLE 2.3

Land Conflicts and Associated Deaths: Pará, 1981–1989

Year	Conflicts	Deaths
1981	33	13
1982	38	26
1983	53	42
1984	119	69
1985	103	143
1986	177	113
1987	144	66
1988	48	33
1989	44	28

Source: Barata (1995).

about the lack of productive use of the land.[52] Valuation of the land and improvements is based on price data held by banks, registered at *cartorios*, or known to rural extension offices or real estate brokers. If the price is contested by the farmer, the judge handling the case determines the final value. INCRA will pay for the land with Agrarian Debt Bonds TDA (*Titulos de divida agraria*) and compensate for improvements with cash payments. The final decree of expropriation is issued by the central INCRA office and the president of Brazil. This process is complex, subject to dispute, and can take a long time. Indeed, the expropriation process can be extended several years if the landowner appeals to the courts contesting the suggested compensation for the land and improvements or challenging the claim that the land was unproductive.[53]

In the 1980s the pressures for land reform had been so intense and the conflicts in certain areas so protracted that the federal government created special agencies to resolve disputes because of INCRA's inability to resolve the issues. Between 1980 and 1985, GETAT (Executive Group of Land of Araguaia-Tocantins) was created with jurisdiction in southeastern Pará, where INCRA had been comparatively ineffective and violent conflicts extensive.[54] GETAT was abolished in May 1986. Between 1985 and 1989 another federal agency, a special Ministry of Agrarian Reform (MIRAD) was created to implement the first national plan for agrarian reform, or PNRA. The first PNRA had a goal of the progressive elimination of latifundia and minifundia, large and small unproductive properties, through settlement of 75,200 families on 5 million hectares in Pará alone. For a time, MIRAD took over INCRA's duties, but the land-reform objectives were not achieved; MIRAD was dismantled in 1989 and INCRA was reestablished, but with reduced budgets and staffing.[55] INCRA's experience with losing an administrative mandate and then being reinstated with diminished appropriations indicates the costs that a government agency can incur if it is ineffective in addressing land conflict issues. Squatters' organizations are aware of this political pressure on the agency and make use of it in lobbying the agency to intervene in a particular conflict.

Violent conflict over land is politically costly to INCRA and prompts its action because violence attracts media attention. This attention, in turn, embarrasses federal politicians, particularly the president, who can punish INCRA with reduced agency budgets. This notion is supported by the fact that 85% of the farm expropriations by INCRA in Pará between 1986 and 1992 followed violent conflict between squatters and farmers.[56]

To empirically investigate the incidence of violence on the Brazilian frontier, Alston et al. developed a model to isolate the motives of the various parties involved and tested it using data from the Brazilian census and the Pastoral

Land Commission, an agency that collects information on land conflicts in Brazil.[57] Here we report the estimation of an equation describing the determinants of deaths due to land conflicts:[58]

Deaths/Rural Population = $\alpha_0 + \alpha_1$ Squatting + α_2 Increase in Land Values + α_3 Land Concentration + α_4 INCRA + α_5 Clearing + e (2)

Data are at the *município* level for the state of Pará. Deaths/Rural Population is a proxy for squatter and farmer violence and comes from data that we assembled from the Pastoral Land Commission, MIRAD, and the Brazilian census.[59] Cumulative deaths from 1978 to 1985 are used as the dependent variable because conflicts take time to develop and can be spread over several years. By using cumulative deaths over an eight-year period we avoid the problem of predicting the precise time that deaths will occur without diminishing the ability to examine the important relationships between deaths and the specified independent variables. Moreover, deaths are a straightforward measure of violent conflict over land.

The data for the independent variables are from the Brazilian census. The Squatting variable is the percentage of farms in a *município* operated by squatters in 1975. This variable places squatters on site, occupying both private and government land. Their presence is a precondition for conflict with farmers, and where squatters are most numerous, property rights to land will be less secure. Large farms are more likely to have insecure property rights, both because they often have extensive forested areas and because monitoring the boundaries of large farms is more costly. Indeed, large farms, not small ones, are the target of land redistribution efforts. Our measure of the incidence of large farms in a *município* is a Land Concentration variable, which is the sum of the area in farms larger than or equal to 5,000 hectares divided by the total area in farms in the *município*. As defined by the constitution, beneficial use is an essential requirement for property rights to be secure, and forest clearing in the Amazon is accepted evidence of beneficial use. More cleared areas in a *município* would increase property rights security. Our Clearing variable is the mean farm area cleared in a *município*.[60] Accordingly, *municípios* with highly concentrated farm sizes and with more forest cover are more likely to be characterized by violent conflict between farmers and squatters over land.

Increases in land value stimulate greater competition for land, and hence greater use of violence by farmers to protect their claims by evicting squatters. Our Increase in Land Values variable is the change in average *município* land values between 1975 and 1985.[61]

We have emphasized the importance of the presence of the land reform agency, INCRA, as a factor in violent land conflict. The possibility of an INCRA expropriation makes it easier for squatters to organize, invade a farm, and resist the farmer's eviction. INCRA is a (0,1) measure of the agency's jurisdiction in a particular *município*.[62] Having INCRA jurisdiction in a *município* makes expropriation more likely, a factor that should lower the costs of squatter organization and associated use of violence. As noted above, INCRA jurisdiction was determined by Decree 1164 in 1971. Therefore it is not the case that the INCRA variable is endogenous with jurisdiction being assigned to areas where there is more violence. In terms of the courts, our analysis is cross-sectional, and as such we assume that the procedural rules affecting the position of the courts toward land reform are constant across *municípios*.

The estimation results are reported in Table 2.4. Significant explanatory power (at better than the 90% level) comes from squatting. The high incidence of squatting in a *município* sets the stage for the subsequent use of violence by farmers to remove squatters from their lands. The estimation results suggest that high levels of squatting in 1975 contributed to violent conflict between squatters and farmers between 1978 and 1985. By contrast, those *municípios* characterized by high levels of forest clearing tended to have fewer violent deaths. The estimated coefficient is negative, but significant only at the 85% level. Cleared areas are considered in beneficial use and are likely to be occupied by the farmer as well. We also argue that large farms are more likely to have insecure property rights than are small ones. The coefficient on the Land Concentration variable is positive, although insignificant at the usual levels. The weak positive relationship indicates that *municípios* characterized by high concentrations of land holdings of 5,000 hectares or more were somewhat more likely to have fatal land conflicts. A rise in land values also contributed to some degree to violent conflicts. The coefficient on the Land Value Increase variable is positive and significant at the 85% level. As land values rose, farmers attempted to solidify their property rights through violence, and squatters attempted to resist eviction. The coefficient on the INCRA variable is positive and significant at the 99% level. *Municípios* with INCRA jurisdiction had more fatalities in land conflicts between 1978 and 1985 than did those without. The presence of INCRA made intervention in land conflicts more likely, and this possibility appears to reduce squatter costs of organizing and resisting farmer evictions. Given high transportation and information costs on a frontier, squatter lobbying of INCRA and the agency's response to an invasion are more likely if there is an INCRA office nearby. The estimation result suggests that where INCRA intervention was probable, squatters were more apt to invade large farms and to resist the eviction efforts of farm owners. Ironically, then, the likelihood of

TABLE 2.4

Deaths Due to Land Violence on the Amazon Frontier

A. Descriptive Statistics

	Mean	Standard Deviation	Minimum	Maximum
Cumulative Deaths/Rural Pop.	0.083	0.229	0.000	1.170
1975 Squatting	0.482	0.238	0.084	0.921
1975 Land value	0.606	0.500	0.057	2.897
1985 Land value	0.630	0.432	0.074	2.173
Increase in land value, 1975–1985	0.024	0.566	−2.389	1.316
Clearing	0.351	0.165	0.018	0.806
INCRA	0.662	0.476	0.000	1.000
Land concentration	0.134	0.177	0.000	0.770

Source: See text.

B. Tobit Estimation

Variable	Estimated Coefficient
Constant	−0.50
	−(2.28)
Squatting	0.49
	(1.72)
Land value increase	0.18
	(1.38)
INCRA	0.43
	(2.51)
Land concentration	0.08
	(0.23)

Notes: t-statistics in parentheses; $n = 71$; log-likelihood ratio = 13.40 ($X^2_{5, .10} = 9.24$).

an INCRA expropriation as a means of forestalling violence could itself increase the strategic use of violence by squatters.

Organization is essential for successful expropriation of the property rights of large landowners. Invasions may appear chaotic, but they must be well prepared in order to obtain INCRA's response. This organization can be provided by the Landless Peasant Movement or other organizations. Our surveys indicate that invasions not linked to any group or rural union tend to be too disorganized to attract a government response and result in eviction and enforcement of the titleholder's rights.

CONCLUSION

In this paper we have examined two frontiers where conflict over land has occurred: the U.S. West, near and beyond the 100th meridian, and the Brazilian Amazon. In both the U.S. and Brazilian cases the inconsistent enforcement of property rights specifications encourages potential violence. In the U.S. West, the failure of the federal government in the late nineteenth century to recognize and enforce the informal specification of the land rights of ranchers created conditions for competition between ranchers and home-steaders. Even so, relative to the Brazilian Amazon, there was less violence between the two antagonists. The reason for this appears to be that the General Land Office was never sufficiently funded to adequately intervene on behalf of homesteaders. Since ranchers had an advantage in the use of force and were organized to do so, homesteaders tended to avoid their lands. Had the agency received more funding so that homesteaders formed expectations of assis-tance, they most likely would have established competing claims on rancher lands, and more violence may have resulted.

In Brazil, conflicts over land result from a failure of the federal government to clearly enforce the property rights of titleholders and its inconsistent sup-port of squatters as they follow the constitution's invitation to invade unused land. Although large farms have titles that are respected by civil law, the title is not enforced against encroachment by squatters when the land is not placed in beneficial use. This provision is called for by the Brazilian Constitution in an effort to promote a more equal distribution of landholdings. Land cannot be held in large tracts that are not placed in production and still have the proper-ty rights of the owner enforced. Although the goal may be laudable from a pol-icy perspective for land reform, the effect is to weaken the enforcement of property rights and to encourage conflict over land. Whether or not squatters are successful in obtaining a transfer of the rights to the land depends on orga-nization. INCRA has a limited budget and staff and reacts to lobbying efforts by organized groups. Indeed, the unanticipated result seems to be that because INCRA is sensitive to violence and its political costs, squatters engage in vio-lence in order to force the agency to intervene on their behalf.[63] This strategy, of course, encourages more violence. Homesteaders on the western U.S. fron-tier appear not to have had such an opportunity or motivation.

The effects of land conflict remain to be determined. In the case of the U.S. West, although there was less short-term violence because the General Land Office did not enforce the rights of homesteaders, there appear to be long-term costs from the failure to clearly define property rights to land. The federal gov-ernment reserved many of the contested lands under the Taylor Grazing Act of

1934 and assigned their administration to the Bureau of Land Management (BLM). The BLM is subject to competing political pressures to change land allocation and use as the political influence of constituent groups changes. This condition likely reduces investment in and the value of western arid lands. In Brazil, the weakening of property rights due to expropriations and land conflict may reduce investment, land value, and economic growth. Alston, Libecap, and Schneider found strong support for the role of title and secure property rights in promoting investment and increases in land value in the Amazon.[64] Alston et al. show that violence reduces land values and investment in the Amazon and encourages forest clearing to firm up squatter or landowner claims.[65]

ACKNOWLEDGMENTS

We have benefited from discussion at the 1996 Economic History Meetings in Berkeley, September 1996; the Conference on Comparative Development in Latin America and the United States, Stanford, November 1996; and the Conference on Latin America and the World Economy in the Nineteenth and Twentieth Centuries: Explorations in Quantitative Economic History, Bellagio, Italy, July 1997. We also received helpful comments from John Coatsworth, Alan Taylor, Doug Allen, Tom Nonnenmacher, and David Gerard. We acknowledge gratefully the financial assistance provided by the National Science Foundation, grant SBR9512107.

NOTES

1. For discussion, see Hughes (1977).
2. This contrasts with the dual development in the South of large plantations worked with slaves on the most fertile land and smaller yeoman farms on more marginal land.
3. Obviously, there was conflict between migrants and the native population.
4. See *New York Times,* 21 April 1996 and *Wall Street Journal,* 20 October 1995.
5. A summary of work in the area can be found in Garfinkel and Skaperdas (1996).
6. See Barzel (1989); Libecap (1989); Feder and Feeny (1991); and Alston, Libecap, and Schneider (1996b).
7. See Libecap and Johnson (1979), Anderson and Hill (1991), and Umbeck (1977).
8. Two recent articles that emphasize the difficulty that the U.S. government had in enforcing property rights are Allen (1991) and Kanazawa (1996).
9. See Chapter 1 in Alston, Eggertsson, and North (1996).

10. We are not arguing that governments begin to assign and enforce property rights at the optimal moment, but only that there is economic pressure to do so. Naturally, because governments are involved, the politics of assignment and enforcement of property rights and the resultant redistribution of assets affect the timing of government intervention. For Brazil, see Alston, Libecap, and Schneider (1996b).

11. For discussion of the history of the General Land Office and its mission, see Conover (1923).

12. The GLO did remove rancher fences periodically, but as we argue below, the agency's efforts were quite limited, occurring mostly late in the nineteenth century and early in the twentieth century. Homesteaders appear to have been convinced that they could not depend on GLO intervention against superior rancher efforts to evict them.

13. Most violence takes place when the squatters are being evicted by the farmer or the police and choose to resist. During the invasion there is usually no violence because the invaded farms are almost always empty and unguarded. Incidents of violence as farmer and squatters test each other out and try to intimidate each other also exist but are of less importance.

14. Kanazawa (1996)

15. Homogeneous groups have reached agreement in other contexts to reduce rent dissipation and to raise the returns from cooperative behavior. See Dennen (1976); Umbeck (1977); Libecap (1978); Ostrom (1990); and Alston, Libecap, and Schneider (1995).

16. Allen (1991) argues that the government strategically opened up land for homesteading as a means of reducing its enforcement costs over the public domain against Indian claims.

17. Dennen (1976).

18. U.S. Congress, House of Representatives (1880).

19. Throughout the nineteenth century the government placed a high value on settlement. See for example, Hurst (1956): "We learned to regard settlement as unquestionably a value in itself; government was under constant, almost invariably successful, pressure to bring land to market and, less successfully, to adopt policies that would put it immediately into the hands of small cultivators" (p. 35).

20. Gates (1968), p. 799.

21. Hargreaves (1957).

22. The Kinkaid Act was specific to Nebraska and somewhat of a trial balloon for the Stock Raising Act. The Kinkaid Act allowed settlers 640 acres in western Nebraska provided they resided on the land for five years and undertook improvements.

23. Libecap (1981b).

24. Libecap (1994).

25. The most famous case of conflict between ranchers and homesteaders was the Johnson County War in Wyoming. Ranchers often viewed homesteaders as cattle rustlers, and the penalties for rustling were high. For discussion, see Burt (1938) and Sandoz (1958).

26. Books and articles reviewed include those by Billington (1967); Brown (1975, 1991); Burt (1938); Fletcher (1960); Frink, Jackson, and Scott (1956); Gard (1947); Larson (1965); Pelzer (1936); Price (1967); Rister (1938); Sandoz (1958); and Terrell (1972). *Annual Reports* of the Commissioner of the General Land Office include those between 1883 and 1906.

27. Dunham (1963), p. 182.

28. Dunham (1963), p. 183.

29. U.S. Senate (1884).

30. *U.S. Statutes at Large* 23 (1885): 321.

31. Libecap (1981a). These are large numbers; recall that in the 1880s an average of 20,000,000 acres were transferred yearly from the government to private hands.

32. Unfortunately, we do not have data on illegal enclosures for Nebraska, the western part of which also witnessed considerable conflict between ranchers and homesteaders.

33. We dropped two outlying observations for New Mexico, 1909 and 1911, because they were distorting the reliability of the estimates. Including them in the estimation does not change the estimation results importantly but does lower the significance of the explanatory variables. For instance, including New Mexico for those two years results in a t-statistic of .94 for the coefficient on the Homestead variable.

34. Pelzer (1936), p. 175.

35. See for example, the *Annual Report of the Commissioner*, 1885.

36. Sandoz (1958), pp. 448–449.

37. Appropriations data are from the *Annual Report of the Commissioner* of the General Land Office. Annual appropriations were converted to real dollars using the All-Items CPI index (1967 = 100) in U.S. Department of Commerce (1975), p. 211.

38. Conover (1923), pp. 47–48.

39. Conover (1923), p. 48.

40. Variable or inconsistent support for homesteaders would have created uncertainty and thereby promoted the use of violence by ranchers and squatters alike.

41. As noted by Libecap (1981a, 1994), much of the arid West could never be privately patented under the land laws after 1891, and the land eventually was placed under the administration of the Bureau of Land Management and the Forest Service. These two agencies continually adjust use rights in response to shifts in the political influence of the constituent groups that compete for access and use of western lands. The associated uncertainty of use rights likely contributes to suboptimal investment in and allocation of the land.

42. Minister of Land Reform, 1996.
43. Gasques and Yokomizo (1986), Yokomizo (1989), and Schneider (1994) provide analyses of the impact of the fiscal incentive program.
44. Foweraker (1981), p. 100. This law was repealed in 1987 by Law 2375, but INCRA continued to administer the areas that previously were under its control.
45. IBGE, *Anuário Estatístico do Brasil* (1990), p. 183; IBGE (1991), pp. 180–183.
46. Land values for 1960–1980 are from the *Censo Agropecuário,* published by IBGE (Fundação Instituto Brasileiro de Geografia e Estatística; 1960, 1970, 1975, 1980, 1985). The values are those declared by the proprietor or administrator of the farm to the census interviewer. The agricultural census is administered over the universe of agricultural establishments in each state and the results are presented aggregated at the *município* or county level. The conversion fractions to place land values in constant 1970 prices can be obtained from the authors.
47. For discussion, see Ianni (1979) and Mahar (1989), p. 15.
48. Monteiro (1980); Schmink and Wood (1992), p. 196. The 1988 Brazilian Constitution lowered the size limit for sales without Senate approval to 2,500 hectares. Santos (1984, pp. 452–453) reports considerable sales in Pará of state lands between 1949 and 1963.
49. Because squatters have lower opportunity costs, they would be more likely to settle early on the frontier than would larger landowners with more education and experience (Alston, Libecap, and Schneider 1995). Accordingly, large landholders might rent portions of their unused land. This possibility, however, does not happen because large landowners are concerned that renters might acquire implied property rights to the land they use. This outcome is another example of the problems encountered when property rights are not enforced.
50. For discussion of the characteristics of squatters and other small holders, see Alston, Schneider, and Libecap (1995, 1996b).
51. Deaths from land conflict between 1987 and 1994 are from the Pastoral Land Commission (CPT) *Annual Reports.* The CPT collects data on land conflicts, and we are researching those files in Brasilia. The 1986 data are from IDESP, *Pará agrário,* no. 1, 1986, p. 51. The 1985 data are from MIRAD, *Violencia no campo,* 1985, and the 1983 and 1984 data are from Pastoral Land Commission files in Brasilia. The evidence on the sporadic nature of conflict on the Amazon frontier in Pará conflicts with the claim made by Juan de Onis (1992, p. 7) that rural violence was "endemic."
52. B. Mueller (1994), p. 96.
53. New legislation in Brazil seeks to speed up the *imissão de posse* process so that title can be transferred from the landowner to INCRA within 48 hours of the expropriation decree.
54. Created by Decree-Law No. 1,676.

55. Naturally, various constituent groups have a stake in promoting or blocking land redistribution efforts, and the political pressures are intense. For discussion, see B. Mueller (1994), p. 81.

56. Between 1986 and 1992, 60 farms were expropriated, and 51 of them involved violent conflict. The remaining 9 expropriated farms may also have originated from a conflict, but no data could be found on those farms. The list of expropriated farms is from IDESP, *Pará agrário*, Belém, no. 8, Jan./Dez. 1992, pp. 6–8. Data on conflicts in Pará are from personal correspondence with the Pastoral Land Commission in Goiania and from IDESP, *Pará agrário—Conflitos agrários*, Belém, Edição Especial, 1990.

57. Alston et al. (1997).

58. The estimation procedure used was a Tobit model, given the fact that several observations had no deaths in the period examined. The dependent variable in Equation (2) is (Cumulative Deaths/1980 Rural Population) × 1,000.

59. The data for deaths used in the estimation are not the same as that shown in Table 2.3 because the definition of what constitutes a land-related conflict may vary from one source to another. Although we have data on deaths and conflicts for the years since 1985, data on many of the independent variables were only available for 1985 and earlier because there has not been an agricultural census since that year.

60. Cleared farm area is calculated from the census by dividing the number of hectares of cleared agricultural land by the total amount of agricultural land in the *município*. The area cleared was defined as the sum of the land in permanent crops, annual crops, planted pasture, natural pasture, planted forest, and unused but usable land, as defined by the census.

61. Our price data for 1975 and 1985 are in 1985 cruzados. Land values generally are from the *Censo agropecuário*, published by IBGE as noted earlier. The value of land in 1985 in Pará was not provided in the census. It was estimated by taking the ratio of land value to the value of farms (which included the value of investments, machinery, and animals) for 1970, 1975, and 1980. The growth rates of this ratio were obtained, and an average growth rate calculated. The 1980 ratio was then multiplied by this average growth rate to give the 1985 ratio, which in turn was multiplied by the 1985 agricultural farm value as provided in the census.

62. *Municípios* are considered to be under INCRA's jurisdiction if the capital of the *município* is within 100 km of a federal highway. Under Brazilian law such lands are placed under federal, rather than state, control.

63. Alston et al. (1997) test this hypothesis with survey data.

64. Alston, Libecap, and Schneider (1996b).

65. Alston et al. (1997).

REFERENCES

Allen, Douglas W. "Homesteading and Property Rights; or, How the West Was Really Won." *The Journal of Law and Economics* 34 (April 1991): 1–24.

Alston, Lee J., Thrainn Eggertsson, and Douglass C. North. *Empirical Studies in Institutional Change*. New York: Cambridge University Press, 1996.

Alston, Lee J., Jeffrey R. Fuller, Gary D. Libecap, and Bernardo Mueller. "Competing Claims to Land: The Sources of Violent Conflict in the Brazilian Amazon." Working paper, Karl Eller Center, University of Arizona, 1997.

Alston, Lee J., Gary D. Libecap, and Robert Schneider. "Property Rights and the Preconditions for Markets: The Case of the Amazon Frontier." *Journal of Institutional and Theoretical Economics* 151, no. 1 (1995): 89–107.

Alston, Lee J., Gary D. Libecap, and Robert Schneider. "Violence and the Assignment of Property Rights on Two Brazilian Frontiers." In *The Political Economy of Conflict and Appropriation*, edited by Michelle R. Garfinkel and Stergios Skaperdas. New York: Cambridge University Press, 1996a.

Alston, Lee J., Gary D. Libecap, and Robert Schneider. "The Determinants and Impact of Property Rights: Land Titles on the Brazilian Frontier." *The Journal of Law, Economics and Organization* 12, no. 1 (1996b): 25–61.

Anderson, Terry L., and P. J. Hill. "The Race for Property Rights." *Journal of Law and Economics* 33 (April 1991): 177–197.

Barata, Ronaldo. *Inventario da violencia no campo*. Belém: CEJUP, 1995.

Barzel, Yoram. *Economic Analysis of Property Rights*. New York: Cambridge University Press, 1989.

Billington, Ray Allen. *Westward Expansion: A History of the American Frontier*, 3rd ed. New York: Macmillan, 1967.

Brown, Richard Maxwell. *Strain of Violence: Historical Studies of American Violence and Vigilantism*. New York: Oxford University Press, 1975.

Brown, Richard Maxwell. *No Duty to Retreat: Violence and Values in American History and Society*. New York: Oxford University Press, 1991.

Bunker, Steven G. *Underdeveloping the Amazon: Extraction, Unequal Exchange, and the Failure of the Modern State*. Chicago: University of Chicago Press, 1985.

Burt, Struthers. *Powder River, Let 'er Buck*. New York: Farrar and Rinehart, 1938.

Conover, Milton. *The General Land Office: Its History, Activities, and Organization*. Institute for Government Research, Service Monographs of the United States Government no. 13. Baltimore: The Johns Hopkins University Press, 1923.

Dennen, R. T. "Cattlemen's Associations and Property Rights in Land in the American West." *Explorations in Economic History* 13 (1976): 423–436.

Dunham, Harold H. "Some Crucial Years of the General Land Office, 1875–1890."

Reprinted in *The Public Lands: Studies in the History of the Public Domain,* edited by Vernon Carstensen. Madison: The University of Wisconsin Press, 1963.

Fearnside, Philip M. *Human Carrying Capacity of the Brazilian Rain Forest.* New York: Columbia University Press, 1986.

Feder, Gershon, and David Feeny. "Land Tenure and Property Rights: Theory and Implications for Development Policy." *World Bank Economic Review* 5, no. 1 (1991): 135–153.

Feder, Gershon, and Tongroj Onchan. "Land Ownership Security and Farm Investment in Thailand." *American Journal of Agricultural Economics* 69 (May 1987): 311–320.

Feder, Gershon, Tongroj Onchan, Yongyuth Chalamwong, and Chira Hongladrarom. *Land Policies and Farm Productivity in Thailand.* Baltimore: Johns Hopkins University Press, 1988.

Fletcher, Robert H. *From Free Grass to Fences: The Montana Cattle Range Story.* New York: University Publishers, 1960.

Foweraker, Joseph. *The Struggle for Land: A Political Economy of the Pioneer Frontier in Brazil, 1930 to Present.* New York: Cambridge University Press, 1981.

Frink, Maurice, W. Turrentine Jackson, and Agnes Wright Scott. *When Grass Was King.* Boulder: University of Colorado Press, 1956.

Fuchin, Luiz Edson. "A justica dos conflitos no Brasil." *Reforma Agraria,* April (1991): 87–94.

Garcia Gasques, Jose, and Clando Yokomizo. "Resultados de 20 anos de encentivos fiscais agropecuaria da Amazonia." In ANPEC, Encontro Nacional de Economia, 47–84, 1986.

Gard, Wayne. "The Fence Cutters." *Southwestern Historical Quarterly* 50 (1947): 1–15.

Garfinkel, Michele, and Stergios Skaperdas, eds. *The Political Economy of Conflict and Appropriation.* New York: Cambridge University Press, 1996.

Gates, Paul W. *History of Public Land Law Development.* Washington, DC: Government Printing Office, 1968.

Hargreaves, Mary. *Dry Farming in the Northern Great Plains 1900–1925.* Cambridge: Harvard University Press, 1957.

Hughes, Jonathan R. T. *The Governmental Habit: Economic Controls from Colonial Times to the Present.* New York: Basic Books, 1977.

Human Rights Watch. *Rural Violence in Brazil.* New York: Human Rights Watch, 1991.

Hurst, James Willard. *Law and the Conditions of Freedom in the Nineteenth-Century United States.* Madison: The University of Wisconsin Press, 1956.

Ianni, Octavio. *Colonizao e contra-reforma agrária na Amazonia.* Petropolis, Brazil: Editora Vozes, 1979.

IBGE (Fundação Instituto Brasileiro de Geografia e Estatística). *Censo agropecuário— Pará.* Rio de Janeiro, 1960, 1970, 1980, and 1985.

IBGE (Fundação Instituto Brasileiro de Geografia e Estatística). *Anuario estatístico do Brasil*. Rio de Janeiro, 1990.

IBGE (Fundação Instituto Brasileiro de Geografia e Estatística). *Geografia do Brasil— Região norte*, Vol. III. Rio de Janeiro, 1991.

IDESP. *Pará Agrário*. Belém, 1986 and various years.

IDESP. *Pará Agrário*. "Conflitos rurais." Numero especial. Belém, 1989.

Kanazawa, Mark T. "Possession Is Nine Points of the Law: The Political Economy of Early Public Land Disposal." *Explorations in Economic History* 33 (April 1996): 227–249.

Larson, Taft A. *History of Wyoming*. Lincoln: University of Nebraska Press, 1965.

Libecap, Gary D. "Economic Variables and the Development of the Law: The Case of Western Mineral Rights." *Journal of Economic History* 38 (1978).

Libecap, Gary D. *Locking Up The Range: Federal Land Use Controls and Grazing*. Cambridge: Ballanger, 1981a.

Libecap, Gary D. "Bureaucratic Opposition to the Assignment of Property Rights: Overgrazing on the Western Range." *Journal of Economic History* 41 (1981b): 151–158.

Libecap, Gary D. *Contracting for Property Rights*. New York: Cambridge University Press, 1989.

Libecap, Gary D. "The Political Economy of Institutional Change: Property Rights and the General Revision Act of 1891." In *Capitalism in Context: Essays on Economic Development and Cultural Change in Honor of R.M. Hartwell*, edited by John A. James and Mark Thomas. Chicago: University of Chicago Press, 1994.

Libecap, Gary D., and Ronald N. Johnson. "Property Rights, Nineteenth-Century Federal Timber Policy, and the Conservation Movement." *Journal of Economic History* 39 (1979): 129–142.

Mahar, Dennis J. *Government Policies and Deforestation in Brazil's Amazon Region*. Washington, DC: World Bank, 1989.

MIRAD. *Violencia no campo*. Brasilia, 1985.

Monteiro, Benedito. *Agrarian Law*. Rio de Janeiro: PLG Comunicação, 1980.

Moran, Emilio F. "Pioneer Farmers of the Transamazon Highway: Adaptation and Agricultural Production in the Lowland Tropics." Ph.D. dissertation, University of Florida, 1975.

Moran, Emilio F. *Developing the Amazon*. Bloomington: Indiana University Press, 1981.

Moran, Emilio F. "Colonization in the Transamazon and Rondonia." In *Frontier Expansion in Amazonia*, edited by Marianne Schmink and Charles H. Wood, 285–303. Gainesville: University of Florida Press, 1984.

Moran, Emilio F. "Adaptation and Maladaptation in Newly Settled Areas." In *The Human Ecology of Tropical Land Settlement in Latin America*, edited by Debra A. Schumann and William L. Partridge, 20–39. Boulder, CO: Westview Press, 1989a.

Moran, Emilio F. "Government-Directed Settlement in the 1970s: An Assessment of Transamazon Highway Colonization." In *The Human Ecology of Tropical Land Settlement in Latin America*, edited by Debra A. Schumann and William L. Partridge, 172–197. Boulder, CO: Westview Press, 1989b.

Mueller, Bernardo. "The Political Economy of Agrarian Reform in Brazil." Ph.D. dissertation, University of Illinois, Champaign/Urbana, 1994.

Mueller, Bernardo, Lee J. Alston, Gary D. Libecap, and Robert Schneider. "Land, Property Rights and Privatization in Brazil." *Quarterly Review of Economics and Finance*, Special Issue, 1994.

Mueller, Charles. "Frontier Based Agricultural Expansion: The Case of Rondonia." In *Land, People, and Planning in Contemporary Amazonia*, edited by Francoise Barbira-Scazzocchio. Occasional Publication no. 3, Cambridge University, Center of Latin American Studies, 1980.

Mueller, Charles. "Colonization Policies, Land Occupation, and Deforestation in the Amazon Countries." Working paper no. 15, Department of Economics, University of Brasilia, 1992.

New York Times. "Violence Grows in Brazilian Land Battle." 21 April 1996, p. 8

O'Grady, Mary Anastasia. "Muddled Policies Spark Brazilian Land Wars." *Wall Street Journal*, 20 October 1995, p. A15.

Onis, Juan de. *The Green Cathedral: Sustainable Development of the Amazon*. New York: Oxford University Press, 1992.

Ostrom, Elinor. *Governing the Commons*. New York: Cambridge University Press, 1990.

Pará Pastoral Land Commission. "People Killed in Land Conflicts." Belém, 1989.

Pastoral Land Commission. *Annual Reports*. Brasilia, various years.

Pelzer, Louis. *The Cattlemen's Frontier*. Glendale, CA: Arthur H. Clark, 1936.

Pinto, Lucio Flavio. *Amazonia: No rastro do saque*. São Paulo: Hucitec, 1980.

Price, Eugene H. *Open Range Ranching on the South Plains in the 1890s*. Cambridge: Clarendon Press, 1967.

Republica Federativa do Brasil, Estado do Pará, rodoviario, politico e estatístico, 3rd ed. Goiania: Editora Turistica e Estatística Ltda, 1988.

Rister, Carl Coke. *The Southern Plainsman*. Norman: University of Oklahoma Press, 1938.

Sandoz, Mari. *The Cattleman*. New York: Hastings House, 1958.

Santos, Roberto. "Law and Social Change: The Problem of Land in the Brazilian Amazon." In *Frontier Expansion in Amazonia*, edited by Marianne Schmink and Charles H. Wood, 180–284. Gainesville: University of Florida Press, 1984.

Sawyer, Donald R. "Frontier Expansion and Retraction in Brazil." In *Frontier Expansion in Amazonia*, edited by Marianne Schmink and Charles H. Wood. Gainesville: University of Florida Press, 1984.

Schmink, Marianne, and Charles H. Wood. *Contested Frontiers in Amazonia*. New York: Columbia University Press, 1992.

Schneider, Robert. *Brazil: An Analysis of Environmental Problems in the Amazon*. Washington, DC: World Bank, 1992.

Schneider, Robert. "Government and the Economy on the Amazon Frontier." Latin America and Caribbean Technical Department, Regional Studies Program Report no. 34. Washington, DC: World Bank, 1994.

Terrell, John Upton. *The Land Grab*. New York: Dial Press, 1972.

Umbeck, John R. "The California Gold Rush: A Study of Emerging Property Rights." *Explorations in Economic History* 14 (1977): 197–226.

U.S. Department of Commerce, Bureau of the Census. *Historical Statistics of the United States*. Washington, DC: Government Printing Office, 1975.

U.S. Department of the Interior, General Land Office. *Illegal Fencing of Government Lands: Wyoming*. Washington, DC: Government Printing Office, 1906.

U.S. Department of the Interior, Office of the Secretary of Interior. Letter from the Secretary of the Interior. In answer to Senate Resolution of February 14, letter of the Commissioner of the General Land Office, on the subject of unauthorized fencing of public lands. National Archives, 1884.

U.S. Department of the Interior, General Land Office. *Annual Report of the Commissioner*. Washington, DC: Government Printing Office, selected years.

Wood, Charles, and John Wilson. "The Magnitude of Migration to the Brazilian Frontier." In *Frontier Expansion in Amazonia*, edited by Marianne Schmink and Charles H. Wood, 142–152. Gainesville: University of Florida Press, 1984.

Yokota, Paulo. "Quest o fundiána Brasileira." Brasilia: INCRA, 1981.

Yokomizo, Clando. "Incentivos financeiros e fiscais na pecuarizacao da Amazonia." Texto Para Discussao no. 22, Institute de Planejamento, Outubro, 1989.

3

The Comparative Productivity Performance of Brazil and Mexico, 1950–1994

André A. Hofman
Economic Development Division,
Economic Commission for Latin America and the Caribbean
Nanno Mulder
Centre d'Etudes Prospectives et d'Informations Internationales

We analyze the 1950 to 1994 growth and productivity performance of Brazil and Mexico using a comparative approach at both the aggregate level and the sectoral level. At the sectoral level we use the industry-of-origin methodology developed in the ICOP (International Comparisons of Output and Productivity) project at the Groningen Growth and Development Centre of the University of Groningen.

Brazil and Mexico, two of the largest economies of Latin America, were among the fastest growing countries in the world in the period from 1950 to 1980, reaching growth rates for gross domestic product (GDP) of over 6% per annum. Although some sectors showed an above-average growth performance, such as manufacturing, others grew at a much lower rate, such as agriculture. In addition to varying sectoral growth rates of GDP, both countries experienced a tremendous change in the structure of their workforce and GDP, namely, a sharp fall of the relative importance of agriculture and a large increase in the share of services. The breakdown by sectors in this paper provides an important tool for understanding the underlying dynamics of economic growth.

Growth rates of GDP and productivity only show part of the picture of the dynamics of these countries because they fail to show what the potential of

Brazil and Mexico was for catching up with industrialized economies. For this purpose, we also assessed their productivity performance in an international perspective, comparing them with the international productivity leader, the United States. We found that Brazilian labor productivity was 12% and Mexican productivity 17% of the U.S. level in 1950. A process of catch-up with American productivity levels took place until 1982, after which the gap widened again. The sectoral breakdown demonstrates that agriculture in Brazil and Mexico stagnated relative to U.S. productivity levels, whereas mining and services showed some catch-up with U.S. levels until 1982.

The second part of this paper analyzes the major determinants of economic growth using a growth accounting framework. Increments of the gross non-residential capital stock explain half of the growth of the Brazilian economy in the 1950–1980 period, compared with 40% of Mexican economic growth. The contribution of labor input growth to total GDP growth was also larger in the Brazilian case (37% compared with 30% in Mexico in the same period). Joint factor productivity, generally considered as an approximate measure of the effect of disembodied technical progress (together with other effects), played a rather meager role in Brazilian and Mexican economic growth. Our growth accounting exercise shows high levels of overexplanation for the 1980s and early 1990s, resulting from underutilization of resources.

A similar methodology was applied to disentangle productivity differences between Brazil and Mexico on the one hand and the United States on the other in 1980 and 1990. The higher capital intensity of production in the United States explains roughly half of its superior productivity performance relative to Brazilian and Mexican levels in 1980 and 1990. Schooling levels were another major determinant of productivity differentials, accounting for one-tenth to one-fifth of the productivity gap. Total factor productivity (TFP) accounted for almost 40% of the productivity gap in 1980. From 1980 to 1990, the productivity gap between Brazil and the United States increased and TFP decreased. The productivity gap between Mexico and the United States remained stable and the contribution of TFP to the productivity gap slightly increased from 1980 to 1991.

We start with an assessment of Brazilian and Mexican economic growth from the Latin American perspective, followed by a disaggregation by sector of the economy. In addition to growth rates, we analyze Brazilian and Mexican performances from an international perspective by comparing them with the international productivity leader, the United States. The second part of the paper analyzes the contributions of labor, capital, land, and other resources to economic growth and to differences in the economic performance of the two countries.

ECONOMIC GROWTH AND PRODUCTIVITY PERFORMANCE

Total Economy Performance

To assess Brazil's and Mexico's growth performances, we compare them with four other major Latin American countries and with the average development of six advanced Organization for Economic Cooperation and Development (OECD) countries (France, Germany, Japan, the Netherlands, the United Kingdom, and the United States), whose levels of income and productivity are amongst the highest in the world.

GDP

The GDP growth rates as presented in Table 3.1 show a quite respectable Latin American performance for the whole twentieth century. The slowest growth was in Argentina and Chile, whereas Brazil and Venezuela had the best overall performance. The best period in the twentieth century for half of the countries (Brazil, Colombia, and Mexico) was without any doubt the 1950–1973 period. For Argentina and the United States, the beginning of the century, 1900–1913, was the best period in terms of total GDP growth.

The interwar period was by far the worst for total GDP growth for most countries in the twentieth century. Chile experienced its lowest point in the 1929–1950 period, whereas Mexico had its low period from 1913 to 1929. Latin America, with the exception of Chile and Mexico, experienced its major crisis during the "Lost Decade" of the 1980s.[1]

TABLE 3.1

Latin America: Total GDP, 1900–1994 (average annual compound growth rates)

	1900–1913	1913–1929	1929–1950	1950–1973	1973–1980	1980–1989	1989–1994	1900–1994
Argentina	6.4	3.5	2.5	4.0	3.0	−1.0	6.1	3.5
Brazil	4.5	4.7	5.0	6.9	7.2	2.3	0.9	5.0
Chile	3.7	2.9	2.2	3.6	2.8	2.9	6.4	3.2
Colombia	4.2	4.7	3.6	5.1	5.0	3.3	4.3	4.4
Mexico	2.6	0.8	4.0	6.5	6.4	1.4	3.0	3.7
Venezuela	3.3	8.2	5.9	6.4	4.1	−0.1	3.6	5.2
Total	4.1	4.1	3.9	5.4	4.8	1.5	4.0	4.2
Six OECD[a]	2.2	2.2	1.3	5.7	2.3	2.6	1.8	2.8
USA	4.0	3.1	2.6	3.7	2.1	3.0	1.7	3.1

[a]The six OECD countries were France, Germany, Japan, the Netherlands, the United Kingdom, and the United States.

Sources: Latin America data are from Hofman (1998), and other countries are from Maddison (1995).

GDP per Capita

There is truth in the assertion that the Latin American countries that performed reasonably well during the 1930s were those which had large domestic markets and some pre-1929 industrial base, as was the case for Argentina, Brazil, Colombia, and Mexico. One may conclude that a minimum size in the domestic market plus a minimum degree of autonomy regarding the exchange rate and fiscal and monetary policies were necessary conditions for industrialization in Latin America in the 1930s.

Table 3.2 shows GDP per capita relative to the United States, and demonstrates that the whole period from 1900 to 1950 was, comparatively, a very prosperous period for Latin America. Its GDP per capita increased somewhat compared with the United States. The advanced OECD countries' level had fallen drastically. The detrimental effects of World War II on most countries and the relatively sheltered position of Latin America explains a great part of this performance.

Since 1950, Latin American performance has been systematically much worse than that of the six OECD countries, with the exception of the 1973–1980 period. The 1950–1973 period was one of great expansion in Latin America, when growth per capita averaged 2.6% a year (faster than the 1.8% average for 1929–1950). In the advanced countries, GDP per capita grew 4.2% a year. In 1973 the period of postwar expansion came abruptly to an end. The advanced countries settled on a much lower growth pace. Latin America slowed down its pace in 1973–1980 and collapsed completely in the 1980–1994 period.

TABLE 3.2

Levels of GDP per Capita, 1900–1994 (international 1980 dollars, USA = 100)

	1900	1913	1929	1950	1973	1980	1989	1994
Argentina	52	55	49	41	42	43	29	34
Brazil	10	11	12	15	22	29	24	22
Chile	38	40	39	33	27	28	26	31
Colombia	18	18	19	19	19	22	21	22
Mexico	35	35	27	27	35	42	33	33
Venezuela	10	10	24	38	41	40	26	26
Average	27	28	28	29	31	34	26	28
Six OECD[a]	68	62	60	52	73	76	77	78

[a]The six major OECD countries were France, Germany, Japan, the Netherlands, the United Kingdom, and the United States.

Sources: Latin America data are from Hofman (1998); other countries are from Maddison (1995).

Table 3.3 presents labor productivity for the period from 1913, the earliest year for which data were available, to 1994. One of the most important findings is that the process of accelerating growth and labor productivity had

TABLE 3.3

Latin America: Growth and Productivity, 1900–1994
(average annual compound growth rates)

	1900– 1913	1913– 1929	1929– 1938	1938– 1950	1950– 1973	1973– 1980	1980– 1989	1989– 1994	1900– 1994
GDP per Capita									
Argentina	2.5	0.9	−0.8	1.7	2.3	1.4	−2.5	4.8	1.3
Brazil	2.3	2.5	2.5	2.7	3.9	4.7	0.2	−0.8	2.6
Chile	2.4	1.6	−0.9	1.7	1.4	1.2	1.3	4.6	1.5
Colombia	2.1	2.1	2.1	1.1	2.2	2.7	1.3	2.5	2.0
Mexico	1.8	0.1	0.2	2.6	3.3	3.5	−0.8	1.1	1.7
Venezuela	2.3	7.3	2.1	5.0	2.5	0.5	−2.5	1.2	2.9
Average	2.2	2.4	0.9	2.5	2.6	2.3	−0.5	2.2	2.0

Labor Productivity (GDP per Man Hour)								
	1913	1929	1938	1950	1973	1980	1989	1994
Argentina	1.6	−0.2	2.7	2.6	2.2	−2.1	4.6	1.7[a]
Brazil	5.2	3.0	3.9	3.9	4.0	0.1	−0.6	3.4[a]
Chile	2.3	−0.7	2.0	3.0	1.0	−0.2	3.2	1.8[a]
Colombia	4.2	0.6	2.3	3.0	1.9	1.3	2.1	2.5[a]
Mexico	2.4	1.0	3.4	4.2	2.7	−1.1	0.4	2.2[a]
Venezuela	11.1	1.4	4.9	3.5	−0.9	−1.8	0.2	2.7[a]
Average	4.5	0.9	3.2	3.4	1.8	−0.6	1.6	2.4[a]

Levels of Labor Productivity (USA = 100), Using Expenditure PPPs for Currency Conversion								
	1913	1929	1938	1950	1973	1980	1989	1994
Argentina	53	51	44	41	40	45	32	38
Brazil	9	15	17	18	24	30	26	24
Chile	42	46	38	32	35	35	30	33
Colombia	18	26	24	21	23	24	24	25
Mexico	37	34	32	33	45	52	41	39
Venezuela	24	37	37	45	53	48	35	33
Average	33	35	32	32	37	39	31	32
USA	100	100	100	100	100	100	100	100

Note: Value added per person was converted by the expenditure PPPs for the total economy.
[a]Refers to the 1913–1994 period.

Source: Hofman (1998).

already started in Latin America around 1938, when GDP per capita and productivity growth accelerated with growth rates about 3 times as high as the previous period from 1929 to 1938. It should be noted that growth was more homogeneous as compared with the 1913–1929 period, when average per capita growth was also relatively high in Latin America.

Especially in Argentina, Chile, Mexico, and Venezuela, growth accelerated from 1938 onward. It is during this period that the combined effects of expansionary fiscal and monetary policies and import substitution resulted in a high growth of productivity per man hour and per capita GDP. Some countries also benefited from the positive effect of World War II.

The growth performance during the 1973–1980 period in Latin America is remarkable. Although GDP per capita continued to grow almost as rapidly as during the 1950–1973 period, labor productivity growth had already slowed down beginning in 1973, announcing the crisis to come.

Sectoral Performance, 1950–1993

Economic growth performance varied across sectors, as demonstrated in Table 3.4. In Brazil mining showed the highest growth in the period from 1950 to 1973, followed by construction, transport, and communications in the 1973–1980 period. Agriculture was the slowest growing sector in this period. After 1980, growth rates of all sectors fell, except those of mining and public utilities. Although economic policy in Brazil focused on rapid development of the manufacturing sector, construction, mining, and certain parts of the service sectors grew faster in the 1950–1980 period.

Growth rates of value added by sector were linked to employment series to derive labor productivity growth (see Table 3.5). Sectoral productivity growth differed strongly from the growth rates of GDP. Labor productivity in services grew at a much lower rate than GDP due to the rapid expansion of employment in this part of the economy in the two countries. Thanks to the massive outflow of surplus labor in Brazil and Mexico, agriculture experienced relatively high productivity growth. From 1950 to 1973 mining was the productivity growth leader in Brazil, compared with public utilities in Mexico. After 1980 productivity growth became negative in both Brazil and Mexico. From 1989 to 1993 productivity continued to decrease in Brazil, but recovered in Mexico.

In the period from 1950 to 1993, labor productivity grew at an average rate of 2% in Brazil and Mexico. Over the whole period, mining, transport, and communications were the fastest growing sectors in Brazil, compared with mining and public utilities in Mexico. Construction, distribution, and other services represented the slowest growing sectors. It is surprising that manufac-

TABLE 3.4

GDP Growth by Sector of the Economy: Brazil and Mexico, 1950–1993
(average annual compound growth rates)

	Brazil				Mexico			
	1950–1973	1973–1980	1980–1989	1989–1993	1950–1973	1973–1980	1980–1989	1989–1993
Agriculture	3.8	4.8	3.2	0.7	3.5	3.4	0.5	1.8
Mining	10.3	8.0	7.3	1.3	3.7	11.3	2.7	1.6
Manufacturing	8.8	6.8	0.9	−2.2	7.2	6.0	1.5	2.9
Construction	8.3	12.0	−0.3	−3.9	7.7	6.9	−1.5	5.0
Public utilities	5.6	7.3	6.5	2.8	11.0	8.7	6.3	3.2
Wholesale and retail trade	6.8	6.3	1.1	−0.9	7.0	9.2	0.6	2.2
Transport and communications	8.5	11.9	3.3	1.3	6.9	8.8	1.4	5.8
Finance and real estate	6.9	7.7	3.2	−4.5	5.1	4.6	4.0	4.0
Other services	8.2	6.4	2.6	3.4	6.7	6.0	1.5	2.5
Total (All branches)	7.2	7.1	2.1	−0.6	6.2	6.7	1.4	2.9

Source: Mulder (1998).

turing showed a very average performance even though economic policy focused on this part of the economy.

Level Comparisons of GDP and Labor Productivity by Sector of the Economy

It was shown that Brazil and Mexico were among the fastest growing economies in Latin America and in the world until the debt crisis of 1982. In addition to rapid growth, labor moved out of agriculture, a low-productivity sector, to mostly services, showing an above-average productivity for the entire postwar period. As such, the structure of the Brazilian and Mexican workforce converged to match that of industrialized countries. The growth rates presented earlier show only part of the dynamics of these countries. They fail to show whether Brazil and Mexico increased the efficiency at which they deployed their factor inputs. To answer this question we compare their productivity with the country of "best practice" in terms of factor utilization, the United States, using a production approach.

International comparisons of output and productivity have been the research focus of the International Comparisons of Output and Productivity (ICOP) project of the University of Groningen since 1983. Following the production

TABLE 3.5

Labor Productivity Growth by Sector of the Economy: Brazil and Mexico, 1950–1993 (annual average compound growth rates)

	Brazil				Mexico			
	1950–1973	1973–1980	1980–1989	1989–1993	1950–1973	1973–1980	1980–1989	1989–1993
Agriculture	2.1	4.8	3.9	−5.7	2.8	3.5	0.3	2.6
Mining	8.0	1.4	4.6	−1.4	1.5	8.4	1.7	6.1
Manufacturing	4.9	4.3	−4.4	0.9	2.5	0.7	−0.3	3.7
Construction	2.6	3.4	−1.1	−6.8	2.2	−0.9	−2.8	−1.3
Public utilities	2.7	5.8	5.0	1.1	6.3	2.2	1.8	3.1
Wholesale and retail trade	1.2	4.3	−6.2	−4.1	2.6	3.2	−3.3	−0.4
Transport and communications	4.8	9.6	0.2	1.2	2.8	0.8	−0.2	3.3
Finance and real estate	−0.6	0.6	−1.3	−6.4	0.9	0.4	1.9	3.8
Other services	1.6	1.7	−3.5	2.1	2.5	−1.4	−0.8	0.6
Total (All branches)	3.7	4.5	−1.6	−2.9	3.6	2.4	−0.4	1.9

Source: Mulder (1998).

approach, ICOP derives purchasing power parities (PPP) or so-called unit value ratios from values of output and quantities produced. Using labor and capital input data, ICOP subsequently compiles measures of labor productivity, capital productivity, and total factor productivity. Most ICOP comparisons have been bilateral, with the United States as the benchmark country, although some ICOP studies have also applied multilateral techniques to manufacturing and agriculture comparisons. ICOP has focused on manufacturing,[2] although some studies have been conducted on agriculture[3] and mining.[4] Mulder's 1998 study is the first to apply the ICOP approach to services in a systematic and detailed way, focusing on Brazil and Mexico. The production approach followed by ICOP is complementary to the expenditure approach adopted by the International Comparisons Project of Eurostat, United Nations and World Bank (ICP).[5]

1975 was the benchmark year for our sectoral comparisons. For the derivation of PPPs, data were required on the value of output and the quantity of goods or services produced. For the goods-producing sector, it is relatively easy to determine what is being produced. However, this is not the case for services. The physical output of services is defined, in line with Hill,[6] as the change in the condition of the person or good affected. This can be very complex for at least three reasons. First, it is often not clear what exactly is being changed, and even when it is, it may not be possible to measure it. In this respect it is useful to distinguish between comparison-resistant and non-comparison-resistant services. Education, health care, and government are included in the former category. For example, on a macro level it is almost impossible to assess the impact of physician services on the health status of a population. As an alternative, proxy indicators of the production process are used, such as the number of patient-days in a hospital adjusted for case-mix differences of medical treatments. The unit of output for many non-comparison-resistant services is also not clear-cut. For example, passenger kilometers, a commonly used output measure for rail passenger transport, fails to account for differences in the proportionate importance of terminal services across countries and for quality in terms of speed, reliability, and safety.

Second, the physical output of many services cannot be captured by a single indicator. Transport is a combination of moving and loading and unloading services. Banking services consist of maintaining deposits, cashing checks, and issuing loans. Third, many output indicators fail to account for quality differences. The quantity indicators used in our binary comparisons of services are presented in Mulder.[7] Where possible an adjustment was made to account for the lower quality of services produced in Brazil and Mexico relative to the United States.

Brazilian labor productivity was only 5% of the U.S. level in agriculture in 1975, and was much below the relative performance of other parts of the commodity-producing sector. Services turned out to be a very heterogeneous sector, showing relatively low productivity in communications and public utilities and relatively high productivity in transport and wholesale and retail trade. In Brazil and Mexico, the relative productivity in services was more than twice that of the commodity-producing sector. Mexico performed relatively better than Brazil in agriculture, communications, finance and real estate, public utilities, and transport, but worse in mining and manufacturing.[8]

The 1975 benchmark results were extrapolated to the period from 1950 to 1993 using time series of GDP at constant prices and employment (see Table 3.6). In this period the performance of Brazilian and Mexican agriculture worsened vis-à-vis the United States. Until 1982 the relative productivity of Brazilian mining, manufacturing, and construction converged to U.S. productivity levels; after that time their performance deteriorated. Transport and communications and other services were the only branches of services showing some catch-up with U.S. levels, whereas the relative performance of distribution and finance and real estate in Brazil deteriorated. The overall productivity performance almost doubled relative to the United States from 1950 to 1982, but subsequently dropped 5 percentage points until 1993. In

TABLE 3.6

ICOP Results: Value Added per Person Engaged—Brazil and Mexico as Percentages of the United States, 1950–1993

	1950	1973	1980	1989	1993
Panel A: Brazil as Percentage of the United States					
Agriculture	6.7	5.1	6.8	6.6	4.4
Mining	12.7	28.0	54.1	60.6	44.9
Manufacturing	26.8	44.0	57.0	27.2	25.2
Construction	32.4	50.0	75.3	70.5	51.8
Public utilities	28.1	14.7	23.3	30.4	30.0
Wholesale and retail trade	45.2	39.7	53.2	25.3	19.9
Transport and communications	15.6	24.3	40.4	33.3	30.7
Finance and real estate	57.4	34.6	37.1	33.6	24.6
Other services	29.3	37.5	42.7	31.0	34.2
Total (All branches)	12.3	18.4	25.4	20.0	17.0
Panel B: Mexico as Percentage of the United States					
Agriculture	10.4	9.0	11.1	7.8	7.3
Mining	53.6	27.9	85.8	75.0	74.5
Manufacturing	24.7	23.8	24.2	16.9	17.5
Construction	36.5	51.0	57.2	45.7	42.3
Public utilities	14.1	16.4	20.4	20.1	21.5
Wholesale and retail trade	25.9	31.4	39.1	24.5	22.4
Transport and communications	31.4	31.5	29.0	23.0	23.1
Finance and real estate	74.0	63.8	67.6	81.0	89.6
Other services	23.1	36.6	33.4	31.3	32.6
Total (All branches)	16.9	24.7	29.7	25.9	26.7

Source: Mulder (1998).

Mexico, mining, construction, distribution, and public utilities and other services show a catch-up process with U.S. productivity levels in the 1950–1982 period. From 1950 to 1982 overall productivity increased almost 13 percentage points, but decreased 4 percentage points afterward. Manufacturing shows no catch-up with U.S. levels, despite the fact that government policy focused on this sector of the economy.

EXPLAINING PRODUCTIVITY GROWTH AND LEVELS

This section links the economic performance of Brazil and Mexico to factor inputs in a simple growth accounting framework. On an aggregate level GDP growth is explained through the growth of factor inputs and the growth of output per unit of input using a Cobb-Douglas production function. Factor inputs consist of quantitative and qualitative measures of labor and physical capital. Several measures of single and joint factor productivity are presented. We also analyze labor productivity differentials by sector of the economy between Brazil and Mexico on the one hand and the United States on the other by looking at the human and physical capital content of production using a level accounting approach.

Explaining Productivity Growth

The growth accounts presented here cover the period from 1950 to 1994 because the availability of data does not permit analysis of previous periods. We have selected 1973, 1980, and 1989 as benchmarks. Growth accounting exercises may serve different purposes, such as explaining differences in growth rates and levels between countries, illuminating processes of convergence and divergence, assessing the role of technical progress, and calculating potential output losses. The growth accounts go successively through the main features that may have significant explanatory value.

The results with respect to the most traditional explanatory factors, that is, changes in the quantity and quality of labor inputs and changes in the quantity and quality of capital inputs, are presented. We also include natural resources as an explanatory factor because, although difficult to measure, Brazil and Mexico have abundant resources.

We have included the quality effects in the factor inputs because in the case of labor inputs the level of education can be related rather directly to improvement of the labor force. In the case of capital, the idea of embodying technical progress in the form of quality improvement in successive vintages of capital was first put forward by Robert Solow in 1962. The basic argument is that physical investment is the prime vehicle by which technical progress is realized. This capital embodiment effect is not a "catch-all" effect of technical progress (as suggested initially by Solow) because a large portion of technical progress is embodied in the labor force and organizational and other improvements. The quality effect is the result of three forces: embodied technical progress, changes in the average age of the stock, and changes in its composition. If the average age of the capital stock goes down, this raises the embodiment effect because newer vintages will have more weight in the total capital stock.

Maddison[9] finds Solow's basic point extraordinarily illuminating. Inclusion of a modest element of technical progress in the analysis does help explain the nature of the growth process and clarifies the impact of changes in the age of capital in a way that is not possible outside the vintage context.

It has been argued that existing differences in technology between advanced countries are increasingly related to differences in work practice and shop-floor organization, these being typically features of disembodied rather than embodied technological change.[10] However, in the case of the Latin American countries the difference between their capital stock and that of the technological leader is still very substantial, and it seems reasonable to assume that technological advance in Latin America will take place, at least partially, through the embodiment of technology in the capital stock.

The age of capital is the basic argument for the inclusion of a vintage element. Direct measurement of the vintage effect is very difficult, but the empirical information on age gives us a clue as to the importance of this effect. However, the age effect is only one factor in the embodiment effect. A recent article by Hulten[11] shows that the failure to adjust capital explicitly for changes in quality diverts the quality effects into the conventional total-factor-productivity residual. Hulten found that approximately 20% of the residual growth of quality-adjusted output could be attributed to embodied technical change.

In order to explain in more detail the complex developments that have occurred since 1950, measures of total factor productivity have been prepared that are different from the traditional labor productivity indicator. The increases of the different factor inputs are measured in average annual compound growth rates. Labor input is derived by multiplication of employment and annual hours per person. The quality effect of labor results from the growth of equivalent years of education, with the assumption that a 1% increase in education causes a 0.5% proportionate gain in labor quality.[12] The quantity and quality effects have been weighted by the relevant factor shares to give the augmented labor input. The average annual compound growth rates of the gross capital stock and of the quality of the capital stock (vintage effect) were weighted by the respective factor share to give the augmented capital input.[13] The sum of the augmented capital and labor inputs plus the growth rate of the natural resources input weighted by 0.1 gives the augmented joint factor input, which is an indication of the impact of factor inputs in economic growth. The following sections present the derivation of the labor, capital, and land inputs in some more detail.

Labor

Labor input was estimated in hours worked and not in terms of employment because the average annual hours worked per employee varies substantially between Brazil and Mexico.[14] The main trends in labor quantity and quality are summarized in Table 3.7. Employment grew rapidly, but annual hours per person declined steadily during the whole postwar period. Labor quality, which is reflected by educational level, shows a steady increase over the whole period.[15] The augmented labor input estimates are weighted by the factor share of labor in GDP and by the sum of the labor quantity and quality growth rates.

In Table 3.7 the quantitative and qualitative changes discussed above have been combined into a measure of "augmented" total labor input. Both changes have been weighted by 0.6, and we have additionally assumed that a 1% increase in education causes a 0.5% proportionate gain in labor quality. From Table 3.7 it becomes clear that no uniform tendency can be distinguished. From the 1950–1973 to the 1973–1980 period, Brazil and Mexico show slow to marked acceleration. In 1980–1989 growth decelerated. In 1989–1994 Brazil experienced a marked deceleration, whereas growth increased somewhat in Mexico.

Total Fixed Capital Stock

Growth accounting only becomes possible if reliable estimates of the flow of services of physical capital are available; for example, in analogy with labor, one would like to know the amount of machine hours used in production during the period of reference. However, data availability normally does not permit this procedure and we therefore used the generally accepted proxy for this calculation, namely, the estimation of the capital stock based on the perpetual inventory method developed by Raymond Goldsmith. The capital stock has been disaggregated into residential structures, machinery and equipment, and nonresidential structures, with respective service lives of 50, 15, and 40 years.[16] The perpetual inventory model produces a "capacity stock" of capital. This includes all capital assets, but some of these may be temporarily idle and others may have been withdrawn from production and held in reserve in case they may be needed to meet an unexpected rise in demand. Therefore this model will not produce estimates of the "utilized" stock.

To produce a capital-augmented joint factor productivity, we have augmented the capital stock. This quality effect is the result of three forces: embodied technical progress, changes in the average age of the capital stock, and changes in the composition of the capital stock. If the average age of the capital stock goes down, it raises the embodiment effect because newer vintages receive more weight in total capital stock. The basic argument is that physical investment is the prime vehicle by which technical progress is realized. The rates of vintage improvement chosen here are rather low, 1.5% per year for machinery and equipment and 0.5% for nonresidential structures. For residential structures we assumed no vintage improvement.

Table 3.7 also shows the rates of growth of the total capital stock in the 1950–1994 period. Brazil and Mexico experienced high growth of the capital stock in the 1950–1973 period. During the 1973–1980 period, capital stock growth showed no tendency to slow down. In the 1980–1994 period, growth rates decelerated drastically.

The quality effect of capital inputs is also presented in Table 3.7. Average growth in Brazil was 0.7% during the 1950–1973 period, 1.1% from 1973 to 1980, and fell substantially below 1% in the 1980–1990 period. Table 3.7 presents the augmented capital input that results from adding the impact of the increments of quantity and quality of capital. The combined effect of quantity and quality makes clear that capital inputs grew at a very high pace, especially from 1950 to 1980. Since then growth has been much slower. In the augmented capital input the quality and quantity effects are combined and weighted by capital's factor share in GDP, and reflect the tendencies described above.

Land

Land has been used as an indicator of natural resource endowment. Natural resources have been measured as the amount of land in use, weighting arable and permanent crop land 1.0, permanent pasture 0.3, and forest land 0.1. At this stage it has not been possible to include more sophisticated measures of natural endowments, which undoubtedly have had a great impact in economic growth, especially in Brazil and Mexico. The factor share used for weighting land was 0.10 for all countries. Table 3.7 shows clearly that the expansion of the agricultural frontier slowed down after 1950 and that since the 1980s agricultural land has been diverted from agricultural uses.

In Table 3.7 a comparison is made between GDP and joint factor productivity. The interpretation of joint factor productivity is still a matter of major debate. Here a step-by-step approach has been followed, starting with a measurement of joint factor productivity that includes the quality improvement of the factor inputs. The final remaining residual can be considered as an approximate measure of the effect of disembodied technical progress on long-term growth, but other unmeasured influences, as well as statistical and other errors, are also included in it. In comparing different kinds of growth account-

TABLE 3.7

Explaining Economic Growth of Brazil and Mexico, 1950–1994
Factor Inputs and Joint Factor Productivity

	Brazil				Mexico			
	1950–1973	1973–1980	1980–1989	1989–1994	1950–1973	1973–1980	1980–1989	1989–1994
GDP	6.91	7.18	2.26	0.90	6.50	6.43	1.36	2.99
Labor								
Quantity	2.90	3.01	2.11	1.54	2.22	3.66	2.46	2.60
Quality	1.33	1.83	1.27	1.28	1.59	2.70	1.08	1.08
Augmented	2.96	2.77	1.93	1.63	1.63	3.46	1.17	1.31
Capital								
Quantity	8.50	10.35	4.99	2.25	8.14	7.85	4.57	3.70
Quality	0.74	1.06	0.44	−0.02	0.61	0.86	0.63	0.52
Augmented	1.85	3.78	1.82	0.72	4.14	3.11	2.51	2.30
Land	2.07	1.37	0.49	0.52	0.36	0.99	−1.05	−0.06
Doubly augmented total factor productivity	1.90	0.50	−1.53	−1.50	0.70	−0.24	−2.52	−0.62
% Explained	69	91	168	267	89	102	284	120

Source: Hofman (1998).

ing, one must be aware that the residual may be quite different with different authors. A joint factor productivity without quality augmentation is what is very often presented in this kind of study.

For the 1950–1973 period, 31% of GDP growth in Brazil and 11% of Mexican growth cannot be explained by increases in factor inputs. The "Lost Decade" of the 1980s caused the residual to become highly negative, indicating that total factor productivity growth was negative.

One of the most prominent writers in this tradition, Abramovitz, stresses social capability and technological congruence. The first term is defined as "the state of a country's political, commercial and financial institutions, its level of general and technical education, and the experience of its entrepreneurs and managers with large scale organization and practice"[17]; the second term refers to the adaptation of the leader country's technology for use in the follower country.

Overexplanation in the 1980–1989 and 1980–1994 periods also increased substantially by adding these factors, contributing little to the understanding of GDP growth. However, the results of the crisis period of the 1980s have to be analyzed with caution. The negative growth of total factor productivity can be attributed partly to demand-side distortions, which cause a fall in economic growth. The debt crisis of the 1980s caused stagnation of economic growth. Negative total factor productivity growth has to be attributed partly to this difference between potential and actual growth. Because Brazil and Mexico were far off their transformation curves, the results for the 1980s have to be interpreted with caution.

When analyzing total factor productivity in a comparative perspective, at least two striking results become clear.[18] First is the similarity of total factor productivity growth rates between Asia and the advanced and Iberian countries, especially in the 1950–1980 period. From 1980 onward, Asian total factor productivity growth rates are much higher than in Iberia and the advanced countries. Latin America's total factor productivity growth rates are much lower than those of Asia or the other countries of our sample.

The second striking result is the relatively small differences in total factor productivity growth, measured as a percentage of GDP growth, between Latin America and the Asian group for the 1950–1980 period, both in regard to total factor productivity and doubly augmented total factor productivity. In very general terms, there is less than a 10 percentage point difference between the Latin American and Asian group (Asia being higher), along with a difference of equal or somewhat higher magnitude between Asia and the advanced countries.

Krugman (1994) generated a lively debate about the Asian growth performance by asserting that "Asian growth seems to be driven by extraordinary growth in inputs like labor and capital rather than by gains in efficiency."[19] He considered Singapore in particular, using the data of Young,[20] showing that total factor productivity growth was zero. However, although factor accumulation explains a great part of the growth performance in the Asian case, as Table 3.8 shows, it also shows very respectable growth rates of total factor productivity.[21]

One could apply the Krugman argument to the cases of Brazil and Mexico and use doubly augmented total factor productivity as he does. Table 3.8 shows that since 1973 the growth of inputs explains, and in some periods overexplains, a great part of economic growth. It becomes clear that not much space is left for efficiency gains.

Finally, it is again important to stress the interdependency of growth factors, either in the proximate or the ultimate sphere, or in combination. The

TABLE 3.8

International Comparison: GDP and Total Factor Productivity, 1950–1994
(average annual compound growth rates and % of GDP)

	GDP				Total Factor Productivity				Doubly Augmented Total Factor Productivity			
	1950–1973	1973–1980	1980–1989	1989–1994	1950–1973	1973–1980	1980–1989	1989–1994	1950–1973	1973–1980	1980–1989	1989–1994
Brazil	6.9	7.2	2.3	0.9	2.6	2.2	–0.5	–0.7	1.9	0.5	–1.5	–1.5
Mexico	6.5	6.4	1.4	3.0	2.7	1.9	–1.5	0.3	0.7	–0.2	–2.5	–0.6
Arithmetic averages												
Latin America	5.4	4.8	1.5	4.0	2.5	1.1	–0.9	1.8	1.5	0.1	–1.8	1.0
Asia	8.4	7.7	8.0	6.9	4.4	1.6	3.9	3.4	2.9	–0.1	2.5	2.0
Iberian countries	5.8	2.7	2.7	1.8	4.1	1.1	1.3	0.8	2.9	0.0	–0.2	0.1
Advanced countries	5.3	2.2	2.6	1.8	3.5	1.0	1.3	1.1	2.8	0.3	0.6	0.8
Explanatory Power of Total Factor Productivity (as % of GDP)												
Brazil					38	31	–22	–77	28	7	–65	–166
Mexico					42	30	–107	10	11	–3	–178	–20
Arithmetic averages Latin America					46	23	–60	45	28	2	–120	25
Asia					52	21	48	50	35	–2	31	29
Iberian countries					71	41	48	44	50	0	–7	6
Advanced countries					66	45	50	61	53	14	23	41

Note: Latin America refers to Argentina, Brazil, Chile, Colombia, Mexico, and Venezuela. Asia refers to Korea and Taiwan. Iberian countries are Spain and Portugal, and advanced countries include France, Germany, Japan, the Netherlands, the United Kingdom, and the United States.

Sources: Hofman (1998); see also note 8.

growth accounting framework, even in its extended version, is not able to specify the interrelationships that exist among the different factors. As Abramovitz (1993) stated, "Standard growth accounting is based on the notion that the several proximate sources of growth that it identifies operate independently of one another. The implication of this assumption is that the contributions attributable to each can be added up. And if the contributions of every substantial source other than technological progress has been estimated, whatever of growth is left over—that is, not accounted for by the sum of the measured sources—is the presumptive contribution of technological progress."[22]

Latin America's "Lost Decade" of the 1980s caused the residual to become highly negative, indicating that total factor productivity growth was negative. This was not, however, the case in the Asian or the developed countries (although doubly augmented total factor productivity was also negative in some periods in those countries), since their total factor productivity remained positive, albeit with declining growth rates.

Explaining Productivity Levels

In addition to explaining growth rates of GDP and productivity, we analyzed differences in productivity levels between Brazil and Mexico on the one hand and the United States on the other.[23] For this purpose we used a level accounting approach, as developed by van Ark.[24] This approach is also based on a Cobb-Douglas function, with constant returns to scale, and factor inputs that are paid according to their marginal product. Joint factor productivity (A) is derived by

$$\ln \frac{A^x}{A^v} = \ln\frac{Y^x}{Y^v} - \alpha^*\ln \frac{L^x}{L^v} - (1-\alpha)^*\ln\frac{K^x}{K^v} \tag{1}$$

Formula (1) can be rewritten as

$$\ln \frac{A^x}{A^v} = \ln\frac{(Y^x/L^x)}{(Y^v/L^v)} - (1-\alpha)^*\ln\frac{(K^x/L^x)}{(K^v/L^v)} \tag{2}$$

where Y is output; L, labor input; and K, capital input. The share of labor compensation in value added is referred to, and X and U are countries X (Brazil and Mexico) and U (United States), respectively. Labor productivity differentials are thus explained by looking at capital intensity of production and the quality of human capital. The results are summarized in Table 3.9 for the Brazil/United States comparison and in Table 3.10 for the Mexico/United States comparison.

Brazilian value added per working hour in agriculture and mining was the lowest of all sectors compared with the United States in 1980. Services showed the highest relative productivity level, namely, 32% of the U.S. level. Labor productivity in the total economy was 25% of the U.S. level. The economic crisis of the 1980s had a large impact on the relative productivity performance of Brazilian manufacturing, construction, and services, and to a lesser extent on that of agriculture. Labor productivity of the total economy fell by 6 percentage points.

Differences in the capital intensity of production explain almost half of the large productivity gap between Brazilian and U.S. agriculture in 1980 (see

TABLE 3.9

Effects of Capital Intensity and Labor Quality on Comparative Labor Productivity
Levels: Brazil/United States (USA = 100), 1980 and 1990

	Value Added per Hour Worked	Total Gap with U.S. Level (%)	Contribution to Gap (%)			
			Capital Intensity	Labor Quality[a]	Final Residual	Total
1980						
Agriculture and mining	7.7	92.3	39.9	7.1	53.0	100.0
Manufacturing and construction	31.0	69.0	18.0	21.9	60.2	100.0
Services	32.1	67.9	29.9	18.3	51.8	100.0
Total (All sectors)	24.7	75.3	40.2	18.0	41.9	100.0
1990						
Agriculture and mining	5.9	94.1	56.6	4.8	38.6	100.0
Manufacturing and construction	21.4	78.6	58.6	13.6	27.8	100.0
Services	21.3	78.7	61.9	10.5	27.6	100.0
Total (All sectors)	18.6	81.4	63.1	11.8	25.0	100.0

[a]Adjustment based on the number of general years of schooling. Its effect on labor productivity was multiplied by 0.6 because schooling has only a partial effect on productivity.

Source: Available upon request from the authors.

Table 3.9). The relatively large explanatory value of capital intensity in agriculture results from the relatively high capital productivity in this part of the economy. Brazilian agricultural workers disposed only 5% of the volume of fixed tangible capital compared with their American colleagues. Differences in capital intensity were less pronounced in manufacturing and construction and services, and its contribution was therefore smaller (21% and 32% of the gap, respectively). Capital intensity differences between Brazil and the United States increased between 1980 and 1990, and as a result so did its contribution to explaining the productivity gap (see the bottom panel of Table 3.9).

Differences in the intensity of human capital are another important variable explaining productivity differentials. The largest difference in schooling levels of employees was in agriculture and mining: 2.5 years of formal schooling in Brazil compared with 11 years in the United States in 1980. Brazilian productivity would have risen if its working population had enjoyed the same quantity of schooling as their U.S. colleagues. Schooling, however, is not the only determinant of labor productivity levels. We assumed that the schooling differential affects the relative labor productivity level by only 50%.[25] When corrected for schooling differentials in 1980, the relative performance of agriculture almost doubled, that of manufacturing and construction increased by 70%, and that of services rose by more than half. The contribution of human capital to explaining the productivity differential decreased from 1980 to 1990, as differences in schooling levels between Brazil and the United States narrowed over time.

Deducting the contribution of differences in capital intensity and schooling from the labor productivity gap yields the final residual (penultimate column of Table 3.9), which represents all determinants of labor productivity unaccounted for in the present approach as well as measurement errors. The residual is often referred to as joint factor productivity, for example, the combination of two partial productivity measures—labor and capital productivity. The largest residual was found in agriculture and mining in 1980 and 1990, and results partly from the high relative capital productivity in Brazil. Services had the lowest contribution of joint factor productivity, resulting from a relatively low level of capital productivity.

The labor productivity gap between Brazil and the United States widened between 1980 and 1990. The drop in relative productivity was strongest in services. The widened productivity gap is explained in large part by the relative decline in the capital intensity, capital productivity, and labor productivity of Brazil. As a result, the contribution of joint factor productivity, the joint effect of labor and capital productivity, also decreased.

Table 3.10 demonstrates the major results of the level accounting approach for the Mexico/United States comparison. Services was also the best-performing sector in Mexico, in terms of relative productivity in 1980 and 1991, as in Brazil, followed by manufacturing and construction and agriculture and mining. The relative performance of agriculture and mining decreased in the 1980–1991 period, whereas that of the other two sectors slightly increased.

The difference in capital intensity of production contributed 58% to the productivity gap in agriculture and mining in 1980 and resulted also from high capital productivity. Mexican agriculture and mining was more capital intensive than its Brazilian counterpart, due to the large oil and gas extraction sector. The smallest contribution of capital intensity differences was in services, both in 1980 and 1991.

Though schooling differentials between Mexico and the United States were smaller than those between Brazil and the United States, they explained a sub-

TABLE 3.10

Effects of Capital Intensity and Labor Quality on Comparative Labor Productivity
Levels: Mexico/United States (USA = 100), 1980 and 1991

	Value Added per Hour Worked	Total Gap with U.S. Level (%)	Contribution to Gap (%)			
			Capital Intensity	Labor Quality[a]	Final Residual	Total
1980						
Agriculture and mining	11.3	88.7	57.8	9.6	32.6	100.0
Manufacturing and construction	24.7	75.3	51.6	14.4	33.9	100.0
Services	30.3	69.7	27.2	16.7	56.1	100.0
Total (All sectors)	24.7	75.3	46.2	16.2	37.7	100.0
1991						
Agriculture and mining	6.3	93.7	73.9	4.5	21.6	100.0
Manufacturing and construction	26.3	73.7	46.5	12.5	41.0	100.0
Services	32.1	67.9	16.0	13.5	70.5	100.0
Total (All sectors)	24.7	75.3	42.2	13.8	44.0	100.0

[a]Adjustment based on the number of general years of schooling. Its effect on labor productivity was multiplied by 0.6 because schooling has only a partial effect on productivity.

Source: Value added from appendix by authors.

stantial share of the productivity differential of all sectors. The counterfactual analysis shows that the relative labor productivity performance of Mexican agriculture would have increased 75% in 1980 if Mexican workers had enjoyed the same number of years of education as their American colleagues. Productivity in manufacturing and construction would have increased 44% and that of services 38%. As the number of years of schooling for Mexican workers increased more rapidly in the 1980s than that for Americans, its contribution decreased in all sectors in 1990.

The largest contribution of joint factor productivity in 1980 and 1991 was in services, and originated from the relatively high levels of labor and capital productivity. This result differs from the Brazil/United States comparison, where we found the highest contribution of joint factor productivity in agriculture. Another major difference between the Brazil/United States and Mexico/United States comparison is the small increase in joint factor productivity from 1980 to 1991 in the latter case and a decrease in the former. The contribution of joint factor productivity decreased from 1980 to 1991 in agriculture for both Brazil and Mexico, a result of a fall in labor productivity and a fall in capital intensity.

CONCLUDING REMARKS

The growth accounting exercise presented in this paper shows that increments in the capital stock were the major force behind economic growth in Brazil and Mexico. Similarly, differences in the capital intensity of production explain a large share of the productivity differentials between Brazil and Mexico on the one hand and the United States on the other. Joint factor productivity plays a more important role in explaining productivity differentials across countries than in explaining growth over time. The sectoral breakdown provided in the level comparison shows that the role of capital intensity and joint factor productivity strongly varies across sectors in both the Brazil/United States and Mexico/United States comparisons.

It should be stressed that growth and level accounting can only explain part of the process of economic growth and productivity differentials across countries because it does not deal with other factors such as economic policy, the national and international environment, and noneconomic factors such as natural disasters and war. These belong to the realm of what now generally is known as the ultimate causes of growth or productivity differentials in comparison with the proximate causes of growth analyzed here. The ultimate sources of Latin American performance are less clearly established than its proximate causes. The most important ultimate causes in Latin America's economic performance are probably economic policies, institutions, and historical events.

In the past decades, the literature on technology has increasingly moved away from the neoclassical framework used in this paper. In this approach knowledge is assumed to be completely exogenous and equally accessible to all firms as a public good. Recent models of technological change focus on the firm's searching process for new techniques in an environment that is characterized by incomplete information. These models also point more clearly in the direction of ultimate causes, such as institutional and organizational factors, which determine the pace of technological change.

ACKNOWLEDGMENTS

Nanno Mulder's research for this paper was conducted at the University of Groningen, The Netherlands. Financial support of the Dutch Foundation for Scientific Research (NWO) is gratefully acknowledged.

NOTES

1. This result is dependent on the periods chosen. The Great Depression in Latin America was rather short-lived; by 1938 most countries were approaching or above the previous total GDP peak level. In the 1980s the crisis was much more extended in time, and several countries only recovered precrisis levels at the end of the decade.
2. See van Ark (1993).
3. Maddison and van Ooststroom (1993).
4. Houben (1990).
5. See also van Ark (1993).
6. Hill (1977).
7. Mulder (1998).
8. See Mulder (1998).
9. Maddison (1991).
10. van Ark (1993).
11. Hulten (1992).
12. See Maddison (1987) for the rationale of the education adjustment.
13. These factor shares were estimated by the authors using national accounts and population census information. The most important adjustment made was for own-account workers, who make up a significant part of the labor force in both countries.
14. Brazilians worked 2,042 hours on average in 1950, and Mexicans worked 2,154 hours. Working hours in Brazil dropped to 1,860 in 1994, and in Mexico to 2,032 hours.
15. The educational level was estimated by the years of formal education of the population. In this growth accounting exercise, primary education has a weight of 1, secondary education a weight of 1.4, and higher education a weight of 2. It seems fair to assume that a rise in the level of education improves the quality of the labor force and therefore its productivity. The average level of education increased rapidly during the 1950–1990 period: from 2.0 years to 6.7 years in Brazil, and from 2.2 years to 8.75 years in Mexico.
16. The service lives used in this method refer to the total length of time from the initial installation of assets to the moment when they are finally scrapped. Clearly these lives may include periods during which the assets are not being used to produce anything.
17. Abramovitz (1991), p. 20.
18. The growth accounting exercise presented here for the 6 Latin American countries was also done for a sample group of 16 countries. Because this paper is about Latin American economic development we did not present the whole database for

all countries, but this is available from the authors upon request. Most of the data with respect to GDP and employment come from Maddison (1995) and were updated using the same sources. If necessary, national sources or databases of international organizations such as the OECD, IMF, the World Bank, or the United Nations were used. The capital stock estimates come from Maddison (1993) for the advanced countries and were updated to 1994 using the same methodology as that for the Latin American countries. Specific estimates were prepared, again using the same methodology, for the Asian and Iberian countries.

19. Krugman (1994), p. 70.

20. Young (1994).

21. The results of Young (1995), which is an updated version of Young (1994), presenting slightly higher total factor productivity growth estimates, coincide to a great extent with the results of this study. His estimates for Korea and Taiwan for the 1960–1990 period are 1.7% and 2.6%, respectively. Our estimates for the 1950–1990 period are 1.7% and 3.0%, respectively.

22. Abramovitz (1993), p. 220.

23. An appendix containing the underlying data of the level comparisons is available from the authors upon request.

24. van Ark (1993).

25. See Maddison (1987).

REFERENCES

Abramovitz, Moses. "The Postwar Productivity Spurt and Slowdown: Factors of Potential and Realisation." In *Technology and Productivity: the Challenge for Economic Policy,* edited by the OECD, 19–36. Paris: OECD, 1991.

Abramovitz, Moses. "The Search for the Sources of Growth: Areas of Ignorance, Old and New." *The Journal of Economic History* 53 (June 1993): 217–243.

Dowrick, Steve, and Duc-Tho Nguyen. "OECD Comparative Economic Growth 1950–1985: Catch-Up and Convergence." *American Economic Review* 79, no. 5 (1989): 1010–1030.

Hill, Peter. "On Goods and Services." *Review of Income and Wealth* 123, no. 4, (1977): 315–338.

Hofman, André A. *The Economic Development of Latin America in the Twentieth Century.* Aldershot, England: Edward Elgar, 1998.

Houben, Aerdt. "An International Comparison of Real Output, Labor Productivity and Purchasing Power in the Mineral Industries of the United States, Brazil and

Mexico for 1975." Research Memorandum no. 368, Institute of Economic Research, University of Groningen, 1990.

Hulten, Charles R. "Growth Accounting When Technical Change Is Embodied in Capital." *American Economic Review* 82, no. 4 (1992): 964–980.

Krugman, Paul. "The Myth of Asia's Miracle." *Foreign Affairs* 73, no. 6 (November/December 1994): 62–78.

Maddison, Angus. "Growth and Slowdown in Advanced Capitalist Countries: Techniques of Quantitative Assessment." *Journal of Economic Literature* 25, no. 2 (1987): 648–708.

Maddison, Angus. *Dynamic Forces in Capitalist Development: A Long-Run Comparative View.* Oxford: Oxford University Press, 1991.

Maddison, Angus. *Monitoring the World Economy, 1820–1992.* Paris: OECD Development Centre, 1995.

Maddison, Angus, and Harry van Ooststroom. "The International Comparison of Value Added, Productivity and Purchasing Power Parities in Agriculture." Research Memorandum no. 36 (GD-1), Groningen Growth and Development Centre, University of Groningen, 1993.

Mulder, Nanno. "The Economic Performance of Brazil, Mexico and the United States in Comparative Perspective, with Particular Reference to the Role of Services." Ph.D. dissertation, University of Groningen, 1998.

Mulder, Nanno, and Angus Maddison. "The International Comparison of Performance in Distribution: Value Added, Labor Productivity and Purchasing Power Parities in Mexican and US Wholesale and Retail Trade 1975/5." Research Memorandum no. GD-2, Groningen Growth and Development Centre, Faculty of Economics, University of Groningen, 1993.

Solow, Robert M. "Technical Progress, Capital Formation and Economic Growth." *American Economic Review* 52, no. 2 (May 1962): 648–708.

van Ark, Bart. "International Comparisons of Output and Productivity: Manufacturing Performance of Ten Countries from 1950 to 1990." Monograph Series, no. 1. Groningen: Groningen Growth and Development Centre, University of Groningen, 1993.

van Ark, Bart, and Angus Maddison. "The International Comparison of Real Product and Productivity." Research Memorandum no. 567 (GD-6), Groningen Growth and Development Centre, University of Groningen, 1994.

Young, Alwyn. "The Tyranny of Numbers: Confronting the Statistical Realities of the East Asian Growth Experience." Working Paper Series no. 4680, National Bureau of Economic Research, March 1994.

Young, Alwyn. "The Tyranny of Numbers: Confronting the Statistical Realities of The East Asian Growth Experience." *The Quarterly Journal of Economics* 110, no. 3 (August 1995): 641–680.

PART II

Patterns of Investment and Growth

The study of investment as a determinant of economic growth has a long and distinguished place in the annals of economics, as well as in economic history. The understanding that the accumulation of physical capital could play a fundamental role in growth, via capital deepening, stands at the center of many seminal contributions from scholars such as Kuznets, Solow, and Abramovitz.[1] This being the case, it has also been natural for scholars to seek out a better understanding of the process of capital formation by examining the functioning of capital markets in history; this research in turn has encouraged the study of evolving financial systems, intermediaries, banks, stock markets, and other institutions. The key development problem here is the creation of more efficient systems to allocate and mobilize the aggregate savings of a society for use in productive investment. There are many well-known studies of this kind in the economic history of the core economies, as in the works of Davis, Sylla, and Neal on Britain and the United States.[2] But work that examines the development of financial systems and capital markets in developing countries, either contemporary or historical, has been rare. Thus the essays in this volume that make a contribution to our understanding of Latin American financial development are a very welcome addition to the literature.

Hanley's essay (Chapter 4) is a probing analysis of the functioning of the São Paulo Bolsa, or stock market, in the pre-1914 period. Her study is built from detailed archival groundwork and seeks to confront the essential questions: How did the market function, and how well did it serve the financing needs of the Paulistas? These are important questions, and not just for Brazilian history. The answers are of broader interest because this was an era in which many developing countries at the periphery established stock markets (including, in the Latin American arena, major markets in Rio de Janeiro, Mexico City, and Buenos Aires). It is important to know whether these fledgling exchanges could indeed deliver a finance capitalism as efficient and sophisticated as the core economies claimed to have. Hanley's evidence overwhelms earlier attempts to categorize the impact of the São Paulo Bolsa and documents its mercurial rise from a modest and informal exchange into a major source of finance capital after 1900.

The essay by della Paolera and Taylor (Chapter 5) takes a look at a different set of financial institutions, banks, in a different country, Argentina, in a different era, the interwar period. They aim to confront an outstanding puzzle in the historical literature. The optimist view argues that the retreat of foreign capital after 1914 in Argentina created a golden opportunity, allowing domestic banks to expand and fill the void and thus keep the previously spectacular Argentine accumulation and growth performance on track. The pessimist view counters that domestic Argentine financial development after 1914 was slow and inefficient, a poor substitute for the foreign institutions, and prone to crisis, thus impairing long-term growth prospects. Using a newly developed database of monthly activities of the banking sector, the authors first attempt to document the ups and downs of the industry from the early 1900s to the late 1930s. With data broken down into domestic and foreign banks, econometric tests reveal very different loan dynamics and leverage choices by local and foreign banks, supporting the pessimistic view that domestic financial development faced substantial challenges once overseas banks took a back seat.

The essay by Twomey (Chapter 6) analyzes the allocation of capital on a global level for developing countries for the entire twentieth century. The main question here is how exactly the ebb and flow of foreign investment has varied over time, and across countries and sectors, and how this informs our view of Latin American development. This is indeed an important question, since the impact of foreign capital in the region has been at the heart of many a political argument in the twentieth century. No previous study has ever managed to quantify capital flows or provide as thorough a comparative analysis as Twomey's laborious data collection now allows. The data illuminate some critical issues: how foreign investments have evolved from mostly railroad stocks to a much broader array of assets; how total foreign investment collapsed in the autarkic years from the 1920s on, only to recover very recently; how Latin America in particular suffered a very big collapse in foreign investment; and how the exposure to foreign investment often correlated with positive growth or income outcomes. The data in this study will no doubt be pored over for many years to come, as it represents a spectacular advance on what we previously knew about that most encompassing set of financial intermediaries, the global capital market.

Notes

1. See Kuznets (1952, 1971), Abramovitz (1956, 1986), and Solow (1956).
2. Davis (1963, 1965), Sylla (1975), Neal (1990).

References

Abramovitz, Moses. "Resource and Output Trends in the United States Since 1870." *American Economic Review* 46 (May 1956): 5–23.

Abramovitz, Moses. "Catching Up, Forging Ahead, and Falling Behind." *Journal of Economic History* 46 (June 1986): 385–406.

Davis, Lance E. "Capital Immobilities and Finance Capitalism: A Study of Economic Evolution in the United States." *Explorations in Economic History* 1 (Fall 1963): 88–105.

Davis, Lance E. "The Investment Market, 1870–1914: The Evolution of a National Market." *Journal of Economic History* 25 (1965): 355–399.

Kuznets, Simon, ed. *Income and Wealth of the United States: Trends and Structure.* London: Bowes and Bowes, 1952.

Kuznets, Simon, ed. *The Economic Growth of Nations.* Cambridge: Harvard University Press, 1971.

Neal, Larry. *The Rise of Financial Capitalism: International Capital Markets in the Age of Reason*. Cambridge: Cambridge University Press, 1990.

Solow, Robert M. "A Contribution to the Theory of Economic Growth." *Quarterly Journal of Economics* 70 (February 1956): 65–94.

Sylla, Richard E. *The American Capital Market, 1846–1914: A Study of the Effects of Public Policy on Economic Development*. Dissertations in American Economic History. New York: Arno Press, 1975.

4

Business Finance and the São Paulo Bolsa, 1886–1917

Anne Hanley
Northwestern University

Scholars have long studied the relationship between formal financial intermediation and economic modernization to assess the latter's importance to the development process. In theory, the emergence of a formal capital market can more efficiently allow for the transfer of resources among the productive sectors of the economy. The state of the financial sector in early stages of development can be of particular importance to the initial shift from agriculture to industry. From the seminal hypothesis of Alexander Gerschenkron on the importance of financial institutions in overcoming economic "backwardness" to recent work on the central role of kin-based financial networks in New England's industrialization, historians have been teasing out these relationships and their impact on the shape of economic change.[1]

Brazil is an area of "recent settlement" in this enterprise of financial sector research. For three decades scholars have labored at the task of understanding why and how Brazil's most important agricultural region, São Paulo, went from a pure export agricultural economy in the 1880s to Brazil's industrial leader by the end of the First World War. The focus of this research had been on the linkages between coffee and urban sectors within the economy, the role of foreign entrepreneurs and capital in São Paulo, and the importance of tariff protection and international economic shocks to industrial investment.[2] Only recently, however, has attention turned to the financial institutions that allowed the transfer of resources from the agricultural to the modern sector to occur.[3]

This new avenue of research has produced mixed findings on the importance of the Brazilian capital markets to the economic transformation taking place at the turn of the twentieth century. Banks appeared to provide little or no investment credit to the new urban commercial and industrial sectors that were popping up and growing quickly.[4] This would lay the modernization burden at the feet of the stock and bond exchange. Research has heretofore been limited to the Rio de Janeiro stock exchange and has yielded mixed results. One scholar found important productivity gains realized by joint-stock companies relative to privately financed companies,[5] whereas another found little benefit to the economy from the emergence of a securities exchange because of the long-run failure of the exchange to keep pace with business formation.[6]

This paper contributes to the debate by using the São Paulo case to suggest that the long-term importance of the securities market to modern sector growth may not be the crucial test. I argue that for the São Paulo Bolsa, a short, sharp burst of activity was enough to have a profound and lasting effect on the region's economic development. After a decade of slow structural maturation in the 1890s, the Bolsa by 1917 had experienced a series of marked changes. First, the exchange was party to brand-new capital formation, principally among urban utilities businesses and industrial companies. Second, the Bolsa financed primarily medium to large companies, directly aiding businesses that were beyond the reach of traditional kin group or community finance. Third, the Bolsa diversified into debt issues after 1909 to the direct benefit of the new urban infrastructure and industrial companies. Finally, this was a domestic phenomenon. Although foreign capital had a sizable presence in the São Paulo economy, it did not compete with or supplant the domestic capital formation taking place in São Paulo's urban areas through the sale of equity and debt. This brief, intense period in the beginning of the century gave São Paulo the institutional framework vital to its early and rapid modernization.

THE EARLY BROKERAGE PROFESSION

The early history of the stock and bond exchange dates from a comprehensive piece of business legislation written in 1850. This legislation, known as the Commercial Code, was prompted by the sudden boom in international demand for Brazil's coffee. The relatively rapid growth of the planter, factor, merchant, and exporter population involved in the coffee trade made the standardization of businesses' practices critical to facilitate exchange and minimize fraud. The Commercial Code began as a set of regulations surrounding the acceptance of various types of commercial paper but went on to form the basis for a body of laws written in the 1860s and 1870s to regulate the legal forms of brokerage activity and business organization, including the fiscal responsibilities of partners and investors in the case of failure, and the legal means to invest in and trade shares of companies. The result was the growth, however modest, of the joint-stock company format, the emergence of a regulated brokerage profession, and, ultimately, the organization of the São Paulo Bolsa.

From 1850 to 1890 the joint-stock format was of limited usefulness to the São Paulo business community due to the regulatory roadblocks set up by the Commercial Code and its offspring. These regulations required that joint-stock companies apply to the imperial government for a charter, something which required an act of Congress to obtain, and that they have a fairly substantial portion of social capital paid in before starting up operations. Most onerous of all the provisions, however, was the one saddling investors with unlimited liability. Under the law, investors bore unlimited liability for the debts of the companies in which they invested for five years from the date of stock purchase, even if the shares had been traded away in the interim. This provision was recognized at the time as antibusiness, earning it the nickname "Law of Impediments." The Brazilian economy at the time was predominantly agricultural, however, and businesses earned little compassion from the government.

The only companies able to attract investors in this relatively hostile business regulatory environment were banks, railroads, and public service companies. Because of the size of their capital requirements, these companies were not easily funded through traditional kin-based or community-based sources of funding and had to rely on a pool of investors to supply them with their capital. They were able to attract investors, where other types of companies could not, in two ways. The first was the route the banks took. These began as closely held companies that proved themselves to be consistently profitable by sticking to low-risk, lucrative commercial banking practices. The sector was able to expand during the era of unlimited liability by enticing investors with an established track record.[7] One publicly owned bank was founded in São Paulo in the 1870s and four new joint-stock banks followed in the 1880s. These five banks together represented a potential 9,500 contos of capital, or about $5 million, distributed in 47,500 shares by 1889.[8]

Railroads and utilities followed a second route for attracting investors: government backing. The railroads all received profit guarantees from the government during the 1870s to 1890s for the explicit purpose of attracting investors.[9] The guarantees worked. The railroad companies underwent dramatic expansion during the 1870s and 1880s, and found a seemingly endless domestic pool of investors on which to draw. The Mogiana railroad grew from 15,000 shares worth 3 million milreis in 1874 to 81,000 shares worth 16 million milreis in 1887.[10] The equity investment in the railroad sector as a whole was worth 91 million milreis by 1886, or approximately $45 million, distributed to investors in 278,000 shares.

The public service companies, urban transportation and utilities, did not receive the same explicit profit guarantees as the railroads, but were granted monopolies. Furthermore, it was the provincial government that set the rates these utilities were allowed to charge. When utilities companies got into financial trouble, the provincial government either authorized a fare increase or bailed them out, much to the chagrin of consumers, who were vocal in criticizing the bad service and high prices. One such company, the Companhia Cantareira e Esgotos (CCE), which held the monopoly for water and sewer service, eased its financial straits with new capital from investors as well as a government bailout.[11] It was clear that this utility had an important safety net that protected it, and its investors, from the liability associated with failure.

Interestingly, capital formation among the largest and most important business ventures during this period appeared to be a domestic phenomenon. Just one foreign-owned railroad and three foreign banks existed in the state of São Paulo during this period. The foreign banks had a combined value of less than 10% of total bank assets for the majority of the period.[12] Additionally, there was only one domestic bank in São Paulo at this time that was *not* organized as a joint-stock company. By the height of the coffee boom in 1886, at least 23 companies raised funds through the sale of close to 450,000 shares, representing $35 million of equity investment.[13] Use of the joint-stock format for business organization helped São Paulo found a regional bank sector and raise capital for a large railway system that opened up São Paulo's agricultural frontier and made possible the expansion of the coffee boom.

1890 TO 1905

The period from 1890 to the early twentieth century began with one of the most aggressive periods of business expansion in Brazilian history and ended with the sharpest recessionary policies of the era. This recession acted as a brake on business formation. The boom to bust cycle is most starkly illustrated by the fact that the same number of stocks were listed on the exchange in 1905 as in 1886. In spite of the uneven terrain of these 15 years, a profound transformation of the Bolsa occurred. This transformation was articulated in three major trends: the emergence of new urban and industrial firms formed as joint-stock companies, a dramatic growth in shareholding, and the first uses of the bond market as a financial tool. In spite of the Bolsa's small size in 1905, the experiences of the 1890s would leave the institution ready for a new, sustained economic boom that lasted up to World War I.

The first São Paulo Bolsa was organized in 1890 as the result of legislative changes that came on the heels of the birth of the new republic. The new government, politically centered in the economically booming Rio de Janeiro–São Paulo region, left behind the guarded policies of the monarchy and actively favored the expansion of domestic enterprise. To the business community, the most important reforms were those which lifted the unlimited liability that for decades had dampened investor interest in joint-stock companies. The reforms of January 1890 lowered the capital threshold required for operation and virtually eliminated all shareholder responsibility for the value of their shares.[14] This legislative reform, coupled with expansive new monetary policies, initiated a flurry of investment and speculation known as the Encilhamento. Over 200 joint-stock companies were founded in São Paulo in the first six months after the reforms, compared with 30 in operation in late 1887. By August of 1890 a prominent broker, Emilio Rangel Pestana, cited the need to provide a forum for such voluminous trading and founded the first formal stock and bond exchange in São Paulo.

The euphoria of the Encilhamento would not last, for the consequences of the liberal business and monetary policies were speculation, fraud, and inflation. The period was plagued by inflation rates that caused the exchange rate to depreciate. This, in turn, made everything denominated in foreign currency more expensive. Imports, the taxes on which were the government's primary source of revenue, declined while the debt service ballooned. The government responded by refocusing on the single goal of restoring the value of the milreis, principally by curtailing the money supply. In pursuing this goal, the government put pressure on the ability of the existing companies to survive and discouraged new investment.[15] Annual report after annual report cited the sluggishness of the economy and new taxes on commercial transactions as the causes behind depressed profits. The late 1890s were as hostile to business as the early 1890s had been inviting.

In spite of the economic malaise, the government left the centerpiece of the new business legislation untouched: Investors continued to remain free of virtually all liability associated with investing in a joint-stock company.[16] A small number but broad range of new companies were organized using the joint-stock format throughout the 1890s. Many of these were commercial and urban utilities firms taking advantage of the accelerated circulation of goods and services prompted by the coffee boom. Several were industrial companies, listed publicly for the first time in São Paulo's history. Limited liability meant that the types of companies that had previously been too new or unproved to attract anything other than private pools of capital, either from kin groups or communities, could now tap a much larger source for their funding.

Many, if not most, of these companies were transitory due to the sharp recessionary policies of the central government after the early 1890s. In any single year the number of joint-stock companies listed on the Bolsa was small, giving the impression that little development took place. This impression is mistaken, however. At least 87 companies were formed through the Bolsa during this decade, representing such businesses as machinery and metalworking, furniture making, textiles, hat and shoe production, food processing, beer brewing, paper production, printing, rudimentary chemical production, and other manufacturing and commercial activities.[17] Although these companies made up a minuscule percentage of all firms in São Paulo, it appears that the industrial firms among them came to constitute a sizable portion—almost 19%—of São Paulo's industrial capital by the end of the period.[18]

The second major trend in the Bolsa's structural transformation during this period was the dramatic growth in shareholding. Although just 28 stocks were listed in both 1886 and 1905, the volume and value of shares listed on the exchange tripled.[19] Several factors contributed to this expansion. First, the banks founded after 1890 were significantly larger than those operating in the 1880s. Second, two of the railway companies, the Paulista and Mogiana, underwent dramatic expansions. By 1905 each had an individual capital value greater than the entire railroad sector in 1886, and their combined worth contributed two-thirds of the Bolsa's paid-in value in 1905. Third, the industrial companies that joined the exchange after 1890 were larger than the infrastructure companies that had dropped off by 1905.

At the same time that the total number of shares was growing, a sort of democratization was taking place within the capital market. The growth in the number of outstanding shares listed on the exchange was accompanied by an increase in the number of individuals investing in the stock market. Evidence from the two largest railway companies, which were also far and away the largest companies listed on the Bolsa, confirms this. The number of investors in the Companhia Paulista doubled from 1893 to 1905, as did the number of investors in the Companhia Mogiana from 1891 to 1903. Each company had approximately 1,100 shareholders in the early 1890s and more than 2,100 shareholders a decade later.[20] The growth in shareholders far outstripped the population growth of the state, meaning the increase in shareholders was not a simple demographic phenomenon.[21] The records of the two railroads also show that the concentration of shares in the hands of large shareholders declined from 1890 to 1905. Both the Paulista's and Mogiana's largest shareholders owned about 14% of the company's stock in the 1890s and just 8% after 1905.[22] The expansion of the Bolsa, then, took the form of drawing more small investors into the capital market.

The third element of the Bolsa's structural transformation during this period, albeit the most timid element of the three, was the early signs of a market for new types of bonded debt. Before 1890, all bond issues were tied to the service and physical infrastructure companies that accompanied the boom in the export sector, such as banks, railroads, public utilities and transportation, and processing mills for agricultural products. After 1890, however, manufacturing and real estate development companies began tapping the bond market for their funding. The first bond issued by a company outside the infrastructure group was for the Companhia Industrial de São Paulo, a manufacturing firm involved in textiles, graphics, and match making. A paper manufacturing firm, the Companhia Melhoramentos de São Paulo, issued a debenture bond in 1895. In 1897 an urban real estate firm that also built electrical substations to power its buildings issued a bond on the São Paulo Bolsa. Although the bond market was not used extensively by industrial and other urban companies, its departure from the infrastructure profile of 1887 demonstrates that investors were beginning to consider funding long-term loans to new types of economic ventures. This new interest was to become an extraordinarily important avenue of business finance less than a decade later.

This apparently static decade, then, was actually one of significant steps toward a mature, diversified exchange. The lack of growth in the 1890s was due to macroeconomic conditions, not to an innate failure of the marketplace. The severe recession purposely provoked by the central government to stabilize foreign exchange rates had the effect of braking new business investment. This was reflected in the Bolsa's inability to expand during this period, spending its time instead changing its profile to accommodate new lines of business.

1905 TO 1917

The changes experienced by the stock and bond exchange between 1905 and 1917 were multiple and bold. There was a rapid growth in the number and types of stock and bond listings after 1905, a dramatic increase in the portion of regional industrial capital financed through the sale of equity, and a boom in bond issues that was important to the surge of development taking place. This was a purely local phenomenon divorced both from the influence of the Rio de Janeiro capital market and from the domination of foreign capital. The domestic nature of this dramatic period of growth goes against the strong undercurrent in Brazilian historiography that assumes that a robust and stable economic environment after 1906 was so attractive to foreign capital that it washed in in waves, lifting Brazil's economy on its rising tide. My research supports an alternative picture of the era for the region of São Paulo—one of

Brazilian (native and immigrant) entrepreneurship, capital, investment, growth, and diversification. The Bolsa was the locus of growth in urban industrial, commercial, and public utilities sectors for a brief but critical period in the prewar economy. The speed with which the joint-stock format was being adopted for new business formation, and the proportion of capital formation that took place as a result, made a significant contribution to the modernization of the São Paulo economy.

The renaissance of the São Paulo Bolsa was directly related to new macroeconomic vigor produced by government policy after 1906. The coffee boom of the 1880s and 1890s had prompted an expansion of coffee planting far beyond the existing market demand for coffee, provoking a crisis in the coffee sector. Overproduction placed pressure on international coffee prices, and export revenues from coffee fell at the rate of 10% per year from 1901 to 1904. The São Paulo government decided to intervene in the market by purchasing excess coffee stocks in order to support prices.[23] In addition, the government instituted a fixed exchange rate that provided stability to domestic prices. These measures protected the income of São Paulo's most important economic sector and ushered in a new era of growth and prosperity.

This new infusion of wealth in São Paulo, however artificial, shook loose the recessionary policies of the turn of the century and drew entrepreneurs and investors back to the market. From 1905 to 1906 alone, the number of equity-funded companies listed in São Paulo rose by 25%. The growth in joint-stock company formations was particularly robust during the five-year period from 1909 to 1913, the year that the market peaked, and was particularly dramatic for public utilities companies and urban industrial and commercial enterprise. Of all companies listed on the Bolsa by 1913, between 65% and 70% of the public utilities companies, textile firms, and other industrial and commercial firms had been founded during this booming five-year period. By 1913, some 167 of 185 companies were public service infrastructure and urban industrial and commercial enterprises outside the traditional offerings of banks, railroads, and insurance companies (Table 4.1).

If we look at the changes to the São Paulo economy introduced by new joint-stock company formations on the basis of their capitalization rather than the firm size of the market, the advances of the post-1905 period become somewhat muted. This is because of the overwhelming volume of railroad capital historically raised through the sale of equity relative to all other business pursuits. Although the railroads accounted for just a handful of the market listings in the 1890s and early 1900s, their capital dominated the Bolsa. Through 1909 over half of all shares in the hands of investors and from 60%

to 70% of all paid-in capital listed on the Bolsa was invested in the railroad companies. These had been the most capital-hungry ventures in the early years of brokerage activity, and their aggressive expansion in the 1880s and 1890s gave them near total dominance of the market's capital.[24]

Although it is true that no sector emerged by 1917 to dislodge the railroads as the largest single sector represented on the Bolsa, there are clear indications of the significant growth of the urban public service, industrial, and commercial firms after 1905. These groups together laid claim to just under 15% of total paid-in equity capital represented on the exchange in 1905, most of it in industrial firms. By 1909 the growth in the number of urban-sector firms doubled their share of listed equity capital to 30%. In real terms, the capital invested in public utilities companies almost tripled from 1909 to 1913, while the capital of industrial-sector firms doubled. The real equity investment of the nonindustrial companies grew by 3.5 times. Meanwhile, the equity value of railroads and banks, the traditional companies to first use public markets for finance, stayed flat or declined in real terms. Their combined share of the market fell from 85% of total paid-in equity in 1905 to just 47% in 1917, whereas 53% of all paid-in equity was invested in urban firms (Table 4.1).

The growth in these new business sectors was stimulated in good part by the demographic and geographic growth of São Paulo. The coffee boom of the

TABLE 4.1

Sectoral Composition of the São Paulo Bolsa
by Number of Firms and Paid-In Capital

	Companies (% of total)				Capital[a] (% of total)			
	1905	1909	1913	1917	1905	1909	1913	1917
Totals[b]	28	73	185	158	228,200	265,851	391,533	280,351
Railroads	18	12	5	2	70	60	41	41
Banking	29	10	4	3	16	10	7	6
Public services	18	18	24	27	4	6	11	14
Textiles	4	14	13	12	1	7	10	9
Other industrial firms	25	18	22	24	9	9	13	13
Nonindustrial firms	7	28	32	32	8	8	18	18

[a] The index used to deflate these capital values was generated by Catão (1992). Because Catão's index only goes to 1913, it was necessary to find an appropriate deflator for the period 1914–1917. Here I chose the price index developed by Haddad (1974).

[b] Total companies are the number of companies quoted on the Bolsa in that year. Total capital is expressed in real contos.

Source: O Estado de São Paulo, Bolsa summary page, January 1906, 1910, 1914, and 1918.

1880s and 1890s had generated a local population boom by importing European laborers to man the plantations. At the same time, the seemingly unending demand for coffee had motivated planters to push out the coffee frontier into previously unsettled areas of São Paulo.[25] The population of the state almost tripled, to over 2 million inhabitants, from the 1870s to 1900.[26] An additional 700,000 immigrants flowed into São Paulo between 1900 and 1915, most drawn by the spread of agriculture and most ending up in the interior of the state, particularly in the areas of recent settlement.[27] The urban centers of these new areas required infrastructure services, which acted as a catalyst for the formation of new utilities companies, while the influx of settlers in São Paulo, as both rural and urban laborers, created demand for domestic-quality goods.[28]

The importance of this new domestic demand to urban and industrial development, and of the use of equity capital to fund that development, is clearest in the example of the textile industry. Here, the ground gained by new joint-stock companies relative to the traditional joint-stock companies is particularly striking. The textile industry grew impressively between 1905 and 1913.[29] Just one textile firm was quoted on the Bolsa in 1905, valued at less than 1% of the Bolsa's total paid-in equity capital. By 1913 there were 24 textile firms, listing equity worth 10% of all São Paulo Bolsa stocks (Table 4.1).

More important, the joint-stock format gained importance in total textile business finance during this period. Just one cotton textile firm was publicly financed before the turn of the century, although we know of at least 18 in existence in the state of São Paulo up to 1905.[30] The single cotton textile firm listed on the Bolsa in 1905 contributed 7% of all capital invested in São Paulo's cotton textile firms.[31] By 1915, just under half of São Paulo's 41 cotton textile companies were financed through stock issues, and more than half of all capital invested in this industry was raised through the sale of stock[32] (Table 4.2). Moreover, the growth in the industry from 1905 to 1915 took place almost entirely through the joint-stock format. Wilson Cano found that the industry grew from 18 to 41 firms between 1905 and 1915, a difference of 23 firms. My stock market data show that 20 new joint-stock cotton textile firms were founded between 1905 and 1915, meaning that virtually all growth in textiles was through market finance.[33] It is clear that the Bolsa played a critical role in the expansion of the textile industry.

When we use the aggregate figures for all São Paulo industry, we find that a much smaller proportion of total industrial firms was listed on the exchange compared with cotton textiles, but that this represented a sizable portion of the total capital employed in São Paulo's industrial sector. Using Cano's estimates

TABLE 4.2

Equity Finance in the Cotton Textile Industry

	Companies Listed	Total São Paulo Companies	Listed as % of Total Companies	Listed Capital (contos)	Total Capital (contos)	Listed K as % of Total K
1905	1	18	5.6	2,000	29,600	6.8
1909	9	24	37.5	17,600	46,700	37.7
1915	21	41	51.2	42,600	81,500	52.3

Note: Capital is quoted in nominal terms. Cano's figures for total companies and total capital are for 1905, 1910, and 1915.

Sources: *O Estado de São Paulo*, Bolsa summary page, January 1906, 1910, and 1916; Cano (1981), p. 292.

of the size of the industrial sector in 1907 and my own calculations for the public equity market, I found that just 1% of industrial firms and close to 20% of total São Paulo industrial capital was represented on the Bolsa in that year.[34] By 1919, according to Cano, joint-stock firms still constituted just 3% of all industrial companies but accounted for 52% of all industrial capital in São Paulo.[35]

That 3% of industrial firms accounted for over half the industrial capital gets to the very heart of the significance of the Bolsa's contribution to economic modernization: It tended to finance the medium and large industrial companies that were probably beyond the means of traditional financing avenues. Published data on the size distribution of Brazilian firms are scarce, but one good source shows that Brazil in 1912 was a nation of very small industrial firms whose average value was 51 contos (about U.S. $16,000), while the median was just 1 conto ($320).[36] São Paulo's 64 joint-stock companies that year averaged 1,324 contos of capital ($424,000); the median was around 1,000 contos ($320,000). This source further shows that just 800 out of more than 9,000 total Brazilian industrial firms were valued at 25 contos or more of capital ($8,000). All São Paulo's joint-stock industrial firms sat above that threshold. In fact, São Paulo's smallest listed industrial firm that year was worth 40 contos, and the next smallest was worth 100 contos. Clearly, the Bolsa played an important role in bringing to life the medium and large firms so important to São Paulo's emerging industrial base.

In the traditional historiography, the importance of local capital formation in the development process has been downplayed and the emphasis has traditionally been placed on the role of foreign capital. Scholars have long held that the phenomenal spurt of economic development experienced by São Paulo and Brazil in the prewar era was a result of the massive influx of foreign capital stimulated by the improved macroeconomic conditions after 1906.[37] My findings on the Bolsa's contribution to business formation are at odds with this interpretation. I argue an alternative scenario in which foreign capital, while sizable, merely played a supporting role in the domestic business formation that was the cornerstone of São Paulo's development. Foreign capital was huge in volume and of great importance to certain sectors of the economy, but neither competed with nor supplanted the type of capital formation experienced through the Bolsa during this period.

In magnitude, foreign capital loomed large. A detailed review of British investment in Latin America from 1865 to 1913 confirms this.[38] British investment in Brazil doubled between 1905 and 1913. The distribution of this investment was highly concentrated in just three sectors, however. Of the 132 million pounds sterling of new investment in Brazil during this period, 120 million pounds went to railways, public utilities, and government loans. In 1909, the year their value peaked in São Paulo, foreign-issued railway bonds were worth almost the full value of the entire Bolsa and two times the value of the domestic equity capital invested in the railroads. In 1911, a huge Canadian transport and electricity conglomerate had holdings in São Paulo valued at an estimated 65 to 80 million milreis.[39] The full value of the domestically financed joint-stock utilities companies in São Paulo at the time was a mere 25 million milreis. Foreign capital was clearly dominant in these sectors.

In addition to direct investment in business enterprise, foreign capital figured importantly in government loans. Government loans were the single largest destination of funds in the history of British lending to Brazil. These loans were particularly relevant to São Paulo's development after 1906. The São Paulo government's decision to undertake the coffee support program meant raising significant sums of capital. It raised one loan valued at close to 4 million pounds sterling by leasing the state-owned Sorocabana railway. It raised an additional 17 million pounds sterling in 1907 and 1908 to pay for the coffee purchases. These loans clearly had general benefits to the state of the economy. It was largely the prosperity of the coffee economy after the 1906 Coffee Conference, when the price support plan was created, that permitted São Paulo's burst of development.

The sheer size of foreign capital in São Paulo has led scholars to accept its dominance of regional finance, but there is ample room to challenge this interpretation. The industrial and utilities sectors are cases in point. Both sectors, whose development is attributed to foreign participation, actually found their financial base in the domestic capital market. The traditional story of foreign investment in industry, for example, is fed by the fact that the majority of industrial establishments in São Paulo in 1920 were foreign owned. Most of these firms, however, were small single-proprietorships owned by permanent immigrants to Brazil and accounted for just 14% of all capital invested in São Paulo industry. This compares with the 52% of industrial capital raised through the sale of equity.[40] There is no question that a few prominent examples of foreign industrial involvement were to be found in Brazil, but these examples were almost entirely absent from São Paulo.[41] Paulista industrial finance was, first and foremost, a domestic phenomenon, and the Bolsa was its primary vehicle.

A similar case can be made for the utilities sector. The huge size of the Canadian-owned São Paulo Tramway, Light, and Power Company, known to this day as "Light," has overshadowed the fact that its investments were limited to the greater São Paulo metropolitan area. "Light" modernized the capital city's transportation to the benefit of 10% of the state's population. The cities of the interior, however, did not gain from Light's presence. The municipal utilities companies for São Paulo's secondary and tertiary cities were financed through the Bolsa. At least 42 separate municipalities outside the capital city raised the money for their urban improvements, including water, electricity, sewer, and gas projects, through the sale of equity. Foreign capital was overwhelming in its sum relative to domestic capital formation, but it was narrowly targeted and did not dominate the development of São Paulo's urban commercial and industrial base to the extent that has been upheld in the literature. Rather, it played an important complementary role.

In addition to championing the importance of foreign capital, traditional studies of Brazilian development have credited large personal family fortunes as the source of domestic-financed enterprise. Indeed, recent research on the Rio de Janeiro Bolsa has found that companies there were too closely held to cultivate an investor pool, and that this tendency toward family ownership undermined the long-term importance of that exchange to business formation.[42] The São Paulo case, by contrast, appears to demonstrate a great deal of impersonal, unrelated investment. To test this, I looked at the Bolsa from the investor's point of view by asking whether there were compelling reasons for unrelated individuals to risk their capital in market investments. I examined the premiums investors could expect to earn and the trading activity the Bolsa generated to develop a proxy for impersonal interest.

As a first pass at the question of investor interest in the securities market, I looked at the behavior of stock prices over time. I compared the quoted price of a given stock against its paid-in value to see what sorts of returns investors could expect in a given year.[43] Up to 1914, all banks traded at or above their par value, and the oldest and largest bank commanded the highest premium of all.

The two largest railroads also commanded huge premiums, anywhere from 1.2 to 2 times the par value.[44] The banks and railroads were the blue chips of their day. Although textile stocks did not trade at prices as high as these older sectors, they routinely traded at or above their par values (Table 4.3). This exercise shows that investors had a reasonable expectation of realizing a profit on their investment in just about any sector they chose, particularly during the boom years between 1909 and 1913. The trading ratio of market to par values rose sharply after 1909 and peaked sometime between 1911 and 1912 for most sectors, corresponding to the pace of new company formations.

The price premiums that stocks earned suggest that investors had a good reason to be interested in the stock exchange. This interest appears to be born out by stock ownership and trading data. I calculated the number of shares in the hands of investors during this period and found that joint-stock company shares in circulation doubled from 1.2 million in 1905 to 2.4 million by 1913. The huge volume of shares that came on the market in less than a decade suggests that this was not a phenomenon of family ownership or closely held companies.[45] Furthermore, I found that there was an active secondary market for shares during this time period. Using published buy-bid quotes and transaction prices as a proxy for investor interest in stocks, I found that a market existed for between half and two-thirds of all stock issues listed in every year from 1906 through 1912.[46]

Investor interest in the market is even more pronounced when we look at the bond market. The number of bonds on the market tripled from 1905 to 1909 and nearly quadrupled again between 1909 to 1914, when the market peaked (Table 4.4). The most striking element is the fact that all the bond mar-

TABLE 4.3

Stock Trading Ratios: Market to Par Values

Equity Shares	1907	1909	1910	1911	1912	1913	1917
Banking	1.40	1.58	1.67	1.48	1.69	1.37	1.68
Railroads	1.42	1.68	1.83	1.84	1.89	1.45	1.62
Public services	1.21	.85	1.26	1.17	1.14	1.08	.58
Textiles	1.06	1.07	1.31	1.48	1.25	.93	.39
Other industrial firms	.76	.88	1.19	1.30	1.35	1.38	.91
Nonindustrial firms	1.03	1.36	1.14	1.02	1.11	1.14	.54
Total	1.34	1.52	1.68	1.64	1.62	1.35	1.41

Source: *O Estado de São Paulo*, Bolsa summary pages and daily stock price columns for January and July.

ket growth came from the new urban and industrial companies. A significant portion of industrial and urban commercial firms—18 of 28 textile companies, 21 of 51 other industrial firms, and 21 of 74 nonindustrial firms—issued bonds during the period from 1909 to 1914. An even greater rise in debt issues took place among the public service companies. Debenture bonds issued by public utilities firms increased fivefold from 1909 to 1912. Of 58 utilities that traded on the exchange at some point between 1905 and the peak year of 1914, 46 had issued debenture bonds. Two-thirds or more of all bonds had a market during this period. In 1910 and 1911, virtually every bond on the Bolsa had a buy bid quoted in the paper.[47]

The figures in Table 4.4 show that of all the sectors of business activity in São Paulo, debenture bonds were issued the most aggressively by public utilities and textile firms. Constructing rough debt–equity ratios for the entire market bears this out.[48] Table 4.5 shows that the public utilities sector had the highest or second-highest level of indebtedness of all business sectors after 1909, followed by the textile manufacturers. These sectors consistently had two to four times the level of indebtedness of publicly traded companies as a whole. Interestingly, the ability of textile firms to issue debt eventually extended to other industrial firms. By 1914 they too had become more highly leveraged.

Although the overall debt levels were low for publicly traded companies as a whole, they nonetheless indicate a significant change in the financing methods available through the formal capital market. Not only did these bonds represent a whole new avenue of finance to the urban industrial and

TABLE 4.4

Bonds of Corporate Debt by Sector

	1886	1905	1909	1912	1914	1917
Banks	1	2	2	1	—	—
Railroads	7	1	2	3	2	1
Public utilities	5	3	6	32	39	38
Textiles	—	1	6	16	16	11
Other industrial firms	—	1	3	17	21	14
Nonindustrial firms	4	1	4	9	18	13
Total bonds	17	9	23	78	96	77

Sources: *Correio Paulistano* (1886) and *O Estado de São Paulo* (1905–1917).

TABLE 4.5

Total Debt to Total Equity for Publicly Traded Companies

	1909	1912	1914
Textiles	.43	.49	.40
Other industrial firms	.17	.27	.40
Nonindustrial firms	.05	.29	.28
Public utilities	.26	.84	.57
Railroads	.04	.11	.06
All stocks	.16	.27	.24

Note: These figures reflect domestic capital only. The low debt levels for the railroads reflect the fact that they went almost exclusively to the foreign markets for their bond issues.

Source: O Estado de São Paulo, Bolsa summary page, January 1910, 1913, 1915.

infrastructure companies, but most of these bonds were also issued by companies that themselves were brand new. Fifteen of eighteen bonds floated by textile companies during this period were for companies founded after 1907. The same is true for the public utilities. These new urban companies were founded in one year and expanding in the next, all but eliminating the need to rely on the relatively slow path of reinvesting profits for their growth.

CONCLUSION

The meteoric rise of the São Paulo Bolsa came to a halt after 1913. Announcements of company bankruptcies began to appear in the stock columns in the following year, and trading appeared to grow thin. The number of observations in any given year became fewer, while the market-to-par ratio of stock prices declined across the board[49] (Table 4.3). The daily stock price columns in the paper grew much shorter and the level of investor interest in the market was low. Fewer than one in five stocks was priced after 1914, compared with better than one in two for the years 1905 to 1912.[50] The market shrank by some 27 companies between the 1913 peak (185) and 1917 (158). The São Paulo Bolsa today is the principal stock and bond exchange in Brazil, yet it listed just 574 companies in the early 1990s, a mere three and a half times the number of companies as in 1917. New issues are rare, and trading is highly concentrated among a handful of stocks.[51] Relative to the importance it bore to the economy in the prewar era, the market appears to have seriously slumped.

The failure of the Bolsa to sustain itself over the long term goes to the heart of scholars' doubts about the importance of the capital market in the modernization of Brazil. One scholar argues that the growth of the 1910–1912 period on the Rio exchange was unimportant because the Bolsa's long-term performance was poor.[52] This macrolevel interpretation of the institution potentially misses its contribution to economic development. I suggest that the long-term health of the institution matters less than the long-term health of the firms that were funded because of its existence. The contraction the Bolsa suffered after 1913 disproportionately affected the smaller listed companies.[53] The larger companies remained intact, and many that date from this era, such as Antartica and Votorantim, are among the largest industrial conglomerates in modern Brazil. The significant contributions of this market in this era are these: The São Paulo Bolsa significantly broadened its reach beyond the traditional sectors that used equity finance to become an important institution for industrial and urban finance, it matured beyond equity issues to become a booming market for corporate debt by 1914, and it provided investors and capital to the medium to large companies that typified the region's rapid development and that were beyond the reach of the traditional means of finance.

The vast contrast between the circumscribed modern Bolsa and the expansionary Bolsa of the early twentieth century supports the view that the development process is neither smooth nor uninterrupted. In the case of São Paulo's development, it appears that a confluence of positive macroeconomic conditions coupled with demographic-stimulated growth in domestic demand and a pool of eager investors created a type of financial Big Bang. In the span of a decade this securities market produced a large, publicly funded industrial sector and provided secondary cities with the infrastructure to support the investment in or modernization of their own industrial and commercial pursuits. The ability of the largest of these companies to withstand the market contraction of the war years ensured that the Bolsa had a lasting effect on economic development.

ACKNOWLEDGMENTS

Research for this paper was made possible through the Fulbright dissertation research program and a grant from the Stanford University Center for Latin American Studies. Additional financial support was generously provided by the Stanford University History Department and the National Endowment for the Humanities dissertation grant program.

NOTES

1. Gerschenkron (1962), Baumol (1965), Cottrell (1979), Michie (1987), Lamoreaux (1994).
2. Dean (1969), Fishlow (1972), Mattoon (1977), Katzman (1978), Silva (1978), Versiani (1979), Cano (1981), Suzigan (1986), Topik (1987).
3. Triner (1994), Hanley (1995).
4. Hanley (1995)
5. Haber (1996).
6. Triner (1994).
7. Hanley (1995).
8. The milreis, expressed as 1$000, was the national currency. One milreis was worth approximately 50 cents in the 1880s, depreciating to about 30 cents in 1890 and fluctuating between 15 and 33 cents up to World War I. One thousand milreis were known as a *conto*. All exchange rates employed in this paper are from Barreto (1977).
9. The guarantees were awarded to each branch line to pay returns to investors during the years of losses. Once a line began to earn a profit above a set threshold, usually 7%, it used the excess profits to repay the government for the guarantee funds it had received.
10. Companhia Mogiana, 25 January 1874 and 1887.
11. Government documents from 1886 show that the CCE also raised a loan from the provincial government of São Paulo. This loan was illustrative of the protection the utilities received. The advance was to be paid back with a credit the company earned from the São Paulo government for every house the utility serviced. At the end of the transaction, the government, which had fronted both the loan and the funds for "repayment," owed the company an additional 2,000 milreis (São Paulo, "Obras Publicas").
12. The founding of a third foreign bank in 1889 pushed the foreign proportion to 20%.
13. Mello (1985) examined inventories to study the structural changes in wealth from the period 1845 to 1895 and found that "the declining participation of slaves corresponds to the increase in real property. But this was not the only thing that increased its share of wealth; new forms, . . . particularly company stocks, increased their participation" (p. 87).
14. Companies could operate once 10% of capital was paid in; stocks could be traded at 20%; and shareholders, previously held liable for the value of their stock for up to five years, were absolved of all responsibility every time the company's financial statements were approved by the yearly stockholders' meeting (Brazil, Decree 164, 17 January 1890).

15. Peláez and Suzigan (1976).

16. A counterreform to the January 1890 business legislation raised the minimum level of paid-in capital necessary for operations from 10% to 30% and the level of paid-in capital necessary for trading from 20% to 40% (Brazil, Decree 850, 13 October 1890).

17. In order to capture the development of São Paulo business, I compiled a list of all companies known to exist during the period 1890–1905 to compare it with the Bolsa listings. This list was gleaned from several monographs on the industrialization of Brazil and compiled with São Paulo newspapers' stock price listings for a total universe of between 113 and 139 firms (Dean 1969; Cano 1981; Suzigan 1986; O Estado de São Paulo; Correio Paulistano). At least 87 of them were organized as joint-stock companies. There are an additional 26 firms identified by industry but not by name for which I cannot determine their trading status.

18. Cano (1981) estimates the number of firms operating in 1907 to be 1,114, with total industrial capital valued at 131,900 contos. My research found the capital value of publicly financed industrial firms in 1907 to total 24,876 contos, or 18.9% of total São Paulo industrial capital.

19. There were 430,612 shares outstanding in 1886 and 1,216,042 in 1905. The 1886 issues totaled 70,312,400 milreis (nominal) of paid-in capital. The 1905 issues totaled 213,025,000 milreis (nominal) of paid-in capital. In real terms, paid-in capital slightly more than doubled.

20. The Paulista listed 1,069 shareholders in 1893 and 2,119 in 1905 (Companhia Paulista 30 April 1893 and 30 June 1905). The Mogiana listed 1,093 shareholders in 1891 and 2,163 in 1903 (Companhia Mogiana 25 October 1891 and 21 June 1903).

21. São Paulo's population was 1.4 million in 1890 and 2.3 million in 1900, an increase of 64%. Shareholders in these companies rose 90% in roughly the same period (Cano 1981).

22. My definition for what determined a large shareholder changed over time as the number of shareholders grew. For the Mogiana, the percentage of shareholders owning 200 or more shares of stock was 20% in 1891 and 17% in 1894. The percentage of shareholders owning 300 or more shares of stock was 13.6% in 1899, 10% in 1903, and 8.2% in 1907. For the Paulista, the number of shareholders owning 500 or more shares of stock was 13.8% in 1893 and fell to 7.9% by 1905. A clear pattern of decline is evident in both cases.

23. Holloway (1975) provides a detailed analysis of the coffee support plan.

24. This dominance was typical of the U.S. and British cases as well, because of the large, indivisible capital requirements and the inability to begin operations before construction was completed. These characteristics made it impossible to rely on profits as a source of finance.

25. The areas closest to the capital city of São Paulo and its port city, Santos, were settled first for transportation reasons. Railroads were initially built into these areas to improve access to the port, but later (1890s to early 1900s) were used to open up new areas for cultivation.

26. Population and immigration figures are from Cano (1981), Tables 71, 72, and 73. The state population was approximately 800,000 in 1872 and 2.2 million in 1900.

27. The classic work by Camargo (1981) regarding the growth and distribution of São Paulo's population identifies 10 distinct zones. Zones 3 through 5 represent the classic Paulista Oeste coffee-growing region. Zones 6 to 9 were opened to coffee production after the turn of the century. Zones 6 and 8 were the fastest growing regions between 1900 and 1920.

28. Tellingly, the production of cotton cloth, hats, and shoes, presumably to clothe this population, doubled from 1905 to 1910 (Cano 1981).

29. "Textiles" includes all firms producing wool, silk, and cotton goods. When I refer specifically to cotton textiles, I have adjusted the figures to remove the wool and silk firms from my totals.

30. Cano (1981).

31. We know from Cano (1981) that there were 18 cotton textile firms in São Paulo in 1905, with a total capitalization of 29,600 contos. The single firm listed on the Bolsa, Companhia Industrial de São Paulo, had equity capital worth 2,000 contos and a debenture bond worth 1,200 contos. A second firm, the Banco União de São Paulo, worth 5,000 contos, was almost exclusively dedicated to its Votorantim textile business at this time, but still figured as a bank among the stock exchange listings. If we include the capital of this second firm, the value of listed cotton textile capital relative to total cotton textile capital in 1905 rises to almost 38%.

32. I compared the capital value of the joint-stock cotton textile firms in 1905, 1909, and 1915 with the capital values calculated by Cano (1981) for all firms in 1905, 1910, and 1915.

33. Cano (1981) reports that the capital value of cotton textile industry grew by 51,900 contos from 1905 to 1915. Of this, 40,600 contos, or 78%, were raised on the Bolsa.

34. Using the 1907 industrial census, Cano (1981) estimates that there were 1,114 industrial establishments in the state of São Paulo, valued at a total of 131,900 contos. I identified 14 industrial companies quoted on the Bolsa in 1907, worth 24,876 contos, or 18.9% of total industrial capital. By 1912, according to Cano, São Paulo's 64 joint-stock industrial firms contributed 18% to the total of Brazilian industrial capital for that year.

35. The total universe in the 1920 census was 4,145 industrial firms, of which roughly 128 were joint-stock companies (Cano 1981).

36. Cano (1981), Table 68.

37. Dean (1969) and Topik (1987) are good examples of this.

38. Stone (1987).

39. The Canadian-owned São Paulo Tramway, Light, and Power Company was formed in 1899 to electrify São Paulo's mule-drawn tramway system. It merged with the Canadian-based Rio de Janeiro Tramway, Light, and Power Company and The São Paulo Electric Company in 1911 to form the Brazilian Traction, Light, and Power Company (Castro 1978).

40. Cano (1981) simply lists the remaining 34% of industrial capital as "Other." The third common type of business format in Brazil in this era was the limited partnership.

41. A company-by-company review of foreign business in Brazil by Barreto (1977) finds that most foreign firms invested in cattle raising, mining, and extractive and transportation endeavors.

42. Triner (1994).

43. I do not measure returns over time for the simple reason that the sample would be too small. Although I have stock prices for one-half or more of the companies in a given year, the prices from year to year are not always for the same companies. If I threw out all companies for which I did not have consecutive years' data, the sample would be so small as to be meaningless. Therefore, I compare the market value against the paid-in value of individual stocks in individual years.

44. Most company stocks were fully paid up to their par value by this time. In the case of a stock that was not fully paid for, I adjusted the par value downward to reflect only the paid-in value.

45. My information on railroad ownership through 1905 indicated that shareholding was in fact becoming less concentrated over time.

46. By all accounts, the economy tapered off after 1913. In that year buy-bid quotes fell to one in three, and fell below one in five for the remainder of the period.

47. Domestic railroad bond issues were historically few, numbering just one or two. During the period 1909–1917, between three and five railroad bonds were denominated in foreign currency. Just one or two issues of bank mortgage-backed notes were in circulation at this time. Therefore, all growth in the bond market was through utilities, industrial companies, or other nonindustrial companies.

48. I lack the financial statements for individual companies after 1905 that would allow me to construct a true debt–equity analysis. Up to 1905, however, my work shows that retained earnings and bank lending were of very small significance to corporate finance. The bank failures of the 1900–1905 period make it unlikely that lending patterns quickly adjusted thereafter to higher-risk lending, and so it seems safe to assume that bank lending remained at very low levels. Therefore, using debt bonds and equity capital as a proxy is reasonable.

49. These trends are self-reinforcing. My market-to-par ratios reflect only companies with a price quote. The low level of trading activity meant that only a few companies were now driving these ratios. Other companies went untraded altogether.
50. As a testament to investor interest in bonds, these were still quoted at a rate of one in two.
51. Dias (1993).
52. Triner's (1994) argument for the insignificance of the Bolsa to economic development is based on the declining proportion of firms funded through the sale of equity relative to total economic growth through 1930.
53. The market contraction involved 15% of companies but just 9% of capital.

REFERENCES

Barreto, Antônio Emílio Muniz. "Relaçoes econômicas e o novo alinhamento internacional do Brasil (1870–1930)." Thesis of Livre-Docencia, University of São Paulo, 1977.

Baumol, William J. *The Stock Market and Economic Efficiency.* New York: Fordham University Press, 1965.

Brazil. *Coleção de Leis e Decretos,* 1849–1906.

Camargo, José Francisco de. *Crescimento da população no estado de São Paulo e seus aspectos econômicos.* 2 vols. São Paulo: Instituto de Pesquisas Econômicas, 1981.

Cano, Wilson. *Raízes da concentração industrial em São Paulo.* São Paulo: T. A. Queiroz Editora, 1981.

Castro, Ana Célia. *As empresas estrangeiras no Brasil, 1860–1913.* Rio de Janeiro: Zahar Editores, 1978.

Catão, Luis A. V. "A New Wholesale Price Index for Brazil During the Period 1870–1913." *Revista Brasileira de Economia* 46, no. 4 (October/December 1992): 519–535.

Companhia Mogiana Estrada de Ferro. Relatórios, 1884–1888, 1891, 1893–1906.

Correio Paulistano, 1886–1906.

Cottrell, Philip L. *Industrial Finance, 1840–1914: The Finance and Organization of the English Manufacturing Industry.* London: Methuen & Co., 1979.

Dean, Warren. *The Industrialization of São Paulo, 1880–1945.* Austin: University of Texas Press, 1969.

Dias, Andre Pires de Oliveira. "Brazil." In *The World's Emerging Stock Markets: Structure, Developments, Regulations and Opportunities,* edited by Keith K. H. Park and Antoine W. Van Agtmael. Chicago: Probus Publishing Company, 1993.

Estrada de Ferro da Companhia Paulista. Relatórios, 1870–1889, 1891–1898, 1900–1906.

Fishlow, Albert. "Origins and Consequences of Import Substitution in Brazil." In *International Economics and Development: Essays in Honor of Raul Prebisch*, edited by Luis Eugenio di Marco. New York: Academic Press, 1972.

Gerschenkron, Alexander. *Economic Backwardness in Historical Perspective*. Cambridge: Harvard University Press, 1962.

Goldsmith, Raymond W. *Financial Structure and Development*. New Haven: Yale University Press, 1969.

Haber, Stephen. "The Efficiency Consequences of Institutional Change: Capital Market Regulation and Industrial Productivity Growth in Brazil, 1866–1914." Department of History, Stanford University, 1996.

Haddad, Cláudio L. S. "Growth of Brazilian Real Output, 1900–47." Ph.D. dissertation, University of Chicago, 1974.

Hanley, Anne G. "Capital Markets in the Coffee Economy: Financial Institutions and Economic Change in São Paulo, Brazil, 1850–1905." Ph.D. dissertation, Stanford University, 1995.

Holloway, Thomas H. *The Brazilian Coffee Valorization of 1906: Regional Politics and Economic Dependence*. Madison, WI: The State Historical Society of Wisconsin for the Department of History, University of Wisconsin, 1975.

Katzman, Martin T. "São Paulo and Its Hinterland: Evolving Relationships and the Rise of an Industrial Power." In *Manchester and São Paulo: Problems of Rapid Urban Growth*, edited by John D. Wirth and Robert L. Jones. Stanford: Stanford University Press, 1978.

Lamoreaux, Naomi R. *Insider Lending: Banks, Personal Connections, and Economic Development in Industrial New England*. New York: Cambridge University Press, 1994.

Levi, Darrell E. *The Prados of São Paulo, Brazil: An Elite Family and Social Change, 1840–1930*. Athens: University of Georgia Press, 1987.

Mattoon, Robert H. Jr. "Railroads, Coffee, and the Growth of Big Business in São Paulo, Brazil." *Hispanic American Historical Review* 57, no. 2 (1977): 273–295.

Mello, Zélia Maria Cardoso de. *Metamorfoses da riqueza: São Paulo, 1845–1895*. São Paulo: Editora Hucitec, 1985.

Michie, Ranald C. *The London and New York Stock Exchanges: 1850–1914*. London: Allen and Unwin, 1987.

O Estado de São Paulo, 1890–1917.

Pelaez, Carlos Manuel, and Wilson Suzigan. *História monetária do Brasil: Análise da política, comportamento e instituiçoes monetárias*. Rio de Janeiro: IPEA/INPES, 1976.

Saes, Flávio Azevedo Marques de. *Crédito e bancos no desenvolvimento da economia paulista: 1850–1930*. São Paulo: Instituto de Pesquisas Econômicas, 1986.

São Paulo. Arquivo do Estado, Seção de Manuscritos. "Bancos" and "Obras Publicas."

Silva, Sérgio. *Expansão cafeeira e origens da indústria no Brasil.* São Paulo: Editora Alfa Omega, 1978.

Stone, Irving. *The Composition and Distribution of British Investment in Latin America, 1865 to 1913.* New York: Garland Publishing, 1987.

Suzigan, Wilson. *Indústria brasileira: origem e desenvolvimento.* São Paulo: Editora Brasiliense, 1986.

Topik, Steven. *The Political Economy of the Brazilian State, 1889–1930.* Institute of Latin American Studies, Monograph no. 71. Austin: University of Texas Press, 1987.

Triner, Gail D. "Banks and Brazilian Economic Development: 1906–1930." Ph.D. dissertation, Columbia University, 1994.

Versiani, Flávio Rabelo. "Industrial Development in an 'Export' Economy: The Brazilian Experience Before 1914." Institute of Latin American Studies Working Papers, University of London, 1979.

5

Finance and Development in an Emerging Market: Argentina in the Interwar Period

Gerardo della Paolera
Universidad Torcuato Di Tella
Alan M. Taylor
Northwestern University and NBER

The economic history of Argentina, a melancholy tale of long-term retardation throughout most of the twentieth century, is understandably something of a fascinating curiosity for scholars with any interest in growth, development, and history. A country that promised in the 1900s and 1910s to enter the league of the developed nations simply could not make it. The 1914–1939 period thus defined a critical transition in Argentine economic history, yet signs of future retardation and recurring crises were not obvious. Even scholars with the most cursory acquaintance with the historical record can point to this key period as a regime shift, when the move from convergence and relative prosperity to divergence and relative backwardness began. All histories single out the interwar period, perhaps even the very year 1929, as the decisive breaking point.[1]

However, in her economic performance Argentina fared no worse than other settler economies in the transition to the interwar period.[2] That is, despite important and violent shifts in the terms of trade and the virtual state of autarky in international capital markets, the Argentine economy managed to overcome both the depths of the 1914–1918 and 1929–1931 crises.[3] How was this possible in an economy that at the turn of the century was still a primary production economy? How should it affect our view of the origins of Argentine relative retardation? Is it fair to say that autarkic forces in capital markets prevented an efficient allocation of investment to new endeavors? Or should we seek alternative or, at least, complementary explanations?

Few scholars have tackled the importance of financial and capital markets as a means to promote and enhance economic growth. Very little has been written on the interaction in Argentina between financial development and aggregate economic activity for the 1913–1939 period.[4] A vague consensus suggests that some financial development took place, but it was not all that might have been hoped for. This was recognized by Díaz Alejandro, who noted that "While the financial history of Latin America remains to be written, it appears that by the 1920s most countries had succeeded in establishing commercial banks of the (then) traditional sort. . . . Although there was no 'financial repression,' critics pointed to a lack of medium and long-term credit, particularly to finance industry and non-export agriculture."[5]

In his landmark history, Díaz Alejandro offers further evidence for significant financial deepening in the interwar period.[6] The domestic debt market featured an expanding array of debt instruments in fixed money terms, and mortgage activity grew. There was an increase in bank channels of mobilizing finance, notably via rapidly expanding savings accounts, which expanded from 8% of gross domestic product (GDP) in 1913–1914 to 22% in 1928–1929. Monetization also expanded, and a traditional indicator, the ratio of monetary assets to GDP, rose from 46% in 1913–1914 to 55% in 1928–1929. Not all signs were good, however. The equity market remained thin, "companies relied primarily on bank credit for short-term financing and on retained earnings and ad hoc arrangements for long-term financing," and activity on the Bolsa was dominated by trades in mortgage paper and state and national government bonds.[7] Only around 10% of trades were in stocks of corporations. Even in bank finance, one institution loomed large, the Banco de la Nación Argentina, which accounted for more than two-fifths of the assets of the commercial banking system and which, in the absence of a central bank, had a quasi-public function. Still, despite these caveats, the evidence looked favorable to Díaz Alejandro. He argued that "[t]he domestic contribution to financing pre-1930 capital accumulation was large and tended to grow" and suggested that by 1930 Argentina had become a "highly monetized" economy with an "expanding [domestic] capital market."[8]

Almost 30 years after Díaz Alejandro's essay, a pioneering work built on scarce data, we think it is time to reexamine these issues and search for new evidence. In this paper we focus on the relationship between the development of domestic financial markets and economic growth for the 1913–1939 period. This is our emphasis because it so often appears as a central redeeming feature of Argentine interwar history, yet it has received little attention from quantitative economic historians. Many economic historians have stressed the pre-1914 struggle of Argentina to adopt monetary regimes that would ensure macroeconomic stability and, in turn, facilitate access to international capital markets.[9] But we have so far lacked a detailed analysis of the linkages among financial development, inside-money deepening, credit creation, the efficiency and level of investment, and economic growth. For the emerging economy of Argentina, the role of financial development—in mobilizing domestic and foreign savings, allocating productive resources, facilitating risk management, and easing trading of goods—is an essential element in understanding what happened after 1914.

The Argentine economy suffered an immediate shock at the onset of World War I: The British supply of financial services proved to be unreliable when international capital markets dried up; thus, there was a need to substitute for foreign mobilization and accumulation of resources with domestic sources that would have to rely on a domestic financial technology.[10] As Levine observes, "England's financial system did a better job at identifying and funding profitable ventures than most countries in the mid-1800s. . . . Indeed, England's advanced financial system also did a good job at identifying profitable ventures in other countries, such as Canada, the United States, and Australia during the 19th Century. England was able to 'export' financial services (as well as financial capital) to many economies with underdeveloped financial systems."[11] The very same process was at work in parts of Latin America, notably Argentina— and there perhaps to an even greater extent given her extreme degree of dependence on foreign capital. Thus did an Anglo-Argentine elite dominate the financial landscape of turn-of-the-century Buenos Aires. About one-half of Argentine capital in 1913 was foreign owned, either directly or indirectly, a far higher percentage than in any other major borrowing nation at the time, and the bulk of that foreign capital was British in origin.[12] International political and economic engagements started to dissolve in the autarkic atmosphere after World War I, with ramifications for world markets and especially for international capital mobility.[13] Savings-scarce countries, such as Argentina, with a heavy dependence on foreign lending were bound to feel a tightening of capital constraints unless they could mobilize and allocate domestic supplies of capital as effectively as the rapidly receding supplies of foreign capital. How did Argentina respond to this challenge?

Our aim in this paper is to address two sets of major questions about these events. First, exactly how remarkable was interwar financial development relative to previous and subsequent trends in Argentina and relative to other countries' long-term experience? What were the financial magnitudes involved? How much capital was mobilized and allocated? And what can we infer about the capacity of financial development to significantly improve Argentina's long-term rates of saving, investment, and economic growth?

Second, what independent sources of macroeconomic instability were originated by financial shocks in this evolving domestic financial system? This question requires us to assess the inherent fragility of the domestic financial system: Could it produce financial shocks that could influence business cycles?[14] In addition, the economy soon faced one of the worst international depressions ever, which wrought worldwide financial panics and collapses. How did the institutional features of the emerging financial markets propagate (or dampen) shocks that originated in the real-sector economy?

FINANCE AND DEVELOPMENT IN THEORY

The influence of the development of financial and capital markets on economic growth and the emergence of market economies has been debated by economists and economic historians since Adam Smith's seminal piece.[15] Theoretical and empirical studies have focused on the role of financial deepening in the process of economic growth. As early as 1912, the Austrian Joseph Schumpeter in his *Theory of Economic Development* argued that finance scarcity was a serious obstacle to development. Economic historians such as Davis, Cameron et al., Gerschenkron, and Goldsmith made pioneering empirical contributions showing that financial markets were "necessary" institutions in the early stages of the industrialization of today's developed countries.[16] By following a comparative approach, these studies claim that a lack of well-functioning capital markets institutions is central in explaining the relative backwardness of some continental European countries.[17]

Two contributions that organize an analytical framework for studying the finance-growth nexus and assessing the quantitative importance of the financial system for economic development are the works of Robert Townsend and Ross Levine.[18] They note that in an Arrow-Debreu world, with perfect information and no transaction costs, there will be basically no need for financial intermediaries. Otherwise, intermediation provides a potentially valuable service. A straightforward question about the functional role and usefulness of capital markets, and especially banks, was posed by Bradford De Long in his paper "Did J. P. Morgan's Men Add Value? An Economist's Perspective on Financial Capitalism." The same question might be asked of any intermediary, in any country, at any time. The value-added characteristics of financial institutions, some of which were listed by Levine,[19] are key functions that could increase the prospects for economic development:

1. The deepening in the use of money and near-monies for transaction purposes to move beyond the technology of a barter-exchange system (i.e., the development of stable and credible monetary and financial institutions).

2. Easing the trading, hedging, and pooling of risk by reducing the uncertainty about the timing and settlement of intertemporal economic transactions (i.e., innovation in the creation of liquid financial instruments).

3. Easing the linkages between savers and investors by reducing the need for information so that available short-term funding from surplus economic units will flow to those short-of-funds investors who can promise a higher expected rate of return for their long-term projects (i.e., improved efficiency in allocating resources by transforming the maturity of assets).[20]

4. The mobilization of savings, which involves the pooling of capital from disparate savers for investment to obtain efficient scales of operation in firms (i.e., a mobilization of savings can produce a fall in the cost of external finance for firms and entrepreneurs, allowing them to choose their first-best techniques).

5. The fall in the cost of finance and interest rates, and the resiliency of financial institutions to systemic fragility, can provide for the flourishing of new entrepreneurs and new firms that otherwise could not have existed.

When all the factors mentioned above are in operation, financial intermediation will enhance capital accumulation and, most important, technological adaptation and innovation, which will, in turn, translate into economic growth. Let us now turn to a preliminary inspection of the available macrodata for Argentina to establish some links between measures of financial deepening and economic performance.

ARGENTINE FINANCIAL DEVELOPMENT AND ECONOMIC GROWTH: A PRELIMINARY SKETCH

In Table 5.1 we offer some preliminary macroeconomic indicators of financial development and economic growth from 1900 to 1939. Let us examine the broad development indicators in the upper panel. The figures show that the Argentine economy suffered a significant slowdown in economic growth after World War I. From an average per capita real growth rate of about 3.5% per year for the first decade of the century, Argentina only rebounded in the 1920s to a growth rate of 1.7% per year. The 1915–1919 period is characterized by a dismal performance of the real economy, even by international standards, but the depression years 1930–1935 show relatively little decline by the same yardstick.[21] Instrumental in both recessions were dramatic declines in investment activity, which never recovered its 1905–1914 level. Several open economy indicators provide evidence of the increased autarky of the Argentine economy in this period: a big reduction in capital inflows measured by the ratio of current account to GDP, and a dramatic worsening in the terms of trade. Despite a modest terms of trade recovery in the mid-1920s, exports as a share of GDP gradually decline after peaking during the later years of World War I (more due to a collapse in the denominator than a rise in export quantum), and fall even further in the 1930s.

We would like to examine the association, if any, between economic development and several measures of financial development. The typical two candidates to be used as proxies for the degree of financial intermediation are (1) monetary aggregates such as the money stock, M3, defined as the sum of currency in the hands of the public plus demand deposits and interest-bearing deposits and liabilities of the banks and nonbank intermediaries (or DEPTH, following King and Levine 1993); and (2) the level of credit activity provided by the banking system as a ratio of GDP (or CREDIT, following De Gregorio and Guidotti 1995). We have constructed, on the basis of a consolidated monetary database, annual and monthly data for a monetary aggregate that resembles M3. We have also collected monthly data on the loan activities of the Argentine banking system for the second definition, relying on the pioneering work of Baiocco.[22]

The usual caveats concerning the variable DEPTH and the use of M3 as an indicator of financial and capital market depth arise. Any definition of monetary aggregates or banking credit might be a weak indicator of capital markets development if it is the case that a significant percentage of industrial finance occurs outside the financial system. We only have fragmentary evidence concerning the quantitative importance of alternative domestic channels of investment such as the Buenos Aires Stock Exchange Market, which we will discuss shortly.[23] Notwithstanding conceptual difficulties, the ratio of M3 to GDP is the traditional indicator of the financial or monetary sophistication of an economy in most of the relevant historical studies. In different studies, it has been shown that higher per capita incomes in developing economies are associated with higher degrees of monetization and secular declines in money velocity.[24]

The variable CREDIT is perhaps a more accurate indicator of financial development, because it measures the amount of credit effectively intermediated by banks. In Table 5.1 we include the ratio of total loans of the financial system to GDP (CREDIT). As banks develop their capacity to create banking,

TABLE 5.1

Finance and Development, 1900–1939

	1900–1904	1905–1909	1910–1914	1915–1919	1920–1924	1925–1929	1930–1934	1935–1939
(A) Broad Development Indicators								
A Per capita GDP (1913 = 100)	76	93	98	83	98	109	99	106
B Savings/GDP (%)	7	10	4	10	4	11	6	11
C Investment/ GDP (%)	9	16	15	7	10	13	9	11
D Current account/GDP (%)	–1	–6	–11	3	–6	–2	–3	0
E Terms of trade (1913 = 100)	88	103	104	88	64	83	73	95
F Exports/ GDP (%)	27	27	24	30	24	24	16	17
(B) Financial Development Indicators								
G DEPTH = M3/ GDP (%)	35	38	40	43	49	47	50	41
H CREDIT = Loans/ GDP (%)	—	27	34	29	37	36	43	29
I NETCREDIT = Non-BNA loans/GDP (%)	—	19	24	18	22	21	23	16
J Savings accounts/ GDP (%)	—	5	7	10	15	18	21	17
K Stock market turnover/GDP (%)	26	19	10	6	11	7	7	10
L Bank stocks price index (start of period, Dec. 13 = 100)	70	104	62	73	65	74	46	—
M Stock market price index (start of period, Dec. 13 = 100)	57	77	94	140	107	142	—	—
N Relative price of bank stocks	122	135	66	52	61	52	—	—

Sources: Nominal GDP, A, G: della Paolera et al. (1996), with population from *Anuario Geográfico* (1941); B, C, D: Taylor (1997); E: pre-1914 from Di Tella and Zymelman (1967), post-1914 from IEERAL (1986); F: Balboa (1972); H, I, L: Baiocco (1937); J: *Revista de Economía Argentina* (February 1938); K: *Anuario Geográfico* (1941); M: Nakamura and Zarazaga (1996); N: L divided by M.

money should increase. Related to this indicator, we want to analyze the credit to the private sector net of the loans of the most important official (quasi-state) bank, the Banco de la Nación Argentina (BNA). We then use the ratio of credit net of BNA to GDP as an indicator. Thus, we abstract from a bank that was the financial agent of the government, and this indicator should be effectively related to the level and efficiency of privately financed investment (NET-CREDIT).

We also include in the lower panel of Table 5.1 some other financial variables covering various aspects of bank and nonbank financial activity. We have a measure of the growth of savings accounts relative to GDP. From the Buenos Aires Bolsa we show an indicator of stock market turnover volume relative to GDP, an index of banks' stock prices (derived from our monthly data set), and an index of all stock prices (from Nakamura and Zarazaga 1996). These indices allow us to get a sense of how banking performed relative to the rest of the equity market in price terms, and how the two finance channels, debt and equity, performed in terms of activity.

From our monetary and financial data we can infer that all was not well in the Argentine financial system. The DEPTH measure is certainly misleading. Although it is the case that the traditional indicator of money deepening measured by the ratio of M3 to GDP increased in a sustained fashion from 35% at the beginning of the century to reach a high of 50% at the onset of the Great Depression, the optimistic picture changes when we observe the behavior of more detailed statistics of banking credit, and even the DEPTH measure drops back to 41% by 1935. However, when financial development is proxied by credit to the economy—and especially by net credit as a proxy of privately created loans for investment—the vitality of the emerging financial system is more questionable. Total credit did rise appreciably prior to the slump, from a low of 27% in 1905 to a high of 43% in 1930. But net credit as a fraction of GDP fell during World War I, recovered a little in the middle of the 1920s, only to plunge, together with output, during the years of the Great Depression. Thus, the widely used M3/GDP measure depicts a monetizing economy, but one that nonetheless did not deliver financial development in the form of a bank credit expansion to the same degree. By either measure, trough-to-peak gains never amounted to more than increases from 27% to 37% (DEPTH) and 18% to 24% (NETCREDIT), but even these modest gains were reversed.

It is not just the credit data that suggest the banking sector had its problems. If banks were the best available technology to channel savings to investments, then their situation as perceived by market participants did not flourish during the interwar period: From 1913 to 1935, the "value" of the industry declined by more than 50% as shown by the quotation of an index of bank stock prices. The relative value of banking as an industry had declined dramatically even by 1930, the first year in which the deflationary effects of the Depression were felt domestically. Relative to other stocks, bank stocks had fallen in price by about 60% relative to their pre-1914 peak. This decline in the market value of banks calls into question whether banks were an effective technology to channel savings to investments in interwar Argentina, an issue that will receive further scrutiny.

As for alternative sources of finance, there was little relief from the equity market either, and stock market turnover suggests a stock market of dwindling importance: Turnover relative to GDP fell by more than half from 1900 to the 1930s. Turnover is not the same as new capitalization, but even so, the data are suggestive of a weak stock market unable to deliver a dynamic and growing source of industrial and commercial finance when such funding was exactly the type needed by the Argentine interwar economy. Further research is surely warranted on the evolution of the Bolsa to uncover its workings in this period.[25]

However, to be fair, not all signs were disappointing, and certainly the expansion of savings accounts in particular, from 5% to 21% in 1905–1930, has attracted attention. It was this trend, and the increase in monetization (DEPTH), that led Díaz Alejandro to see an "expanding capital market."[26] But more concrete measures of financial development results (in terms of credit delivered and the health of bank stocks) do not seem to justify this rosy view. Most tellingly of all, more savings accounts and more monetization, at the end of the day, could not by themselves deliver large and sustained increases in loan activity and thus deliver an impact on the private finance of investment via the credit channel, the ultimate benchmark for financial development. Hence, the standard measures of "financial development"—DEPTH and CREDIT—need always to be interpreted with caution in this and other historical contexts. On the face of it, increases in DEPTH or CREDIT of about 15 percentage points (as seen in interwar Argentina) would deliver impressive gains in growth performance. According to King and Levine or De Gregorio and Guidotti,[27] these changes would be worth about 0.5% per annum in growth performance via improved mobilization and allocation of capital.

Such results failed to materialize in Argentina. The figures in the upper panel of Table 5.1 on savings and investment show the disappointing bottom line. In the absence of foreign savings during the interwar years, the dwindling current account deficits meant that Argentina had to finance most domestic investment out of domestic savings. Yet the home financial system could not respond to the challenge. After 1914, savings rates climbed only modestly, averaging just 8% of GDP; investment rates declined to average about 10% of GDP, much less than the investment rates of 15% to 16% seen in 1905–1914 and so heavily financed by foreign capital inflows. After 1914, foreign capital only contributed an inflow of about 2% of GDP on average. Economic retardation was the result of this new capital constraint.[28] The financial system failed in its two core *microeconomic* tasks: It could neither successfully mobilize more capital (quantities did not increase appreciably), nor improve the efficiency of the allocation of capital (indeed, bank stock price declines suggest a shift to poorer-quality assets over time). The *macroeconomic* results were predictable, but to understand why the domestic system failed we need to understand its own institutional shortcomings and thus why it faced a much harder task than the foreign financial intermediaries it was seeking to replace.

ARGENTINE FINANCIAL DEVELOPMENT: AN INTERNATIONAL PERSPECTIVE

To recall some of the key motivating questions for this study, we ask again how remarkable was interwar financial development in Argentina? What were the magnitudes involved? And what can we infer about the capacity of financial development to significantly improve Argentina's prospects for long-term economic development? These questions are, at least in part, comparative questions: If we assess Argentine growth relative to that of other countries, so also must we seek international benchmarks for financial development. This is very much the spirit of the studies by King and Levine and De Gregorio and Guidotti, who use large cross-sectional databases covering scores of countries. We cannot hope to match this sample size given the availability of historical data before 1945, but we can compare Argentine experience with a sample of a few well-chosen developed and developing countries in Figure 5.1.

The figure shows two measures of financial development, both using M3, the only monetary aggregate available for this purpose (we were unable to obtain currency in the hands of the public for such a broad sample). The first measure is the DEPTH measure, the ratio of M3 to GDP for seven countries from 1913 to 1939. The second measure is *real* M3 per capita, measured in 1928 prices and converted to U.S. dollars at 1928 parities. The sample includes Argentina plus three benchmark rich "core" countries (Britain, the United States, and Germany) and three developing "periphery" countries (Italy, Portugal, and Spain). In 1913, Argentina was one of the five or so richest countries in the world and would have been considered a good candidate for comparison with the first reference group. But by the postwar decades Argentina's

FIGURE 5.1 INTERNATIONAL COMPARISONS OF MONETARY AND FINANCIAL DEEPENING

(a) ln(M3/GDP)

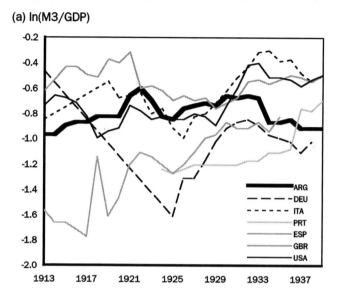

(b) ln(real M3 per capita in 1928 U.S. dollars)

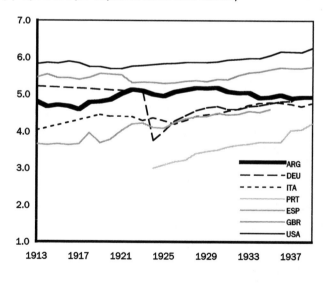

Sources: Data for Argentina from della Paolera (1996); other data from Mitchell (1992, 1993) and Bordo (unpublished data).

position had certainly lapsed into the developing country sample and fell behind the three European periphery countries included in the second reference group. Can we find evidence of such a reversal of fortunes in these financial data?

The first chart (Figure 5.1a) shows that in 1913, Argentina's DEPTH measure was only just behind that of the three core countries. After the shocks associated with World War I, Argentina briefly surpassed all countries in the sample on this measure of financial deepening. This success proved short-lived. A brief financial crisis in Argentina in the mid-1920s brought the DEPTH measure down to its initial level. The only core country by then below Argentina was Germany, whose own financial system had been wrecked by chaos and financial repression during the hyperinflation. There was then some stability up to 1929, but other periphery countries saw very rapid increases in DEPTH over the same years, which Argentina could not match. In the 1930s, Argentina faced further financial crises, reducing the DEPTH measure below that of *all* other countries in the sample by the late 1930s, excepting Germany, an economy with serious problems, financial and otherwise (heavily controlled currencies, an increasingly command-type economy, and crowding out via militarization—all serving to strain the private financial system). A similar story is told by the evolution of real M3 per capita in the second chart (Figure 5.1b). Again, Argentina started near the top of the financial league in 1913, and her relative position improved a little by the early 1920s. But after 1920 almost nothing happened to change the Argentine level of real M3 per capita, whereas in *all* other countries this measure of real financial activity per person was continually increasing, even in the 1930s. The core countries all surpassed Argentina in the level of this variable by the 1930s, and only Portugal and Italy (barely) had a lower level, though they were converging rapidly.

Both of these measures indicate that in terms of financial development Argentina began in a very strong position in 1913, consistent with its claim to be one of the richest economies in the world. However, this position was continuously eroded in relative terms in the interwar period, such that by the late 1930s, Argentina had experienced virtually no net increase in financial depth. Despite wars and the Great Depression, most other countries posted gains in the same period. It is very telling that Argentine financial development looks good only in comparison with a financial disaster case like Germany.

This sequence of events suggests that we examine the Argentine interwar financial system and economic growth in more detail. Figure 5.2 provides a starting point. The charts depict time series of output per capita GDP/POP, and two measures of financial development: currency in the hands of the

FIGURE 5.2 FINANCIAL DEEPENING AND ECONOMIC DEVELOPMENT

(a) Real GDP per capita index–GDP/POP

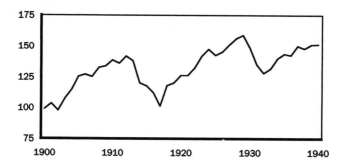

(b) Currency in the hands of the public/GDP–CPUB/GDP

(c) Banking money/GDP–(M3–M0)/GDP

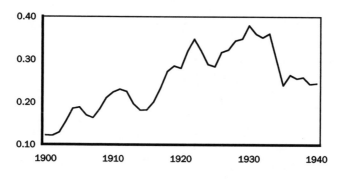

Source: della Paolera et al. (1996).

public as a share of GDP (CPUB/GDP) and banking money (M3 minus M0) as a share of GDP (M3–M0/GDP). According to the established theories of finance and development, the level of CPUB/GDP should remain constant or even fall, and the level of M3–M0/GDP should rise as development proceeds, reflecting an increase in sophistication through the public's substitution of assets in the financial system (banking money) for simple cash in hand.[29]

The time path of output per capita shows the two major crises: World War I and the Great Depression, with the latter *less* severe than the former. There are also minor recessions in 1906–1907 (as in the United States) and in 1924–1925. These cyclic events, both big and small, can be seen to have parallels in financial activity in the second and third charts. CPUB/GDP is seen to be declining dramatically from a high of 15% to about 6% in 1920, albeit with some reversal at the beginning of the 1914 crisis. But thereafter CPUB/GDP holds steady and even increases slightly, reaching a level of 9% to 10% in the 1930s. Thus, the substitution of banking system assets for cash seems to grind to a halt in Argentina soon after World War I. This trend break is also evident in the path of M3–M0/GDP, which shows volatility around an upward trend before 1920 (almost doubling from 15% to 30%), no trend at all from 1920 to 1929 (with a minicollapse in the mid-1920s), and a marked decline in the 1930s (almost falling back to 20%, comparable with pre-1914 levels).[30]

In fact, one can argue that there is even evidence of financial retardation or involution after 1920, as the public substitutes back toward currency and away from financial assets in the banking system. The interwar trends are certainly disturbing, and they may shed more light on the beginnings of Argentina's long-term retardation. However, the macroeconomic data gathered so far can only provide weak evidence of the failure of the Argentine financial system between the wars. We are still poorly equipped to trace the causal relationship between, on the one hand, the institutional structure of the Argentine economy and its position in a changing international economy and, on the other hand, internal developments in the financial system and their relationship to economic development. To understand these linkages better, we now aim to provide an integrated view of the macroeconomic and microeconomic workings of the interwar Argentine financial system.

FINANCIAL MARKETS IN THE INTERWAR PERIOD: INSTITUTIONAL AND ECONOMIC FRAGILITIES

Macroeconomic Twin Risk:
Exchange Rate Regime and Financial Structure

What were the institutional and economic impediments to the establishment of a full-fledged, resilient financial system during the interwar period? In well-documented studies, Calomiris and Bordo argued that the "industrial organization of banking affected the propensities for panics and for nonpanic waves of bank failures."[31] They put special emphasis on the advantages of a branch banking system as a mechanism that could systematically avert financial panics and crises. Yet Argentina, a country not included in their studies but which had extensive bank branching, did not avoid such panics.

To understand why Argentina suffered recurrent financial distress, it is important to introduce here the concept of intertwined macroeconomic monetary and financial risk for a small, open economy under, mostly, a fixed exchange rate monetary standard (i.e., the gold or gold-exchange standard). Crucial here is the fact that until 1935 the Argentine monetary and financial regime operated without a central bank. Until that time, a potential cause of a suboptimal financial structure came from the existence of a different kind of monetary authority, the Caja de Conversión. The Caja had the exclusive macroeconomic responsibility of guaranteeing the external value of the domestic currency. However, the Caja could not, *at the same time*, for all possible macroshocks, guarantee the internal convertibility of banking deposits (a multiple of the currency issue) into cash in the event of general bank runs. That is, the Caja de Conversión could not act as a lender of last resort for the financial system without threatening its macroeconomic responsibility of defending the external value of the domestic currency.

The almost simultaneous problems of exchange rate crises and financial crises were a recurrent problem for Argentina, and this type of economic phenomenon is now better understood.[32] The complicated dynamics of a regime that combined a high ratio of inside to outside money (i.e., a fractional reserve financial system) and a fixed exchange rate regime (e.g., the gold standard) became apparent by the end of 1913. The "world central banker," the Bank of England, decided on successive and dramatic increases in its discount rate. The outbreak of World War I was a devastating foreign shock for the Argentine economy and for the monetary and financial regime in particular. In Table 5.2 we show the anatomy of several financial crises to highlight the main channels of transmission to the real economy. We include three important financial

TABLE 5.2

Anatomy of Financial Crises

	Baring Crisis 1890	Baring Crisis 1891	World War I 1913	World War I 1914	Great Depression 1930	Great Depression 1931
A Real Activity						
Real output (% change)		−10.9		−11.0		−3.9
B Monetary Variables						
Money supply (% change, M0)		−25.9		−10.7		−8.3
Money base (% change, M3)		6.7		−3.6		1.3
Bank-created money (% change, M3 − M0)		—		−17.5		−11.3
International reserves backing (%)	21.0	4.0	72.6	66.3	82.1	47.6
Devaluation (% change in $mn/$oro)		45.0		1.7		25.0
Inflation (% change, WPI)		56.0		1.2		−3.3
C Banking Variables						
Deposits (% change)		−47.2		−15.4		−8.6
Banking fractional reserves (%)	20.0	27.0	32.4	33.8	11.6	14.9
Money multiplier (M3/M0)	2.3	1.6	2.1	1.9	3.7	3.3
D Financial Market Variables						
Ex post real interest rate (%, internal bonds)		—		6.5		10.8
Nominal interest rates (%)						
High month	—	10.3	8.1	8.8	7.7	7.9
Low month	—	—	7.5	7.5	6.4	6.7
Bank stock prices (Dec. 1913 = 100)	—	—	100	62	69	64
Stock price index (Dec. 1913 = 100)	—	—	100	94	147	
Paid-in capital (millions $mn)	—	—	513	449	498	485

Sources: della Paolera et al. (1994), Baiocco (1937), and Nakamura and Zarazaga (1996).

crises: the Baring crash (as a reference point), the financial crash of 1913–1914, and the 1930–1931 financial distress.

A common characteristic of real financial crises is that the fall in bank money or in the ratio of inside to outside money (due to a persistent run on bank deposits) is translated into a severe loss in output. By focusing on the 1913–1914 crisis we can see that, although a major devaluation of the currency was avoided (a major cost during the Baring crash), the banking industry was devastated. Bank stock prices fell by 38% in one year. There was an intense process of capital crunch (the use of capital to pay out depositors when assets fail). Paid-in capital fell by more than one-tenth in less than 12 months.

It is important to notice that the destruction in the banking industry, measured by the price of bank stocks, was far worse than the (expected) behavior of overall stocks, which declined by a "mere" 6%. Suppose that the quotation of bank stocks reflected the expected net present value of the future stream of income of the industry. Then, judging by what happened ex post facto in the years subsequent to 1930–1931, one is tempted to say that investors and economic agents had a very accurate perception that World War I had had a devastating effect on the health of financial and capital markets institutions. By 1930–1931, prices of bank stocks were at the same level as 1914 and general stocks were up by 47%, whereas nominal paid-in capital was below the 1913 level! In other words, it seems that financial markets were losing strength at each successive stage of financial distress. Even when a recovery was in place after a shock hit the system, investment in the industry never recovered its previous level.

To show the links between the expected solvency of the banks as determined, simultaneously, by monetary and real factors, we have regressed the logarithm of bank stock prices on (1) the logarithm of bankruptcies that is used as a proxy for the distress of borrowers or the state of affairs in the real sector and (2) on the logarithm of current and lagged values of the gold stock, variables used as a control for the domestic money market situation and possibly to be interpreted as a proxy for country macroeconomic risk. The results are reported in Table 5.3. The principal inferences to be drawn are as follows:

1. An increase in bankruptcies lowers the market value of banks: The long-term elasticity is –0.2, so an increase of 10% in bankruptcies lowers the price of bank stocks by 2% in the long run.
2. A gold inflow (an improvement in the balance of payments) eases the monetary liquidity of the economy and has a positive impact on the financial intermediation industry: A rise of 10% in the stock of gold increases the monthly price of bank stocks by 3.6% in the long run.

TABLE 5.3

Bank Stock Prices, Bankruptcies, and Macroeconomic Risk

Dependent Variable	ln Bank Stock Price
Constant	−0.015
	(0.23)
Trend	0.000
	(0.07)
ln Bankruptcies	−0.009
	(2.28)
ln Gold Stock	−0.302
	(2.18)
ln Gold Stock (−1)	0.517
	(2.12)
ln Gold Stock (−2)	−0.199
	(1.42)
ln Bank Stock Price (−1)	0.956
	(47.8)
Long-term elasticities	
ln Bankruptcies	−0.20
ln Gold Stock	0.36
R^2	.957
NOBS	222
SEE	0.03

Notes: Monthly data, May 1907 to January 1936. ln Bank Stock Price = ln bank stock price index; ln Bankruptcies = ln value of bankruptcies in million pesos moneda nacional; ln Gold Stock = ln of domestic gold stock in million pesos oro.

Sources: Baiocco (1937), except bankruptcies from *Revista de Economía Argentina* (various issues).

In the equation presented in Table 5.3, it is seen that the solvency of banks is crucially linked to a principal macroeconomic variable: the level of gold stock, mostly international reserves at the Caja de Conversión. From the point of view of individual bankers and investors, who set the "price" of banks, this variable, like the bankruptcy level, would be seen as exogenous—hence our choice of specification. The gold stock, in turn, is related to the choice and stability of the level of the exchange rate.

The above transmission mechanism distinctly parallels the seminal ideas of Bernanke, who argued that the financial system constituted an additional channel through which monetary crises could cause havoc in the real economy.[33] The above model is fairly simple and describes the first-order effect by which the terms of Argentina's deviation from gold standard rules could have a definite impact on the "pricing" of banks by exacerbating gold outflows. As it stands, we can trace out important independent effects of the real and monetary sectors on the perceived solvency of banks.[34]

The story for 1913–1914 is compelling. Let us suppose that, as in 1914, a foreign shock hits the economy and starts a financial crisis when economic agents begin to panic and try to convert all their deposits into currency. If the monetary authority, the Caja de Conversión, acts as a lender of last resort to finance the drain of deposits, the money market could at first absorb the fall in the nominal quantity of money. However, if the intervention is of a magnitude such that the relationship between the monetary base and international reserves increases significantly, this would exacerbate the expectation of an eventual devaluation of the currency. This, in turn, would feed a new run on bank deposits, but this time to convert peso deposits into specie.[35]

Microeconomics of Banking

Thus, one might now ask what was the "effective" cost, in terms of lending, of having a fragile financial regime subject to these twin macroeconomic shocks. This is a difficult question to tackle without examining the microeconomic behavior of banks. Thanks to the construction of a new data set based on the monumental work done by Baiocco, we can assess the microeconomic behavior of bankers and banks (by origin of capital) and see how such behavior affected the availability of credit in the economy.

In Figure 5.3 we display the share in the financial system of the Banco de la Nación (BNA, the most important official bank), domestic banks (founded domestically by coalitions of migrants: Banco Frances del Río de la Plata, Nuevo Banco Italiano, Banco Español, etc.), and foreign banks (international banks). One striking aspect is that from 1910 until 1930, domestic banks' share in total loans declined from almost 50% to less than 35%, foreign banks could hardly maintain a share of 20%, and the Banco de la Nación jumped from 28% to 45%. In short, it appeared that the private sector was losing ground in the capital market.

In Figure 5.4, the evolution of paid-in capital of banks is reported. It is interesting to note the dramatic capital crunches suffered by domestic banks during financial crises or distress. In the 1914 crisis, the domestic banks lost almost half their capital; again, in the short-lived drain of 1922–1923 they lost 25%; and in 1934, as we said previously, their nominal paid-in capital was almost the same as in 1913. In a virtually unregulated banking environment, the bankers could optimize their asset holdings and portfolios, and we could think of the level of lending in terms of its assets or capital as being the most important choice variable in the industry.

FIGURE 5.3 SHARE OF TOTAL LOANS OF BANKS, BY BANK TYPE

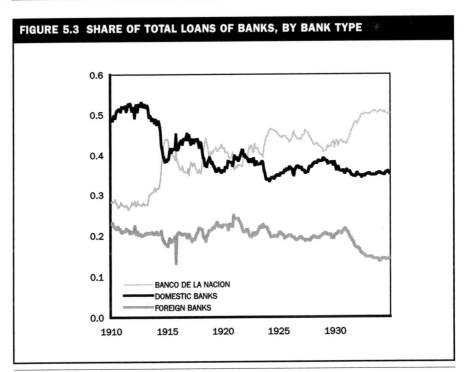

Source: Baiocco (1937).

In Figure 5.5, we observe that, excluding the Banco de la Nación, domestic-owned banks had a leverage ratio of risky loans to paid-in capital much lower than the leverage of foreign-owned banks. Differences in capital constraints and in attitudes toward the tolerated riskiness of assets might explain the microeconomic differences in lending. We speculate that foreign-owned banks, which after the Baring crash accounted for more than half of lending activities despite losing relative importance, could choose a higher loan-to-capital ratio because (1) they could rely more on their international headquarters to avert and overcome financial crises (remember, there was no such thing as a lender of last resort in Argentina until 1935) and (2) they were lending to "safer" assets, giving them a mix of risk and returns that allowed them to carry a higher leverage (they specialized in trade financing, where exchange rate risk, self-liquidating characteristics, and collateral risk are all well hedged).

Our interpretation of the differences in observed leverages across banks of different type follows that of the *Censo Bancario de la República Argentina 1925*.[36] In the census, the disparity between the loan–capital ratios is *not* attributed to systematic differences in fractional banking reserves. For example, in December 1925, foreign banks maintained a loan–capital ratio of 7.3

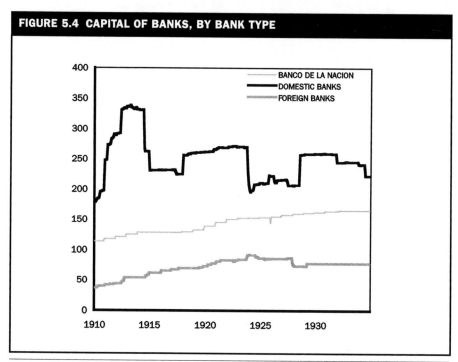

FIGURE 5.4 CAPITAL OF BANKS, BY BANK TYPE

Note: Figure shows paid-in capital only.

Source: Baiocco (1937).

while having a reserve–deposit ratio of 29%; domestic banks had a loan–capital ratio of 5.3 and a reserve–deposit ratio of 21%. Following Calomiris' model, one can infer that this is fully consistent with domestic banks having greater portfolio risk than foreign banks.[37] That is, domestic banks had to hold more "capital" because they were "longer" in riskier and more illiquid assets; foreign banks had high liquidity but more lending intermediation too. How can this be reconciled? First, not surprisingly a large share of funding comes through deposits, and deposit–capital ratios, as a first approximation, explain the observed differences in loan–capital ratios. However, on top of this, domestic banks relied exclusively on capital, reserves, and deposits to effect lending. Meanwhile, foreign banks could rely on profits generated internationally and, especially, on easy access to open letters of credit from international correspondent banks. In other words, foreign banks could leverage more easily by using international credit.

The evidence suggests that only foreign banks could have a net indebtedness position vis-à-vis correspondents in the rest of the world. That is, they could

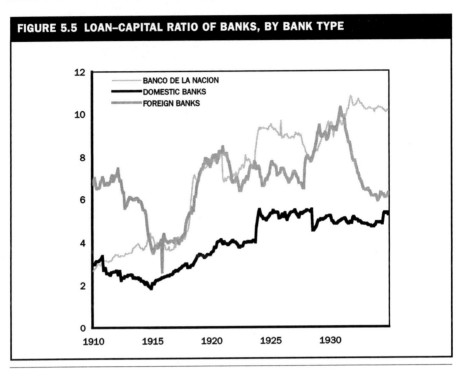

FIGURE 5.5 LOAN–CAPITAL RATIO OF BANKS, BY BANK TYPE

BANCO DE LA NACION
DOMESTIC BANKS
FOREIGN BANKS

Source: Baiocco (1937).

channel resources from abroad but only for investing in very safe and short-term assets. For example, long-term loans and mortgage loans represented 16% of assets in domestic banks, but only 4% in foreign banks. Conversely, short-term loans accounted for 22% in domestic banks versus 45% in foreign banks.[38]

The second important behavioral consideration is that changes in leverage are more important as a response to changing business cycle conditions in the case of foreign banks. This is apparent from the data presented in Figure 5.5. By combining Figures 5.4 and 5.5 we can see that when financial crises or exchange rate crises arise, severe capital crunches occur in domestic banks, but no severe curtailment of paid-in capital occurs in the other banks. Therefore, it was principally the domestic banks, who were more prone to long-term lending, that were exposed to capital crunches. We argue that this was because they could not rely on international diversification to smooth out financial runs or crises. Under stressful conditions, domestic banks might have been forced to call back loans, but a total transformation of assets to pay back short-term debt was, in general, neither sufficient nor feasible: Therefore, capital was squeezed out. In contrast, foreign banks could immediately call up loans, and they could decide not to open up new letters of credit. Idiosyncratic risks could

TABLE 5.4

Lending by Type of Bank as a Reaction to Gold Flows and Bank Stock Prices

Type of Bank Dependent Variable	Domestic ln Loans	Foreign ln Loans
Constant	0.059 (1.31)	−0.082 (1.34)
Trend	0.000 (0.77)	0.000 (0.30)
ln Gold Stock	0.025 (2.72)	0.046 (3.26)
ln Bank Stock Price	0.023 (1.93)	0.026 (1.60)
ln Loans (−1)	1.048 (17.2)	0.689 (13.1)
ln Loans (−2)	−0.083 (1.41)	0.274 (5.28)
Long-term elasticities		
ln Gold Stock	0.70	1.22
ln Bank Stock Price	0.66	0.70
R^2	.996	.990
NOBS	343	343
SEE	0.02	0.04

Notes: Monthly data, February 1917 to December 1935. ln Bank Stock Price = ln bank stock price index; ln Gold Stock (−1) = lagged ln of domestic gold stock in million pesos oro; ln Loans = ln loans in million pesos moneda nacional.

Sources: Baiocco (1937), except bankruptcies from *Revista de Economía Argentina* (various issues).

not be bypassed by domestic banks and the adjustment mechanism during a downturn in the business cycle was a capital crunch. In the case of foreign banks, lending was immediately curtailed to effect adjustment.

To reinforce the argument, in Table 5.4 we use an econometric analysis to illustrate the differences in lending behavior as a function of (1) gold flows, to show how inflows and outflows of capital are channeled to lending by bank type; and (2) bank stock prices, to assess the performance of the industry and how bankers react to the "pricing" of banks by the market. The results are consistent with theory: In a monetary, small, open economy, gold inflows and increases in the expected net present value of the banking industry should be conducive to an increase in the amount of lending. Note also the long-term elasticities of lending by type of bank to the level of gold stock of the economy: If the economy experiences an increase of 10% in the gold stock, foreign

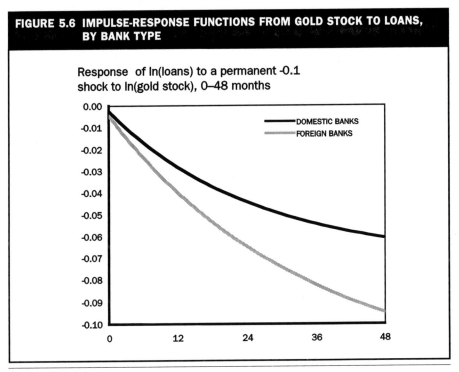

FIGURE 5.6 IMPULSE-RESPONSE FUNCTIONS FROM GOLD STOCK TO LOANS, BY BANK TYPE

Source: Table 5.4

banks increase lending by 12.2%, but domestic banks by only 7%. It is important to notice how elastic is the reaction of foreign banks to liquidity considerations and to the situation of the balance of payments of Argentina.[39]

To display these effects more clearly, Figure 5.6 displays impulse-response functions for the two types of banks based on the dynamic equations estimated in Table 5.4. It is apparent that full adjustment by the banks takes a number of years. Even after 36 months, a 10% decline in gold stocks translates into only a 5.4% and 8.2% fall in loans for domestic and foreign banks, respectively, whereas the long-term adjustment would be 10% and 12.2%, respectively. Evidently, banks could not adjust their loan portfolios overnight, so external shocks had long-lasting effects as banks continued to adjust their lending activity over several years.

The finding of structural differences in lending behavior as a response to macroeconomic and microeconomic events from different types of banks, domestic and foreign, is an extremely important result, one that has not been identified in previous studies of banking in emerging markets in a historical perspective, or in contemporary studies.

FINANCE AND DEVELOPMENT IN ARGENTINA:
SUCCESS OR FAILURE?

A review of the existing literature on Argentine financial development suggests a much more optimistic view of the interwar period than the one we have just presented. Marshaling new evidence both for Argentina in time series and relative to other countries in cross section, we have shown the weakness of the financial system between the wars. According to this new view, we have reason to suspect the financial system as one cause of Argentina's relative retardation after 1914.

Our study highlights two important institutional features of the interwar financial system as they interacted with the behavior of two types of intermediaries: domestic and foreign banks. First, we highlighted the macroeconomic twin risk: Under a quasi-fixed exchange rate regime, with a currency board but without a lender of last resort, the fractional reserve financial system was prone to systemic risks triggered by external shocks via gold flows. Second, we examined the microeconomic behavior of banks under such monetary and financial institutions and found significant differences between domestic and foreign banks. Adverse external shocks damaged the value of all banks, but elicited a larger and swifter adjustment of lending by foreign banks. However, in terms of capital adjustment, it was only the domestic banks that suffered capital crunches.

The two types of banks differed in asset risks and type of lending, and they served different niches after 1914. Foreign banks narrowed their lending activities to specialize in liquid short-term commercial loans, leaving domestic banks to supply longer-term loans in firms and real estate. They also crucially differed in terms of exposure to risk. Other things being equal, a foreign bank was less likely to fail. First, it could pool risk via international diversification: In a time of crisis foreign banks could call on overseas partners for liquidity, for example, a bank's London headquarters. Second, it could avoid systemic risk by its link to a monetary authority that acted as a lender of last resort. If the crisis was very severe, central banks would intervene—for example, the London headquarters of the bank would enlist the support of the Bank of England (as indeed happened during the 1890 Baring crisis).

Given these considerations, Argentine domestic banks were forced to choose a lower leverage: They had to maintain a higher capital cushion. Therefore, domestic banks could not fill the void left by the retreat of foreign capital after 1914; the lower leverage meant that they could not mobilize finance to the same extent and thus could not facilitate so easily the accumulation and allocation of capital in this emerging economy.

ACKNOWLEDGMENTS

Gerardo della Paolera is Rector and Professor of Economics at Universidad Torcuato Di Tella.

Alan M. Taylor is Assistant Professor at Northwestern University and Faculty Research Fellow at the National Bureau of Economic Research.

This paper was prepared while Taylor was a Visiting Scholar at the Universidad Torcuato Di Tella and while della Paolera was a Visiting Scholar at the IMF and at Northwestern University; we thank these institutions for their hospitality. We gratefully acknowledge financial support from the National Science Foundation, the Center for International and Comparative Studies at Northwestern University, and the Centro de Investigación en Finanzas y Mercado de Capitales (CIF) at the Universidad Torcuato Di Tella. For their research assistance we thank Sandra Amuso, Marcela Harriague, and Laura Ivanier. For help, comments, and suggestions we thank Pablo Martin Aceña, Michael Bordo, Charles Calomiris, Carlos Newland, Anna Schwartz, Carlos Zarazaga, and seminar participants at the Universidad Torcuato Di Tella.

NOTES

1. Díaz Alejandro (1970), Di Tella and Zymelman (1967), Cortés Conde (1979), Taylor (1994).
2. Díaz Alejandro (1984), Taylor (1994).
3. della Paolera et al. (1996).
4. See, however, della Paolera et al. (1996).
5. Díaz Alejandro (1985), p. 2.
6. Díaz Alejandro (1970), pp. 28–35.
7. Díaz Alejandro (1970), p. xx.
8. Díaz Alejandro (1970), pp. 33–34.
9. della Paolera (1994), Bordo and Rockoff (1996).
10. Taylor (1992).
11. Levine (1996), p. 14.
12. Taylor (1992).
13. Obstfeld and Taylor (1997).
14. In particular, banking intermediaries have an inherent instability under the so-called Diamond-Dybvig (1983) framework. Since banks insure the nominal value in deposit contracts and create high-powered deposits, they are subject to runs from investors. In a scenario of generalized runs, the expectation of the bank-

ruptcy of an otherwise safe institution is self-fulfilling.

15. Smith (1776).

16. Davis (1963), Cameron et al. (1967), Gerschenkron (1962), and Goldsmith (1969).

17. More recently, authors such as McKinnon (1973), Shaw (1973), and Fry (1995) have studied the recent experience of a large sample of developed and developing countries. They examine the channels of transmission from financial intermediation to growth by inspecting institutional and economic forces such as legal regulation and the influence of interest rates on savings and investments. The literature on endogenous growth has produced a renewed interest in the effect of financial development on the allocation of capital, expanding and formalizing these ideas even further (see Fry 1995).

18. Townsend (1983), Levine (1996).

19. Levine (1996).

20. Levine (1996) notes that "the link between liquidity and economic development arises because some high-return projects require a long-term commitment of capital, but savers do not like to relinquish control of their savings for long periods. Thus, if the financial system does not augment the liquidity of long-term investments, less investment is likely to occur in the high (risk-adjusted) return projects." This is a crucial function because when performed in an efficient manner it enables entrepreneurs to overcome the problem of borrowing or credit rationing. Following Calomiris (1993), if financial intermediation did not develop beyond short-term credit and lending practices, the allocation of resources and the nature and speed of economic growth would be affected because the choice of inputs in production would be biased toward variable-cost inputs and against investment in fixed capital.

21. Taylor (1992).

22. Baiocco (1937).

23. See the work in progress by Nakamura and Zarazaga (1996). However, in their paper they attempt to construct a preliminary index of the prices of stocks in the Buenos Aires Stock Exchange, which we include in Table 5.1, not the size of the market capitalization. The issue of exactly how much finance was raised via equity instruments is a subject for future research.

24. For the monetary economic history of the United States and the United Kingdom, see Friedman and Schwartz (1982); for monetary history episodes of different European countries, see Bordo and Jonung (1987); and for recent experiences, see Fry (1995) and King and Levine (1993).

25. See Nakamura and Zarazaga (1996).

26. Díaz Alejandro (1970).

27. King and Levine (1993), De Gregorio and Guidotti (1995).

28. Taylor (1992).

29. Townsend (1983).

30. We also examined correlations of real output per person and the two financial variables. The correlations are striking. Before 1920, the economy appears to be developing as per the standard economic model: Real economic growth moves in parallel with the relative expansion of the financial system and the substitution away from cash. After 1920, these correlations completely break down.

31. Calomiris (1993), Bordo (1987). The quote is from Calomiris (1993), p. 25. Calomiris and Bordo discuss U.S. banking structure from an international perspective that includes the causes of panics and crises.

32. Kaminsky and Reinhart (1996).

33. Bernanke (1983).

34. A second-order effect (of expected depreciation of the currency) via the behavior of depositors (investors) in a fractional reserve banking system also deserves comment here. But our data still preclude a detailed econometric analysis of this effect, usually referred to as twin exchange rate and financial crises.

35. della Paolera et al. (1996), p. 28.

36. Republica Argentina (1926).

37. Calomiris (1993).

38. Republica Argentina (1926), p. 39. In the census it is shown that foreign-owned banks typically had a net debtor position; that is, they were recipients of financial capital from correspondent banks abroad that was applied to trade lines. Domestic banks and the Banco de la Nación had a net creditor position vis-à-vis such *corresponsales en el exterior*. For 1925, the net debtor position for foreign banks was equivalent to 60% of total paid-in capital of those banks (Republica Argentina 1926, pp. 26–27, 44).

39. There are no significant differences in the elasticity of loans to changes in the bank stock prices, but it is worth noting that the elasticity is again very high.

REFERENCES

Baiocco, Pedro J. *La economía bancaria argentina*. Buenos Aires: Universidad de Buenos Aires, 1937.

Bernanke, Ben S. "Non-Monetary Effects of the Financial Crisis in the Propagation of the Great Depression." *American Economic Review* 73 (June 1983): 257–276.

Bordo, Michael D., and Lars Jonung. *The Long-Run Behavior of the Velocity of Circulation*. Cambridge: Cambridge University Press, 1987.

Bordo, Michael D., and Hugh Rockoff. "The Gold Standard as a 'Good Housekeeping Seal of Approval.'" *Journal of Economic History* 56 (June 1996): 389–428.

Cain, Peter J., and Anthony G. Hopkins. *British Imperialism: Innovation and Expansion, 1688–1914*. London: Longman, 1993.

Calomiris, Charles W. "Regulation, Industrial Structure, and Instability in U.S. Banking: An Historical Perspective." In *Structural Change in Banking*, edited by Michael Klausner and Lawrence J. White. Homewood, IL: Business One Irwin, 1993.

Cameron, Rondo, et al. *Banking in the Early Stages of Industrialization: A Study in Comparative Economic History*. New York: Oxford University Press, 1967.

Cortés Conde, Roberto. *El progreso argentino*. Buenos Aires: Editorial Sudamericana, 1979.

Davis, Lance E. "Capital Immobilities and Finance Capitalism: A Study of Economic Evolution in the United States." *Explorations in Economic History* 1 (Fall 1963): 88–105.

De Gregorio, José, and Pablo E. Guidotti. "Financial Development and Economic Growth." *World Development* 23 (1995): 433–448.

della Paolera, Gerardo. "Experimentos monetarios y bancarios en Argentina: 1861–1930." *Revista de Historia Económica* 12 (Fall 1994): 539–590.

della Paolera, Gerardo, et al. *Dinero, intermediación financiera y nivel de actividad en 110 años de historia económica argentina*. Buenos Aires: ADEBA, 1996.

De Long, J. Bradford. "Did J. P. Morgan's Men Add Value? An Economist's Perspective on Financial Capitalism." In *Inside the Business Enterprise: Historical Perspectives on the Use of Information*, edited by Peter Temin. Chicago: University of Chicago Press, 1991.

Diamond, Peter A., and Phillip H. Dybvig. "Bank Runs, Deposit Insurance, and Liquidity." *Journal of Political Economy* 91 (June 1983): 401–419.

Díaz Alejandro, Carlos F. "Stages in the Industrialization of Argentina." Centro de Investigaciones Económicas, Instituto Torcuato Di Tella, 1966.

Díaz Alejandro, Carlos F. *Essays on the Economic History of the Argentine Republic*. New Haven, CT: Yale University Press, 1970.

Díaz Alejandro, Carlos F. "Latin America in the 1930s." In *Latin America in the 1930s: The Role of the Periphery in World Crisis*, edited by Rosemary Thorp. New York: St. Martin's Press, 1984.

Díaz Alejandro, Carlos F. "Good-Bye Financial Repression, Hello Financial Crash." *Journal of Development Economics* 19 (September–October 1985): 1–24.

Di Tella, Guido, and Manuel Zymelman. *Las etapas del desarrollo económico argentino.* Buenos Aires: Editorial Universitaria de Buenos Aires, 1967.

Friedman, Milton, and Anna J. Schwartz. *Monetary Trends in the United States and United Kingdom: Their Relation to Income, Prices, and Interest Rates, 1867–1975.* Chicago: University of Chicago Press, 1982.

Fry, Maxwell J. *Money, Interest, and Banking in Economic Development,* 2nd ed. Baltimore: Johns Hopkins University Press, 1995.

Gerschenkron, Alexander. *Economic Backwardness in Historical Perspective.* Cambridge, MA: Harvard University Press, 1962.

Goldsmith, Raymond W. *Financial Structure and Economic Development.* New Haven, CT: Yale University Press, 1969.

Kaminsky, Graciela L., and Carmen M. Reinhart. "The Twin Crises: The Causes of Banking and Balance-of-Payments Problems." Board of Governors of the Federal Reserve System, September 1996. Photocopy.

King, Robert G., and Ross Levine. "Finance and Growth: Schumpeter Might Be Right." *Quarterly Journal of Economics* 108 (1993): 717–738.

Levine, Ross. "Financial Development and Economic Growth: Views and Agenda." Policy Research Working Papers no. 1678, World Bank, October 1996.

McKinnon, Ronald I. *Money and Capital in Economic Development.* Washington, DC: The Brookings Institution, 1973.

Nakamura, Leonard I., and Calos E. J. M. Zarazaga. "Economic Growth in Argentina in the Period 1905–1930: Some Evidence from Stock Returns." Federal Reserve Bank of Dallas, 1996.

Obstfeld, Maurice, and Alan M. Taylor. "The Great Depression as a Watershed: International Capital Mobility in the Long Run." Working Paper Series no. 5690, National Bureau of Economic Research, April 1997.

Ortiz, Javier. "Essays on the Early History of Latin American Central Banking." Ph.D. dissertation, University of California at Los Angeles, 1993.

República Argentina. *Censo bancario de la República Argentina 1925.* Buenos Aires, 1926.

Shaw, Edward S. *Financial Deepening in Economic Development.* Oxford: Oxford University Press, 1973.

Smith, Adam. *An Inquiry into the Nature and Causes of the Wealth of Nations.* London: W. Strahan & T. Cadell, 1776.

Taylor, Alan M. "External Dependence, Demographic Burdens and Argentine Economic Decline After the *Belle Époque.*" *Journal of Economic History* 52 (December 1992): 907–936.

Taylor, Alan M. "Tres fases del crecimiento económico argentino." *Revista de Historia Económica* 12 (Otoño 1994): 649–683.

Taylor, Alan M. "Argentina and the World Capital Market: Saving, Investment, and International Capital Mobility in the Twentieth Century." *NBER*, 1997.

Townsend, Robert M. "Financial Structure and Economic Activity." *American Economic Review* 73 (December 1983): 895–911.

6

Patterns of Foreign Investment in Latin America in the Twentieth Century

Michael J. Twomey
University of Michigan, Dearborn

This chapter presents initial results of a study of the size and evolution of foreign investment in the Third World during the twentieth century, centering on the countries of Latin America. I will address three related, essentially descriptive questions: How large was foreign investment in these countries at the start of this century? where was it large? and how has it evolved over time? The analysis will be presented for total foreign investment and its two components, portfolio and direct investment. Size will be judged by comparisons of foreign investment stocks with primarily two indicators: population and gross domestic (or national) product (GDP). This leads to a discussion of the degree to which these indicators serve as useful proxies for a third variable, foreign investment as a fraction of total capital—or foreign ownership of national capital.

Before beginning, let me clarify some key terms. Foreign investment (FI) will refer to loans to the government and loans and equity investment (including reinvested profits) into private-sector enterprises in the host country. It is customary to disaggregate total foreign investment as the sum of portfolio and foreign direct investment (FDI); the latter implies control, whereas the former is typically exemplified by fixed-interest-paying bonds. The railroad sector falls somewhere between the categories of portfolio and direct when the identifying characteristic is control over production or even assuredness of interest payments, particularly at the start of the century. When referring to direct investment in sectors outside of railroads, I will speak of other foreign direct investment (OFDI).

For most countries or colonies before 1950, estimates of the aggregate stocks of foreign investment are more available and reliable than estimates of annual flows of the type that are reported in balance of payments statistics, so this paper will only refer to stocks of foreign investment. How to scale the investment variables will be determined by practical considerations—essentially the availability of data—as well as theoretical concerns. Population data are quite accessible. As indicators of the size of the economy, and indeed as proxies for the capital stock, the estimated GDP figures are preferable, even though these data are less precisely measured and the question of the appropriate exchange rate arises. The value of exports is another obvious scalar, which could be attempted in future work.

Although the outlines of the description of the pattern of per capita levels of foreign investment can be gleaned from the literature, there would appear to be very little work presenting calculations of foreign investment as a fraction of GDP for Third World countries. This is perhaps surprising, given that contemporary analyses of foreign investment levels typically include size of the market as a major determinant. Although his interests were somewhat different from mine, Pamuk, in his landmark study of the Ottoman Empire, specifically considers the possibility of comparing the ratio of foreign investment with national income, but then rejects the idea as infeasible due to data limitations.[1] Drawing especially on the work of Angus Maddison and the recent historical work on GDP to which he leads, I hope to show that this conclusion is incorrect.

FOREIGN INVESTMENT ON THE EVE OF WORLD WAR I

According to the estimates for 1913–1914 in Woodruff, today's Third World countries received less than 40% of global foreign investment.[2] Just over half of that amount was directed toward Latin America, where 80% of it was concentrated in Argentina, Brazil, and Mexico. These three countries had received amounts of a similar order of magnitude to that of Canada and Australia. Each of the United Kingdom, France, and Germany was more important than the United States as a source for Third World countries. Challenging an earlier stereotype of pre–World War I foreign investment as being dominated by passive, rentier participants, Svedberg estimates that 44% to 60% of foreign investment in Third World countries in 1913–1914 was direct investment (including directly controlled railroads).[3] Overall, direct investment in Latin America was about average; the fraction was lower in India, Turkey, and Africa, and higher in China and Southeast Asia.

Data for 1913–1914 of foreign investment for several Third World areas are presented in Table 6.1. In per capita terms, Argentina and South Africa have

TABLE 6.1

Foreign Investment and GDP, 1913–1914

	GDP	Per Capita, in 1900 US$			As Percentage of GDP		
		FI	Portfolio*	OFDI	FI	Portfolio*	OFDI
Argentina	107	279	229	50	260	213	47
Brazil	23	68	49	18	296	215	81
Chile	58	122	70	52	211	121	90
Colombia	38	10	7	4	27	17	10
Cuba	127	175	83	93	138	65	73
Guatemala	38	62	58	4	166	154	12
Honduras	32	50	36	13	156	114	42
Mexico	49	90	42	48	183	86	97
Paraguay	41	35	21	15	86	50	36
Peru	33	40	25	15	121	76	45
Uruguay	106	172	138	35	162	129	33
Venezuela	18	17	13	4	98	73	25
China	13	3	1	2	23	4	19
India	24	8	5	3	34	23	11
Indochina		9	5	4			
Indonesia	11	11	1	10	95	8	87
Korea				1			3
Malaya	45	66	15	52	148	33	115
Philippines	58	10	1	9	17	2	15
Taiwan			6		21		
Thailand	16	6	4	2	38	23	15
Turkey	40	40	35	5	101	88	13
Egypt	78	71	35	35	90	45	45
Algeria	47	48	33	15	102	70	32
Morocco	23	14	5	9	59	22	37
U. South Africa	96	210	70	140	220	73	147
Zaire		17					
British W. Africa		6	0	6			
French W. Africa		6	3	3			
French Equatorial Africa	21	16	5				
Australia	344	289	217	72	84	63	21
Canada	252	375	302	73	161	135	26

Note: *Includes investment in railroads.

Source: See appendix.

very high levels, between $200 and $300 per capita (US$, 1900 prices), approx-imating those of Canada and Australia. The next largest level corresponds to Cuba and Uruguay, at $150 to $200, followed by a more heterogeneous group, including Chile, Mexico, Egypt, and Malaya; the high investment in these last two countries has been noted in the literature. Not surprisingly, the per capita levels of investment in China and India at $3 to $5 are only 1% to 2% of those in the high-investment countries. Colonial areas in sub-Saharan Africa are only slightly higher.

Table 6.1's ranking of countries by the relative size of foreign investment changes markedly when, instead of per capita investment, we consider invest-ment as a percentage of GDP. Using this measure, the familiar group of coun-tries of recent settlement—Australia, Canada, and Argentina—are no longer outliers, because countries such as Brazil and Chile now have comparable ratios. Furthermore, the ratios for Cuba, Mexico, Guatemala, and Honduras are much closer to those leaders. Asian colonies such as Malaya and Indonesia also have similarly high levels of foreign investment, while even the low num-bers corresponding to China and India are now within a factor of 5 or at most 10, as opposed to the earlier 50.[4]

Disaggregating foreign investment, we note that loans and funds for rail-roads tended to be larger than foreign direct investment in Latin America—as also in Australia and Canada—and that this was not typically the case in Asia and Africa. Where there was large portfolio investment, it resulted from loans for infrastructure such as railroad construction, either directly through private interests or utilizing the government as intermediary. There was less external funding of railroads in Asia and Africa than in Latin America.

Turning to foreign direct investment outside railroads (OFDI), we see in Table 6.1 that when measured relative to GDP, there is an even more drastic modification of rankings by countries. In Latin America, each of Brazil, Chile, Cuba, and Mexico has a higher level of OFDI/GDP than Argentina. Moreover, Canada and Australia now have rather small amounts of nonrailroad OFDI/GDP—around 25%. Malaya has the highest estimated ratio of OFDI/GDP at 115%, followed closely by Indonesia at 87%, which is the level for Chile and Mexico. Levels in India and China would now seem to lie about one-third and one-half below those of Australia and Canada, far from the dif-ferentials of 50 or 100 that we saw initially with foreign investment per capita. Although the numbers presented in Table 6.1 appear with more precision than is merited, there can be little doubt that in 1914 the countries of recent settle-ment had *lower* levels of nonrailroad OFDI/GDP than did many countries or colonies now referred to as the Third World.

Let us pause for a simple but important comment on the differences in rankings according to the denominator being used. As an arithmetical identity, investment divided by income is simply investment per capita divided by income per capita, so the same level of investment per capita will appear to be larger in poorer countries, and conversely. The above reversals of rankings, when moving from FI per capita to FI/GDP across countries at a single point in time, result from the greater differences in GDP per capita than in FI per capita. For our purposes, the most noteworthy example is the 1914 ratio of per capita incomes between neighboring Argentina and Brazil, which both Maddison and Bulmer-Thomas put at over four.[5] The gap in Table 6.1 between the per capita income of Brazil and, say, Australia and Canada, is larger than that reported in Maddison; however, even using Maddison's data, the conclusion about the rankings of OFDI/GDP still holds.

A REGRESSION ANALYSIS OF THE DETERMINANTS OF FOREIGN INVESTMENT IN 1913–1914

With the goal of more rigorously identifying the countries where foreign investment was large or small, some regressions were estimated on this data for 1913–1914. This year was chosen because of data availability, of course, but it also should represent the maximum impact of fin de siècle liberalism. The dependent variables are foreign investment as a fraction of GDP (FI/GDP), and its two components, portfolio and nonrailroad direct investment (PORT/GDP and OFDI/GDP, respectively).

The primary explanatory variable was per capita income (GDP/CAP), reflecting a hypothesized positive link to the size of the market. Because it was clear that financing railroads had been important in several countries, an indicator RR/GDP (kilometers of operational railroad divided by GDP) was used. Furthermore, because mineral exports were associated with higher foreign direct investment, an indicator MIN (minerals as a fraction of total exports) was used. With this minimal set of variables one can incorporate motivations for foreign investment involving domestic market as well as foreign trade considerations. Finally, dummy variables reflecting colonial status were utilized. The literature provides conflicting hints about the expected sign on the estimated coefficient for this variable; investment might be larger in colonies because of reduced risk in terms of the legal and institutional framework, to which a nationalist might append a story of greater ease of exploitation. However, with equal facility one could cite stories about colonialism's defenders' disappointment with investment levels, most pointedly in comparison with independent Argentina.

Observations were not available for at least one of FI, OFDI, or GDP for Indochina, Taiwan, Korea, or sub-Saharan Africa, leaving us with data on 25 countries. Because Australia and Canada were outliers in the regression on direct investment, observations for those two countries were omitted, and the results in Table 6.2 refer to 23 countries. The regressions were run as ordinary least squares. Specification on levels actually did slightly better than semilogarithmic or double-logarithmic equations, and additive dummies produced the same results as composite variables generated by multiplying the dummies by other explanatory variables. Fortunately, this makes interpretation of the results very easy.

As can be seen in Table 6.2, the coefficient of GDP/CAP in the regression on total investment (FI/GDP) is the sum of the coefficients for that variable in the equations on portfolio (PORT/GDP) and other direct investment (OFDI/GDP); the estimated coefficients are generally positive and statistically significant. Portfolio investment responded about as strongly to per capita income as did direct investment. The presence of railroads also had a strong

TABLE 6.2

Regression Results

Dependent Variable	Constant	GDP/CAP	MIN	RR/GDP	D1	R^2
FI/GDP	13.7	0.47	−0.10	5.39		0.83
	(1.01)	(2.25)	(0.33)	(0.61)		
PORT/GDP	−2.67	0.19	−1.11	4.99		0.89
	(0.30)	(1.43)	(5.19)	(2.61)		
OFDI/GDP	16.4	0.27	1.00	0.39		0.45
	(1.34)	(1.46)	(3.38)	(0.71)		
FI/GDP	22.6	0.44	−0.22	5.83	−20.1	0.84
	(1.52)	(2.15)	(0.67)	(8.53)	(1.31)	
PORT/GDP	−6.10	0.20	−1.07	4.83	7.77	0.88
	(0.61)	(1.49)	(4.75)	(10.5)	(0.76)	
OFDI/GDP	28.7	0.24	0.89	0.99	−27.9	0.53
	(2.30)	(1.36)	(2.99)	(1.73)	(2.19)	

Notes: Estimated t coefficients are in parentheses. There were 23 observations.

Variables: FI/GDP is total foreign investment divided by GDP, PORT/GDP is portfolio investment—which incorporates loans to the government and financing for railroads—divided by GDP, and OFDI/GDP is direct foreign investment in other enterprises divided by GDP. GDP/CAP is gross domestic product per capita, in U.S. dollars at 1900 prices. MIN is the share of mining exports in total exports. RR/GDP is kilometers of railroads in operation in 1913 divided by GDP. D1 is a dummy variable equal to 1 if the area was an independent country (all of Latin America, China, Thailand, and Turkey).

effect on portfolio investment, as expected from how portfolio investment was measured; its positive, albeit small, effect on direct investment would be consistent with an explanation focusing on railroads opening up the economy, making the area more attractive to investors. The negative coefficient of mining on portfolio investment was not expected, and may capture an indirect effect via income and perhaps savings.

The results from both excluding and including the dummy variables are reported. Being an independent country (dummy variable D1 equal to unity— Latin American countries, Thailand, China, and Turkey) had a small, positive, but statistically insignificant effect on the level of portfolio investment. More interesting, the estimated coefficient on D1 is negative for other foreign direct investment: Independent status lowered OFDI/GDP by about 28% of GDP, which was about half of the average value of that variable. Following some suggestions in the literature, an additional dummy variable was inserted for the self-governing members of the British Empire, which did not cause major changes. Of course, independence is relative; it is difficult to argue that Canada was in fact less independent than Cuba in 1913, and a more complex representation of political status would certainly be preferable to this dichotomous dummy variable.

One can use the econometric results to assess whether countries had more or less investment than "normal" by looking at the residuals in the equations discussed above (without the dummy variable), which are presented in Table 6.3. With regard to direct foreign investment in other enterprises, the largest positive residuals occur for Malaya, Brazil, and South Africa; the most negative ones occur for Chile, Peru, and Turkey. A very different set of countries stand out with regard to government loans and railroads: The largest positive residuals occur for Honduras, Guatemala, and Turkey, whereas the most negative ones are for Paraguay, Mexico, and India. It should be added that the residuals from the regressions that incorporated the dummies have a relatively similar distribution. The residual on total investment is the sum of the other two residuals. However, notice that in over half the cases, the residuals from the regressions on portfolio and direct investment have the opposite sign. Evidently the omitted factors determining the two types of investment worked differently in the several cases.

LONG-TERM TRENDS

The other major goal of this paper is description of the long-term trends of foreign investment and its components. The data for Latin American countries are presented in Table 6.4 and illustrated in Figures 6.1 and 6.2, which suggest

TABLE 6.3

Observed and Residual Levels of FI/GDP, PORT/GDP, and OFDI/GDP

	FI/GDP		PORT/GDP		OFDI/GDP	
	Observed	Residual	Observed	Residual	Observed	Residual
Argentina	260	−19	−213	−4	47	−15
Brazil	296	27	−215	−12	81	39
Chile	211	−37	121	9	90	−46
Colombia	27	−33	17	−12	10	−21
Cuba	138	−2	65	−16	73	14
Guatemala	166	14	154	37	12	−24
Honduras	156	55	114	44	42	12
Mexico	183	4	86	−24	97	27
Paraguay	86	−22	50	−24	36	3
Peru	121	−28	76	3	45	−31
Uruguay	162	−4	129	16	33	−20
Venezuela	98	−22	73	−16	25	−6
China	23	−6	4	−5	19	−2
India	34	−41	23	−23	11	−18
Indonesia	95	31	8	−7	87	38
Malaya	148	−57	33	6	115	51
Philippines	17	−35	2	−17	15	−18
Thailand	38	−19	23	1	15	−21
Turkey	101	12	88	34	13	−22
Egypt	90	14	45	10	45	4
Algeria	102	−3	70	−1	32	−2
Morocco	59	16	22	3	37	13
South Africa	220	41	73	−3	147	44

Note: Residuals are from the regressions that omit dummy variables for political status, as reported in Table 6.2.

a characterization of the long-term trend as a U-shaped curve, hitting a low point in midcentury, with differing subsequent degrees of recovery. The initial high point of investment as a percentage of GDP occurred prior to 1900, whereas that of investment per capita was closer to 1913, reflecting the increase in per capita income during those years. Note that exclusion of Argentina has only a marginal effect on the size and timing of the initial phase, indicating

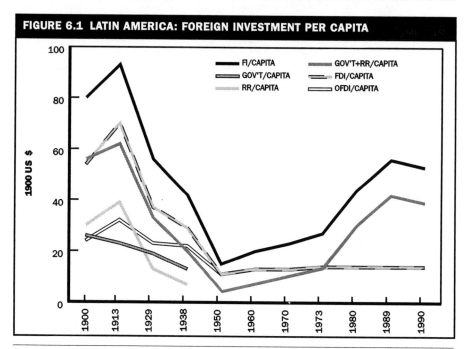

FIGURE 6.1 LATIN AMERICA: FOREIGN INVESTMENT PER CAPITA

Sources: See appendix.

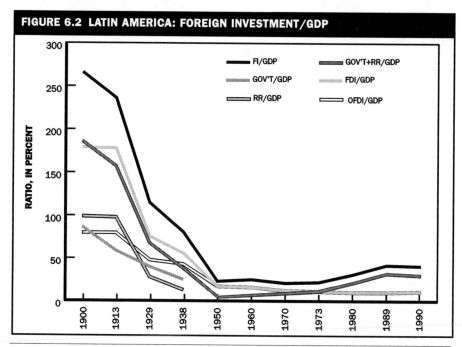

FIGURE 6.2 LATIN AMERICA: FOREIGN INVESTMENT/GDP

Sources: See appendix.

that this U-shaped pattern was not merely the result of numerical dominance by a relatively large Argentina.[6] The more recent upswing in total investment per capita has nearly regained the levels achieved at the start of the century. However, because the long-term trend of real per capita income has been positive, especially after World War II, the comparison of foreign investment with real income lowers the more recent figures, compared with the per capita data. As can be seen in Figure 6.2, the ratio of foreign investment to GDP rises only slightly after 1950; perhaps the image of a flat reverse S is more appropriate than that of a U for this ratio.

The question arises as to the trends in investment before the turn of the century. In the original version of this work (available from the author on request), it is argued that the high absolute and per capita levels in Argentina and Uruguay go back at least to 1875, as do those for Cuba and Peru also. The River Platte countries may have actually peaked before 1900, whereas investments in Cuba rose after the Spanish American War, and direct investments in Peru rose in sectors such as mining and agriculture.

To understand more fully the twentieth-century experience, it is necessary to separate direct from portfolio investment and to isolate railroads. In 1990, government loans constituted 75% of the regional total, other direct investments were still about 25%, and of course foreign interest in railroads had disappeared. However, as is clear from Table 6.4, these components have evolved along quite distinct paths.

Relative to either population or GDP, loans to governments (and other portfolio funds) trace a marked U shape during this century, hitting a low point at midcentury. Indeed, for several years foreign aid was the major source of new funds. The subsequent increase in loans during the 1970s and 1980s is familiar, particularly as a proximate cause of the Third World debt crisis; the very recent activity in emerging stock markets is not reflected in this data.

With regard to foreign investment in railroads, the story is quite different. This declined relatively—and eventually absolutely—both because the host countries' domestic savers and entrepreneurs (including their governments) learned the railroad business and displaced foreigners and because the growth of railroad lines was stymied, by 1930 or earlier, by the exhaustion of good routes and the expanded use of the motor car. The United States had invested significantly in railroads in only Canada, Mexico, and Central America, and the governments of the first two countries had already progressed significantly in the purchase of those investments by the mid-1920s. British railroad ownership, which was larger and more widespread geographically, also declined during this period, and her last major holding in this sector in Latin America was purchased by Argentina's Perón in the late 1940s.

The major long-term contributors to the relative changes in foreign investment were therefore changes in government loans and the disappearance of foreign participation in railroads. Let us now turn to the behavior of foreign investment in sectors outside of railroads and government loans, that is, to what I am calling other foreign direct investment. Although levels of foreign investment in private enterprises were high in certain countries at the start of the century, this was fundamentally due to high foreign involvement in railroads. Taking out railroads, the price adjusted per capita level of other direct investment in 1900 was only about a third higher than the level it consistently maintained after 1950, having reached a somewhat higher plateau in 1913–1929. Big growth occurred in some familiar cases, each related to an exported raw material: mining in Chile, sugar in Cuba, and petroleum in Venezuela. In Mexico, increased investment in petroleum counterbalanced the reduction in other sectors due to the Revolution. Note that the implicit model before 1950 is that of nonrailroad FDI growth determined by availability of an exported natural resource; foreign investment in manufacturing for domestic markets came after World War II, whereas foreign investment into export-oriented manufacturing awaited the 1970s.

Foreign direct investment per capita was flat in Latin America after 1950. It actually declined when measured as a fraction of GDP, as can be seen in Figure 6.2. There was a fall of two-thirds between 1929 and 1950, which was again cut in half subsequently. Once again, note that although the cross-sectional ranking of countries varies tremendously depending on the use of population or GDP as the scalar, the longitudinal stories that these two indicators provide are quite similar until after about 1960, when per capita income starts to rise appreciably.

For all the countries covered in the regressions presented above, the ratio OFDI/GDP fell from 47% in 1914 to 11% in 1970, remaining at 12% in 1990. This result does not correspond to the familiar image of strong contemporary growth of foreign investment, perhaps because such stories do not distinguish direct from portfolio investment—and loans to many governments have certainly been rising recently—or merely because many observers, such as the UN Conference on Trade and Development (UNCTAD), are content to gauge the strength of foreign investment by reference to its nominal value, which of course has been increasing.[7]

TABLE 6.4

Foreign Investment in Latin America, Twentieth Century

	1900	1913	1929	1938	1950	1970	1973	1980	1989	1990
Total										
FI/capita	80	93	56	42	15	23	27	44	56	53
(G + RR)/capita	56	62	33	20	4	10	13	30	42	39
RR/capita	30	39	13	7						
OFDI/capita	24	32	23	22	11	13	14	14	14	14
FI/GDP	266	236	115	81	23	21	22	31	42	41
(G + RR)/GDP	186	157	68	38	6	9	11	21	32	30
RR/GDP	99	98	28	13						
OFDI/GDP	80	80	48	43	17	12	11	10	10	11
Total, without Argentina										
FI/capita	59	72	45	33	15	22	27	44	52	
FI/GDP	227	227	117	79	27	23	24	32	40	
(G + RR)/GDP	146	134	61	31	7	10	12	22	30	28
RR/GDP	73	82	21	4						
OFDI/GDP	81	93	56	47	20	13	12	10	10	
Argentina										
FI/capita	337	279	140	104	16	28	30	45	101	
FI/GDP	415	260	112	87	12	14	14	23	64	
(G + RR)/GDP	337	213	83	57	5	7	7	15	56	49
RR/GDP	197	138	44	37						
OFDI/GDP	78	47	29	30	7	7	6	8	8	
Brazil										
FI/capita	49	68	28	23	7	13	21	39	45	43
FI/GDP	255	296	92	70	18	17	20	32	35	36
(G + RR)/GDP	207	215	64	58	6	8	10	22	25	25
RR/GDP	84	109	13	7						
OFDI/GDP	48	81	28	12	12	9	10	9	10	11

TABLE 6.4 (CONT.)

Foreign Investment in Latin America, Twentieth Century

	1900	1913	1929	1938	1950	1970	1973	1980	1989	1990
Chile										
FI/capita	80	122	131	122	47	54	48	41	68	67
FI/GDP	188	211	156	163	49	38	34	27	41	40
(G + RR)/ GDP	117	121	80	68	18	26	29	23	28	25
RR/GDP	55	51	14	12						
OFDI/GDP	71	90	76	95	31	12	5	4	13	15
Colombia										
FI/capita	22	10	16	19	15	18	18	16	30	30
FI/GDP	74	27	34	35	24	19	18	13	21	21
(G + RR)/ GDP	21	17	14	19	6	12	12	10	17	17
RR/GDP	12	8	2	0						
OFDI/GDP	52	10	20	16	18	8	6	3	4	4
Cuba										
FI/capita	160	175	171	115	42					
FI/GDP	133	138	213	188	47					
(G + RR)/ GDP	86	65	67	67	4					
RR/GDP	37	43	40	27						
OFDI/GDP	47	73	146	121	43					
Guatemala										
FI/capita	45	62	31	34		9	8	7		
FI/GDP	136	166	73	63		12	11	8		
(G + RR)/ GDP	128	154	53	17	0	5	4	7	17	17
RR/GDP	90	141	44	0						
OFDI/GDP	7	12	19	46		8	7	1		
Honduras										
FI/capita	44	50	51	28		18	17		36	
FI/GDP	158	156	119	88		38	35		69	
(G + RR)/ GDP	113	114	33	27	1	12	14	41	64	69
RR/GDP	0	0	0	0						
OFDI/GDP	45	42	87	61		26	22		6	

TABLE 6.4 (CONT.)

Foreign Investment in Latin America, Twentieth Century

	1900	1913	1929	1938	1950	1970	1973	1980	1989	1990
Mexico										
FI/capita	63	90	67	44	14	18	22	50	70	68
FI/GDP	155	183	128	79	17	12	14	23	34	32
(G + RR)/ GDP	100	86	78	41	7	7	9	18	25	23
RR/GDP	79	62	33	24						
OFDI/GDP	55	97	50	39	10	5	5	5	9	9
Paraguay										
FI/capita	25	35	17			11	11		31	
FI/GDP	70	86	36			18	18		31	
(G + RR)/ GDP	66	50	21	7	14	13	16	28	22	
RR/GDP	42	38	17	0						
OFDI/GDP	4	36	15	22		5	5		3	
Peru										
FI/capita	47	40	31	24	12	20	24	34	36	36
FI/GDP	178	121	64	46	22	22	24	32	45	48
(G + RR)/ GDP	125	76	37	30	7	12	14	28	41	44
RR/GDP	124	66	17	14						
OFDI/GDP	53	45	27	16	14	10	10	4	4	4
Uruguay										
FI/capita	258	172	76	67	25	21	22		62	
FI/GDP	314	162	67	59	18	13	14		31	
(G + RR)/ GDP	229	129	54	32	10	10	11	16	27	26
RR/GDP	88	58	19	0						
OFDI/GDP	85	33	14	27	8	3	3		4	

TABLE 6.4 (CONT.)

Foreign Investment in Latin America, Twentieth Century

	1900	1913	1929	1938	1950	1970	1973	1980	1989	1990
Venezuela										
FI/capita	33	17	58	49	62	73	65	67	83	78
FI/GDP	252	98	105	73	55	36	39	32	52	47
(G + RR)/ GDP	161	73	6	0	0	6	12	28	46	41
RR/GDP	85	37	5	0						
OFDI/GDP	90	25	99	73	55	30	27	4	6	6

Notes: Per capita data are U.S. dollars in 1900 prices; other data are foreign investment components as a percentage of GDP. FI = total foreign investment. G + RR = loans to the government and external funding for railroads. RR = funds for railroads only. OFDI = other foreign direct investment.

Sources: See appendix.

TRENDS IN CANADA AND AUSTRALIA

One standard comparison for Latin America is the cases of Australia and Canada, for which some data are presented in Table 6.5. One basic similarity with Latin America is the midcentury decline in foreign investment relative to population or GDP; another is the smallness of investment in sectors other than government and railroads. A third parallel is the relative constancy of nonrailroad OFDI/GDP. One minor difference we would highlight here is the rise of OFDI/GDP in Canada during the 1920s due to investments from the United States, whereas that ratio fell in Latin America and apparently stayed constant in Australia.

Note the different paths of portfolio and direct foreign investment over the century, particularly the relative constancy of OFDI/GDP, and the decline in portfolio investment between 1929 and 1950. There is also a suggestion of two peaks in the ratio of foreign investment to GDP, the earlier one in 1895—during another recession, to be sure—and the second in 1913, at the end of a remarkable expansion. Patching together disparate sources for Australia generates a similar pattern, in which OFDI as a fraction of GDP remains slightly larger than in Canada, although still smaller than in Latin America. Of course, today both Canada and Australia are major sources of both direct and portfolio foreign investment, as was Canada even before World War I, but pursuit of this topic would take us too far afield.

TABLE 6.5

Foreign Investment in Australia and Canada, Twentieth Century

Australia

	1900	1914	1929	1930	1938	1947	1960	1970	1980	1989
1900 US$/CAP										
FI/CAP	308	275	286	300	282	138	143	144	276	646
PORT/CAP	>232	>208	221	235		100	56	58	131	419
OFDI/CAP	< 75	< 67	64	65		38	87	86	145	227
Percentages										
FI/GNP	124	84	91	103	85	61	32	28	32	69
PORT/GNP	>93	>64	70	80		42	11	11	15	45
OFDI/GNP	< 31	<21	20	22		17	19	17	17	24

Canada

	1900	1914	1926	1930	1939	1950	1960	1970	1980	1990
1900 US$/CAP										
FI/CAP	226	375	313	337	359	225	329	438	647	969
PORT/CAP	162	302	226	263	242	134	151	208	410	703
OFDI/CAP	63	73	87	114	117	90	178	231	237	266
Percentages										
FI/GDP	140	161	120	133	126	53	64	58	57	69
PORT/GDP	108	135	87	93	85	32	29	28	36	50
OFDI/GDP	32	26	32	40	41	21	34	31	21	19

Note: FI is total foreign investment, PORT (portfolio) includes government and railroads, and OFDI is all direct foreign investment outside of railroads.

Sources: Standard sources for these countries; the precise listing is available on request from the author.

THE RELATIVE SIZE OF RAILROADS

Because railroads occupied such an important role in the early phase of foreign investment, and in turn represented one of the first major accumulations of capital, their story should perhaps be sketched out in more detail. For the canonical case of the United Kingdom, railroads reached their peak relative size around 1875, when the value of the system was equivalent to about 40% of a year's GDP and 25% of total fixed nonresidential capital. In all the countries of interest in this paper, the railroads attained their highest relative size later in chronological terms. For example, in the United States the peak was one or two decades later, at about the same relative size according to either measure. By contrast, in Japan, the only other country for which elaborate, authoritative, published estimates appear to be available for the late nineteenth century, the growth of railroads started later and peaked in the second decade of this century at a level less than half that of the United Kingdom and the United States.

The expectation of railroads playing a bigger role in Argentina, Australia, Canada, and South Africa are supported by the calculations based on the available data. By my rough estimates, net railroad stock reached over 60% of GDP and 30% to 40% of nonresidential capital, making the railroad system relatively larger in these countries than in those discussed in the previous paragraph. Virtually all the countries in Asia and Africa with available estimates of national income present similarities in both size and timing to the pattern described above for Japan, which we might label one of "lesser importance" for railroads.

Given this contrasting experience between the countries of recent settlement and the "lesser importance" pattern, it is also worth commenting that in several Latin American countries the railroads attained levels fully comparable with that of Argentina, at least when measured by railroad mileage/GDP (capital stock data not being available). Specifically, this is the case for Brazil and Mexico, and nearly so for Chile and Peru, whereas the level in Costa Rica was actually much higher.

THE DEGREE OF FOREIGN OWNERSHIP
OF THE TOTAL CAPITAL STOCK

The evidence reviewed indicates a widespread fall in the ratio of foreign direct investment to GDP. Can we infer that foreign ownership of the means of production also decreased? There are several reasons to study trends of FDI—as a provider of foreign exchange, capital, technology, etc.—but many analysts' primary interest focuses on knowing about trends in foreign ownership, which some favor and others do not. There are both direct and indirect approaches for answering the question of the evolution of foreign ownership.

The information available from directly estimated capital stock data is presented in Table 6.6. In terms of levels of foreign ownership in 1914, there were marked differences. Argentina, Mexico, and South Africa had ratios that were two or three times that of Canada, whereas that of India was again much lower. This did not correspond to my expectation.

With regard to trends in Latin America, the work of the United Nations Economic Commission for Latin America (ECLA) of the early 1950s estimated the constant price values of both foreign investment (apparently including loans) and the domestic capital stock (fixed reproducible capital, apparently including residential) for several countries. The ECLA estimate for the region

TABLE 6.6

Foreign Direct Investment as a Percentage
of the Domestic Capital Stock, Twentieth Century

Argentina	1900	1913	1929	1940	1950	1957		
FI/K	32	48	32	20	5	6		
FDI/K	21	34	21	16	3			
OFDI/K	6	9	8	7	3			
RR/K	18	16	11	7				

Mexico		1910	1930	1940	1950		1970	1985
FDI/K		49	47	32	26		9	13
OFDI/K		31	30	26				

Latin America			1929	1940	1950	1955		
FI/K			25	17	11	12		

India		1913	1929	1939	1950	1960	1970	1975
FDI/K		9	9	11	2	2	1	0

Australia	1900	1914	1929	1938				
FDI/K	9	7	8	6				

South Africa		1913		1936	1956		1970	
FDI/K		66		42	16		13	

Canada	1900	1914	1926	1930	1951	1960	1970	1980
FDI/K	36	28	12	15	8	13	12	7
OFDI/K	17	10	12					

Sources: Argentina: United Nations Economic Commision for Latin America (1958), Cuadros 27 and 32, Cuadro 11
of Annex 3 of Addendum 4, combined with the breakdown of FI in Table 6.5. Mexico: Twomey (1993)
Tables 5-5a and 5-5c, as reflected in Graph 5-3; K is nonresidential capital. Latin America: Ganz (1959, p.
232). India: FDI 1913–1939 from Goldsmith (1983), pp. 24, 81, 222; breakdown of FI for 1913 follows
Howard's estimate reported in Svedberg (1978, p. 774). 1950–1975 from Reserve Bank of India (1964, 1985).
Capital stock for 1913–1939 are Bina Roy's estimates, and 1950–1975 are official data, all reported in
Goldsmith (1983). Australia: FDI and K are described in the appendix available from the author. South
Africa: FDI 1913 and 1936 from Frankel (1938), 1956 and 1970 from *Statistical Abstract*. Capital stock from
Franzsen and Willers (1959), and de Jager (1973). Canada: FDI 1900 and 1914 combine the unpublished
estimates for the United Kingdom of Davis and Gallman with those for the United States from Lewis (1938).
Both sources allow separation of funds for railroads. Subsequent years from *CIIP*. Capital stock 1900–1913
estimated as discussed in the appendix. 1926–1990 from Statistics Canada, *Fixed Capital Flows and Stocks*,
adjusting upward the 1926 and 1930 figures for residences, and using the ratio of total to nonresidential
for 1936.

as a whole indicates a decline in this ratio from 25% in 1929 to 11% in 1950, with a slight recovery to 12% in 1955.[8] With specific regard to Argentina, the ECLA reports that the ratio of foreign investment to total capital reached a very high 48% in 1913, falling to 6% in 1957.[9] The importance of railroads as a determinant of the total trend is evident in the table. Making a very rough adjustment for loans also suggests that both FDI/K and OFDI/K declined after 1913 in Argentina. While the ECLA did not provide the ratio for any other Latin American country, its data do at least permit a calculation for the regional total minus Argentina, which indicates that for the other countries, foreign investment also fell relatively after 1929.[10] The author's own work on Mexico suggests a strong drop in direct foreign ownership, in which changes in railroads account for much of the decline.[11]

A very useful set of official measurements of foreign ownership and control comes from Canada. On an aggregate level, foreign control of nonresidential capital declined between the late 1920s and the 1950s, rose slightly during the 1950s and 1960s, and has fallen since the early 1970s (see Figure 6.3). Although there were fluctuations in the estimated ratio of direct foreign investment to

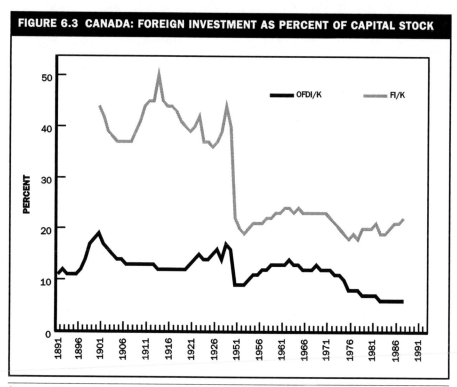

FIGURE 6.3 CANADA: FOREIGN INVESTMENT AS PERCENT OF CAPITAL STOCK

Sources: See appendix.

the capital stock prior to 1926, they pale in size compared with the variation of portfolio investment reported earlier in Table 6.5. Although no official estimate of the capital stock exists for Australia before World War II, my own estimates, also included in that table, suggest that FDI was a small and declining share of total capital in that country.

As a complement to the above-mentioned work on Latin America, data that had been generated using reasonably similar methodologies were sought on capital stocks and FDI for the post-1950 period. Two published estimates of the real value of capital stock are those of Hofman, and King and Levine.[12] Calculations for Latin America comparing annual real growth rates of total capital stock and total or U.S.-originating foreign direct investment are presented in Table 6.7. For Mexico and Brazil, the real value of the stock of foreign direct investment essentially grew as fast as the total stock of capital; for Argentina, Chile,[13] Colombia, Ecuador, Peru, and Venezuela, the latter grew faster. When the comparison is restricted to direct investment originating in the United States for the period 1950–1989 (for which the data are more homogeneous), calculations also indicate that the domestic capital stock grew faster than FDI for all the countries.

For an explanation of the apparent contradiction between perceptions of increased foreign control and the general finding of a decline in the ratio of

TABLE 6.7

Annual Growth Rates of Foreign Direct Investment and the Capital Stock

	1970–1989		1950–1989	
	Total FDI	Total Capital	U.S. FDI	Total Capital
Argentina	−0.4	2.7	0.9	3.7
Brazil	7.3	7.8	3.7	8.5
Chile	13.2	1.7	−2.6	3.3
Colombia	4.1	4.9	1.7	4.2
Ecuador	2.2	6.0	4.2	n.a.
Mexico	5.8	5.6	3.0	6.5
Peru	−0.2	4.0	0.5	n.a.
Venezuela	1.7	5.7	−3.2	6.5

Notes: The time period for Argentina is 1976–1989; for Chile it is 1981–1989. For the second column, the time period is 1973–1989. The original data in Hofman (1992) and King and Levine (1994) was expressed in per capita terms. The series chosen from Hofman is nonresidential physical capital, whereas that from King and Levine would appear to include residential capital.

Sources: Author's calculations. Total FDI is from UNCTAD (1994a), which is based on national sources. U.S. FDI is from U.S. Department of Commerce (1960) and *Survey of Current Business* (1992), deflated by the U.S. GDP deflator. Capital stock is from Hofman (1992), except for Ecuador and Peru, for which the source is King and Levine (1994).

FDI to the capital stock, one is once again drawn to focus on individual sectors. One finds, scattered in the literature, different studies of foreign ownership in individual Latin American countries, which often study specific sectors. Important recent examples on Brazil and Mexico are Fritsch and Franco, and Peres Nuñez, respectively.[14] They suggest that the cases of relative increases of foreign ownership are not generalized throughout the entire economies, but rather are limited to certain sectors, such as manufacturing or mining, and even to specific subsectors, such as pharmaceuticals and motor vehicles. The vision of a limited sectoral extension of foreign ownership also informs Evans' landmark analysis of "dependent development."[15]

WHAT DETERMINED LONG-TERM TRENDS IN FDI/GDP?

The long-term trends of portfolio and direct investment in Latin America differed markedly. Evidently factors in both the sending and the receiving countries contributed to this evolution; I will focus on direct investment.

The downward secular trend of foreign direct investment in Latin America clashes with the expectation, bolstered by the regression exercise above, of a positive link between FDI and per capita income. Conventional wisdom attributes a midcentury decline of FDI in Latin America to nationalist policies which were part of a general rejection of Manchesterian liberalism. The heterogeneity of policy approaches followed by individual countries, in Latin America as elsewhere, cautions against the attribution of that fall simply to nationalist policies, however strong such policies were in specific contexts.[16] For example, one component of that nationalist orientation was the widespread use of high tariffs to stimulate import substitution industrialization during the middle of the century, which would have had the opposite effect, according to the theory of tariffs as attractors of direct investment, for which Canada is a prime example. Nor has the neoliberal rejection of nationalistic import substitution policies led uniformly to increases in foreign investment, as recently documented by Bleischowsky and Stumpo.[17]

Without denying the political element, I will search for economic explanations. The 1930s depression and World War II evidently affected capital exporters, but it is the postwar economic recovery that leads me to look for an acceleration of investment flows. I suggest going beyond national macroeconomic conditions to more sector-specific variables, using what economists call an industrial organization approach, whose extension into the study of foreign investment has been led by John Dunning.[18] For example, it is well documented that the sectoral composition of outward FDI from the United States has gone through several phases: The pre–World War I predominance of infrastructure and services was ceded to raw materials—agriculture, mining, and petroleum—which after World War II were surpassed by manufacturing. Investment in services is once again on the rise. Many commentators explain the recent decline in U.S. investment as resulting from the U.S. corporations' loss of a competitive edge compared with entrepreneurs from host countries or other investing countries. Petroleum is an important case; in several countries these enclaves have been replaced by joint ventures or other licensing arrangements. In most other primary products, such as rubber, sugar, or nonferrous metals, these swings of the product cycle are even starker. Another obvious case would be railroads, discussed earlier. Some new investments follow strategies that reflect the branch plant mentality of U.S. manufacturers less and return to modernized versions of the holding company, such as the *sogo shosha* and *keiretsu*.

The agricultural sector certainly has its own unique dynamic. The infamous Latin American examples of foreign-controlled plantation crops such as bananas, henequen, and sugar have disappeared with modernization of the countryside.

The official Canadian data on foreign direct investment illustrate very well how markedly different were the level and evolution of ownership ratios by economic sectors. Figure 6.4 illustrates that the overall trend in the foreign presence is an average of several disparate sector-specific changes: Foreign control of manufacturing and minerals has risen since World War II, whereas that in service sectors is lower and follows a declining trend. Less complete data from Australia provide a similar message. My analysis of the situation in Mexico, summarized in Figure 6.5, actually portrays more extreme sectoral variations. Indeed, the combination of marked sectoral differences not only in foreign ownership ratios but also in growth rates in capital—in favor of services—leads to the paradoxical situation, in Canada and perhaps elsewhere, of small increases in foreign ownership in each sector being overwhelmed by the faster growth of the sectors with low foreign participation, so that the ownership ratio for the entire economy is measured as falling.

CONCLUSIONS

The long-term U-shaped pattern of foreign investment relative to income was seen to arise predominantly because of changes in loans. The general trend of direct foreign investment has been downward relative to income and, probably, total capital stock. The contemporary policy implication would be that factors *reducing* direct foreign investment, such as a more rapid transfer of technology in product cycles, the spread of nonmajority ownership linkages such as

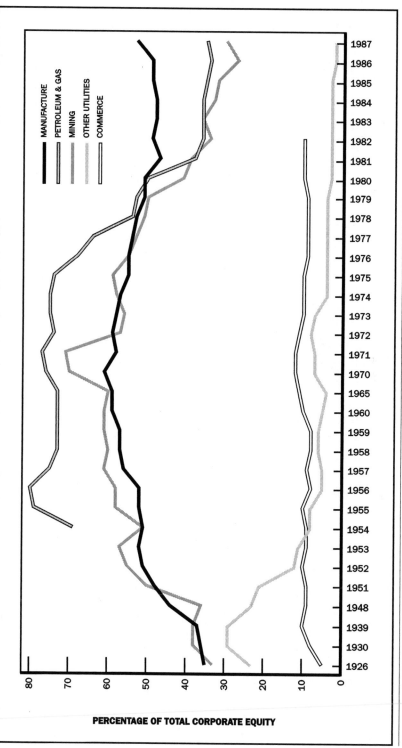

FIGURE 6.4 CANADA: FOREIGN CONTROL, BY SECTORS

MANUFACTURE
PETROLEUM & GAS
MINING
OTHER UTILITIES
COMMERCE

PERCENTAGE OF TOTAL CORPORATE EQUITY

Sources: See appendix.

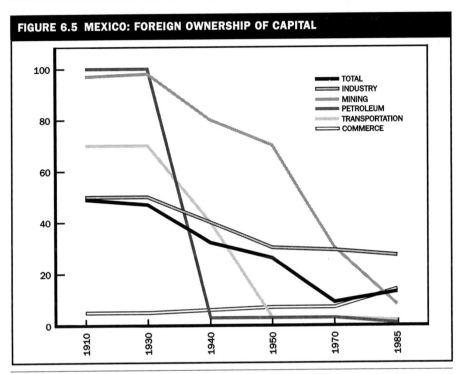

FIGURE 6.5 MEXICO: FOREIGN OWNERSHIP OF CAPITAL

Sources: See appendix.

joint ventures, the relative growth of sectors such as services, and perhaps trade liberalization, are outweighing factors *increasing* foreign direct investment, such as the relaxation of foreign investment restrictions and privatization of state-owned enterprises. Moreover, the divergence in the trends of different types of foreign capital argues in favor of sector-specific explanations, something beyond macroeconomic variables such as interest rates, savings propensities, or exchange rates. The dramatic reversal of pre–World War I country rankings, responding to the shift from investment per capita to investment over GDP, fundamentally implies that the key question is not where was foreign investment large, but why did income levels vary so much.

ACKNOWLEDGMENTS

For their helpful comments on earlier versions, the author would like to thank, without implication, Gabriel Tortella and the other participants of the Bellagio Conference, as well as Victor Bulmer-Thomas, Lance Davis, Steffany Ellis, Robert Gallman, Sevket Pamuk, Alan Taylor, M. C. Urquhart, and members of the Economic History seminar at UM-Ann Arbor. Special thanks to Lance Davis and André Hofman for generously providing unpublished data.

Appendix

DATA FOR LATIN AMERICA

GDP

The core of the estimates is from ECLA (1978). For early years of this century, GDP was estimated from population and GDP per capita. The sources for the latter were as follows: Maddison (1995) for Chile and Peru, 1900–1913; for Brazil and Colombia, 1900–1929; and for Venezuela, 1900–1938; Bulmer-Thomas (1994) for the period 1913–1929. A 1% rate of growth of per capita income was assumed for Honduras (1900–1913) and Paraguay (1900–1929). For Mexico, the pre-1938 estimates of Cárdenas (1987) were used. Current value estimates of NNP for Cuba were also taken from Mitchell (1993) and deflated by the U.S. CPI. For the period after 1973, I used the ECLA's 1985 *Anuario Estadístico*, and their 1994 *Anuario Estadístico* for the period 1989–1990.

Population

Estimates are from the *Statistical Abstract of Latin America*, Vol. 28, for the period from 1900. Data for earlier years are my extrapolations, using rates of growth calculated from official censuses, reported in the same source.

Foreign Debt of the Government

For 1900, it is estimated as the sum of that from France (Rippy 1948) and from the United Kingdom (Stone 1987), averaging the data for 1895 and 1905. Note that Lewis (1938) does not indicate any portfolio investment for the United States for 1897. For 1913, data are from ECLA (1965, p. 16). For Mexico for 1900 and 1911, data are from Turlington (1930, pp. 229, 246). For 1929, data are from ECLA (1965, p. 27). For Cuba, data are from Rippy (1959) and the U.S. Department of Commerce (1960, p. 16) for 1928 and 1930, respectively. For 1938, data are from Lewis (1948), and, for Venezuela, Marichal (1989). For 1950–1960, data are from ECLA (1965, p. 203), reporting results of Avramovic and the IBRD. The 1950 datum for Cuba utilized the total (1951) from Foreign Bondholders (1954). For 1970 on, the data are those of the World Bank's *World Debt Tables* for public and publicly guaranteed long-term debt.

Foreign Direct Investment

From the United Kingdom: Data up through 1928 are from Rippy (1959) and ECLA (1965, p. 9). For 1938, Lewis (1948). For 1950, Bank of England (1950) and Mikesell (1955, p. 10)—the former referring to 1948, and the latter to 1951. Data for investment in Colombia in 1950 are from ECLA (1957, p. 65). Subtotals for railroads and nonrailroads are from Rippy (1959) and various issues of the *South American Journal* for 1928 and 1938. The breakdown of Peruvian investments in railroads and others follows Rippy (1959, p. 69) in assigning most of the Peruvian Corporation's investment into the railroad sector. For 1938, U.K. holdings in railroads in Brazil, Chile, and Peru were extrapolated from the values for 1929 and 1950.

From the United States: Data for 1897 through 1929 are from Lewis (1938), supplemented by ECLA (1965, p. 32) and U.S. Department of Commerce (1960). Data for 1911 in Mexico are from D'Olwer (1965); his data for French investment (p. 1115) were added to the sums from the United Kingdom and the United States for 1900. For 1938, Lewis (1948). For 1950, U.S. Department of Commerce (1960). For 1960 and 1970, the source for U.S. FDI is the *Survey of Current Business*. 1902 and 1913 business and railroad investments from France were taken from Rippy (1948).

Total private foreign investment was calculated summing the separate totals for the United Kingdom, the United States, and France for the period up through 1950. The 1960 total was expanded from the U.S. total, using the average of the United States to total investment in 1950 and 1971. For 1971–1978, data were used from UNCTC (1983, 1988) and UNCTAD (1993, 1994a); the total for 1980 was estimated on the basis of the countries given in UNCTC (1988, p. 129). Data for the total for Latin America and the Caribbean for the 1980s are from UNCTAD (1993) and earlier numbers of the *World Investment Report*. Individual country totals for the 1980s are from UNCTAD (1994a, 1994b). Linear extrapolation was used to approximate totals for reference years. Current U.S. dollar values for GNP or GDP, foreign investment, etc., were deflated to a base of 1900 using the U.S. GNP deflator.

Total Capital and Railroad Capital

The major source of estimates of Argentine capital stock (total, railroads, residential, etc.), as well as real GDP and foreign ownership, is ECLA (1958). For Mexico, the source is Twomey (1993). Railroad length is from the series in *International Historical Statistics*, edited by B. R. Mitchell.

DATA FOR OTHER COUNTRIES

A data appendix is available from the author. For Third World countries, I relied heavily on Maddison (1995) and his sources for real GDP, and on the sources in Svedberg (1978) for foreign investment.

NOTES

1. Pamuk (1987), p. 136.
2. Woodruff (1967).
3. Svedberg (1978).
4. Curiosity led me to look for the corresponding data for some other countries. (Sources are listed in the original version of this paper.) In Russia, FI/GDP was over 70%, and OFDI/GDP was closer to 10%. In Japan, FI/GDP was 39%. The world's largest debtor in 1913 was the United States, for whom total external obligations were 17% of its GNP (down from 25% in the 1870s), while OFDI/GDP was only 4%. In 1994 the same country had the world's largest amount of external obligations, amounting to some 47% of GNP; of this, nearly one-fifth is (inward) direct investment and about the same amount is "foreign official assets."
5. Maddison (1995), p. 202; Bulmer-Thomas (1994), p. 444.
6. This U-shaped pattern was noted, but not further analyzed, by Maddison et al. (1992) in their studies on Brazil and Mexico.
7. United Nations Conference on Trade and Development (1993).
8. Ganz (1959), p. 232.
9. United Nations Economic Commission for Latin America (1958), p. 28.
10. Using the admittedly weak estimate of capital stock in Goldsmith (1986, p. 154), and this paper's estimated foreign investment (or that reported in Maddison et al. 1992, p. 56), the ratio of total foreign investment to capital would have been constant over 1913–1930 and fallen thereafter, whereas the ratios of FDI and OFDI to capital would have fallen continuously.
11. Twomey (1993).
12. Hofman (1992), King and Levine (1994).
13. The calculated growth rate of total foreign direct investment in Chile appears to be exaggerated, perhaps due to the adoption of a new registration system in 1974. This judgment is supported by the U.S. data, although it is known that Chile's external sources of funds have diversified recently.
14. Fritsch and Franco (1991), Peres Nuñez (1990).

15. Evans (1979).
16. Nationalist rhetoric does not necessarily lead to a reduction in foreign presence. Chapter 3 of Twomey (1993) highlights the contrast between postrevolutionary nationalist rhetoric in Mexico and the gradual opening of the manufacturing and service sectors to foreigners.
17. Bleischowsky and Stumpo (1995).
18. For example, see United Nations Centre on Transnational Corporations (1988).

REFERENCES

Bank of England. *United Kingdom Overseas Investments 1938 to 1948.* London: East and Blades, Ltd., 1950.

Bleischowsky, Ricardo A., and Giovanni Stumpo. "Transnational Corporations and Structural Changes in Industry in Argentina, Brazil, Chile and Mexico." *CEPAL Review* no. 55 (1995).

Bulmer-Thomas, Victor. *The Economic History of Latin America Since Independence.* Cambridge: Cambridge University Press, 1994.

Butlin, Noel G. *Australian Domestic Product, Investment and Foreign Borrowing 1861–1938/39.* Cambridge: Cambridge University Press, 1962.

Cárdenas, Enrique. *La industrialización mexicana durante la gran depresión.* México: El Colegio de México, 1987.

de Jager, B. L. "The Fixed Capital Stock and Capital Output Ratio of South Africa from 1946 to 1972." *South African Reserve Bank Quarterly Bulletin* (1973): 17–29.

D'Olwer, Luis Nicolau. "Las inversiones extranjeras." In *Historia moderna de México: El Porfiriato. La vida económica,* edited by Daniel Cosío Villegas. México: Editorial Hermes, 1965.

Evans, Peter. *Dependent Development: The Alliance of Multinational, State, and Local Capital in Brazil.* Princeton: Princeton University Press, 1979.

Foreign Bondholders Protective Council, Inc. *Report 1951 through 1952.* New York: Lenz & Riecker, 1954.

Frankel, S. Herbert. *Capital Investment in Africa.* London: Oxford University Press, 1938.

Franzsen, D. G., and J. D. Willers. "Capital Accumulation and Economic Growth in South Africa." *Income and Wealth* Series VIII (1959): 293–322.

Fritsch, Winston, and Gustavo Franco. *Foreign Direct Investment in Brazil: Its Impact on Industrial Restructuring.* Paris: OECD, 1991.

Ganz, Alexander. "Problems and Uses of National Wealth Estimates in Latin America."

Income and Wealth Series VIII (1959).

Goldsmith, Raymond W. *Financial Development of India, 1860–1977*. New Haven: Yale University Press, 1983.

Goldsmith, Raymond W. *Brasil 1850–1984: Desenvolvimento financeiro so um século de inflaçâo*. Sâo Paulo: Harper & Row do Brasil, 1986.

Hofman, André. "Capital Accumulation in Latin America: A Six Country Comparison for 1950–1989." *Review of Income and Wealth* 38 (1992): 365–401.

Hofman, André. "Economic Development in the 20th Century—A Comparative Perspective." In *Explaining Economic Growth: Essays in Honour of Angus Maddison*, edited by Adam Szirmai et al. Amsterdam: North-Holland, 1993.

King, Robert G., and Ross Levine. "Capital Fundamentalism, Economic Development, and Economic Growth." *Carnegie-Rochester Conference Series on Public Policy*, vol. 40 (1994): 259–292.

Lewis, Cleona. *America's Stake in International Investments*. Washington, DC: The Brookings Institution, 1938.

Lewis, Cleona. *The United States and Foreign Investment Problems*. Washington, DC: The Brookings Institution, 1948.

Maddison, Angus. *Monitoring the World Economy: 1820–1992*. Paris: OECD, 1995.

Maddison, Angus, et al. *The Political Economy of Poverty, Equity and Growth: Brazil and Mexico*. Oxford: Oxford University Press, 1992.

Maddock, Rodney, and Ian W. McLean. *The Australian Economy in the Long Run*. Cambridge: Cambridge University Press, 1987.

Marichal, Carlos. *A Century of Debt Crises in Latin America*. Princeton: Princeton University Press, 1989.

Mikesell, Raymond F. *Foreign Investments in Latin America*. Washington, DC: Pan American Union, 1955.

Mitchell, B. R. *International Historical Statistics: Africa and Asia*. New York: New York University Press, 1982.

Mitchell, B. R. *British Historical Statistics*. New York: Cambridge University Press, 1988.

Mitchell, B. R. *International Historical Statistics—The Americas 1750–1988*. New York: Macmillan, 1993.

Pamuk, Sevket. *The Ottoman Empire and European Capitalism, 1820–1913*. Cambridge: Cambridge University Press, 1987.

Peres Nuñez, Wilson. *Foreign Direct Investment and Industrial Development in Mexico*. Paris: OECD, 1990.

Reserve Bank of India. *India's Foreign Liabilities and Assets, 1961*. Bombay: Reserve Bank of India, 1964.

Reserve Bank of India. "India's International Investment Position 1977–78 to 1979–80." *Reserve Bank of India Bulletin* (April 1985): 269–292.

Rippy, J. Fred. "French Investments in Latin America." *Inter-American Economic Affairs* (1948): 52–71.

Rippy, J. Fred. *British Investments in Latin America, 1822–1949.* Hamden, CT: Archon Books, 1959.

Statistics Canada. *Canada's International Investment Position* [CIIP]. Ottawa: Information Canada. Annual. Catalogue 67-202.

Statistics Canada. *Fixed Capital Flows and Stocks* [FCFS]. Ottawa: Minister of Supply and Services Canada. Annual. Catalogue 13-568.

Stone, Irving. *The Composition and Distribution of British Investment in Latin America, 1865 to 1913.* New York: Garland Publishing, 1987.

Svedberg, Peter. "The Portfolio-Direct Composition of Private Foreign Investment in 1914 Revisited." *Economic Journal* 88 (1978): 763–777.

Turlington, Edgar. *Mexico and Her Foreign Creditors.* New York: Columbia University Press, 1930.

Twomey, Michael J. *Multinational Corporations and the North American Free Trade Agreement.* Westport: Praeger, 1993. (Spanish translation published by Fondo de Cultura Económica in 1996.)

United Nations Centre on Transnational Corporations (UNCTC). *Transnational Corporations in World Development. Third Survey.* New York: United Nations, 1983.

United Nations Centre on Transnational Corporations (UNCTC). *Transnational Corporations in World Development: Trends and Prospects.* New York: United Nations, 1988.

United Nations Conference on Trade and Development (UNCTAD), Programme on Transnational Corporations. *World Investment Report 1993. Transnational Corporations and Integrated International Production.* New York: United Nations, 1993.

United Nations Conference on Trade and Development (UNCTAD), Division on Transnational Corporations and Investment. *World Investment Directory: Foreign Direct Investment, Legal Framework and Corporate Data. Volume IV Latin America and the Caribbean.* New York: United Nations, 1994a.

United Nations Conference on Trade and Development (UNCTAD), Division on Transnational Corporations and Investment. *World Investment Report 1994: Transnational Corporations, Employment and the Workplace.* New York: United Nations, 1994b.

United Nations Department of Economic and Social Affairs. *Foreign Capital in Latin America.* New York: United Nations, 1995.

United Nations Economic Commission for Latin America (ECLA). *Analyses and Projections of Economic Development III. The Economic Development of Colombia.* Columbia: Departamento Administrativo Nacional de Estadistica, 1957.

United Nations Economic Commission for Latin America (ECLA). *Analisis y proyecciones del desarrollo económico: El desarrollo económico de la Argentina.* Mexico City: United Nations, 1958.

United Nations Economic Commission for Latin America (ECLA). *External Financing in Latin America.* New York: United Nations, 1965.

United Nations Economic Commission for Latin America (ECLA). *Series históricas del crecimiento de América Latina.* Cuadernos de la CEPAL #130. United Nations: Santiago de Chile, 1978.

United States Department of Commerce, Office of Business Economics. *U.S. Business Investments in Foreign Countries.* Washington, DC: Government Printing Office, 1960.

Woodruff, William. *Impact of Western Man: A Study of Europe's Role in the World Economy 1750–1960.* New York: St. Martin's Press, 1967.

Part III

Measuring National and International Integration

The three chapters in this section analyze the extent to which economic activities carried out in distinct regions of the same nation—or in different countries—formed part of a single interactive market. When markets are integrated, price changes produced by supply and demand conditions in one place affect behavior in other places. Standard measures of integration are based on tracking differences in prices for the same commodity or factor (such as capital) across space and time. Where price trends are similar and differences small (or at least constant), markets are said to be integrated. Integrated markets contribute to economic growth because they induce consumers and investors to allocate their expenditures in ways that better reflect relative scarcities across larger geographic areas.

Little is known about the history of market integration in Latin America before the twentieth century. Measures of market integration rely on analyzing price data from different locations. In most regions of Latin America, the history of prices has yet to be studied and the mountains of price data in the archives have yet to be systematically retrieved and made available to researchers.[1] In contrast, economic historians of Europe and the United States can rely on published prices for many commodities going back centuries.[2] Published or readily available data on wages and interest rates are also available from relatively early dates for the United States, England, and much of Europe.[3] Studies of market integration within and across countries in the developed regions are therefore quite common.[4] For Latin America, the lack of data makes them rare indeed.

In this section, Newland's essay (Chapter 7) looks at regional disparities in Argentine economic growth in the decades after independence. He reminds us that market integration does not necessarily imply economic convergence, either for individual nations or the global economy. With independence, Argentina threw off colonial restrictions on trade with other countries. Argentine hides, salted beef, and other cattle (and later sheep) products flowed directly to Europe as well as to Brazil, the United States, and other foreign markets. Meanwhile, Spanish trade regulations that forced colonial Bolivia to export all its silver through Buenos Aires and give preference to Argentine imports also disappeared. The impact of all these changes on Argentina's economy is difficult to gauge in the absence of good data on provincial or regional output and prices. Newland's solution is to use population data from censuses in 1819 and 1869 as a substitute. He exploits this demographic data to document the relative decline of the interior provinces in contrast to the rapid growth of the littoral region. Integration into the Atlantic economy dynamized the Littoral while it crushed the once-prosperous but inefficient producers of the interior. While Newland's account thus emphasizes the unevenness of Argentina's postindependence economic experience, it builds on other recent work that points to the onset of economic growth as early as the 1820s for the country as a whole.[5]

Triner (Chapter 8) makes a similar point in her study of money market integration in Brazil between the fall of the Empire in 1889 and the collapse of the First Republic in 1930. To measure integration, she uses bank data to construct a time series of "interest rate approximations" for the important states of São Paulo and Minas Gerais and compares these local rates to the benchmark interest rate of the Banco do Brasil. Triner finds that the reform legislation of 1905, which placed the Banco do Brasil at the center of the emerging banking system, tended to concentrate the benefits of integration in the São Paulo region. Interest rates in Minas Gerais, in contrast to São Paulo, suggest an "independent dynamism," with higher interest rates that fluctuated mainly in response to local economic and regulatory developments. Triner's conclusions are consistent with those of the two other authors in this book who treat Brazilian financial markets in the same period. Both Hanley (Chapter 4) and Haber (Chapter 10) emphasize the importance of the São Paulo financial sector in the early industrial development of the country.

Latin American financial markets were attracting massive flows of external capital by the end of the nineteenth century. Nakamura and Zarazaga (in Chapter 9) measure the extent of the integration of Argentina's financial market with international financial markets from the turn of the century to 1930. They do so by looking at rates of return on stocks and bonds issued on the Buenos Aires exchange and comparing them to rates of return in the United States and Britain. Their results suggest that the Argentine financial sector was as firmly integrated with world capital markets in the 1920s as in the pre–World War I era. Although Nakamura and Zarazaga's emphasis is different, their finding is consistent with della Paolera and Taylor (Chapter 5) and Taylor's earlier work,[6] namely, that Argentina did suffer from constraints that inhibited external investment in the 1920s. Rates of return were generally higher after the war than before in Argentina, as in world markets, limiting the number of viable investment projects that could be undertaken.

NOTES

1. Exceptions include Borah and Cook (1958), Florescano (1969), and Johnson and Tandeter (1990).
2. For a pioneering example, see Hamilton (1947).
3. For a sampling of what is available, see the various editions of B. R. Mitchell's compendia of historical statistics for various parts of the world (e.g., 1992).
4. See the essays in Goldin and Rockoff (1992), for example.
5. See the works cited by Newland. The conclusion that Argentina experienced early and sustained growth after independence is consistent with Coatsworth's claim in Chapter 1 that Argentina inherited fewer entrenched institutional obstacles to growth.
6. Taylor (1992, 1994).

REFERENCES

Borah, Woodrow W., and Sherburne F. Cook. *Price Trends of Some Basic Commodities in Central Mexico, 1531–1570*. Berkeley: University of California Press, 1958.

Florescano, Enrique. *Precios del maíz y crisis agrícolas en México (1708–1810)*. Mexico: El Colegio de México, 1969.

Goldin, Claudia, and Hugh Rockoff, eds. *Strategic Factors in Nineteenth-Century American Economic History: A Volume to Honor Robert W. Fogel*. Chicago: University of Chicago Press, 1992.

Hamilton, Earl J. *War and Prices in Spain, 1651–1800*. Cambridge: Harvard University Press, 1947.

Johnson, Lyman L., and Enrique Tandeter, eds. *Essays on the Price History of Eighteenth-Century Latin America*. Albuquerque: University of New Mexico Press, 1990.

Mitchell, B. R. *International Historical Statistics*. New York: Stockton Press, 1992.

Taylor, Alan M. "External Dependence, Demographic Burdens, and Argentine Economic Decline After the Belle Epoque." *Journal of Economic History* 52 (1992): 907–936.

Taylor, Alan M. "Tres fases del crecimiento económico argentino." *Revista de Historia Económica* 12 (Otoño 1994): 649–683.

7

Economic Development and Population Change: Argentina, 1810–1870

Carlos Newland
Universidad Torcuato Di Tella

The evolution of the Argentine economy between 1810 and 1870 has been difficult to evaluate due to the scarcity of relevant statistics, particularly for the first decades of the nineteenth century. Recent studies offer new series and magnitudes that shed more light on some basic characteristics of the period, such as the evolution of exports, the terms of trade, the productivity of the rural sector, and the height of the inhabitants.[1] These studies imply the existence of economic growth prior to the traditionally assumed 1870. The external sector, for example, shows strong growth between 1810 and 1870: Total exports grew at 5% or 6% per year and per capita exports at approximately 3%. To this could be added an improvement in the terms of trade in the first decades of the century, with a positive effect on welfare. Productivity in the pastoral sector also seems to have increased: While pastoral production grew (in the Littoral) at an annual rate of 5.1%, total factor productivity was 2%, a superior amount to that observed in the following period. This change in productivity was parallel to an intensification of labor inputs caused by the relative increase of sheep with respect to cows. The positive vision of this period is reinforced by an anthropometric study showing an increase in the height of the population, a result of nutrition and health improvements. That economic growth started early should not be surprising: The addition of labor and capital to an empty country will have initial high returns, which will fall gradually as land becomes less abundant.

The aim of this paper is to complement recent research and to describe some aspects of Argentine general and regional development using population statistics. This contribution is especially useful in the analysis of regional development, since past and recent studies concentrate mainly on data from Buenos Aires or the Littoral, for which greater statistical information exists.[2] The Interior has been less attended to, in part due to the lack of homogeneous sources of data at the provincial level. The use of population data in this paper assumes that they reflect structural change and the long-term evolution of the economy. The correlation of some of these variables with economic development can be questioned, as with population growth. However, I believe that for the nineteenth century the inferences are correct, specially considering the evolution of all the variables in unison.[3] Besides population growth, other variables used are urbanization, internal migration, immigration, and the distribution of labor by economic activity. The paper mainly compares figures for the years 1819 and 1869, which were selected because they coincide with the years of some early provincial censuses and the first national census. The paper also includes discussion of the validity of the classic division of Argentina into two distinct regions: the Interior and the Littoral.

In this paper only the population living inside the frontier has been considered. Aborigines living outside the frontier (in the Chaco, pampas, and Patagonia) have not been included. Their numbers are difficult to estimate; probably their population did not increase between 1820 and 1870, due to the violence exercised against them, the impact of epidemics, and migrations. The indigenous population can be estimated to be around 15% of the total Argentine population in 1820, and 5% in 1870.[4]

THE DIFFERENCES BETWEEN
THE INTERIOR AND THE LITTORAL REGIONS

Argentina during the period 1810–1870 presents a typical case of growth based on exports of pastoral land-intensive products, such as hides, tallow, wool, and salted meat. The Argentine littoral region, which includes the provinces of Buenos Aires, Entre Ríos, Corrientes, and Santa Fé, was suited for this type of development for several reasons. First, its natural endowments were favorable to pastoral production: It had abundant fertile plains and natural prairies, low altitude, plenty of rainfall evenly distributed over the year, and a temperate climate. Second, its access to the rivers of the Río de la Plata Basin permitted an easy and cheap outlet for its production—an important factor before the development of railroads. This meant that approximately 90% of Argentine exports during this period originated in the Littoral.[5] The provinces traditionally classified as part of the interior region—Córdoba, San

Luis, Mendoza, San Juan, Catamarca, La Rioja, Santiago del Estero, Tucumán, Salta, and Jujuy—were not particularly suited to cattle production. In the Interior, land was less abundant and less fertile, climatic differences between seasons were sharper, and rainfall was scarce, especially during the winter. The high and mountainous terrain of the provinces closest to the Andes hindered the transport of goods. In addition, the lack of navigable rivers made the export of goods less viable, given that land freight was five times more expensive than river freight for a similar distance and load.[6]

Given the distribution of its resources between regions, it would be expected that in 1819 the majority of the population would have been located in the Littoral. However, at that time only 38.7% of the population lived in the Littoral, whereas 61.3% lived in the Interior. The reason the majority of the population was located in the less productive zone was that during colonial times the Interior depended on the sale of transport services, livestock, food, and other goods to the mining economy of Alto Perú. Also, the commercial traffic along the Buenos Aires–Potosí route permitted the cities of the Interior to finance themselves by means of taxes on the transit of goods. At the end of the eighteenth century, however, Bolivian mining activity began to decline. Bolivian silver production during the 1820s was less than half the level achieved at the end of the previous century.[7] Although trade with the Interior did not disappear, it declined significantly and became limited to the sale of cattle to Bolivia and Chile.[8] Finally, the liberalization of the Atlantic trade after independence meant that local artisanal production declined with the competition of cheap imports, as was the case with textiles. The reduced level of economic activity in the Interior had important demographic effects. By 1869 the share of the population in the Interior had fallen to 51.2%, whereas the share in the Littoral had increased to 48.8%, a trend that would continue in the future.

Before analyzing the evolution of population indicators, the validity of the division of Argentina into two distinct regions is examined. A test was performed to determine how homogeneous or different the provinces of the interior and the littoral regions were among themselves. Values for the following variables for each of the 14 provinces around the year 1870 were used: urbanization, value of livestock per capita, migration from other provinces, immigration, share of the labor force in the primary sector, and migration to other provinces.[9] The first four variables should increase with the level of economic development of the province, and the latter two variables should diminish. An analysis of the correlation between the different variables for each province shows that they behave according to expectations. For example, a province that attracted migrants from other places expelled few local inhabitants, had a high level of urbanization, employed a relatively small proportion of the labor force in primary activities, and had a high level of livestock per capita (see Appendix Table 7.2).

To determine the validity of the classic division of the Argentine provinces into the Interior and the Littoral, for each of these variables the provinces were ordered from highest to lowest and assigned a value corresponding to their rank. Then the values of the ranking orders obtained for each province were added. The sum was used as an indicator of each province's level of development: Higher values were related to the most developed provinces and lower values to the least developed ones. The results of the exercise show that Buenos Aires was the province with the highest level of development, followed closely by Entre Ríos; Santa Fé occupied the third place. Corrientes (normally included in the Littoral), San Juan, and Tucumán all had intermediate levels of development. The remainder of the provinces received inferior values. Catamarca and Santiago del Estero stand out as having especially primitive economies.

Cluster analysis was also used to classify the provinces, although the scarce number of observations limits its usefulness.[10] When the provinces are divided into three groups, one group is made up of Buenos Aires, Entre Ríos, and Santa Fé; the rest of the provinces are included in the other two groups, a result which confirms the previous conclusions.[11] In spite of these results, Corrientes was grouped with the other more dynamic provinces of the Littoral in order to respect the traditional regional division based on a geographic criterion and on the importance of pastoral production in the province's economy.

GROWTH AND POPULATION MOVEMENTS

The first population indicator of economic growth is the rate of population increase. There is an especially close relationship between these variables for the nineteenth century because greater wealth promoted fertility, reduced mortality, lowered the age of marriage, and induced immigration and migration. The availability of population data for the year 1856 enables us to determine how population growth rates changed over the subperiods of 1819–1856 and 1856–1869 (Table 7.1).

Between 1819 and 1869 the Argentine population increased at an average annual rate of 2.6%, a magnitude superior to that experienced by most other countries in the same period, as can be seen in the following comparison of population growth for the period 1820–1870:[12]

Argentina	2.6%
Belgium	0.3%
Brazil	2.0%
France	0.5%
Germany	1.1%
Italy	0.7%
Mexico	0.7%
Peru	1.1%
Spain	0.6%
Great Britain	1.2%
United States	2.9%

Brazil, a nation that imported slaves until the 1850s, had an annual rate of population growth of only 2%, whereas Mexico's population grew by only 0.7% per year. Argentina's rate of population growth, however, was inferior to that of other countries with abundant amounts of land, such as the United States. The high rate of population growth in Argentina is explained largely by the reception of foreigners, who represented 6% of the population in 1819 and 12.2% in 1869.[13] Population growth, in fact, accelerated during 1856–1869, compared with 1819–1856, due to immigration.

The regional comparison shows that the rate of population increase during 1819–1869 was greater in the littoral region, at 3.1%. The provinces with the highest rates of population growth were Entre Ríos and Santa Fé. Over the same period the population of the Interior grew at an average annual rate of 2.2%. Population growth rates did not vary markedly between the provinces of the Interior, although growth rates were somewhat higher in Mendoza, San Juan, and Salta. As in the littoral region, population growth in the Interior accelerated after 1856. There were also regional differences in the importance of immigration and internal migration. In 1869, 28.6% of the population of the Littoral was nonlocal, of which 5.9% came from the Interior and 22.7% came from other countries, most importantly Spain, France, and Italy. Only 2% of the population of the Interior was nonlocal, of which about 0.2% came from the littoral region and the remainder from Bolivia and Chile.

Internal migration over this period reflects the regional disequilibrium: The inhabitants of the Interior were expelled by the surrounding poverty and simultaneously attracted by the high salaries and abundant employment in the littoral region. The big beneficiaries of internal population movements were Buenos Aires and Santa Fé, where migrants typically went to work in seasonal agricultural and pastoral tasks. According to one author, at harvest time a "cloud of Santiagueños" invaded Buenos Aires.[14] Workers moved not only between regions, but also within them. In the littoral region 4.1% of the native population in 1869 had moved to another province of the region. The most important migrations were among bordering provinces, for example, of Correntinos to Entre Ríos and of Santafesinos to Buenos Aires. Intraregional migration was even more important in the Interior; the proportion of the population that had moved to another province within the same region was 6.5%. Here, however, precise tendencies are not found. Workers moved in all directions, especially to bordering provinces. Santiago del Estero and San Luis were important expellers, losing 15.1% and 14.8% of their native populations, respectively.

The great attraction of both internal migrants and foreigners to the Littoral had existed since the beginning of the century. A province that was especially receptive to external workers was Buenos Aires, where 37% of the population was nonlocal in 1810. Buenos Aires received Santiagueños, Misioneros, Cordobeces, Mendocinos, Tucumanos, Spaniards, and Spanish Americans. The province of Entre Ríos, where 12% of the population was nonlocal, received Misioneros, Paraguayans, Santafesinos, and Bonaerenses. Corrientes, where only 3% of the population was nonlocal, received Spaniards, Brazilians, Misioneros, and Paraguayans.[15]

URBANIZATION

Urbanization can be considered another indicator of economic development for the nineteenth century because it reflected the level of agricultural productivity and the size of the secondary and tertiary sectors. Table 7.1 shows that in 1819, 25.3% of the Argentine population lived in urban areas (i.e., urban centers with more than 1,000 inhabitants). The entire urban population lived in 16 cities, which were almost exclusively provincial capitals. Buenos Aires, the largest city, had 54,000 residents in 1819, accounting for 46.1% of the urban population.

TABLE 7.1

Population and Urbanization, 1819–1869

	Annual Increase of Population (%)			Urbanization (%)	
	1819–1856	1856–1869	1819–1869	1819	1869
Littoral	2.7	4.3	3.1	36.8	45.7
Interior	2.1	2.5	2.2	18.1	15.9
Total	2.4	3.3	2.6	25.3	30.4

Source: See Appendix Table 7.1.

The next largest cities were Córdoba, which had 13,000 inhabitants, and Santiago del Estero and Salta, which each had more than 7,000 inhabitants.

By 1869 the rate of urbanization of the country was 30.4%. The most notable factor that contributed to the increase in the degree of urbanization was the multiplication of towns and cities, which increased to a total of 103 in 1869. Buenos Aires continued to be the most important city, although its 177,000 inhabitants only accounted for 33.4% of the total urban population: The rate of population growth in Buenos Aires was similar to that of the total population. Córdoba remained the second largest city with 28,500 inhabitants, followed by Rosario, which had become Argentina's second port, with 23,000 inhabitants. The next largest city was Tucumán, which had 17,500 inhabitants. There were several other cities that had around 10,000 inhabitants; many of these cities were river ports that provided outlets for exportables, such as Paraná, Santa Fé, Gualeguaychú, and Corrientes. The degree of urbanization of each province was undoubtedly related to its participation in pastoral exports. The Spearman correlation coefficient (see Appendix Table 7.2) between the rate of urbanization and the value of livestock per capita circa 1869 is 0.82.[16]

How does the level of urbanization in Argentina contrast with contemporaneous levels in other countries? The degree of urbanization in Argentina was superior or at least similar to that of both Canada and the United States, in which the rate of urbanization had not surpassed 25% in 1850.[17] The pace of urbanization in Argentina was higher than in other Latin American countries when based on the growth of the capital cities. Whereas the population of Buenos Aires grew at an average annual rate of 2.4%, Rio de Janeiro grew by only 1.8%, and Mexico City by less than 1%.[18]

A significant difference in the level of urbanization is noted between regions. The littoral region in 1819 had a high rate of urbanization of 36.8%, rising to 45.7% in 1869. The high figure for 1819 was due not only to the importance of Buenos Aires but also to the high degree of urbanization in Entre Ríos. In 1869 the degree of urbanization was high in all the provinces of the Littoral. In contrast, in the Interior region the rate of urbanization was 18.1% in 1819 and only 15.9% in 1869. Witnesses described the cities of the Interior at that time as demolished and decadent, evidence of the effect of the loss of the Altoperuvian market and the low rural productivity.[19] The most striking example is the city of Santiago del Estero, which saw its population diminish in absolute terms. It was described as a "town recently plundered."[20] The situation of the provinces of the Interior was relatively homogeneous; none had a rate of urbanization greater than 22% in 1869.

DISTRIBUTION OF THE LABOR FORCE BY ECONOMIC ACTIVITY

Together with the rates of urbanization and population growth, the distribution of the labor force by economic activity is another indicator of the degree of economic development. In this paper the analysis is restricted to male workers due to the well-known lack of information on female participation in the labor market. Table 7.2 presents the distribution of the labor force by economic sector in 1819 and 1869 for the sum of five provinces for which information is available. Although the estimates for 1819 are tentative, the figures do show that over the half century there was no notable change in the sectoral distribution of the labor force, a fact that is also reflected in the low degree of increase in urbanization for the country as a whole. There were certainly differences at a regional level. Although the high level of productivity in the rural sector in the Littoral allowed it to continuously absorb local and external workers, the high initial level of urbanization, and its subsequent growth, implies that there was a positive structural change. In the Interior, the fall in the rate of urbanization is evidence of an increase in the size of the primary sector, an increase not based on the market but on self-consumption.

A detailed disaggregation of the labor force by economic sector based on the 1869 Argentine census is presented in Table 7.3. Taking the country as a whole, the primary sector accounted for 58.9% of workers, the secondary sector for 17.2%, and the tertiary sector for 23.9%. The proportion of the labor force employed in primary activities was somewhat superior to that of Canada (51.3%) or the United States (53%), but inferior to that of other Latin American countries, such as Brazil (65–70%) and Mexico (79%), and to that of countries from which workers immigrated to Argentina, such as Spain (66%) and Italy (61%).[21]

Although Argentina before 1870 is typically characterized as a pastoral economy, the distribution of employment within the primary sector shows the

TABLE 7.2

Distribution of the Labor Force by Economic Sector, 1819 and 1869

Sector	1819	1869
Primary	57.1%	54.2%
Secondary	14.1%	17.2%
Tertiary	28.8%	28.6%

Sources: The table only includes the provinces of Buenos Aires, Córdoba, Corrientes, Entre Ríos, and Mendoza. The proportions for 1869 were calculated based on the sources and criteria used in Appendix Table 7.1. The sources for 1819 are as follows, listed by province. Buenos Aires: García Belsunce (1976). Entre Ríos and Corrientes: Maeder (1969a). Mendoza: Comadrán Ruiz (1973). Córdoba: Information on the 1813 census for Córdoba was generously provided by Anibal Arcondo. The magnitudes for the early censuses were projected to 1819 according to the population growth of the province.

TABLE 7.3

Labor Occupation by Economic Activity in 1869

	Littoral (%)	Interior (%)	Total (%)
Primary			
Pastoral	27.1	17.9	23.0
Agriculture	23.0	49.4	34.9
Other	1.3	0.6	1.0
Total	51.4	68.0	58.9
Secondary			
Construction	4.3	2.0	3.2
Textile	1.4	2.1	1.7
Leather	3.1	6.6	4.7
Wood	3.7	2.9	3.3
Other	5.1	3.4	4.3
Total	17.5	16.9	17.2
Tertiary			
Transport	8.7	4.1	6.6
Servants	4.2	2.7	3.5
Trade	11.3	4.6	8.3
Other	7.0	3.9	5.6
Total	31.2	15.2	23.9
Total workers	299,113	247,112	546,225

Source: See Appendix Table 7.1.

prevalence of agriculture, fundamentally the cultivation of wheat, corn, alfalfa, and, to a lesser degree, vineyards. The prevalence of agriculture was most marked in the Interior, where for each cattleman there were almost three agricultural workers. In the Littoral the proportion was one to one. Although some agricultural products such as flour were imported, the sectoral distribution of the labor force suggests that a large share of local consumption was being satisfied by local production. In fact, after 1870 Argentina went from being an importer to an exporter of wheat. What explains the greater importance of agriculture in the Interior? First, agricultural activities required comparably less land than cattle raising. The scarcer lands of the Interior were used in irrigation-based agriculture. Second, the high wages paid in the Littoral made labor-intensive agricultural production unprofitable in that region. As for the type of crops cultivated, wheat was the dominant crop in the Littoral in terms of sown area. In the Interior, large shares of the cultivated area were devoted to vineyards and to alfalfa, which was used to feed livestock as a complement to the scarce natural grasses.[22]

In the littoral region half of the rural labor force was employed in cattle raising. This was because cattle ranching was land-intensive, a resource with which the region was generously endowed. The differences between the two regions are even more evident when comparing the value of livestock per capita (see Appendix Table 7.1). In the 1870s the littoral region had nearly six times the livestock per capita as the interior region. Cows and sheep were the most important farm animals in both regions; the famous mules of colonial times only accounted for 5.1% of the total livestock of the Interior.[23]

The proportion of workers employed in the secondary sector was similar in the littoral and the interior regions. Within the secondary sector, construction workers and leather and wood artisans stand out for their importance. Labor in construction, which mainly included masons, painters, and blacksmiths, was more important in the Littoral, undoubtedly because of the greater degree of urbanization. Leather artisans, such as shoemakers and to a lesser degree tanners and saddlers, were more frequent in the Interior. Woodworkers, who were primarily carpenters, were slightly more important in the Littoral. Other important members of the secondary sector were tailors, cigar makers, bakers, silversmiths, and soap makers.

The importance of the tertiary sector, which accounted for 23.6% of the total labor force, differed greatly between the two regions. The proportion of the labor force employed in the tertiary sector in the Littoral was double that in the Interior. This was undoubtedly a reflection of the higher income levels in the littoral region and the fact that its economy was more oriented toward the market. The most important service sectors were transport and commerce. The former included cattle and product transporters, such as cart drivers, sailors, and distributors. The latter included merchants and salespersons, such as wholesalers, grocers, and butchers. The tertiary sector also employed innkeepers, soldiers, sailors, musicians, teachers, priests and members of religious orders, and servants.[24]

CONCLUSION

The analysis of Argentine economic development between 1819 and 1869 is complicated by the lack of economic time-series data. This paper attempts to describe important economic changes over the period using population data. The analysis reveals the existence of two distinct regions. The littoral region, which enjoyed low costs of transport and abundant land, was the source of most pastoral product exports. It had a relatively modern economic structure, similar to that of the United States or Canada, a relatively small primary sector for the time, an important pastoral sector, and a substantial tertiary sector. It also had a relatively high and growing degree of urbanization. The Littoral received nearly all immigrants, as well as many internal migrants from the rest of Argentina; the consequence was a notable rate of population growth. The interior region, conditioned by its scarce land and lack of navigable rivers, was similar to other Latin American countries in terms of the distribution of its labor force by economic activity. It had a large primary sector, mainly devoted to agricultural activities. The degree of urbanization in the Interior was not only low but also seems to have diminished over the period. This region lost part of its population to the Littoral and was unable to attract either workers from the littoral region or immigrants from nonbordering countries.[25]

ACKNOWLEDGMENTS
I thank Cristina Corti Maderna, Colin Lewis, John Coatsworth, Alan Taylor, Ann Mitchell, and Tamara Burdisso for their help and advice.

Appendix

APPENDIX TABLE 7.1

Demographic and Economic Variables, 1819–1869

	A	B	C	D	E	F	G	H	I	J
Entre Ríos	134,271	3.9	27.7	39.7	25.9	2.4	53.0	20.4	145	12
Buenos Aires	495,107	3.0	49.2	52.7	37.1	2.6	46.5	18.2	199	7
Santa Fé	89,117	3.5	7.3	40.9	45.7	11.7	56.8	14.7	126	21
Corrientes	129,023	2.6	14.9	28.7	7.8	7.3	70.0	11.5	90	34
Littoral	847,518	3.1	36.8	45.7			51.4	17.5	182	
Mendoza	65,413	2.6	28.6	12.4	17.3	9.0	62.1	15.8	21	42
San Juan	60,319	2.7	24.6	13.8	13.3	8.6	50.8	15.8	23	37
Catamarca	79,962	2.4	9.2	12.2	6.6	9.7	72.5	15.3	39	52
La Rioja	48,746	2.3	22.2	21.4	6.2	11.6	67.0	10.9	38	44
Córdoba	210,508	2.1	17.1	21.5	4.4	12.4	68.3	14.8	43	45
Santiago	132,898	2.1	18.0	6.9	1.5	15.1	78.0	15.6	19	69
Tucumán	108,953	2.4	14.4	18.2	9.2	8.4	60.7	25.5	44	31
San Luis	53,294	2.1	9.9	17.1	8.7	14.8	65.2	16.1	38	45
Salta	88,933	2.8	31.6	17.1	11.8	5.9	68.4	18.1	14	43
Jujuy	40,379	1.2	13.8	15.4	15.7	5.1	73.9	18.4	27	41
Interior	889,405	2.2	18.1	15.9			68.0	16.9	32	
Total	1,736,923	2.6	25.3	30.4			58.9	17.2	99	

Note: Variables are as follows: (A) population in 1869; (B) annual rate of growth of population, 1819–1869; (C) urbanization rate in 1819; (D) urbanization rate in 1869; (E) nonlocal population (share of migrants and immigrants in total population) in 1869; (F) expulsion of local population in 1869 (share of original local population); (G) percentage of population in the primary sector in 1869; (H) percentage of population in the secondary sector in 1869; (I) value of livestock per capita (in silver pesos), 1873–1874; and (J) summation of the ranks of variables B, D, E, F, G, and I (see text).

Sources: Population and urbanization: 1819 estimates are based on Maeder (1969b). The population of Mendoza in 1819 was taken from Comadrán Ruiz (1973). 1869 estimates are from *Primer censo* (1872). Urbanization in 1869 for La Rioja and Santiago del Estero was corrected according to the warning given in *Segundo censo* (1898), vol. II, pp. 339 and 450.

Occupational variables: Day laborers who did not live in the capitals were assigned entirely to the primary sector. Residents in the capital cities were assigned to the secondary and tertiary sectors. Given that in the occupations in which both sexes worked, female participation was not indicated; the original figures were corrected according to the female participation rates given in the *Segundo censo* (1898), vol. II.

Other variables corresponding to 1869 are from *Primer censo* (1872).

Livestock per capita: In general the data were taken from Napp (1876), p. 311. The figures given for Córdoba, Jujuy, San Luis, and Santiago del Estero had to be corrected with projections of those given by Latzina (1888), pp. 544–546, since they included obvious errors. For the per capita estimates, projections of the 1869 population were used, with the rate of increase of the period 1856–1869.

APPENDIX TABLE 7.2

Spearman Correlation between Variables

	D	E	F	G	I
D		.43	−.36	−.54	.82
E	.43		−.59	−.67	.36
F	−.36	−.59		.31	−.31
G	−.54	−.67	.31		−.49
I	.82	.36	−.31	−.49	

Note: Spearman correlation, the nonparametric alternative to the Pearson coefficient, was used due to the limited number of observations. The variables are defined as follows: (D) urbanization rate in 1869; (E) nonlocal population (share of migrants and immigrants in total population) in 1869; (F) expulsion of local population in 1869 (share of original local population); (G) percentage of population in the primary sector in 1869; and (I) value of livestock per capita (in silver pesos), 1873–1874.

Source: See Appendix Table 7.1.

NOTES

1. See Amaral (1997), Newland (forthcoming), Newland and Poulson (forthcoming), and Salvatore (1997).
2. This is the case of the otherwise excellent works by Burgin (1975) and Brown (1979).
3. Livi-Bacci (1992), p. 132.
4. Martínez Sarasola (1996), pp. 254, 305.
5. Mulhall (1885), p. 77; Parish (1958), pp. 522–523.
6. Burgin (1975), p. 161.
7. Klein (1988), p. 356.
8. On the continuity of the economic relations between the Interior and the Alto Perú after 1820, see Conti (1989).
9. The figures are included in Appendix Table 7.1.
10. The same variables were used for the cluster analysis as were used for the rankings.
11. When the provinces were divided into two and three groups, modal groups did not appear.
12. The sources for the figures are Boyer and Davies (1973), U.S. Bureau of the Census (1960), and Mitchell (1975).
13. The proportion for 1869 is from *Primer censo* (1872). The proportion for 1819 is a conjecture based on figures for foreigners of 23% for Buenos Aires (with a majority being Spaniards), 3.2% for Entre Ríos, and 1.6% for Corrientes. I arbitrarily assigned 2% to Santa Fé and 0.5% to the Interior. These estimates were based on Maeder (1969a) and García Belsunce (1976).

14. Quesada (1942), p. 338.
15. The sources for these proportions are Maeder (1969a) for Entre Ríos and Corrientes, and García Belsunce (1976) for Buenos Aires.
16. See Appendix Table 7.2.
17. The comparison with the United States is problematic since in that country urbanization was measured as the share of the population living in towns with more than 2,500 inhabitants. Urbanization in the United States was 10.8% in 1840 and 19.8% in 1860. Urbanization in Canada was measured in the same way as in this paper and was 13% in 1851. See Poulson (1981), p. 324, and Marr and Paterson (1980), p. 185.
18. Boyer and Davies (1973).
19. See the descriptions of cities at the time in Sarmiento (1845) and Quesada (1942). Also see Romero (1978).
20. Hutchinson (1945), p. 252.
21. See Bairoch (n.d.); INEGI (1994), vol. I, p. 348; and Poulson (1981), p. 247.
22. Napp (1876), pp. 426–443.
23. Livestock per capita figures are in general taken from Napp (1876), p. 311. The figures for Córdoba, Jujuy, San Luis, and Santiago del Estero had to be corrected with projections of the figures given by Latzina (1888), pp. 544–546, since they contained obvious errors.
24. See a detailed description of occupations in Buenos Aires in Sabato and Romero (1992).
25. In his excellent paper on the evolution of the height of the Argentine population, Salvatore (1997) finds that in the first half of the nineteenth century soldiers of the Interior in Buenos Aires had higher average stature than the *porteños* and also made greater gains in height during the period. However, due to truncation problems, traditional regression analysis has not confirmed his results, nor has Salvatore been able to detect if mechanisms of self-selection existed. Additional tests are needed to confirm or reject the existence of significant differentials in height between regions.

REFERENCES

Amaral, Samuel. *The Rise of Capitalism on the Pampas.* Cambridge: Cambridge University Press, 1997.

Bairoch, Paul, et al., eds. *La population active et sa structure.* Brussels: Centre d'Economie Politique, Université Libre de Bruxelles, 1968.

Boyer, Richard, and Davies, Keith A. *Urbanization in 19th Century America: Statistics and Sources.* Los Angeles: Latin American Center, University of California, 1973.

Brown, Jonathan. *A Socioeconomic History of Argentina, 1776–1860.* Cambridge: Cambridge University Press, 1979.

Burgin, Miron. *Aspectos económicos del federalismo Argentino.* Buenos Aires: Solar, 1975.

Comadrán Ruiz, Jorge. "Algunos aspectos de la estructura demográfica y socio-económica de Mendoza hacia 1822–24." In *Primer congreso de historia Argentina y regional,* compiled by Academia Nacional de Historia, 405–422. Buenos Aires: Academia Nacional de Historia, 1973.

Conti, Viviana. "Una periferia del espacio mercantil andino: El norte argentino en el siglo XIX." In *Avances de investigación antropología e historia,* 39–62. Salta, 1989.

García Belsunce, Cesar, dir. *Buenos Aires: Su gente 1800–1830.* Buenos Aires: 1976.

Hutchinson, Thomas. *Buenos Aires y otras provincias argentinas.* Buenos Aires: Editorial Huarpes, 1945.

Instituto Nacional de Estadística, Geografía e Informática (INEGI). *Estadísticas históricas de México.* 2 vols. Aguascalientes: Instituto Nacional de Estadística, Geografía e Informática, 1994.

Klein, Herbert. *Historia general de Bolivia.* La Paz, 1988.

Latzina, Francisco. *Geografía de la República Argentina.* Buenos Aires: F. Lajouane, 1888.

Livi-Bacci, Massimo. *A Concise History of World Population,* translated by Carl Ipsen. Cambridge, MA: Blackwell Publishers, 1992.

Maeder, Ernesto. "La estructura demográfica y ocupacional de Corrientes y Entre Ríos, en 1820." *Cuadernos de Historia* 1, no. 4 (1969a): 1–42.

Maeder, Ernesto. *Evolución demográfica Argentina desde 1810 a 1869.* Buenos Aires: Eudeba, 1969b.

Marr, William L., and Donald Paterson. *Canada: An Economic History.* Toronto: Macmillan of Canada, 1980.

Martínez Sarasola, Carlos. *Nuestros paisanos los indios.* Buenos Aires: Emece, 1996.

Mitchell, B. R. *European Historical Statistics 1750–1970.* New York: Columbia University Press, 1975.

Mulhall, M. G. *Handbook of the River Plata.* London: Trubner and Co., 1885.

Napp, Ricardo. *La República Argentina.* Buenos Aires: Impr. du Courier de la Plata, 1876.

Newland, Carlos. "Exports and Terms of Trade in Argentina, 1811–1870." *Bulletin of Latin American Research.* Forthcoming.

Newland, Carlos, and Barry Poulson. "Purely Animal, Pastoral Production and Early Argentine Economic Growth." *Explorations in Economic History.* Forthcoming.

Parish, Woodbine. *Buenos Aires y las provincias del Río de la Plata*. Buenos Aires: Hachette, 1958.

Poulson, Barry. *Economic History of the United States*. New York: Macmillan, 1981.

Primer censo de la República Argentina. Buenos Aires, 1872.

Quesada, Vicente Gregorio. *Memorias de un viejo. Escenas de costumbres de la República Argentina*. Buenos Aires: Ediciones Argentinas Solar, 1942.

Romero, Luis A. "Decadencia regional y declinación urbana en el Interior argentino." *Revista Paraguaya de Sociología* 15, no. 42/43 (1978): 47–56.

Sábato, Hilda, and Romero, Luis Alberto. *Los trabajadores de Buenos Aires. La experiencia del mercado 1850–1880*. Buenos Aires: Editorial Sudamericana, 1992.

Salvatore, Ricardo. "Heights and Welfare in Post-Independence Argentina." Paper presented at the Conference on Economic Development and the Biological Standard of Living, Munich, 1997.

Sarmiento, Domingo F. *Facundo*. Buenos Aires: Losada, 1845.

Segundo censo de la República Argentina. 2 vols. Buenos Aires, 1898.

Semanario de Agricultura, 8 August 1802.

U.S. Bureau of the Census. *Historical Statistics of the United States. Colonial Times to 1957*. Washington, DC: Government Printing Office, 1960.

8

Banking and Money Markets in Brazil, 1889–1930

Gail D. Triner
Rutgers University

The preponderance of existing research on national economic consolidation focuses on economies that experienced significant industrialization and sustained growth by the twentieth century.[1] Despite a rich diversity in the specific means by which local markets became integrated into national economies, this research collectively concludes that the State and formal financial systems were crucial to the process. An examination of financial systems therefore presents a fruitful starting point for exploring the dynamics of national economic consolidation among a wider variety of countries.

Brazil offers an interesting opportunity to examine these issues in an important "underdeveloped" economy. The difficulties of forging a national unit from autonomous regional groups riddled nineteenth- and early-twentieth-century Brazil. Regional autonomy resulted in a hierarchical system of local oligarchies that hindered political cohesion.[2] Economically, regional autonomy had equally profound, if less studied, effects.[3] The means by which Brazil evolved from a loose aggregation of fragmented local markets to a large, complex and strongly centralized economy by the middle of the twentieth century remain quite mysterious.

Evidence suggests that during the First Republic from 1889 to 1930, the economies of diverse regions were becoming increasingly interrelated and that formerly local markets were coalescing into markets of national scope. Regional banking systems reflected their local economies, and the financial structures of banking in these regions reflected their interrelationships in logically consistent manners. But trends of growth, liquidity, and risk protection practices suggest that the dynamism of banking systems may also have been related to changing strengths among regions.[4]

Also during the First Republic, one of the overriding political and economic concerns of the governmental system under each political regime was to establish its authority on a national level. In these efforts, the federal Treasury fashioned monetary and financial policy to mediate multiple goals and to accommodate a wide variety of political regimes. A cohesive, responsive banking system of national scope was considered integral to this process.[5] However, the competing and more urgent requirements of debt servicing and of existing strong interest groups also depended on the tools of money and banking.[6] The Banco do Brasil orchestrated the most wide-ranging and complex activities to mediate these goals. Shifts of monetary policy and uses of the bank illustrated the manners in which various economic interests competed with, and accommodated, each other. The bank's centrality in the financial system very effectively served to link public and private sectors.

This paper examines the mechanisms by which banking participated in the consolidation of regional finance. Two perspectives inform this evaluation. First, the paper examines the national infrastructure for financial transactions that the Banco do Brasil created after 1905. Then, within a limited but important geographic scope, the paper explores the behavior of local bank interest rates in relation to the effective interest rates earned by the Banco do Brasil and the resulting relationships between local prices of money and the national scope of money markets. The conclusions are mixed. Nevertheless, two developments demonstrated the emerging role of the federal government and the nature of the national banking system. The banking system reinforced the pre-existing economic dominance of the state of São Paulo and increasingly linked it with the federal government. Further, the Banco do Brasil constructed a national financial infrastructure network in anticipation of transactional needs. In contrast to the experience of many other economies, the construction of a banking system of national scope may have served to concentrate, rather than spread, its benefits among economic agents. The manner in which the banking system evolved had lasting consequences for the Brazilian economy.

BANKING SYSTEM AND MONETARY POLICY IN THE FIRST REPUBLIC

Financial expansion was an immediate priority of the first republican governments in 1889. The abolition of slavery and expansion of export agriculture created conditions for rapid growth. In an attempt to accommodate the financial requirements for this growth, earliest republican monetary policy granted banks widespread and easy rights to issue money, along with other measures loosening financial regulation.[7] During these years, known as the Encilhamento, rapid formation of banks and corporations led to frenzied stock market activity. Policymakers believed that regional money issuance was necessary because of the disparities of local markets.[8] The first postemancipation efforts to provide for local monetary needs through regional banks met with the inability of the regional economies to support them. By 1890, expansive note-issuing rights and the ensuing inflation induced the Treasury to limit the right to issue currency to three regional banks.[9] In 1891, the Encilhamento cracked and the financial markets collapsed. The absence of national financial markets to meet the economy's needs during this period of transition prevented a smooth recovery from the failure of regional money markets.

Attempting to stabilize the economy, the federal government tried to impose the orthodox policies of balanced budgets and fixed currency values, resulting in a period of financial stagnation that continued until 1906. Financial reform was slow and uneven while the government consolidated its political authority during the 1890s. A broad package of fundamental changes to economic and financial management was initiated from the end of 1905 through 1908. Reforms included a coffee valorization (price-support) program[10] and new international borrowing, with the reinstitution of the metal standard to maintain the value of the milreis.[11] For the domestic banking system, the most important changes were the reconstitution of the Banco da República as the newly chartered Banco do Brasil and the emergence of a conservative system in which a diminished number of banks limited their risk-related business activity to deposit taking and short-term credit.

From the reforms of 1905, currency had a single centralized source of issue, facilitating the emergence of a common unit of exchange and value for money in Brazil. Although organizational arrangements continued to shift during the remainder of the First Republic, the Treasury Ministry maintained direct management of the money supply. From the time of its rechartering in 1905, the Treasury implemented changes in monetary policy through the Banco do Brasil by managing its funding of the bank.[12] From the time of its new charter in 1906 through the remainder of the First Republic, the Banco do Brasil served as the Treasury's proxy for the State in the banking system. Beyond its role in monetary policy, the bank also acquired a dominant position in the national distribution of financial services. It was also the largest bank serving the private sector. Financial flows and services were heavily concentrated within the bank. The Banco do Brasil held between 10% and 37% of total deposits in Brazilian banks (excluding deposits of Treasury funds) between its reconstitution in 1906 and 1930.[13] Although the bank's concentration of deposits fluctuated over the period, it was always a significant financial player and its dominance in providing services to other banks was never challenged.

Perhaps the most obvious mechanism for consolidating banks into a national system, as well as the most obvious legacy of banking during the First Republic for subsequent economic structure, was the use of the banking system to create a strong centralized role for the national government in the economy. Monetary policy continued to fluctuate rapidly and severely after the changes of 1905 and largely determined both price level changes and the size of the banking system.[14] Despite their effects on expansion and contraction, political expediency and the immediate financial needs of the federal government, rather than the needs of the private sector, motivated monetary policy.[15] The most visible actions of monetary policy and State finance that the Banco do Brasil undertook were in 1906, 1921, and 1923.[16] Soon after its opening in 1905, the bank began to administer the currency and exchange transactions to facilitate the return to a metal standard. After a short-lived rediscount facility in 1915, the Treasury funded a vastly enlarged Rediscount Office within the bank in 1921 to finance a domestic expansion by purchasing government notes and notes from other banks. The contractionary closing of the Rediscount Office, with the opening of a central banking office and a reconstituted metal standard, took place in 1923. The bank withdrew from formal monetary management in 1926.

The reforms marked the initiation of the modern Brazilian banking system. In contrast to earlier years, banks engaged solely in financing short-term commercial transactions with rigorous procedures to protect against the risks of borrower defaults. They funded their short-term investments with their own capital and deposits, rather than issuing notes that created insecure future liabilities.[17] Amended bank statutes and regulation precluded direct engagement in long-term finance and the issuance of unfunded notes.[18] Enhanced stability and legitimacy accompanied the reforms that restructured the banking system in 1906. Private-sector banking remained unregulated by the federal Treasury and was relatively unregulated by state-level authorities. However, the multiple uses of the Banco do Brasil in both public and private sectors ensured that privately owned banks were both subject to and instruments of public policy.

The increasing importance of banking in the monetary system indicated its enhanced credibility in the private sector. The banking system increasingly accumulated and reallocated financial resources of the private sector at the expense of either personal or other institutional channels. Money increasingly took the form of bank deposits, rather than currency. In 1930, bank deposits represented 34% of the money supply, compared with 17% in 1906. Between 1906 and 1930 real (inflation-adjusted) bank deposits increased ninefold, while the economy and the real money supply (M_2) increased 2.6 and 3.6 times, respectively.[19] Although these aggregate data imply the development of a cohesive and monetized economy, the effects spread unevenly.

FINANCIAL INFRASTRUCTURE

Efforts to develop a nationwide infrastructure for overtly conducting financial transactions attempted to construct a consolidated national banking system that would integrate regional economies and smooth seasonal bottlenecks.[20] Expansion of the geographic reach of banking was a consistent goal for the federal government, dating back to its earliest efforts in allowing regional banks to issue their own money.[21] The low volume of financial services needed in regional locations constrained the viability of local banks. By the same token, however, the absence of financial services hindered the development of local commerce. After its opening, the Banco do Brasil actively pursued regional expansion. It established a national network of branches, served as correspondent for regional banks, opened check-clearance facilities, and rediscounted the notes of other banks.

The Banco do Brasil's national charter allowed it to establish an interstate network of branches, which other banks could emulate only with greater cost and difficulty.[22] By 1921, the bank had branches in every state;[23] in 1928, 73 branches were open.[24] The Banco do Brasil network transferred financial resources from the head office in the Federal District to branch locations. From 1908 to 1916 (the years for which data are available), the volume of credit that the branches extended exceeded the deposits they collected locally.[25] The volume of finance flowing between regions through the Banco do Brasil's interstate network remained low. Total credit extended by the branches did not exceed 4% of total private-sector credit in Brazil during these years.[26] Nevertheless, the existence of the network contributed to the role of the Banco do Brasil as a centralizing force for the national banking system as the need for an extensive branch system subsequently developed.

Other efforts to expand the geographic reach of the banking system through the Banco do Brasil franchise had similarly ambiguous results. The Banco do Brasil served as a correspondent for other banks to facilitate the transactions between small local banks and financial centers. The volume of balances involved in correspondent relationships remained small.[27] These relationships created connections directly between regional banks and the Banco do Brasil without fostering a dense weave of relationships among banks in closely aligned markets. In 1921, the Banco do Brasil began to establish check-clearing facilities in regional centers, providing for the automatic transfer of funds from the account of one bank to another based on the payment orders (checks) of clients. This distribution function enhanced the bank's role of moving funds among private banks. But the function of easing interregional flows of funds developed slowly. A national clearing facility to settle checks that transferred resources between regions still did not exist at the end of the First Republic.

One of the goals of the rediscount facilities was to expand credit outside the major financial centers of Rio de Janeiro and São Paulo.[28] In addition to financing federal expenses by buying Treasury notes, the rediscount facility was to buy commercial paper from publicly chartered banks. Eligible banks established accounts with the Rediscount Office.[29] In effect, the Banco do Brasil facilities formed the apex of a rediscounting network. State-supported banks routinely purchased the notes of smaller and privately held banks within their states, which they resold to the Banco do Brasil.[30] Even so, it remained difficult to change the geographic distribution of credit in practice. Rediscounts were only slightly more geographically dispersed than private credit. Rio de Janeiro and São Paulo received the largest proportion of this funding.[31] In 1921, 23% of note rediscounting occurred in São Paulo, for coffee valorization, and 54% of notes rediscounted were in the Federal District (preponderantly rediscounts of treasury bills); the concentration in the Federal District increased to 63% in the following year.[32]

In the absence of local financial markets responding to private sector credit demands, these additional centrally orchestrated facilities neither created nor redistributed private sector credit. However, the modest volume of transactions understates the importance of these facilities. Where they appeared, the financial distribution facilities may have significantly eased local commercial bottlenecks. Anecdotal evidence suggests that to have been the experience.[33] In doing so, capabilities that appeared small at the national level could have significant local effect. Further, these facilities defined the infrastructure for banking development and facilitated an emerging national financial system. The importance of the network was to consolidate the role of the Banco do Brasil as a centralizing force for the national banking system. The Banco do Brasil provided important institutional stability to the banking system for the first time in Brazil's history.[34] This stability and reliability allowed the monetized portion of the economy to grow rapidly after 1905. The financial infrastructure anticipated its demand and shaped the mechanisms by which subsequent activity would be accommodated.

The use of the Banco do Brasil to establish a banking system of national scope had an ironic effect. One of the bank's goals was to establish banking facilities nationally; its effect was to concentrate the national financial system within one organization. The bank was influential in establishing national standards for banking practices and initiating during the First Republic the mechanisms to connect regional financial markets. The simultaneous importance of the Banco do Brasil in the banking system and in the federal government's economic policy firmly entrenched the State in the financial system.

THE NATURE OF THE MONEY MARKETS

Financial distribution on a national scope and increasing interrelations among regional markets generate expectations of an equalization of the cost of money across regions. An established literature on the formation of a national money market in the United States compares interest rates on short-term bank credit across regions in order to assess financial integration.[35] This material hypothesizes that, in an economy that is in the process of integrating financially, resources shift from resource-rich to resource-scarce areas and uses. Increased interaction both requires and reinforces commensurate improvements in information flows, ease of conducting transactions, and broadening groups of economic agents. Such conditions should lead money to respond to opportunities throughout an enlarging geographic region with greater facility and to reflect equilibrating conditions of supply, demand, risk, and transactions costs.

Money market integration, viewed through the prism of the banking system, is a logical place to assess early dynamics of the consolidation of national economic markets. Studies of the U.S. experience explain the importance of banks in consolidating the use of capital over wider areas through a variety of mechanisms. Banks efficiently pool information about borrowers' financial structures and business prospects, serving as a storehouse of investment information.[36] They also separate financial risk from production and market risks in new and innovative activities. As a result the allocation of resources to investment opportunities becomes more efficient, maximizing the return to investments. Consolidating information networks over larger areas should diminish the costs of assessing risks.[37] In addition, larger market areas enhance competition and erode local monopolies.[38] These were the circumstances that Brazilian authorities hoped to achieve in building an effective national banking system in Brazil at the beginning of the twentieth century.

Two results are expected to characterize a money market that enlarges by consolidating markets that had previously been smaller in scale. First, interest rates should display a pattern of converging toward a single national rate. The differential between interest rates of different regions and institutions should narrow with time. Convergence results from diminished transaction costs and enhanced allocational efficiency. The trend in the differential between a given rate and a benchmark rate, identified as the "center" of the money market, measures convergence. Second, to the extent that interest rate differentials remain, signifying underlying differences in economic structure, the fluctuations of regional interest rates should become increasingly uniform. Such a trend would indicate that conditions affecting the price of money appeared throughout an enlarging market area. This consideration recognizes that financial integration may occur where economic structures remain different. Structural differences affect interest rates through their effects on transaction costs, risk premia, time differentials, local investment options, and organizational management. Therefore, differences in the level of interest rates may remain, but increasing interaction results in more uniform fluctuation. The trend and persistence of rate differentials reflect underlying regional and institutional variation. Bank structure, interest rate differentials, and fluctuations among banks reveal much about regional economic difference and integration.

These hypothesized relationships between local interest rates, fluctuations, and differentials can be expressed as

$$\Delta r_{it} = a + b_1 \, \Delta BB_t + b_2 (r_{it-1} - BB_{it-1})$$

where r_{it} is the proxy interest rate for bank i in period t, BB_t is the proxy benchmark money market (Banco do Brasil) interest rate in period t, and $(r_{it-1} - MM_{it-1})$ is the lagged differential between local and central money market rates. (All measures are in natural logarithms; Δ indicates change from prior period.) A positive value of b_1 confirms that rates fluctuated together. The lagged differential between the rates specifies the convergence relationship over time. A negative relationship ($b_2 < 0$) suggests that rate changes (Δr_{it}) were mitigated by the extent of the (lagged) rate differential, influencing movement toward a more uniform rate structure.[39] In a perfectly integrated money market, a single interest rate would prevail for money instruments of similar structure, and rate fluctuations would be uniform throughout the market ($b_1 = 1$ and $r_{it-1} - MM_{it-1} = 0$).

The interest rate approximations in this paper represent the first attempt to construct interest rate histories for domestic Brazilian money instruments as early as the First Republic.[40] The ratio of (adjusted) gross earnings to average credit measures the gross return on bank credit and serves as a proxy for the effective average interest rate.[41] In a strictly commercial banking system, this ratio approximates the prevailing interest rate for short-term credit. Credit is measured as loans plus discounted notes (on an average semiannual basis). Credit and other bank balance data are from balance sheet reporting in the local financial press.[42] This source also provides the data for the size, structure, and regional distribution of banking on a national basis.

The measure of credit excludes holdings of assets for the banks' own investment accounts—bonds, equity shares, and public debt and other non-credit earning assets. Brazilian banks held only low volumes of these assets. For privately owned banks, this category of assets seldom reached 5% of earning assets (and then only for short periods). Gross earnings, as reported on bank income statements, are adjusted to exclude imputed earnings on other (non-credit) assets. Income on these assets is imputed to be 5% per annum throughout the period.[43] Because of the low volumes of these balance categories, the measures presented here are insensitive to the imputed rate.

Unlike balance sheet information, gross earnings from published semiannual income statements are not available for many banks. Public reporting requirements for bank earnings were less comprehensive than for balance sheets. After 1912, only São Paulo banks published income statements in the commercial press. Income statements also became less comprehensive with time. By 1921, income statements in bank annual reports did not identify interest income or expense. Further, foreign banks did not publish income statements in a consistent manner or on a sustained basis. Therefore, on a consistent basis, income statements are currently available only for the Banco do Brasil, private domestic banks in the state of São Paulo, and the "state banks" (those for which annual reports covering the period are available are the Banco de Crédito Hypothecário de Agrícola de São Paulo/Banco do Estado de São Paulo (Banespa) and the Banco de Crédito Real de Minas Gerais). Figure 8.1 charts the calculated proxy interest rates.

Data on the states of São Paulo and Minas Gerais are the most useful for assessing questions of early national money markets.[44] As discussed later, the economic structures of these two states were quite different from each other. They experienced changes during these years that demonstrate many of the fundamental tensions within the Brazilian economy. They also emerged during the twentieth century as the largest and perhaps most developed state economies in Brazil. Further, both state governments actively developed roles in their state banking systems. Therefore they offer interesting circumstances for assessing the earliest consolidation of diverse financial markets.[45]

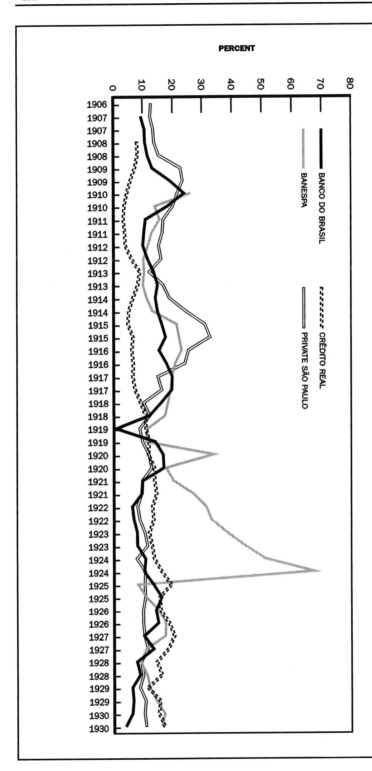

FIGURE 8.1 PROXY INTEREST RATES ON CREDIT

The proxy interest rate on Banco do Brasil credit provides the benchmark against which local bank interest rates are compared. The bank's dual roles as the federal Treasury's monetary agent and the largest commercial bank, combined with its unique position in providing financial infrastructure, suggest that it was the financial institution with the ability to mediate between dispersed local banking systems. The average price at which the Banco do Brasil extended credit offers the best information available for the price of money in the First Republic. A standard discount rate at which the Banco do Brasil acquired notes would offer an ideal benchmark rate. That rate is not available, however, and cannot be derived reliably from the data.

Interest rate patterns emerging from this analysis document center and regional economic dynamics that reflect specific local circumstances during the first third of the twentieth century (see Table 8.1). Local banking structures mirrored regional economic patterns. The level and trends of interest rates at varying organizations differed sufficiently to suggest that financial markets recognized, and instituted through price mechanisms, differential values to money instruments (see Figure 8.1). Because this model looks at the relationship between interest rates, it offers only limited explanation of interest rate levels.[46] Nevertheless, the interest rate differences among institutions and regions yield important conclusions about the nature of the early national money market. They demonstrate that in São Paulo banking was becoming more closely integrated with the center of the money market, whereas this was not the case in Minas Gerais.[47]

TABLE 8.1

Interest Rate Convergence Benchmarks

Dependent Variable:

Change in Proxy

Interest Rate	Constant	BB	Convergence Term	R^2	D-W	n
Crédito Real	0.02	0.03	−0.002	0.01	1.65	45
	(.61)	(.64)	(−.08)			
Banespa	0.10[a]	0.14[a]	−0.23[c]	0.12	2.03	41
	(1.18)	(1.25)	(−2.26)			
Private São Paulo banks	0.02	0.15[c]	−0.11[a]	0.13	2.16	47
	(.55)	(2.59)	(−1.39)			

Note: BB = Banco do Brasil, change in proxy interest rate. D-W = Durbin-Watson statistic.
Convergence term = $(r_{it-1} - BB_{it-1})$. t-statistics are in parentheses.
[a]Significant at .20 level (two-tailed).
[b]Significant at .10 level (two-tailed).
[c]Significant at .05 level (two-tailed).

The Crédito Real was the only publicly chartered bank in Minas Gerais until 1911; from then until the end of the First Republic, it held an average of 60% of bank deposits in the state.[48] Essentially, the bank defined credit and money conditions in the state. The real economy of Minas Gerais relied on a relatively diversified balance between coffee for international trade and agricultural products supplying a wide market area throughout Brazil.[49] Growth, diversification, and production of domestically oriented agriculture and consumer manufacturing appeared strong during the 1920s,[50] a period of slow progress for the country as a whole.[51] Despite its rapid growth, small family-held enterprise remained predominant in the Mineiro economy, with a tendency toward using internally generated capital to finance expansion.[52] The state government took an active role in regional economic development earlier than elsewhere, and the financial sector provided important mechanisms for its involvement.

As a result of these conditions, the regression results assessing integration trends in the money markets are extremely weak in Minas Gerais (see Table 8.1). The correlation coefficients, though in the hypothesized directions, are very low and not statistically significant. Instead, the structure of the state banking system demonstrated signs of independent dynamism. These financial indicators included a long-term shift from low to relatively high interest rates (Figure 8.1), very rapid growth in the size of the banking system that resulted in an increase of the state's share of total deposits from 2% in 1906 to 6% in 1930[53] (Figure 8.2), and declining liquidity needs, as measured by the reserve ratio of cash relative to deposits (Figure 8.3). These results reflected the long-term increasing value of money in this rapidly developing region.[54] The accelerated growth of banking and increasing interest rates stabilized in the early 1920s, when the state Treasury recapitalized and enlarged the bank. The state government's participation in the bank contributed to strong growth in the size of the banking system and may have mitigated, though not eliminated, rising interest rates during the 1920s. Rooted in the real growth of domestic markets (apparently stronger growth than otherwise observed in Brazil), and beginning the period with a very small banking system, effective interest rates reflected the scarcity of bank funds relative to demand.

In São Paulo, banking structure and the relationship between region and center were clearly different than in Minas Gerais. The banking system in São Paulo was the largest state system in Brazil, representing 40% of deposits in 1906 and 34% in 1930.[55] The financial structure of Paulista banking clearly demonstrated the characteristics of its stagnation during the 1920s that are generally attributed to Brazil as a whole. Proxy interest rates for privately

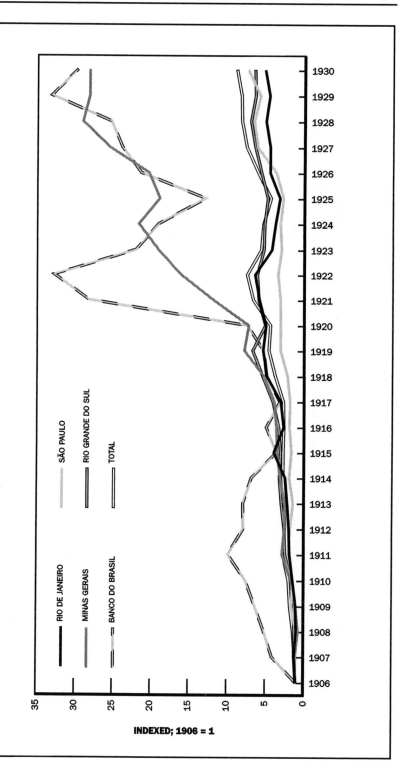

FIGURE 8.2 REGIONAL DEPOSIT GROWTH

INDEXED; 1906 = 1

RIO DE JANEIRO

MINAS GERAIS

BANCO DO BRASIL

SÃO PAULO

RIO GRANDE DO SUL

TOTAL

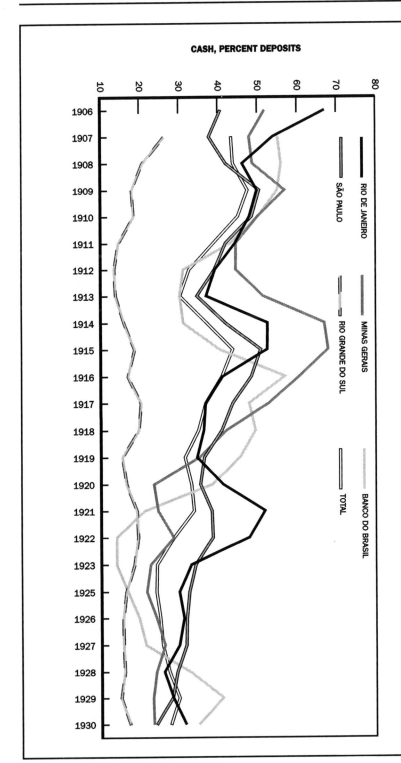

FIGURE 8.3 RESERVE RATIOS, BY REGION

owned domestic banks fell from high to low levels in comparison with other rates (see Figure 8.1). Growth of the banking system was slow until the state recapitalized Banespa in 1926 (Figure 8.2), and the average reserve ratio in the state declined only moderately (Figure 8.3).

The São Paulo banking system had two distinct components: a relatively mature network of privately owned organizations, and Banespa, the agricultural finance bank in which the state acquired majority ownership in 1926. For practical purposes, Banespa's agricultural financing was designed to meet the needs of the coffee trade. The level of their proxy interest rates testifies to the difference between Banespa and the privately owned banks (see Figure 8.1). The regression statements for both, however, suggest much similarity in interest rate trends (see Table 8.1). For both, rate fluctuation was in step with the Banco do Brasil and their rates converged toward the benchmark, although at a slow pace. For São Paulo banks, the results are much stronger than for Minas Gerais, with respect to both the strength of the effects (size of coefficient) and their statistical significance (t-statistics).

These findings reflect the importance of the São Paulo economy and the financial condition of the federal Treasury during the First Republic. They also demonstrate the limits of the third leg of the policy rhetoric, the development of a responsive national banking system, in anticipation of the need for such a system.[56] The sharp inversion of interest rates between the Banco do Brasil and Banespa in the early 1920s, with windfall gains accruing to Banespa during the 1921–1923 rediscount program (Figure 8.1), corresponded with the period of coffee price supports and the rapid and strong manipulation of federal monetary policy and credit conditions.[57] These rate conditions ceased immediately with the end of the rediscount program in 1923. The subsequent expansion of Banespa in 1926, with equity from the state government, countered the contractionary federal monetary policy. Previous research has found that Banco do Brasil monetary actions, especially during the 1921–1923 rediscount program, did not realize their intended effects on the national financial system.[58] Further, the debates surrounding the state capitalization of the Crédito Real in Minas Gerais emphasized the belief that Banco do Brasil policies and programs benefited São Paulo in preference to other states.[59] Cumulatively, these findings add specificity to those earlier conclusions. The interest rate histories suggest that the effects of the federal policies included enriching Banespa shareholders and integrating a financial nexus between Paulista banking and federal finance that exceeded the experience in Minas Gerais.

The money markets reflected the interests of competing strategies and agents during the latter 25 years of the First Republic. The specific interests of

Paulista economic agents certainly found strong representation in national financial and monetary policy. However, to interpret these results entirely as an expression of political will overstates that argument. Federal policy and practice did not overtly discriminate by region. Monetary policy and Banco do Brasil programs had their largest effects in the geographic area where they had the most opportunity to be exercised. Further, state-financed banks often countermanded the Banco do Brasil activities in deference to local interests. Two results of these activities are important for the evolution of the national banking system. First, multiple layers of monetary management constrained the importance of privately owned banks responding freely to the demands for banking in the productive sectors. Second, they proved an effective, if slow, mechanism for reinforcing the financial nexus between the dominant regional economy of São Paulo and the federal government.

CONCLUSION

On both a national scale and in specific regional settings, the banking system facilitated the economic (and political) relationships that banking historiography hypothesizes. The findings here do not contradict other research that banking, or more generally, finance, dynamically supported economic development in Brazil during the First Republic.[60] Here, we see some of the long-term implications of the specific course of banking development in Brazil. These results reflect an important shift of relative regional economic strength emanating from Minas Gerais, but also demonstrate that the national financial network reinforced preexisting economic conditions.

These countervailing forces of national consolidation and strong regionalism were often in contention during the First Republic. The processes of building a national banking system were neither smooth nor unidirectional. They continued to reflect strong differences in local conditions. Two conclusions emerge from the examination of these processes. The institutional character of the financial system was established during these years. The monopoly of the Banco do Brasil in the transactional infrastructure connecting banks entrenched the bank, and by implication the federal Treasury, at the center of the banking system. This dominance has not been challenged in subsequent years. Second, efforts to spread the benefits of banking to wider geographic areas had the ironic result of concentrating the banking sector and reinforcing incipient regional patterns of distribution rather than mitigating them. Both the use of financial infrastructure and available information on the cost of money demonstrate this conclusion. In this sense, finance and the State were important for establishing the patterns of economic modernization, as the early historiography hypothesizes for "latecomers" to modernization. However, the results may not have been as expansive as that historiography would have predicted.

The end of the First Republic in 1930 coincided with years of significant economic and political upheaval. The effects of the Great Depression exacerbated problems caused by a severe domestic recession that began in 1927. Politically, the overthrow of the Republic by Getúlio Vargas laid the groundwork for the imposed and economically nationalistic policies of the *Estado Nôvo*, including an international debt moratorium in 1932. Future studies of national economic consolidation during the transitional years of the 1930s face the task of separating effects endogenous to economic processes from exogenous political and economic circumstances. Nevertheless, during the years of the Vargas political administration, a fully consolidated economy of national scope emerged.[61] The economy was highly centralized and featured an activist State. The federal government owned and operated large companies that produced crucial industrial goods, and it orchestrated private-sector production and prices. The Banco do Brasil was crucial to the management of this economy. The model of hierarchical and centralized economic management depended on the State's use of the Banco do Brasil in the private financial sector and mirrored earlier strategies in the financial sector with respect to State ownership and management. The consolidation of a national economy relied on a dynamic balance of regional and sectoral differentiation and interaction. The financial system reinforced emerging patterns of concentration. Although development experience and State centralization partially mitigated regional differences, the nationally integrated economy that emerged incorporated and formalized patterns seen in money and banking during the First Republic.

ACKNOWLEDGMENTS

This paper is a significant revision of the paper originally presented at the "Latin America and the World Economy in the Nineteenth and Twentieth Centuries: Explorations in Quantitative Economic History" Conference. The participants of the conference provided many useful suggestions, both in and outside of the meetings. I would also like to thank Michael Edelstein, Stanley Engerman, Kerry Odell, Steven Topik, Eugene White, and the participants at the All-University of California Economic History/Stanford University Conference on Comparative Development in Latin America and the United States, November 1996. Special thanks go to Catalina Vizcarra and Richard Sicotte. None of the above are implicated in any remaining problems.

NOTES

1. Gerschenkron (1962), Cameron (1967, 1972), Sylla (1975).
2. Graham (1990), Fausto (1989).
3. C. Prado (1993), Furtado (1993), L. C. Prado (1991), Leff (1982).
4. Triner (1997).
5. Ministério da Fazenda, *Relatório*, 1905.
6. Fritsch (1988), Peláez (1971).
7. Easy credit and rapid money creation were specific policies enacted to ameliorate the conditions of former slave owners, who lost their primary store of capital by virtue of emancipation. See Franco (1987) and Levy (1980) for more on this little-understood episode in Brazilian economic history.
8. Franco (1987), pp. 101–109; Neuhaus (1974), pp. 5–7; Peláez and Suzigan (1976), pp. 277–281.
9. These three banks were the Banco dos Estados Unidos do Brasil, the Banco Nacional, and (the third) Banco do Brasil. By December 1890, the Banco dos Estados Unidos and the Banco Nacional merged into the Banco da República. This further concentrated note-issuing rights; it also resulted in an institutional structure that lasted until 1900, when the Banco da República failed (to be reorganized as the fourth Banco do Brasil in 1905).
10. The coffee valorization of 1906 initiated a long series of coffee price-support programs throughout much of the remainder of the First Republic (Topik 1987, chap. 3).
11. Neuhaus (1974), pp. 18–23.
12. Triner (1996a), pp. 58–63.
13. Triner (1994), Table A.9.
14. Peláez and Suzigan (1976), pp. 148–155; Triner (1994), chap. 3.
15. Fritsch (1988); Topik (1987), chap. 2.
16. Neuhaus (1974), chaps. 1–3; Peláez and Suzigan (1976), chap. 6; Topik (1987), chap. 2; Villela and Suzigan (1973), chaps. 3–5.
17. Triner (1994), pp. 101–108.
18. Bankers did effectively convert short-term finance into medium- and long-term facilities, but with a structure that allowed them to revert to the benefits of short-term lending (Triner 1994, pp. 105–106).
19. Money supply is measured as M_2 for reasons of data consistency. The reliability of price indices for the period should not be overestimated; however, a wide variety of assumptions about price fluctuations does not change the relative conclusion (Triner 1994, pp. 55–56).
20. Ministério da Fazenda, *Relatórios*, 1905, p. xii, and 1914, p. 12.
21. Goldsmith (1986), p. 100; Banco do Brasil, *Relatórios*, 1915, pp. 41–42, and 1922,

pp. 10–11.

22. In principle, any bank could engage in interstate banking. Separate charters could be obtained from the states in which banks wished to establish branches. Domestic banks began to establish branches in more than one state routinely during the 1920s, and then the practice spread slowly.

23. Banco do Brasil, *Cartas*, 26 October 1921.

24. Triner (1994), p. 66. In 1928, the cumulative operating loss of the branches consumed 11% of the bank's net income (Banco do Brasil, *Relatório*, 1928, p. 13).

25. Banco do Brasil, *Relatórios*, annually 1908–1916.

26. Triner (1994), p. 122.

27. Between 1922 and 1930 (the years for which data are available), the volume of balances in domestic correspondent accounts was less than 1% of the bank's total volume of credit and deposits (Banco do Brasil, *Relatórios*, annually 1922–1930). (Correspondent balances are not included in credit and deposit volumes, presented elsewhere.)

28. Triner (1997).

29. The major criterion for eligibility was a capital base of 5,000 contos (Banco do Brasil, *Relatório*, 1920).

30. See, for example, da Costa (1988), p. 68.

31. Triner (1994), p. 122.

32. Banco do Brasil, *Cartas*, 8 July 1921, 26 August 1921, and 16 September 1921; Triner (1994), Table 3.6.

33. Banco do Brasil, *Relatórios*, 1921 and 1922; *Retrospecto comercial*, 1921.

34. I thank Anne Hanley for suggesting this phrasing.

35. Davis (1965), Sylla (1969), Smiley (1975), James (1976), Odell (1989), Bodenhorn (1992, 1995).

36. James (1976), p. 880; Odell (1989), p. 298.

37. Odell (1989).

38. Sylla (1969).

39. Malley (1990) and Kennedy (1993, pp. 250–254) offer further discussion of the technical aspects of the model. More sophisticated time-series models can also test these hypotheses, as could factor-analysis models. However, the quantity and specificity of the currently available data mitigate their usefulness.

40. Only one other attempt at constructing a time series of domestic interest rates exists. Neuhaus (1974, Table 40) presents *apólice* yields (domestic debt instruments of the federal government, structured like consuls). These represent the domestic cost of federal Treasury long-term debt, rather than short-term private-sector borrowing. Further, Neuhaus is not entirely clear on how the data have been constructed: For the early portion of that time series he reports semiannual

yields, but reports annual yields from 1922. The data are from a variety of sources. Neuhaus calculates the gains and losses from price change in his yield calculation (without giving the time period of the underlying data). To my knowledge, the Neuhaus data have not been used in analytic work.

41. Economic historians of the United States have debated the appropriate measure to use for this purpose. Davis (1965), Smiley (1975), and James (1976) have explored the possibilities of using net rates of return rather than gross rates. Consensus has consolidated around the measure of gross returns. Good (1977, p. 898) further emphasizes matters of expediency for using the gross return on earning assets—an extremely applicable consideration in the Brazilian case. It should be noted that this is an average realized interest rate, rather than a marginal rate on specific loans. For short-term lending, the difference between the average and the marginal rates should be relatively small. The measure also includes fee income that banks earn (not strictly part of an interest rate). For commercial banks, these differences from a marginal interest rate on a short-term instrument should be relatively small. Further research and data availability should ultimately make possible an alternative measure of interest rates, based on net profits, for a wider group of banks.

42. Triner (1994), appendix.

43. Five percent was the nominal rate on the federal Treasury's domestic notes (*apólices*) during the First Republic. *Apólices* were the major category of noncredit earning assets that banks held.

44. Even so, it should be pointed out that using state-level data assumes that state boundaries provided operative definitions of markets in First Republic Brazil. That assumption can certainly be debated. But state-level regulation and, to some extent, economic activity suggest that states are not an unreasonable unit for assessing banking systems.

45. Were data available, it would be possible to test the hypothesis that enhancing local financial mechanisms aided money market integration of remote areas, as demonstrated by interest rate experience, to a greater extent than financial development in the larger and more established regions of São Paulo and Minas Gerais.

46. This explains the low R^2's in the regression statements.

47. An earlier version of this paper in which the *apólice* yield (the domestic cost of borrowing by the federal Treasury) served as the benchmark concluded that regional bank rates converged toward the central rate. This result seems to reflect the relative stability of the *apólice* yield, in comparison with the greater fluctuation of bank rates, as much as it reflects actual convergence. The dynamics of Brazilian money markets and the term structure of the financial instruments suggest that the Banco do Brasil rate is the more appropriate, if still imperfect, bench-

mark.
48. Triner (1997).
49. da Costa (1978), pp. 22–60.
50. da Costa (1978), p. 53.
51. Baer (1995), pp. 32–35.
52. Eakin (1997).
53. Triner (1997).
54. This corresponds with the experience in the U.S. West of higher rate differentials and lower sensitivity to fluctuations in the financially developed center (Odell 1989, p. 306).
55. Triner (1997).
56. Topik (1987), chap. 3; Fritsch (1988), chap. 1.
57. Peláez and Suzigan (1976), pp. 176–181; Neuhaus (1974), chap. 2.
58. Triner (1994), chap. 3.
59. da Costa (1978), pp. 75–78.
60. Hanley (1995), Haber (1997), Triner (1996b).
61. Baer (1995), chaps. 3 and 4.

REFERENCES

Baer, Werner. *The Brazilian Economy: Growth and Development.* 4th ed. Westport, CT: Praeger, 1995.

Banco do Brasil. *Relatório do Banco do Brasil apresentado à Assembléia Geral dos Accionistas na Sessão Ordinaria.* Banco do Brasil Archives, Rio de Janeiro, 1898–1932.

Banco do Brasil. *Cartas Particulares dos Presidentes.* Banco do Brasil Archives, Rio de Janeiro, 1909–1930.

Banco do Brasil. "Projeto dos Estátutos do Banco do Brasil." elaborado pelo Sr. Daniel de Mendonça e depois discutido pela Commissão redigido pelo Sr. Affonso Celso. Banco do Brasil Archives, Rio de Janeiro. Rio de Janeiro: Typ. Leuzinger, 1920.

Bodenhorn, Howard. "Capital Mobility and Financial Integration in Antebellum America." *Journal of Economic History* 52, no. 3 (Sept. 1992): 585–610.

Bodenhorn, Howard. "A More Perfect Union: Regional Interest Rates in the United States, 1880–1960." In *Anglo-American Financial Systems: Institutions and Markets in the Twentieth Century,* edited by Michael D. Bordo and Richard Eugene Sylla. Burr Ridge, IL: Irwin Professional Publishing, 1995.

Bodenhorn, Howard, and Hugh Rockoff. "Regional Interest Rates in Antebellum

America." In *Strategic Factors in Nineteenth-Century American Economic History: A Volume to Honor Robert Fogel*, edited by Claudia Goldin and Hugh Rockoff, 159–188. Chicago: University of Chicago Press and National Bureau of Economic Research, 1992.

Cameron, Rondo E., ed. *Banking in the Early Stages of Industrialization: A Study in Comparative Economic History*. With the collaboration of Olga Crisp, Hugh T. Patrick, and Richard Tilly. New York: Oxford University Press, 1967.

Cameron, Rondo E., ed. *Banking and Economic Development: Some Lessons of History*. New York: Oxford University Press, 1972.

da Costa, Fernando Nogueira. "Bancos em Minas Gerais (1889–1964)." Tese de Mestrado, Universidade Estadual de Campinas, 1978.

da Costa, Fernando Nogueira. "Banco do Estado: O Caso Banespa." Tese de Doutoramento, Universidade Estadual de Campinas, 1988.

Davis, Lance E. "The Investment Market, 1870–1914: The Evolution of a National Market." *Journal of Economic History* 25 (1965): 355–399.

Eakin, Marshall C. "The Formation of a Business Elite: Belo Horizonte, Brazil, 1890s–1940s." Conference on Latin American History, New York, January, 1997.

Fausto, Boris. *A Revolução de 1930: Historiografia e história*. São Paulo: Editora Brasiliense, 1989.

Franco, Gustavo Henrique Barroso. *Reforma monetária e instabilidade durante a transição republicana*, 2d ed. Rio de Janeiro: Banco Nacional de Desenvolvimento Econômico e Social, 1987.

Fritsch, Winston. *External Constraints on Economic Policy in Brazil, 1889–1930*. Pittsburgh: University of Pittsburgh Press, 1988.

Furtado, Celso. *Formação econômica do Brasil*, 40th ed. São Paulo: Editora Brasiliense, 1993.

Gerschenkron, Alexander. *Economic Backwardness in Historical Perspective*. Cambridge, MA: Harvard University Press, 1962.

Goldsmith, Raymond W. *Brasil 1850–1984: Desenvolvimento financeiro sob um século de inflação*. São Paulo: Banco Bamerindus e Ed. Harper Row do Brasil, 1986.

Good, David F. "Financial Integration in Late Nineteenth-Century Austria." *Journal of Economic History* 37, no. 4 (Dec. 1977): 890–910.

Graham, Richard. *Patronage and Politics in Nineteenth-Century Brazil*. Stanford, CA: Stanford University Press, 1990.

Haber, Stephen. "Financial Markets and Industrial Development: A Comparative Study of Governmental Regulation, Financial Innovation and Industrial Structure in Brazil and Mexico, 1840–1930." In *How Latin America Fell Behind: Essays on the Economic Histories of Brazil and Mexico, 1800–1914*, edited by Stephen Haber, 146–178. Stanford, CA: Stanford, University Press, 1997.

Hanley, Anne Gerard. "Capital Markets in the Coffee Economy: Financial Institutions and Economic Change in São Paulo, Brazil, 1850–1905." Ph.D. dissertation, Stanford University, 1995.

James, John A. "Banking Market Structure, Risk and the Pattern of Local Interest Rates in the United States, 1893–1911." *Review of Economics and Statistics* 53, no. 4 (Nov. 1976): 453–462.

Kennedy, Peter. *A Guide to Econometrics.* 3d ed. Cambridge, MA: MIT Press, 1993.

Leff, Nathaniel H. *Underdevelopment and Development in Brazil.* 2 vols. London and Boston: Allen & Unwin, 1982.

Levy, Maria Bárbara. "O Encilhamento." In *Economia Brasileira: Uma visão histórica,* edited by Paulo Neuhaus, 194–204. Rio de Janeiro: Editora Campus, 1980.

Malley, James R. "Dynamic Specification in Econometric Estimation." *Journal of Agricultural Economics Research* 42, no. 2 (1990): 52–55.

Ministério da Fazenda. Brasil. *Relatório apresentado ao Presidente da República dos Estados Unidos do Brasil pelo Ministro de Estado dos Negócios da Fazenda.* Annual series. Rio de Janeiro: Imprensa Nacional, 1898–1930.

Neuhaus, Paulo. "A Monetary History of Brazil, 1900–1945." Ph.D. dissertation, University of Chicago, 1974.

Odell, Kerry A. "The Integration of Regional and Interregional Capital Markets: Evidence from the Pacific Coast, 1883–1913." *Journal of Economic History* 49, no. 2 (June 1989): 297–309.

Peláez, Carlos Manuel. "As conseqüências econômicas da ortodoxia monetária, cambial e fiscal no Brasil entre 1889–1945." *Revista Brasileira da Economia* 5, no. 3 (July–Sept. 1971): 5–82.

Peláez, Carlos Manuel, and Wilson Suzigan. *História monetária do Brasil: Análise da política, comportamento e instituições monetárias.* Instituto de Planejamento Econômico e Social/Instituto de Pesquisas, Monografia no. 23. Rio de Janeiro: IPEA/INPES, 1976.

Prado, Caio, Jr. *História econômica do Brasil.* 1961. Reprint. São Paulo: Editora Brasilense, 1993

Prado, Luiz Carlos T. D. "Commercial Capital, Domestic Market and Manufacturing in Imperial Brazil: The Failure of Brazilian Economic Development in the Nineteenth Century." Ph.D. dissertation, University of London, 1991.

Retrospecto comercial de Journal do Commércio. Annual series. Rio de Janeiro: *Jornal do Commércio* de Rodrigues e Cia, 1898–1932.

Smiley, Gene. "Interest Rate Movements in the United States, 1888–1913." *Journal of Economic History* 35 (Sept. 1975): 591–620.

Sylla, Richard E. "Federal Policy, Banking Market Structure and Capital Mobility in the United States, 1863–1914." *Journal of Economic History* 29, no. 4 (Dec. 1969): 657–686.

Sylla, Richard E. *The American Capital Market, 1846–1914: A Study of the Effects of*

Public Policy on Economic Development. Dissertations in American Economic History. New York: Arno Press, 1975.

Topik, Steven. *The Political Economy of the Brazilian State, 1889–1930.* Latin American Monographs no. 71, Institute of Latin American Studies, University of Texas at Austin. Austin: University of Texas Press, 1987.

Triner, Gail D. "Banking and Brazilian Economic Development: 1906–1930." Ph.D. dissertation, Columbia University, 1994.

Triner, Gail D. "The Formation of Modern Brazilian Banking, 1906–1930: Opportunities and Constraints Presented by the Public and Private Sectors." *Journal of Latin American Studies* 28 (Feb. 1996a): 49–74.

Triner, Gail D. "Banking, Economic Growth and Industrialization: Brazil, 1906–1930." *Revista Brasileira de Econômia* 50, no. 1 (Jan. 1996b): 135–154.

Triner, Gail D. "Banks, Regions and Nation in Brazil, 1889–1930." *Latin American Perspectives.* Forthcoming.

Villela, Annibal V., and Wilson Suzigan. *Política do governo e crescimento da econômia Brasileira, 1889–1945.* Instituto de Planejamento Econômico e Social/Instituto de Pesquisas, Monografia no. 10. Rio de Janeiro: IPEA/INPES, 1973.

9

Economic Growth in Argentina in the Period 1900–1930: Some Evidence from Stock Returns

Leonard I. Nakamura
Federal Reserve Bank of Philadelphia
Carlos E. J. M. Zarazaga
Federal Reserve Bank of Dallas

This paper is a preliminary report on stock market returns to equity issues in Argentina in the period from 1900 to 1930. It is part of an ongoing project aimed at recovering aggregate financial data for Argentina for the entire twentieth century. This particular part of the project is an effort to shed some light on the controversy surrounding the economic growth trends prevailing in that country at the beginning of the twentieth century, especially after World War I.

Di Tella and Zymelman have argued that Argentina experienced a significant slowdown in economic growth after World War I.[1] However, in one of the most thorough studies of Argentina's economic history, Díaz Alejandro argued that that country's performance in the 1920s was one of continued strong growth.[2] In particular, he showed that, accounting for the understandable and temporary disruptions associated with World War I, Argentina did well in this period in comparison with Australia and Canada. His work is in line with that of Prebisch, who argued that real economic activity in the late 1920s had exceeded that of the prewar period.[3] More recent work, however, has come to dispute this view. Using the performance of OECD countries after World War I as a benchmark, Alan Taylor has argued in an influential study that 1913 marks the high tide of Argentine economic performance.[4] Recent revisions of estimates of Argentina's gross domestic product (GDP) at the beginning of the twentieth century by Cortés Conde point in the same direction.[5]

The question of what marked the end of Argentina's Belle Époque—the period of rapid growth from the turn of the century to the eve of the First World War—holds implications for the politically charged issue of the wisdom of government policies in response to the challenges Argentina faced in the interwar years: the exhaustion of economically useful land to continue the expansion of the primary sector, and the decline of England, Argentina's chief financier. The collapse of the international gold standard hindered not only international trade but also the inflow of capital to settler economies such as Argentina, Australia, and Canada. Were these temporary factors responsible for Argentina's poor economic performance during the interwar years? Or, as maintained by Di Tella and Zymelman, were misguided policies responsible for a "Great Delay" that lasted until 1933? The answers to these questions hold the key to the critical evaluation of the inward-looking policies and import-substitution policies adopted after the Great Depression. After all, as Taylor pointedly notes, "If economic failure can be said to predate the adoption of import-substitution doctrines, the structuralist camp can evade responsibility for decline and implicate the liberal, export-oriented policy regime prevailing until 1929."[6]

The preliminary results presented in this paper are part of a wider research project that attempts to answer the questions above and related ones with the use, to our knowledge for the first time, of a large data set that will eventually make it possible to compute rates of return to equity in Argentina from 1900 to the present. The motivation for the part of our project presented here is that corporate equity prices and dividends tend to reflect the actual and prospective changes in the rate of expansion of the economy. Thus, stock returns may, in principle, serve as an additional indicator of contemporary sentiment on the expected return to capital during the interwar periods. This may indirectly shed light on the economic development and long-term growth prospects of the Argentine economy in this period, as Sylla et al. have shown for the U.S. economy and financial markets.[7]

Particularly important for the controversy surrounding Argentina's growth after World War I is that the pricing and other characteristics of financial assets can provide crucial information on Argentine firms' access to international capital markets. Taylor has argued that credit constraints in the international capital markets after World War I forced Argentina to slow down its domestic investment to rates sustainable with its relatively low domestic savings capacity. A break of this type in Argentina's linkage with international capital markets would be reflected, in principle, in higher ex ante real interest rates and returns to equity relative to those prevailing in international markets.

The evidence from stock returns does not point in that direction. In particular, real rates of return to equity and dividend–price ratios in Argentina were not obviously different from those prevailing, for example, in the United States. The stock market data confirm, as is well known, that Argentina, along with other settler economies, did take an unusually big hit in the Great War and that economic conditions in its aftermath were perhaps not as rosy as Díaz Alejandro believed. But the financial data clearly indicate that Argentina was by no means excluded from international capital markets. On the contrary, the data indicate that Argentina was better integrated into world capital markets in the last half of the 1920s than it was before the Great War.

THE SLOWDOWN CONTROVERSY

Between 1900 and 1930, total Argentine output grew at 4.6% per annum. Most of this growth can be explained by standard neoclassical growth accounting. In that period, capital grew at an annual rate of 4.8%, and unadjusted labor input at the annual rate of 3.1%. Giving to the contribution of capital a weight between one-half and one-third, and to that of labor a weight between one-half and two-thirds, the unexplained residual would be limited to between 14% and 20% of the growth rate. Total factor productivity, thus crudely measured, would lie between 0.6% to 0.9% annually. This residual is not very far from the annual rate of 0.9% that Solow found in his original study of the United States for the period 1909 to 1929.[8]

Di Tella and Zymelman claimed that Argentine growth slowed down significantly after World War I. They reported data from the Economic Commission for Latin America (ECLA), according to which the average annual growth rate in the period 1900–1904/1910–1914 was 6.3%, whereas it was only 3.5% in the period 1910–1914/1925–1929 (these are growth rates between levels of five-year averages).[9] But Díaz Alejandro argued that the slowdown in the second period disappears if one excludes the period 1913–1917, during which GDP fell almost 20%. The decline in this period reflected unusual circumstances rather than a permanent change in the dynamic forces propelling the Argentine economy: the European monetary tightness of the second half of 1913, which reduced capital inflows, the crop failures of 1914, and finally the outbreak of the war. Otherwise, the expansion for the period 1917–1929, as reported by Díaz Alejandro, was brisk:

1918–1920: 9.8% per annum
1921–1923: 7.2% per annum
1924–1926: 4.1% per annum
1927–1929: 6.0% per annum

Although GDP growth was highest in the early recovery years, the figures on th previous page do not lend much support to the idea of a clear-cut slowdown with respect to the period 1900–1914.

The slowdown hypothesis resurfaced, however, after Cortés Conde reestimated GDP for the period 1875–1935, correcting the shortcomings allegedly present in the ECLA methodology. According to his figures, real GDP grew at an average annual rate of 8.3% between 1900–1913 and at the much slower rate of 4.3% in the period 1917–1929. The slowdown also shows up, albeit less dramatically, in the figures for real GDP per capita: 4.3% annual growth in the first period against 3.3% in the second.

Cortés Conde's findings, however, do not necessarily lend support to Di Tella and Zymelman's hypothesis that the slowdown was the result of misguided policies. After all, as Díaz Alejandro has pointed out, if Argentina's growth slowed down after World War I, the same was true of Canada and Australia, all three countries reflecting the worldwide economic conditions of low British economic growth and low European population expansion between 1913 and 1929.

Alan Taylor, however, has questioned that comparison on the grounds that it entails "mutual flattery among a group of poor performers" because those three countries (along with Mexico and the Philippines) were the five hardest hit by the effects of World War I.[10] He goes on to show that the closest Argentina got to the income per capita of the OECD countries was in 1913. Taylor points out that Argentina's domestic savings rate was low even relative to Canada and Australia and attributes the ultimate decline of Argentina's growth after World War I to Argentina's dependence on foreign capital. Thus, Taylor seems to side with Di Tella and Zymelman in that a "vulnerable growth strategy," that is, excessive reliance on foreign savings before World War I, was ultimately responsible for the slowdown of Argentina's economic growth.

From this argument, it is not clear what fraction of the common fates of Argentina, Canada, and Australia is attributable to a lower demand for capital and what part to a lower supply of it. In this regard, the decline of England as an international supplier of capital coincided with factors, such as changing patterns of world trade and the closing of the Argentine frontier, that would qualify as downward shifts in the demand for capital.

The transition from Western European capital suppliers to American ones could be easily associated with at least some form of temporary market incompleteness (Taylor's maintained hypothesis) and, therefore, with a rise in the cost of capital to Argentina above the one prevailing in the world financial markets. In particular, Argentina's financial markets after World War I should have been associated with higher required returns to capital relative to the rest of the world. We argue below that that was not the case.

Savings and Investment

According to the ECLA, gross fixed capital formation represented on average 40% of GDP between 1900 and 1914 and about 30% between 1920 and 1929.[11] Thus, it is clear that a lower equilibrium rate of investment occurred in the latter period. But it is important to identify whether this decline resulted from a fall in the supply of capital or in the demand for capital, or both.

High rates of investment associated with a rising capital–labor ratio during a growth spurt need not be sustainable in the long run. The capital–labor ratio in 1925–1929 was indeed 46% higher than in 1900–1904.[12] Consistent with these figures, Taylor reports that capital stock per person was 36% higher in 1913 than in 1890.[13] Thus, the evolution of investment rates in Argentina in the period 1900–1930 is not inconsistent with the predictions of many standard models of economic growth.[14] In other words, it may have been unrealistic to expect that the investment boom that characterized the years prior to the Great War would continue much longer. In this sense, the investment slowdown of the 1920s could also be regarded as the natural course of economic development and therefore does not provide any evidence that Argentina's economic policies prior to the Great Depression were misguided.

It is interesting to compare the estimates of investment rates reported above with the savings rates calculated by Taylor. He reports savings rates of about 5% between 1900 and 1930, which suggests that a substantial fraction (about 85%) of capital accumulation after World War I was still being financed from abroad. It is hard to see how Argentina could have been credit constrained in international capital markets when it was able to finance abroad such a large proportion of domestic investment. Although it is true that placing debt on European markets remained difficult, Argentine placements on both domestic and the New York markets were considerable.

If there was a credit constraint in the late 1920s, it was not clearly evident to at least one well-placed observer. In the *Economist* of 24 March 1928, the Argentine correspondent, after noting the successful placement of US $41 million in bonds of the Province of Buenos Aires on the New York market at an average rate of 6.5% (replacing loans with average interest rates of 7.9%), asserted that Argentine domestic investors had a lending capacity appearing to be "without a limit.... In round figures, the Argentine investor during the past ten years has absorbed at least 1,500,000,000 paper [pesos] in the form of locally issued bonds."[15] The magnitude of this figure may be compared with that of Argentina's national debt, reported as 2.6 billion paper pesos in December of 1927,[16] and Argentina's nominal GDP, which averaged 7.4 billion paper pesos in the decade 1918–1927. The correspondent's report suggests that domestic savings rates may not have been so low after all, perhaps more in line with Díaz Alejandro's estimate that domestic gross savings amounted to around 10% of GDP in most years before 1930. But even this implies that about 60% of postwar capital accumulation was financed abroad, still a large percentage for a country that may have been credit constrained. Unfortunately, savings rates are notoriously difficult to measure accurately, so additional evidence on domestic channels for capital is of value in this controversy. Lacking a direct resolution of this issue, we must rely on other evidence to assess whether Argentina had difficulties in accessing international capital markets after World War I.

In that respect, there is another important difference between Taylor and Díaz Alejandro. According to Díaz Alejandro, international capital markets for Argentina after World War I were free of any significant frictions. He reports that Argentina's creditworthiness, as measured by the market yield of her bonds, was not very different from that of Canada and Australia during the 1920s. As late as 1931 Argentina was able to roll over a loan at an interest rate only 90 basis points above the average rate paid by the government of the United Kingdom. Díaz Alejandro reports that, according to Wortman, in 1927 Argentina's creditworthiness was ranked by British experts as seventh among foreign countries.[17]

By contrast, Taylor reports that according to Harold Peters and Vernon Phelps,[18] Argentina had limited success trying to raise funds from the New York money market and that prior to 1923 advances could be obtained only over the short term and at high interest rates. In Taylor's words, "Unsuccessful attempts to raise funds in New York for several years and the inability to attract new foreign additions to the capital stock caused Argentine accumulation to limp along, relying on low rates of domestic accumulation to drive new investment."[19]

As emphasized earlier, the completeness of capital markets is important for the resolution of this controversy because the efficient markets hypothesis underlies the arbitrage condition and similar conditions typically used in models of asset pricing and analysis of financial asset returns. If markets are complete, arbitrage should result in equalization of expected rates of return across capital markets and financial instruments, and the rate of domestic investment should be unaffected by the local savings rate. On the other hand, informational or political barriers to international capital mobility could prevent full arbitrage and lead to a relative scarcity of capital in the credit-constrained economy, raising real expected returns to capital above those observed in international financial markets.

The data on stock returns used in this paper can shed some light on this controversy. In a frictionless world, the arbitrage condition implies that expected returns to equity and to other capital instruments in Argentina should have been approximately the same as in the world stock markets, especially in the stock markets of the emerging economies of the time. Substantial differences would be consistent with the existence of significant frictions in international capital markets. With that goal in mind, in the next sections we report measures of real returns to equity in Argentina in the period 1900–1930 and other relevant stock market indicators.

Inflation Rates and Purchasing Power Parities

To measure real returns, we have to consider the reference market baskets of alternative investors, as purchasing power parity is not reliable. Table 9.1 shows consumer and wholesale prices for Argentina (columns 1 and 2), and consumer price indexes for the United States and the United Kingdom (columns 3 and 4). It also shows these price indexes for the United States and United Kingdom in terms of Argentine paper pesos, based on exchange rates (columns 5 and 6).

Note that the period from 1900 to 1913 is generally an inflationary one for Argentina. Using prices in the United States and United Kingdom measured in pesos, we see that U.S. and U.K. investors lose less of their peso returns in translating them into home goods than do Argentine investors, but the trend is also generally inflationary. Thereafter, inflation in Argentina is relatively slower than abroad, and the Argentine exchange rate vis-à-vis the pound and dollar is trendless through 1929. Worldwide, the wartime inflation boom crests in early 1920. There follows a sharp decline in prices and a stabilization beginning around 1922. Broadly speaking, comparing the prewar period with the postwar period, purchasing power held its own better in the 1920s than in the earlier period.

DATA AND METHODOLOGY

The sources of the primary data collected were *The Review of the River Plate*, the *Boletín Oficial de la Bolsa de Comercio de Buenos Aires*, and *El Monitor de Sociedades Anónimas*. These sources contain monthly observations on transaction prices on the Argentine Bolsa, dividends paid, volumes traded, and firms' capitalization. These comprise all listed shares, including common equity and preferred shares, with dividends paid in notes convertible in gold (gold pesos) as well as in fiat money (pesos moneda nacional).

Statistics for each stock were constructed as follows: $P(t)$ = price at the end of the year (last transaction price reported in the year), and $D(t)$ = dividends

TABLE 9.1

Price Indexes

Year	Argen. WPI	Argen. CPI	U.K. CPI	U.S. CPI	U.K. PPP	U.S. PPP
1900	100		100	100	100	100
1901	88		99	100	99	100
1902	96		99	104	100	105
1903	91		100	108	98	106
1904	93		101	108	99	106
1905	101		101	108	99	106
1906	107		102	108	100	106
1907	110		104	112	103	110
1908	106		102	108	100	106
1909	116		103	108	102	106
1910	125		106	112	104	110
1911	124		107	112	105	110
1912	127		110	116	108	114
1913	127	100	112	119	110	117
1914	128	100	113	120	112	121
1915	137	107	136	122	132	120
1916	156	115	161	131	154	127
1917	194	135	194	154	179	145
1918	212	170	224	180	203	168
1919	219	160	237	207	205	198
1920	229	187	274	240	215	253
1921	182	167	249	214	255	278
1922	165	140	201	201	210	230
1923	172	137	192	204	216	246
1924	184	140	193	205	211	247
1925	187	136	194	210	198	216
1926	168	132	190	212	193	216
1927	165	131	184	208	179	203
1928	166	132	183	205	178	200
1929	161	131	181	205	178	202
1930	154	132	174	200	196	226

Sources: Argentina: before 1914, della Paolera (1988); thereafter, Domenech (1986). United Kingdom: Feinstein (1972). United States: Bureau of the Census (1975).

during year (issued before last reported transaction price). The dividend–price ratio is $D(t)/P(t)$.

Price indexes were constructed by taking the ratio of average stock prices in year t and dividing by the average stock prices in year $t-1$. These unweighted averages give the stock a weight equal to its share price, so we call these share-price weighted indexes.

If a stock does not have a reported trade in both years (or months, for the eventual monthly indicator), its rate of return is not calculated. Thus, we implicitly assume that reported stocks reflect the return for stocks not reported. This assumption is not too bad inasmuch as reported stocks are likely to be those stocks that are more widely held. However, it is likely to be biased in that stocks with bad news or in bankruptcy are not included.

RATES OF RETURN ON ARGENTINE DEBT ISSUES

Table 9.2 shows rates of return from a long-term instrument, the 1886–1887 Argentina 5% custom loan regularly quoted on the London stock exchange market, from 1900 to 1913[20] and from June 1920 to June 1928.[21] This custom loan was secured by Argentine custom receipts and was the largest loan ever floated abroad by the Argentine government. The third column shows the yields on Argentine government consols on the domestic market from 1900 to 1913. The first column shows the Argentine prime rate from 1901 to 1930. Columns 4 and 5 show rates of return on British consols and on U.S. 20-year corporate bonds.

Broadly speaking, both world and Argentine interest rates were roughly the same or somewhat higher in the period after 1922 than before 1914. From 1901 to 1913, the custom loan yielded just under 5.0%, and from 1922 to 1928 it yielded an identical amount. Similarly, in the earlier period the prime rate averaged 6.3% and in the later period 6.9%. Over the period, the spread between the custom loan and the British consol narrowed. Thus, while it is evident that there was some upward drift in the real interest rate in Argentina, its magnitude appears small and in keeping with changes in the world market-place, rather than suggesting an abrupt change in Buenos Aires' role therein. For example, in New York, 20-year corporate bonds yielded between 3.25% and 4% from 1901 to 1913, whereas they yielded between 4% and 5% from 1922 to 1929. Indeed, if anything, we see that the British consol rate was drifting higher with respect to long-term rates for U.S. issues, whereas the Argentine custom loan and prime rate were holding their own. Thus, the transition from British to U.S. dominance of the capital markets appears to have been a relatively smooth one for Argentine borrowing.

TABLE 9.2

Interest Rates on Argentine, U.K., and U.S. Debt Issues

Year	Prime Rate	Custom Loan	Domestic Bonds	U.K. Consols	U.S. 20-Year Corporate
1900	6.3	5.4	8.0	2.8	3.30
1901	7.1	5.2	7.8	2.9	3.25
1902	6.7	5.2	7.7	2.9	3.30
1903	5.3	5.0	6.4	2.8	3.45
1904	4.3	4.9	6.0	2.8	3.60
1905	4.7	4.9	5.9	2.8	3.50
1906	5.5	4.9	5.3	2.8	3.55
1907	6.5	4.9	5.6	3.0	3.80
1908	6.8	4.8	5.7	2.9	3.95
1909	6.3	4.8	5.4	3.0	3.82
1910	6.4	4.8	5.1	3.1	3.87
1911	7.0	4.8	5.2	3.2	3.94
1912	7.6	4.8	5.4	3.3	3.91
1913	7.7	4.9	5.4	3.4	4.02
1914	7.9	4.9		3.3	4.16
1915	7.6			3.8	4.20
1916	7.1			4.3	4.05
1917	6.8			4.6	4.05
1918	6.3			4.4	4.82
1919	7.2			4.6	4.81
1920	7.8	5.6		5.3	5.17
1921	7.7	5.4		5.2	5.31
1922	6.5	5.0		4.4	4.85
1923	6.5	5.0		4.3	4.68
1924	7.4	5.0		4.4	4.69
1925	6.9	5.0		4.4	4.50
1926	6.9	5.0		4.6	4.40
1927	6.3	4.9		4.6	4.30
1928	6.9	4.9		4.5	4.05
1929	6.9			4.6	4.45
1930	6.9			4.5	

Sources: Argentina: before 1914, della Paolera (1988); after, *Boletín de la Bolsa de Comercio de Buenos Aires* for prime rate and the *Economist* for custom loan. U.K. consols: Mitchell and Deane (1962). U.S. corporates: Bureau of the Census (1975).

The Size of the Argentine Bolsa

The Buenos Aires Bolsa had a market capitalization of between US $350 and $400 million in 1929, when the GDP was roughly US $4 billion. The market capitalization was thus roughly 10% of GDP. In that same year, the market capitalization of the New York Stock Exchange (NYSE) was $65 billion when U.S. gross national product was $103 billion; thus, U.S. market capitalization represented over 60% of U.S. GDP. But the U.S. stock market bubble in 1929 exaggerates the size of the U.S. market capitalization with respect to the economy. For the NYSE, 1924 is perhaps more representative, and in that year, market capitalization was 32% of GDP. To offer another comparison, the Italian stock market in 1992 had a capitalization of less than 15% of Italian GDP.

Two further points should be noted. First, the Argentine stock market did not list the major railway issues—the Southern, the Western, the Pacific, and the Central. Together, the Argentine railway issues had a market capitalization in 1929 of 92.5 million British pounds, or somewhat more than the market capitalization of the entire Argentine Bolsa. If we were to add these issues to the Argentine stock market, its capitalization would rise to above 20% of GDP. Second, we have included only ordinary stock, whereas the NYSE figures include preferred stock as well.

Table 9.3 offers a more formal comparison with modern emerging markets. The table gives market capitalization-to-GDP ratios for 18 non-OECD countries. The median ratio is 21%, which is similar to the capitalization of Argentina's equity issues, including the railway shares, in 1929.

In sum, the market capitalization of the Argentine stock market was reasonably substantial for an emerging market. Although it did not represent Argentina's foremost industrial concerns, the railroads, it represented a high proportion of the remaining ones and a substantial amount of asset values.

Turnover on the Argentine Bolsa

Turnover—the extent to which outstanding shares are actively traded—varies considerably across stock markets and within stock markets over time. Trading on the Argentine Bolsa represented some 5% of market capitalization during the 1920s; that is, on average only 1 share in 20 turned over in a given year. Again, this figure does not include the most heavily traded issues, the railroads. In the hectic New York market of the 1920s, trading volume sometimes more than equaled the market capitalization. However, in the 1950s and 1960s, trading volume on the NYSE was more like 15% to 20% of market capitalization, and today it is roughly 50%. In 1992, trading on the Italian stock market was 20% of market capitalization. Table 9.3 shows that the trading turnover on

TABLE 9.3

Modern Non-OECD Country Stock Market Indicators, 1986–1993

Country	Market Capitalization to GDP	Turnover
Argentina	.06	.34
Brazil	.11	.48
Chile	.52	.08
Colombia	.07	.07
Hong Kong	1.36	.44
India	.16	.50
Indonesia	.06	.23
Israel	.21	.72
Jordan	.57	.22
Korea, Republic of	.40	.93
Malaysia	1.28	.24
Nigeria	.04	.01
Pakistan	.11	.08
Philippines	.24	.23
Singapore	1.04	.34
South Africa	1.54	.05
Thailand	.36	.70
Venezuela	.10	.15
Zimbabwe	.18	.03
Median, Non-OECD	.21	.235
Median, 23 OECD	.24	.31

Source: Demirguc-Kunt and Levine (1996).

modern emerging markets is about 20% to 25%.

Thus, the Argentine Bolsa's trading rate in the 1920s was relatively slow, either by contemporary standards or past ones, but by no means trivial. Although the Bolsa cannot be considered highly liquid, it would be a mistake not to take this market seriously as a channel of finance.

Table 9.4 shows estimates of the volume of paper peso equity transactions on the Argentine Bolsa from 1914 to 1930. In nominal terms, volume peaked in 1918. But the latter part of this period was one in which the price level was falling, so in real terms, volume was close to trendless. It should be noted that the shares of the largest firms on the exchange traded regularly, to the extent that a trade was recorded in virtually every week for which we have records. This rate of trade is certainly sufficient to provide a reasonable record of valuations.

TABLE 9.4

Trading Volume on the Buenos Aires Bolsa

Year	Annual Transactions Volume	Real Transactions Volume
(million paper pesos)	(1914 = 100)	
1914	7.35	100
1915	5.44	69
1916	7.41	87
1917	19.02	191
1918	40.04	323
1919	27.48	233
1920	20.81	150
1921	31.05	253
1922	32.50	314
1923	30.04	296
1924	16.02	157
1925	12.39	123
1926	21.80	223
1927	27.83	288
1928	27.30	280
1929	22.29	231
1930	11.65	119

Source: *Boletín de la Bolsa de Comercio de Buenos Aires.*

Rates of Return on Equity

Dividend–Price Ratio

One measure of the expected return to stocks is the dividend–price ratio. If price movements are difficult to forecast, as one expects on an equity market, movements in the dividend–price ratio may reflect changing ex ante returns to the market. In this respect, there do not appear to have been enormous changes in the ex ante returns on the Argentine Bolsa. Table 9.5 reports dividend–price ratios for a group of common stocks with nominal capitalizations in excess of 10 million paper pesos. Generally speaking, these represent the bulk of the Bolsa's market capitalization.

Dividend–price ratios for the Argentine stocks were roughly 6% from 1906 to 1912, in the Belle Époque, not far above the 4.7% average for U.S. stocks in the same period. From 1926 to 1930, Argentine dividend–price ratios were roughly 5%, a narrower spread than the 4.4% average for U.S. stocks in the same period. The Argentine dividend–price ratios in the late 1920s are also

TABLE 9.5

Dividend–Price Ratios for Large-Capitalization Argentine Stocks and U.S. Stocks

	Argentine Large-Cap. Stocks		U.S. Common Stock
Year	Mean	No. of Stocks	Cowles Commission
1906	.03	7	.040
1907	.09	7	.054
1908	.08	7	.049
1909	.06	7	.043
1910	.05	7	.048
1911	.06	7	.049
1912	.06	7	.049
1913	.08	7	.054
1914	.07	16	.050
1915	.08	16	.050
1916	.06	16	.056
1917	.12	16	.078
1918	.09	16	.072
1919	.09	16	.058
1920	.12	27	.061
1921	.07	27	.065
1922	.08	27	.058
1923	.06	27	.059
1924	.07	27	.059
1925	.06	27	.052
1926	.05	27	.053
1927	.04	27	.048
1928	.05	27	.040
1929	.05	27	.035
1930	.05	27	.043

Sources: Argentina: Authors' calculations. United States: Bureau of the Census (1975).

lower relative to returns on debt, both domestically and abroad, than in the Belle Époque.

There are two possible interpretations. One is that ex ante required returns had fallen, if price expectations were low. Such an interpretation, of course, is inconsistent with the view that costs of capital were unusually high for Argentina with respect to world markets during this period. The alternative is that Argentina's stock prices were expected to appreciate substantially. Let us now turn to ex post returns.

TABLE 9.6

Argentine Stock Market, 1906–1930: Share-Weighted Stock Indexes

Year	Price Index, Nominal	Price Index, Real	No. of Companies
1906	100	100	7
1907	94	92	7
1908	100	101	7
1909	117	108	7
1910	123	105	7
1911	119	102	7
1912	123	103	7
1913	104	87	7
1914	83	70	7
1915	81	63	16
1916	82	56	16
1917	92	51	16
1918	117	59	16
1919	109	53	16
1920	86	40	16
1921	64	38	27
1922	63	41	27
1923	66	41	27
1924	65	38	27
1925	67	39	27
1926	73	47	27
1927	79	51	27
1928	87	56	27
1929	81	54	27
1930	67	47	27

Sources: Authors' calculations, real prices deflated by PPI.

Price Indexes

Table 9.6 shows Argentine stock prices based on high market capitalization stocks. This index is constructed like the Dow Jones stock index, with the shares included weighted by their share value. From 1906 to 1912, in the Belle Époque, the real value of shares on the Argentine stock market was roughly stable. After 1912, however, the stock market dropped for two years and continued to sink until 1920. Beginning in 1920, however, the stock market stabilized and then rallied spiritedly from 1925 to 1928. In 1930, the stock market was still well above its level in the first half of the decade. There are thus grounds for suspecting that, although over the period as a whole the trend of stock prices was downward, expectations of price appreciation might have become a factor in investment decisions in the latter part of the 1920s. Such expectations of rising prices, with implied increases in market valuations of firms, would not appear to be consistent with dismal economic prospects.

Table 9.7 shows the comparable price levels for the U.S. stock market, as measured by the Standard & Poor's (S&P) 500 index and deflated by the U.S. consumer price index (CPI). The comparison between the two series is made graphically in Figure 9.1. Note that the U.S. stock market price level fell, in real terms, slightly more than the Argentine market from 1906 to 1920. Thus, the equity market slide in Argentina was mirrored in the United States, yet the performance of the U.S. economy during this period can hardly be characterized as dismal.

We have also constructed a stock price index where the high-capitalization stocks are weighted by their market capitalization, as they are in the U.S. S&P 500 index. However, the capitalization data were not reported as systematically before 1912 as they were thereafter. Moreover, a single entity, the Provincial Bank of Buenos Aires, represents most of the capitalization of the stock market reported here from 1906 to 1914. As a consequence, we view the data, reported in Table 9.8, as primarily confirming the trends reported in Table 9.6.

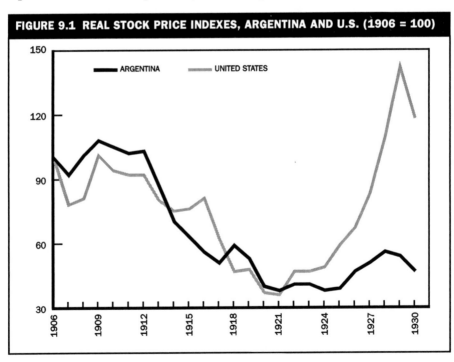

FIGURE 9.1 REAL STOCK PRICE INDEXES, ARGENTINA AND U.S. (1906 = 100)

TABLE 9.7

U.S. Stock Prices, Standard & Poor's 500

Year	Nominal	Real
1899	65.25	70.47
1900	63.80	68.90
1901	81.33	87.83
1902	87.34	90.70
1903	74.79	74.79
1904	73.13	73.13
1905	93.26	93.26
1906	100.00	100.00
1907	81.33	78.42
1908	80.71	80.71
1909	100.73	100.73
1910	96.99	93.53
1911	95.85	92.43
1912	98.86	92.04
1913	88.28	80.12
1914	83.82	75.44
1915	86.20	76.31
1916	98.24	80.99
1917	88.17	61.84
1918	78.22	46.93
1919	91.08	47.52
1920	82.78	37.25
1921	71.16	35.91
1922	87.24	46.88
1923	88.90	47.06
1924	93.88	49.46
1925	115.66	59.48
1926	130.60	66.53
1927	159.13	82.62
1928	206.95	109.03
1929	269.92	142.20
1930	218.15	117.80

Source: Bureau of the Census (1975).

TABLE 9.8

Argentine Stock Prices: Major Companies Weighted by Market Capitalization

Year	Nominal	Real (1906 = 100)	No. of Companies
1899	56.65	68.10	6
1900	61.70	66.02	6
1901	56.87	69.15	6
1902	57.00	63.53	6
1903	71.33	83.87	6
1904	80.99	93.19	6
1905	105.57	111.84	6
1906	100.00	100.00	6
1907	115.01	111.87	9
1908	131.47	132.71	9
1909	145.82	134.51	9
1910	176.78	151.32	9
1911	172.91	149.21	9
1912	162.74	137.12	12
1913	140.87	118.68	12
1914	123.95	103.62	12
1915	98.89	77.24	12
1916	99.33	68.13	12
1917	108.28	59.72	13
1918	127.94	64.57	13
1919	118.36	57.83	13
1920	102.78	48.02	16
1921	100.18	58.90	16
1922	107.35	69.61	16
1923	107.27	66.73	16
1924	111.14	64.63	16
1925	114.64	65.59	20
1926	121.88	77.63	20
1927	130.62	84.71	22
1928	146.77	94.60	24
1929	145.19	96.49	24
1930	127.92	88.88	24

Real Rates of Return

Table 9.9 presents real rates of return to common stock denominated in domestic currency. The figures reveal that, on average, real rates of return were substantially higher in the 1920s than in the period from 1906–1913. However, far from suggesting isolation of Argentina from international capital markets in the 1920s, these figures are consistent with Díaz Alejandro's view that in the late 1920s Argentina was as firmly integrated with international capital markets as ever: The increase in real rates of return to equity paralleled the one experienced by the United States, as evidenced by the decade averages reported from Sylla et al. reproduced in Table 9.9.[22]

TABLE 9.9

Average Annual Rates of Return to Argentine Stocks

Year	Real Return (%)	Prior Decade Average Argentina	Prior Decade Average United States
1907	−0.3		
1908	19.6		
1909	13.1		
1910	3.1		
1911	2.7		
1912	7.0		
1913	−9.1		
1914	−14.8		
1915	−2.1	1.7	3.4
1916	−5.3		
1917	0.1		
1918	27.6		
1919	−2.0		
1920	−14.7	−1.7	−4.0
1921	0.5		
1922	15.4		
1923	7.0		
1924	−1.1		
1925	7.8	2.9	3.7
1926	26.7		
1927	14.6		
1928	14.1		
1929	1.8		
1930	−9.9	7.3	14.2

Sources: Argentina: Authors' calculations. United States: Sylla et al. (1994).

British-Owned Argentine Railways

In 1929, on the eve of the collapse of the international commodity prices, the Argentine railways continued to trade at or above par on the London market, having, if anything, risen in price over the past several years.[23] Thus, Argentine equity issues appeared remarkably robust well after the end of Britain's role as the main supplier of capital and despite the rising pressure of increased real rates of interest on world capital markets in the 1920s.

CONCLUSION

A preliminary analysis of returns to common stock in the Argentine Bolsa in the period from 1900 to 1930 suggests that rates of return to capital, be they in nominal or real terms, reflected worldwide capital market conditions. Real rates of return in the period 1920–1930 were above those of the Belle Époque (1906–1912), but the implied increase in the cost of capital was not out of sync with international capital markets. That is, stock yields right before the Great Depression suggest that returns to capital investment in Argentina were not far from those that investors would have obtained in world capital markets. This finding is consistent with Díaz Alejandro's view that World War I left Argentina convalescent but firmly integrated in world financial markets and ready to grow at a healthy pace without any need of drastic changes in the outward-oriented, foreign-capital-friendly policies pursued until the Great Depression.

It is our hope that the research agenda initiated with this paper will shed some light not only on a particular period of Argentina's economic growth but also on the sources of growth in general, as well as make a contribution to the better understanding of the so-called emerging economies and their often puzzling capital markets.

ACKNOWLEDGMENTS

The views expressed here are those of the authors and do not necessarily reflect those of the Federal Reserve Bank of Philadelphia, the Federal Reserve Bank of Dallas, or the Federal Reserve system. Victoria Kruglikov and John Benedetto provided excellent research assistance. Comments and assistance from our discussant, Colin Lewis, were much appreciated. Comments from Alan Taylor, John Coatsworth, Loretta Mester, Gerardo della Paolera, Richard Sylla, Gail Triner, and participants in the Conference on Latin America and the World Economy in the Nineteenth and Twentieth Centuries and the Columbia University Seminar on Economic History are gratefully acknowledged. We have heavy institutional debts, including to the Center for Latin American

Economies of the Federal Reserve Bank of Dallas, the Bellagio Study and Conference Center of the Rockefeller Foundation, and to Marta Gutierrez and the staff of the Tornquist Library at the Central Bank of Argentina, but we are particularly grateful to the president of the Federal Reserve of Dallas, Robert McTeer Jr., without whose support this project would not have been possible.

Notes

1. Di Tella and Zymelman (1967).
2. Díaz Alejandro (1975).
3. Prebisch (1928).
4. Taylor (1992).
5. Cortés Conde (1994).
6. Taylor (1992), p. 147.
7. Sylla et al. (1994).
8. Solow (1957).
9. ECLA (1959).
10. Taylor (1992), p. 10.
11. ECLA (1959), Cuadro 85, p. 71.
12. ECLA (1959), Table XV of Appendix II.
13. Taylor (1992), p. 919.
14. For example, Koopmans (1965).
15. *Economist*, 24 March 1928, vol. 106, p. 599.
16. *Economist*, 4 August 1928, vol. 107, p. 234.
17. Wortman (n.d.), cited in Díaz Alejandro (1975).
18. Peters (1934) and Phelps (1938), cited in Taylor (1992).
19. Taylor (1992), p. 922.
20. della Paolera (1988).
21. *Economist*, last issue in June of each year for 1920–1928.
22. Sylla et al. (1994).
23. Lewis (1974, 1983).

REFERENCES

Brown, Stephen J., William Goetzmann, and Stephen A. Ross. "Survival." *Journal of Finance* 50 (July 1995): 853–873.

Bureau of the Census, U.S. Department of Commerce. *Historical Statistics of the United States: Colonial Times to 1970.* Washington, DC: Government Printing Office, 1975.

Cortés Conde, Roberto. "Estimaciones del producto bruto interno de Argentina, 1875–1935." Documento de Trabajo no. 3, Universidad de San Andres, Buenos Aires, Argentina, 1994.

della Paolera, Gerardo. "How the Argentine Economy Performed during the International Gold Standard: A Reexamination." Ph.D. dissertation, University of Chicago, 1988.

Demirguc-Kunt, Asli, and Ross Levine. "Stock Market Development and Financial Intermediaries: Stylized Facts." *The World Bank Economic Review,* May 1996.

Díaz Alejandro, Carlos F. *Essays on the Economic History of the Argentine Republic.* New Haven, CT: Yale University Press, 1975.

Di Tella, Guido, and M. Zymelman. *Las etapas del desarrollo económico argentino.* Buenos Aires: EUDEBA, 1967.

Di Tella, Guido, and M. Zymelman. "Argentina, Australia, and Brazil Before 1929." In *Argentina, Australia and Canada: Studies in Comparative Development, 1870–1965,* edited by D. C. M. Platt and Guido Di Tella. New York: St. Martin's Press, 1985.

Domenech, Roberto L. "Estadísticas de la evolución económica de Argentina, 1913–1984." *Estudios de IEERAL* 9, no. 39 (1986): 103–185.

ECLA (United Nations Economic Commission for Latin America). "El desarrollo econ—mico de la Argentina." In *Analisis y proyecciones del desarrollo económico,* vol. 5. Mexico: United Nations Department of Social and Economic Affairs, 1959.

Feinstein, C. H. *National Income Expenditure and Output of the United Kingdom, 1855–1965.* Cambridge: Cambridge University Press, 1972.

Koopmans, Tjalling. "On the Concept of Optimal Economic Growth." In *The Econometric Approach to Developing Planning* by Tjalling Koopmans. Amsterdam: North Holland, 1965.

Lewis, Colin M. "British-Owned Railways in Argentina, 1857–1947." Ph.D. dissertation, University of Exeter, 1974.

Lewis, Colin M. *British Railways in Argentina, 1857–1914.* London: Athlone, 1983.

Mitchell, B. R., and Phyllis Deane. *Abstract of British Historical Statistics.* Cambridge: Cambridge University Press, 1962.

Peters, Harold E. *The Foreign Debt of the Argentine Republic.* Baltimore: The Johns Hopkins Press, 1934.

Phelps, Vernon L. *The International Economic Position of Argentina.* Philadelphia: Oxford University Press, 1938.

Prebisch, Raul. "La posición de 1928 y las variaciones económicas de la última década." *Revista Económica* 2 (Jan. 1928): 1–8.

Solow, Robert M. "Technical Change and the Aggregate Production Function." *Review of Economics and Statistics* 39 (1957): 312–321.

Sylla, Richard, Jack W. Wilson, and Charles P. Jones. "U.S. Financial Markets and Long-Term Economic Growth, 1790–1989." In *American Economic Development in Historical Perspective,* edited by Thomas Weiss and Donald Schaefer, 28–52. Stanford, CA: Stanford University Press, 1994.

Taylor, Alan M. "External Dependence, Demographic Burdens, and Argentina Economic Decline After the Belle Époque." *Journal of Economic History* 52 (1992): 907–936.

Wortman, Charles. "Argentina, Australia, and Brazil: Bonds in the London Capital Market, 1929–39." Unpublished manuscript, Yale University.

PART IV

Institutions and Economic Growth

Most of the chapters in this book contribute to knowledge about institutions and their impact on economic growth. Coatsworth (Chapter 1), for example, assesses the relative weight of differing institutional configurations in shaping nineteenth-century trends, whereas Alston, Libecap, and Mueller (Chapter 2) compare the effects of differing frontier property rights regimes in Brazil and the United States. Several chapters analyze the role of financial institutions in Argentina and Brazil to assess their effectiveness in promoting market integration and channeling capital to industrial development. Later chapters in the concluding section of this book analyze government policies in key areas of economic activity. Cliometricians take politics, legislation and regulation, formal rules of the economic game as well as unwritten customary practices, and all manner of cultural norms very seriously.[1]

The three chapters in this section take particular institutions and institutional changes as their main focus. Each of them develops quantitative tests for hypotheses about the impact of institutions on productivity or welfare. Haber's essay (Chapter 10) takes a new look at a topic which has occupied him for some time, that is, the importance of government regulations that shape financial markets and thus help or hinder the flow of capital to finance industrial development.[2] In this chapter, Haber goes a step further. The legislative reforms introduced by Brazil's new republican government in 1890, including laws that established limited liability and mandatory disclosure of financial data for shareholders, dramatically increased the flow of capital through expanding securities markets to industrial firms. However, other government policies also tended to promote industrial development. To assess whether the 1890 legislative changes had an independent effect, Haber tests the hypothesis that publicly traded companies contributed disproportionately to productivity advance, using data from the textile industry. He shows that companies that raised funds in the market tended to adopt new technology more rapidly, in contrast to companies that retained the old partnership or family organization and thus faced constraints on their ability to raise money for such purposes.

Dye's essay (Chapter 11) makes the point that important institutional changes can occur without direct government intervention, through trial and error in the marketplace.[3] The Cuban sugar industry grew rapidly between 1898 and the late 1920s. The standard account points to the creation of huge, highly efficient sugar mills with a voracious appetite for cane as a key factor in the industry's growth. But the standard account also charges that the new *centrales* succeeded only by imposing rigid controls over cane production—either by buying up land to manage it directly, or through long-term contracts with independent or tenant producers, called *colonos*, that deprived them of any decision-making power. Thus the Cuban sugar industry became more efficient, but the growers of the cane actually suffered. Dye tests this part of the standard account by taking a fresh look at the history of the *colono* contract and by deconstructing its terms. He concludes that both parties to the stricter contracts benefited from the productivity increases the *centrales* made possible. Dye's work on the *colono* contract is an excellent example of what is sometimes called the "new institutional history," a growing body of work that tackles the thorny task of modeling and measuring the impact of institutional change.

Sometimes institutional changes come in huge bundles all at once. Revolutions, like the great upheaval in Mexico between 1911 and 1917, often generate new political leaders and alter both the basis of political power and the institutions through which it is exercised. They can transform society by displacing old interest groups and social classes, and they can certainly play havoc with economic activity and organization. Economic historians tend to be skeptical, however, about the extent to which such processes can actually alter the parameters of economic life. Gómez-Galvarriato's essay (Chapter 12) uses new wage and price data she has collected to assess the impact of the Mexican Revolution on real wages. She also contributes to the debate over the causes of the Revolution, with new wage series for the decade prior to the conflict.

NOTES

1. For a theoretical discussion, see Douglass North's Nobel Laureate lecture (1994).
2. See, for example, Haber (1997).
3. See also Dye (1998).

REFERENCES

Dye, Alan. *Cuban Sugar in the Age of Mass Production: Technology and the Effects of the Sugar Central, 1899–1929.* Stanford: Stanford University Press, 1998.

Haber, Stephen. "Financial Markets and Industrial Development: A Comparative Study of Governmental Regulation, Financial Innovation, and Industrial Structure in Brazil and Mexico, 1840–1930." In *How Latin America Fell Behind: Essays on the Economic Histories of Mexico and Brazil, 1800–1914,* edited by Stephen Haber, 146–178. Stanford: Stanford University Press, 1997.

North, Douglass C. "Economic Performance Through Time." *American Economic Review* 84 (1994): 359–368.

10

The Efficiency Consequences of Institutional Change: Financial Market Regulation and Industrial Productivity Growth in Brazil, 1866–1934

Stephen Haber
Stanford University

In recent years economists and economic historians have become increasingly interested in the role of institutional change in the process of economic growth. One of the major variants of the recent research on institutions, most commonly associated with Douglass North, holds that economic growth is the outcome of productivity increases that are brought about by the more efficient allocation of the factors of production through more smoothly functioning markets. At the core of increases in the efficiency of markets is the reform of institutions—the rules and regulations enforced by the state that both permit and bound the operation of markets. Institutional reform, these scholars argue, makes credible commitments possible, property rights more secure, and contracts enforceable, thereby lowering transactions costs and increasing the range of exchanges that are mediated through the market.[1]

This view is advanced not as a set of necessary truths, but as a set of hypotheses to be tested. Unfortunately, operationalizing the testable implications of these hypotheses has proved somewhat elusive: It is extraordinarily difficult to develop econometric evidence that demonstrates that changes in institutions make markets function more smoothly, and that changes in the efficiency of markets have any demonstrable effect on productivity growth.

Attempts to create such econometric evidence have largely been unsuccessful for four reasons. First, most scholars operating within the new institutional economics (NIE) have looked at economies in which institutional change has taken place gradually. This has meant that it is difficult to pinpoint particular institutional reforms that have been crucial for the growth of productivity. Second, most scholars operating within the NIE have looked at economies that have had long histories of well-developed markets. In these economies the market has anticipated institutional changes, meaning that it is difficult, if not impossible, to use the history of developed countries as a laboratory to assess the impact of institutional reforms.[2] Third, endogeneity may exist between the market and institutional development: As markets become more efficient they may affect the process of institutional development, which, in turn, feeds back into markets, and so on. Fourth, there are numerous technical difficulties in the measurement of productivity, which are made even more difficult still by the problem of tying any change in the growth of productivity to some exogenous change in institutions.

The most unambiguous results in institutional analysis are therefore to be found in those historical cases where there have been dramatic changes in institutions, where markets were not well developed prior to those institutional changes, and where there is sufficient quantitative data available to measure the productivity consequences of institutional change.[3] An ideal laboratory for this kind of research is the economic history of less-developed economies during the early stages of their economic development.

This paper offers a contribution to this literature through the examination of the history of capital market regulation and industrial productivity growth in Brazil during the period 1866 to 1934. I focus on capital market regulation because capital markets are especially crucial for economic growth and are also notoriously subject to government regulation. Indeed, it is widely accepted that the details of such regulation have profound effects on the structure of banking and securities markets. What is less clear is whether these differences in the structure of capital markets have any discernible impact on the performance of the rest of the economy.[4]

I focus on the case of Brazil during the period 1866–1934 for the following reasons. First, Brazil provides a counterfactual test of the proposition that the specific features of government regulation have a profound effect on the development of securities markets because the overthrow of the Brazilian monarchy in 1889 and the founding of a federal republic brought about a dramatic revision of the preexisting laws. Second, by focusing on the early stages of the development of the securities markets the problem of simultaneity is eliminated: The market could not anticipate changes in institutions because the market was poorly developed prior to these changes in regulation. Third, Brazil is unusual in that there is abundant data at the firm level that permit the estimation of productivity growth by firm type and size. It is therefore possible in the Brazilian case to estimate the efficiency gains afforded to manufacturers by calculating the differences in the levels of total factor productivity between those firms that mobilized capital by selling debt and equity to the investing public and those that used more traditional, personalized channels.

I carry out this analysis using panel data techniques, which involve linking together 18 censuses covering the period 1866–1934 with production, financial, and dummy variable information for 558 textile firms. I estimate time-series, cross-sectional regressions for the census years following the institutional reforms of the 1890s (the years 1905–1927) that permit the measurement of the impact of the ability of firms to take the joint-stock corporate form, sell equity on the public markets, and issue bonded debt on their level of total factor productivity.

I argue that changes in government regulations had a profound effect on the growth and performance of industry. The first reform was the establishment of limited liability. Limited liability overcame a fundamental asymmetry in incentives: Before 1890 the law created disincentives for entrepreneurs to issue debt and disincentives for investors to purchase equity because an investor was held to be fully liable for a firm's debts in the case of insolvency, even if the investor had traded away the stock. From the point of view of founding groups of investors, the new limited-liability law meant that they could go out to the debt markets and not be personally liable for those debts if the company failed. From the point of view of potential investors from outside the founding groups, limited liability meant that they could purchase equity shares in firms and not have to be concerned that they would be held personally liable for the firm's debts if it went bankrupt.

The second crucial reforms in securities markets were those related to mandatory disclosure. The 1890 regulatory law required firms to produce financial statements, reprint at least the balance sheets in public documents, such as a newspaper or state gazette, and include a statement in the report about the identities of each stockholder and the number of shares owned. In the early stages of the use of the market it is likely the case that investors made decisions about which firms to invest in based on the reputations of the founding group of entrepreneurs. Over time, however, potential investors had far more information to go on: They knew who held controlling interest in the firm and they had a great deal of financial information available, including the firm's history of dividend payments, its level of indebtedness, the size of its reserves, and the liquidity of their investment.

The effects of these regulatory reforms were to reduce transaction and monitoring costs, thereby lowering the cost of capital to firms that adopted the joint-stock limited-liability form. First, mandatory disclosure made it easier for investors to monitor managers. Second, limited-liability eliminates the need for investors to monitor one another. In a situation in which liability is not limited, investors must create costly covenants that restrict the transferability of ownership rights to individuals with sufficient wealth to cover their share of any liability resulting from insolvency. Alternatively, investors must engage in costly monitoring to verify the liquidity of their partners.[5] In the absence of these reforms, access to capital could have served as a barrier to entry because some firms could have used the reputational capital or personal connections of their owners to obtain investment funds from third parties, whereas most other firms would not have been able to do so.

Prior to these reforms few firms utilized the market to mobilize capital, and Brazilian industry was small in size—even by Latin American standards. After the reforms, large numbers of firms were financed through the sale of stocks and bonds to the investing public. The result of lower capital costs was that already-existing firms were able to grow faster than they could have otherwise, and new firms could enter the market because their cost of capital was lower than their expected, risk-adjusted rate of return. Not only did industry grow by leaps and bounds (capacity, as measured by spindlage, grew nearly 30-fold from 1881 to 1925), but limited-liability joint-stock companies became the dominant form of corporate organization. In the case under study here—the cotton textile industry—70% of the industry's installed capacity in 1925 was located in joint-stock firms.

The use of the securities markets had similarly unambiguous effects on the performance of industry. There was a sizable difference in absolute levels and rates of growth of productivity between firms that used the markets to obtain finance and those that continued to mobilize capital through traditional informal avenues. These differences in total factor productivity (TFP) hold regardless of firm size. The primary impact of the securities markets on productivity was not, therefore, that joint-stock firms could take advantage of economies of scale in production. The increase in TFP was produced by the fact that limited-liability joint-stock companies were able to move into the market for fine-weave, high-quality output, which earned a price premium. Because the production of high-quality output requires machines to be run more slowly, it necessitates more machines per worker than the production of low-quality cloth. Under these conditions, firms with access to low-cost capital had a distinct advantage. Thus, limited-liability joint-stock companies were able to use their access to relatively less expensive capital to move into this market, whereas privately owned firms, which tended to be more capital constrained, were not. The result was increased allocative efficiency: Those entrepreneurs who could best combine the factors of production and choose the optimal output mix were able to mobilize capital that otherwise would not have been available to them. The implication is that had it been difficult for smaller entrepreneurs to use the securities markets to obtain investment capital, the growth of TFP in Brazilian cotton textile manufacturing would have been significantly lower.

One might argue that causality ran the other way: Firms did not have high TFP because they were publicly owned; rather, they were publicly owned because they had high TFP or because they were founded by entrepreneurs with a proven track record of business success in other areas. There are two problems with this line of reasoning. The first is that most limited-liability joint-stock companies did not start out as privately owned firms that at some point in their life cycle decided to change corporate form. In the vast majority of cases, publicly owned firms were entirely new enterprises without track records in the textile industry: Their initial finance came from the sale of equity to the investing public. The second problem is that from the point of view of economic growth it does not matter whether entrepreneurs were screened in some way by brokers or other intermediaries based on their previous record. Had the securities markets not existed, or had access to them been limited in some way, these more able entrepreneurs would have been capital constrained. They therefore would have directed smaller enterprises, or perhaps not founded firms at all. The result would have been a deadweight loss to the Brazilian economy.

This is not to argue that the only constraint faced by Brazilian industry was access to capital and that the only relevant policy change in Brazil related to the regulation of financial markets. Coterminous with the reform of financial market regulations were increases in tariff protection and the expansion of the railroad network, which had begun to develop in the 1880s but which now grew rapidly under the combined influence of federal subsidies and the availability of foreign capital.[6] It is to argue, however, that one crucial piece of the puzzle explaining the lack of industrial development before 1890 and rapid industrial growth after 1890 was access to capital. Changes in the rules and regulations governing the operation of banks and capital markets were a necessary, but not a sufficient, condition for the expansion of Brazilian industry.

This paper is organized into four sections. Section I explains the choice of the textile industry as a test case and discusses the data sources and their limitations. Section II discusses the institutional history of financial market regulation in Brazil. Section III examines the effects of regulatory reforms, paying particular attention to the impact of greater use of the financial markets on industrial productivity. The final section contains conclusions.

I: STUDY PARAMETERS

Cotton Textiles as a Test Case

This paper focuses on the cotton textile manufacture, but I would expect that the relationships between access to capital, firm size, and TFP growth would extend to a broad range of industries in early-twentieth-century Brazil. In fact, Brazil's securities markets were used to mobilize capital for urban tramways and municipal railroads, utility companies, navigation companies, banks, insurance companies, and sugar refineries, as well as a diverse range of industrial enterprises, including beer breweries, food processors, glassworks, and cement manufacturers.

I focus on the cotton textile industry for both practical and theoretical reasons. First, cotton textiles were the most important manufacturing industry in Brazil during the period under study.[7] Second, both the Brazilian government and Brazil's various manufacturers' associations regularly gathered systematic census-type data on the textile industry that permit the estimation of TFP. Third, there are compelling theoretical reasons to focus on cotton textiles. Textile manufacturing is characterized by capital divisibilities and modest scale economies. Thus, the minimum efficient scale of production is small enough that firms may be financed through traditional sole-proprietor and partnership arrangements, as well as through the use of impersonal financial markets. This permits productivity comparisons across various firm types and sizes that would not be possible in most other mechanized industries, such as cement, beer, chemicals, or steel, where there were few firms that were not financed through the sale of equity.[8]

The Data

The analysis presented here rests on three bodies of evidence. The first is the censuses that cover all the mechanized cotton textile companies—both privately and publicly owned—operating in Brazil. Prior to the 1890s this was roughly 20 firms, growing to 117 firms by 1907, to 205 firms by 1914, and to 228 firms in 1927. In addition to carrying information about each firm's output (by both value and volume), machinery, and workforce, these censuses also identify the owners of each mill and (from 1905 to 1934) include detailed financial information about each firm. I have retrieved and put into machine-readable form the censuses from 1866, 1875, 1881, 1883, 1895, 1898, 1901, 1905, 1907, 1908, 1914, 1915, 1923 to 1927, and 1934.[9] Because the data are presented in each census at the firm level, it is possible to cross-check individual firm's reported data from census to census in order to isolate errors in variables. The detailed nature of the censuses also permits the calculation of ratios of factor inputs to one another and to various types of output in order to isolate firms that clearly under- or overreported inputs and outputs. Following earlier researchers, I culled these observations from the data sets used to estimate production functions and factor productivity.[10] One caveat holds for all the censuses: Many of the smallest privately owned firms provided only partial responses to the census. Since these very small firms tended to account for a small percentage of output but a correspondingly high percentage of factor inputs, their exclusion from the estimation of production functions and total factor productivity likely biases the TFP estimates for small, privately owned firms upward. This biases the results against the hypotheses advanced in this paper.

The second body of evidence analyzed here is the semiannual financial statements of 15 publicly traded cotton textile manufacturing firms, covering the years 1895 to 1940. These 15 firms are not a random sample, but were chosen because it was possible to retrieve complete sets of their financial statements.[11] These 15 firms controlled 42% of the industry's installed capacity in 1905 and 24% even as late as 1934. It is clear from comparing the financial data in the censuses with the financial data in these reports that these firms were more likely to have significant long-term bonded debt than was the norm, even for publicly traded joint-stock companies. These financial statements permit, however, a more detailed study of the structure of debt and equity than do the censuses.

The third body of evidence is data on the secondary markets for textile firm securities that were retrieved from the major newspapers for Rio de Janeiro and São Paulo. In addition, small regional stock exchanges operated in Bahia, Pernambuco, Minas Gerais, and other states as well, and it appears that, similar to the Rio de Janeiro and São Paulo exchanges, these served as secondary markets for the debt and equity of nearby cotton mills.[12] No data have been retrieved on these smaller markets.

II: FINANCIAL MARKET REGULATION IN BRAZIL

Textile Finance Before 1890

Throughout most of the nineteenth century, institutions designed to mobilize impersonal sources of capital were largely absent in Brazil. An organized stock exchange had functioned in Rio de Janeiro since early in the century, but it was small and was seldom used to finance industrial companies. Brazil's mill owners could also not appeal to the banking system to provide them with capital: As late as 1888 Brazil had only 26 banks, whose combined capital totaled only 145,000 contos—roughly U.S. $48 million. Only 7 of the country's 20 states had any banks at all, and half of all deposits were held by a few banks in Rio de Janeiro.[13] The absence of banks not only restricted the amount of credit available to textile entrepreneurs but also meant that banks could not underwrite securities trading or finance securities speculation the way they did in the United States or Western Europe.

The slow development of these institutions can be traced in large part to public policies designed to restrict entry into banking and limit abuses of the public by unscrupulous corporate promoters. The imperial government, which held the right to charter banks, was primarily concerned with creating a small number of super-banks that could serve as a source of government finance and that would promote monetary stability. Unfortunately, the government's continual shift in regulatory policies prevented the development of even a tightly controlled centralized banking system along the lines of many Western European countries.[14]

The imperial government also created regulations designed to discourage the corporate form of ownership. Brazil's 1860 incorporation law required the promoters of joint-stock companies to obtain the special permission of the imperial government, prohibited investors from purchasing stocks on margin, and restricted banks from investing in corporate securities. In addition, it did not permit limited liability. In fact, under Brazilian law an investor could be held liable for a firm's debts for a period of five years after he had sold the stock.[15]

Given these constraints on the formation of financial intermediaries, the securities markets were rarely used to mobilize capital for industry. Not coincidentally, the textile industry remained small. In 1866 the entire modern sector of the industry numbered nine firms, none of which were joint-stock companies. The early 1870s witnessed the creation of two joint-stock companies that raised their initial capital through public offerings in Rio de Janeiro.[16] Even with these two joint-stock companies, the capacity of the Brazilian cotton textile industry was only 85,000 spindles in 1881 (see Table 10.1).[17] Not only was this minuscule by the standards of the United States, which in 1880 had an industry of some 10.6 million spindles, but it was also small by Latin American standards. Circa 1880, Mexico's cotton textile industry was more than three times the size of Brazil's (249,000 spindles) even though Mexican national income was only 55% that of Brazil.[18]

Regulatory Reforms and Outcomes

In the last decades of the nineteenth century, a dramatic reform of the regulations governing Brazil's capital markets took place. These changes began in 1882, when the government removed the requirement that joint-stock companies obtain special charters from Parliament. This reform also lowered, from 25% to 20%, the amount of paid-in capital required before the stock could be traded. Investors were still liable for the firm's debts, in the case of insolvency, however, even if those shares had been traded away as long as five years before.[19] As one might imagine, the lack of limited liability meant that these reforms had very little effect on the use of the stock and bond markets as sources of industrial investment.

The real impetus to regulatory reform did not get underway until 1888, when the imperial government abolished slavery. The end of slavery produced a series of unexpected and unintended outcomes that set in motion both the overthrow of the monarchy and the complete reform of banking and securities market regulation. Abolition drove a wedge between Brazil's planter class, which historically had been the mainstay of the monarchy, and the imperial government. In an effort to placate the planters by making credit more easily available to them, the imperial government awarded concessions to 12 banks of issue and provided 17 banks with interest-free loans. The easy credit policies of 1888 were not enough, however, to stem the tide of Brazil's republican movement, which saw the monarchy and its policies as inimical to the creation of a modern economy and society. In November of 1889 Dom Pedro II, Brazil's emperor, was overthrown and a federal republic was created.

The newly created federal system shifted the weight of political power away from the Northeast and toward the richer, faster-growing South, particularly the states of São Paulo and Rio de Janeiro, which used their newly found political power to push through regulatory reforms that would maximize economic growth within their borders. Three reforms were especially crucial. First, the government deregulated the banking industry: Banks could now engage in whatever kind of financial transactions they wished, including extending long-term loans and investing in corporate securities. Second, the government

TABLE 10.1

Participation of Limited-Liability Joint-Stock Firms
in the Brazilian Cotton Textile Industy, 1866–1934

			Number of Joint-Stock Firms			
Year	Total Firms	Total Spindles	Rio de Janeiro[a]	São Paulo	All States[b]	% of Total
1866	9	14,875				
1875	11	45,830	1		1	9
1881	24	84,956	2		2	8
1883	24	78,908	2		2	8
1885[c]		66,466[c]				
1895[c]	22	260,842	9	2	13	—
1898[d]	18	279,666[d]	14		14	—
1905	90	778,224	17	3	25	28
1907	117	823,343	19	5	30	26
1908[c]	119	761,816[c]	10	6	16	13
1914	205	1,634,449	25	29	66	32
1915	170	1,598,568	25	25	63	37
1921[c]	242	1,621,300[c]				
1923[c]	243	1,700,000[c]				
1924	184	2,200,612	23	27	69	38
1925	183	2,397,380	25	34	80	44
1926	215	2,558,433	23	44	92	43
1927	228	2,692,077	25	41	94	41
1934	203	2,507,126	26	32	83	41

[a] Includes Distrito Federal firms.
[b] This is a national count of limited-liability joint-stock companies, including Rio de Janeiro and São Paulo firms.
[c] Estimate based on partial information.
[d] Includes only Rio de Janeiro and Distrito Federal firms.

Sources: 1866   Borja Castro, "Relatório," pp. 3–73.
    1875   Commissão (para) Exposição Universal (em) Philadelphia, *Empire of Brazil*, pp. 285–287 and statistical tables.
    1881   Bibliotheca da Associação Industrial, *Archivo da Exposição*, pp. xcvi–xcvii.
        Commissão de Inquerito Nacional, *Relatório*, p. 15.
    1883   Branner, "Cotton in the Empire of Brazil—1883."
    1885   Consul Ricketts, *Report*, C4657, 1xv (1886), pp. 187–188, as cited by Stein, *Brazilian Cotton*, Appendix I.
    1895   dos Santos Pires, *Relatório*, pp. 24–25.
    1898   de Carvalho, "Cafe." Also, de Carvalho, "Algodão."
    1905   Cunha Vasco, "Industria de Algodão".
    1907   Censo Industrial do Brasil, *Industria de Transportes*. Prefeitura do Distrito Federal, *Noticia*.
    1908   Graham Clark, *Cotton Goods*; Cunha Vasco, "Fabrica de Fiação"; Bandeira, *Industria no Estado de São Paulo.*

TABLE 10.1 (CONT.)

Participation of Limited-Liability Joint-Stock Firms
in the Brazilian Cotton Textile Industy, 1866–1934

| Year | Capacity of Joint-Stock Firms (measured in spindles) | | | |
	Rio de Janeiro[a]	São Paulo	All States[b]	% of Total
1866				
1875	20,000		20,000	44
1881	29,660		29,660	35
1883	25,500		25,500	32
1885[c]				
1895[c]	164,405	8,204	192,275	—
1898[d]	255,578		255,578	—
1905	316,310	27,606	358,740	46
1907	321,783	65,329	402,863	49
1908[c]	267,011	62,857	329,867	—
1914	512,387	384,206	983,404	60
1915	517,757	358,096	972,935	61
1921[c]				
1923[c]				
1924	821,682	521,934	1,475,982	67
1925	870,226	668,710	1,689,357	70
1926	890,902	700,261	1,751,761	68
1927	880,561	719,871	1,788,244	66
1934	796,696	624,314	1,618,310	65

1914 Centro Industrial do Brasil, *Relatório da Directoria*, 1915.
1915 Centro Industrial do Brasil, *Centro na Conferencia Algodeira.*
1921 Centro Industrial de Fiação e Tecelagem de Algodão (hereafter CIFTA), *Relatório da Directoria*, 1921–1922.
1923 CIFTA, Exposição de Tecidos CIFTA, *Relatório de Directoria*, 1923.
1924 CIFTA, *Relatório da Directoria*, 1924.
1925 CIFTA, *Relatório da Directoria*, 1925.
1926 CIFTA, *Fabricas Filiadas.*
1927 CIFTA, *Relatório da Directoria*, 1928.
1934 CIFTA, *Fiação e Tecelagem.*

dramatically reduced shareholder liability. Shareholders were still liable for the face value of their shares, but only until the annual shareholder's meeting when the financial records were approved. This effectively limited their liability to a 12-month period.[20] Third, the government instituted a set of mandatory disclosure laws that were highly unusual for the time. Brazil's publicly owned corporations were required to produce financial statements annually (many in fact produced them twice per year) and reprint them in public documents, such as state or federal gazettes or the newspaper. In addition, their annual reports had to list the names of all shareholders and the number of shares they controlled. Finally, the annual report had to list the number of shares that had changed hands during the year, including information on the number of shares that traded in each transaction. Investors could thus obtain reasonably good information on the health of firms, the potential liquidity of their shares, and the identities of a firm's major shareholders.[21]

The results of these reforms were dramatic. The nominal capital of corporations listed on the Rio de Janeiro and São Paulo exchanges, which had stood at 410,000 contos (roughly $136 million) in May of 1888, doubled to 963,965 contos by December 1889 under the impact of the new banking laws, and then doubled again by December 1890 when the use of the markets spread to other areas of economic activity. By December 1891, it reached 3,778,695 contos, a fourfold increase in just three years.[22]

In the short term, the speculative bubble created by the Encilhamento financed large numbers of banks. Although many of the banking enterprises failed during the collapse of the bubble and the recurrent financial crises over the following decade, in the short run they provided loans to Brazil's textile industry. In some cases, banks directly organized and ran textile companies.

Bank-financed industrial development was not, however, to be long lasting in Brazil. The boom created by the Encilhamento created a speculative bubble that burst in 1892, bringing down many of the banks. The government therefore decided in 1896 to once again restrict the right to issue currency to a single bank acting as the agent of the treasury. These more restrictive regulations, coupled with the already shaky financial situation of many of the banks, produced a massive contraction of the banking sector. In 1891 there were 68 banks operating in Brazil. By 1906 there were only 10, and their capital was only one-ninth that of the 1891 banks.[23] The banking system then began to expand, led and controlled by a semiofficial super-bank, the third Banco do Brasil, which acted both as a commercial bank and as the treasury's financial agent.

After the contraction of the banking system in 1896, Brazil's banks appear to have lent very little money for long-term investment.[24] Banks played an important role, however, in providing short-term working capital to manufacturers by discounting commercial paper. As Table 10.2 shows for the 15 firms whose balance sheets I have retrieved, during the period 1895–1915 short-term debt accounted for from 29% to 42% of their total indebtedness, depending on the year.

The more important, long-run effect of the Encilhamento was that the regulatory reforms of the securities markets gave rise to the widespread sale of equity and bonded debt to the investing public in order to mobilize long-term capital. Essentially, corporate finance took the following form: A group of entrepreneurs tied through kinship or established business relationships would come together and found a joint-stock company. They would then issue a prospectus, find a broker or bank to act as an intermediary, and sell shares to the public. These offerings would often be advertised in newspapers or state gazettes. As a firm's capital requirements grew, it would either issue new shares, which would be advertised in a public offering and handled by a broker, or it would issue bonds, which would also be subscribed by the public through the services of a broker or a bank. Over time, therefore, stock ownership grew more diversified and individuals could choose between owning equity or owning debt. In the early stages of the development of the market this looked much like the Boston Stock Exchange: Stocks tended to be closely held by the founding groups. Gradually, however, stock ownership became more diversified, particularly for the larger, more successful companies. By the 1920s, larger companies typically had more than 100 shareholders, and the rate of turnover of shares in the secondary markets was roughly 10% per year. It was also generally the case that no individual stockholder controlled more than 10% of a firm's shares. In fact, in the country's largest firm, the Companhia America Fabril, the minority shareholders actually banded together in the early 1920s and forced a reform of the board of directors, removing the founding group of entrepreneurs from their control of the firm.[25]

The overall process is reflected in Table 10.1. In 1866 there were no joint-stock companies in the cotton textile industry. By the early 1880s there were 2, accounting for 32% of the industry's installed capacity. By 1895, 13 joint-stock firms had been founded, and their capacity was seven times that of the joint-stock companies in 1883. This mushroomed to 66 joint-stock firms (accounting for 60% of industry capacity) by 1914, and to 80 joint-stock firms (accounting for 70% of capacity) by 1925.

By the standards of other countries during the early stages of industrialization this is an impressively high percentage of firms mobilizing capital through the sale of equity. Even as late as 1860, when the Boston Stock Exchange was at its peak importance as a source of capital for New England's mechanized mills, only 40 firms were listed on the exchange, out of a total of 1,091 firms in operation in the United States.[26] Perhaps the most relevant example is Mexico, a nation of similar per capita income and level of industrial development. Only 4 of Mexico's 100 operating textile firms in 1912 sold equity on the Mexico City Bolsa. Moreover, in Mexico there was little entry and exit from the

TABLE 10.2

Debt–Equity Ratios and Sources of New Capital for 15-Firm Sample, 1895–1940
(estimated from balance sheets, includes short-term debt)

Panel I.   Liabilities (millions of milreis)

Year	Paid Capital	Retained Earnings	Short-Term Debt	Bond Debt	Total Liabilities
1895	10	1	2	5	19
1900	53	16	9	19	96
1905	61	30	7	16	115
1910	76	28	19	26	149
1915	81	30	26	38	175
1920	115	43	21	45	224
1925	145	118	54	39	357
1930	137	100	65	78	380
1935	135	124	66	64	389
1940	145	143	74	46	409

Panel II.   Sources of New Capital (weighted by total liabilities)

Period	Growth of Debt + Equity	Share of Short-Term Debt	Share of Bond Debt	Share of Retained Earnings	Share of Paid Capital
1895–1900	410.8%	8.1%	17.1%	18.9%	55.9%
1900–1905	19.3%	−6.2%	−13.0%	77.5%	41.8%
1905–1910	30.3%	33.2%	28.8%	−5.0%	43.0%
1910–1915	16.9%	28.8%	45.2%	5.9%	20.1%
1915–1920	28.1%	−11.3%	14.8%	27.5%	69.0%
1920–1925	59.4%	25.1%	−4.2%	56.3%	22.8%
1925–1930	6.5%	46.1%	170.1%	−78.8%	−37.3%
1930–1935	2.5%	13.5%	−145.2%	251.0%	−19.3%
1935–1940	4.9%	41.3%	−96.0%	100.9%	53.8%

Source: See note 11 in the text.

financial markets. The same 4 firms listed on the exchange in Mexico in the late 1890s were the only 4 publicly owned cotton textile producers listed on the exchange until the 1940s.[27] In Brazil, on the other hand, there was a high degree of entry and exit.

Moreover, it was not the case, as it was in the mid-nineteenth-century United States, that Brazilian firms issued equity once and then funded their

TABLE 10.2 (CONT.)

Debt–Equity Ratios and Sources of New Capital for 15-Firm Sample, 1895–1940
(estimated from balance sheets, includes short-term debt)

Panel I.   Composite Debt–Equity Ratios (weighted by total liabilities)

Debt–Equity Ratio	Short-Term/Total Debt	Bond Debt/ Debt + Equity	Retained Earnings/ Debt + Equity	Paid Capital/ Debt + Equity
0.68	0.29	0.29	0.06	0.53
0.39	0.31	0.19	0.16	0.55
0.26	0.31	0.14	0.26	0.53
0.43	0.42	0.18	0.19	0.51
0.57	0.41	0.22	0.17	0.46
0.41	0.32	0.20	0.19	0.51
0.35	0.58	0.11	0.33	0.41
0.60	0.45	0.21	0.26	0.36
0.50	0.51	0.17	0.32	0.35
0.42	0.62	0.11	0.35	0.36

subsequent growth out of retained earnings.[28] Rather, firms regularly went back to the financial markets to seek new equity to fund their rapid expansion. Fourteen of the 15 firms whose balance sheets I have studied in detail raised additional equity capital from the investing public after they had been in business for some time.

As important as the development of the equities markets in Brazil was the simultaneous development of markets for long-term debt. As was the case with equities, debt issues came in small denominations: Virtually all had a par value of 200 milreis (about $50 at the rate of exchange at the turn of the century), implying that they could be held by medium-sized savers. These debts took the form of general obligation bonds, were callable, carried nominal interest rates of from 5% to 8%, and had terms of 20 years or more.

These debt issues raised significant amounts of capital. A comparison of the 1905 and 1915 censuses indicates that firms located in Rio de Janeiro or the Distrito Federal, where the market was well developed, financed 69% of their growth in total capitalization through the sale of new debt. For the country as a whole, 29% of new investment came in the form of long-term debt (see Table 10.3). In 1915 the average (weighted) debt–equity ratio for firms in Rio de

TABLE 10.3

Sources of New Capital for Brazilian Cotton Textile Firms, 1905–1934
(does not include short-term debt)

Period	Location	Growth of Total Firms	Share of New Paid Capital (%)	Share of Long-Term Debt (%)	Share of New Reserves (%)	Share of Capital plus Reserves(%)
1905–1915	All Brazil	174	88	—	29.2	—	70.8
	Firms located in RJ or DF	30	45	—	68.9	—	31.1
	Firms located in SP	43	272	—	14.4	—	85.6
	Joint-stock firms in RJ	25	55	—	53.6	—	46.4
	Joint-stock firms in SP	25	834	—	13.5	—	86.5
	Joint-stock firms in other states	12	208	—	31.1	—	68.9
	Total joint-stock firms	62	135	—	29.1	—	70.9
	Total private firms	112	35	—	29.8	—	70.2
1915–1925	All Brazil	189	137	37.5	4.2	58.3	—
	Firms located in RJ or DF	28	118	36.1	3.5	60.4	—
	Firms located in SP	53	244	39.2	6.9	53.9	—
	Joint-stock firms in RJ	25	136	35.9	6.5	57.6	—
	Joint-stock firms in SP	33	270	37.9	7.0	55.1	—
	Joint-stock firms in other states	20	109	33.9	1.1	65.0	—
	Total joint-stock firms	78	181	36.9	6.4	56.7	—
	Total private firms	111	54	41.3	−10.2	68.9	—
1925–1934	All Brazil	244	19	80.3	64.7	−45.1	—
	Firms located in RJ or DF	35	7	67.4	89.6	−56.9	—
	Firms located in SP	98	13	127.1	147.7	−174.7	—
	Joint-stock firms in RJ	25	2	18.2	243.9	−162.1	—
	Joint-stock firms in SP	31	1	578.4	2215.3	−2693.7	—
	Joint-stock firms in other states	25	102	65.9	26.5	7.6	—
	Total joint-stock firms	81	9	84.0	158.7	−142.7	—
	Total private firms	163	56	78.3	12.2	9.5	—

Note: RJ=Rio de Janeiro; DF=Distrito Federal; SP=São Paulo.

Sources: Estimated from Borja Castro, "Relatório," pp. 3–73; Commissão de Inquerito Industrial, *Relatório*; Branner, "Cotton in the Empire of Brazil"; Ministerio da Industria Viação e Obras Publicas, *Relatório*; Vasco, "Industria de Algodão"; Centro Industrial do Brasil, *O Brasil*; Centro Industrial do Brasil, *Relatório* 1915; Centro Industrial do Brasil, "O Centro Industrial"; Centro Industrial de Fiação, 1925, 1926; Centro Industrial de Fiação e Tecelagem de Algodão, *Estatisticas da industria*; Centro Industrial de Fiação e Tecelagem; Stein, *Brazilian Cotton*, Appendix 1.

Janeiro or the Distrito Federal was 0.43:1.00, three times its level in 1905. For the country as a whole, the debt–equity ratio in 1915 was 0.27:1.00, nearly twice its level in 1905 (see Table 10.4).

This analysis based on census data significantly understates the importance of debt financing because it does not include trade debt from suppliers, short-term liabilities (mostly commercial paper), and the small quantity of mortgage debt owed to banks. For that reason, I have estimated financial ratios for the 15-firm sample of publicly owned companies from their balance sheets. In 1915 the average (weighted) debt–equity ratio for these 15 firms was 0.57:1.00 (see Table 10.2). The balance sheet data also corroborate the census data in regard to the pattern of bond finance: The use of the bond market was most important during the periods 1905–1910, when new bond debt accounted for 29% of all new investment, and 1910–1915, when new bond debt accounted for 45% of all new investment (see Panel II of Table 10.2).

The use of long-term bond debt and the high percentages of capital coming from debt issues were quite remarkable by the standards of other countries. In the case of the early industrial United States, debt played a minimal role. In 1860 the large integrated textile manufacturers of New England typically had debt–equity ratios of 0.20:1.00—roughly one-third that of their large-scale Rio de Janeiro counterparts in 1915. All this debt was short-term accounts payable and commercial paper.[29] As late as 1910, the average debt–equity ratio of large-scale firms in the United States textile industry (those listed in *Moody's Industrials*) was 0.40:1.00, roughly one-third lower than the debt–equity ratios for comparable Brazilian firms. Virtually all the debt of U.S. firms, however, was short term. Long-term bonded debt was so scarce as to be nonexistent.[30] Even by 1920, when a few of the largest U.S. firms began to issue long term bonds, the average debt–equity ratio was still 0.29:1.00. Most U.S. textile firms, of course, were not able to make use of the bond market and had to resort to the less-optimal option of issuing preferred shares when they wanted to grow faster than was possible through the reinvestment of retained earnings.[31]

Mexico, a country that was much closer to Brazil than the United States in terms of its level of industrial development, per capita income, and other features of its nineteenth-century economic history, provides an even more striking comparison. Mexico's large, publicly owned joint-stock cotton textile companies (similar in many ways to the 15 Rio de Janeiro firms analyzed in table 10.2) had an average ratio of debt to equity of 0.18:1.00 during the period 1900–1910, less than one-third of their Brazilian counterparts.[32]

Perhaps equally notable is the almost total absence of foreign direct investment in Brazil's textile industry. At their peak in 1915, foreign-owned

TABLE 10.4

Financial Structure of Brazilian Cotton Textile Firms, 1905–1934
(does not include short-term debt)

						(millions of current milreis)		
Year	Location	Firms	Paid Capital	Long-Term Debt	Reserves	Capital Plus Reserves	Total Capital	Debt–Equity Ratio
1905	All Brazil	90	—	28	—	177	205	0.16
	Firms located in RJ or DF	19	—	13	—	93	106	0.14
	Firms located in SP	17	—	4	—	24	28	0.16
	Joint-stock firms in RJ	17	—	13	—	77	91	0.17
	Joint-stock firms in SP	3	—	4	—	6	10	0.68
	Joint-stock firms in other states	4	—	—	—	7	8	0.06
	Total joint-stock firms	24	—	18	—	90	108	0.20
	Total private firms	66	—	11	—	87	97	0.12
	Joint-stock firms as % of Brazil		—	62.8	—	51.1	52.7	
1915	All Brazil	174	264	81	41	305	386	0.27
	Firms located in RJ or DF	30	87	46	21	108	154	0.43
	Firms located in SP	43	79	15	8	88	103	0.17
	Joint-stock firms in RJ	25	79	40	21	100	140	0.40
	Joint-stock firms in SP	25	67	15	8	75	90	0.20
	Joint-stock firms in other states	12	17	6	2	19	24	0.30
	Total joint-stock firms	62	163	60	31	194	255	0.31
	Total private firms	112	101	21	9	111	131	0.19
	Joint-stock firms as % of Brazil		61.6	74.5	76.8	63.7	65.9	
1925	All Brazil	189	463	103	350	813	916	0.13
	Firms located in RJ or DF	28	152	52	131	284	336	0.18
	Firms located in SP	53	178	32	143	321	353	0.10
	Joint-stock firms in RJ	25	148	52	131	279	331	0.19
	Joint-stock firms in SP	33	159	32	142	300	332	0.11
	Joint-stock firms in other states	20	26	6	19	45	51	0.13

Note: RJ = Rio de Janeiro; DF = Distrito Federal; SP = São Paulo.

Source: See Table 10.3.

TABLE 10.4 (CONT.)

Financial Structure of Brazilian Cotton Textile Firms, 1905–1934
(does not include short-term debt)

Year	Location	Firms	Paid Capital	Long-Term Debt	Reserves	Capital Plus Reserves	Total Capital	Debt–Equity Ratio
				(millions of current mil-reis)				
	Total joint-stock firms	78	332	90	292	624	714	0.14
	Total private firms	111	130	14	58	188	202	0.07
	Joint-stock firms as % of Brazil		71.8	86.9	83.4	76.8	78.0	
1934	All Brazil	244	605	218	271	875	1093	0.25
	Firms located in RJ or DF	35	168	73	118	286	359	0.25
	Firms located in SP	98	235	98	65	300	398	0.33
	Joint-stock firms in RJ	25	149	73	118	267	340	0.27
	Joint-stock firms in SP	31	176	98	61	237	335	0.42
	Joint-stock firms in other states	25	60	20	23	84	103	0.24
	Total joint-stock firms	81	385	191	202	587	778	0.32
	Total private firms	163	219	27	69	288	315	0.10
	Joint-stock firms as % of Brazil		63.7	87.4	74.5	67.1	71.1	

or foreign-affiliated firms (broadly defined to include any firm in the census that listed any of its capital in foreign currency or any firm whose name indicated possible foreign participation) numbered only four and accounted for only 2.8% of installed capacity.

The absence of foreign investment in textiles is explained by three factors. First, Brazil did not have a comparative advantage in producing textiles; thus, Brazilian firms sold all of their output domestically (behind a high tariff wall) and earned their revenues in Brazilian milreis. Brazil was not on the gold standard, and thus the milreis continually depreciated as silver lost value against gold. A foreign investor would therefore have seen the (gold-denominated) value of his assets decline. Perhaps equally important, foreign investors had no way of knowing which way the silver milreis was headed, thus creating uncertainty about the future value of assets.

Second, as a general rule foreigners tended to invest abroad only in those lines of economic activity where they had some distinct advantage over local entrepreneurs. When foreign entrepreneurs or corporations had knowledge of specialized technology that local capitalists did not, or where the scale of enterprise was larger than domestic financial markets could fund, foreign direct investment dominated the industry. Thus, foreign investment characterized industries such as railroading, electric power generation, and deep-shaft mining. In the textile industry none of these factors came into play.

Third, the high tariff wall necessary to protect the industry against foreign competition imposed a high cost on Brazilian consumers and by extension made it necessary for Brazilian industrialists to continually lobby the federal government to maintain their protection.[33] Overseas investors would have been poorly placed politically to press the case for protection. Domestic industrialists, including foreign-born Brazilians, on the other hand, were an important political constituency and could therefore make the case for protection.

III: Effects of Regulatory Reforms

The reform of the regulations governing the operation of the securities market had significant impacts on the growth in size, industrial structure, and productivity of the textile industry. The most obvious change in the industry was its size. As Table 10.1 demonstrates, a small industry that appears to have been stagnating in the 1880s began to grow rapidly. Even according to the partial census of 1895, which seriously undercounted the industry's installed capacity, the industry had tripled in size since 1885. From 1895 to 1905 the industry tripled in size again, and then doubled from 1905 to 1915, making it the largest cotton textile industry of any Latin American country. It then grew an additional 70% up until 1927, when the Depression cut short its growth.

This rapid rate of growth, it should be pointed out, was not confined to the cotton textile industry. According to Nathaniel Leff's estimates, real agricultural output increased from 1900 to 1909 by 3.5% per year, industrial output by 5.6% per year, and aggregate real output at a rate of 4.2% per year. From 1900 to 1947, the annual rate of growth of aggregate real output rose at 4.4%, and per capita real output grew by 2.3% per year. This impressive rate of aggregate growth was accompanied by a process of structural transformation in which industry came to be the fastest growing sector of the economy. Indeed, the period after 1900 marked the rapid expansion of a wide variety of manufacturing industries in Brazil, including steel, cement, glass, beer, food processing, and machine tools.[34]

This is not to argue that the only obstacle to growth prior to the 1890s was capital immobilities and that the only relevant policy change in Brazil related to the regulation of financial markets. Coterminous with the reform of financial market regulations were increases in tariff protection and the expansion of the railroad network, which had begun to develop in the 1880s but which now grew rapidly under the combined influence of federal subsidies and the availability of foreign capital. It is to argue, however, that one crucial piece of the puzzle explaining the lack of industrial development before 1890 and rapid industrial growth after 1890 was access to capital. Indeed, had problems in the mobility of capital not been an issue prior to 1890 it would be hard to explain the vast change in the way that firms used the securities markets to obtain their investment funds: The industry could simply have grown using the traditional sole-proprietor and partnership forms of business organization.

There are two ways that one can at least partially control for these other changes in the Brazilian economy, thereby measuring the marginal effects of the capital market reforms. One is to look at firm size. Panel I of Table 10.5 looks at 62 firms that appear in both the 1905 and 1915 censuses, segmenting them into five categories: private firms (partnerships or sole proprietorships), nontraded joint-stock companies, publicly traded joint-stock companies, private firms that switched to nontraded joint-stock companies, and private firms that switched to publicly traded joint-stock companies. Panel II of the same table repeats the operation, this time looking at 111 firms that appear in both the 1915 and 1925 censuses. The results of both panels are unambiguous. First, joint-stock firms were anywhere from 2.5 to 4 times the size of private firms (the exact ratio depending on the year). Second, the rate of growth of new investment (as measured by spindlage) in joint-stock companies was consistently faster than in private firms. Third, firms that switched from sole proprietorships or partnerships to publicly traded joint-stock companies consistently grew faster than firms that did not switch. In fact, from 1905 to 1915 private firms that became traded joint-stock companies outgrew the other traded firms by three to one and outgrew private firms by four to one. The implication is clear: Privately owned firms were capital constrained. Their growth was limited by the rate at which they could plow back retained earnings or the rate at which their owners could divert their wealth from other sources into their textile mills. Limited-liability joint-stock companies, on the other hand, were not as constrained. They could mobilize capital from a broad range of individual and institutional investors through a variety of financial instruments, including stocks, bonds, and commercial paper.

Brazilian industry would therefore have been smaller had there not been financial markets to mobilize capital—but how much smaller? One way to get

TABLE 10.5

Growth in Installed Capacity by Firm Type, 1905–1915 and 1915–1925

Panel I.   Firms that appear in both the 1905 and 1915 censuses

Firm Type	Firms	Total Spindles in 1905	Total Spindles in 1915	Average Spindles per Firm in 1905	Average Spindles per Firm in 1915	Percent Change in Average Firm Size
Private	41	291,334	402,824	7,283	9,825	35%
Nontraded joint stock						
Traded joint stock	13	244,812	369,278	18,832	28,406	51%
Firms that switched						
Private to non-traded joint stock	1	31,884	36,000	31,884	36,000	13%
Private to traded joint stock	7	69,712	171,292	9,959	24,470	146%

Panel II.   Firms that appear in both the 1915 and 1925 censuses

Firm Type	Firms	Total Spindles in 1915	Total Spindles in 1925	Average Spindles per Firm in 1915	Average Spindles per Firm in 1925	Percent Change in Average Firm Size
Private	72	549,332	613,155	7,630	8,516	12%
Nontraded joint stock	3	72,180	109,860	24,060	36,620	52%
Traded joint stock	32	634,292	1,001,784	19,822	31,306	58%
Firms that switched						
Private to non-traded joint stock	3	28,900	36,108	9,633	12,036	25%
Private to traded joint stock	1	7,000	10,000	7,000	10,000	43%

Source: See Table 10.1.

a first-order approximation is to assume that the same number of firms would have existed, but that the publicly owned firms would have been as capital constrained as the privately owned firms. They therefore would have been the same size as privately owned firms. The total size of the industry in any year would therefore have been the actual number of firms censused multiplied by the average size of privately owned firms. Table 10.6 presents the results of these calculations. Had all firms been privately owned, in 1905 the industry would have been 28% smaller; in 1915, 32% smaller; and in 1925, 49% smaller.

One might argue that the absence of joint-stock limited-liability companies would have opened up the possibility for investments in the industry by existing and potential private firms, and thus the industry would not in fact have been any smaller. Doubtless this would have happened. The implication, however, is that these potential firms would have been less efficient than the joint-stock firms they would have replaced; otherwise, they would have come into existence anyway and out-competed the joint-stock companies. Either way there would have been a loss for Brazil: a smaller, but equally efficient industry or a less efficient, but equal-sized industry. I will return to this latter possibility in some detail shortly.

The second way to control for factors other than the capital market reforms would be a counterfactual exercise comparing Brazil with another late-industrializing country that had similar tariff reforms and railroad-building programs. Mexico is such a case.[35] Mexico did not, however, undertake the kinds of financial market regulatory reforms that Brazil did, and where its legal reforms did mirror those of Brazil, it did not enforce the new laws. The result was that the Mexican textile industry grew slowly. In the early 1880s the Mexican cotton textile industry was three times the size of Brazil's. By 1907 the industries were roughly the same size, and by circa 1915, Brazil's industry was twice the size of Mexico's, even though Mexican and Brazilian national incomes were roughly equal.[36]

The second impact of the institutional reforms that allowed for the creation of limited-liability joint-stock companies in Brazil was an increase in productivity: Joint-stock firms were more efficient than those that were privately owned. These results are indicated by estimates of Cobb-Douglas production functions on the panel data set and by estimates of firm-level total factor productivity derived from those production functions. Let us first look at TFP across each census where there are sufficient observations to estimate mean TFP by firm type, and then turn to multivariate regression analysis to decompose the differences between firm types.

Tables 10.7 and 10.8 present estimates of mean (weighted by firm size) factor productivity by firm type and size covering the years 1905 to 1927. I measure output two ways, by real value and by physical units (meters of cloth). Each measure of output has its advantages and disadvantages: Real output is sensitive to the price index constructed to measure changes in the price of cloth; physical output eliminates the price index problem, but understates output because it cannot capture differences in the quality of cloth over time (which was significant).

The real-value estimates require first the estimation of a price index for cotton textile goods. I assume that Brazilian manufacturers priced their products at the milreis price of foreign imports plus the tariff. It then follows that the

TABLE 10.6

Average Capacity by Firm Type, 1866–1934

| | Number of Firms | | | |
Year	Total[a]	Private	Joint Stock Traded	Joint Stock Not Traded
1866	9	9	0	0
1875	11	11	0	0
1881	24	22	2	0
1883	24	22	2	0
1905	90	72	16	2
1907	117	95	21	1
1914	204	152	49	3
1915	170	120	45	5
1924	184	132	42	10
1925	183	122	44	17
1926	214	141	50	23
1927	228	146	48	34
1934	203	131	41	31

[a] Includes only those firms with spindle data.

Source: See Table 10.1.

rate of change of domestic prices is equal to the sum of the changes in the nominal exchange rate, the tariff, and the value of foreign cotton goods. Since most Brazilian imports were from Great Britain, I employ the British cotton goods price series.

I then estimate TFP by combining the capital and labor inputs using weights from the first specification of the production functions presented in Table 10.9 (normalizing the capital and labor coefficients to 1).[37] Following Kane's work on the United States, I employ the number of spindles as a proxy for the capital input of each company.[38] Following Atack and Sokoloff on productivity in the United States, and of Bernard and Jones on international productivity comparisons, I employed the number of workers as the measure of the labor input.[39]

The estimates presented here break firms into two categories, joint-stock and privately owned, and into two sizes, those smaller than 13,500 spindles and those larger than 13,500 spindles. This size was chosen as the break point because 13,500 spindles was the median firm size observed in the panel data set. Conveniently, it also represents a firm size equivalent to a capacity share of 0.5% at the time of the last census under analysis. As will be seen later on when

TABLE 10.6 (CONT.)

Average Capacity by Firm Type, 1866–1934

Average Number of Spindles			Industry Size		
Private	Joint Stock Traded	Joint Stock Not Traded	If All Firms Private	Actual	Difference (%)
1,653	—	—	14,875	14,875	0
4,166	—	—	45,830	45,830	0
2,513	14,830	—	60,323	84,956	29
2,428	12,750	—	58,264	78,908	26
6,210	11,932	20,270	558,900	778,224	28
4,790	15,758	37,340	560,430	823,343	32
5,495	16,608	6,346	1,120,980	1,634,449	31
6,355	16,701	16,874	1,080,350	1,598,568	32
6,610	31,320	17,685	1,216,240	2,200,612	45
6,720	30,010	15,120	1,229,760	2,397,380	49
6,391	26,578	14,594	1,367,674	2,558,433	47
6,702	27,820	11,126	1,528,056	2,692,007	43
7,491	26,828	13,739	1,520,673	2,507,126	39

I use survivor methods to cross-check the TFP regressions, 0.5% turns out to be the minimum efficient scale of production. The results for one public firm, the Companhia America Fabril, are reported separately. This firm controlled roughly 12% of the industry's capacity and 26% of the capacity of joint-stock firms. Because the estimates presented here are weighted averages, the inclusion of this firm can potentially drive the results. Note that the number of firms analyzed here does not correspond to the total number of firms in the industry in any given year. Only those firms that reported all the necessary variables to estimate TFP are included.

A number of features of the data are immediately obvious. The first, as Table 10.7 indicates, is that average output per worker is anywhere from 29% to 53% higher in joint-stock firms. This relationship holds across time and across size categories. The reason for this difference in labor productivity is not hard to fathom when one looks at a second feature of the data: the capital–labor ratio. On average, joint-stock firms had anywhere from 18% to 49% more spindles per worker than their privately owned competitors (depending on the year), owing, no doubt, to the lower cost at which they could obtain capital. Not surprisingly, large joint-stock firms appear to have

TABLE 10.7

Average Total Factor Productivity (in real value of output) by Firm Type and Size,
Brazilian Cotton Textile Industry, 1907–1927

Output Proxied by Real Value of Production (1913 milreis)

Year	Firm Sizes	Reporting Firms			Average Output per Worker		
		JS	Private	Total	JS	Private	Diff.
1907	Total	18	52	70	3,656	2,503	46%
	<13,500	9	49	58	3,152	2,497	26%
	>13,500	8	3	11	3,847	2,545	51%
	America Fabril	1		1	3,030		
1914	Total	39	84	123	3,856	2,895	33%
	<13,500	21	75	96	2,970	2,868	4%
	>13,500	17	9	26	4,246	2,948	44%
	America Fabril	1		1	3,896		
1915	Total	41	98	139	3,945	2,945	34%
	<13,500	22	88	110	3,805	2,812	35%
	>13,500	18	10	28	3,997	3,257	23%
	America Fabril	1		1	3,871		
1924	Total	50	111	161	7,996	5,889	36%
	<13,500	29	95	124	7,216	6,532	10%
	>13,500	20	16	36	8,277	4,762	74%
	America Fabril	1		1	8,769		
1925	Total	57	98	155	10,498	6,859	53%
	<13,500	36	85	121	10,398	7,149	45%
	>13,500	20	13	33	10,542	6,240	69%
	America Fabril	1		1	7,770		
1926	Total	65	104	169	8,918	6,890	29%
	<13,500	39	88	127	9,288	6,911	34%
	>13,500	25	16	41	8,782	6,860	28%
	America Fabril	1		1	7,214		
1927	Total	73	110	183	8,571	6,499	32%
	<13,500	45	93	138	8,439	6,711	26%
	>13,500	27	17	44	8,621	6,235	38%
	America Fabril	1		1	6,429		

Note: TFP estimated using normalized capital and labor weights from production functions reported in Table 10.9
(weighted by firm size).

Source: See Table 10.1.

TABLE 10.7 (CONT.)

Average Total Factor Productivity (in real value of output) by Firm Type and Size,
Brazilian Cotton Textile Industry, 1907–1927

Output Proxied by Real Value of Production (1913 milreis)

Average Output per Spindle			Average Spindles per Worker			Average Total Factor Productivity			Average TFP All Firms
JS	Private	Diff.	JS	Private	Diff.	JS	Private	Diff.	Firms
150	153	-2%	24	16	49%	1,194	941	27%	1,053
232	169	37%	14	15	-8%	1,264	974	30%	1,028
135	91	48%	29	28	2%	1,190	794	50%	1,117
145			21			1,045			
153	135	13%	25	21	18%	1,246	991	26%	1,109
151	156	-3%	20	18	6%	1,048	1,034	1%	1,038
153	109	41%	28	27	2%	1,327	928	43%	1,180
141			28			1,218			
167	164	2%	24	18	31%	1,305	1,071	22%	1,175
203	174	17%	19	16	16%	1,364	1,061	29%	1,133
158	147	7%	25	22	14%	1,289	1,100	17%	1,224
141			28			1,213			
382	363	5%	21	16	29%	2,759	2,222	24%	2,759
454	452	0%	16	14	10%	2,740	2,566	7%	2,616
364	247	48%	23	19	18%	2,775	1,690	64%	2,419
214			41			2,391			
472	430	10%	22	16	39%	3,546	2,603	36%	3,127
604	507	19%	17	14	22%	3,840	2,832	36%	3,191
431	314	37%	24	20	23%	3,444	2,192	57%	3,103
214			36			2,210			
433	415	4%	21	17	24%	3,094	2,577	20%	2,872
534	452	18%	17	15	14%	3,418	2,660	28%	2,943
404	370	9%	22	19	17%	2,988	2,468	21%	2,835
176			41			1,966			
385	374	3%	22	17	28%	2,894	2,393	21%	2,675
496	428	16%	17	16	8%	3,130	2,560	22%	2,779
356	321	11%	24	19	25%	2,825	2,207	28%	2,626
157			41			1,752			

TABLE 10.8

Average Total Factor Productivity (in physical volume) by Firm Type and Size, Brazilian Cotton Textile Industry, 1905–1927

Output Proxied by Meters of Cloth

Year	Firm Sizes	Reporting Firms JS	Reporting Firms Private	Total	Average Output per Worker JS	Average Output per Worker Private	Diff.
1905	Total	16	48	63	8,957	6,875	30%
	<13,500	8	43	51	6,882	6,109	13%
	>13,500	7	5	12	9,814	8,869	11%
	America Fabril	1			7,576		
1907	Total	18	51	68	9,138	5,499	66%
	<13,500	9	48	57	8,098	5,319	52%
	>13,500	8	3	11	9,533	6,764	41%
	America Fabril	1			7,576		
1924	Total	49	107	155	6,088	5,973	2%
	<13,500	29	91	120	5,736	5,890	-3%
	>13,500	19	16	35	6,216	6,111	2%
	America Fabril	1			4,571		
1925	Total	57	96	152	6,208	5,941	4%
	<13,500	35	83	118	6,141	5,587	10%
	>13,500	21	13	34	6,235	6,637	-6%
	America Fabril	1			4,069		
1926	Total	61	91	151	6,183	5,763	7%
	<13,500	36	78	114	6,200	5,976	4%
	>13,500	24	13	37	6,177	5,474	13%
	America Fabril	1			4,571		
1927	Total	71	92	162	6,088	5,890	3%
	<13,500	45	74	119	5,864	5,728	2%
	>13,500	25	18	43	6,182	6,062	2%
	America Fabril	1			4,008		

Note: TFP estimated using normalized capital and labor weights from production functions reported in Table 10.9 (weighted by firm size).

Source: See Table 10.1.

TABLE 10.8 (CONT.)

Average Total Factor Productivity (in physical volume) by Firm Type and Size,
Brazilian Cotton Textile Industry, 1905–1927

Output Proxied by Meters of Cloth

Average Output per Spindle			Average Spindles per Worker			Average Total Factor Productivity			Average TFP All
JS	Private	Diff.	JS	Private	Diff.	JS	Private	Diff.	Firms
375	387	–3%	24	18	35%	3,045	2,586	18%	2,780
481	403	19%	14	15	–5%	2,784	2,425	15%	2,503
353	362	–3%	28	25	14%	3,167	2,989	6%	3,104
361			21			2,692			
374	340	10%	24	16	51%	3,083	2,134	44%	2,562
595	366	62%	14	15	–6%	3,333	2,142	56%	2,366
334	242	38%	29	28	2%	3,050	2,181	40%	2,890
361			21			2,692			
313	365	–14%	19	16	19%	2,220	2,309	–4%	2,262
361	404	–11%	16	15	9%	2,239	2,368	–5%	2,328
300	317	–5%	21	19	7%	7,686	2,234	244%	2,223
111			41			1,293			
282	367	–23%	22	16	36%	2,170	2,305	–6%	2,223
359	386	–7%	17	14	18%	2,339	2,252	4%	2,281
260	338	–23%	24	20	22%	2,116	2,413	–12%	2,195
112			36			1,199			
303	341	–11%	20	17	21%	2,218	2,204	1%	2,210
366	382	–4%	17	16	8%	2,369	2,345	1%	2,354
286	295	–3%	22	19	17%	2,172	2,028	7%	2,129
111			41			1,293			
277	334	–17%	22	18	25%	2,128	2,221	–4%	2,164
356	365	–2%	16	16	5%	2,263	2,247	1%	2,254
254	308	–18%	24	20	24%	2,088	2,201	–5%	2,124
98			41			1,134			

been the most capital intense. The third striking feature of the data is the sizable differences in TFP across firm type: The weighted mean of TFP for all joint-stock firms was anywhere from 20% to 36% higher than for all privately owned firms.

In Table 10.8 I estimate TFP using the same procedures employed in Table 10.7, but substituting meters of cloth as the proxy for output in the TFP calculations. The results obtained are dissimilar from those obtained when output was measured by its real value. First, the gap in average output per worker between firm types disappears in the 1920s. Second, average output per spindle is much lower in joint-stock companies than in privately owned companies in the 1920s. Third, on average, there is little difference in TFP between private and joint-stock firms in the 1920s. Fourth, average TFP estimates indicate no productivity growth at all in this industry from 1905 to 1927, which is difficult to reconcile with the fact that the industry was expanding rapidly. It is also difficult to reconcile with the rapid TFP growth when one proxies output by the real value of production (see Table 10.7). The most reasonable interpretation is that joint-stock firms in the 1920s were moving into the production of small runs of high-value products, whereas private firms tended to continue the old practice of producing large volumes of low-quality cloth. I will return to this issue shortly, when I turn to multivariate analysis.

In order to decompose these differences in factor productivity by firm type and size and to measure the impact of access to low-cost capital from the securities markets on the margin, I turn to multivariate regression analysis. I used an unbalanced panel procedure to estimate basic pooled and fixed-effects specifications of regressions for the years 1905–1927 of the following type:

$$Y_{it} = \alpha + \beta \cdot X_{it} + u_{it}$$

where Y_{it} is the dependent variable of firm i at time t, α is the overall intercept term for all firms, β is a vector of coefficients corresponding to the X_{it} vector of independent variables, and u_{it} is a stochastic term.[40] I assume usual normality and independence conditions to obtain least-squares estimates of β.[41]

I assume a Cobb-Douglas production function of the form $Y = A \cdot K^\gamma \cdot L^{1-\gamma}$ with constant returns to scale, where K and L represent the capital and labor inputs and A is a function that captures improvements in technology over time. In order to use linear estimation procedures, I take natural logarithms of a normalized production function of the form $y = k^\alpha$, where $y = Y/L$ and $k = K/L$, and add explanatory variables to arrive at the following model:

$$\text{Ln } y = \alpha + \beta_1 \cdot \text{Ln } k + \beta_2 \cdot \text{Ln } L + \beta_3 \cdot \text{Time Trend} + \delta \cdot \textbf{Dummies}$$

This specification allows one to test for economies of scale as well as to obtain the rate of total factor productivity growth, the coefficient on the time trend. I use variations of this equation to estimate the impact of other features of firms (location, traded status, vintage, and other relevant variables) for the specifications whose results are reported in Table 10.9.[42]

Specification 1 of Table 10.9 indicates that, as predicted, there were negligible scale economies in the Brazilian cotton textile industry (the coefficient on firm size is negative, of small magnitude, and is not statistically significant). The industry was, however, characterized by rapid productivity growth: The time trend was 6.1% per year. As expected, newer firms (those founded after 1905) had higher productivities than their older competitors (the coefficient translates into roughly an 8% TFP advantage for newer firms, everything else being equal).[43] Perhaps most striking is the sizable impact of the joint-stock corporate form. The coefficient of .226 on the joint-stock dummy translates into a 25% TFP advantage over non-joint-stock firms.

One might think that firms that were actively traded on an organized exchange might have been more efficient than joint-stock firms that were not traded. The notion is that firms that were regularly traded were monitored more closely by large investors. Ideally, one would add a traded dummy to specification 1 to measure the marginal impact of being publicly traded. Traded firms were, however, a subset of joint-stock firms, meaning that there is collinearity between the two variables. I therefore estimate the impact of being traded in specification 2 by substituting a traded dummy for the joint-stock dummy. One can reject the hypothesis that traded status explains the advantage that joint-stock firms had over their competitors: The coefficient is large and statistically significant, but it is of a smaller magnitude than that on joint-stock firms alone. It may have been the case that the secondary markets for equity were too thin to serve as efficient monitors. Or it may have been that some of the most productive joint-stock companies' shares were closely held by their original investors.

What was the impact of being able to issue bonds on productivity growth? One view would hold that there should be a positive correlation between being able to sell debt and higher levels and rates of growth of productivity. In this view, firms that have established track records for being well managed will be the most likely to succeed in selling debt to the investing public. In turn, this reduces their cost of capital and further increases their growth of productivity. An alternative view, associated with Brander and Spencer, is that if an owner-manager substitutes borrowed funds for equity, then the effort of the owner

TABLE 10.9

Alternate Specifications of Cobb-Douglas Production Functions, Brazilian Cotton Textile Industry, 1905–1927

Dependent Variable	Log (real value of production/worker)[a]				
	Spec 1	Spec 2	Spec 3	Spec 4	Spec 5
1) Intercept	6.502 (39.678)	6.389 (38.909)	6.268 (38.652)	6.154 (40.351)	6.256 (37.689)
2) Ln(Spindles/Worker) —Proxy for capital	0.316 (8.765)	0.331 (9.100)	0.348 (9.603)	0.304 (8.607)	0.298 (8.336)
3) Ln(Workers)— Proxy for firm size	−0.012 (−0.613)	0.002 (0.088)	0.018 (0.985)	0.034 (1.958)	0.019 (0.978)
4) Time	0.061 (21.310)	0.062 (21.545)	0.063 (21.376)	0.061 (21.627)	0.061 (21.435)
5) Vintage—Dummy for firms founded on or after 1905	0.076 (2.037)	0.089 (2.344)	0.087 (2.284)	0.065 (1.756)	0.059 (1.583)
6) Joint stock— Dummy for limited-liability joint-stock company	0.226 (5.770)				
A) Joint stock out— Dummy for joint-stock firm outside of competitive region					0.285 (2.248)
7) Traded—Dummy for firms listed in stock exchange markets		0.165 (3.872)			
8) Bonds—Dummy for bonded debt			0.093 (1.842)		
9) Region—Dummy for firms in MG, RJ, DF, SP				0.300 (8.281)	
A) Privately owned in MG, RJ, DF, SP					0.279 (6.394)
B) Joint stock in MG, RJ, DF, SP					0.354 (8.138)
N	1017	1017	1017	1017	1017
Adjusted R^2	0.40	0.39	0.39	0.42	0.43

Notes: Unbalanced panel regressions on entire sample. Total ordinary least squares. T statistics in parentheses.
[a] Sample runs from 1907 through 1927.
[b] Sample runs from 1905 through 1927.

Source: See Table 10.1.

TABLE 10.9 (CONT.)

Alternate Specifications of Cobb-Douglas Production Functions, Brazilian Cotton Textile Industry, 1905–1927

	Log (meters of output/worker)[b]			
Spec 6	Spec 7	Spec 8	Spec 9	Spec 10
8.240	8.290	8.162	8.077	8.181
(48.685)	(49.408)	(49.651)	(51.001)	(46.686)
0.307	0.301	0.322	0.299	0.289
(7.236)	(7.145)	(7.710)	(7.077)	(6.732)
−0.060	−0.068	−0.052	−0.039	−0.051
(−3.094)	(−3.493)	(−2.731)	(−2.916)	(−2.529)
−0.008	−0.008	−0.007	−0.007	−0.007
(−3.103)	(−3.012)	(−2.921)	(−2.916)	(−2.953)
0.019	0.030	0.025	0.016	0.020
(0.475)	(0.755)	(0.625)	(0.421)	(0.500)
0.096				
(2.432)				
				−0.052
				(-0.459)
	0.147			
	(3.447)			
		0.080		
		(1.566)		
			0.126	
			(3.323)	
				0.088
				(1.922)
				0.153
				(3.389)
785	785	785	785	785
0.09	0.10	0.09	0.10	0.10

declines and the firm's output falls. The reason for this is that bondholders have less incentive than equity holders to monitor managers.[44] Specification 3 tests these hypotheses by introducing a dummy variable for firms whose bonds were traded on either the Rio de Janeiro or São Paulo exchanges. The magnitude of the coefficient is much smaller than that for being a joint-stock company, indicating that although firms that issued bonds were roughly 10% more productive than the average firm, they were less efficient than joint-stock firms as a group.

One might argue that the differences in TFP between joint-stock and privately owned firms are due purely to regional productivity differences. Perhaps it was the case that all of the low TFP firms were located in isolated markets where transport barriers protected them from competition. Specifications 4 and 5 test this hypothesis. Specification 4 introduces a dummy variable for firms located in the highly integrated, rapidly growing, four-state market of Rio de Janeiro, the Distrito Federal, Minas Gerais, and São Paulo. The coefficient on region (0.300) indicates that there were in fact sizable regional productivity differences. Specification 5 decomposes the effects of region and joint-stock status by introducing dummy variables for joint-stock firms located outside of the competitive region, joint-stock firms located in the region, and all other firms in the region.[45] The results indicate that even if one controls for regional effects, there is still a positive residual for firms that took the joint-stock form (note that the coefficient in line 9B is of greater magnitude than line 9A, and both are significant at the 1% level). The regressions also indicate that joint-stock firms outside of the competitive region had a sizable productivity advantage against their privately owned competitors. The coefficient of 0.285 (line 6A, specification 5) translates into a 33% productivity differential.

What advantage was conferred on joint-stock firms that created such sizable productivity differences? Table 10.8 indicates that joint-stock firms had higher capital–labor ratios, owing, no doubt, to the relative ease with which they could raise capital. One might imagine that this might have either allowed them to produce more cloth per worker or allowed them to specialize in high-value cloth, whose production required more capital-intensive techniques. Panel II of Table 10.9 tests these hypotheses by substituting the volume of cloth produced (in meters) for the real value of output (specifications 6, 7, 8, 9, and 10 mirror specifications 1 to 5, except that the proxy for output changes). With the exception of the time trend, the qualitative results of the relationship among vintage, region, capital–labor ratio, firm size, joint-stock status, and other relevant variables are similar to those obtained when output was proxied by real value. Joint-stock firms were more productive than their private competitors. Although there are a number of minor differences between the results in the two panels (such as the stronger impact of being publicly traded when output is proxied by volume), the only glaring difference is that when output is proxied by meters of cloth the time trend is negative. Thus, one can reject the hypothesis that joint-stock firms were able to produce more cloth per input than their private competitors.

The most reasonable interpretation of the variance of the time trend across the two panels is that joint-stock firms tended to produce more fine-weave, high-quality goods than private firms. Generally speaking, the production of such cloth requires that machines be run more slowly, because fine yarns are more subject to breakage. The result is that firms need to purchase larger numbers of machines to produce the same volume of cloth, resulting in more machines per worker than in firms that produce low-value cloth. These results are consistent with information on the value of various types of output in the 1907 and 1915 censuses. The census data indicate that joint-stock firms tended to produce more high-value goods than their private counterparts.

A skeptical reader might respond that the use of physical inputs of capital and labor in the production functions means that although public firms might have been more technically efficient, they were not necessarily more economically efficient. It might have been the case, for example, that the different techniques of production between joint-stock and private firms meant that joint-stock firms actually had higher unit costs because they had to purchase more expensive skilled labor or because they had to purchase more expensive types of raw cotton. Stigler's survivor method allows us to test this hypothesis. In a competitive market the most economically efficient firms survive, whereas those firms that are economically inefficient go out of business. Firm types or firm sizes that are inefficient will therefore grow more slowly than firm types or sizes that are efficient.

A glance at Table 10.10 demonstrates that the fastest growing type of firm was limited-liability joint-stock companies, and the fastest growing size category was small firms (capacity shares of less than 0.5%). Fastest growing of all were small joint-stock firms. Over the 30 years from 1905 to 1934, the number of joint-stock limited-liability companies more than tripled, whereas the number of private firms did not even double. The number of small joint-stock firms grew nearly fivefold (from 8 in 1905 to 47 in 1934). These results corroborate the findings in Tables 10.7, 10.8, and 10.9 that scale economies were exhausted at small firm sizes. They also corroborate the findings that joint-stock companies, regardless of size, were more efficient than private firms. In short, technical efficiency and economic efficiency were one and the same in the case under study.

TABLE 10.10

Survivorship, by Capacity and Firm Type, 1895–1934

	Number of Firms			Percentage of Firms		
	Joint Stock	Private	Total	Joint Stock	Private	Total
1905 Share of Capacity						
<.5%	8	33	41	9	37	46
.5–1.00%	3	15	18	3	17	20
1.01–3.00%	6	15	21	7	17	23
3.01–5.00%	6	3	9	7	3	10
>5.01%	1	0	1	1	0	1
Total	24	66	90	27	73	100
1915 Share of Capacity						
<.5%	23	87	110	14	51	65
.5–1.00%	19	16	35	11	9	21
1.01–3.00%	16	5	21	9	3	12
3.01–5.00%	2	1	3	1	1	2
>5.01%	1	0	1	1	0	1
Total	61	109	170	36	64	100
1925 Share of Capacity						
<.5%	44	96	140	24	52	77
.5–1.00%	10	8	18	5	4	10
1.01–3.00%	16	5	21	9	3	11
3.01–5.00%	3	0	3	2	0	2
>5.01%	1	0	1	1	0	1
Total	74	109	183	40	60	100
1934 Share of Capacity						
<.5%	47	105	152	23	52	75
.5–1.00%	11	13	24	5	6	12
1.01–3.00%	20	5	25	10	2	12
3.01–5.00%	1	0	1	0	0	0
>5.01%	1	0	1	0	0	0
Total	80	123	203	39	61	100

Source: See Table 10.1.

IV: CONCLUSIONS AND IMPLICATIONS

Changes in the regulations governing financial markets in Brazil allowed the capital markets to function more smoothly. It was not just that it was difficult to form a joint-stock company. Indeed, even after these restrictions were removed in 1882, capital did not quickly flow into the textile industry. Nor did legal restrictions on the operation of banks turn out to be important. Even after restrictions on the operations of banks were removed in 1890 there was little long-term investment by banks in the textile industry. Rather, the most important reforms were those related to limited-liability and mandatory disclosure. These reforms lowered the costs of monitoring managers and eliminated the need for shareholders to monitor one another. This allowed entrepreneurs to mobilize capital from beyond their founding kinship and business groups. Indeed, secondary markets developed in Rio de Janeiro and São Paulo that made these investments liquid.

These institutional changes meant that many firms (and potential firms) were no longer capital constrained. Not every firm could tap the capital markets, because it was necessary to either have a well-established reputation or have access to an intermediary who could signal investors that a firm was a good investment. It was the case, however, that large numbers of firms were able to take advantage of the joint-stock limited-liability form and mobilize capital from beyond their founding groups. The fall in the cost of capital meant that those firms had more flexibility in their choice of the capital–labor ratio. The result was an increase in the size of the industry and an increase in the rate of growth of productivity.

ACKNOWLEDGMENTS

Research for this paper was made possible through support provided by National Science Foundation grant number SBR-9515222 administered through the National Bureau of Economic Research. Research assistance was ably provided by Armando Razo and Moramay Lopez Alonso. This paper has benefited from comments by Charles Calomiris, John Coatsworth, Stanley Engerman, Avner Greif, Herbert Klein, Anne Krueger, Naomi Lamoreaux, Robert Packenham, Armando Razo, Jean Laurent Rosenthal, Kenneth Sokoloff, William Summerhill, Richard Sylla, Peter Temin, and Barry Weingast. Earlier versions were presented at the Summer Institute of the DAE Group of the NBER, the All-University of California Group in Economic History, the Research Division of the World Bank, the Social Science History Workshop at Stanford University, and the Conference of the Economic History Association. The usual caveats apply.

NOTES

1. The literature on institutions and growth suggests various avenues through which institutional reform can enhance productivity growth. For example, the definition of institutions also include the rules governing contracts within firms. Changes in labor laws, to cite one example, can produce significant changes in work rules, which may allow for organizational innovation by firms, thereby increasing productivity. This paper only considers one variant of the institutional literature and therefore concentrates on how changes in the institutions governing markets enhance productivity growth. For the most succinct statement of this view, see North (1991). For a survey and analysis of the different institutionalist approaches, see Greif (1997).

2. The notion here is that economic agents realize that there is about to be a reform of institutions and so bid asset prices up or down accordingly (see Clark 1996).

3. An example of such an analysis is Rosenthal's (1992) study of the impact of the French Revolution on the institutions that constrained agricultural productivity growth prior to 1789.

4. The term *capital markets* is used here to mean the organized process by which banks, brokers, and exchanges raise, securitize, distribute, trade, and continually value investment funds. Although the exact mechanisms are rarely examined empirically, one can infer from the literature that there are four channels through which the development of capital markets increases the efficiency of the rest of the economy. First, by eliminating the need for savers and investors to have direct knowledge of one another, capital markets increase allocative efficiency: Funds flow to those entrepreneurs who can provide savers with the highest risk-adjusted rate of return. Second, by lowering the cost of capital to firms (and potential firms), capital markets allow entrepreneurs greater flexibility in their choice of the capital-to-labor ratio. Third, by allowing firms the ability to grow far more rapidly than they would be able to otherwise, capital markets permit firms to rapidly reach the size at which they can take advantage of potential scale economies in production. Fourth, by lowering the cost of capital to entrepreneurs and potential entrepreneurs, new firms come into existence that would not have existed otherwise. The result is an increase in the rate of technical change (because new firms are putting physical plants of more recent vintage into service) and increased competition, which intensifies entrepreneurial efforts to raise productivity through new technological and organizational innovations. For a comparison of the U.S. and German cases, arguing that Germany had a more efficient financial system because of differences in the regulation of banking, see Calomiris (1994).

5. Carr and Mathewson (1988).

6. On the impact of Brazil's inefficient railroad system, see Summerhill (1997). On the myriad problems constraining growth in nineteenth-century Brazil, see Leff (1982, 1997).

7. As Kuznets pointed out, textiles tend to be the first manufacturing industry to develop as economies modernize. Brazil conformed to this general pattern. At the time of Brazil's first full-scale industrial census in 1920, cotton textiles accounted for 24.4% of manufacturing value added, a higher percentage than any other manufacturing activity. See Kuznets (1971), pp. 111–113; see also Haber (1992).

8. This does not mean that there were no scale economies in cotton textile production. Indeed, had the minimum efficient scale of production been extremely small—such as that found in industries like beeswax candle making—differences in access to low-cost capital could not have played a role in raising productivity. It does mean, however, that economies of scale were exhausted in textiles at relatively small firm sizes compared with industries such as steel, cement, or chemicals. Indeed, the estimates of firm-level TFP later in this paper indicate a minimum efficient scale equivalent to a market share of less than 0.5%.

9. Some of these are only partial censuses: The 1895 census only reports the returns from large firms, the 1901 and 1908 censuses are strongly biased toward São Paulo firms, and the 1923 census only reports large firms that were members of the Rio de Janeiro cotton textile manufacturer's association. The others are all nationwide censuses of all mechanized firms.

10. See, for example, Griliches and Ringstad (1971).

11. The 15 firms are as follows: Companhia de Fiaçao e Tecidos Alliança, Companhia America Fabril, Companhia Brasil Industrial, Companhia de Fiaçao e Tecelagem Carioca, Companhia de Fiaçao e Tecidos Industrial Campista, Companhia de Fiaçao e Tecidos Cometa, Companhia de Fiaçao e Tecidos Confiança Industrial, Companhia de Fiaçao e Tecidos Corcovado, Companhia de Fiaçao e Tecidos Industrial Mineira, Companhia de Fiaçao e Tecidos Mageénse, Companhia Manufactora Fluminense, Companhia Petropolitana, Companhia Progresso Industrial do Brasil, Companhia de Fiaçao e Tecidos Santo Aleixo, and Companhia Fabrica de Tecidos São Pedro de Alcantara.

Some of these reports were located in the Bibliotheca Nacional in Rio de Janeiro, filed erroneously in the periodicals section. Most were retrieved from the *Jornal do Commercio* (Rio de Janeiro's major financial daily) and the *Diario Official* (Brazil's equivalent of the *Federal Register*). In theory, it would be possible to retrieve the reports of all publicly traded companies from these and similar sources—such as the *Diario Official* for each state and the major financial dailies of all the major cities—because under Brazilian law, firms had to reprint abbreviated versions of their financial statements in public venues. In practice, however, this is a costly procedure because none of the relevant publications is indexed and each runs to roughly 20,000 pages per year. I therefore concentrated on the months of January, February, March, April, July, and August (when most firms produced their financial statements) for the *Jornal do Commercio* and the *Diario Official*. Research in progress is retrieving reports published in *O Estado de São Paulo* (São Paulo's major newspaper) and the *Diario Official do Estado de São Paulo*. Even restricting analysis to these four publications and concentrating solely on the months listed earlier requires the researcher to look at roughly 1 million frames of microfilm to cover the 60 years from 1880 to 1940.

12. Ridings (1994), p. 294.
13. Topik (1987), p. 28.
14. Topik (1987), p. 28; Peláez and Suzigan (1976), chaps. 2–5; Saes (1986), pp. 22, 73, 27–86; Levy (1977), pp. 109–112; Stein (1957), pp. 25–27; Sylla (1975), pp. 52, 209.
15. Presumably this provision of the law was meant to protect individuals and enterprises doing business with joint-stock companies, as well as to protect outside investors from being fleeced by unscrupulous corporate promoters. The fear evidently was that individuals would found a firm, take on large amounts of debt, sell virtually all of the stock to outsiders, transfer the wealth of the firm to themselves, and then leave their creditors holding unrepayable debts and the outside investors holding watered stock. See Levy (1977), p. 117; Peláez and Suzigan (1976), pp. 78–83, 96–97; Saes (1986), pp. 22, 86; Hanley (1995); and Ridings (1994).
16. Borja Castro (1869); Commissão de Inquerito Industrial (1882).
17. Spindlage is used as the index for capacity because it is widely agreed that it provides the best proxy for physical capital.
18. Mexican textile data from Haber (1997). National income data from Coatsworth, (1978), p. 82. Note that Mexico and Brazil had roughly similar population sizes in the early 1880s: 9.1 million and 9.9 million, respectively.
19. Hanley (1995), pp. 24, 27.
20. Hanley (1995), pp. 24–28; Topik (1987), pp. 28–32; Peláez and Suzigan (1976), pp. 141–143; Stein (1957), p. 86.
21. Shareholder lists were not always published in the abbreviated reports reprinted in the newspapers, but they were published in the original reports.
22. 1888 data are from Neuhaus (1975), p. 19ff. Data for 1889, 1890, and 1891 were calculated from consolidated stock tables in *O Estado de São Paulo* and *Jornal do Commercio* (see Table 10.1). A conto was equal to 1,000 milreis, the basic unit of Brazilian currency. There were roughly three milreis to the dollar in 1890.
23. Neuhaus (1975), p. 22. For a discussion of bank portfolios see Hanley (1995) and Triner (1994).
24. Triner (1994), Hanley (1995).

25. Weid and Rodrigues Bastos (1986).

26. On the financing of the New England textile industry, see McGouldrick (1968) and Davis (1957).

27. Haber (1989), chap. 5.

28. McGouldrick (1968).

29. On the early industrial United States, see Davis (1957) and McGouldrick (1968).

30. Debt–equity ratios were calculated from *Moody's Industrials* for 1900, 1910, and 1920.

31. Preferred shares are less favorable for firms than bonds because, like bonds, they carry the requirement of guaranteed interest payments, but at the same time they afford the firm much less flexibility. Unlike bondholders, preferred shareholders have the right to make claims on profits beyond the guaranteed interest rate. In addition, bonds are amortized, whereas preferred shares are not. Unless repurchased from shareholders, preferred shares require the payment of guaranteed returns to their holders in perpetuity. Finally, any such repurchase must be done at the market value of the shares, unlike callable bonds, which are repurchased at their par value. Since preferred shareholders have the right to a share of profits beyond the guaranteed interest rate, this means that the profitability of the firm becomes capitalized in their market value. Thus, almost by definition, a firm that has the ability to buy back its preferred shares is going to have to pay a price significantly above the par value of the shares to do so.

32. Haber (1989), chap. 5.

33. For a history of the struggle by industrialists to obtain protective tariffs, see Vilela Luz (1978).

34. Leff (1997), Suzigan (1986).

35. Graham Clark (1910), p. 38.

36. Haber (1997).

37. When output is measured in real values, this produces capital and labor weights of .35 and .65, respectively. When output is measured in physical units (meters of cloth), this produces capital and labor weights of .34 and .66.

38. See, for instance, Kane (1988).

39. See Atack (1985), Sokoloff (1984), and Bernard and Jones (1996).

40. For ordinary least-squares (OLS) estimates, this coefficient would be the same for all firms; for fixed effects, it was not estimated because it was allowed to vary freely among cross sections. Both models, the basic pooled and fixed effects, produced the same qualitative results with minor differences in the magnitude of the estimated coefficients. In some cases, as with the time trend, the estimates were nearly identical. Thus, to avoid repetition, I report only results from the basic pooled model.

41. In the construction of time series for each observation unit, it is evident that plain OLS techniques would result in biased estimates because some of the variables in latter periods could be predicted from earlier years (e.g., spindles at time t could very well be equal to spindles at time t +1). The panel procedure individually identifies each company over time to correct for potential autocorrelation in its variables.

42. This specification provides a simple test for economies of scale, following the methodology of Atack (1985). The sign of β_2 would indicate whether, if negative, there are decreasing returns to scale or, if positive, increasing returns to scale. The magnitude of β_2 would indicate the level to which production deviates from the standard case of constant returns to scale. A coefficient of small magnitude, that is not statistically significant, would corroborate the hypothesis of constant returns to scale. The additional variables, **Dummies** and **Interaction Terms**, are vectors of dummy explanatory variables (including limited-liability status, trading in the stock market, and location in the central region), respectively; δ and γ are correspondingly the coefficient vectors. I use these to further decompose the rate of growth (β_3) of TFP. The same results are obtained if one uses a specification where the variables are not normalized by the labor input, but in that case one would not be able to test for economies of scale. Whether or not one normalizes by labor, β_3 remains the rate of total factor productivity growth because, in both cases, the contribution of the two inputs would have been accounted for by the estimates of β_1 and β_2.

43. Intercept coefficients can be translated into percentages through the following formula: $e^{\beta_1} - 1$.

44. Brander and Spencer (1989).

45. The fact that virtually all the joint-stock companies were located in the four-state region means that these variables are likely to be collinear. Thus, one cannot simultaneously introduce dummy variables for region and joint-stock to measure the marginal impact of being traded taking region into account.

REFERENCES

Atack, Jeremy. *Estimation of Economies of Scale in Nineteenth Century United States Manufacturing and the Form of the Production Function*. New York: Garland Publishers, 1985.

Bandeira, Antonio F., Jr. *A industria no estado de São Paulo*. São Paulo, 1908.

Barjau Martinez, Luis, et al. "Estadísticas económicas del siglo XIX." *Cuadernos de*

Trabajo del Departamento de Investigaciones Históricas, INAH, no. 14 (July 1976).

Bernard, A. B., and C. I. Jones. "Productivity Across Industries and Countries." *The Review of Economics and Statistics* 78, no. 1 (1996): 135–146.

Bibliotheca da Associacão Industrial. *Archivo da Exposicão da Industria Nacional de 1881*. Rio de Janeiro: Tipographia Nacional, 1982.

Borja Castro, Agostino Vioto de. "Relatório do segundo grupo." In *Relatório da segunda Exposição Nacional de 1866*, edited by Antonio José de Souza Rego, 3–73. Rio de Janeiro, 1869.

Brander, James A., and Barbara J. Spencer. "Moral Hazard and Limited Liability: Implications for the Theory of the Firm." *International Economic Review* 30, no. 4 (1989): 833–849.

Branner, John C. "Cotton in the Empire of Brazil." U.S. Department of Agriculture Special Report no. 8. Washington, DC, 1885.

Brazil. Commissão [para] Exposicão Universal [em] Philadelphia. *The Empire of Brazil at the Universal Exhibition of 1876 in Philadelphia*. Rio de Janeiro: Typ. e Lithographia do Imperial Instituto Artistico, 1876.

Brazil. Commissão de Inquerito Industrial. *Relatório ao Ministerio da Fazenda*. Rio de Janeiro, 1882.

Brazil. Instituto Brasileiro de Geografia e Estatística. *Estatísticas históricas do Brasil*. Rio de Janeiro, 1890.

Brazil. Ministerio da Industria, Viação e Obras Publicas. *Relatório, 1896*. Rio de Janeiro, 1896.

Brazil. Prefeitura do Distrito Federal. *Noticia sobre o desenvolvimento da industria fabril no Distrito Federal e sua situação actual*. Milano: Tipografia Fratelli Trevos, 1908.

Calomiris, Charles W. "The Costs of Rejecting Universal Banking: American Finance in the German Mirror, 1870–1914." In *The Coordination of Economic Activity within and between Firms*, edited by Naomi Lamoreaux and Daniel Raff. Chicago: University of Chicago Press, 1994.

Carr, Jack L., and G. Frank Mathewson. "Unlimited Liability as a Barrier to Entry." *Journal of Political Economy* 96, no. 4 (1988): 766–784.

Centro Industrial do Brasil. *O Brasil: suas riquezas naturaes, suas industrias*. Vol. 3, *Industria de Transportes, Industria Fabril*. Rio de Janeiro, 1909.

Centro Industrial do Brasil. *Relatório da Directoria para ser Apresentado a Assemblea Geral Ordinaria do anno de 1915*. Rio de Janeiro, 1915.

Centro Industrial do Brasil. *O Centro Industrial na conferencia algodoeira*. Rio de Janeiro, 1917.

Centro Industrial de Fiação e Tecelagem de Algodão (CIFTA). *Relatório da Directoria 1921–1922*. Rio de Janeiro, 1922.

Centro Industrial de Fiaçao e Tecelagem de Algodão (CIFTA). *Exposição de Tecidos de Algodão*. Rio de Janeiro, 1923.

Centro Industrial de Fiaçao e Tecelagem de Algodão (CIFTA). *Relatório da Directoria 1923*. Rio de Janeiro, 1924.

Centro Industrial de Fiaçao e Tecelagem de Algodão (CIFTA). *Relatório da Directoria.* Rio de Janeiro, 1924.

Centro Industrial de Fiaçao e Tecelagem de Algodão (CIFTA). *Relatório da Directoria do Centro Industrial de Fiação e Tecelagem de Algodão do anno 1925.* Rio de Janeiro, circa 1925.

Centro Industrial de Fiaçao e Tecelagem de Algodão (CIFTA). *Fabricas filiadas.* Rio de Janeiro, circa 1926.

Centro Industrial de Fiaçao e Tecelagem de Algodão (CIFTA). *Estatísticas da industria, commercio e lavoura de Algodão relativos ao anno de 1927.* Rio de Janeiro, 1928.

Centro Industrial de Fiaçao e Tecelagem de Algodão (CIFTA). *Fiaçao e Tecelagem: Censo Organizado pelo Centro Industrial de Fiaçao e Tecelagem de Algodão.* Rio de Janeiro, 1935.

Clark, Gregory. "The Political Foundations of Modern Economic Growth, England, 1540–1800." *The Journal of Interdisciplinary History* 26, no. 4 (1996): 563–588.

Coatsworth, John H. "Obstacles to Economic Growth in Nineteenth-Century Mexico." *American Historical Review* 83, no. 1 (1978): 80–100.

Consul Ricketts. *Report.* C4657, 1xv, 1886, pp. 187–188.

Cunha Vasco. "A Industria de Algodão." *Boletim do Centro Industrial do Brasil.* Fasciculo 111. Rio de Janeiro, 1905.

Cunha Vasco. *Fabrica de fiação e tecelagem de Algodão.* Rio de Janeiro, 1908.

Davis, Lance. "Sources of Industrial Finance: The American Textile Industry, A Case Study." *Explorations in Entrepreneurial History* 9 (1957): 189–203.

Davis, Lance. "Capital Immobilities and Finance Capitalism: A Study of Economic Evolution in the United States, 1820–1920." *Explorations in Economic History* 1 (1963): 88–105.

Davis, Lance. "The Capital Markets and Industrial Concentration: The U.S. and U.K., A Comparative Study." *The Economic History Review* 19 (1966): 255–272.

Davis, Lance E., and H. Louis Stettler III. "The New England Textile Industry, 1825–1860: Trends and Fluctuations." In *Output, Employment, and Productivity in the United States after 1800.* Conference on Research on Income and Wealth. New York: National Bureau of Economic Research, 1966.

de Carvalho, José Carlos. "O Algodão: sua historia." In *Sociedade Nacional de Agricultura.* Fasciculo No. 7. Rio de Janeiro, 1900.

de Carvalho, José Carlos. "O Cafe: Sua historia." In *Sociedade Nacional de Agricultura.* Fasciculo No. 7. Rio de Janeiro, 1900.

De Long, J. Bradford, et al. "Did J. P. Morgan's Men Add Value? An Economist's Perspective on Financial Capitalism." In *Inside the Business Enterprise: Historical Perspectives on the Use of Information*, edited by Peter Temin, 205–236. National Bureau of Economic Research Report. Chicago and London: University of Chicago Press, 1991.

Diario Official do Estado de São Paulo. São Paulo, 1891–1940.

Diario Official da Federacão. Rio de Janeiro, 1890–1940.

dos Santos Pires, Antonio Olyntho. *Relatório apresentado ao Presidente da Republica dos Estados Unidos do Brasil pelo Ministerio de Estado dos Negocios da Industria, Viacão e Obras Publicas.* Rio de Janeiro, 1896.

El Economista Mexicano. Mexico City, 4 July 1914.

García Cubas, Antonio. *Cuadro geográfico, estadístico, descriptivo é histórico de los estados unidos mexicanos.* Mexico City, 1884–1885.

García Cubas, Antonio. *Mexico: Its Trade, Industries and Resources.* Mexico City, 1893.

Graham Clark, William A. *Cotton Goods in Latin America Part I: Cuba, Mexico, and Central America.* Washington, DC, 1910.

Greif, Avner. "Micro Theory and Recent Developments in the Study of Economic Institutions through Economic History." In *Advances in Economic Theory*, edited by David M. Kreps and Kenneth F. Wallis. Cambridge University Press, 1997.

Griliches, Zvi, and Vidar Ringstad. *Economies of Scale and the Form of the Production Function: An Econometric Study of Norwegian Manufacturing Establishment Data.* Amsterdam: North Holland Publishing Co., 1971.

Haber, Stephen H. *Industry and Underdevelopment: The Industrialization of Mexico, 1890–1940.* Stanford: Stanford University Press, 1989.

Haber, Stephen H. "Industrial Concentration and the Capital Markets: A Comparative Study of Brazil, Mexico, and the United States, 1830–1930." *Journal of Economic History* 51, no. 3 (1991): 559–580.

Haber, Stephen H. "Business Enterprise and the Great Depression in Brazil: A Study of Profits and Losses in Textile Manufacturing." *Business History Review* 66, no. 2 (1992): 335–363.

Haber, Stephen H. "Financial Markets and Industrial Development: A Comparative Study of Governmental Regulation, Financial Innovation, and Industrial Structure in Brazil and Mexico, 1840–1930." In *How Latin America Fell Behind: Essays on the Economic Histories of Brazil and Mexico, 1800–1914*, edited by Stephen Haber. Stanford: Stanford University Press, 1997.

Hanley, Anne. "Capital Markets in the Coffee Economy." Ph.D. dissertation, Stanford University, 1995.

Jornal do Commercio. Rio de Janeiro, 1880–1940.

Kane, Nancy Frances. *Textiles in Transition: Technology, Wages, and Industry Relocation in the United States Textile Industry 1880-1930*. New York: Greenwood Press, 1988.

Kuznets, Simon. *Economic Growth of Nations: Total Output and Production Structure.* Cambridge: Belknap Press of Harvard University Press, 1971.

Lamoreaux, Naomi. "Banks, Kinship, and Economic Development: The New England Case." *Journal of Economic History* 46 (1986): 647–667.

Leff, Nathaniel. *Underdevelopment and Development in Brazil*. London: George Allen & Unwin Publishers, 1982.

Leff, Nathaniel. "Economic Development in Brazil, 1822–1913." In *How Latin America Fell Behind: Essays on the Economic Histories of Brazil and Mexico, 1800–1914*, edited by Stephen Haber. Stanford: Stanford University Press, 1997.

Levy, Maria Bárbara. *História da bolsa de valores do Rio de Janeiro*. Rio de Janeiro, 1977.

McGouldrick, Paul F. *New England Textiles in the Nineteenth Century*. Cambridge, MA: Harvard University Press, 1968.

McKinnon, Ronald I. *Money and Capital in Economic Development*. Washington, DC: Brookings Institution, 1973.

Mexico. Archivo General de la Nación. "Extracto de las Manifestaciones presentadas por los fabricantes de hilados y tejidos de algodón para el semestre de enero a junio de 1913." Caja 31, Exp. 2, Mexico City, n.d.

Mexico. Archivo General de la Nación. "Extracto de las Manifestaciones presentadas por los fabricantes de hilados y tejidos de algodón para el semestre de enero a junio de 1912." Caja 5, Exp. 4, Mexico City, n.d.

Mexico. Dirección General de Estadística. *Anuario estadístico de la República Mexicana 1893–94*. Mexico, 1894.

Mexico. Gobierno del Estado de México. *Estadística del Departamento de México*. Mexico, 1980.

Mexico. Ministerio de Fomento. *Memoria 1865*. Mexico, 1866.

Mexico. Secretaría del Estado. *Memoria de la Secretaría del Estado y del Despacho de Fomento, Colonización, Industria y Comercio de la República Mexicana*. Mexico, 1857.

Mexico. Secretaría de Fomento. *Boletín Semestral de la República Mexicana*. Mexico City, 1890.

Mexico. Secretaría de Fomento, Colonización e Industria. *Memoria que la dirección de colonización e industria presentó al Ministerio de Relaciones en 17 de Enero de 1852, sobre el estado de estos ramos en el año anterior*. Mexico, 1852.

Mexico. Secretaría de Hacienda. *Estadísticas de la República Mexicana*. Mexico City, 1880.

Mexico. Secretaría de Hacienda. *Estadística de la República Mexicana*. Mexico, 1896.

Mexico. Secretaría de Hacienda. *Memoria de la Secretaría de Hacienda*. Mexico, 1896.

Mexico. Secretaría de Hacienda y Crédito Público (SHCP). *Boletín de la Secretaría de*

Hacienda y Crédito Público. Mexico City, 1917–1932.

Mexico. Secretaría de Hacienda y Crédito Público (SHCP). *Documentos para el estudio de la industrialización de México, 1837–1845*. Mexico City, 1977.

Mexico. Secretaría de Hacienda y Crédito Público (SHCP). Departamento de Estadística. "Estadísticas del ramo de hilados y tejidos de algodón y de lana." Obras Raras Collection. Library of Banco de México. Mexico City, n.d.

Neuhaus, Paulo. *História monetária do Brasil, 1900–45*. Rio de Janeiro: Instituto Brasileiro de Mercado de Capitais, 1975.

North, Douglass C. *Institutions, Institutional Change, and Economic Performance*. Cambridge University Press, 1991.

O Estado de São Paulo. São Paulo, 1888–1921.

Patrick, Hugh. "Financial Development and Economic Growth in Underdeveloped Countries." *Economic Development and Cultural Change* 14 (1966): 174–189.

Peláez, Carlos Manuel, and Wilson Suzigan. *História monetária do Brasil: Análise da política, comportamento e institucões monetárias*. Brasilia: IPEA/INPES, 1976.

Pérez Hernandez, José Maria. *Estadística de la República Mexicana*. Guadalajara, 1862.

Retrospecto Commercial do Jornal do Comercio. Rio de Janeiro, 1911–1930.

Ridings, Eugene. *Business Interest Groups in Nineteenth-Century Brazil*. Cambridge University Press, 1994.

Rosenthal, Jean Laurent. *The Fruits of Revolution: Property Rights, Litigation, and French Agriculture, 1700–1860*. Cambridge University Press, 1992.

Saes, Flávio Azevedo Marques de. *Crédito e bancos no desenvolvimento da economia paulista, 1850–1930*. São Paulo: Instituto de Pesquisas Economicas, 1986.

Semana Mercantil. Mexico City, various dates.

Smith, George David, and Richard Sylla. "The Transformation of Financial Capitalism: An Essay on the History of American Capital Markets." *Financial Markets, Institutions and Instruments* 2, no. 2 (1993): 1–61.

Sokoloff, Kenneth L. "Was the Transition from the Artisanal Shop to the Non-Mechanized Factory Associated with Gains in Efficiency? Evidence from the U.S. Manufacturing Censuses of 1820 and 1850." *Explorations in Economic History* 20 (1984): 351–382.

Stein, Stanley J. *The Brazilian Cotton Textile Manufacture: Textile Enterprise in an Underdeveloped Area*. Cambridge, MA: Harvard University Press, 1957.

Summerhill, William R. "Transport Improvements and Economic Growth in Brazil and Mexico." In *How Latin America Fell Behind: Essays on the Economic Histories of Brazil and Mexico, 1800–1914*, edited by Stephen Haber. Stanford: Stanford University Press, 1997.

Suzigan, Wilson. *Indústria brasileira: Origem e desenvolvimento*. São Paulo: Editora Brasiliense, 1986.

Sylla, Richard E. *The American Capital Market, 1846–1914.* New York: Arno Press, 1975.

Topik, Steven. *Political Economy of the Brazilian State, 1889–1930.* Austin: University of Texas Press, 1987.

Triner, Gail D. "Banks and Brazilian Economic Development: 1906–1930." Ph.D. dissertation, Columbia University, 1994.

Vilela Luz, Nicia. *A luta pela industrialização do Brasil.* São Paulo: Editora Alfa Omega, 1978.

Weid, Elisabeth Von der, and Ana Marta Rodrigues Bastos. *O fio da meada: Estrategoa de expansão de uma industria têxtil, Companhia América Fabril, 1878–1930.* Rio de Janeiro: FCRB, 1986.

11

Why Did Cuban Cane Growers
Lose Autonomy? 1889–1929

Alan Dye
Barnard College

In the 1880s, technical change and organizational adaptation permitted Cuba to recover from the crisis of emancipation and the aftermath of the Ten Years' War (1868–1878) to answer the competitive threat of European beet sugar and to reemerge, after 1898, as the world's leading sugar-producing country. Key to the recovery was the abandonment of the age-old organizational practice of the vertically integrated plantation and the successful innovation of raw material provision by contracting with outside cane growers. The innovation resulted in a high rate of growth for the industry between the 1890s and 1929, averaging 4.5% annually and increasing its share of the world sugar market from about 10% in the 1890s to over 20% in the 1920s.[1]

Interestingly, the historiography has often ascribed little importance to the growth consequences of innovation and has focused instead on its impact on the industrial structure in Cuba—the concentration of ownership and control over land and other key resources. Conventionally, the story is told of the rise of a Cuban rural middle class of independent cane growers, which was afterward arrested by enormous, foreign-owned, land-hungry mills that, using superior financial power, subdued small and medium-sized rural proprietors into a feudal-like relationship within colossal sugar latifundia.[2] The sugar latifundium became a symbol of the North American subordination of Cuban industry, the prelude to the Revolution of 1959.[3]

The conventional story of the demise of the independent cane grower follows the work of Ramiro Guerra y Sánchez. His seminal work argued that the diminished control of cane growers was caused by *latifundización* accomplished by two means: acquisition of land and imposition of long-term contracts on both owner-operator and tenant growers. He criticized the long-term contract as an instrument of coercion that converted the cane grower into a "serf of the mill, tied down by contract and impeded from freely selling his produce," and he argued that a cane market free of cane-growing contracts would have been a superior arrangement for growers.[4] Other discussions have closely followed Guerra y Sánchez's analysis; for example, see Nelson, Chonchol, Bianchi, CERP, and Pino Santos.

This paper focuses on one of the two means by which *latifundización* was accomplished—the contract. An examination of the evolution of the cane contract demonstrates that modifications in the contract became more restrictive and reduced the autonomy of the cane grower over time. But what caused the loss of autonomy? Guerra y Sánchez and others have ascribed it to the greater financial power of North American companies that entered the industry in large numbers after independence in 1898. The new institutional economics, although it does not challenge the importance of financial resources, can provide a better understanding of why the contracts became more restrictive to *colonos*. Using a theoretical framework developed by Oliver Hart and Sanford Grossman, I conclude that a key reason for the reduced autonomy of the Cuban cane grower was that the reassignment of rights of control over locationally specific assets reduced the transaction costs the mills incurred when they contracted for cane.[5] The lost autonomy did not necessarily mean a worsening of terms since it contributed to increased productivity, but this also depended on whether growers received additional compensation. Evidence shows that some of the productivity gains were passed on to growers in the forms of higher rates of pay and an increase in the number of contracts offered.

Guerra y Sánchez, the principal author of the conventional view, argued that the terms of the contract were essentially coercive—imposed unilaterally by the mill onto the grower. A more careful analysis of the evidence demonstrates that the contracts actually served to protect growers against opportunism. Some key features of the cane contract cannot be explained except as guarantees to the grower against possible opportunism of the mill. If the grower was coerced to accept whatever contractual conditions the mills offered, as the *latifundización* thesis has come to imply, it is difficult to explain why key features that spoke directly to the growers' interests were so deeply embedded in the cane contract.

Central to understanding the loss of autonomy is the process of evolution of the contracting arrangements known as the *colono* system. The *colono* system was an organizational response to technical change in sugar manufacturing that altered the benefits and costs of integrated versus specialized production of the raw material, sugar cane.[6] The contracts evolved gradually as agents learned how to reduce transaction costs by modifying the specific rights assigned by the contracts. As they did, the autonomy of *colonos*, or their control over the operations of their businesses, diminished because the stipulations of the contracts transferred more specific rights of control to the mill management. A sample of contracts written in the 1890s and 1920s, discussed below, permits direct examination of these changes in stipulations and the specific rights they transferred.

THE EARLY *COLONO* CONTRACT

The cane contracting relationship had originated in Cuba prior to the 1870s, but it was not until the 1880s and 1890s that it was adopted widely and relied on for providing a significant portion of the mills' raw material needs. Its earliest appearance came about at midcentury as some planters experimented with contracting out for cane as a means of attracting free laborers to replace the diminishing slave population.[7] Contracting out for cane became more widely practiced by the 1880s, as planters' needs changed with the emergence of continuous-process milling technology. Those plantations that did not install new machinery were threatened with bankruptcy. Meanwhile, the Ten Years' War (1868–1878) and emancipation (1870–1886) had been costly for sugar producers in Cuba. Many emerged from these events in debt and unable to raise capital to invest in new machinery. But because the new optimal scale of production was much greater, those who were able to raise the funds to install the new large-scale mills had much greater demands for cane than they had previously. To supply these new mills, some innovating mill owners contracted with former planters, who agreed to cease grinding and commit to supply their cane to the neighboring incipient central mill.[8] From that point, the lands of many former plantations were contracted out to provide cane, often divided up into smaller parcels. *Colono* arrangements eventually became the main source of cane supplies to Cuban mills.[9]

Table 11.1 illustrates some of these trends quantitatively. The number of mills fell from 1,190 to 163 between 1877 and 1929 as the average capacity of mills increased by more than 72 times. The overall outcome of these inverse trends was a huge increase, about twelvefold, in Cuba's annual sugar export crop. By 1894, just before the outbreak of the Cuban War for Independence (1895–1898), it is estimated that *colonos* provided about 30% of the cane supplies to mills on the island. By 1929, *colonos* provided about 82% of all cane supplied to mills.

TABLE 11.1

Sugar Production in Cuba, 1877–1929

Year	Active Mills	Sugar Produced (thousands of metric tons)	Price of Sugar, Net of U.S. Duties (cents/lb.)	Sugar per Mill (thousands of metric tons)	Cane Land per Mill (thousands of acres)	Ratio of Sugar to Cane (%)	Percentage of Cane Produced by Colonos
1877	1190	526.8	—	0.4	0.5	6.1	—
1894	450	1110.9	2.87	2.5	—	—	30.0
1905	174	1078.7	2.93	6.2	3.5	9.9	—
1913	172	2515.1	2.16	14.6	7.8	10.9	69.7
1916	189	3104	4.78	16.5	8.0	11.5	—
1929	163	5352.6	1.94	32.8	14.8	12.4	81.7

Sources: See Dye (1998), Tables 6.1 and 6.2.

The relative uniformity of the later contracts, of the 1920s, contrasted great-ly with the considerable variation in the forms of early, 1890s contracts. From the 1880s forward, the contracts that formalized the *colono*-mill exchange rela-tionship evolved considerably from heterogeneous, rudimentary, and experi-mental forms to a mature standard-form contract by the 1920s. Still, some features were uniform throughout their existence. *Colono* contracts were agreements between a mill owner and a grower that provided for the planting, cultivation, harvest, and delivery of cane. Generally, the mill was given the exclusive right to grind the cane grown on the contracted *colonia* in exchange for the commitment to grind it. Duration was for a period of several years, typically 6 to 10. Payment was typically specified as *x* arrobas of sugar per 100 arrobas of cane delivered to the mill. (An arroba = 25 lbs.) Additionally, the agreements often involved lease and credit agreements, though not always. *Colonos'* tenure and access to credit varied. Many *colonos* owned their own land or had independent sources of credit; in such cases the lease or credit agree-ments might not apply.

The heterogeneity in early *colono* contracts is understandable since, as an innovation in how mills' cane provisions were organized, there was a need to experiment to learn about the problems of using contracts to procure cane. Some contracts were more complete, some less. Table 11.2 gives the frequency of selected features of a sample of 38 contracts written between 1889 and 1897. Clauses specified the sale and grinding commitment, the payment, planting of cane, some conditions on deliveries, lease, the provision of credit for plantings and other scheduled gang work, and right-of-way (to permit passage by the other *colonos*). Some contracts more completely specified how other contin-

TABLE 11.2

Inclusion of Selected Provisions of *Colono* Contracts, 1889–1897

	Count	Percentage
Number of Contracts in Sample	38	
Defining Features		
Provisions for plantings (new or existing)	38	100
Duration	36	95
Payment specified in sugar or equivalent[a]	34	89
Exclusive grinding commitment	30	79
Tenure and Credit		
Leased from mill	17	45
Owner-operated	12	32
Leased from third party	2	5
Provisions for credit to be provided by mill	12	32
Deliveries		
Provision that cane must be delivered in proper condition[b]	30	80
Rights-of-way for railroad or for other *colonos*	13	32
Obligations of grower to suspend cutting and delivery	10	26
Rights of mill to suspend delivery and grinding	9	24
Nonperformance		
Rights of mill if grower fails to fulfill obligations of the contract	7	18
Rights of grower if mill fails to fulfill obligations of the contract	5	13

[a] In 15 out of 35 contracts, payment was specified in kind at a rate of x arrobas of sugar per 100 arrobas of cane delivered, with provisions for where the sugar was to be delivered and which party would bear the ancillary costs. In 9 contracts, payment was stated to be the "cash equivalent" of x arrobas of sugar per 100 arrobas of cane. In 4 contracts, the price was stated to be in money scaled to the price of sugar.

[b] The standard provision, which was present in 80 percent of the sample contracts (28 contracts), was that the cane must be delivered "mature and free of straw, shoots, and roots." In three cases, some additional restrictions either on the time between cutting and delivery or the specific gravity of the cane juice at delivery were included.

Source: Compiled from documents collected from USNA, R.G. 76, Entry 352.

gencies, such as machinery breakdowns and cane fires, were to be treated. Examples of different styles of contract are found in Dye (1997).

The heterogeneity of early contracts might also be explained, in part, by the heterogeneity of wealth, status, experience, and bargaining power of *colonos*. Those who became *colonos* ranged from former planters to ex-foremen, oxcart drivers (who worked on contract), and so forth. The success of early *colonos* attracted urban middle-class investors to become *colonos*—as one observer noted, "lawyers, merchants, physicians and in short all those who ... knew how to evaluate the payoff the first-comers received."[10] Their social class, education, and agricultural and business experience differed considerably. Sizes of *colonias* varied according to wealth and access to credit, ranging usually from 30 acres to a few thousand acres.

In contrast with these early contracts, a perusal of the later, more uniform, 1920s contracts gives an overall impression that they granted broad powers to the mill and imposed numerous specific requirements on the *colono*. In particular, they provided in-contract guarantees against nonperformance of the *colono*, but they did not provide for similar guarantees to the *colono*. Selected clauses of the contract are summarized in Appendix 2. (See Dye 1997 for the complete contract.) Guerra y Sánchez attacked contracts such as this as "inflexible and unfair," forced on the *colono*, containing whatever conditions the mill desired.[11] Consistent with his criticism, the stipulations on the *colono* in the later contracts gave the mill rights to make many of the important decisions regarding planting, cultivation, and harvesting. Also, in contrast with earlier contracts, later contracts consistently provided for supervision and penalties if the conditions were not met (see Appendix 2).

DEFINING CHARACTERISTICS
OF THE *COLONO*-MILL RELATIONSHIP

Implicit in Guerra y Sánchez's criticism of the latifundium is the counterfactual premise that cane could have been supplied to mills through a free market by independent *colonos* free of contractual obligations.[12] Notwithstanding his belief, examination of the technical requirements of sugar production shows that a spot market was not a viable way to organize cane provisions to mills. Evidence from the late nineteenth century points to the ubiquitous use of multiple-year contracts, and the few growers without contracts indicate that a contract was preferred.[13] Furthermore, the organization of sugar enterprises in the rest of the world attested that some form of complex contractual arrangement or vertical integration were the only choices. Indeed, Cuba's principal competitors, in Hawaii and Java, were vertically integrated.

First, the cane transaction depended on investments by both parties in location-specific assets.[14] From the grower's standpoint, the establishment of a cane *colonia* implied a long-term physical commitment to a nearby mill because once cane was cut, it had to be ground immediately to avoid substantial losses of sucrose and water. It deteriorated too rapidly to be shipped except a short distance; therefore, it could only be ground at a mill within close proximity of the cane field. Furthermore, a cane planting was a durable investment, which produced usually between 6 and 10, and sometimes more, annual crops. This meant that the grower would require a reasonably secure arrangement for selling the cane for several years before he would be willing to incur the investment of planting a cane field.

From the mill's standpoint, capital-intensive sugar mills made daily demands for cane highly inelastic. First, because fixed costs had become a larger component of total milling costs, costs per unit were sensitive to capacity utilization. Hence, mills wanted assurances that the planned cane supplies would be available because the risks of relying entirely on proximate lands and the transaction-cost hazards of bargaining with small numbers of suppliers were greater. To complicate matters, the large-scale mills of the latest technology serviced such a large area that efficient deliveries to the mills usually required investment in railroads to cover distances quickly. Because railroads were site-specific assets, their builders (the mills) would want assurances that, once they were built, they would be used for their intended purpose—to haul cane.

The rapid deterioration of cut cane created further reason to establish contractual terms of exchange. Besides the long-term commitment, it was also necessary to coordinate the exchange on a daily basis. The cane could not be permitted to accumulate as inventory at the mill, yet delays in deliveries that left the mill idle raised unit costs. Delivery quotas had to be adaptable to uncertainties of weather, the use of machinery, or the progress of the work at any stage of production. The cane contract functioned so as to encourage cooperation and mitigate transaction costs.

Consequently, the fixity and locational specificity of the physical investments in sugar mills, railroads, and cane fields, combined with the time limitations for processing cut cane, created a mutual benefit to contractual commitments between mill managers and cane growers.[15] Neither set of investments would have been undertaken without some assurance of a commitment of sufficient duration.[16] Any criticism made against the inflexibility of the terms of the *colono* contract should be evaluated in light of this coordination requirement. Also noteworthy is that other highly efficient producers, such as Hawaii and Java, had solved these problems through vertical integration. That experience suggests that the plausible counterfactual situation, if the contractual solution in Cuba had not been found viable, would likely have been greater, not less, concentration of ownership of the sugar industry's assets. Why the contracting choice was preferred in Cuba but not among some of its competitors is addressed in Dye (1995).

The three defining features of *colono* contracts outlined earlier—the exclusivity, the term of duration, and the payment in kind—were permanent features of *colono* contracts because they mitigated some of these problems.

The exclusivity provided reciprocal assurances to the mill and *colono* that the cane would be supplied and purchased, both of which were needed to evoke investments in specific cane field and railroad assets.

Setting the duration mitigated one of two potential holdup problems. As noted, investment in fixed assets included relationship-specific physical investments in cane fields and railroads. Because of the diminished value of his investments if the planned transactions were not carried through, the *colono* sought contractual protection against any contingencies that might give the mill reason to withdraw its original offer to purchase the cane. The usual 6- to 10-year duration of the *colono* contract is explained by this motive. The expected life of a cane field in Cuba, from the initial planting through each profitable annual crop, was usually between 6 and 10 years.

Strategic selection of the contract's duration might have protected the mill against similar problems of opportunism. However, the life of the railroad was considerably longer than the life of the cane field. The advantages of fixing the duration of the contract to suit the life of the railroad were offset by a need for flexibility in revising agreements to purchase cane according to long-run changes in needs, soil fertility, and other uncertainties. Despite the reason, the duration was set to the advantage of the *colono*'s, rather than the mill's, specific investments. Elsewhere, I have argued that this was the source of mills' incentives to acquire land.[17]

The payment in kind—*x* arrobas sugar per 100 arrobas cane delivered—accomplished two things. First, it divided the price risk (of sugar and inputs) between grower and mill. Second, it divided the residual claims functionally into separate claims on cane production and its processing. Relative to, say, a fixed price per unit, this payment method introduced built-in incentives for the mill and *colono* to cooperate in coordinating harvest and grinding. Therefore, it reduced the transaction costs of an arm's-length series of exchanges and made contracting out more viable.

Because cane was upstream to raw sugar, the mill had to distribute a portion of the overall profits to the grower as an incentive for him to grow cane. In principle, the possible ways of dividing profits between mill and grower were infinite. The arrangement chosen was characterized by a payment in kind (sugar) that took the following form:

$$\Pi_{Gi} = p\alpha_i g_i - C_{Gi} \quad i = 1, \ldots, n$$
$$\Pi_M = p(r - \alpha)g - C_M \tag{1}$$

where p is the price of sugar, C_j are costs, α is the amount (arrobas) of sugar paid to the *colono* per arroba of cane delivered, g_i is the amount of cane produced by *colono* i, r is the "yield," or sugar-to-cane ratio, Π_{Gi} and Π_M are profits that went to *colono* and mill, respectively, i represents the ith *colono*, $g = \sum g_i$, and α is a weighted average of α_i.

Some measure to evoke coordination was to their mutual benefit, since a complete coordination failure would have eliminated contracting out for cane as an option. The alternative, as the experience of Hawaii, Java, and other producers showed, was vertical integration, not the free exchange of cane. Nonetheless, the *colono* payment method was not the only possibility. Other plausible pricing arrangements, such as revenue or profit sharing, could also build-in incentives to reduce transaction costs relative to a fixed price. Why was the *colono* method of payment—x arrobas sugar per 100 arrobas cane—chosen over other possible built-in mechanisms for reducing transaction costs?

COMPARING CONTRACTUAL ARRANGEMENTS

Central to managing cane supplies, the design of the contract, and the payment method was the better coordination of cane deliveries with grinding. In an article in the *Revista de Agricultura* in 1890, José de la O. García remarked that "the delivery of cane is one of the true cores of discord between the *colonos* and mill owners."[18] Managers' reports of the Rionda mills and United Fruit Company indicate that, even when the enterprise was well organized, mills were idle about 30% of the grinding season, 20% of which was caused by delayed cane deliveries, 5% by machinery breakdowns, and 5% by routine cleaning.[19] When operations were less well organized, the costs of coordination failure could be much greater. For example, in 1885, the general manager of the Central Soledad lamented over its *colono* arrangements with the Ingenio Josefa because of the tardiness and poor condition of the deliveries, which took up his attention almost every day of that season.[20] Such failures were costly both to the sucrose content in the cane and to unit fixed costs.

To incorporate the coordination efforts between growers and millers of cane, the model represented in Equations (1) requires an additional feature. If coordination failed, it resulted in poorer-quality cane; therefore, the functional relationship between cane and sugar production needs cane quality to be made explicit. The sugar-to-cane ratio was dependent on the quantity of available sucrose per unit of cane, s, and on the efficiency at which the mill extracted the available sucrose from the cane, *m*. Sucrose content, *s*, was measured as a percentage of the total cane weight, and the mill's efficiency (recovery rate), *m*, was measured as the percentage of the available sucrose that was extracted and crystallized. Raw sugar was the product of these two components and the quantity of cane ground: $Q = msg$.

One might think that the sucrose content was the sole responsibility of the grower, but this was not true. Deliveries of cane to the mill typically consisted of two stages—the delivery of cane by oxcart to the railroad loading station and the shipment of the cane by rail to the mill. The grower's employees were responsible for delivering the cane to the loading station and loading it into the railcars. But the mill's personnel were responsible for delivering the railcars to be loaded and for shipment from the loading station to the mill. Further, the mill was responsible for coordinating the deliveries from all the growers with whom it contracted so that cane did not queue up at the mill and for preventing breakdowns in mill machinery to minimize bottlenecks in grinding. This meant that, for a given sucrose content at the time of cutting, the functional responsibility for maintaining the sucrose content lay with both the grower and the mill. I model this interaction between producers in the following way: Raw sugar output is

$$Q = m(y)s(x,y)g(x) \qquad\qquad (2)$$

in which *x* and *y* represent actions that grower and mill, respectively, took (or could take) as managers that were complementary to the assets they each owned or controlled—the cane fields, the railroad, and the mill.

The overlapping management of sucrose content meant that both grower and mill could potentially shirk in the maintenance of sucrose. The grower could harvest cane to maximize weight rather than sucrose content, or he could neglect solving delays in deliveries to focus on other tasks. The mill could provide inadequate numbers or timing of delivery of railcars to the loading sites, or cause queuing at the mill because of machinery breakdowns, or give inadequate notification when suspension of grinding was unavoidable. Either party might have an incentive to so shirk if the costs could be spread partially to the other party. Less effort or resources expended in sucrose maintenance could be redirected into other income-producing activities. Of course, contractual incentives could redress some of the potential for opportunism.

As a means of understanding how the payment method affected the incentives for diverting efforts elsewhere, suppose the grower could redirect some of the contracted *x* into alternative activities, resulting in a reduction in the sucrose content of γs and an alternative income $u(\gamma x)$, where $0 \le \gamma < 1$. Similarly, suppose the mill could redirect some of the contracted y into other activities, which would reduce the sucrose content by μs and produce an alternative income of $v(\mu y)$, $0 \le \mu < 1$. Equation (2), then, represents the special case when γ and μ are zero. More generally, $\gamma \ge 0$ or $\mu \ge 0$, the sucrose content is $(1 - \mu)(1 - \gamma)s(x, y)$, and sugar output is $Q = m(y)(1-\mu)(1-\gamma)s(x,y)g(x) \le m(y)s(x,y)g(y)$. Although artificial, this abstraction helps us to look at the effects of the shared responsibility for managing sucrose content.

Incorporating the effects of redirected efforts into the *colono* payment method when $\gamma > 0$ or $\mu > 0$ results in a division of profits between the grower and mill of the following form:

$$\text{Grower:} \quad \Pi_G = p\alpha\,g - C_G(x) + u(\gamma x) \tag{3}$$
$$\text{Mill:} \quad \Pi_M = p[(1 - \mu)(1 - \gamma)ms - \alpha]g - C_M(y) + v(\mu y) \tag{4}$$

The grower would have chosen x to maximize Equation (3), and the mill management would have chosen y to maximize Equation (4). (I have omitted the index for *colono i* to simplify notation.)

What incentives did this method of compensation give to the parties to commit their resources and efforts voluntarily as agreed? First, it is obvious that the *colono*'s payment was independent of μ. There was no guarantee that $\mu = 0$, but if not, both the gains and costs of the diversion of resources were incurred internally by the mill. In other words, the *colono* payment was designed so that potential opportunism by the mill, such as shirking in the delivery of cane cars or other aspects of the coordination of deliveries, would not harm the income of the *colono*. The same cannot be said of γ. The *colono* payment externalized the costs of diverting attention or resources from coordinating deliveries and grinding—the *colono* enjoyed the gains from a positive γ, but the mill incurred all the costs.

This observation that the *colono* was protected from opportunistic actions of the mill that caused $\mu > 0$, but the mill was not protected from similar $\gamma > 0$, raises some important questions about Guerra y Sánchez's interpretation of *latifundización* and the coercion of the *colonos*. If mills were so powerful vis-à-vis the *colonos* that they could virtually impose the terms of the contracts unilaterally, why would they have accepted terms such as these? Mills were powerful enough so that they would not have accepted such terms unwillingly. Why would the mill have agreed to such an arrangement? To understand the motives better, it is useful to place them in a comparative context by outlining some plausible options in payment methods that were not chosen.

One alternative to the existing arrangements was a payment to the *colono* based on the sucrose content rather than solely on the weight of the cane. Such a reform in the payment method was actively proposed in the 1890s by mill owners.[21] Comparing payment by cane weight and sucrose content, what is noteworthy is that payment by sucrose content would have done more than enhance the *colono*'s incentive to attend to cane quality: It would also have made the *colono* vulnerable to opportunism by the mill from redirecting efforts, $\mu > 0$, whereas the payment by weight protected him. To see this, observe how γ and μ are reallocated in Equations (5) and (6) relative to Equations (3) and (4). Under the alternative sucrose-based arrangement, the *colono* would have chosen x to maximize:

$$\text{Grower:} \quad p\hat{a}(1 - \gamma)(1 - \mu)s(x, y)g(x) - C_G(x) + u(\gamma x) \tag{5}$$

The mill would have chosen y to maximize:

$$\text{Mill:} \quad p[m(y) - \hat{a}](1 - \mu)(1 - \gamma)s(x, y)g(x) - C_M(y) + v(\mu y) \tag{6}$$

where $\hat{a}$ is the amount of sucrose paid to the grower per unit available sucrose. What is most significant is that by making γ appear in the grower's profits, μ also appears. The attempt to make the grower partially internalize the costs of neglecting sucrose content also partially externalizes those costs for which the mill is responsible. The incentive for the mill to redirect attention to other activities would have been greater because the costs of $\mu > 0$ would have been borne partially by the *colono*.

Admittedly, this outcome depended on the costs of measurement. Measuring sucrose content involved the use of specialized scientific instruments and formal training. Mills employed professionally trained chemists to take these measurements in laboratories at the mill.[22] In actual practice, when paid by cane weight, *colonos* had a representative to monitor the weighing of their cane at the mill.[23] If paid by sucrose content, they could not have verified the measurements taken by the mill without employing their own chemists, yet such skills were scarce in rural Cuba. A comparable employee competent to supervise the measurement of sucrose content would have been too costly for most *colonos*.[24] *Colonos* had enough influence over the terms of the contract to resist this change.

Other plausible alternative payment methods would have had the same effect. For example, consider profit sharing as an alternative. One of the charges against *latifundista* mills was that they could set *colonos*' compensation at the minimum necessary to cover costs and did not award them a share in the surplus. Advocates of *colono* autonomy might have considered a profit-sharing arrangement to be a more equitable arrangement because it forced a sharing of any increases in productivity. But what effect would profit sharing have had on the incentive structure?

It is easy to show that, like the effects of payment by sucrose content, profit sharing, revenue sharing, or similar arrangements would have made the grower more vulnerable to opportunism by the mill because any change in μ would affect the grower's income. Therefore, it is clear that one effect of the *colono* payment method was that it protected the *colono* against opportunism by the mill. *Colonos* were well aware that any change in that payment method would not be to their advantage.

In short, with these alternative payment methods, if the mill suffered frequent breakdowns, if it scrimped on the provision of cane cars, or if it failed to coordinate and notify *colonos* of changes in delivery schedules due to unexpected contingencies, the costs were spread to the growers. Relative to the alternatives, the *colono* payment method protected the *colono* from any reduction in sucrose content that might result from negligence or opportunism of the mill. In the same stroke, the *colono* payment method permitted growers to externalize the costs of neglecting sucrose content and impose them on the mill. But given these tensions in early contracts, one would expect subsequently to see mills expend some energy to shift the moral hazard costs of $\gamma > 0$ onto their originators.

TRANSFERRING RIGHTS OF CONTROL

The tensions inherent in the *colono* payment method are key to understanding the inclusion of the other conditions of the *colono* contract. If not by the pricing method, the mill could seek to reduce coordination failures by providing that specific actions be taken to reduce γ.

Contracts were preferred to spot transactions because they established the rules of governance of the exchange relationship and a long-term commitment to it. The contracts were not complete, however. Identifying, negotiating, and enforcing the additional provisions were costly activities; therefore, the contracts typically failed to mention many contingencies.[25]

Despite their omission, when rights are left unspecified by a contract, they are not left entirely ambiguous because law and custom often recognize implicit rights of control. In particular, some unspecified rights regarding physical assets are often bestowed by law or custom upon the legal owner. For example, suppose person A leases her house to person B. If person B wishes to remove a wall from the interior, person A has the right to decide on any such permanent alteration, even if the right was not specified in the contract. Such rights have been referred to in the theoretical literature as the residual rights of control.[26] The person who holds the residual rights of control over an asset is usually the legal owner. In this frame, there are two distinct kinds of property rights: the specific rights of control, or those assigned explicitly by the contract, and the residual rights of control, or those left unspecified, generally bestowed on the owner of the asset(s).

The *colono* payment method separated the claims, or rights, to the income from the quantity and quality (sucrose content) of the cane and assigned the claims to income from increased quality to the mill. But the *colono*, as owner and possessor of the cane, retained residual rights of control over the cane's quality. Grossman and Hart would predict that ownership would reside with the party that could most affect the productive outcome, but in this case both parties had a significant effect on cane quality.[27] The language of the contracts and, later, statutory law (in 1922) identified the grower as owner of the cane.[28] Hart suggests that the failure to locate control firmly with the single party that most influenced production led to poorer coordination and dissipation of their joint income.[29] One can interpret the additional restrictions of later contracts (see Appendix 2) as a reassignment of rights from residual to specific, which were then transferred from the *colono* to the mill, to reduce the tensions inherent in the *colono* method of payment.[30] The direction of transfer of the specific rights—toward the mill—is consistent with the theory because the mill was in the best position to act as a central coordinator to ensure the continuity of the daily deliveries of many growers with its grinding operations. Performance of this function affected both the yield (sugar-to-cane ratio) and the volume of cane the mill could grind in a season; therefore, it affected the incomes of both the mill and all its *colonos*.[31]

But assigning specific rights to the underlying asset did not come about automatically. The movement from heterogeneous to standardized sets of clauses in the long run reflected a process of learning how to make the *colono* contract work. As experience from using it accumulated, producers learned about the causes of coordination failures or other transaction costs. Learning by using led producers to modify the contracts over time to incorporate clauses to address specific discovered needs. In this way, the variety of clauses, that had characterized the early contracts, reflected in Table 11.2, converged into a standardized set of clauses by the 1920s.

In the process, one observes a transfer of rights from *colonos* to mill management. One does not see a reciprocal transfer of rights of control from mill to *colono*. By the above model, one would not expect the reciprocal transfer because the payment method provided built-in incentives to ensure the mill's performance.

As evidence of these claims, compare the clauses pertaining to deliveries and grinding in the early and later contracts. Two features in particular can be underlined. First, the conditions placed on deliveries to ensure cane quality were nominally similar, but in later contracts, a provision was added for enforcing the condition that made the effectiveness of the clause in assigning specific rights substantially different. Refer to Appendix 2, clause D.1. The first sentence is almost identical to clauses used in the 1890s (Appendix 1, clauses A.1, B.1, and C.3), but the second sentence added the stipulation that if the *colono* failed to meet the conditions specified, the mill could either refuse the cane or apply a discount to the agreed price.

Second, early contracts varied in whether they restricted mills' rights to suspend grinding or provided for compensation to growers, but later contracts commonly assigned to mills broad rights to suspend grinding for machinery breakdowns or for any other contingency without compensation to the growers (see Appendices 1 and 2, clauses C.2, C.5, C.6, and D.3). Similarly, delays in deliveries caused by growers were penalized if they affected the freshness of the cane at delivery (Appendix 2, clause D.1). The modification and standardization of the terms of the contract reflect a transfer of specific rights to the mill. This transfer was reinforced by clauses D.4 to D.7 of Appendix 2 in later contracts, which granted mills specific rights of supervision, reporting, and general enforcement of the contract. Particularly remarkable is clause D.7: If the *colono* did not give proper attention to the cane fields, the mill could take over the operation of the *colonia* at the *colono*'s expense. Depending on how it was applied or enforced in the courts, this clause potentially transferred to the mill a large portion of the *colono*'s previous residual rights. The assignment of specific rights to the mill to delay grinding, to supervise, and to enforce was conspicuously unequal, but was to be expected, not only because the mill was more powerful but also because the payment method established a stronger incentive for the mill to perform as the grower desired regardless of the assignment of specific rights.

RATES OF PAYMENT

Were growers forced to accept this reduced autonomy? They may have accepted it willingly if they were compensated by increased income. So how did growers fare as the terms of the contracts changed? Productivity improvements from technical and organizational improvements were reflected in the yields, that is, the sugar-to-cane ratio, r of Equation (1). If the contracted rate of payment, α, were not renegotiated upward, then all the gains from increased productivity would have gone to the mill. If the gains were shared equally, then the share of sugar that growers received would have remained steady in the long run.

Did growers receive a share of the increase in productivity in exchange for giving up some rights of control? Table 11.3, which gives estimates of rates of payment, yields, and growers' shares for the 1890s and 1917, shows that they did. The average rates of payment increased from 4.28 to 6.11 arrobas of sugar per 100 arrobas of cane from the 1890s to 1917.

TABLE 11.3

Growers' Shares of Sugar Output

Period		Payment to Grower (lb. sugar/100 lbs. cane)	Yields (Sugar–Cane Ratios) (lb. sugar/100 lbs. cane)		Growers' Share (%)	
			Best Practice	Average	Best Practice	Average
1890s	Mean	4.28	9.39		45.6	
	(Std. dev.)	(0.78)	(1.10)			
	N	37	10			
1917	Mean	6.11	12.24[a]	10.40	49.9	58.8
	(Std. dev.)	(0.95)	(0.28)	(1.26)		
	N	23	10	199		
1925	Mean	6.11[b]		11.51		53.1
	(Std. dev.)			(0.81)		
	N			183		

[a] The best-practice yield in 1917 is estimated by the average yield of the top 10 mills. This approach introduces a slight downward bias in the difference between the 1917 and 1890s growers' shares since the 1890s sample includes 10 high-productivity mills, but not necessarily the top 10.

[b] Scattered evidence suggests that average rates of payment rose slightly in the 1920s. Assuming the same rate in 1917 and 1925 will be a lower bound estimate of the growers' share in 1925.

Sources: Author's calculations using data collected from USNA, STCC; BB Ser. 127; Iglesias García (1996), pp. 88–94; Cuba, Secretaría de Hacienda, *Industria azucarera* (1917, 1925); and U.S. Department of Commerce (1917).

Growers' shares were sensitive to the mills' yields. For the 1890s, the shares growers received are best approximated by assuming the higher yields of best-practice mills because it was those mills that were contracting with *colonos*. By 1917, all active mills had advanced beyond the 1890s milling technology, and *colonos* were employed throughout the industry. Therefore, the share by 1917 is best approximated by using the average yield for all active mills. By this standard, growers' share of sugar from their cane increased from 46% to 59% between the 1890s and 1917. It dropped slightly afterward, but was not lower than 53% by 1925. Comparison of shares received at the best-practice mills understates the increase because by 1917 the average *colono* did not supply cane to such efficient mills. Therefore, it can be concluded that on average growers received a greater share of the increase in productivity than did mills when comparing the 1890s and 1917 or 1925.

As an additional effect, the productivity of Cuban mills permitted a flourishing of opportunities for contracting out under these new terms. The amount of cane supplied by *colonos* increased 10 times from 1894 to 1929, and a lower bound estimate of the increase in cane produced by landowning *colonos* indicates that it more than doubled during that period (see Table 11.4). Much of

TABLE 11.4

Aggregate *Colono* Production and Revenues

Cane Produced, in Quantity (millions of metric tons) and Percentage				Aggregate Revenues in Sugar (millions of metric tons) and Thousands of $U.S. (1913 = 100)		
Year		By Colonos	By Landowning Colonos		By Colonos	By Landowning Colonos
1894	Quantity	3.55	—	In sugar	0.15	—
	Percentage	30.0		In $U.S.	90.4	
1905	Quantity	7.59	3.98	In sugar	0.42	0.22
	Percentage	69.6	36.5	In $U.S.	246.1	129.1
1917	Quantity	24.03	5.65	In sugar	1.47	0.50
	Percentage	86.6	29.7	In $U.S.	996.9	341.9
1929	Quantity	35.16	6.80	In sugar	2.12	0.41
	Percentage	81.2	15.7	In $U.S.	478.7	92.6

Sources: Tables 11.1, 11.3; Dye (1998), Table 6.4; and Moreno Fraginals (1978), Vol. 3, Cuadros 2, 3.

that growth meant new opportunities for landowners and tenants to become *colonos* as the industry expanded its geographical boundaries. Meanwhile, opportunities in other agricultural sectors were not flourishing, so the employment opportunities provided by the growing sugar industry were likely an irreplaceable source of income to the population.

Growers' monetary incomes were more variable than their receipts of sugar because of a volatile sugar price. The price of sugar was high during World War I, averaging 5.5 cents U.S. per pound. Afterward, it returned to historically normal rates, averaging 3.25 cents between 1921 and 1928. In 1929 it fell to the unprecedented low level of 1.94 cents, and it continued to fall until 1933. Satisfaction with the contract seems to have been associated more with the price of sugar than the transfer of rights of control. Although the terms of the *colono* contract had taken their more restrictive form by 1917, enthusiasm over the lucrative prospects of investing in *colonias* was at its height then, according to Thomas. Opposition to the contracts and other practices grew as the market price of sugar fell in the latter 1920s, but the cane growers' association that arose later to defend growers' interests neither opposed the residual-claim nature of their income nor sought to eliminate risk sharing.[32]

CONCLUSION

Early *colono* contracts imposed fewer restrictions and awarded considerable autonomy to growers, but the built-in adverse incentives of the payment method resulted in tensions between grower and mill. Over time the tensions were reduced by awarding more specific rights of control to the mill. Learning how to design the contract was key to the transfer of those rights. Rights of control were transferred through the development of effective clauses to convert residual rights to specific rights and to reassign them. The lost autonomy does not necessarily imply a worsening of contract terms for growers because, in the longer run, they benefited from productivity gains that were passed on to growers. In addition, the global competitiveness of Cuban sugar, to which this innovation contributed, permitted a great expansion of the industry and created many more opportunities for contracting out. The demand for *colonos* grew and became the principal source of income for many Cubans. *Colonos'* prospects soured with the collapse of the price of sugar at the onset of the world crisis; the long-term contract with its unequal transfer of specific rights was not the cause.

The contract, rather than being an instrument that coerced the grower, was in some aspects an instrument to protect him. The growers' interests were embedded in the long-term commitment and, in particular, in the payment method, and it is difficult to explain the contract's form except as a guarantee to the grower against opportunism by the mill. Nonetheless, the terms of the contract evolved so that the mill was granted increased control over growers' businesses. The cause of this was not simply the superior financial resources of mills. More immutable was the technical and logistical advantages that accrued to those mills that acquired more residual rights of control over deliveries to coordinate better with grinding. Those mills that achieved better coordination through improved contractual arrangements and could report better mill performance were better able to attract the needed financial resources.

ACKNOWLEDGMENTS

I wish to thank Margaret Levenstein, Richard Sicotte, and participants of the Conference on Latin America and the World Economy in the Nineteenth and Twentieth Centuries, Bellagio, Italy, 1997.

Appendix 1

EXAMPLES OF STIPULATIONS FOR DELIVERIES IN EARLY CONTRACTS

Contract A: José Antonio Mesa (mill owner) and Juan Cejas (lessee), 1893

A.1 *Colono* must sell all the cane to the owner at the "generally accepted price which might be paid in Sabanilla" for every 100 arrobas of cane placed in the railcars.

Contract B: Francisco Machado (mill owner) and Simón Díaz (*colono*), 1894

B.1 *Colono* must "put on the conductor free of straw, shoots and roots," and it must arrive "in time to grind it."

Contract C: Messrs. E. Atkins & Co. (mill owner) and Messrs. Peter M. Beal, et al. (*colono*), 1899

C.1 Mill is obligated to receive cane from the day grinding begins at the Soledad mill in the amount determined by the management of the mill.

C.2 Mill is obligated to provide the number of railcars needed so that the loading and hauling of the cane to the mill suffer no delay.

C.3 *Colono* is obligated to deliver the cane clean of straw and shoots; the density of its juice must be below 8" Baumé; and the cane, once loaded into carts, must not be allowed to stand more than 48 hours in the fields.

C.4 Mill is obligated to weigh the cane on the scale of the mill and deliver a voucher for the amount delivered.

C.5 Mill may not suspend delivery of cane except in cases of *fuerza mayor*, or for ordinary causes such as for cleaning the machinery and those cases in which the machinery does not function.

C.6 *Colono*, in case of rain that makes the operations of cutting and hauling difficult or other *fuerza mayor*, is not obligated to deliver the quota required by the mill management.

Appendix 2

STIPULATIONS FOR DELIVERIES AND SUPERVISION AND ENFORCEMENT IN THE LATER CONTRACT

The example is the standard *colono* contract of the Washington Sugar Company, circa 1917.

Deliveries

D.1 *Colono* must deliver cane free of straw and roots, in proper maturity and condition. The company can refuse to accept or require a discount of cane that does not meet these conditions.

D.2 The company will specify the date at which grinding begins and the quota to be delivered to the loading stations daily.

D.3 Any interruptions in grinding due to the fault of the company will be resolved in a manner "mutually beneficial" to both parties of the contract.

Supervision and Enforcement

D.4 Establishes the company's right to inspect the planting.

D.5 Gives the company the right to inspect all operations on the *colonia*.

D.6 Requires of the *colono* an account of all expenses for each operation during the season.

D.7 If the obligation is not fulfilled, the company has the right to take charge at the *colono*'s expense. Lack of attention to the cane fields gives the company the right to cancel the contract.

NOTES

1. Dye (1998).
2. Guerra y Sánchez (1944).
3. Benjamin (1974), Bianchi (1964), Rodríguez (1987).
4. Guerra y Sánchez (1944), pp. 92–93.
5. See Grossman and Hart (1986), Hart (1988, 1989), and Hart and Moore (1990).
6. Dye (1998).
7. Scott (1984).
8. Mills that contracted out for cane were called central mills because they provided services as centers of processing to other cane growers.
9. Dye (1998); *Revista de Agricultura* (1888–1892), passim.
10. *Revista de Agricultura* 9, no. 36, 8 September 1889, p. 423. These investors sometimes operated their *colonias* in absentia or sublet them, establishing a *subcolono* agreement. See, for example, USNA, Spanish Treaty Claims Commission, Entry 352, PI 177, Claims 6, 35; and BB, Record Group II, Series 10A.
11. Guerra y Sánchez (1944), pp. 92–93.
12. Guerra y Sánchez (1944), pp. 108, 110.
13. See growers' depositions of USNA, STCC, and in *Revista de Agricultura*, 1889–1891, passim.
14. See Williamson (1985).
15. For the theoretical arguments, see Klein, Crawford, and Alchian (1978); and Williamson (1985).
16. The degree to which mills were vulnerable to holdup depended on other factors, including the relative importance of a *colono* to a mill, cooperation between *colonos*, and whether they had options of selling cane to neighboring mills. On this issue, see Dye (1994a, b).
17. See Dye (1994a, b).
18. *Revista de Agricultura* 10, no. 15, 13 April 1890, p. 172.
19. Dye (1998), p. 117; Zanetti and García (1976), p. 137.
20. ANC, ICEA—Libros, Book No. 740. See also related *Revista de Agricultura*, 11, no. 24 (1891), p. 293.
21. *Revista de Agricultura* 10, no. 15, 13 April 1890, p. 172.
22. Heitmann (1987), Deerr (1950).
23. USNA, STCC.
24. See Barzel (1982). Even the costs of measuring the cane weight were not negligible. Reflecting economies of scale, some contracts provided that the mill would build a weighing platform (for railcars) on a *colonia* only after its annual deliveries exceeded a million arrobas (implying plantings of between 400 and 650 acres).

Most *colonias* were not this large, and their cane was weighed at the mills with a representative present (USNA, STCC).

25. Williamson (1985).
26. Hart (1988, 1989).
27. Grossman and Hart (1986).
28. Usátegui y Lezama (1938).
29. Hart (1988)
30. Compare Langlois and Robertson (1995), p. 29.
31. Compare Alchian and Demsetz (1972).
32. CERP (1965), pp. 336–342.

REFERENCES

Archival Sources

Archivo Nacional de Cuba (ANC). Havana, Cuba. Fondos consulted were the Instituto Cubano del Estabilización de Azúcar (ICEA), Protocolos Notariales (PN), and Secretaría de la Presidencia (SP).

Braga Brothers Collection (BB), University Archives, University of Florida at Gainesville. Gainesville, Florida.

U.S. National Archives (USNA). Washington D.C. Record Group 76. Spanish Treaty Claims Commission (STCC).

Published Sources

Alchian, Armen, and Harold Demsetz. "Production, Information Costs, and Economic Organization." *American Economic Review* 62 (1972): 777–795.

Barzel, Yoram. "Measurement Costs and the Organization of Markets." *Journal of Law and Economics* 25 (1982): 27–48.

Benjamin, Jules. *The United States and Cuba: Hegemony and Dependent Development, 1880–1934.* Pittsburgh: University of Pittsburgh Press, 1974.

Bianchi, Andrés. "Agriculture—The Pre-Revolutionary Background." In *Cuba: The Economic and Social Revolution*, edited by Dudley Seers, et al. Chapel Hill: University of North Carolina Press, 1964.

CERP (Cuban Economic Research Project). *A Study on Cuba: The Colonial and Republican Periods, The Socialist Experience.* Coral Gables, FL: University of Miami Press, 1965.

Chonchol, Jacques. "Analisis crítico de la reforma agraria cubana." *Revista Trimestre*

Económico 30, no. 117 (1963): 69–143.

Cuba, República de, Secretaría de Hacienda. *Industria azucarera y sus derivados.* Annual series. Havana: [various publishers], 1903/04–1930.

Deerr, Noel. *The History of Sugar.* Vol. 2. London: Chapman and Hall, Ltd., 1950.

Dye, Alan. "Avoiding Holdup: Asset Specificity and Technical Change in the Cuban Sugar Industry, 1899–1929." *Journal of Economic History* 54 (1994a): 628–653.

Dye, Alan. "Cane Contracting and Renegotiation: A Fixed Effects Analysis of the Adoption of New Technologies in the Cuban Sugar Industry, 1899–1929." *Explorations in Economic History* 31 (1994b): 141–175.

Dye, Alan. "Factor Endowments and Contract Choice: Why Were Cane Supply Arrangements Different in Cuba and Hawaii? 1900–1929." Stanford: Mimeo, 1995.

Dye, Alan. "Organizational Innovation and the Latifundium: The Meaning of the Colono Contract in Cuban Sugar, 1889–1929." Working Paper Series #98-xx, Department of Economics, Barnard College, September 1997.

Dye, Alan. *Cuban Sugar in the Age of Mass Production: Technology and the Economics of the Sugar Central, 1899–1929.* Stanford, CA: Stanford University Press, 1998.

Grossman, Sanford, and Oliver Hart. "The Costs and Benefits of Ownership: A Theory of Vertical and Lateral Integration." *Journal of Political Economy* 94, no. 4 (1986): 691–719.

Guerra y Sánchez, Ramiro. *Azúcar y población en las Antillas*, 3rd ed. Havana: Cultural, 1944.

Hart, Oliver. "Incomplete Contracts and the Theory of the Firm." *Journal of Law, Economics and Organization* 4, no. 1 (1988): 119–139.

Hart, Oliver. "An Economist's Perspective on the Theory of the Firm." *Columbia Law Review* 89 (1989): 1757–1774.

Hart, Oliver, and John Moore. "Property Rights and the Nature of the Firm." *Journal of Political Economy* 98, no. 6 (1990): 1119–1158.

Heitmann, John Alfred. *The Modernization of the Louisiana Sugar Industry 1830–1910.* Baton Rouge: Louisiana State University Press, 1987.

Iglesias García, Fe. "De *El ingenio* al central." Instituto de Historia de Cuba, Havana, Cuba, unpublished manuscript, 1996.

Klein, Benjamin, Robert G. Crawford, and Armen A. Alchian. "Vertical Integration, Appropriable Rents, and the Competitive Contracting Process." *Journal of Law and Economics* 21 (1978): 297–326.

Langlois, Richard, and Paul Robertson. *Firms, Markets and Economic Change.* London: Routledge, 1995.

Martinez-Alier, Juan. "The Cuban Sugar Cane Planters, 1934–1960." *Oxford Agrarian Studies* 2, no. 1 (1974): 1–29.

Moreno Fraginals, Manuel. *El Ingenio: Complejo Economico Social Cubano del Azucar.*

Vol. 3. Havana: Editorial de Cienrias Sociales, 1978.

Moreno Fraginals, Manuel. "Plantaciones en el Caribe: El caso de Cuba—Puerto Rico—Santo Domingo (1860–1940)." In *La historia como arma*, by Manuel Moreno Fraginals. Barcelona: Editorial Crítica, Grupo Editorial Grijalbo, 1983.

Nelson, Lowry. *Rural Cuba*. Minneapolis: University of Minnesota Press, 1950.

Pino Santos, Oscar. *El asalto a Cuba por la oligarquía financiera yanqui*. Havana: Casa de las Américas, 1973.

Rodríguez, José Luís. "Agricultural Policy and Development in Cuba." In *Cuba's Socialist Economy Toward the 1990s*, edited by Andrew Zimbalist. Boulder, CO: Lynne Reinner Publishers, 1987.

Scott, Rebecca. "The Transformation of Sugar Production in Cuba After Emancipation." In *Crisis and Change in the International Sugar Economy 1860-1914*, edited by Bill Albert and Adrian Graves. ISC Press, 1984.

Thomas, Hugh. *Cuba: The Pursuit of Freedom*. London: Eyre and Spottiswoode, 1971.

Usátegui y Lezama, Angel. *El colono cubano*. La Habana: Jesus Montero, 1938.

U.S. Department of Commerce, Bureau of Foreign and Domestic Commerce. *The Cane Sugar Industry: Agricultural, Manufacturing, and Marketing Costs in Hawaii, Porto Rico, and Louisiana, and Cuba*. Washington, DC: Government Printing Office, 1917.

Williamson, Oliver E. *The Economic Institutions of Capitalism*. New York: Free Press, 1985.

Zanetti Lecuona, Oscar, and Alejandro García Alvarez. *United Fruit Company: Un caso del dominio imperialista en Cuba*. Havana: Editorial de Ciencias Sociales, 1976.

12

The Evolution of Prices and Real Wages in Mexico from the Porfiriato to the Revolution

Aurora Gómez-Galvarriato
Centro de Investigación y Docencia Económicas A.C.

What is the impact of popular revolutions on workers' standards of living? This paper seeks to answer this question for the case of the Mexican Revolution (1910–1920). In terms of economic history two important conclusions are often made about this period. First, that workers' living standards deteriorated during the last decade of the Porfiriato, despite remarkable economic growth, because of markedly rising prices. Second, the Revolution is believed to have improved living standards for workers and peasants. The first of these beliefs has been supported quantitatively by the work of Fernando Rosenzweig and the group he coordinated at the Colegio de México to build a price index for the Porfiriato and obtain statistics for wages (El Colegio de México 1965). According to these researchers, although there was a sharp increase in prices in this period, wages remained fixed at the same level, and thus real wages fell. This has been considered an important factor in explaining the collapse of the Porfirian regime.[1] But the price index and the nominal wage series are ambiguous and have been criticized, although no satisfactory alternative has been developed.

The idea that living standards for workers and peasants improved as a result of the Revolution has generally been supported by the fact that important pro-labor legal reforms were made in the Constitution of 1917 (e.g., the legalization of unions). The Constitution of 1917 also set the basis for an agrarian reform, which was carried out most significantly between 1935 and 1938. Yet, many revisionist studies have questioned the fruits of the Revolution in concrete case studies, looking at how a specific town fared from the Porfiriato to some year after the Revolution[2] or questioning the general results of the Revolution, either the nature of the event itself or arguing that at some point it was betrayed.[3]

The question of what happened to the living standards of workers during the Revolution itself is one that has never been posed.[4] It is traditionally viewed as a transition period in which the economy was totally disrupted. Therefore it would seem useless to try to determine the evolution of real wages during this period. However, more recent studies show that industrial production did not stop during the Revolution and that most industrial workers continued to work in their factories.[5] During the years from 1910 to 1920 most Mexicans carried on their lives—working, studying, making businesses, building families. The war generated new circumstances that made the struggle for survival more difficult but which also opened up new opportunities.

During this decade, labor organized at an unprecedented level in Mexico's industrial regions, in part due to the Revolution and in part due to general tendencies of the labor movement throughout Latin America. At the same time an inflationary process started in 1914 that reached hyperinflationary levels in 1916 as a result of the anarchic printing of money by several different revolutionary armies. Therefore, it is extremely interesting to look at the effects of the strengthening of the labor movement and the inflationary process on workers' living standards during this period.

The purpose of my work is to give some quantitative substance to these contentions by looking at the evolution of industrial real wages from 1900 to 1920. The first task of this research was to build a consumer price index for this period. The second step was the construction of a series for wages, which I obtained from a specific textile mill, the Santa Rosa factory, owned by the Compañía Industrial Veracruzana S.A. (CIVSA).

Since CIVSA documents run continually for the period of my study, I can be certain that I am comparing similar information. Yet, by using information from one company, although I gain certainty in my calculations, I lose generality in my results. However, I believe it is better to set a solid stone on which we can stand confidently than to build a flimsy bridge.

CIVSA workers can be considered as an upper bound of industrial workers' living standards, both during the Porfiriato and afterward, for several reasons.[6] They belonged to a factory more modern and productive than most textile mills in Mexico in this period, and their union was in the forefront of the nation's labor movement.[7] Veracruz was an important revolutionary arena, and many labor laws were applied in Veracruz before they were put into practice in the whole nation.[8]

Since the sources and the specific methodology I used changed through different periods, and since the economic history of each period is also very different, I will divide the study of prices and wages into three parts. The first, which runs from 1900 to 1913, was a period of relative price stability, for which the sources are continuous and of good quality. The second, which extends from 1914 to 1916, was an inflationary period in which the economy was most disrupted. Practically the only information available for these years are CIVSA documents. The third extends from 1917 to 1920, when a new era of economic stability and reconstruction started but when political stability had not yet been achieved. World War I had important effects on the Mexican economy that generated a particular economic environment. In the appendix, I give a general description of the methodology used to calculate prices and wage series.

FROM THE PORFIRIATO TO THE REVOLUTION: 1900–1913

Prices

Inflation from 1900 to 1910 was between 41% and 52%, depending on the index used,[9] which would represent an annual average inflation of 4% (compared with 2.4% in the United States). From 1908 to 1910 there was a substantial increase in inflation; prices increased in these two years by approximately 18%, compared with a 24% price increase in the previous eight years.[10]

Figure 12.1 displays my consumer price indexes for Mexico compared with an index of the peso-dollar exchange rate and the U.S. consumer price index for the same period. We can see a great volatility in the exchange rate until 1904, with a general trend toward depreciation of the peso. Although legally Mexico was a bimetallist country, gold disappeared from circulation from 1873 to 1905 and the value of the peso was based on the price of silver, whereas the dollar's value was based on gold.[11] From the mid-nineteenth century on the general tendency was for silver to depreciate relative to gold.[12] However, this tendency was reversed from April 1903 to September 1907.[13] In March 1905, Mexico adopted the gold standard through a policy of progressively replacing silver with gold pesos.[14] This change in monetary policy can be seen in Figure 12.1 in the greater stability in the exchange rate after 1905. In 1907 a new depreciation of the peso took place due to the world financial crisis, but although the exchange rate was more variable from then on compared with 1905–1907, it was more stable than in the period before 1905.

From 1900 to 1907 prices closely follow movements in the exchange rate.

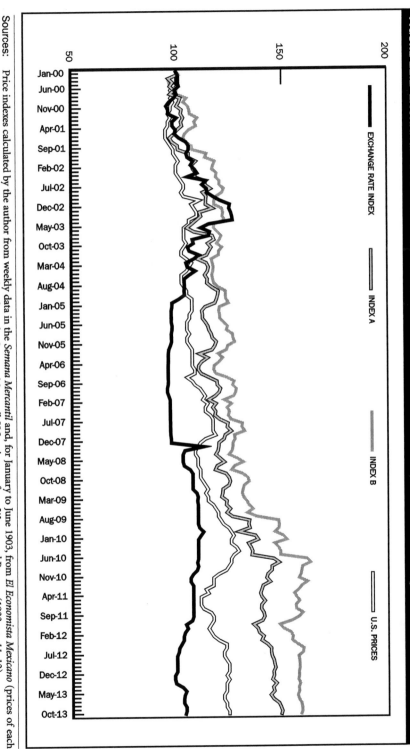

FIGURE 12.1 EXCHANGE RATE AND MEXICAN AND UNITED STATES PRICE INDEXES (JAN 1900 = 100)

Sources: Price indexes calculated by the author from weekly data in the *Semana Mercantil* and, for January to June 1903, from *El Economista Mexicano* (prices of each fourth week of the month). Exchange rates are taken from the *Semana Mercantil*. U.S. prices are from Warren and Pearson (1933, pp. 11–12).

However, from 1908 to 1910, despite a stable exchange rate, there is an important increase in prices parallel to that in the United States.[15] From 1907 on, the government had to relax its financial policy in order to face the delicate financial situation brought on by the 1907 crisis and the fall in the price of silver. By the end of 1908 the Monetary Commission succeeded in stabilizing the exchange rate using resources from foreign loans. The Mexican government also expanded credits (Comisión Monetaria 1909). The monetary history of Mexico from 1907 to 1910 needs to be further developed to enable us to better understand the price movements we find for this period.

Figure 12.2 compares my new price indexes on an annual basis with the Colegio de México (Colmex) index. As can be seen, the new indexes are less volatile than the Colmex one and describe a smaller increase in prices, although they show the same general trend. The new indexes move more in accord with what we know about monetary policy during the Porfiriato. The spurt in inflation that the Colmex index shows from 1904 to 1906, for instance, is hard to understand, given the fact that it was in those years that Mexico adopted the gold standard, while the exchange rate was very stable.

The new price indexes give less credence than the Colmex one to the argument that the last decade of the Porfiriato was a period when "rampant inflation was an important cause of the Revolution."[16] However, they do show the important spurt in inflation during the last years of the Porfiriato that is commonly mentioned in the literature.[17]

Wages

From 1900 to 1910, nominal wages rose by 41% and real wages declined by 3.8% (see Table 12.1). As can be seen in Figure 12.3, from 1900 to 1907 there is evidence of real wage stability. However, from 1907 to 1911 there is a reduction in real wages of 18%, most of which took place between 1909 and 1910, due mainly to the enormous increase in prices that took place in these years. This qualifies the results of the Colegio de México study that show "a constant erosion of real wages from 1900 on, in which the increase in prices was greater than the increase in nominal wages, due to the less dynamic conditions in economic growth that weakened the labor market."[18] At the same time, it supports the view that worsening economic conditions might have added to other causes of popular discontent in the advent of the Revolution.

From 1911 to 1913 CIVSA real wages grew by 19%, almost redressing the previous loss in workers' purchasing power. This resulted from important nominal wage increases (22.9%) coupled with a low inflation rate of only 3.2%. Yet, by 1913 real wages were still 2.4% below their highest point in 1907.

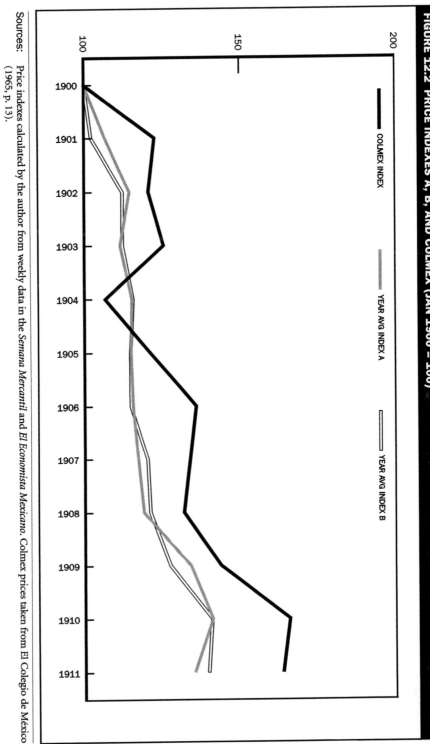

FIGURE 12.2 PRICE INDEXES A, B, AND COLMEX (JAN 1900 = 100)

COLMEX INDEX

YEAR AVG INDEX A

YEAR AVG INDEX B

Sources: Price indexes calculated by the author from weekly data in the *Semana Mercantil* and *El Economista Mexicano*. Colmex prices taken from El Colegio de México (1965, p. 13).

TABLE 12.1

Prices and Real Wages (1900–1913)

	Prices	Nominal Wages (pesos)		Real Wages (pesos of 1900)	
	Average Index[a]	Average Weekly Earnings	Avg. Wkly. Earnings[b] (72-hr wk)	Average Weekly Earnings	Avg. Wkly. Earnings[b] (72-hr wk)
1900	100	$4.89	$4.89	$4.89	$4.89
1901	104.72	$5.62	$5.62	$5.37	$5.37
1902	114.89	$5.95	$5.95	$5.18	$5.18
1903	115.30	$5.76	$5.76	$5.00	$5.00
1904	116.57	$6.31	$6.31	$5.41	$5.41
1905	117.94	$6.04	$6.04	$5.12	$5.12
1906	117.79	$6.19	$6.19	$5.26	$5.26
1907	122.35	$6.74	$6.74	$5.51	$5.51
1908	123.97	$6.62	$6.62	$5.34	$5.34
1909	132.25	$6.91	$6.91	$5.23	$5.23
1910	146.50	$6.90	$6.90	$4.71	$4.71
1911	146.07	$6.60	$6.60	$4.52	$4.52
1912	148.73	$7.72	$9.27	$5.19	$6.23
1913	150.76	$8.11	$9.73	$5.38	$6.46
1900–1907	22.3%	37.7%	37.7%	12.6%	12.6%
1907–1911	19.4%	−2.0%	−2.0%	−17.9%	−17.9%
1911–1913	3.2%	22.9%	47.4%	19.0%	42.9%
1900–1910	46.5%	41.0%	41.0%	−3.8%	−3.8%

[a]The average price index is derived from the geometric average of growth rates from indexes A and B.
[b]Wages are CIVSA's average wages from the departments of spinning, weaving, bleaching, and printing. Weekly working hours were reduced from 72 to 60 in January 1912.

Sources: Price index calculated by the author from weekly data in the *Semana Mercantil, El Economista Mexicano,* and CIVSA documents; wages taken from CIVSA documents.

Wages increased as the result of several strikes,[19] coupled with the support of the newly created Department of Labor, which intervened between workers and manufacturers to end strikes and support negotiations for the benefit of workers. In January 1912 working hours were reduced from 12 to 10,[20] and in July, a set of rules to be followed nationwide inside the mills (*Reglamento*) and a minimum wage schedule that set standard pay rates throughout the industry (*Tarifa Mínima*) were established.[21] If we take into account the reduction in the length of the shift, real wages for a 72-hour work week increased by 42.9% between 1911 and 1913. And in 1913, they were 17% above their level in 1907. But it was leisure, rather than income, that workers gained. They could, of course, employ this free time to complement their wages with another job.

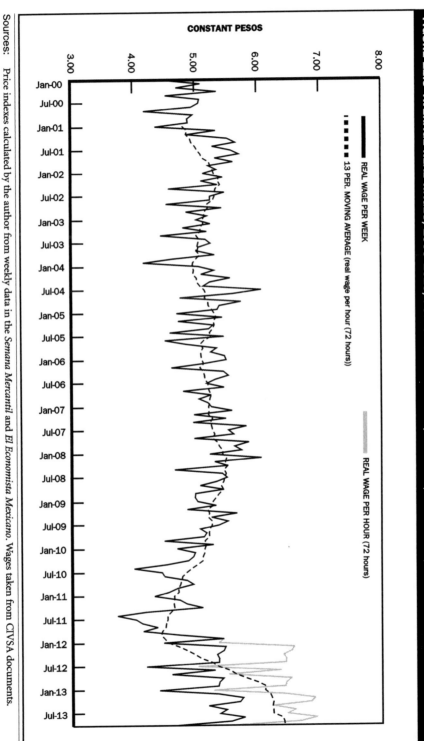

FIGURE 12.3 AVERAGE REAL WAGES, 1900–1913, FOR CIVSA'S SPINNING, WEAVING, BLEACHING, AND PRINTING DEPARTMENTS

Sources: Price indexes calculated by the author from weekly data in the *Semana Mercantil* and *El Economista Mexicano*. Wages taken from CIVSA documents.

Apparently during this period, wages at Santa Rosa increased less than in most textile mills because its wages before the minimum wage was established were higher than those of other mills. The minimum wage schedule gave the Santa Rosa board of directors an opportunity "to level their wages" to wages paid in the industry.[22]

MONETARY ANARCHY AND INFLATION: 1914–1916

Prices

These are the most violent years of the Revolution, and a period for which little economic data of any kind exist. From the fall of Huerta, on August 12, 1914, to the final entrance of the *Constitucionalistas* into the capital on August 2, 1915, it is hard to talk about the existence of a Mexican government. All governmental publications ceased to exist, as well as almost all other publications of any kind. Yet, in terms of price movements this is perhaps the most interesting period in Mexican history. As Edwin Kemmerer points out, "Mexico in the brief period of a dozen years ending in 1916, ran almost the entire gamut of monetary experiences of civilized man,"[23] and between 1914 and 1916 it lived the most extraordinary ones of all.[24]

When Victoriano Huerta came to power after overthrowing democratically elected President Francisco I. Madero in February 1913, he had to finance war against a great number of revolutionary armies that revolted against him. To obtain the necessary money, he forced Mexico's major emission banks to give him credit, and to enable them to do so, he lowered their reserve limits. The credibility of paper money fell, and people rushed to the banks to change their banknotes into specie. Huerta passed a law that allowed banks to end the convertibility of paper money into metallic coins on November 5, 1913.[25] The inflationary process reached new levels.

At the same time revolutionary armies realized that if Huerta could finance his government through the emission of paper money, they could do the same. An anarchic printing of paper money started throughout the Republic, with each revolutionary group's paper money being effective only in the area under its control.

In June 1916, Carranza put into effect a sort of "stabilization program" by which he tried to restore the confidence of citizens in paper money by taking out of circulation all types of paper money that his army had printed previously, replacing them with a new kind of currency, the *infalsificable*. The problem was that his government printed more than seven times the number of *infalsificables* necessary to replace the paper money then in circulation.[26] The *infalsificables* were originally convertible to gold. However, by the end of June the population realized the emission was too large and started exchanging *infalsificables* for gold, so the fund established to back the paper money ran out, ending the convertibility of *infalsificables* to gold. From this moment on, the *infalsificables* depreciated at an impressive rate.[27]

The peso ceased to serve as a unit of value and most prices were set in dollars or gold pesos even as early as mid-1915. In April 1915, CIVSA documents record a meeting of merchants and industrialists in which they decided to set their prices in terms of dollars.[28] Sales were made according to the exchange rate of the date of purchase, although paid in Mexican paper money.

By 1916 all prices of articles announced in newspapers were set in gold pesos.[29] Only wages, taxes, and the prices of a few articles such as newspapers and tramway rides were set in *infalsificables*. By October, the government also started collecting a portion of taxes in metallic coins in order to avoid a total collapse in its real tax revenues.[30] By the end of November, even newspapers were priced in gold pesos.[31]

In December, the government finally realized that it was better to abandon the *infalsificable* policy, and Carranza decreed that all wages, as well as taxes, had to be paid in gold pesos.[32] By the end of December, all payments were made in metallic coins, which people had been hoarding.

Figure 12.4 shows the evolution of the textile price index in pesos from 1914 to 1916, compared with the exchange rate. These figures show how the textile index followed the exchange rate closely. Taking January of 1914 as 100, the textile index in December 1916 is equal to 90,859.05, showing the greatest increases in the period from August to December of 1916.

The exchange rate was relatively stable until December 1914. From this month on CIVSA's prices fell behind until July 1915, when its owners found this trend unsustainable and decided to set their prices in dollars. The fact that they decided to do so in coordination with many other merchants and industrialists was an indicator that this pattern must have occurred elsewhere in the economy.

During the same period the prices of raw cotton in dollars and the price index of textile products in the United States were both increasing due to World War I. As the international prices of cotton and textiles grew, prices rose in Mexico even in terms of dollars. In Figure 12.4 we can see that from December 1915 on, the textile price index grew faster than the exchange rate. However, most of the price climb in terms of pesos can be explained by the change in the exchange rate.

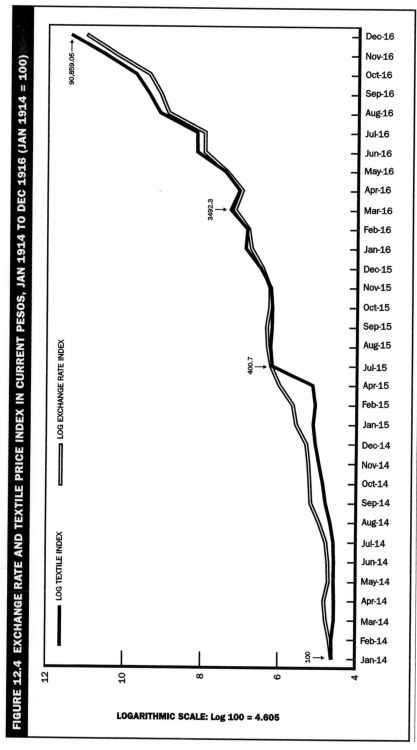

FIGURE 12.4 EXCHANGE RATE AND TEXTILE PRICE INDEX IN CURRENT PESOS, JAN 1914 TO DEC 1916 (JAN 1914 = 100)

LOG TEXTILE INDEX

LOG EXCHANGE RATE INDEX

LOGARITHMIC SCALE: Log 100 = 4.605

90,859.05

3492.3

400.7

100

Sources: CIVSA documents; exchange rates from Kemmerer (1940). The period should be divided in two parts, but I have unified them using a specific exchange rate (7.5) that is between the *infalsificables* and "Veracruz" money.

Wages

From January 1914 to December 1915, nominal wages rose by approximately 153%. Yet CIVSA prices rose by 560% in the same period. Real wages deflated by the textile index fell from $8 pesos in June and August 1914 to less than $2 pesos in May 1916, when they reached their lowest level.

In 1915 there were no strikes, but nominal wages were increased several times, amounting to a 99.7% increase for the year.[33] Some of these increases were the result of Carranza's decrees, while others were granted by the company "given the high cost of the products of the most basic need."[34] In August the maximum legal working hours were reduced from 10 to 9 hours.[35]

In January 1916 a further 50% wage increase was granted to workers on the condition that they promised not to strike.[36] However, every increase in wages was followed by a greater increase in prices, and wages in gold pesos kept falling, as can be seen in Figure 12.5. This made workers aware that the only solution was to be paid in gold pesos. In February 1916, the Executive Committee of the Union of Free Workers of Spinning, Weaving and Printing of CIVSA sent a letter demanding the factory managers pay wages in gold pesos or their equivalent since,

> given that daily wages are not enough to cover our living necessities, because merchants have raised their prices by 2000% and given that we will never be able to get even with them by asking for an increase in wages, ... and to avoid abuses, we have agreed with all the unions of the State of Veracruz that from the 24th of this month, our wage should be paid in "national gold" or its equivalent in paper money calculated by the exchange rate at New York, in order to put ourselves on equal terms with capital that charges in "American gold" for its merchandise.[37]

From May 20 to 26, 1916, CIVSA workers again joined a strike that had reached national levels.[38] To end this strike, companies and workers reached a compromise by which wages in *infalsificables* were set at the same nominal amount that they had been paid in the "Veracruz" paper money, despite the fact that an *infalsificable* was worth at least four times more than a "Veracruz" note.[39] This caused the 281% wage increase in terms of gold pesos that we see in Figure 12.5.

Although nominal wages were increased again in September and October, the real wages kept deteriorating.[40] In November, workers finally gained the right to be paid in gold pesos, after an important strike in all the Orizaba valley mills that lasted more than two weeks.[41] They were the first workers in

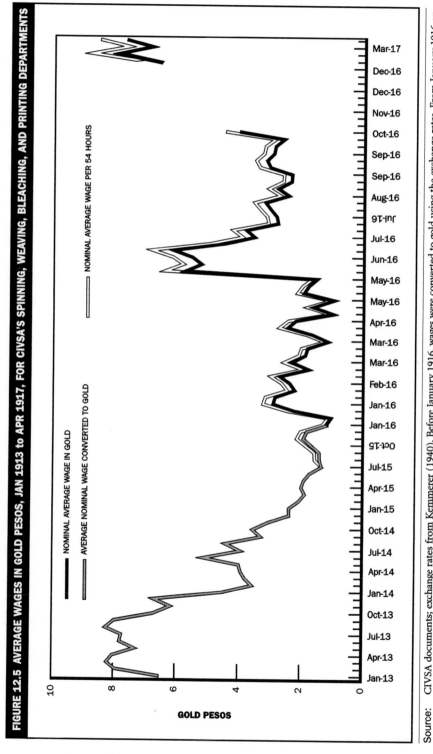

FIGURE 12.5 AVERAGE WAGES IN GOLD PESOS, JAN 1913 to APR 1917, FOR CIVSA'S SPINNING, WEAVING, BLEACHING, AND PRINTING DEPARTMENTS

Source: CIVSA documents; exchange rates from Kemmerer (1940). Before January 1916, wages were converted to gold using the exchange rates. From January 1916 on, the graph shows weekly data. In August 1915, weekly working hours were reduced from 60 to 54.

Mexico to obtain payment in specie, an event that made newspaper head-lines.[42] As can be seen in Figure 12.5, labor regained the gold peso wages of the first semester of 1913 through this measure. Workers experienced a reduction in wages of 698% in terms of gold compared with the average wage of 1912 to May 1916, when wages reached their nadir. By the end of 1916 and early 1917, wages had regained their 1912–1913 gold value.

THE DIFFICULT RETURN TO STABILITY: 1917–1920

Prices

The return to price stability was not a soft landing. The impact of World War I on international financial markets produced an extensive rise in the price of silver after August 1915. By March 1916 the silver peso was worth more as mer-chandise than as money. This situation created incentives to melt down and export silver coins and, as a result, created a tremendous scarcity of metallic money.[43] According to Torres Gaytán, in December 1916 there were $35 mil-lion pesos in metallic coins in circulation, and a year later there were close to $56 million pesos.[44] This is a small amount compared with the $173.5 million metallic coins plus more than $130 million pesos in bank bills that circulated in early 1914.[45] Carranza instituted a bank seizure in September 1916 that last-ed until January 1921 and created a further contraction in the supply of mon-ey. In November 1918, following Edwin Kemmerer's advice, the Mexican government started reminting the existing silver coins in order to reduce their metallic content.[46] The continued appreciation of silver made it necessary to remint silver pesos again on October 27, 1919.[47]

The scarcity of money would lead us to expect deflation in the indexes. This is what Espinosa de los Monteros believed.[48] Yet, this is not what the new indexes show, nor what newspapers and company documents of the period recount.[49] As can be seen in Figure 12.6, there is a sharp price increase in 1917, after which prices follow the trend of the Bach and Reyna (1943) price index until 1920.[50] Prices rose from March to December of that year between 47% and 60%, depending on the index used. If we consider only the last semester of 1917, for which better price data exist, they increased between 26% and 29%. CIVSA's textile prices also show an increasing trend during this period.

The enormous increase in prices in this year, despite monetary contraction, was the result of a supply contraction generated by a decrease in production due to the Revolution, coupled with an increase in demand caused by World War I. The backward shift of the supply curve was not only the result of wartime destruction, but also and primarily of the disruption of the railway

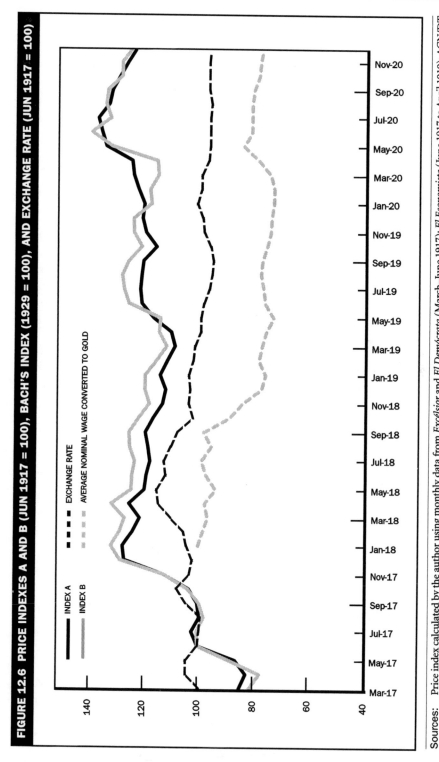

FIGURE 12.6 PRICE INDEXES A AND B (JUN 1917 = 100), BACH'S INDEX (1929 = 100), AND EXCHANGE RATE (JUN 1917 = 100)

INDEX A

INDEX B

EXCHANGE RATE

AVERAGE NOMINAL WAGE CONVERTED TO GOLD

Sources: Price index calculated by the author using monthly data from *Excelsior* and *El Demócrata* (March–June 1917); *El Economista* (June 1917 to April 1919); AGN/DT boxes 144, 184, and 187 (April 1919 to July 1920); and Boletín de Industria Comercio y Trabajo, 1919, vols. I and II, Gaceta Mensual del Departmento del Trabajo, (September–December 1920). Exchange rates taken from Ortíz Mena (1972). Bach's index taken from Bach and Reyna (1943).

and financial systems.[51] To this we should add the bad weather that damaged agriculture, described in accounts of the period.[52]

On the demand side, World War I generated an outward shift that created worldwide inflation. Prices in the United States, Mexico's main commercial partner, rose dramatically in 1917, which must have pushed price increases in Mexico.[53] Furthermore, trade restrictions arose due to the war that inhibited Mexico from supplementing its reduced production with imports. *El Economista* attributed the rise in corn and sugar prices in part to a United States law that prohibited the export of these two products.[54]

In 1918 the contractionary monetary forces that I have described must have prevailed, since the price indexes indicate a price deflation of between 3.9% and 5.9%, depending on the index used.[55] In this year, the situation in the commodities market changed, as the government and the various merchant associations made major efforts to import the goods that had been scarce during 1917. From January 1918 on, shipments of sugar, wheat, flour, and corn were brought from the United States, Cuba, Guatemala, El Salvador, and Argentina.[56] The abundance of goods combined with the scarcity of money to reduce prices in this year, but as the monetary situation stabilized and domestic production increased, the economy returned to a more stable path and faced a moderate increase in prices in the next two years.[57]

Wages

Conflicts over wage increases did not end in Mexican industry when wages were finally set in gold pesos at the end of November 1916. The tremendous decline in purchasing power that workers had faced in the previous years finally ended. Yet prices continued to rise during 1917, even in terms of gold pesos. The difference is that by this time workers no longer had any "monetary illusion"; they had built a strong labor movement, and they could count on the support of the government in ways previously unimagined.

On May 1, 1917, the workday was officially reduced from nine to eight hours in compliance with the new Mexican Constitution signed in February. The constitution also included legislation that required companies to provide coverage for accidents, sickness, pensions, and so forth. CIVSA managers reported that these supplementary expenditures would increase labor costs for the factory by at least 15%.[58]

On May 3, CIVSA workers went on strike,[59] together with 15 factories in Mexico City and all textile mills in Veracruz and Michoacán, representing a workforce of more than 3,000.[60] On May 15, the government of Veracruz decided to give workers an increase over the minimum wage rates of 1912 of 80% for work paid per piece and of 65% for work paid per shift.[61] Figure 12.7 shows this substantial wage increase, which took place between May and June 1917.

This wage increase was higher for Veracruz mills than for those of the rest of the country. CIVSA managers claimed that this put them at a disadvantage with other factories since Puebla factories increased wages only by 16% per shift and by 20% per piece, whereas factories in Mexico City increased wages by 55% and 20%, respectively.[62]

The huge nominal wage increase that took place from May to June of 1917 was completely wiped out in real terms by the great price increases of this period (see Figure 12.7). In 1917 real wages per week fell by 10.5%, and hourly wages by a little less due to the shift reduction (see Table 12.2). This time the causal relationship between price and wage increases seems to be different. Whereas in 1912, 1915, and 1916 inflation preceded wage increases, now wages moved before prices did. There were no further important wage increases until the end of 1920, except a 10% increase that occurred in August 1919 as a byproduct of an important strike whose principal motive was to obtain a collective contract.

In 1918 real wages recovered as a product of the price deflation, although not enough to recover the purchasing power lost by workers in the previous year. From 1917 to 1920 real wages fell by 3.29%, while real wages per hour fell by 1.74%. Wages at the beginning of 1917 were similar to those of 1912–1913 in terms of gold (see Figure 12.5). The decline in real wages experienced from 1917 to 1920 shows how difficult it was for workers to maintain the purchasing power they had in 1912–1913.

TABLE 12.2

Prices and Real Wages (1917–1920)

	Prices	Nominal Wages (pesos)		Real Wages (pesos of 1917)	
	Average Index[a] (June 1917 = 100)	Average Weekly Earnings	Avg. Weekly Earnings[b] (48-hr week)	Average Weekly Earnings	Avg. Weekly Earnings[b] (48-hr week)
1917	99.11	$10.54	$7.80	$10.63	$7.86
1918	121.36	$11.56	$8.64	$9.52	$7.14
1919	115.40	$11.99	$9.00	$10.39	$7.80
1920	125.59	$12.92	$9.66	$10.29	$7.74
1917–1918	22.4%	9.7%	10.8%	−10.5%	−9.2%
1918–1919	−4.9%	3.7%	4.2%	9.1%	9.2%
1919–1920	8.8%	7.8%	7.3%	−1.0%	−0.8%

[a]The average price index is derived from the geometric average of growth rates from indexes A and B.
[b]Wages are CIVSA's average wages from the departments of spinning, weaving, bleaching, and printing. Weekly working hours were reduced from 54 to 48 in May 1917.

Sources: Wages taken from CIVSA documents. For price index sources, see Figure 12.6.

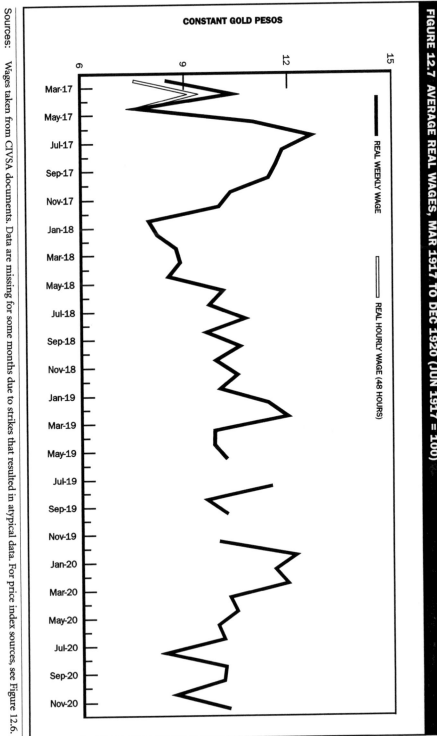

FIGURE 12.7 AVERAGE REAL WAGES, MAR 1917 TO DEC 1920 (JUN 1917 = 100)

CONSTANT GOLD PESOS

REAL WEEKLY WAGE

REAL HOURLY WAGE (48 HOURS)

Sources: Wages taken from CIVSA documents. Data are missing for some months due to strikes that resulted in atypical data. For price index sources, see Figure 12.6.

CONCLUSIONS

This paper gives evidence of a bitter struggle between industrial workers and inflation between 1908 and 1920. Although until 1907 there was relative stability in real wages, from 1907 to 1911 they fell by almost 18%. It is difficult to tell what impact this erosion in real wages had on the growing popular discontent that gave way to the Mexican Revolution.[63] Yet the deterioration of real wages, not in the last decade but in the last four years of the Porfirian regime, might have contributed to the regime's demise.

The general trend of real wages at CIVSA during the Porfiriato can be safely generalized to industrial workers of at least the central region of Mexico during this period.

During the first years of the Revolution, workers started being able to fight back against inflation through the surge of the labor movement and the support the new government provided through the Department of Labor. The minimum wage for the textile industry negotiated at the Convention of Industrialists of July 1912 was the most significant result of this process. From 1911 to 1913 real wages per shift grew by 19% and hourly wages increased by 42.9%. It is likely that real wages increased even more in most textile mills, since Santa Rosa wages were already high before the setting of the minimum wage schedule. Those factories that had lower wages prior to that year must have increased wages by a greater amount.

However, these gains proved to be short-lived. After Huerta seized power and the war took on greater proportions, political chaos gave way to monetary anarchy, and inflation struck with great intensity. From 1914 to 1916, hyperinflation caused an impressive decline in workers' purchasing power, which fell to its worst point in May 1916, to a seventh of what it had been in 1912 in terms of gold pesos. Evidence exists showing that companies were pricing their merchandise in gold as early as December 1915, which would imply a transfer of income from workers to company owners. In December 1916 to after several strikes, workers finally won the battle for payment of wages in gold pesos.

We can be fairly sure that workers' real wages faced a similar overall decline during this period. CIVSA workers were, to a certain extent, able to check the deterioration of their purchasing power caused by inflation through strikes. This appears to have been the case for most textile workers, since CIVSA workers were not alone in their strikes, but were part of a broader labor movement that organized and coordinated workers of several trades and industries from several regions in central Mexico.

Other workers lacking an equally powerful labor movement would have experienced a further deterioration of their real wages. However, those workers who received a significant portion of their payment in kind must have fared better, since they were less subject to the ravages of inflation. Furthermore, workers who faced subsistence wages prior to 1914 could not have experienced as dramatic a fall in their wages as CIVSA workers.

In 1917 workers were able to regain the real wages they earned in 1913, which had been lost during the inflationary period from 1914 to 1916. The purchasing power achieved from 1917 to 1920 was an improvement over the final years of the Porfiriato, yet it was not very different from the real wage earned in 1907. However, in hourly terms, real wages increased in this period relative to those of 1913 because the workday was reduced from 10 to 8 hours. Furthermore, the labor laws of Veracruz in 1914 and 1915 and the Constitution of 1917 brought other nonwage benefits to workers, such as sickness and accident compensation and retirement pensions, which CIVSA directors valued as an additonal 15% increase in wages.

It was very difficult for workers to maintain the purchasing power just recovered. From 1917 to 1920 the effects of World War I on the Mexican economy and the destruction of economic institutions and infrastructure caused by the Revolution made the return to price stability a difficult task. In 1917 an important inflationary process took place despite the enormous monetary contraction generated by the collapse of the *infalsificables*. Despite great nominal wage increases, real weekly wages diminished by more than 10%, a loss that was almost recovered during the following year due to the price deflation. By 1920 workers' weekly real wages were almost 4% below those of 1913. CIVSA's real wage increase from 1917 to 1920 cannot be generalized to other industries or regions since we know that textile mills in other states increased their wages by a much lower rate.

The high inflation after 1914 must have been an important factor in strengthening the labor movement, one that gave workers an immediate and relevant motive to unite and to fight. Most of the strikes carried on during this period were highly effective, and this imparted great prestige to unions as well as additional strength. At the same time, inflation enabled employers to cope with the additional costs implicit in the new labor legislation.

By 1913 workers had won most of what the Revolution would give them. The fall of Madero and the intensification of war imposed high costs on workers in terms of living standards. The war years were times of penury and hunger. The labor movement grew stronger, and by 1917 workers had recovered the purchasing power they had achieved in 1913, working less and with higher nonwage benefits. Yet, despite the vigorous unions, workers were not able to retain this level of real wages through the period 1917–1920. This paper shows that it was leisure rather than income that workers obtained from the Revolution relative to their earnings before real wages started collapsing in the last two years of the Porfiriato.

These results provide an explanation for the controversial role that industrial workers played during the Revolution.[64] It does not seem strange that workers joined the *Constitucionalista* armies against *Zapatista* peasants, as they did after 1915, given that the war was now costing them so dearly and that they had already obtained benefits from the constitution.

Given that in Mexico the Revolution came about together with a strengthening of the labor movement, it is impossible to separate their effects as independent processes. The Revolution certainly contributed to the growth of the labor movement and the speed and depth of its gains. Yet, by no means can we conclude that if the Revolution had not taken place, these gains would not have taken place anyway. A comparative study with other Latin American countries could help to clarify this counterfactual premise.

ACKNOWLEDGMENTS

Research support for this paper was provided by the *Instituto Tecnológico Autónomo de México*, the *Social Science Research Council*, and the *Tinker* and *México en Harvard* Foundations. Research assistance was ably provided by Julieta Almeida and Aldo Musacchio. The author benefited from comments on an earlier draft of this paper by Jonathan Brown, John Coatsworth, Claudia Goldin, Colin Lewis, Graciela Márquez, Jeffrey Williamson, and John Womack. All errors are my own.

Appendix

A GENERAL METHODOLOGICAL PERSPECTIVE

Prices

Two price indexes exist for the period of this study, but both have important limitations. The first is an annual consumer price index for Mexico City for the Porfiriato (1877, 1886–1911) created in the 1960s by a group of historians led by Fernando Rosenzweig at El Colegio de México.[65] It has been criticized mainly for weighting its shares by production instead of apparent consumption data.[66] The few articles it includes and the fact that it is annual create additional problems for its use to deflate wages for this period.

The second index covers the period 1918–1928 and was constructed by Frederico Bach and Margarita Reyna from the Oficina de Barómetros Económicos in 1943.[67] Its problem is also related to the weights employed, since they are based on production estimates that were recognized as not being very reliable.[68] A further problem is the absence of an explanation of the methodology the authors followed.

Instead of an index weighted by production, I decided to build a new price index based on laborers' budgets.[69] Fortunately, an effort to build estimates of workers' consumption baskets based on direct questionnaires answered by families was undertaken in 1930 by the Comité Reorganizador de los Ferrocarriles Nacionales de México (The Railways Reorganization Office). Unable to distribute their questionnaire among railway workers, they handed it out among workers of the Ministry of Finance. There is a full description of the methodology used, which makes this information reliable.[70] The basket I used refers to consumption patterns in Mexico City and is based on 1,189 completed questionnaires. I call this the "1930 basket," which I used to calculate index A.

The problem with this basket is that it pertains mainly to public employees, who had incomes higher than most industrial workers.[71] Also, consumption patterns are likely to have changed between 1900 and 1930. Fortunately, it was possible to construct an alternative basket from a series of questionnaires distributed in 1914 to families in Mexico City by the Office of Legislation and Labor of the Department of Labor. There were 18 questionnaires which detailed the income and expenditures of very low income families.[72] I refer to the shares obtained from this source as the "1914 basket." They were used to calculate index B (see Appendix Table 12.1).

A lower and an upper bound price index can be built with these two baskets since they pertain to families either poorer or richer than the average industrial worker. At the same time, since one is from 1914 and the other from 1930, they embody the changes in consumption patterns over time.

I constructed Laspeyres price indexes specific to Mexico City. This city is the only one for which I have enough price data. This does not pose a big problem because the price data that I have for the Orizaba region for some years correlates closely with prices in the capital.[73] Yet this price index cannot be generalized for the whole country. Further efforts at building price indexes for other Mexican regions need to be undertaken.[74]

I took prices of textiles from CIVSA price lists. Santa Rosa prices give a good idea of textile prices in the market since the company documents show that they were continually checking competitors' prices in order to fix theirs, generally at the same level.

Since I did not have prices for some goods included in the original baskets, I excluded them, recalculating the shares for the items I had. The shares actually used to calculate the indexes are shown in the right side of Appendix Table 12.1 Since I have a different set of products for the 1900–1913 period than for the 1917–1920 one, the weights accorded to products in the two periods differ.

Wages

The most significant effort to collect data for wages for the Porfiriato was also undertaken by the Colegio de México group. However, the data are not very reliable because they combine wage data for different occupations from disparate sources. A further problem is the difficulty in comparing them with data for other periods, for which this kind of series was never built.

My main sources for wage data were CIVSA payrolls and accounting books.[75] This company, located in the Orizaba valley of the state of Veracruz, has been in continuous operation since 1898. During the Porfiriato it operated with the Compañía Industrial de Orizaba S.A. (CIDOSA), one of the most modern textile mills. Together they produced 20% of Mexican cotton textiles in the last decade of the Porfiriato.[76] The textile industry was the most important manufacturing industry in these years; in 1930 it employed approximately 30% of manufacturing labor.[77] The series of average weekly nominal wages used includes the wages of all workers in the spinning, weaving, bleaching, and printing departments of Santa Rosa, representing 83% of the total labor force at the mill.[78] From CIVSA documents I obtained weekly wages per worker, not wages per hour of work. Since most of the workers of the factory were paid for piecework rather than on a daily basis, wages varied depending on the number of hours and days per week actually worked. This adds volatility to the wages actually obtained.

APPENDIX TABLE 12.1

Consumer Price Index Shares

	Observed (%)		Used 1900–1913 (%)		Used 1917–1920 (%)	
	(A) 1930	(B) 1914	(A) 1930	(B) 1914	(A) 1930	(B) 1914
Expenditures						
Food	38.8	61.6	62.5	79.3	55.1	86.7
Clothing	14.6	7.0	23.6	10.4	20.8	3.2
Rent	14.8	14.8				
Personal Expenses	7.3	6.0	11.8	8.9	10.4	0.4
Alcoholic Beverages	4.9	4.0	8.09	5.59		
Soap	1.5	1.2	2.39	1.65	10.4	0.4
Tobacco	0.9	0.8	1.52	1.05		
Fuel and Lighting	9.7	7.5	2.10	1.4	13.8	9.7
Firewood					4.3	3.0
Coal		5.0			4.3	3.0
Paraffin oil		1.6			3.4	2.4
Candles		0.9	2.10	1.4	1.9	1.3
Other Expenditures	14.7	3.1				
Total	100	100	100	100	100	100
Food						
Rice	1.5	2.4	2.4	2.1	1.9	1.9
Sugar & sugar loaf	3.7	5.1	5.8	4.7	4.7	4.3
Coffee	3.0	4.5	4.8	4.7	3.9	4.3
Meat	15.3	17.5	24.2	24.1	19.6	21.7
Chocolate	1.2		2.0			
Beans	3.7	6.7	5.8	6.3	4.7	5.6
Fruit	3.6					
Chickpea	1.4	0.1	2.2			
Eggs	7.4	0.4				
Milk	18.5	5.5			23.8	7.3
Vegetables	3.4	6.2				
Fat	5.9	7.7	9.3	8.2	7.6	7.4
Butter	1.2					
Bread	18.2	22.3	28.8	22.7	23.4	20.5
Potatoes	1.2	1.4				
Fish	1.4					
Cheese	1.2	1.3	1.9	10.6		
Tortillas	6.3	14.2	9.9	12.3	8.0	11.0
Salt		1.9		2.2		2.0
Chili	1.8	2.9	2.8	2.0	2.3	14.1
Total	100	100	100	100	100	100

Sources: Luna Arroyo, *Estudio del costo de la vida en México*, 1931, and Presupuesto de familias de obreros, Departamento de Legislación y Trabajo, Fondo del Departamento del Trabajo, AGN, Caja 368, exp. 2 and 3.

NOTES

1. Rosenzweig (1989), p. 247; Reynolds (1970), p. 25; Katz (1981), pp. 3–49; Clark (1934), p. 9; Knight (1990), pp. 127–130; Tobler (1994), pp. 137–139.
2. Friedrich (1970), Ronfedlt (1973), Warman (1976).
3. Gilly (1971), Córdoba (1973), Meyer (1991).
4. An exception to this would be Ulloa (1981), pp. 17–25.
5. Womack (1978), Haber (1989).
6. In 1912, the average daily wage of workers in the textile industry of Veracruz was the highest in the country, reaching 3.19 pesos, whereas in other important industrial centers, such as Mexico City or Puebla, average daily wages were 2.48 and 2.36 pesos, respectively. An even greater disparity is seen in 1921: The national average daily wage in textile industries was 2.63 pesos, whereas the CIVSA average daily wage was almost double, or 5.08 pesos (Boletín Estadística Fiscal, *Anuario del año fiscal 1912–13; Fábricas de hilados y tejidos en la República en el año 1921,* AGN/DT, box 399, folder 1).
7. García Díaz (1981), Anderson (1976).
8. De la Cueva (1938).
9. I calculate two price indexes. Index A is constructed using a basket that reflects the patterns of consumption in 1930 of families marginally wealthier than the average industrial worker. Index B's basket corresponds to families in 1914 poorer than the average industrial worker (see appendix).
10. Throughout the paper, I calculate the average index using the geometric average of the growth rates of the two price indexes. Given that both indexes show the same trend, doing this does not modify the general argument and provides simplicity.
11. Kemmerer (1940).
12. Secretaría de Fomento, Colonización, Industria y Comercio (1886), p. 29.
13. Kemmerer (1917).
14. For the best description of how Mexico adopted the gold standard, see Kemmerer (1916), pp. 471–553.
15. The correlation between the average price index and U.S. monthly prices (Warren and Pearson 1933) is .89.
16. Katz (1981), p. 10.
17. Tobler (1994), p. 138; Knight (1990), p. 130.
18. El Colegio de México (1965), p. 17.
19. In 1911 there were two major strikes at Santa Rosa that included all mills in the Orizaba region. CIVSA archive (henceforth CV), copiadores de cartas (correspondence) between Santa Rosa (SR) and Mexico City offices (MX), September 28 and 29, and October 4, 7–10, 12–14, and 16, 1911.

20. CV correspondence SR–MX, January 1 and 19, 1912.

21. *Boletín del Archivo General de la Nación* (1984), pp. 3–4.

22. CV correspondence SR–MX, July 16, 1912.

23. Kemmerer (1940), p. 3.

24. For the sake of brevity, this paper does not include a full explanation of the monetary events that took place in these years. For a more detailed account, see Kemmerer (1940), Manns (1986), Cárdenas and Manns (1992), Manero (1926, 1957), and Ortíz Mena (1972).

25. Secretaría de Hacienda y Crédito Público (1959).

26. Cárdenas and Manns (1992), p. 457.

27. Cárdenas and Manns (1992), p. 458.

28. CV, "Actas de deliberaciones del Consejo de Administración," April 27, 1915. CIVSA price lists show prices in dollars starting July 1915. They probably had changed in May, but there are no price lists available for May and June of that year.

29. The most important national ones are *El Demócrata* and *El Nacional*.

30. Boletín de la Secretaría de Hacienda (1917); Carranza decrees of October 5, 22, 23, 27, and November 1, 15, 16 of 1916.

31. *El Nacional*, November 30, 1916, and November 15, 1916.

32. Decrees of December 9 and 13, 1916.

33. CV correspondence SR–MX, February 20, 1915, and April 7, 1915. CIDOSA archive (henceforth CD), telegram of Marcos López Jiménez to CIDOSA, April 2, 1915.

34. CV correspondence SR–MX, October 19, 1915.

35. Ibid., August 23, 1915, and CD letter from Río Blanco to the Department of Labor of Veracruz, August 10, 1915.

36. CV correspondence SR–MX, January 18, 1916.

37. Ibid., February 21, 1916 (translation from Spanish done by myself).

38. Newspapers reported that bakers, electricians, and tramway, telephone, and potable water workers in Mexico City were also part of this strike (*El Nacional*, May 23, 1916).

39. There is a problem in defining the equivalence between "Veracruz" notes and *infalsificables*. A government decree in May 19, 1916, sets its equivalence as 4 to 1. However, CIVSA documents set the equivalence as 5 to 1 during the first week of June, as 8 to 1 during the second week, and as 10 to 1 thereafter.

40. CV correspondence SR–MX, September 12, 1916, and October 24, 1916.

41. CD correspondence Mexico–Río Blanco, October 27 and 30, November 1 and 17, 1916.

42. *El Nacional*, November 1, 1916.

43. *El Economista*, June 4, 1918, p. 2.

44. Torres Gaytán (1986), p. 145.
45. Kemmerer (1917), p. 32.
46. Kemmerer (1917), p. 24; Torres Gaytán (1986), p. 150.
47. Espinosa de los Monteros (1928), p. 14.
48. Espinosa de los Monteros (1928), p. 9.
49. *El Pueblo*, January 21, 1917, p. 10, and March 6, 1917, p. 1; *El Economista*, November 23, 1917, p. 3; and CV, letter from J. Michel, MX, to the Comité Consultatif in Paris, October 9, 1917.
50. Bach and Reyna (1943).
51. Gómez (1990).
52. CV, letter from J. Michel, MX, to the Comité Consultatif in Paris, October 9, 1917.
53. The inflation rate for 1917 in the United States was 37% (U.S. Bureau of the Census 1975, p. 200).
54. *El Economista*, October 5, 1917, p. 10.
55. This is the price change of the annual average index of each year. If we calculate the December to December index, deflation in 1918 was 11.4% or 9.2%, depending on the index used.
56. *El Economista*, December 3, 1917; February 6 and 23, March 18, April 18 and 23, and May 11, 1918. Notices of the shipment arrivals appeared on February 16, March 22, May 6, and June 12, 1918.
57. Between 3.2% and 5.5% in 1919 and between 1.6% and 0.7% in 1920, using indexes A and B respectively (December to December price changes).
58. CV, letter from J. Michel, MX, to the Comité Consultatif in Paris, April 30, 1917.
59. CV, telegram SR–MX, May 3, 1917.
60. *El Pueblo*, May 9, 1917, p. 1.
61. CV, correspondence SR–MX, May 15, 1917.
62. CV, letter from J. Michel, MX, to the Comité Consultatif in Paris, May 15, 1917.
63. Alan Knight (1990, p. 130) criticizes the argument that the real drop in living standards during the 1900s be considered an important cause of the Revolution since it is very difficult to establish a causality between the two events.
64. Carr (1976), Clark (1934).
65. El Colegio de México (1965). The index includes prices of 13 items.
66. Craig (1993), pp. 51–67; Cerda (1993). Luis Cerda and Marc Gilly (1993) have recalculated the Colmex index by adding imports and subtracting exports from the production figures to calculate the shares of each item. The resulting index is not very different from the Colmex one.
67. It included prices of 33 articles.
68. Bach and Reyna (1943).
69. Fisher (1926), p. 207.

70. Arroyo (1931), Ferrocarriles Nacionales de México (1931).
71. The average annual wage of CIVSA's workers ($1,038.59 for 1930) fell in the Comité's lowest earning category of less than $1,200 pesos annually.
72. Archivo General de la Nación, Fondo del Departamento del Trabajo, 91/4 and 68/1 (first number indicates box; the second, folder).
73. The average correlation of prices between Córdoba and Mexico City for 1918–1930 is .72. Unfortunately, there are not enough prices from Orizaba. However, this city lies between Mexico City and Córdoba, which is only 13.7 miles away from Orizaba and can be considered part of the same region.
74. The price index for Guadalajara during the Porfiriato that Craig (1993) presents seems, for instance, to be very different from the one for Mexico City.
75. CIVSA employed an average of 2,100 workers. Weekly total payments to labor per department are taken from the *Libro de Caja* (cashier's book). The number of workers per department comes from CIVSA payrolls. I obtained weekly wages by dividing total payments per department between the number of workers per department.
76. Haber (1989), pp. 57, 94.
77. Dirección General de Estadística (1930).
78. This leaves out workers from three departments: dyeing, general merchandises, and workshops.

REFERENCES

Archives

Archivo de la Compañía Industrial Veracruzana, Ciudad Mendoza, Veracruz, México (abbreviated in notes as CV).

Archivo de la Compañía Industrial de Orizaba, Río Blanco, Veracruz, México.

Archivo General de la Nación, Fondo del Departamento del Trabajo (abbreviated in notes as AGN/DT).

Newspaper Sources

La Semana Mercantil, financial weekly, Mexico City, several volumes, 1900–1913.

El Economista Mexicano, financial weekly, Mexico City, several volumes, 1900–1914.

El Nacional, daily newspaper, Mexico City, several volumes, 1915–1918.

El Demócrata, daily newspaper, Mexico City, several volumes, 1915–1917.

El Pueblo, several volumes, 1917–1920.

El Economista, several volumes, 1917–1930.

Books and Articles

Anderson, Rodney. *Outcasts in Their Own Land. Mexican Industrial Workers 1906–11.* Dekalb: Northern Illinois University Press, 1976.

Archivo General de la Nación. "Las primeras tarifas (salarios) mínimas en la industria textil (1912)." In *Boletín del Archivo General de la Nación,* Tercera Serie, VIII, 3–4, July–December, 1984.

Arroyo, Luna. *Estudios del costo de la vida en México.* México, 1931. Mimeographed.

Bach, Frederico, and Margarita Reyna. "El nuevo índice de precios al mayoreo en la Ciudad de México de la Secretaria de la Economía Nacional." *El Trimestre Económico* 10, no. 37, 1943.

Boletín de la Secretaría de Hacienda. *Decretos y Circulares 1913–1917.* Several volumes. México: SHCP, 1917.

Cárdenas, Enrique, and Carlos Manns. "Inflación y estabilización monetaria en México durante la revolución." In *Historia económica de México,* Vol. 3, edited by Enrique Cárdenas, 447–470. México: Fondo de Cultura Económica, 1992.

Carr, Barry. *El movimiento obrero y la política en México 1910–1922.* México: SEP, 1976.

Cerda, Luis. "¿Causas económicas de la revolución mexicana?" *Revista Mexicana de Sociología* 27 (1993): 172–191.

Cerda, Luis, and Marc Gilly. "Indices de precios durante el Porfiriato." Unpublished manuscript, Mexico, 1993.

Clark, Ruth. *Organized Labor in Mexico.* Chapel Hill: The University of North Carolina, 1934.

Comisión Monetaria. *Informe de la Comisión de Cambios y Moneda.* In *La reforma monetaria,* by Enrique Martínez Sobral. México: Tipografía de la Oficina Impresora de Estampillas, 1910.

Córdoba, Arnaldo. *La ideología de la revolución mexicana. La formación del nuevo régimen.* México: Era, 1973.

Cosío Villegas, Daniel. *Historia moderna de México. El Porfiriato. La vida económica.* 2 vols. México: Hermes, 1965.

Craig Antebi, Marc Christopher. "Los índices de precios en México: El caso del Porfiriato." B.A. thesis, Instituto Tecnológico Autónomo de México, México, 1993.

De la Cueva, Mario. *Derecho mexicano del trabajo.* México: Porrúa, 1938.

Dirección General de Estadística. *Primer censo industrial.* México, 1930.

El Colegio de México. *Estadísticas económicas del Porfiriato. Comercio exterior.* México: El Colegio de México, 1965.

El Colegio de México. *Estadísticas económicas del Porfiriato. Fuerza de trabajo y actividad por sectores.* México: El Colegio de México, n.d.

Espinosa de los Monteros, Antonio. "La moneda en México desde 1910." In *Revista mexicana de economía,* Vol. I. México, 1928.

Ferrocarriles Nacionales de México. Oficina de Estudios Económicos, Jesús Silva Herzog. *Un estudio del costo de la vida en México.* México: Facultad de Economía UNAM, 1931.

Fisher, Irving. *The Purchasing Power of Money.* New York: The Macmillan Company, 1926.

Friedrich, Paul. *Agrarian Revolt in a Mexican Village.* Englewood Cliffs, NJ: Prentice Hall, 1970.

García Díaz, Bernardo. *Un pueblo fabril del Porfiriato: Santa Rosa, Veracruz.* México: CONAFE y FCE, 1981.

Gilly, Adolfo. *La revolución interrumpida.* México: El Caballito, 1971.

Gómez-Galvarriato, Aurora. "El primer impulso industrializador en México: El caso de Fundidora Monterrey, México." B.A. thesis, ITAM, 1990.

Haber, Stephen. *Industry and Underdevelopment: The Industrialization of Mexico 1890–1940.* Stanford: Stanford University Press, 1989.

Katz, Friedrich. *The Secret War in Mexico.* Chicago: The University of Chicago Press, 1981.

Kemmerer, Edwin. *Modern Currency Reforms.* New York: The Macmillan Co., 1916.

Kemmerer, Edwin. *Sistema monetario de México. Reformas propuestas.* México: Palacio Nacional, 1917.

Kemmerer, Edwin. *Inflation and Revolution: Mexico's Experience 1912–1917.* Princeton: Princeton University Press, 1940.

Knight, Alan. *The Mexican Revolution.* Vol. I. Nebraska: University of Nebraska Press, 1990.

Manero, Antonio. *El Banco de México. Sus orígenes y fundación.* New York: F. Mayans, 1926.

Manero, Antonio. *La revolución bancaria en México 1865–1955.* México: Instituto Nacional de Estudios Históricos de la Revolución Mexicana, 1957.

Manns, Carlos. "Inflación y estabilización en México: La experiencia de 1916." B.A. thesis, Universidad de la Américas, Puebla, 1986.

Meyer, Jean. *La revolución mexicana.* México: JUS, 1991.

Ortíz Mena, Raúl. *La moneda Mexicana: Análisis de sus fluctuaciones, las depreciaciones y sus causas.* México: Banco de México, 1972.

Ramírez, Elia B. *Estadística bancaria.* México: INAH, 1985.

Reynolds, Clark. *The Mexican Economy: Twentieth Century Structure and Growth.* New Haven: Yale University Press, 1970.

Ronfeldt, David. *Atencingo: The Politics of Agrarian Struggle in a Mexican Ejido.* Stanford: Stanford University Press, 1973.

Rosenzweig, Fernando. *El desarrollo económico en México 1800–1910.* México: El Colegio Mexiquense A.C. and ITAM, 1989.

Secretaría de Fomento, Colonización, Industria y Comercio. *La crisis monetaria. Estudios sobre la crisis mercantil y la depreciación de la plata.* México: Oficina Tip. de la Secretaría de Fomento, 1886.

Secretaría de Hacienda y Crédito Público. *Legislación monetaria.* Tomo I. México: SHCP, 1959.

Secretaría de la Economía Nacional. *Trimestre de Barómetros Económicos.* Numbers 6 and 7. December 1947, México.

Tobler, Hans Werner. *La revolución mexicana. Transformación social y cambio político.* México: Alianza, 1994.

Torres Gaytán, Ricardo. *Un siglo de devaluaciones del peso mexicano,* 4th ed. México: Siglo XXI, 1986.

Ulloa, Berta. *Historia de la revolución 1914–1917.* México: El Colegio de México, 1979.

Ulloa, Berta. *Historia de la revolución mexicana 1914–1917. La Encrucijada de 1915,* 1a reimp. México: El Colegio de México, 1981.

U.S. Bureau of the Census. *Historical Statistics of the United States, Colonial Times to 1970.* Washington, DC: U.S. Government Printing Office, 1975.

Warman, Arturo. *. . . Y venimos a contradecir. Los campesinos de Morelos y el Estado Nacional.* México: Secretaría de Educación Pública, 1976.

Warren, George F., and Frank A. Pearson. *Prices.* New York: Wiley, 1933.

Womack, John. "The Mexican Economy during the Revolution 1910–20." *Marxist Perspectives* 1, no. 4 (1978): 80–123.

PART V

Government Policies and the External Sector

E ven in the long nineteenth century of (relatively) unfettered markets and diminutive public sectors, governments mattered. At the margin, relatively small doses of government intervention could yield powerful results. The three chapters in this final section analyze the role of government policy where it has always mattered most in Latin America—taxing and regulating the region's external economic relations. In the aftermath of independence, for example, the last power even the weakest of governments gave up before succumbing to the next revolt or coup was the capacity to tax imports and exports. By the end of the century, the major countries of the region had developed cadres of sophisticated technicians and ministers, who worked assiduously to manage capital flows, exchange rates, money supplies, and tariff rates to serve national economic policy goals.[1]

The most powerful symbol of nineteenth-century modernization and government intervention was the railroad. As Summerhill points out in his essay on railroads in imperial Brazil (Chapter 13), foreign investors poured money into railroad construction and operation only after the Brazilian government guaranteed a fixed rate of return on their investment. Any time a (mostly foreign-owned) Brazilian railroad company failed to earn the guaranteed rate, the Brazilian government sent a check. The results of such meddling could be seen belching smoke all over Latin America. Though few governments were as generous as that of the Emperor Dom Pedro II, all provided subsidies or guarantees sufficient to attract more foreign capital to railroad construction in the era between 1850 and World War I than to all other forms of foreign direct investment combined.[2] Brazilian railroads, as Summerhill points out, produced respectable social returns—higher than in countries such as the United States and Britain, where a high proportion of railroad freight could have shifted to water routes, but lower than in Mexico, where the railroad contributed to stimulating rapid economic growth.[3] Summerhill concludes that in an era when the Brazilian economy did not grow much, if at all, railroads helped prevent decline. Perhaps, as Leff has argued, the imperial government should either have intervened with even greater incentives to attract even more railroad investment or liberated the provinces to do so, as republican governments did after 1889.[4]

Government nurturing and protecting of domestic-use industries has declined in favor among economists and publics in the past two decades. As every student of Latin American economic history knows, conscious government promotion of import substituting industrialization (ISI) did not occur before the 1930s depression.[5] Most countries that adopted it as an official strategy did not do so until the 1940s or 1950s. On the other hand, as Márquez shows clearly (Chapter 14), some Latin American governments, in this case Mexico, adopted protectionist policies well before 1900. Márquez's essay is especially helpful because she develops a method for measuring the relative importance of tariffs and such nontariff factors as the depreciation of Mexico's silver-based currency. She finds that ad valorem tariff rates declined between 1890 and 1905, while the protection provided by depreciation of the exchange rate increased. Once Mexico adopted the gold standard with the monetary reform of 1905, depreciation stopped and tariff rates suddenly became important again as the main instrument for protecting domestic producers.

The Revolution of 1910 drove Mexico off the gold standard. Most of the other Latin American countries abandoned it along with the great powers during World War I. After the war, as Díaz Fuentes points out (Chapter 15), the countries with the three largest economies (Argentina, Brazil, and Mexico) all worked to return to the gold standard, but only succeeded in doing so for a short time on the eve of the Great Depression. Only Argentina, however, sought to restore the prewar exchange rate. Díaz Fuentes discounts the influence of foreign economic consultants, the "money doctors" of the 1920s, in his three cases. He concludes by showing that the relative exchange rate stability that had characterized the pre–World War I era did not return to Latin America until after the U.S. devaluation of 1933 and the creation of the "managed floating system" that reigned until the onset of World War II.

Notes

1. The Brazilian case is well treated in Topik (1987).
2. See United Nations Economic Commission for Latin America (1965).
3. See Coatsworth (1981), Fogel (1964), Hawke (1970), and Metzer (1977).
4. Leff (1982).
5. Bulmer-Thomas (1994), chap. 7.

References

Bulmer-Thomas, Victor. *The Economic History of Latin America Since Independence.* Cambridge: Cambridge University Press, 1994.

Coatsworth, John H. *Growth Against Development: The Economic Impact of Railroads in Porfirian Mexico.* DeKalb: Northern Illinois University Press, 1981.

Fogel, Robert William. *Railroads and American Economic Growth: Essays in Econometric History.* Baltimore: Johns Hopkins University Press, 1964.

Hawke, Gary. *Railways and Economic Growth in England and Wales, 1840–1870.* London: Oxford University Press, 1970.

Leff, Nathaniel. *Underdevelopment and Development in Brazil.* London: Allen and Unwin, 1982.

Metzer, Jacob. *Some Economic Aspects of Railroad Development in Tsarist Russia.* New York: Arno Press, 1977.

Topik, Steven. *The Political Economy of the Brazilian State, 1889–1930.* Austin: University of Texas Press, 1987.

United Nations Economic Commission for Latin America. *External Financing in Latin America.* New York: United Nations, 1965.

13

Railroads in Imperial Brazil, 1854–1889

William R. Summerhill
University of California, Los Angeles

The economic consequences of railroads in the nineteenth century have long been of interest to historians. Imperial Brazil was slow to pursue internal improvements, despite its remarkable stability among the Latin American nations, and entered the railway age relatively late. By the time the first railroads opened for operation in the 1850s and 1860s, Brazil's planter class eagerly sought the benefits that cheap transport conferred. Railroads expanded rapidly under government promotion after 1870, and by the time the Empire succumbed to the Republic in 1889, Brazil had passed through its first stage of railroad development.

Many historians would find much to agree with in the claim that "the plantation- and mine-to-port pattern of Latin American railroad construction did little to provide political integration, to serve local, regional, or national markets, and to encourage industrialization," and that railroads merely "linked Brazil to world markets and thereby deepened dependency."[1] The general impression of railroads in nineteenth-century Brazil is that they were extraordinarily efficient at squandering and draining resources, enriching a small planter class while impoverishing the country. Enjoying similarly wide currency is the view that foreign financing of development projects like railroads necessarily meant that "even the largest, the most stable, and the potentially wealthy countries saw their control over their own economies dissipate."[2] In spite of the testable implications embedded in the historiography, for Brazil in particular there are surprisingly few evaluations of the economic consequences of railroads or government policy.[3]

The process of railroad development in imperial Brazil warrants assessment in terms of its measurable consequences. This paper proceeds in four sections. The first discusses the failure of markets to supply railroad transport services, the operation of Brazil's railroad subsidy arrangements, and the growth of the railroad sector from the 1850s until 1887. The second assesses the direct impact of railroad development. It specifies the principal consequences of railroads by measuring the savings on transport costs that the iron horse created. The third section examines indirect effects from railroad development, the most important of which were the differential impact on the export sector and dependence on foreign inputs. The final section concludes.

The main findings of the study are two. First, by the end of the Empire the gains from railroads were appreciable. Conservative estimates of the railroad's social savings on freight in 1887 run in excess of 10% of gross domestic product (GDP). In an economy undergoing relatively little per capita income growth, the railroad substantially boosted the level of economic activity. Second, the costs of using foreign capital and inputs in constructing and operating railroads were a good deal less than the benefits. Brazil's integration into world product and capital markets enabled it to obtain railroads more quickly and inexpensively than would have otherwise been possible. Had it been otherwise, the pace of railroad expansion would have been much reduced, given the absence of domestic industries and capital market institutions required to provision transport improvements.

These conclusions differ sharply from prevailing characterizations in several ways. Arguments that stress the costs of the railroad's role in producing underdevelopment fail to square with the evidence. In that scenario, reliance on the international market for finance, inputs, and export earnings is viewed as fostering business activities that benefited foreign investors disproportionately at the expense of the national economy.[4] Dependency perspectives that view foreign investment as inimical because it was exploitative, misallocated resources, skewed growth, and drained off surplus value, impoverishing the country and reducing Brazil to a neocolony, rest on a fragile empirical edifice.[5] In fact, the gains Brazil secured from railroads easily outweighed the costs. The distribution of those gains within Brazil was no doubt skewed to favor the enfranchised, the wealthy, and the powerful, thanks mainly to prevailing features of the polity. It seems unlikely that any regressive consequences of railroads were an inherent feature of either railroad technology or foreign finance. Foreigners neither captured the surplus that railroads created, nor controlled policies related to subsidy or pricing. Policymakers responded not to Brazil's presumed peripheral position in the world economy, but rather to the imperatives of domestic political constituencies. The course of economic change fostered by railroads reflected less a pattern of dependent development than it did the ordinary actions of domestic interest groups seeking transport improvements because they prized the private benefits thereby created.

FROM MARKET FAILURE TO RAILROAD DEVELOPMENT

Private markets failed to supply railroad transport services in Brazil, in spite of the fact that the potential return to the economy's producers and consumers from reducing transport costs was large. The first government railroad concessions in Brazil arose during the Regency (1831–1840), under the tutelage of Feijó. Attempts to construct railroads before 1850 foundered on the complexity, cost, and uncertainty inherent in large, capital-intensive investment projects. Railroad development began in Brazil only in 1852, when the government created a guaranteed minimum dividend for investors, many of whom were foreigners.[6] During Brazil's Second Reign (1840–1889), railroad investments accounted for the bulk of foreign finance that flowed into the country, almost all of which was British in origin.

Several factors made railroads expensive and risky and delayed their appearance in Brazil. First, the start-up capital requirements of a railroad were hefty. Railroads differed from other businesses requiring relatively large investments, such as a coffee *fazenda* or a textile mill. Unlike a factory or farm, which could begin small and build up incrementally by adding another loom or planting another hectare, railroads were lumpy. Individual railroads had to be built on a scale sufficient to let them tap enough traffic to cover the costs of operation and finance. By the mid-1880s, the capital stock of a relatively modest railroad, such as the Recife to Caruarú line, although less than 12 million mil-réis, nonetheless exceeded that of Brazil's entire cotton textile industry.[7] If mobilizing capital for industrialization was difficult, then doing so for railroads proved challenging in the extreme.

Second, much uncertainty attached to the viability of a railroad. Investors were naturally skittish about projects with uncertain returns, and it was difficult for them to know just how much revenue the railroad stood to earn. Brazil's early railroad concessions set the maximum rates that could be charged for freight and passenger services yet did nothing to secure returns to shareholders.[8] Until the expected private return to the owners of railroad capital could be pulled more closely in line with the returns to the shippers benefiting from cheap transport, investors proved unwilling to undertake a railroad, no matter how great the overall gains to the economy. Potential investors, either at home or abroad, were naturally wary of a government that could regulate in a way that potentially pushed rates below costs. Risk of expropriation figured among the early obstacles to accumulating railroad capital.

Compounding the obstacles common to all railroads were two more found in the Brazilian setting. The first was a severely underdeveloped capital market. The government restricted banking and stock market activities for much of the imperial era. Moreover, savings rates were undoubtedly low. It was simply difficult to find enough investors with the right preferences toward risk that had sufficient funds to undertake a railroad. The second obstacle was political conditions. Instability under the Regency and the first decade of the Second Reign (1840–1889) further discouraged investment. The resources required to quell the separatism of the 1830s and early 1840s rendered subsidies for internal improvements unfeasible. Although regional revolts waned by 1845, it was only with the first provision of guaranteed dividends by the imperial government in 1852 that investment was forthcoming.[9] Thereafter, both central and provincial governments in Brazil worked to satisfy landowners' demands for cheap transport by offering guaranteed minimum dividends to railroad projects. Early guarantees were project specific, but follow-up legislation in the 1870s and 1880s expanded central government guarantees, making them accessible, in theory, to all of the provinces.[10]

Guaranteed dividends overcame two negative perceptions of Brazil's prospects on the part of investors. The subsidies implicit in the guarantee policy reduced risk and permitted the railroad either to obtain capital that it would not have received or to obtain it more cheaply than would otherwise have been possible.[11] The guarantee arrangement with each railroad set a minimum dividend rate on an agreed-upon value of the firm's capital. When the railroad's net earnings failed to attain the prescribed level, the government aided the company by paying to it the difference between its profits and the legislated rate of return. When the company achieved net earnings in excess of the prescribed dividend level by a sufficient margin, the additional profits were divided with the government in order to reimburse any guarantee payments. Even-higher dividends occasioned the lowering of freight and passenger rates. Although the specific arrangements adopted in Brazil varied from line to line, the gist of the dividend guarantees was that they provided subsidized loans to railroads.

Brazil's first railroad opened in 1854, yet the growth of the railroad sector proceeded slowly until after the war with Paraguay (1864–1870). Railroad development accelerated thereafter, with both track and output expanding at a steady pace through the end of the Empire. By the early 1880s, the government owned and operated a growing share of railroad capacity. In 1887 Brazil

TABLE 13.1

Track and Output on Brazilian Railroads, 1855–1887

Year	Total Track	Railroad Output
1855	15	0.2
1860	223	2.1
1865	498	3.6
1870	744	6.6
1875	1,801	14.3
1880	3,398	26.7
1885	6,930	35.0
1887	8,400	37.4

Note: Track is route kilometers. Output is expressed in millions of mil-réis of 1887, deflated by the extended wholesale price index for Rio de Janeiro.

Source: Summerhill (1997), Tables 6.1 and 6.2.

had some 8,400 kilometers of line open for service. Table 13.1 sketches the growth of the railroad sector in Brazil through 1887 by reference to two basic indicators. The first is track route kilometers, a crude index of sectoral capacity and capital formation.[12] The second index is total railroad operating revenues, deflated to 1887 prices using the extended wholesale price index for Rio de Janeiro.[13] It provides a rough measure of railroad output. The bulk of those revenues came from railroad freight and passenger services. Both indicators show sustained growth in railroad activity during the Empire. Transport capacity and freight traffic grew especially rapidly after 1875. Increases in route mileage resulted from the increase in Brazilian government subsidies to new railroad projects and the dramatic fall in the price of rails and rolling stock occasioned by advances abroad in the iron and steel industries. Between 1855 and 1887 the average increase in output was almost 15% per year. Increases in traffic levels resulted from falling transport costs that both supplanted nonrail modes of shipment and induced a shift in the demand schedule for transport services.

DIRECT EFFECTS

Gains on Freight Services

The railroad's ability to transform nineteenth-century economies depended on the strength of its relationship to production in other sectors, and scholars have found it useful to partition these into two separate sets of linkages. The first is the railroad's forward linkage to transport-using activities. The second is the railroad's backward linkage to activities that produced inputs employed by the railroad (discussed below). In Brazil the railroad's forward linkage was strong. Its magnitude depended on two features of the setting into which the railroad was introduced. The first was the savings on the cost of producing a unit of transport services that the railroad provided; this depended on the relative efficiency of other forms of transport. The second was the quantity of transport services that Brazil's railroads produced. Quantity in turn depended on two factors: the share of transportables in the economy's total output, and that share's sensitivity to changing transport costs. The composite of these cost and quantity effects provides upper and lower limits on the benefits of railroad transport, that is, the social savings.

Railroads in imperial Brazil created an economic surplus because they were more efficient than other modes of overland shipment, namely animal-drawn carts, mule trains, and in some cases human porters.[14] Throughout much of Brazil, high overland transport costs posed a formidable obstacle to the extension and integration of product markets. Although the far north was well served by rivers, by the end of the eighteenth century most of the population was well south of the Amazon basin. There was little substitution between water shipment and railroads. Regions of the country with rich agricultural endowments did not possess navigable inland waterways, and freight moved overland. Geography joined with tropical conditions to hinder the construction and maintenance of sorely needed turnpikes and wagon roads.[15] Before the opening of railroads the best-practice technology of overland shipment in Brazil was animal-drawn wagons operating on improved, macadamized roads. The cost of freight shipment by road was a good deal higher than transport by rail. In 1864, before the disruptions of the war with Paraguay, the typical unit charge to carry goods on mules and in carts over the roads in central and eastern São Paulo, where a large portion of Brazil's railroad traffic would ultimately originate, was 0.393 mil-réis per ton-kilometer.[16] This was one of the lowest freight charges in all of Brazil at the time.[17] In most areas of Brazil, where mules hauled freight over unimproved trails, freight charges far exceeded those of São Paulo. The São Paulo rate provides a conservative measure of the alternative cost of freight shipment. Adjusted for changes in the price level, the nonrail freight charge was 0.478 mil-réis in 1887 prices.

The social saving is the difference between the cost of hauling freight by rail and the cost of shipping it by the next-best alternative. Table 13.2 presents two estimates. In 1887, railroads produced 221.1 million ton-kilometers of freight service, charging on average 0.123 mil-réis per ton-kilometer.[18] This was well less than the best-practice prerail charge of 0.478 mil-réis. The measures in Table 13.2 take the difference between these two charges as the unit savings

TABLE 13.2

Direct Social Savings on Freight Services in Brazil, 1887

Upper Bound	
Total freight services	221.1 ton-kilometers
Cost of shipment by road	105.7 mil-réis
Cost of shipment by rail	27.3 mil-réis
Direct social savings	78.4 mil-réis
Lower Bound	
Direct social savings	3.9 mil-réis (for price elasticity of demand equal to -1.0)

Note: All units are in millions

that railroads provided on freight shipment. The first measure assumes that, in the absence of the railroad, all freight service would be handled by improved roads, carrying the same freight over the same lengths of haul. In that case the social savings on railroad freight shipment come to 78.4 million mil-réis in 1887, nearly 12% of Brazil's gross domestic product.[19] Because of capital subsidies under the government's dividend guarantees, the rail charges do not include the full resource costs of shipment. Nonetheless, this is more than offset by assuming, as the estimate does, that Brazil would have had improved wagon roads sufficient to handle all the railroad's freight in 1887. Providing the counterfactual economy with a more efficient mode of nonrail shipment than Brazil possessed balances the lack of downward adjustment in the social savings to account for the impact of government subsidies.[20]

The first measure ignores the possibility that, at the higher freight charge that would have prevailed in the absence of the railroad, less freight service would have been demanded. The second measure in Table 13.2 controls for the economy's sensitivity to changing freight costs. It adjusts the level of freight service that would have been demanded in the face of higher nonrail charges. Table 13.3 estimates the price elasticity of demand for freight services using a cross section of railroads in Brazil in 1887. On those lines, the price of freight transport varied from a low of 90 réis to a high of 370 réis. Demand functions for railroad freight service in Table 13.3 suggest that long-term demand for freight services was relatively inelastic. Both take the price of freight service to be exogenous, since public authorities set rates. By working in cross section, the demand elasticities here may be taken as those for long-term changes in price.[21] Both specifications employ a logarithmic transformation and thus assume a constant-elasticity demand curve. Price, of course, was only one determinant of the quantity of freight services demanded. Other factors bearing

TABLE 13.3

Estimates of the Long-Term Price Elasticity
of Demand for Railroad Freight Services in Brazil, 1887

1. $\ln Q = 177 - 0.42 \ln P + 1.3 \ln K - 0.09\, O$

       (4.7) (−1.3)   (5.7)   (−4.5)

    Adj $R^2 = 0.7$ $F = 34.5$

2. $\ln Q = 169 - 0.7 \ln P + 1.2 \ln K - 0.09\, O + 0.44\, CS$

       (4.4) (−1.7)   (5.2)   (−4.3) (1.2)

    Adj $R^2 = 0.7$ $F = 26.5$

Note: Q is freight service in ton-kilometers, P is the unit price, K is track in service, O is opening year of the line, and CS is a dummy for the four provinces of the center south. t-statistics are in parentheses.

on the level of demand aid in identifying the demand schedule. The first of these is trackage, which as a measure of capacity affects the level of freight service. The second is the opening date of the railroad. This aids in controlling for endogenous effects that stem from the induced demand for freight services that each railroad created in the region it served. All things else being equal, railroads that had been open for longer periods of time would have generated their own demand and would exhibit higher levels of output. Finally, railroads served distinct regions, where production possibilities varied and where the transport requirements of local production varied as well. To try to control for these regional differences, the second specification includes a dummy variable for railroads in Brazil's south center (Minas Gerais, Espírito Santo, Rio de Janeiro, and São Paulo), where income is believed to have been higher than in the rest of Brazil.

The results of the second equation in Table 13.3, where the elasticity of demand equals −0.7, are statistically more significant than those of the first. Given the crude nature of the estimate, the second measure of the social savings increases this elasticity by more than 40%, assuming long-term unit-elastic demand.[22] This parameter is applied in Table 13.2 to establish a lower bound on the railroad's benefits. The social savings in this case come to about 36.9 million mil-réis, still more than 5% of Brazil's GDP in 1887. Combined with the relatively modest nonrail freight charge, the assumption of unit-elastic demand in the second measure no doubt understates the true social savings. Nonetheless, even this lower-bound estimate represents an important increment to the level of economic activity.

The significance of these results may be judged by means of comparison. The direct impact of the railroad in Brazil places it comfortably within the top tier of the cases for which economic historians have constructed social savings estimates. Railroads in England and Wales provided resource savings on freight in 1865 that came to 4.1% of national income at most.[23] In the antebellum United States, which like Brazil in 1887 was a little more than three decades into its first stage of railroad development, the upper-bound social savings on freight services were about 3.7% of national income in 1859.[24] Throughout western Europe in the late nineteenth century, with the exception of Spain, upper-bound estimates of freight social savings based on prevailing alternatives to the railroad were under 6% of national income.[25] The Brazilian measure comparable to these other countries is the upper-bound estimate in Table 13.2, which is more than double that for either of the major North Atlantic cases. Indeed, the lower-bound estimate for Brazil is at or above the upper-bound measures in the advanced industrializing economies. Estimates that rival those obtained for Brazil are found in the Spanish and Mexican cases. Both were relatively backward economies that relied heavily on overland freight services before railroads were constructed.[26] In Brazil, where market integration was limited by high overland freight charges and inland waterways were poorly located, railroads no doubt proved to be the single most important force at work in raising output per capita, accounting for at least one-fourth of the increase in per capita output in the post-*conciliação* era of the Second Reign.[27] It is unlikely that any other single resource-saving technology or change in economic organization in Brazil contributed even half this much to the nation's economy before the fall of the Empire.

Savings on Railroad Passenger Services

The benefits that railroads provided for travelers turned on two factors: the reduction in direct outlays on fares, and the value of the time saved due to the higher speed of travel by rail. Tables 13.4 and 13.5 provide details of the estimated savings for passengers traveling in first class. In 1887, Brazilian railroads produced some 70 million passenger-kilometers of first-class service, at a per passenger-kilometer charge of 56.8 réis.[28] The stagecoach fare from São Paulo to Santos in 1865 was 190 réis per passenger-kilometer. Had all first-class rail passengers shifted to stagecoaches in the absence of railroads, the outlay on fares would have been almost 14.5 million mil-réis in 1887 prices. The estimates of Table 13.4 show that first-class railroad passengers enjoyed fare savings equal to 10.5 million mil-réis. This is an exaggeration because it allows for no adjustment to the demand for first-class travel services at the higher nonrail fare.

TABLE 13.4

Total Savings on First-Class Fares and Time

Rate Differential	
a. First-class rail passenger-kilometers in 1887	70.2
b. Stagecoach passenger revenues (at $206.5 per passenger-kilometer)	14.5
c. First-class passenger rail revenues ($056.8 × a)	4.0
d. Savings on travel fares (assuming inelastic demand) (b − c)	10.5
e. Total savings on fares and time for first-class passengers (d + bottom line from Table 13.5)	11.4

Note: All units are in millions.

Evaluating the savings on travel time is necessarily conjectural given the dearth of information required to construct detailed measures of wages, passenger occupations, and the value of leisure time. Passenger statistics do not reveal how many passengers were traveling for reasons of work. Table 13.5 applies the assumption that Brazilians in 1887 traveled in proportion to their participation in the labor force, and further divides passengers into three categories: leisure travelers, passengers who worked in agriculture, and passengers employed in nonagricultural activities.[29] First-class passengers in nonagricultural pursuits are assumed to have valued their time at twice the wage for a skilled worker, such as those employed in manufacturing.[30] Manufacturing wages in nineteenth-century Brazil, not available to researchers, are further assumed to have equaled those of carpenters in Rio de Janeiro.[31] Monthly wages are converted to hourly wages under the assumption of a 28-day work month and 10-hour workdays. Passengers assigned to agricultural pursuits are assumed to have valued their time at twice the hourly wage in agriculture; this figure is imputed from daily rental rates on agricultural slaves, converted to hourly levels based on a 10-hour day.[32] Over improved roads through hilly terrain, the average speed of the stagecoach between São Paulo and Santos was 13 kilometers per hour, whereas the average Brazilian rail speed in the late nineteenth century was around 30 kilometers per hour. Based on these figures, the value of the time saved by first-class working passengers was under 1 million mil-réis. Total first-class passenger benefits (time and fare savings) come to 11.4 million mil-réis in 1887, equal to 1.7% of GDP.

Table 13.6 presents the savings on second-class passenger rail service and proceeds in a similar fashion, with two exceptions to the underpinning

TABLE 13.5

Travel Time Savings on First-Class Passenger Services in 1887

Time Savings	
a. Passenger-kilometers	70.2
b. Passenger-kilometers by agricultural workers (32.25% of a)	22.7
c. Passenger-kilometers by nonagricultural workers (26.17% of a)	18.4
d. Time required for agricultural workers to travel by stagecoach (at 13 kilometers per hour)	1.7
e. Time required for nonagricultural workers to travel by stagecoach (at 13 kilometers per hour)	1.4
f. Time required for agricultural workers to travel by rail (at 30 kilometers per hour)	0.75
g. Time required for nonagricultural workers to travel by rail (at 30 kilometers per hour)	0.6
h. Travel time savings for agricultural workers (d − f)	0.95
i. Travel time savings for nonagricultural workers (e − g)	0.8
j. Value of time saved in agriculture ($099.6 × h)	0.1 mil-réis
k. Value of time saved in nonagriculture ($415.2 × i)	0.33 mil-réis
l. Total first-class time savings (2 × (j + k))	0.86 mil-réis

Note: All units are in millions.

assumptions. The first of these is that in the absence of railroads, these passengers would have found the pecuniary costs of commercial travel prohibitively expensive and would have walked instead. As a result, savings on travel fares here are negative, since the alternative to buying a second-class ticket would involve no cash outlay. Second, these passengers would have valued their time at the hourly wage in their respective sectors of employment. In 1887 railroads produced an estimated 192 million passenger-kilometers of second-class services, earning 26.5 réis per passenger-kilometer. Adjusting for the value of travel time saved and the outlays on fares gives savings on second-class services equal to 3 million mil-réis.

TABLE 13.6

Savings on Second-Class Passenger Services in 1887

a. Second-class passenger-kilometers	192.1
b. Passenger-kilometers by agricultural workers (32.25% of a)	62
c. Passenger-kilometers by nonagricultural workers (26.17% of a)	50.3
d. Time required for agricultural workers to travel by foot (at 3 kilometers per hour)	20.7
e. Time required for nonagricultural workers to travel by rail (at 3 kilometers per hour)	16.8
f. Time required for agricultural workers to travel by rail (at 39 kilometers per hour)	2.1
g. Time required for nonagricultural workers to travel by rail (at 39 kilometers per hour)	1.7
h. Travel time savings for agricultural workers (d − f)	18.6
i. Travel time savings for nonagricultural workers (e − g)	15.1
j. Value of time saved in agriculture ($099.6 × h)	1.9
k. Value of time saved in nonagriculture ($415 × i)	6.3
l. Total second-class time savings (j + k)	8.1 mil-réis
m. Second-class rail passenger revenues ($026.5 × a)	5.1 mil-réis
n. Total second-class passenger savings (l − m)	3 mil-réis

Note: All figures are in units of millions.

Together, the material advantages that railroads provided travelers were small, totaling less than 2.2% of GDP. This figure no doubt overstates the gain, thanks to the assumptions attached to the value of travel time and the completely inelastic demand applied to first-class travel. It is true that, had Brazil not enjoyed the cheap transport provided by the railroad, many fewer people would have chosen to travel even over the relatively short distance of the average rail journey, or people would have traveled less frequently. Labor market integration would have been poorer, the opportunities for migration more tightly constrained, and the resources devoted to travel greater. Nonetheless, the losses to the economy would have been slight. Although passenger services certainly created benefits to travelers and improved the mobility of the working class and the elite alike, in the aggregate, passenger benefits had less impact on the economy than those provided by freight services.

INDIRECT EFFECTS

Railroads and Economic Structure

The forward linkage that the railroad forged by reducing transport costs clearly created appreciable gains. The character of that linkage (along with other less direct effects) in Brazil, where the expansion of agricultural and pastoral exports to overseas markets is often believed to have posed negative implications for development, may nonetheless be questioned. In the context of a relatively backward economy, plantation agriculture, and slavery, railroads might well have reinforced tendencies toward monoculture, dependency, and institutional and social rigidity. Since Brazilians constructed railroads during the Empire precisely to link plantations to ports, it is no surprise that early in the railway age exports loomed large in freight shipments.

Table 13.7 shows the sectoral distribution of freight on Brazil's railroads in 1868 and 1887. In 1868 coffee, cotton, and sugar together accounted for one-half of freight shipments on the six railroads in operation.[33] The share of freight accounted for by exports was no doubt greater than this, since tobacco and hides were not enumerated. Surprisingly, for railroads designed to promote export agriculture, the share of exports in total freight declined by 1887.[34] This is less surprising in light of two additional features. First, freight rate structures mandated by the government discriminated heavily in favor of domestically produced and consumed agricultural products in the 1870s and 1880s.[35] Second, the domestic sector of the economy—the internal market—responded flexibly to the opportunities to ship goods over longer distances. Exports, with their high value-to-weight ratios, were no doubt more transport intensive, traveling by rail and land over greater distances. At the same time,

TABLE 13.7

Distribution of Freight on Brazilian Railroads, 1868 and 1887

	1868	1887
Export-sector freight	139.9 (50)	549 (35)
Nonexport freight	141.9 (50)	999 (65)

Note: Freight is given in units of one thousand metric tons. Figures in parentheses are percentages.

Sources: MACOP 1870, 1887.

nonexport products, often exhibiting lower value per unit, were far more dependent than exports on the opportunities provided by cheap transport. In what is often believed to have been predominantly an export economy, railroads served to boost the production of goods for the domestic market even more dramatically than they did exports.

The Costs of Foreign Provision

If the railroad provided an unexpectedly large and diverse stimulus to transport-using activities, its impact on enterprises that produced the inputs it required was weak. The strength of the backward linkage depended on two factors. First was the derived demand for materials, namely products of manufacturing, required to build and operate railroads. Second was the share of these inputs supplied domestically. In Brazil this share was low. Most locomotives, rolling stock, track, and even fuel came from overseas. By importing railroad materials and financial services, Brazil exported abroad the employment and development effects that other nations had successfully channeled to domestic industry. Under assumptions intentionally designed to cast Brazilian railroad development in the costliest light possible, the outlays on these inputs may be taken as the losses from pursuing railroad development with foreign provision. This is an admittedly implausible counterfactual, one in which Brazil could have provisioned its own railroads at no greater cost while maintaining the pace of railroad development without reducing the social savings. Nonetheless, the outlays on foreign inputs are treated in this manner under the purposely unrealistic assumption that Brazilian industry could have supplied them. That Brazilian industry in fact supplied so little meant that the outlays by railroads for industrial inputs accrued to foreigners, and are treated as a cost. Estimating the backward "leakage" in this way overstates the burden of dependence on railroad imports.

In 1887 the major railroad companies reported to the Ministry of Agriculture the origins of their equipment.[36] All of their locomotives came from overseas, as did most wagons and passenger cars. This is unsurprising given that Brazil lacked foundries and steel mills of the type required to produce rails and rolling stock. Hundreds of miles separated coalfields from deposits of iron ore, which merely exacerbated the need for transport improvements. Coking coal used to forge the iron and steel required by railroads was scarce.[37] Similarly bereft of deposits of coal of sufficient quality to fuel trains, railroads relied on a mix of imported coal and local wood. Capital, subscribed in both equity and debt, often came from Britain.

Neither government nor company sources present a detailed accounting of overseas payments by railroads. The costs of foreign materials in sterling were relatively stable for much of the Second Reign, thanks to the modest character of exchange rate fluctuations. On Brazil's largest railroad, the Dom Pedro II, the value of imported inputs was probably high. The company's report from 1887 provides enough detail to estimate upper-bound outlays on foreign materials. The ratios for the Dom Pedro II are applied in Table 13.8 to the sector as a whole. These rest on two main assumptions: First, all additions to rolling stock came from abroad, as did all the materials used in repairing wagons, cars, locomotives, and road (rails, sleepers, and spikes); second, all coal was imported. The first of these is exaggerated, since both wood and basic hardware of Brazilian origin were used in repairs. The second is more accurate, given the limited amount of domestically mined coal suitable for locomotives. The value of inputs that can be considered foreign in origin in 1887 on the Dom Pedro II railroad was almost 2.6 million mil-réis, nearly 25% of gross operating revenues. Using this ratio for all railroads puts the foreign exchange costs of importing capital goods and operating inputs at more than 9.7 million mil-réis.

To this cost is added the charges incurred overseas in the course of financing railroad construction and operation. By 1887 Brazilian railroads had issued more than 14.5 million pounds sterling of equity and debt on the London Exchange.[38] Assuming that all these shares and bonds were held abroad means that capital expenditures totaling more than 10.5 million mil-réis flowed out of the country.[39] Additionally, the imperial government's loan of 1883 had been issued to finance government railroads, among other internal improvements, and the interest and amortization on the loan leaked abroad.

TABLE 13.8

Leakage Overseas of Interest, Profits, and Payments for Railroad Inputs, 1887

Railroad dividends and interest	10.5
Interest and amortization on loan of 1883	2.6
Imported railroad inputs	9.7
Total	22.8

Note: Units are in millions of mil-réis.

Sources: See text; *Investor's Monthly Manual*; Carreira (1980), p. 715; Estrada de Ferro Dom Pedro II, *Relatório*, 1888.

The sum of the components of income leakage equals 22.9 million mil-réis. This was almost 56% of gross railroad revenues in 1887, and 3.5% of GDP. Had Brazil been able to staunch that flow, redirecting demands for railroad inputs to domestic sources of supply while simultaneously maintaining the pace of railroad development without raising its costs, it would clearly have been better off. For reasons unrelated to railroad development, this proved impossible. However, even under the strong assumption that leakage somehow translated into a real resource cost to Brazil, the losses would be more than off-set by the gains that railroads created by reducing transport costs. It is quite improbable that domestic resources would have been adequate for Brazil's railroads under the Empire.

CONCLUSIONS AND EXTENSIONS

This paper casts the developmental role of railroads in imperial Brazil in a new light by elaborating measures of the impact of the iron horse on key sectors of the economy. For a relatively backward, export-oriented country dependent on foreign product and financial markets, Brazil received an unambiguous boost from railroad construction and operation in the decades before the fall of the Empire. Many of the measures of that boost are necessarily static, and occasionally arbitrary in their assumptions, yet altering the key parameters in any reasonable manner would leave the qualitative results unchanged. Although the gains to the economy from railroad passenger services and from the demands for railroad inputs were of limited importance, the estimates of freight benefits reveal the railroad's clear advantage over wagon roads.

The additional range of effects often ascribed to the railroad in the advanced industrializing nations appeared only in attenuated form in Brazil. The development of capital market institutions depended in part on railroad shares and bonds, but by 1889 also rested on the banking sector and some manufacturing enterprises and ultimately stemmed from the nature of government financial repression.[40] Managerial expertise, required eventually to coordinate modern mass production, could be glimpsed on those railroads operated by Brazilian firms, but was channeled increasingly to the public sector on state-owned lines, or abroad in the case of British-owned railroads.

The character of the railroad's linkages did not deform the economy. The composition of freight shifted in the opposite direction from what one would predict in the widely caricaturized process of Latin American export-led growth. Because Brazil lacked the manufacturing sector and institutions the more advanced economies enjoyed at the time they built railroads, it could not exploit the railroad's backward linkages. If it had been otherwise, then a course of railroad development reliant on domestic inputs could easily have generated an appreciable array of gains independent of cheap transport services. Only under very restrictive conditions can the cost of such a lost opportunity be charged against the gains from the extension and integration of markets that railroads actually provided. Measuring the social savings of the railroad in the context of high overland transport costs and a clear technological alternative is one thing. Assuming that Brazil could have provisioned its own railroads is a historical alternative that can only be guessed at. Pursuing transport improvements did not necessarily require technology and capital from abroad, but any alternative would have generated substantial costs in terms of opportunities foregone. Following a different path that forced Brazil alone to provision and finance its own transport improvements might well have provoked wide-ranging transformations in economic institutions and even in its political structure. More probably, it would have merely raised the returns to scarce capital, vastly reduced the pace of railroad development, further hobbled economic growth, and institutionalized backwardness under the Empire.

ACKNOWLEDGMENTS

Lee Alston, John Coatsworth, Stephen Haber, Colin Lewis, Jean-Laurent Rosenthal, and Alan Taylor, along with participants in informal groups at UCLA and Stanford and in workshops at Northwestern University and the University of Illinois, generously provided comments on this paper. Research support came from the U.S. Department of Education Fulbright-Hays Program and the Joint Committee on Latin American and Caribbean Studies of the Social Science Research Council. All errors are mine.

NOTES

1. The quotations are from Burns (1980), p. 136, and Burns (1993), p. 161, respectively. Assessments that implicate railroads in generating undue costs, permitting foreign control, or deforming the economy can be found in Evans (1979), pp. 61, 85; Frank (1967), pp. 145–174, passim; Graham (1969), pp. 35–36; Ridings (1994), p. 262; and Blasenheim (1994), pp. 347–374.
2. Burns (1980), p. 138, which mainly combines lines of argument found in Frank (1967), Cardoso and Faletto (1979), and dos Santos (1970).
3. For a detailed study of railroad policy in the province of São Paulo, see Lewis (1991). In terms of empirical assessment, the sole exception is Fendt (1977).

4. Cardoso and Faletto (1979), p. xvi; dos Santos (1970), pp. 231–236.

5. Frank (1967), pp. 147, 171–173, 290–296.

6. Lei no. 641, 26 June 1852, reprinted in C. D. R. Pessôa (1886), p. 3. Unless otherwise noted, the discussion of the overall evolution of Brazil's railroad sector derives from this source and from Galvão (1869); Picanço da Costa (1884); Lyon (1885); Branner (1887); Pinheiro (1889), pp. 383–439; Castro (1893), pp. 344–352; Sá (1893); Pessôa (1902); Silva (1904); Cunha (1909); Winer (1913), pp. 53–117; and Duncan (1932).

7. For the value of capital in the cotton textile industry, see Branner (1885), pp. 42–43.

8. Lei no. 101, 31 October 1835; Decreto, 4 November 1840. The annual volumes of *Coleção das leis do império do Brazil* (hereafter *CLB*) published railroad legislation and administrative decrees bearing on railroad policy.

9. The railroad law of 1852 retained for the government the power to set maximum passenger fares and freight charges; the major difference between it and the earlier concession was the guarantee of a minimum dividend (C. D. R. Pessôa 1886, pp. 3–4).

10. *CLB*, Decreto 2450, 24 September 1873; Decreto 6995, 10 August 1878; Decreto 7959, 29 August 1880.

11. Mercer (1982), pp. 19–26.

12. The growth of route kilometers is a lagging indicator of investment because a fair amount of the capital formation occurs in the year or two prior to placing the track in operation. Track as an index of capital formation implies that the average cost of constructing a kilometer of track was the same from year to year, and that outlays on rolling stock, structures, and the like were a constant share of total outlays. None of these assumptions hold strictly, but departures from them would not alter dramatically the measure of capacity.

13. The series of nominal revenues derive from annual figures for individual railroads, taken from C. D. R. Pessôa (1886); Picanço da Costa (1884); MACOP *Relatórios* for 1886 and 1887; and Carreira (1980), pp. 777–830. The output series excludes urban tramways and some smaller railroads that reported only to provincial authorities. The nominal revenues are deflated by the wholesale price index in Catão (1992), pp. 519–533. The index is extended backward from 1870 by regressing it on a related index, that for Rio de Janeiro consumer prices, presented in Lobo (1978), pp. 804–805.

14. On the use of porters to carry freight over long distances in Brazil's backlands, see Benévolo (1953), p. 522.

15. Pack roads were more common than wagon roads in nineteenth-century Brazil, and improvements were limited. Brazil possessed few private turnpike roads at

midcentury. Three of the more prominent roads were the União e Indústria, the Mangaratiba, and the Graciosa. On the União e Indústria, see Giroletti (1980); on the Graciosa, see Tourinho (1882); and on the Mangaratiba, see Soares (1861).

16. This is an unweighted average of monthly spot observations of rates on the five major routes in São Paulo, drawn from the current prices section of the *Correio Paulistano* in 1864. Between 1864 and 1887, the value of the mil-réis in U.S. dollars fluctuated between 38 and 55 cents.

17. This was no doubt attributable to the relatively favorable road conditions, since the province had undertaken improvements. Several sections of these main routes, including that running from the plateau down the sierra to the port of Santos, were paved with macadam or otherwise improved by this time, and the rest very likely would have been in the absence of the railroad (Fletcher and Kidder 1866, pp. 355–356).

18. The output, revenue, and capital of the railroad sector in 1887 come from a variety of sources, including the company reports of the major railroads, the report of the Ministry of Agriculture for 1887, and the annual reports of provincial presidents. For detail on the derivation of output and revenues, see Summerhill (1997), this paper's lengthier ancestor.

19. GDP estimate for 1887 is from Contador and Haddad (1975), pp. 407–440.

20. A detailed discussion of this point, including estimates of the cumulative level of railroad subsidy and the costs of creating an improved wagon road system in Brazil, are found in Summerhill (1997).

21. The long-term elasticity of demand is greater in absolute value than the short-term measure; estimates of the elasticity from cross-sectional data approximate more closely the value of the long-term elasticity (Wilson 1980, pp. 68–69).

22. Under unit-elastic demand, a 10% increase in price leads to a 10% decline in the quantity of freight service demanded. At the higher prerail charge, the quantity of freight services produced in the counterfactual economy is scaled down proportionally. In the lower-bound measure of the social savings, the locus of all price-quantity combinations between the nonrail and railroad-inclusive states is taken to lie along a constant-elasticity Marshallian demand curve, and the social savings simply equals the area to the left of the curve.

23. Hawke (1970), p. 196.

24. Fishlow (1965), pp. 37, 52.

25. O'Brien (1982), p. 347. Direct social savings on freight services were 5.8% of French GNP in 1872, roughly 5% in Germany in the 1890s, and 2.5% in Belgium in 1865.

26. Mendoza (1983). In Mexico, the upper-bound estimates for 1895 ranged between 10% and 15% of GDP (Coatsworth 1981, p. 118). Mexican social savings were

large thanks in part to the high levels of freight service occasioned by Mexico's access to the U.S. railroad network.

27. Based on the rate of growth between 1861 and 1887 (Contador and Haddad 1975).

28. Although government railroad materials did not report revenue by class of service, several of the company reports did. These were supplemented by reference to regulated rates published in Brazilian legislation. Derivation of the passenger output and fares is found in Summerhill (1997).

29. These shares stem from unadjusted figures in the census of 1872, which had changed relatively little by 1900 (IBGE 1990).

30. This conjecture is based loosely on studies of modern travel that find that travelers value their time in transit at as much as 178% of the wage rate and as little as 6% (Winston 1985, p. 77). Using twice the wage rate for first-class passengers, and the wage rate for second-class passengers, merely serves to place an upper limit on the likely value of time spent traveling in nineteenth-century Brazil.

31. Lobo (1978), p. 804.

32. Melo (1992).

33. MACOP, *Relatório,* 1869.

34. MACOP, *Relatório,* 1887. This trend continued well into the twentieth century.

35. Summerhill (1997) provides an analysis of rates and their political determinants.

36. MACOP, *Relatório,* 1887.

37. Callahan (1981), pp. 38–40.

38. Calculated from *Investor's Monthly Manual* for November 1887.

39. One might also add remitted wages and foreign purchases by railroad workers, as done for the Mexican case (see Coatsworth 1981, p. 141). The number of foreign railroad workers in imperial Brazil is unknown, much less the share of their earnings that they remitted. Neither was likely very large. Ignoring remittances and purchases of foreign goods leaves little out of the estimate in Table 13.8.

40. Carreira (1980), pp. 771–776.

REFERENCES

Benévolo, Ademar. *Introdução a história ferroviária do Brasil.* Recife, 1953.

Blasenheim, Peter L. "Railroads in Nineteenth-Century Minas Gerais." *Journal of Latin American Studies* 26 (1994): 347–374.

Branner, John C. *Cotton in the Empire of Brazil.* Washington, DC: Government Printing Office, 1885.

Branner, John C. *The Railways of Brazil, A Statistical Article*. Chicago: The Railway Age Publishing Company, 1887.

Brazil. Ministério da Agricultura, Commércio, e Obras Públicas (MACOP). *Relatório*. Rio de Janeiro, 1861–1889.

Burns, E. Bradford. *The Poverty of Progress: Latin America in the Nineteenth Century*. Berkeley: University of California Press, 1980.

Burns, E. Bradford. *A History of Brazil*, 3rd ed. New York: Columbia University Press, 1993.

Callahan, William Stuart. "Obstacles to Industrialization: The Iron and Steel Industry in Brazil During the Old Republic." Ph.D. dissertation, University of Texas, 1981.

Cardoso, Fernando Henrique, and Enzo Faletto. *Dependency and Underdevelopment in Latin America*. Berkeley: University of California Press, 1979.

Carreira, Liberato de Castro. *História financeira e orçamentária do império no Brasil*. Rio de Janeiro: Fundação Casa de Rui Barbosa, 1980.

Castro, Juan José. *Treatise on the South American Railways*. Montevideo: La Nacion Steam Printing Office, 1893.

Catão, Luís A. V. "A New Wholesale Price Index for Brazil during the Period 1870–1913." *Revista Brasileira de Economia* 46 (1992): 519–533.

Coatsworth, John H. *Growth Against Development: The Economic Impact of Railroads in Porfirian Mexico*. DeKalb, IL: Northern Illinois University Press, 1981.

Contador, Claudio, and Claudio Haddad. "Produto real, moeda, e preços: A experiência brasileira no período 1861–1979." *Revista Brasileira de Estatística* 36 (1975): 407–440.

Cunha, Ernesto Antonio Lassance. *Estudo descriptivo da viação ferrea do Brazil*. Rio de Janeiro: Imprensa Nacional, 1909.

dos Santos, Theotonio. "Structure of Dependence." *American Economic Review* 60 (1970): 231–236.

Duncan, Julian Smith. *Public and Private Operation of Railways in Brazil*. New York: Columbia University Press, 1932.

Estrada de Ferro Dom Pedro II. *Relatório*. Rio de Janeiro, 1888.

Evans, Peter. *Dependent Development: The Alliance of Multinational, State, and Local Capital in Brazil*. Princeton: Princeton University Press, 1979.

Fendt, Roberto Jr. "Investimentos inglêses no Brazil, 1870–1913: Uma avaliação da política brasileira." *Revista Brasileira de Economia* 31, no. 3 (1977): 521–539.

Fishlow, Albert. *American Railroads and the Transformation of the Ante Bellum Economy*. Cambridge, MA: Harvard University Press, 1965.

Fletcher, James C., and D. P. Kidder. *Brazil and the Brazilians*. Boston: Little, Brown & Co., 1866.

Frank, Andre Gunder. *Capitalism and Underdevelopment in Latin America*. New York:

Monthly Review Press, 1967.

Galvão, Manoel da Cunha. *Notícia sobre as estradas de ferro do Brasil*. Rio de Janeiro, 1869.

Giroletti, Domingos. "A Companhia e a Rodovia União e Indústria e o desenvolvimento de Juiz de Fora, 1850–1900." Unpublished manuscript, Belo Horizonte, 1980.

Graham, Richard. "Sepoys and Imperialists: Techniques of British Power in Nineteenth-Century Brazil." *Inter-American Economic Affairs* 23 (1969): 23–27.

Hawke, Gary. *Railways and Economic Growth in England and Wales, 1840–1870*. Oxford: Clarendon Press, 1970.

Instituto Brasileiro de Geografia e Estatística (IBGE). *Estatísticas históricas do Brasil*, 2nd ed. Rio de Janeiro: IBGE, 1990.

Lewis, Colin M. *Public Policy and Private Initiative: Railway Building in São Paulo, 1860–1889*. London: Institute of Latin American Studies, 1991.

Lobo, Eulália Maria Lehmeyer. *História do Rio de Janeiro (do capital comercial ao capital industrial financeiro)*. Vol. 2. Rio de Janeiro: IBMEC, 1978.

Lyon, Max. *Note sur les chemins de fer du Bresil*. Paris, 1885.

Melo, Pedro Carvalho de. "Rates of Return on Slave Capital in Brazilian Coffee Plantations, 1871–1881." In *Without Consent or Contract: Markets and Production. Technical Papers*, vol. 1, edited by Robert William Fogel and Stanley Engerman, 63–79. New York: W. W. Norton & Company, 1992.

Mendoza, Antonio Gómez. "Spain." In *Railways and the Economic Development of Western Europe, 1830–1914*, edited by Patrick K. O'Brien. Oxford: Oxford University Press, 1983.

Mercer, Lloyd J. *Railroads and Land Grant Policy: A Study in Government Intervention*. New York: Academic Press, 1982.

O'Brien, Patrick, "Transport and Economic Growth in Western Europe, 1839–1914." *Journal of European Economic History* 11 (1982): 335–367.

Pessôa, Cyro Diocleciano Ribeiro, Jr. *Estudo descriptivo das estradas de ferro do Brasil*. Rio de Janeiro, 1886.

Pessôa, V. A. de Paulo. *Guia da Estrada de Ferro Central do Brasil*. Vol. 1. Rio de Janeiro: Imprensa Nacional, 1902.

Picanço da Costa, Francisco Barreto. *Viação ferrea do Brazil*. Rio de Janeiro: Machado & Co., 1884.

Pinheiro, Fernandes. "Chemins de fer." In *Le Brésil en 1889*, edited by F. J. de Santa-Anna Nery. Paris: C. Delagrave, 1889.

Ridings, Eugene. *Business Interest Groups in Nineteenth-Century Brazil*. Cambridge, UK: Cambridge University Press, 1994.

Sá, Chrockatt de. *Brazilian Railways, Their History, Legislation, and Development*. Rio de Janeiro: C. Levzinger & Filhos, 1893.

Silva, Clodomiro Pereira da. *Política e legislação de estradas de ferro*. São Paulo Levi, 1904.

Soares, Sebastião Ferreira. *Histórico da Companhia Industrial da Estrada de Mangaratiba e analyse crítica e econômica dos negócios desta companhia*. Rio de Janeiro, 1861.

Summerhill, William R. "Benefits and Costs: The Political Economy of Railroad Subsidy and Regulation in Imperial Brazil." Unpublished manuscript, 1997.

Tourinho, Francisco Antonio Monteiro. "Bosquejo histórico da Estrada de Graciosa." Unpublished manuscript, Curitiba, 1882.

Wilson, George. *Economic Analysis of Intercity Freight Transportation*. Bloomington: Indiana University Press, 1980.

Wiener, Lionel. "The Railways of Brazil." In *The South American Year Book*, edited by C. S. Vesey Brown. London: The Louis Cassier Co. Ltd., 1913.

Winston, Clifford. "Conceptual Developments in the Economics of Transportation: An Interpretive Survey." *Journal of Economic Literature* 23 (1985): 57–94.

14

Tariff Protection in Mexico, 1892–1909: Ad Valorem Tariff Rates and Sources of Variation

Graciela Márquez
Harvard University

In the history of industrial development in Mexico, the last two decades of the Porfiriato have been recognized as a critical period for the growth of manufacturing activities. Along with an expansion in cotton textiles, imports were substituted by domestically produced beer, paper, soap, cement, and steel goods. By the 1890s nascent modern manufacturing industries were benefiting from the rapid changes that had been taking place in the Mexican economy and society since the 1870s. In this process the government also played a significant role in inducing manufacturing growth: Commercial policy and industrial promotion programs produced favorable conditions for industrial development by protecting the domestic market and creating fiscal incentives for producers.

Historians of the Porfiriato have acknowledged the importance of tariff protection for industrial growth. Coupled with the depreciation of silver, tariffs have been identified as factors that protected domestic markets and favored Mexico's industrial success during this period.[1] Yet most works that argue for a positive effect of tariffs on industrial development during the Porfiriato fail to specify the actual level of protection conferred by tariffs. Bulmer-Thomas makes scattered references to tariff rates in Latin America rising by as much as 100% between 1890 and 1914, whereas Salvucci and Haber simply allude to Mexican tariffs at this time as among the highest in the world.[2] More recently, however, an independent paper by Beatty has estimated more precise measures of protection.[3] He finds an average nominal tariff of between 50% and 88%

based on the post-1891 schedule. Consequently, the literature on tariff protection and industrial performance has left many unanswered questions: What were the levels of tariff protection in different industries? Did tariff rates remain at the same level from 1890 to 1910? If not, what were the driving forces behind the changes in tariff rates? Answering these questions would provide a better understanding of the effects of commercial policy in the early phases of Mexican industrialization.

This paper presents a methodology for measuring and decomposing tariff rates for the period 1892 to 1909. Assessing the actual level of tariff rates will allow one to evaluate their impact on protection. It will also shed some light on the factors that shaped the evolution of tariff protection. My analysis yields four important results. First, from 1892 to 1909 a general downward trend in most ad valorem tariff rates reduced the protection conferred by tariffs. Second, sources of variation of the ad valorem rate demonstrate that the exchange rate was responsible for most of the decline in tariff protection, ameliorated, however, by general and individual price trends. Third, in the years prior to the monetary reform in 1905, tariff protection declined in importance vis-à-vis the influence of nontariff protection, primarily in the form of silver depreciation. For the sample of commodities analyzed in this paper, the Mexican government implemented very few changes in tariff rates during the 1890s, allowing price effects to erode the value of ad valorem rates. Fourth, beginning in 1905, tariff policy regained its role as the main source of protection, opening possibilities for securing higher protection levels through negotiations between industrialists and public officials.

The next section describes tariff and price data for 1892 to 1909, making explicit the limitations and assumptions of what are very rich but imperfect statistics. Next, the paper focuses on the decomposition of ad valorem rates encompassing tariff and price effects. The last sections interpret ad valorem rates and their decomposition for Mexican tariff data between 1892 and 1909 and present concluding remarks.

DATA SET AND MEASUREMENT PROBLEMS

Since more than 50% of Mexican federal revenue during the nineteenth century came from foreign trade taxes, customs house officials meticulously gathered records on trade transactions. The result was a highly disaggregated statistical series on foreign trade and taxes. However, foreign trade statistics require a considerable amount of work before they become suitable for historical analysis. From 1870 to 1910 the Mexican government issued five trade ordinances to regulate transportation, storage, internment, and taxes on foreign trade. The last trade ordinance of the Porfirian administration, issued on July 12, 1891, took effect in November of the same year. Several modifications occurred thereafter: New products were added to the original list of 921 items, subdivisions in some categories included more detailed specifications, and most important, import duties changed intermittently. The analysis of tariff rates presented here considers the 1891 schedule, concentrating on a sample that comprises 32 commodities representing six industries: cotton textiles, beer, soap, paper, iron and steel, and cement.

A common practice in the nineteenth century was to set specific tariffs instead of ad valorem tariffs. The former provided industries with better protection from underinvoicing in times of imperfect price information. The 1891 tariff schedule listed specific tariffs, indicating the amount of silver pesos per unit levied in the customs houses. Silver depreciation and foreign financial obligations in gold forced the Mexican government to partially index import duties from January 1903 to August 1905. The collection of import duties was pegged to the gold value of the Mexican silver peso, causing an increase in all specific tariffs of 12.56% for 1902 and 3.85% for 1903. By fixing the value of the peso, the monetary reform of 1905 eliminated the need for such indexation.[4]

Before 1905, the Mexican government collected tariffs in silver pesos, but import values were usually expressed in gold prices. To examine tariffs as a percentage of price, I constructed a compatible price series in silver pesos. After the 1905 monetary reform, trade statistics reported values in domestic currency (*moneda mexicana*), which is compatible with data expressed in silver pesos from 1892 to 1904.

The commodity level of my analysis imposed certain restrictions on the price series. As a proxy for price data I used the unit value data reported in *Estadística Fiscal*. From 1893 to 1904, annual value data reports the invoice value of imports in gold pesos recorded according to fixed exchange rates set in the ordinance of 1891.[5] Given that the dollar exchange rate used to report import values set one peso equal to one dollar, the transformation to silver pesos required only the conversion of dollar values to silver pesos according to the actual exchange rate of silver pesos per dollar.[6] Beginning in 1905, invoice values and import duties were appraised in Mexican currency (*moneda mexicana*), so unit values do not require any further transformation.

DECOMPOSITION OF THE AD VALOREM EQUIVALENT TARIFF RATE

An ad valorem tariff is the ratio of a commodity price to its tariff. The ad valorem equivalent tariff is a specific tariff transformed into an ad valorem tariff. If we define ϖ_{js} as the specific tariff of commodity j in the period of tariff schedule s, and P_{jt} as the price of commodity j in year t, then the ad valorem equivalent tariff of commodity j in period t is

$$\tau_{jt} = \frac{\varpi_{js}}{P_{jt}} \qquad (1)$$

Note that there exists a negative relationship between τ_{jt} and P_{jt}. As the price of commodity j increases, the ad valorem equivalent tariff decreases and vice versa, provided that the specific tariff remains constant. Conversely, changes in the specific tariff of commodity j would cause movements of τ_{jt} in the same direction. Every time specific tariff rates increase, the ad valorem equivalent tariff increases if prices remain at the same level. Yet it is also possible that price fluctuations could compensate for the effect of higher tariff rates.

A close examination of tariff rates and prices enables us to better understand fluctuations in the ad valorem equivalent tariff. This is possible by breaking Equation (1) into different components without altering its original value. Crucini has done this exercise for the United States from 1903 to 1940.[7] Using a sample of 32 products, he finds that major fluctuations in tariff protection resulted from price variation, not from changes in tariff rates. Crucini's decomposition includes three components: a legislative component that describes the ad valorem tariff at the time of tariff revision, a price-level component that portrays the effect of general fluctuations in the prices of all imports, and a relative-price component that measures the effect of changes in the price of a single commodity as compared with the general price index.[8]

Despite Crucini's insightful results, his decomposition leaves out the effects of exchange rate variations. Because a devaluation causes an increase in import prices, silver depreciation contributes changes to the ad valorem tariff rates. In an extension of Crucini's decomposition, I have added a component that explains the contribution of silver depreciation to ad valorem rate variations.

Let SPI_t denote the import price index of silver pesos in period t, and GPI_t denote the import price index in gold pesos in period t.[9] Index zero indicates the year in which legislative changes occurred. Equation (1) can thus be expressed as

$$\tau_{jt} = \left|\frac{\omega_{jo}}{P_{jo}}\right| + \left|\frac{\omega_{jo}}{P_{jo}}\right| \left|\frac{SPI_o}{SPI_t} - \frac{\frac{SPI_o}{GPI_o}}{\frac{SPI_t}{GPI_t}}\right| + \left|\frac{\omega_{jo}}{P_{jo}}\right| \left|\frac{P_{jo}}{P_{jt}} - \frac{SPI_o}{SPI_t}\right| + \left|\frac{\omega_{jo}}{P_{jo}}\right| \left|\frac{\frac{SPI_o}{GPI_o}}{\frac{SPI_t}{GPI_t}} - 1\right| \quad (2)$$

or,

$$\equiv TL_{js} + TP_{jt} + TRP_{jt} + TSD_{jt}$$

where TL_{js} is the tariff's legislative component of commodity j at the time of tariff revision s; and TP_{jt}, TRP_{jt}, and TSD_{jt} are the tariff's price effects of commodity j at time t. Hereafter they are referred to as the price-level, the relative-price, and the silver depreciation components, respectively.[10]

The legislative component indicates the specific tariff and price ratio of commodity j at the time tariff revision occurs. The two variables needed to compute the legislative component specific tariff and price are positive and are defined at the time of tariff revision. Therefore, the value of this component is always positive and is constant over periods where no revisions take place. Note that the legislative component becomes part of each of the remaining components, setting a level around which the ad valorem value fluctuates. Intuitively, the legislative component reveals protection the government intends to provide at the time of tariff changes, remaining constant as long as commodity prices are also constant.

The price-level component isolates the effect of commodity price fluctuations in the world market on ad valorem tariff rates. This is possible by subtracting the changes caused by silver depreciation captured in the exchange rate ratio between period 0 and t from total changes in import prices. The price-level component is positive in two cases: if the increase in the import price index measured in silver is higher than the increase in the exchange rate, and if import prices in silver decrease at a lower rate than the exchange rate. The ultimate cause behind this result is that import prices, measured in gold, varied more than the exchange rate, increasing the ad valorem tariff rate. In a regime of a fixed exchange rate, the price-level component captures price variations denominated in silver. Equation (2) then becomes the same as in Crucini's decomposition, where price variations do not incorporate any exchange rate effect.

The relative-price component measures the difference between variations in individual commodity prices and changes in the general import price index. When individual price variations differ from the import price index, a decrease in an individual price may drive a rise in the ad valorem tariff rate, thus compensating for inflationary pressures in the price of imported commodities. If a commodity's price increase in the period under consideration is greater than the increase in the import price index, the ad valorem tariff rate will rise; if a commodity's price increase is lower, the ad valorem tariff rate will decrease.

The last component of Equation (2) reveals the effect of nominal variation in the exchange rate over the period from 0 to t. A devaluation causes increases in prices of imports measured in domestic currency. Concomitantly, price increases in domestic currency drive reductions in ad valorem tariff rates. Fixed exchange rate regimes eliminate this effect altogether.

NOMINAL PROTECTION AND AD VALOREM TARIFF RATES, 1892–1909

The ad valorem equivalent tariff rate measures specific tariffs as a percentage of individual prices. When added to the price of imports, it represents the nominal protection conferred on domestic producers. Between 1892 and 1909, nominal protection experienced several changes originating in tariff policy, price variations, and exchange rate fluctuations. What were the distinctive features of nominal protection in this period? Did differences across industries remain unchanged?

This section addresses these questions and discusses the patterns of nominal protection for a sample of 32 industrial products. First, I briefly describe the commodities in the sample and the evolution of specific tariffs. Next, I present general trends in nominal protection and discuss cases where patterns diverged from the trends.

Sample and Specific Rates

As mentioned above, this paper focuses on a sample of representative industries: cotton textiles, an example of a traditional industry with modern production dating as far back as the 1830s; paper, beer, and soap manufacturing, which although not new, expanded modern production in the Porfiriato; and steel and cement, which represent industries that emerged in the 1890s and 1900s. In all, the sample consists of 32 commodities that accounted for 14% of total dutiable imports and 29% of dutiable industrial goods in 1892 (see Table 14.1). The number of commodities per industry varies: cotton products include yarns, textiles, and manufactures, totaling 15 commodities; the iron and steel industry follows with 10 products; there are 3 varieties of paper; and finally, the soap, beer, and cement industries have 1 commodity each.[11]

Before presenting the patterns of nominal protection for the commodity sample, it is convenient to examine the evolution of a simpler form of protection: the patterns of change in specific tariffs. A salient feature of the 32-

TABLE 14.1

Industries and Products Included in Sample (percentage of dutiable imports)

Description	1891	1905	%
Cotton Products			
Yarns			
Cotton cord, not exceeding 10 millimeters in diameter	444	325	0.01
Cotton yarn	446	327	0.05
Cotton thread in balls, skeins, and spools	447	328	0.47
Cotton wicks	451	329	0.03
Textiles			
Cotton lace and point lace of all kinds, and manufactures thereof	453	330	0.31
Cloth 1: Cotton fabrics, bleached or unbleached, of smooth texture, not exceeding 30 threads, warp and woof, in a square of 5 mm. side	458	333	2.43
Cloth 2: Cotton fabrics, bleached or unbleached, of smooth texture, exceeding 30 threads, warp and woof, in a square of 5 mm. side	459	334	0.48
Cloth 3: Cotton fabrics, colored, printed, or dyed, of smooth texture, not exceeding 30 threads, warp and woof, in a square of 5 mm. side	460	335	2.79
Cloth 4: Cotton fabrics, colored, printed, or dyed, of smooth texture, exceeding 30 threads, warp and woof, in a square of 5 mm. side	461	336	0.14
Cloth 5: Cotton fabrics, bleached or unbleached or colored, of a texture hat is not smooth	462	337	1.86
Cloth 6: Cotton fabrics of all kinds, embroidered with wool	464	338	0.01
Manufactures			
Rufflings, fringes, galloons, lace trimmings, lace ribbons, and cotton nettings	480	356	0.09
Elastic webbing of cotton and rubber, exceeding 4 centimeters in width	490	367	0.19

TABLE 14.1 (CONT.)

Industries and Products Included in Sample (percentage of dutiable imports)

Description	1891	1905	%
Manufactures (continued)			
Ready-made clothing, not specially mentioned, and separate parts, of cotton fabrics of all kinds	492	368	0.12
Cotton insertions, open worked or embroidered with cotton, wool, or linen	435	370	0.23
Paper Products			
Newsprint: Paper, uncoated or half coated, for newspaper printing	743		0.03
Brown paper, for packing, tarring or not	746	582	0.18
Paper for cigarettes	760		0.17
Soap			
Soap, not perfumed	899	693	0.12
Beer			
Beer, cider, and refreshing beverages in bottles	734	572	1.16
Cement	359	268	0.40
Roman or Portland cement, common and hydraulic lime, and carbonate of lime or Spanish white			
Iron and Steel Products			
Steel in bars, round, square, flat, channel, in an octagonal or hexagonal section of cruciform	305	228	0.11
Iron or steel wire of more than 1 millimeter in diameter	307	229	0.01
Iron or steel wire cables	316	234	0.04
Iron in ingots of first fusion or in fillings or scrap	322	239	0.22
Iron wire for fences, and hoops of iron with their rivets, for packing purposes	311	231	0.22

TABLE 14.1 (CONT.)

Industries and Products Included in Sample (percentage of dutiable imports)

Description	1891	1905	%
Iron and Steel Products			
Plows and loose parts or pieces thereof, spades, scythes, and other agricultural and grading tools	313	232	0.07
Iron piping, of all dimensions, tinned or not	317	235	0.49
Beams and joists of iron and steel, not specially perforated or slotted, for construction purposes	333	251	0.16
Iron, round, square, flat, channel, and T-shaped	323	241	0.25
Iron and steel in sheets, corrugated and in tiles	326	243	0.77
Tinplate in sheets up to 55 centimeters in length by 40 in width	327	244	0.04
Total in sample			13.68
Total dutiable imports			100

Source: Secretaría de Hacienda y Crédito Público, *Estadística fiscal*, various years.

commodity sample is that most of the changes in specific tariff rates took place between 1902 and 1905. Prior to 1902, only 4 commodities altered their tariffs: cotton cord, steel wire, and steel ingots in 1898, and paper for cigarettes in 1901. Moreover, cotton lace, soap, and tinplate sheets maintained their 1892 specific tariff throughout the period.

Propelled by the partial indexation of import duties, tariffs for all products changed in 1902 and 1903[12]; 7 other products changed again in 1904, including cotton cord, cloth 5, and 5 iron and steel products.[13] The monetary reform brought about tariff rate changes aimed at restoring protection levels for domestic producers.[14] As a result, tariffs on 23 commodities were increased between 4% and 100%, whereas for 6 commodities specific rates were kept constant.[15] In sum, tariff changes in the sample occurred mostly in 1902, 1903, and 1905; at any other moment, such as 1898, 1901, or 1904, variations in specific tariffs were limited to a handful of commodities. Even more striking, the years from 1906 to 1909 registered no alteration in specific tariff rates.

Although changes in specific tariffs are essential in understanding tariff protection and commercial policy, they are a poor indicator of protection levels and can lead to distorted conclusions. For instance, looking only at specific tariffs, protection appears to have experienced almost no variation in the 1890s. However, the opposite occurred: Protection levels deteriorated rapidly as prices varied in the years prior to 1901. In this sense, ad valorem rates, which incorporate price fluctuations, offer a much better measure of protection levels.

Ad Valorem Tariff Rates and Nominal Protection

Before presenting the estimates of ad valorem tariff rates, a caveat must be made. This paper concentrates on nominal rates in a first effort to approximate the levels of tariff protection in the Porfirian era. The author recognizes that the effect of protection on industrial development must consider effective rates as well as nontariff factors. Work in progress indicates that, on the one hand, the structure of protection significantly elevated the already high levels of tariff protection. On the other hand, nontariff factors, primarily silver depreciation, played a decisive role in protecting domestic producers from foreign competition.

Table 14.2 presents the evolution of ad valorem tariff rates in the 1892–1909 period. A rather consistent picture emerges indicating that nominal protection declined steadily in the 1890s for almost three-quarters of the commodities in the sample.[16] As shown in the preceding section, given that specific tariffs changed little, the ad valorem tariff rate must have fallen as a result of inflationary pressures. In particular, the stability of specific rates was disturbed by price increases originating in silver depreciation and variation in relative prices. The 1890s, then, represented a period in which tariffs became less important as a source of protection.[17] The most dramatic change occurred in cotton products, for which the ad valorem tariff dropped, on average, by 41% between 1892 and 1900, cloth 6 being the product with the largest decline in the entire sample (–68%). Although it is true that for some products short-term price fluctuations ameliorated the fall in the ad valorem tariff, rates at the beginning of the century were definitely lower than in 1892.

When the Mexican government decided to partially index import duties, it introduced a de facto increase in specific tariffs, thus preventing a further deterioration in the ad valorem rates. In half of the commodities of the sample, the partial indexation was accompanied by a complete reversal of the declining trend, most notably for steel products. In other cases, however, higher tariffs could only ameliorate the fall in the ad valorem rate. For example, the ad valorem rate for newsprint was further reduced in 1902, but both types of tariffs increased in 1903. Finally, in a minority of products not even an elevation of specific tariffs could offset price effects. Such was the case for ready-made clothing, whose ad valorem rate fell below the 1901 level for the rest of the period.

Turning to the years that followed the 1905 monetary reform, the evidence suggests that the decreasing trend of ad valorem tariff rates either disappeared or at least stabilized around the 1905 value. The ad valorem rate weighted average was 59.5% in 1905 and 61.44% in 1909, an increase of only 3%.[18] The shift to a new pattern is apparent in most of the commodities of the sample: More than two-thirds of the sample maintained the 1905 ad valorem rate. Only five types of cotton goods experienced further deterioration in ad valorem rates after 1905: cloth 6, cotton insertions, coarse thread, ready-made clothing, and trimmings.

In sum, the evidence presented here suggests that nominal protection generally declined throughout the 1890s, partially recovered in 1902 and 1903, increased again in 1905, and remained close to the 1905 level during the last years of the Porfiriato. However, the erosion of the 1890s was not fully reversed, generally leaving ad valorem rates below their 1892 level. This pattern is consistent with the evolution of specific tariffs and prices across the sample. The stability of specific tariffs in times of great exchange rate fluctuations and great price variability produced sharp declines in nominal protection. When the instability of import prices in domestic currency disappeared after 1905, changes in the ad valorem tariff rate then stemmed more from variability in individual prices and less from price-level and exchange rate fluctuations. In this sense, the sources of variation observed in the decade from 1892 to 1901 had little explanatory power in the 1900s.

Cement and cotton cloth 3 significantly differ from the general pattern of declining ad valorem rates in the period from 1893 to 1901. Instead, the ad valorem rate for cement surpassed the 1892 rate for almost all years in this period, peaking in 1893 almost 20 percentage points above the rate set in 1892. A steady fall in cement prices relative to 1892, with the exception of 1896, compensated for the inflationary effect of silver depreciation and thus explains the departure from the general trend (see Figure 14.1). A high-bulk, low-value product, cement must have benefited from declining costs in transportation to achieve price reductions at the end of the nineteenth century.

In the case of cotton cloth 3, the deviations occurred primarily in the 1890s. The ad valorem rate described an inverted U shape, surpassing the 1892 rate from 1893 to 1899 and peaking in 1897. In the period from 1905 to 1909, cloth 3 closely followed the pattern of most commodities, but ended up with the highest ad valorem tariff in the sample (see Figure 14.2). The ad valorem tariff decomposition shows, on the one hand, that the relative-price and the

TABLE 14.2

Ad Valorem Equivalent Tariff Rates (percentage of price)

	1892	1893	1894	1895	1896	1897	1898	1899
Cotton Products								
Yarns								
Cord	116.18	103.17	143.20	96.26	97.45	110.61	88.94	94.17
Coarse thread	110.94	83.91	83.90	110.88	95.07	66.60	77.36	63.44
Thread	115.64	88.50	60.80	64.74	63.72	73.12	102.48	73.79
Wick	33.99	15.73	16.30	18.47	16.45	15.10	16.77	14.36
Textiles								
Lace	165.30	123.80	83.55	91.79	82.00	68.06	73.09	68.51
Cloth 1	63.41	54.55	53.46	70.49	61.36	62.35	61.69	52.60
Cloth 2	72.39	52.62	59.74	61.87	74.66	68.99	53.90	51.60
Cloth 3	119.48	112.79	123.85	126.05	131.11	133.14	131.57	128.57
Cloth 4	83.01	70.95	60.79	60.69	45.40	49.70	49.08	55.91
Cloth 5	73.74	56.97	56.92	60.67	59.98	49.22	57.82	54.29
Cloth 6	114.14	37.69	11.06	46.08	32.31	90.49	18.63	37.85
Manufactures								
Trimmings	143.86	87.10	59.42	67.90	74.18	54.76	65.69	59.73
Elastic webbing	29.07	22.36	20.06	23.78	21.94	19.74	21.39	22.03
Ready-made clothing	90.64	67.32	72.91	85.16	111.87	62.38	56.00	50.53
Insertions	37.85	28.52	24.38	22.25	24.47	24.82	21.85	18.05
Paper Products								
Newsprint	43.10	41.27	27.36	44.93	60.42	50.15	41.94	50.80
Brown paper	40.94	36.95	34.63	40.71	36.73	35.87	38.58	40.14
Paper for cigarettes	28.47	22.60	22.46	25.17	22.85	20.39	21.47	19.91
Soap	158.60	142.77	157.81	272.19	283.95	159.85	153.32	145.35
Beer	65.09	53.77	52.77	53.40	48.16	45.62	44.37	43.39
Cement	22.75	42.26	31.81	30.72	22.40	29.19	25.32	23.53

TABLE 14.2 (CONT.)

Ad Valorem Equivalent Tariff Rates (percentage of price)

1900	1901	1902	1903	1904	1905	1906	1907	1908	1909
Cotton Products									
Yarns									
90.53	83.30	87.96	73.48	54.03	73.53	72.89	61.66	70.57	67.89
64.37	72.24	58.91	33.77	57.03	43.77	35.70	38.79	33.32	34.90
54.52	53.00	52.60	49.03	48.38	37.92	48.15	45.13	46.78	45.04
14.44	13.06	15.25	11.53	10.96	18.46	21.47	19.38	19.67	18.92
Textiles									
61.59	49.53	45.10	47.72	47.03	57.72	53.11	49.98	58.11	63.16
47.54	48.82	49.34	45.82	45.69	52.67	48.29	48.72	54.99	58.44
46.67	43.51	49.18	47.72	50.26	52.88	48.16	45.41	48.60	54.12
117.38	119.88	122.71	101.26	101.22	112.96	108.77	101.63	108.97	114.42
44.49	44.30	51.65	55.95	52.83	66.05	58.76	57.99	71.39	76.99
48.33	42.99	43.40	45.74	45.74	51.49	49.14	46.42	50.98	52.45
36.41	35.48	26.74	39.13	36.22	54.15	54.38	43.26	40.89	26.66
Manufactures									
51.22	45.63	46.14	47.48	45.79	55.63	53.67	54.10	52.91	53.26
23.68	21.69	23.77	23.98	26.86	30.45	31.40	29.74	28.63	28.78
55.47	57.08	51.73	43.93	40.65	44.86	44.00	41.31	41.30	40.62
19.06	18.30	19.17	20.56	24.28	28.28	26.24	22.99	26.28	26.05
Paper Products									
43.59	28.59	27.43	34.31	36.75	n.a.	n.a.	n.a.	n.a.	n.a.
36.26	34.80	43.72	40.16	41.87	n.a.	n.a.	n.a.	n.a.	n.a.
20.56	23.64	21.51	24.83	25.83	n.a.	n.a.	n.a.	n.a.	n.a.
134.03	128.54	125.68	134.04	90.34	75.39	89.64	77.49	78.95	75.48
44.68	38.40	39.06	38.76	41.50	54.03	54.21	53.88	52.30	50.95
24.76	22.93	21.12	24.80	27.45	34.99	32.87	32.73	34.15	35.94

TABLE 14.2 (CONT.)

Ad Valorem Equivalent Tariff Rates (percentage of price)

	1892	1893	1894	1895	1896	1897	1898	1899
Iron and Steel Products								
Bars	50.00	36.26	30.17	42.30	33.27	32.71	35.94	27.60
Wire	10.11	5.51	9.14	6.01	11.23	10.15	40.28	31.88
Cable	3.12	2.21	2.58	2.90	2.79	2.88	2.90	2.57
Iron in ingots	34.74	45.70	23.36	32.89	32.06	36.01	62.05	39.15
Iron wire for fences	11.52	10.39	10.92	11.64	12.88	11.38	10.95	8.91
Plows	4.65	3.93	4.32	4.94	4.10	4.30	4.86	4.79
Iron piping	8.55	8.30	7.93	9.06	10.77	9.07	8.50	7.57
Beams and joists	23.98	11.07	20.18	17.9	15.52	11.53	13.22	11.05
Manufactures	79.67	78.80	66.3	120.31	78.59	73.28	75.33	59.07
Sheets	41.4	31.54	43.62	37.95	35.68	34.81	29.79	27.02
Tinplate sheets	10.00	8.25	8.31	10.14	10.49	9.54	8.62	7.34

n.a.:   Insufficient data due to classification changes.

Source: See text.

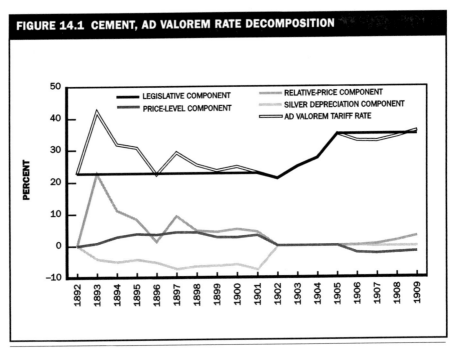

FIGURE 14.1 CEMENT, AD VALOREM RATE DECOMPOSITION

Source: Tables 14.2 to 14.6.

TABLE 14.2 (CONT.)

Ad Valorem Equivalent Tariff Rates (percentage of price)

1900	1901	1902	1903	1904	1905	1906	1907	1908	1909
Iron and Steel Products									
24.48	17.29	19.24	20.57	26.89	26.70	31.04	27.44	32.20	34.44
35.36	36.91	40.57	41.69	55.24	56.04	51.37	54.85	58.61	60.27
1.28	2.38	2.67	2.80	2.66	2.95	3.01	2.98	3.17	3.09
40.35	45.45	35.30	37.63	46.94	39.29	36.57	36.61	39.71	47.79
9.00	8.34	8.72	8.71	18.96	24.77	23.46	22.90	23.77	23.92
4.66	4.13	4.03	4.27	6.57	5.70	5.02	5.18	5.32	5.86
7.54	6.53	6.76	7.64	10.80	20.24	19.77	18.53	17.63	22.42
12.76	10.10	12.18	15.11	17.12	28.05	25.03	25.78	30.62	25.20
61.11	59.21	54.93	56.99	57.67	65.38	62.87	54.71	69.17	60.37
26.69	30.06	31.11	33.30	51.85	55.17	50.20	50.74	56.67	59.60
8.78	7.61	7.23	8.22	8.56	9.69	8.25	8.04	8.83	9.21

price-level components more than compensated for the declining tendency in the silver depreciation component. This result is not surprising for cloth 3 (colored, medium-quality fabric), a fairly common type of cotton product that was likely to experience successive price cuts in the late nineteenth and early twentieth centuries. On the other hand, the high specific tariff reinforced this pattern by providing the third highest rate between 1892 and 1901. Even after the tariff reform of 1905, the legislative rate was 53.5 percentage points above the average. In other words, both prices and tariff policy acted together to erect a barrier to protect domestic production. Evidence suggests that this combination worked, since imports of cloth 3 substantially decreased from 11.6 million square meters in 1892 to only 3.2 million in 1909.

Finally, ad valorem tariffs in 1909 tended to be lower than in the early 1890s, despite the fact that some of them, as discussed above, had been recovering during the early 1900s. Seven iron and steel products—wire, ingots, beams and joists, wire for fences, plows, piping, and sheets—constitute an exception to this pattern. This was in part possible because of a higher specific tariff. By raising the legislative tariff, the government must have tried to support the recently founded cement and steel firms, for which higher tariff protection could have compensated for the loss of nontariff protection caused by silver depreciation.[19]

FIGURE 14.2 COTTON CLOTH 3, AD VALOREM RATE DECOMPOSITION

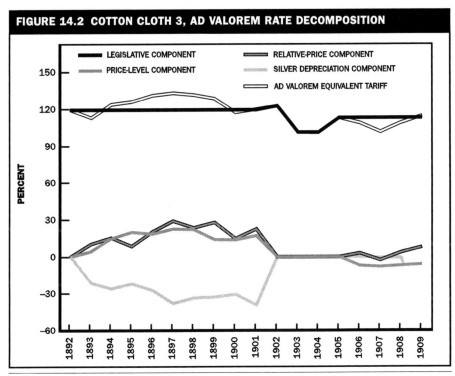

Source: Tables 14.2 to 14.6.

AD VALOREM TARIFF RATE DECOMPOSITION, 1892–1909

This section summarizes the results of decomposing the ad valorem rate for
the 32-commodity sample in the 1892–1909 period. The stability of specific
tariffs in most sampled products during the 1890s allowed price effects a major
role in shaping the behavior of ad valorem rates. When considered together,
values of each component combined different magnitudes and often worked
in opposite directions, producing a falling effect on the ad valorem rate during
the 1890s. Between 1892 and 1901 the silver depreciation component featured,
on average, higher values than the price-level and the relative-price components, and therefore had a greater influence on the price effect outcome. The
silver depreciation component set a strong pattern of declining ad valorem
rates in most of the commodities in the sample. This trend was, of course,
compensated by the price-level component, whose value tended to drive ad
valorem rates upward. Yet the positive influence of the price-level component
was not enough to overcome the depressing force of the silver depreciation
component. The relative-price component, which captures individual price
fluctuations, shaped the ad valorem tariff rate evolution. In most cases in the
sample, the declining trend prevailed from 1892 to 1901, thus implying that

the relative-price component reinforced the effect of the silver depreciation component and, of course, lower ad valorem rates.

A major source of instability in import prices disappeared when Mexico adopted the gold standard in 1905. As a consequence, price effects substantially diminished their influence on the ad valorem tariff. Price effects diminished in magnitude, such that their impact on the ad valorem rate tended to be lower than in periods of great price variability. For instance, between 1905 and 1909 ad valorem tariff rates grew, on average, 3.3%, as opposed to the 25% reduction experienced between 1892 and 1901. The relative-price component, with greater variability and magnitude, defined the direction of changes in ad valorem rates with little modification from the other two price components.

Legislative Component

Prices and specific tariff rates are the two factors that combined to drive movements in ad valorem tariff rates. Following Equation (2), the legislative component determines the contribution of specific tariff rates to ad valorem variations. In this sense, specific rates as a percentage of price, or the legislative component, provide an estimation of the level of tariff protection that the government granted through tariffs. What were, then, the patterns resulting from Porfirian tariff policy from 1892 to 1909?

The legislative component for 32 commodities points out two contrasting tendencies. On the one hand, more than two-thirds of the commodities in the sample had a lower legislative tariff in 1909 than in 1892. Table 14.3 shows this result, featuring a sharp concentration by industry. All cotton products (except for elastic webbing, which increased from 29% to 31%), beer, and soap lowered their legislative tariff rate. On the other hand, a group of 10 products increased the level of legislative rates mostly due to higher specific tariff rates. Cement and 7 steel products (wire, ingots, wire for fences, plows, piping, beams, and sheets) make up most of this group. By providing higher specific tariff rates to this group of products, the government revealed its preference for the promotion of domestic industries that had started production in the early 1900s, including cement and iron and steel.

Price-Level Component

First of all, we should note that the price-level component consists of a common factor that isolates change in prices unrelated to silver depreciation, plus an individual or scale factor. This is why the sign and pattern of the contribution remain the same across the sample, provided that commodities are in the same base year. In other words, for the 29 commodities sharing 1892 as a base

TABLE 14.3

Legislative Component (percentage of price)

	1892	1893	1894	1895	1896	1897	1898	1899
Cotton Products								
Yarns								
Cord	116.18	116.18	116.18	116.18	116.18	116.18	88.94	88.94
Coarse thread	110.94	110.94	110.94	110.94	110.94	110.94	110.94	110.94
Thread	115.64	115.64	115.64	115.64	115.64	115.64	115.64	115.64
Wick	33.99	33.99	33.99	33.99	33.99	33.99	33.99	33.99
Textiles								
Lace	165.30	165.30	165.30	165.30	165.30	165.30	165.30	165.30
Cloth 1	63.41	63.41	63.41	63.41	63.41	63.41	63.41	63.41
Cloth 2	72.39	72.39	72.39	72.39	72.39	72.39	72.39	72.39
Cloth 3	119.48	119.48	119.48	119.48	119.48	119.48	119.48	119.48
Cloth 4	83.01	83.01	83.01	83.01	83.01	83.01	83.01	83.01
Cloth 5	73.74	73.74	73.74	73.74	73.74	73.74	73.74	73.74
Cloth 6	114.14	114.14	114.14	114.14	114.14	114.14	114.14	114.14
Manufactures								
Trimmings	143.86	143.86	143.86	143.86	143.86	143.86	143.86	143.86
Elastic webbing	29.07	29.07	29.07	29.07	29.07	29.07	29.07	29.07
Ready-made clothing	90.64	90.64	90.64	90.64	90.64	90.64	90.64	90.64
Insertions	37.85	37.85	37.85	37.85	37.85	37.85	37.85	37.85
Paper Products								
Newsprint	43.10	43.10	43.10	43.10	43.10	43.10	43.10	43.10
Brown paper	40.94	40.94	40.94	40.94	40.94	40.94	40.94	40.94
Paper for cigarettes	28.47	28.47	28.47	28.47	28.47	28.47	28.47	28.47
Soap	158.60	158.60	158.60	158.60	158.60	158.60	158.60	158.60
Beer	65.09	65.09	65.09	65.09	65.09	65.09	65.09	65.09
Cement	22.75	22.75	22.75	22.75	22.75	22.75	22.75	22.75

TABLE 14.3 (CONT.)

Legislative Component (percentage of price)

1900	1901	1902	1903	1904	1905	1906	1907	1908	1909
Cotton Products									
Yarns									
88.94	88.94	87.96	73.48	54.03	54.03	54.03	54.03	54.03	54.03
110.94	110.94	58.91	33.77	57.03	43.77	43.77	43.77	43.77	43.77
115.64	115.64	52.60	49.03	48.38	37.92	37.92	37.92	37.92	37.92
33.99	33.99	15.25	11.53	10.96	18.46	18.46	18.46	18.46	18.46
Textiles									
165.30	165.30	45.10	47.72	47.03	47.03	47.03	47.03	47.03	47.03
63.41	63.41	49.34	45.82	45.69	52.67	52.67	52.67	52.67	52.67
72.39	72.39	49.18	47.72	50.26	52.88	52.88	52.88	52.88	52.88
119.48	119.48	122.71	101.26	101.22	112.96	112.96	112.96	112.96	112.96
83.01	83.01	51.65	55.95	52.83	66.05	66.05	66.05	66.05	66.05
73.74	73.74	43.40	45.74	45.74	51.49	51.49	51.49	51.49	51.49
114.14	114.14	26.74	39.13	36.22	54.15	54.15	54.15	54.15	54.15
Manufactures									
143.86	143.86	46.14	47.48	45.79	55.63	55.63	55.63	55.63	55.63
29.07	29.07	23.77	23.98	26.86	30.45	30.45	30.45	30.45	30.45
90.64	90.64	51.73	43.93	40.65	44.86	44.86	44.86	44.86	44.86
37.85	37.85	19.17	20.56	24.28	28.28	28.28	28.28	28.28	28.28
Paper Products									
43.10	43.10	27.43	34.31	36.75	n.a.	n.a.	n.a.	n.a.	n.a.
40.94	40.94	43.72	40.16	41.87	n.a.	n.a.	n.a.	n.a.	n.a.
28.47	23.64	21.51	24.83	25.83	n.a.	n.a.	n.a.	n.a.	n.a.
158.60	158.60	125.68	134.04	90.34	90.34	90.34	90.34	90.34	90.34
65.09	65.09	39.06	38.76	41.50	54.03	54.03	54.03	54.03	54.03
22.75	22.75	21.12	24.80	27.45	34.99	34.99	34.99	34.99	34.99

TABLE 14.3 (CONT.)

Legislative Component (percentage of price)

	1892	1893	1894	1895	1896	1897	1898	1899
Iron and Steel Products								
Bars	50.00	50.00	50.00	50.00	50.00	50.00	50.00	50.00
Wire	10.11	10.11	10.11	10.11	10.11	10.11	40.28	40.28
Cable	3.12	3.12	3.12	3.12	3.12	3.12	3.12	3.12
Steel in ingots	34.74	34.74	34.74	34.74	34.74	34.74	62.05	62.05
Iron wire for fences	11.52	11.52	11.52	11.52	11.52	11.52	11.52	11.52
Plows	4.65	4.65	4.65	4.65	4.65	4.65	4.65	4.65
Iron piping	8.55	8.55	8.55	8.55	8.55	8.55	8.55	8.55
Beams and joists	23.98	23.98	23.98	23.98	23.98	23.98	23.98	23.98
Manufactures	79.67	79.67	79.67	79.67	79.67	79.67	79.67	79.67
Sheets	41.40	41.40	41.40	41.40	41.40	41.40	41.40	41.40
Tinplate sheets	10.00	10.00	10.00	10.00	10.00	10.00	10.00	10.00

n.a.:   Insufficient data due to classification changes.

Source: See text.

year, the price-level component displayed the same pattern at different scales and preserved its sign until 1901, when the base year changed.

Table 14.4 shows increases in the ad valorem rate that originated in the price-level component for 29 commodities between 1892 and 1901. In this 10-year period, the inflationary effect of devaluation could not compensate for the overall decreasing trend in import prices measured in gold. In fact, in many cases the positive effect of the price-level component was the only variable that ameliorated the decreasing trend in ad valorem tariff rates. For 3 commodities, however, the price-level component lowered the value of the ad valorem rate. The reforms in specific tariffs for cotton cord, steel wire, and steel in ingots shifted the base year from 1892 to 1898. Consequently, the value of this component turned negative between 1899 and 1901, revealing that, when compared with 1898, exchange rate inflationary pressures dominated total price movements.

The monetary reform of 1905 eliminated the disturbances that had been caused by exchange rate fluctuations, such that total price variation depended only on import prices measured in Mexican currency. Between 1906 and 1909, upward variation in the import price index lowered ad valorem rates. It is

TABLE 14.3 (CONT.)

Legislative Component (percentage of price)

1900	1901	1902	1903	1904	1905	1906	1907	1908	1909
Iron and Steel Products									
50.00	50.00	19.24	20.57	26.89	26.70	26.70	26.70	26.70	26.70
40.28	40.28	40.57	41.69	55.24	56.04	56.04	56.04	56.04	56.04
3.12	3.12	2.67	2.80	2.66	2.95	2.95	2.95	2.95	2.95
62.05	62.05	35.3	37.63	46.94	46.94	46.94	46.94	46.94	46.94
11.52	11.52	8.72	8.71	18.96	24.77	24.77	24.77	24.77	24.77
4.65	4.65	4.03	4.27	6.57	5.70	5.70	5.70	5.70	5.70
8.55	8.55	6.76	7.64	10.80	20.24	20.24	20.24	20.24	20.24
23.98	23.98	12.18	15.11	17.12	28.05	28.05	28.05	28.05	28.05
79.67	79.67	54.93	56.99	57.67	65.38	65.38	65.38	65.38	65.38
41.40	41.40	31.11	33.30	51.85	55.17	55.17	55.17	55.17	55.17
10.00	10.00	7.23	8.22	8.56	9.69	9.69	9.69	9.69	9.69

worth noting, however, that the price-level component effect on the ad valorem tariff rate was more accentuated for the period 1892–1901 than for 1906–1909.

Silver Depreciation Component

At the end of the nineteenth century, monetary regimes tied to silver were continuously disturbed by the secular decline in silver prices.[20] Falling silver prices translated into devaluations of the exchange rate, causing import prices to rise in domestic currency. This inflationary effect on import prices in turn pulled ad valorem rates downward.[21] In Equation (2), the silver depreciation component captures this effect in a common factor, scaling it for each commodity according to individual legislative tariffs in base years, as did the price-level component.

In general, the silver depreciation component tended to reduce the value of the ad valorem rate because the inflationary effect of the declining exchange rate on import prices eroded the constant value of specific tariffs (see Table 14.5). In the years 1892 to 1901, the contribution of the silver depreciation component follows two patterns, depending on the base year. For the com-

TABLE 14.4

Price-Level Component (percentage of price)

	1892	1893	1894	1895	1896	1897	1898	1899
Cotton Products								
Yarns								
Cord	0.00	4.32	14.51	19.48	18.08	21.99	0.00	10.51
Coarse thread	0.00	4.12	13.85	18.60	17.27	21.00	20.58	13.12
Thread	0.00	4.30	14.44	19.38	18.00	21.89	21.45	13.67
Wick	0.00	1.26	4.24	5.70	5.29	6.44	6.31	4.02
Textiles								
Lace	0.00	6.14	20.64	27.71	25.73	31.29	30.67	19.54
Cloth 1	0.00	2.36	7.92	10.63	9.87	12.00	11.76	7.50
Cloth 2	0.00	2.69	9.04	12.14	11.27	13.70	13.43	8.56
Cloth 3	0.00	4.44	14.92	20.03	18.59	22.62	22.17	14.12
Cloth 4	0.00	3.08	10.36	13.91	12.92	15.71	15.40	9.81
Cloth 5	0.00	2.74	9.21	12.36	11.48	13.96	13.68	8.72
Cloth 6	0.00	4.24	14.25	19.13	17.76	21.61	21.17	13.49
Manufactures								
Trimmings	0.00	5.34	17.96	24.12	22.39	27.23	26.69	17.01
Elastic webbing	0.00	1.08	3.63	4.87	4.52	5.50	5.39	3.44
Ready-made clothing	0.00	3.37	11.32	15.19	14.11	17.16	16.82	10.71
Insertions	0.00	1.41	4.73	6.34	5.89	7.16	7.02	4.47
Paper Products								
Newsprint	0.00	1.60	5.38	7.23	6.71	8.16	8.00	5.10
Brown paper	0.00	1.52	5.11	6.86	6.37	7.75	7.59	4.84
Paper for cigarettes	0.00	1.06	3.55	4.77	4.43	5.39	5.28	3.37
Soap	0.00	5.89	19.80	26.59	24.68	30.02	29.42	18.75
Beer	0.00	2.42	8.13	10.91	10.13	12.32	12.08	7.69
Cement	0.00	0.84	2.84	3.81	3.54	4.31	4.22	2.69

TABLE 14.4 (CONT.)

Price-Level Component (percentage of price)

1900	1901	1902	1903	1904	1905	1906	1907	1908	1909
Cotton Products									
Yarns									
10.24	12.80	0.00	0.00	0.00	0.48	−3.09	−3.53	−3.04	−2.61
12.77	15.97	0.00	0.00	0.00	0.00	−2.77	−3.11	−2.73	−2.39
13.31	16.64	0.00	0.00	0.00	0.00	−2.40	−2.70	−2.36	−2.07
3.91	4.89	0.00	0.00	0.00	0.00	−1.17	−1.31	−1.15	−1.01
Textiles									
19.03	23.79	0.00	0.00	0.00	0.42	−2.69	−3.08	−2.66	−2.23
7.30	9.13	0.00	0.00	0.00	0.00	−3.33	−3.75	−3.29	−2.83
8.34	10.42	0.00	0.00	0.00	0.00	−3.35	−3.76	−3.31	−2.84
13.76	17.19	0.00	0.00	0.00	0.00	−7.15	−8.03	−7.06	−6.08
9.56	11.95	0.00	0.00	0.00	0.00	−4.18	−4.70	−4.13	−3.55
8.49	10.61	0.00	0.00	0.00	0.00	−3.26	−3.66	−3.22	−2.77
13.14	16.43	0.00	0.00	0.00	0.00	−3.43	−3.85	−3.39	−2.91
Manufactures									
16.56	20.70	0.00	0.00	0.00	0.00	−3.52	−3.96	−3.47	−2.99
3.35	4.18	0.00	0.00	0.00	0.00	−1.93	−2.16	−1.90	−1.64
10.44	13.04	0.00	0.00	0.00	0.00	−2.84	−3.19	−2.79	−2.41
4.36	5.45	0.00	0.00	0.00	0.00	−1.79	−2.01	−1.76	−1.52
Paper Products									
4.96	6.20	0.00	0.00	0.00	n.a.	n.a.	n.a.	n.a.	n.a.
4.71	5.89	0.00	0.00	0.00	n.a.	n.a.	n.a.	n.a.	n.a.
3.28	0.00	0.00	0.00	0.00	n.a.	n.a.	n.a.	n.a.	n.a.
18.26	22.82	0.00	0.00	0.00	0.80	−5.17	−5.91	−5.10	−4.27
7.49	9.37	0.00	0.00	0.00	0.00	−3.42	−3.84	−3.38	−2.95
2.62	3.27	0.00	0.00	0.00	0.00	−2.22	−2.49	−2.19	−1.88

TABLE 14.4 (CONT.)

Price-Level Component (percentage of price)

	1892	1893	1894	1895	1896	1897	1898	1899
Iron and Steel Products								
Bars	0.00	1.86	6.24	8.38	7.78	9.47	9.28	5.91
Wire	0.00	0.38	1.26	1.70	1.57	1.91	0.00	–3.07
Cable	0.00	0.12	0.39	0.52	0.49	0.59	0.58	0.37
Iron in ingots	0.00	1.29	4.34	5.82	5.41	6.58	0.00	–4.73
Iron wire for fences	0.00	0.43	1.44	1.93	1.79	2.18	2.14	1.36
Plows	0.00	0.17	0.58	0.78	0.72	0.88	0.86	0.55
Iron piping	0.00	0.32	1.07	1.43	1.33	1.62	1.59	1.01
Beams and joists	0.00	0.89	2.99	4.02	3.73	4.54	4.45	2.83
Manufactures	0.00	2.96	9.95	13.36	12.40	15.08	14.78	9.42
Sheets	0.00	1.54	5.17	6.94	6.44	7.84	7.68	4.89
Tinplate sheets	0.00	0.37	1.25	1.68	1.56	1.89	1.86	1.18

n.a.:   Insufficient data due to classification changes.

Source: See text.

modities that take 1892 as a base year, this component reduced the ad valorem rates increasingly up to 1896 as silver lost value in the international market; a moderate recovery in silver prices ameliorated the effect from 1897 to 1901. A base change in 1898 produced a slightly different pattern in the silver depreciation component, affecting cotton cord, steel wire, and iron in ingots. Beginning with increases in the ad valorem rates in 1899 and 1900, the silver depreciation component then decreased in 1901, responding to the sharp decline in silver prices in that year. This case illustrates that a temporary recovery of silver prices stopped its inflationary effect on import prices, thus increasing ad valorem rates. Another fall in 1901 renewed the downward effect, however.

The years from 1905 to 1909 present a completely different picture. By eliminating exchange rate fluctuations, the change in the monetary regime in 1905 stabilized import prices in domestic currency. Consequently, the silver depreciation component caused almost no variation in the ad valorem rates during the last four years of the period.

TABLE 14.4 (CONT.)

Price-Level Component (percentage of price)

1900	1901	1902	1903	1904	1905	1906	1907	1908	1909
Iron and Steel Products									
5.76	7.20	0.00	0.00	0.00	0.00	−1.69	−1.90	−1.67	−1.44
−3.41	−1.30	0.00	0.00	0.00	0.00	−3.55	−3.99	−3.50	−3.01
0.36	0.45	0.00	0.00	0.00	0.00	−0.19	−0.21	−0.18	−0.16
−5.26	−2.01	0.00	0.00	0.00	0.42	−2.69	−3.07	−2.69	−2.22
1.33	1.66	0.00	0.00	0.00	0.00	−1.57	−1.76	−1.55	−1.33
0.53	0.67	0.00	0.00	0.00	0.00	−0.36	−0.41	−0.36	−0.31
0.98	1.23	0.00	0.00	0.00	0.00	−1.28	−1.44	−1.27	−1.09
2.76	3.45	0.00	0.00	0.00	0.00	−1.78	−1.99	−1.75	−1.51
9.17	11.47	0.00	0.00	0.00	0.00	−4.14	−4.65	−4.09	−3.52
4.77	5.96	0.00	0.00	0.00	0.00	−3.49	−3.92	−3.45	−2.97
1.15	1.44	0.00	0.00	0.00	0.00	−0.61	−0.69	−0.61	−0.52

Relative-Price Component

Unlike the price-level and silver depreciation components, the relative-price component varies according to individual price movements and general price fluctuations. Common features can be found across the sample, however, revealing five different patterns. Three of them describe the relative-price component in the period from 1892 to 1901, whereas the other two patterns explain the behavior of the relative-price component after 1905 (see Table 14.6).

In the period from 1892 to 1901, the first pattern shows reduction in ad valorem tariff rates, indicating that individual prices, valued in silver, grew less than the general increase in import prices. The commodities that exhibit this pattern are beer, paper for cigarettes, three steel products (bars, ingots, and beams and joists), and nine cotton products. The latter consist of all cotton manufactures, yarns, and luxury textiles (see Table 14.6). The second pattern reflects the lack of a trend in individual prices, producing mixed results when compared with an ever-increasing price index. Table 14.6 shows a mixed con-

TABLE 14.5

Silver Depreciation Component (percentage of price)

	1892	1893	1894	1895	1896	1897	1898	1899
Cotton Products								
Yarns								
Cord	0.00	−20.81	−25.31	−21.47	−26.61	−36.97	0.00	0.75
Coarse thread	0.00	−19.87	−24.17	−20.50	−25.41	−35.31	−31.22	−30.55
Thread	0.00	−20.72	−25.19	−21.37	−26.49	−36.80	−32.54	−31.84
Wick	0.00	−6.09	−7.41	−6.28	−7.79	−10.82	−9.57	−9.36
Textiles								
Lace	0.00	−29.61	−36.02	−30.55	−37.87	−52.60	−46.52	−45.52
Cloth 1	0.00	−11.36	−13.82	−11.72	−14.53	−20.18	−17.85	−17.46
Cloth 2	0.00	−12.97	−15.77	−13.38	−16.58	−23.04	−20.37	−19.94
Cloth 3	0.00	−21.40	−26.03	−22.08	−27.37	−38.02	−33.62	−32.90
Cloth 4	0.00	−14.87	−18.09	−15.34	−19.01	−26.42	−23.36	−22.86
Cloth 5	0.00	−13.21	−16.07	−13.63	−16.89	−23.47	−20.75	−20.31
Cloth 6	0.00	−20.45	−24.87	−21.09	−26.14	−36.32	−32.12	−31.43
Manufactures								
Trimmings	0.00	−25.77	−31.34	−26.59	−32.95	−45.78	−40.48	−39.62
Elastic webbing	0.00	−5.21	−6.33	−5.37	−6.66	−9.25	−8.18	−8.01
Ready-made clothing	0.00	−16.24	−19.75	−16.75	−20.76	−28.84	−25.51	−24.96
Insertions	0.00	−6.78	−8.25	−6.99	−8.67	−12.04	−10.65	−10.42
Paper Products								
Newsprint	0.00	−7.72	−9.39	−7.97	−9.87	−13.72	−12.13	−11.87
Brown paper	0.00	−7.33	−8.92	−7.57	−9.38	−13.03	−11.52	−11.27
Paper for cigarettes	0.00	−5.10	−6.20	−5.26	−6.52	−9.06	−8.01	−7.84
Soap	0.00	−28.41	−34.56	−29.31	−36.33	−50.47	−44.63	−43.68
Beer	0.00	−11.66	−14.18	−12.03	−14.91	−20.71	−18.32	−17.93
Cement	0.00	−4.08	−4.96	−4.20	−5.21	−7.24	−6.40	−6.26

TABLE 14.5 (CONT.)

Silver Depreciation Component (percentage of price)

1900	1901	1902	1903	1904	1905	1906	1907	1908	1909
Cotton Products									
Yarns									
3.00	−5.90	0.00	0.00	0.00	1.89	1.91	1.54	1.38	1.71
−28.53	−36.51	0.00	0.00	0.00	0.00	0.01	−0.27	−0.40	−0.14
−29.74	−38.06	0.00	0.00	0.00	0.00	0.01	−0.24	−0.35	−0.12
−8.74	−11.19	0.00	0.00	0.00	0.00	0.01	−0.11	−0.17	−0.06
Textiles									
−42.51	−54.40	0.00	0.00	0.00	1.65	1.66	1.34	1.39	1.45
−16.31	−20.87	0.00	0.00	0.00	0.00	0.01	−0.33	−0.27	−0.21
−18.62	−23.82	0.00	0.00	0.00	0.00	0.02	−0.33	−0.27	−0.21
−30.72	−39.32	0.00	0.00	0.00	0.00	0.03	−0.70	−0.58	−0.46
−21.34	−27.32	0.00	0.00	0.00	0.00	0.02	−0.41	−0.34	−0.27
−18.96	−24.27	0.00	0.00	0.00	0.00	0.01	−0.32	−0.27	−0.21
−29.35	−37.56	0.00	0.00	0.00	0.00	0.02	−0.34	−0.28	−0.22
Manufactures									
−36.99	−47.34	0.00	0.00	0.00	0.00	0.02	−0.35	−0.51	−0.23
−7.47	−9.57	0.00	0.00	0.00	0.00	0.01	−0.19	−0.28	−0.12
−23.31	−29.83	0.00	0.00	0.00	0.00	0.01	−0.28	−0.41	−0.18
−9.73	−12.46	0.00	0.00	0.00	0.00	0.01	−0.18	−0.26	−0.11
Paper Products									
−11.08	−14.19	0.00	0.00	0.00	n.a.	n.a.	n.a.	n.a.	n.a.
−10.53	−13.47	0.00	0.00	0.00	n.a.	n.a.	n.a.	n.a.	n.a.
−7.32	0.00	0.00	0.00	0.00	n.a.	n.a.	n.a.	n.a.	n.a.
−40.78	−52.19	0.00	0.00	0.00	3.16	3.19	2.58	2.68	2.78
−16.74	−21.42	0.00	0.00	0.00	0.00	0.02	−0.34	−0.28	−0.17
−5.85	−7.49	0.00	0.00	0.00	0.00	0.01	−0.22	−0.18	−0.14

TABLE 14.5 (CONT.)

Silver Depreciation Component (percentage of price)

	1892	1893	1894	1895	1896	1897	1898	1899
Iron and Steel Products								
Bars	0.00	−8.96	−10.89	−9.24	−11.45	−15.91	−14.07	−13.77
Wire	0.00	−1.81	−2.20	−1.87	−2.32	−3.22	0.00	0.34
Cable	0.00	−0.56	−0.68	−0.58	−0.72	−0.99	−0.88	−0.86
Iron in ingots	0.00	−6.22	−7.57	−6.42	−7.96	−11.06	0.00	0.52
Iron wire for fences	0.00	−2.06	−2.51	−2.13	−2.64	−3.67	−3.24	−3.17
Plows	0.00	−0.83	−1.01	−0.86	−1.06	−1.48	−1.31	−1.28
Iron piping	0.00	−1.53	−1.86	−1.58	−1.96	−2.72	−2.41	−2.35
Beams and joists	0.00	−4.30	−5.22	−4.43	−5.49	−7.63	−6.75	−6.60
Manufactures	0.00	−14.27	−17.36	−14.72	−18.25	−25.35	−22.42	−21.94
Sheets	0.00	−7.42	−9.02	−7.65	−9.48	−13.18	−11.65	−11.40
Tinplate sheets	0.00	−1.79	−2.18	−1.85	−2.29	−3.18	−2.82	−2.76

n.a.:   Insufficient data due to classification changes.

Source: See text.

tribution of the relative-price component to ad valorem rates for cotton cord, cloths 1 and 2, newsprint and brown paper, and most iron and steel products.

The third pattern, including cloth 3, cement, plows, iron piping, and soap, reveals that the decreasing tendency of individual prices dominated the upward movement of the import price index, increasing ad valorem rates for the 1890s.[22] The relative-price effect coupled with increases stemming from the price-level component worked to counterbalance ad valorem rate reductions provoked by the depreciation effect. Yet, like other patterns described here, the final outcome in the ad valorem tariff depended on the combination of magnitudes of these effects. Specifically, for cement and cloth 3 the interaction of specific tariffs and prices yielded a positive effect in their ad valorem rates, as shown in the preceding section.

A shift in the behavior of the relative-price component took place in the years that followed the monetary reform. In the first pattern exhibited after 1905, the relative-price component caused rises in the ad valorem rates of 13 commodities: cement, soap, 5 iron and steel products (cable, fences, bars, ingots, and wire), and 6 cotton goods (wick, thread, lace, trimmings, elastic webbing, and cotton cord). As of the price-level component and the silver depreciation component significantly reduced their influence on the ad val-

TABLE 14.5 (CONT.)

Silver Depreciation Component (percentage of price)

1900	1901	1902	1903	1904	1905	1906	1907	1908	1909
Iron and Steel Products									
-12.86	-16.46	0.00	0.00	0.00	0.00	0.01	-0.17	-0.14	-0.11
1.36	-2.67	0.00	0.00	0.00	0.00	0.02	-0.35	-0.29	-0.23
-0.80	-1.03	0.00	0.00	0.00	0.00	0.00	-0.02	-0.02	-0.01
2.10	-4.12	0.00	0.00	0.00	1.64	1.66	1.34	1.39	1.45
-2.96	-3.79	0.00	0.00	0.00	0.00	0.01	-0.15	-0.13	-0.10
-1.19	-1.53	0.00	0.00	0.00	0.00	0.00	-0.04	-0.03	-0.02
-2.20	-2.81	0.00	0.00	0.00	0.00	0.01	-0.13	-0.10	-0.08
-6.17	-7.89	0.00	0.00	0.00	0.00	0.01	-0.17	-0.14	-0.11
-20.49	-26.22	0.00	0.00	0.00	0.00	0.02	-0.41	-0.34	-0.27
-10.65	-13.63	0.00	0.00	0.00	0.00	0.02	-0.34	-0.28	-0.22
-2.57	-3.29	0.00	0.00	0.00	0.00	0.00	-0.06	-0.05	-0.04

orem tariff, the increases arising from the relative-price component reversed the downward movement of the ad valorem tariff. A second pattern for 1906–1909 exhibited a mix of increases and reductions in the ad valorem tariff. This pattern also features goods from the cotton industry (all textiles, insertions, ready-made clothing, and coarse thread) and the iron and steel industry (sheets, beams and joists, piping, plows, tinplate sheets, and manufactures).

FINAL REMARKS

During the last two decades of the Porfirian era, tariffs diminished in importance as a source of protection for domestic producers. In the first place, the patterns found in my sample highlight a declining trend in ad valorem tariff values up until 1905, provoked in large part by the inflexibility of legislative tariffs and the deteriorating effect of silver depreciation. Second, the relative stability of ad valorem rates after 1905 reveals how tariffs gained importance as policy instruments of protection when the effect of nontariff barriers, mainly silver depreciation, came to an end with the monetary reform.

Falling ad valorem tariff rates imply that domestic products lost the advantages provided by tariff barriers. Yet there is little evidence that indicates a

TABLE 14.6

Relative-Price Component (percentage of price)

	1892	1893	1894	1895	1896	1897	1898	1899
Cotton Products								
Yarns								
Cord	0.00	3.49	37.83	−17.92	−10.20	9.41	0.00	11.25
Coarse thread	0.00	−11.28	−16.72	1.84	−7.72	−30.04	−22.94	−30.07
Thread	0.00	−10.72	−44.08	−48.91	−43.43	−27.61	−2.07	−23.67
Wick	0.00	−13.44	−14.53	−14.94	−15.04	−14.51	−13.96	−14.29
Textiles								
Lace	0.00	−29.61	−36.02	−30.55	−37.87	−52.60	−46.52	−45.52
Cloth 1	0.00	0.14	−4.05	8.17	2.61	7.11	4.36	−0.84
Cloth 2	0.00	−9.49	−5.92	−9.28	7.59	5.94	−11.55	−9.41
Cloth 3	0.00	10.28	15.49	8.62	20.41	29.07	23.55	27.87
Cloth 4	0.00	−0.27	−14.49	−20.89	−31.51	−22.60	−25.97	−14.05
Cloth 5	0.00	−6.30	−9.96	−11.80	−8.34	−15.01	−8.85	−7.85
Cloth 6	0.00	−60.24	−92.46	−66.09	−73.44	−8.93	−84.57	−58.35
Manufactures								
Trimmings	0.00	−36.33	−71.05	−73.49	−59.12	−70.55	−64.38	−61.52
Elastic webbing	0.00	−2.58	−6.31	−4.79	−5.00	−5.58	−4.90	−2.47
Ready-made clothing	0.00	−10.45	−9.30	−3.92	27.89	−16.57	−25.95	−25.86
Insertions	0.00	−3.96	−9.94	−14.94	−10.60	−8.14	−12.36	−13.85
Paper Products								
Newsprint	0.00	4.29	−11.74	2.56	20.48	12.60	2.97	14.47
Brown paper	0.00	1.83	−2.50	0.48	−1.20	0.21	1.57	5.64
Paper for cigarettes	0.00	−1.82	−3.36	−2.81	−3.53	−4.40	−4.27	−4.08
Soap	0.00	6.70	13.96	116.32	136.99	21.70	9.93	11.68
Beer	0.00	−2.07	−6.27	−10.57	−12.15	−11.07	−14.48	−11.47
Cement	0.00	22.74	11.18	8.36	1.32	9.38	4.76	4.36

TABLE 14.6 (CONT.)

Relative-Price Component (percentage of price)

1900	1901	1902	1903	1904	1905	1906	1907	1908	1909
Cotton Products									
Yarns									
6.13	3.14	0.00	0.00	0.00	17.13	20.04	9.61	18.20	14.75
−30.82	−18.16	0.00	0.00	0.00	0.00	−5.32	−1.59	−7.33	−6.33
−44.70	−41.22	0.00	0.00	0.00	0.00	12.62	10.14	11.57	9.32
−14.73	−14.64	0.00	0.00	0.00	0.00	4.17	2.34	2.53	1.53
Textiles									
−42.51	−54.40	0.00	0.00	0.00	1.65	1.66	1.34	1.39	1.45
−6.87	−2.85	0.00	0.00	0.00	0.00	−1.07	0.12	5.88	8.81
−15.44	−15.48	0.00	0.00	0.00	0.00	−1.38	−3.38	−0.69	4.30
14.87	22.53	0.00	0.00	0.00	0.00	2.93	−2.59	3.66	8.00
−26.73	−23.34	0.00	0.00	0.00	0.00	−3.13	−2.95	9.81	14.76
−14.94	−17.09	0.00	0.00	0.00	0.00	0.90	−1.09	2.98	3.94
−61.52	−57.52	0.00	0.00	0.00	0.00	3.64	−6.70	−9.59	−24.36
Manufactures									
−72.22	−71.59	0.00	0.00	0.00	0.00	1.54	2.77	1.26	0.84
−1.26	−2.00	0.00	0.00	0.00	0.00	2.87	1.65	0.36	0.10
−22.29	−16.77	0.00	0.00	0.00	0.00	1.96	−0.08	−0.35	−1.65
−13.42	−12.54	0.00	0.00	0.00	0.00	−0.26	−3.10	0.02	−0.60
Paper Products									
6.61	−6.53	0.00	0.00	0.00	n.a.	n.a.	n.a.	n.a.	n.a.
1.14	1.45	0.00	0.00	0.00	n.a.	n.a.	n.a.	n.a.	n.a.
−3.86	0.00	0.00	0.00	0.00	n.a.	n.a.	n.a.	n.a.	n.a.
−2.04	−0.69	0.00	0.00	0.00	−18.91	1.28	−9.53	−8.68	−13.36
−11.17	−14.63	0.00	0.00	0.00	0.00	3.58	4.03	1.93	0.05
5.24	4.39	0.00	0.00	0.00	0.00	0.08	0.45	1.53	2.97

TABLE 14.6 (CONT.)

Relative-Price Component (percentage of price)

	1892	1893	1894	1895	1896	1897	1898	1899
Iron and Steel Products								
Bars	0.00	−6.65	−15.19	−6.85	−13.06	−10.85	−9.27	−14.54
Wire	0.00	−3.17	−0.03	−3.93	1.87	1.35	0.00	−5.67
Cable	0.00	−0.47	−0.26	−0.17	−0.11	0.16	0.07	−0.07
Iron in ingots	0.00	15.90	−8.15	−1.25	−0.13	5.75	0.00	−18.69
Iron wire for fences	0.00	0.51	0.47	0.32	2.21	1.34	0.54	−0.79
Plows	0.00	−0.06	0.11	0.37	−0.21	0.25	0.66	0.87
Iron piping	0.00	0.96	0.18	0.66	2.85	1.63	0.77	0.36
Beams and joists	0.00	−9.50	−1.57	−5.67	−6.69	−9.36	−8.46	−9.16
Iron manufactures	0.00	10.44	−5.96	42.01	4.77	3.88	3.30	−8.08
Sheets	0.00	−3.98	6.07	−2.74	−2.68	−1.26	−7.64	−7.87
Tinplate sheets	0.00	−0.34	−0.76	0.31	1.23	0.83	−0.42	−1.09

n.a.: Insufficient data due to classification changes.

Source: See text.

disappearance of domestic industrial production. Rather, the 1890s have been considered years of industrial expansion, particularly for the products included in the sample. With tariffs diminishing their role in fostering industrialization, there must have been other forces at work that enabled domestic producers to endure reductions in nominal tariff protection. Evidence points to nontariff factors capable of providing the required protection to nascent Mexican industries. Specifically, silver depreciation seems to have been a crucial factor in providing such protection. By increasing import prices in domestic currency, depreciation erected a barrier favoring domestic producers, whose prices tended to be higher than world prices. Contemporaries contended that this protection was temporary since domestic inflation would compensate for any beneficial effect to producers.[23] More recently, Zabludowsky concluded that, at least in the short run, silver depreciation indeed worked as a barrier against foreign competition, thus widening the margin between prices of domestically produced goods and import prices in domestic currency.[24]

Once exchange rate fluctuations came to an end, Mexican producers lost one important source of nontariff protection. As a consequence, in the last years of the Porfiriato, tariffs recovered their significance as an instrument of industrial promotion, a role they had played for a number of years during the nineteenth century.[25] This did not imply that domestic producers benefited from the same or higher levels of protection; however, such protection

TABLE 14.6 (CONT.)

Relative-Price Component (percentage of price)

1900	1901	1902	1903	1904	1905	1906	1907	1908	1909
Iron and Steel Products									
−18.42	−23.45	0.00	0.00	0.00	0.00	6.02	2.8	7.31	9.28
−2.86	0.61	0.00	0.00	0.00	0.00	−1.14	3.14	6.36	7.47
−1.40	−0.16	0.00	0.00	0.00	0.00	0.25	0.26	0.42	0.32
−18.53	−10.47	0.00	0.00	0.00	−9.71	−9.34	−8.59	−5.97	−1.63
−0.89	−1.05	0.00	0.00	0.00	0.00	0.25	0.05	0.67	0.58
0.68	0.35	0.00	0.00	0.00	0.00	−0.32	−0.08	0.00	0.49
0.21	−0.44	0.00	0.00	0.00	0.00	0.80	−0.15	−1.24	3.35
−7.81	−9.44	0.00	0.00	0.00	0.00	−1.25	−0.10	4.47	−1.23
−7.25	−5.71	0.00	0.00	0.00	0.00	1.60	−5.62	8.21	−1.23
−8.84	−3.67	0.00	0.00	0.00	0.00	−1.49	−0.16	5.24	7.62
0.20	−0.55	0.00	0.00	0.00	0.00	−0.84	−0.90	−0.20	0.08

was granted on an individual basis. A fundamental change, then, came in conjunction with the renewed strength of tariff policy: It offered room for negotiation. If industrialists needed more protection, they would have to negotiate tariff increases with the Porfirian administration.

ACKNOWLEDGMENTS

I would like to thank participants in the conference "Latin American and the World Economy in the 19th and 20th Centuries: Explorations in Quantitative History" for their comments. Special thanks to John Coatsworth, Aurora Gómez-Galavarriato, Hilary Burger, and Gerardo Esquivel for valuable comments and suggestions on earlier versions. All errors are, of course, my own.

The author is a Ph.D. candidate in history at Harvard University. Research support was generously provided by the Mellon Fellowships in Latin American History, and the David Rockefeller Center for Latin American Studies at Harvard University.

NOTES

1. Fernando Rosenzweig's classic work on the Porfirian economy argues that tariffs secured markets for domestic producers in the early days of the Porfirian administration, and that silver depreciation became another significant source of protection. See Rosenzweig (1985), p. 474ff.

2. Bulmer-Thomas (1994), p. 110; Salvucci (1991), p. 722; Haber (1989), p. 38.

3. Beatty (1996).

4. See México, Secretaría de Hacienda y Crédito Público (1903).

5. Exchange rates were set as follows: 1 US dollar = 1 peso; 1 pound sterling = 5 pesos; 1 French franc = 0.20 pesos; 1 German mark = 0.25 pesos.

6. Note that this same procedure was used to report import prices in *Estadísticas Económicas del Porfiriato*. The exchange rate I used is the same one used in that publication to convert dollars to silver pesos. See Colegio de México (1960), p. 36.

7. Crucini (1994).

8. Crucini's decomposition follows:

$$\tau_\pi = \left[\tau_{js} + \frac{\omega_{js}}{P_{js-1}} \right] + \left[\frac{\omega_{js}}{P_{js-1}} \left\{ \frac{P_s}{P_t} - 1 \right\} \right] + \left[\frac{\omega_{js}}{P_{js-1}} \left\{ \frac{P_{js-1}}{P_{jt}} - \frac{P_s}{P_t} \right\} \right]$$

where τ_{jt} is the ad valorem tariff and ω_{js} is the specific duty, index j indicates the commodity, and index s is the revision period.

9. I used gold and silver price indexes from *Estadísticas Económicas del Porfiriato*. These indexes are perfectly comparable since they are based on the same commodity set and weights. See Colegio de México (1960), pp. 1–13.

10. My definition differs from Crucini's beyond the addition of the silver depreciation component. I omitted the combined duty expression in Equation (1) because Mexican tariff rates were limited to specific rates. In Equation (2) I used current prices instead of lagged prices because revisions usually took effect within the same year. See Crucini (1994), p. 734.

11. Table 14.1 presents a complete description of each commodity. To facilitate description, I use shorter terms when referring to them. In the case of cotton textiles, I have adopted the terms cloth 1 through cloth 6, indicating three varieties of cotton fabrics differentiated by thread counts in warp and woof, such that cloths 1 and 2 are coarse fabrics, cloths 3 and 4 are low- to medium-quality colored fabrics, and cloths 5 and 6 are luxury fabrics.

12. In addition to the indexation change, the specific tariff on iron manufactures increased from 0.01 to 0.02 pesos per kilo.

13. The products included are wire for fences, piping, beams and joists, sheets, and plows.

14. U.S. Department of Commerce and Labor (1905), p. 873.

15. Strictly speaking, only lace and soap had the same specific tariff throughout the period. Other commodities, however, experienced only a temporary tariff change and can thus be included in the group with constant tariffs: Cotton cord changed its tariff in 1898, remaining constant ever since; iron manufactures and beams and joists reduced their tariff in 1904, only to return to their former tariff in 1905; and tinplate in sheets also returned to its initial tariff in 1905 after increasing it in 1904.

16. Totaling 23 commodities, this group includes all 15 cotton products, 4 iron and steel products (steel in bars, cable, manufactures, and tinplate sheets), newsprint, brown paper, soap, and beer.

17. Beatty reached a similar conclusion working on a comparison of the 1891 schedule and the reforms of 1905. For a different set of commodities, he found an average decline ranging from 50% to 75%. See Beatty (1996), p. 11.

18. All weighted averages use 1892 dutiable import shares as weights.

19. The fact that three major cement firms were founded between 1906 and 1909 indicates the existence of favorable circumstances, including those incentives provided by tariffs.

20. Despite the pronounced downward trend in silver prices, the instability of the exchange rate rather than the fall in prices was often cited as one of the main reasons to abandon the silver standard. See Casasús (1896) and Limantour (1965), chap. 4.

21. For a discussion of the effects of silver depreciation on domestic inflation, see Zabludowsky (1984), pp. 129–181.

22. I have included plows and soap in this group despite their featuring a reduction in ad valorem tariff rates for two years because their behavior is closer to the third pattern than to the second pattern described earlier (see Table 14.6).

23. See Gurza (1903), p. 67.

24. Zabludowsky (1984).

25. See Salvucci (1991) and Bernecker (1992), chap. 5.

REFERENCES

Beatty, Edward N. "The Political Basis of Industrialization in Mexico Before 1911." Paper presented at the Conference on Governance in Nineteenth-Century Latin America, Harvard University, Cambridge, Massachusetts, November 1996.

Bernecker, Walther. *De agiotistas y empresarios. En torno de la temprana industrialización mexicana (siglo XIX)*. Mexico: Universidad Panamericana, 1992.

Bulmer-Thomas, Victor. *The Economic History of Latin America since Independence.* New York: Cambridge University Press, 1994.

Casasús, Joaquín D. *La cuestión de la plata en México.* Mexico: Tipografía de la Oficina Impresora del Timbre, 1896.

Colegio de México. *Estadísticas económicas del Porfiriato: Comercio exterior de México 1877– 1911.* Mexico: El Colegio de México, 1960.

Crucini, Mario. "Sources of Variation in Real Tariff Rates: The United States, 1900–1940." *American Economic Review* 84 (1994): 732–743.

Gurza, Jaime. "Apuntes sobre la cuestión de la plata en México." In *Datos para el estudio de la cuestión monetaria en México.* Mexico: Tipografía de la Oficina Impresora de Estampillas, 1903.

Haber, Stephen. *Industry and Underdevelopment: The Industrialization of Mexico, 1890–1940.* Stanford, CA: Stanford University Press, 1989.

Limantour, José Y. *Apuntes de mi vida pública.* Mexico: Porrúa, 1965.

Mexico. Secretaría de Hacienda y Crédito Público. *Memoria 1902–1903.* Mexico: Imprenta del Gobierno, 1903.

Mexico. Secretaría de Hacienda y Crédito Público. *Estadística fiscal.* Mexico: Imprenta del Gobierno, various years.

Rosenzweig, Fernando. "La industria." In *Historia moderna de México.* 1965. Reprint, Mexico: Hermes, 1985.

Salvucci, Richard. "The Origins and Progress of US-Mexican Trade, 1825–1884: 'Hoc opus, hic labor est.'" *Hispanic American Historical Review* 71, no. 4 (1991): 697–735.

Zabludowsky, Jaime Enrique. "Money, Foreign Indebtedness and Export Performance in Porfirist Mexico." Ph.D. dissertation, Yale University, 1984.

U.S. Department of Commerce and Labor, Bureau of Statistics. *Customs Tariff of the Republic of Mexico.* Washington, DC: Government Printing Office, 1905.

15

Latin America during the Interwar Period: The Rise and Fall of the Gold Standard in Argentina, Brazil, and Mexico

Daniel Díaz Fuentes
University of Cantabria, Spain

This chapter deals with the diverse exchange rate policies of the three largest Latin American countries, Argentina, Brazil, and Mexico, during the interwar period and, specifically, during the Great Depression. Inheritance of the classic gold standard is a key feature of this period. I will consider the commitment of these Latin American countries to restoring the standard, their reasons for doing so, and how their exchange rates evolved throughout the period.

The chapter is organized in six parts. The first section reviews the historical significance of the interwar period for the Latin American countries and considers the importance of the shift of the exchange rate regimes in their paths of development. The second section contains a synthesis of the evolution of the gold standard in Latin America and presents the main inquiries that are considered in the rest of the paper. The next three sections examine the exchange rate experience in the three case studies, namely, Argentina, Brazil, and Mexico, respectively, in particular in regard to the inquiries outlined. Finally, a comparative analysis allows conclusions to be drawn.

AN OVERVIEW OF THE INTERWAR PERIOD: WAS THE GREAT DEPRESSION THE REAL TURNING POINT?

The economic importance of the Great Depression has been repeatedly pointed out by key economists and does not demand more justification here.

However, there are some major differences in the evolution of the Latin American countries in comparison with the more developed countries that have not been fully analyzed in the literature.

Angus Maddison defined the periodization of the world economy with the following phases: "Liberal" (1820–1913), "Beggar-Thy-Neighbour" (1913–1948), "Golden Age" (1948–1973), and "Phase of Cautious Objectives" (1973 and onward). In the case of Latin American economies, however, the periodization is partially different. Diverse authors[1] have distinguished the following periods: a first phase, lasting from the mid-nineteenth century until the Great Depression, when the countries followed export-led growth models and were becoming increasingly integrated with the international trade and financial system; a second phase, from the Great Depression to the beginning of the 1980s, when these countries adopted inward-looking growth models that applied policies of industrialization by import substitution; and a third phase, marked by the debt crisis of the 1980s, the so-called lost decade, which was a prelude to a return to a phase of outward-looking growth as a result of policies of liberalization, privatization, and integration with external financial markets.[2] The fact that the periodization of Latin America differs from Maddison's classic definition does not imply that the periodizations are antagonistic, since Latin American countries did not suffer in such a direct way some of the effects of the world wars in comparison with Europe and Japan. For Latin America, the Great Depression was economically more significant than the world wars.

The Great Depression was neither an isolated historical episode nor a simple economic discontinuity. From at least the beginning of the First World War there were symptoms that made possible the crisis of the 1930s.[3] In the same way, some elements in the political economy of the Great Depression can help to explain why there was a second war. Economic policymakers in Argentina and Brazil considered the First World War to be a transitory problem. The war's effects were contradictory: International trade and financial restrictions had a negative effect on their export-led growth models, but their productive structures did not change significantly. Once the conflict had come to an end, the aim was to return to the normality of the nineteenth century. In the case of Mexico, it was the Revolution more than the First World War that most affected the economy; however, postrevolutionary economic policies consisted of many elements of orthodox policies similar to those pursued during the Porfiriato, such as the effort to achieve the rule of the gold standard and a balanced budget.

During the 1920s, efforts to return to the liberal normality of the nineteenth century were frustrated. This failure was a result of many factors, but particularly important obstacles for the periphery were fluctuations in the prices of their exports, the terms of trade, and modifications in the practices of major financial centers as a result of the new position of the United States as creditor and the United Kingdom as debtor, which defined a different conditionality in the monetary and fiscal stability of the Latin American economies.[4]

All three Latin American countries could be defined as primary exporters, but there were notable differences in the products exported.[5] They were not mono-exporters, but the evolution of the different commodities defined by the international "lottery of prices"[6] had different consequences for each economy; their individual relations with their main trading partners defined the restrictions of "bilateral trade" when the multilateral payment system collapsed.[7] After the Great Depression, Brazil had a trade surplus with the United States and a deficit with the United Kingdom, but because the United States had a trade surplus with the United Kingdom, the financial flow could compensate the overall balance. The opposite was true in the case of Argentina: It had a trade surplus with the United Kingdom and a deficit with the United States, but because the United States had a surplus with the United Kingdom, the British financial flow to Argentina did not close the triangular relation.[8]

For the Latin American economies, the Great Depression was clearly an imported phenomenon that affected them in four main ways:

1. Financial restrictions as a result of the stringent U.S. monetary policy adopted in June 1928 provoked capital flight and loss of reserves, which obliged countries to leave the gold standard.
2. International trade contracted and protectionism increased.
3. The terms of trade deteriorated and primary commodity prices were weak.
4. General deflation increased the burden of foreign debt.

The importance of the shift in the policy of the United States as an initial impulse is not incompatible with the view of a shared causation in the crisis.[9] Because of the dependence of Argentina and Brazil on capital imports, their adherence to the gold standard required drastic restrictive policies. It is not coincidental that countries such as Argentina, Australia, and Brazil were some of the more important receivers of foreign capital during the 1920s and were among the first to enter into crisis and to abandon the gold standard.

The trade crisis had two harmful direct results: Production fell and deterioration in the terms of trade brought about a loss of income. Evaluation of the impact of both factors for all countries shows that the consequences for their income was more important than the consequences for their production.[10] However, in all cases, the fall in income was less dramatic than in the United States and Canada.

Diverse studies of the consequences of the Great Depression for the Latin American periphery have coincided in presenting it as a turning point in their economic policies and patterns of growth. This change in policies was more important for the larger regional economies such as Argentina, Brazil, and Mexico than for the smaller ones. Broadly speaking, the period has been characterized as a change from passive to reactive policies[11] or from the orthodoxy of the gold standard and balanced budgets to the heterodoxy associated with Keynesianism. Furthermore, some authors consider that the modification of exchange rate policies encouraged the countries to abandon a model of outward-looking growth and to adopt one of import substitution industrialization (ISI).[12]

A deeper understanding of the role of economic policy in the crisis and recovery of the 1930s requires an integrated analysis of both economic policies and their effects. Indeed, the concept of economic policy is a multifaceted one. The policy instruments available to each government could be classified as internal and external. Internal economic measures included monetary expansion and fiscal stimulus, which were constrained by the rules of the game of the gold standard (monetary restriction and a balanced budget). External economic policies included trade measures such as tariff protection, quantitative restrictions, preferences, and discriminatory agreements, and exchange rate measures such as currency depreciation or exchange control.[13]

The shifts in the exchange rate regime in particular, and the international monetary regimes in general, have received widespread attention.[14] The analysis of balance of payment adjustments, based on modified and extended versions of the Mundell-Fleming model, has formed the basis for the discussion of stabilization policies.[15] One of the main conclusions from this model is that the effectiveness of monetary and fiscal policies depends on both capital mobility and the exchange rate regime.

The external policies for both trade and exchange rates adopted in the 1930s are usually described as of the beggar-thy-neighbor type. Eichengreen and Sachs offered a different interpretation of the impact of the changes in exchange rate policies based on a sample of 10 European countries, which reconsidered the idea that depreciation was necessarily a pernicious policy.[16] Although Campa, basing his work on a sample of 10 Latin American countries, generalized the results of Eichengreen and Sachs, he suggested there were positive implications of the depreciation for industrial production and export volume.[17] Based on this evidence, the author concluded that Latin American countries were not structurally constrained in the interwar period, and that these "reactive policies" during the 1930s led them to select a subsequent inward-oriented path of development based on ISI. Considering the diversity of internal and external policies, is it then an oversimplification to point to exchange rate policies as the main factor that explains the shift of growth strategies in Latin America?

THE GOLD STANDARD IN THE INTERWAR PERIOD

The system of the gold standard is an important reference point because all succeeding agreements on fixed exchange rate systems have been inspired by its advantages.[18] In theory, the gold standard rule (fixing the prices of currencies in terms of gold) would limit monetary expansion in the international economy and create stability in price levels. In practice, however, the objective of full employment was subordinated to external objectives.[19]

The international monetary system restored in the 1920s differed from the classic gold standard of 1870–1914. During the First World War, many governments, in particular those of belligerent countries, were forced into inconvertible currency. As happened in previous times of war, the governments financed part of their military expenses by borrowing from their banks, which led to monetary expansion and inflation.[20] Thus, in the early 1920s, price levels were higher in these countries. Some countries continued a policy of monetary expansion to finance reconstruction, which was followed by inflation and hyperinflation.

After the First World War there was an aspiration to return to the rules of the game of the gold standard (Genoa Conference of 1922). But the war had brought about an accumulation of a significant proportion of the world's gold reserves in the hands of the new largest creditor. The United States rapidly restored the gold standard in June 1919, but the United Kingdom delayed restoring it at the prewar parity until April 1925. Although British price levels had been falling since the end of the war, they were still higher than before the conflict began.[21] This was the main reason that Keynes criticized Britain's return to the old parity.[22]

Perceiving that world gold reserves were insufficient after the war, the League of Nations called for the adoption of a "gold exchange standard," in which countries, including those of Latin America, could hold large countries' currencies, such as sterling.[23] Policymakers in Argentina, Brazil, and Mexico belatedly adopted the gold standard (Brazil in December 1926, Mexico in February

1927, and Argentina in August 1927), but their membership was inspired more by circumstance than by conviction. For Brazil and Argentina, this was a way to facilitate access to foreign finance,[24] whereas for Mexico it was the only way to stabilize the discredited postrevolutionary monetary system.

The exchange parity adjustments dominated postwar economic policy debates in many countries. According to some analysts, the maintenance of a fixed parity served as a time-consistent credible-commitment mechanism.[25] Other authors argue that the nations that made the most concerted efforts to restore their prewar parities in the 1920s showed the least hesitation to devalue in the 1930s.[26] The first line of inquiry is the degree of commitment exhibited by the Latin American countries to returning to the old gold parities in the 1920s. To answer this, it will be necessary to analyze the history of the exchange rate systems of each country. Moreover, if such a commitment existed, how did this affect the decision to delay devaluation in the 1930s?

The role of foreign policy advisers in the restoration of the gold standard and the creation of some central banks in the Andean region has been examined by Drake.[27] A second interesting inquiry is the role of foreign advisers in the restoration of the gold standard and the creation of monetary institutions in the three countries under consideration. On the face of it, since Mexico received a Kemmerer mission in 1917 and created a central bank in 1925,[28] and Brazil and Argentina received a British Niemeyer mission in 1931 and 1933, respectively, it would appear that Drake's definition of "money doctoring" is also relevant here.[29] In addition, I examine to what extent policymakers in these countries adopted policies according to their own convictions, or whether they were pushed into decisions against their convictions by force of circumstance.

Convertibility is associated with institutional monetary and financial mechanisms that link different national currencies. Each country's legal tender is accepted at par, or very close to par, by residents of other countries. Under the gold standard, convertibility was bypassed through the material equivalence of currencies in terms of their gold content. Bank money did not necessarily create an additional convertibility problem, but when an issue of notes was granted "legal tender" status, a provision had to be enacted to specify convertibility.[30]

Nineteenth-century experience suggests that convertibility could be defined as an institutional framework. In this system a currency became inconvertible de facto or de jure when the issuing institution ceased to honor its redemption commitment or suspended it by law. This did not mean, however, that currency holders would be unable to convert it into gold or foreign currencies, since they could usually continue to do so through the market. In this sense, inconvertibility could be considered as exchange rate flexibility. With the emergence of bilateralism after the 1930s, the meaning of the term *inconvertibility* changed.

The exchange rate system in the interwar period may be divided into four periods of three regimes: freely floating exchange rates (1920–1925),[31] fixed rates (1926–1931),[32] floating exchange rates again (1931–1933), and managed floating (remainder of the 1930s). As always, the division into periods may seem arbitrary.[33] Bearing these phases in mind, a third line of inquiry is the timing and stability or volatility of the exchange rates, and the extent of depreciation in Argentina, Brazil, and Mexico.

Figure 15.1 summarizes the evolution of exchange rates for Argentina, Brazil, and Mexico, obtained from the League of Nations.[34] These exchange rates are normalized indexes and show the values of each currency in the New York international market in terms of the legal gold parities of each country.[35] The indexes show high fluctuations in Brazil and Argentina and a stable evolution in Mexico prior to the restoration of the gold standard. In the same period, while the Brazilian index fluctuates significantly above and below a new gold parity, the Argentine index reaches a maximum in the restored old gold parity. Meanwhile, the Mexican index follows a consistent path before and after the establishment of a new parity; this stability lasted longer than in the other two countries. Argentina and Brazil, both of which belonged to the group that abandoned the gold standard first, suffered intense devaluations from the end of 1929 to the middle of 1931.

When the United Kingdom abandoned the gold standard in 1931, all three Latin American countries experienced a second round of depreciation. During the next two years, Argentina and Brazil applied exchange controls, although Argentina more successfully established the exchange rate than Brazil. Meanwhile, Mexico suffered a severe depreciation in the floating system. The last round of devaluation was brought about by the United States' suspension of the gold standard in March 1933. The managed floating system applied until the end of the gold standard seems to have been more effective in the stabilization of the exchange rate.

THE RETURN TO THE ARGENTINE "LOST PARADISE"?

The evolution of the exchange rate in Argentina after the passing of the Conversion Law of 1899 would seem erratic to observers.[36] First, Argentina adhered to the gold standard for 14 years between 1899 and 1913. This was followed by 13 years of inconvertibility until 1927. The gold standard was then reestablished for 2 more years until 1929, after which there followed another 2 years of inconvertibility. Finally, after 1931, various types of exchange control were in operation. As regards its monetary institutions, Argentina did not create a central bank with the aim of entering the gold standard prior to the Great Depression.[37]

The Conversion Law of 1899 was made possible by a period of favorable balances of payments. The law stated that the Caja de Conversión was obliged to exchange gold for paper and vice versa at the gold premium then ruling in the market (2.27 pesos per 1 gold peso) and that a redemption fund would be created.[38] On 5 November 1891, Congress created a gold peso of 1,451.61 milligrams fine gold, which was equal to a mint par of US $0.965 per gold peso; this parity was significant because it was to last longer than any other and would be established again in 1927.

During the decade preceding the First World War, foreign investment, the volume and value of exports, and the foreign debt all increased. The outbreak of hostilities brought about a restriction in capital flows, and as a result, there was a net repayment of bank loans.[39] Throughout the war period, gold payments and specie exports were indefinitely suspended. However, the authorities were determined to avoid any fundamental change in the 1899 law, and they also wanted to prevent any decrease in note circulation. During the conflict the peso followed two different trends. Until 1916, restrictions on foreign trade and the difficulties encountered in obtaining and renewing foreign loans caused a slow appreciation of the peso against the inconvertible European currencies and the depreciation in 1915 with respect to the dollar, which was the only important gold currency. From the end of 1916 through the next three years, the peso was at a premium over the currencies of every major country.

As in many other countries, the exchange parity adjustments dominated the economic controversies of the postwar years. From 1920 to the third quarter of 1924, the peso was lowered to its prewar gold parity in two phases (see Figure 15.1). Between 1921 and the last quarter of 1922, it ameliorated its differential, reaching a value around 10% below its gold parity. In the second period, the differential increased, and reached over 30% in the second quarter of 1924. In part, these trends were a consequence of the fiscal deficit, which was financed by external borrowing. This borrowing was facilitated by the availability of external credit due to financial conditions, particularly in New York, which made it possible to avoid a further depreciation of the peso.

In 1921, some groups favored an immediate and complete return to conversion on the pre-1914 basis. Others believed that redundant paper money had been responsible for the depreciation, and they advocated limited redemption.

FIGURE 15.1 NORMALIZED EXCHANGE RATES, 1920–1936 (VALUE OF CURRENCY IS SHOWN AS A PERCENTAGE OF ITS GOLD PARITY)

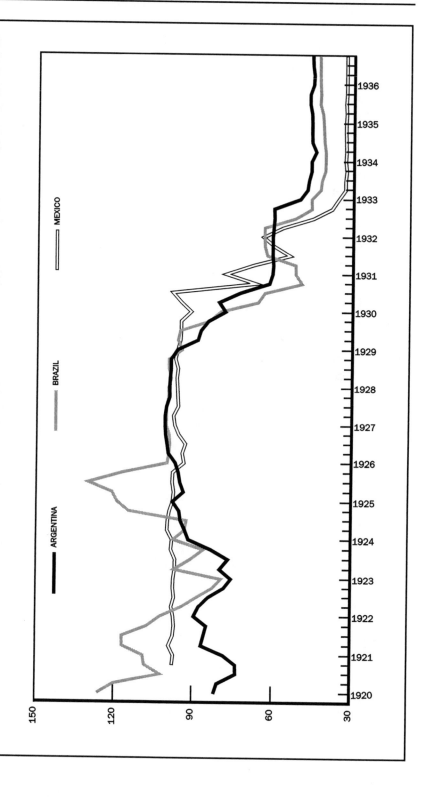

A third group, which represented the interests of importers, wished to differentiate between types of exchange transactions. In their view, exchange difficulties could be remedied by establishing par conversion of paper that would only be applicable to payments for merchandise imports. This debate over the resumption of gold payment did not encourage the government to reopen the Caja de Conversión in the immediate postwar period. In a report to Congress in 1921, it was argued that, given the international monetary conditions of inconvertibility, the restoration of gold payment would result in a loss of gold and the withdrawal of paper pesos in circulation, which would intensify monetary contraction. This situation continued until 1924, when a significant trade surplus and access to foreign capital improved the position of the peso.[40] The peso-to-dollar rate improved from 132.4 in the last quarter of 1923 to 109 in the same period of 1924, and then to 102.3 in the corresponding period in 1925. The peso moved closer to par between 1925 to 1927 and attained parity in March 1927.

The impetus resulting from commercial and financial markets is not enough to explain the political decision to return to the gold standard in 1927. The resumption of gold payments was considered a mechanism to avoid the continued appreciation of the peso, which jeopardized the peso incomes of the exporters. The significance of the return to the old gold parity was momentous, but this did not imply there was a commitment to a long-term equilibrium exchange rate. There was no consensus on the measure, and different observers and policymakers considered the return to gold as erroneous, some claiming it was belated, others, premature.[41]

Stability did not last long; by the end of 1928, the gold parity had already started to diverge slightly. In 1929 the trade deficit did not ameliorate the situation, but, in any case, the monetary position of the country was bound to foreign capital access. In this sense, the determining obstacle to the stability of the peso was the financial restriction brought about as a result of the change of the United States' monetary policy in June 1928.[42] This provoked simultaneous capital flight that replaced the earlier inflows. Most of the reserve drain resulted in a loss of the stock of the Banco de la Nación, whose holdings did not serve as a reserve behind the note circulation. As a result of capital flight and a loss of reserves, the government decreed the closure of the Caja de Conversión on 16 December 1929.

The Federal Reserve Board's change of monetary policy in 1928 could be considered the beginning of the end of the gold standard for the Latin American periphery. Between 1923 and 1930 Argentina increased its foreign debt with the United States from $93 to $340 million.[43] Its reserves had increased from $775 million in 1926 to $1,047 million in 1928; in contrast, by 1929 they had declined by $297 million. When the gold standard was suspended in December 1929, the authorities considered this only a temporary situation.[44] It is important to emphasize that Argentina, in contrast to Brazil and Mexico, maintained significant levels of gold reserves at the moment that it abandoned the gold standard.

The military dictatorship that seized power in Argentina in September 1930 intended to restore the gold standard and establish a central bank. This latter project was continued by the next government, which came into power after fraudulent and partially competitive elections in 1932. With the aim of instituting a central bank, the authorities asked for the advice of the Bank of England, which commissioned Otto Niemeyer as head of a mission that arrived in January 1933.[45] However, the central bank that was eventually established in March 1935 was inspired more by local than by foreign influence, because the proposals of the Minister of Finance, Federico Pinedo, differed profoundly from Niemeyer's recommendations.[46]

After the United Kingdom abandoned the gold standard, the Argentine authorities implemented multiple exchange rate controls in October 1931, with the purpose of allocating the reserves and avoiding fluctuations in the money supply. These measures were considered temporary,[47] although they lasted for a considerable period.

Financial crisis and the collapse of the gold standard both reinforced the arguments that promoted greater governmental intervention in the economy and the creation of a central bank.[48] The preferential exchange rates were used to service foreign debt and to pay for essential imports and remuneration of British investment (as a result of the Anglo-Argentine Treaty of May 1933, which established exchange rates and payment clauses); this implied Argentina's discrimination against the United States and other countries.[49] Argentina was one of the few countries in the world that continued to service foreign public debts, probably conditioned by British pressures and because it hoped that this would give it access to capital.

BRAZILIAN HETERODOXY

Before 1930, Brazilian economic policy was characterized by the stabilization of the exchange rate and a coffee valorization policy.[50] Both policies were supported by the coffee lobby that dominated the national and key state governments, whose purpose was to avoid appreciation of the currency (milreis) and maintain a stable coffee income. The valorization policies were applied in 1906–1907 and from 1921 to 1939. A great proportion of the financial requirements for this policy were obtained from international capital markets.[51] Brazil's dependence on foreign finance for its valorization policy made it accept the requirement that British missions (Montagu in 1923–1924 and D'Abernon in 1929) assess the country's payment capacity and recommend the polices it should follow to assure regular service of debt.[52]

Brazil, like Argentina, did not create a central bank in order to enter the gold standard.[53] However, proposals for exchange rate stabilization through an independent central bank were common in Brazil throughout the 1920s. The first experiment took place from 1923 to 1926 under the Arthur Bernardes presidency, but the Banco do Brasil's functions were suspended when Washington Luíz assumed the presidency. He reestablished a Caixa de Estabilização, similar to the one that had existed from 1906 to 1914, and fixed an exchange rate parity of US $0.11963 per new milreis in December 1926 as a provisional measure to create conditions for a central bank in the near future (1928). The establishment of this new parity did not, in fact, reflect a commitment to restore a prewar parity. Rather, it reflected the average value of the volatile evolution of the flexible exchange rates during the 1920s, as I have estimated (103 of the new gold parity, see Figure 15.1).

The stabilization of the milreis did not last long. The coffee valorization policy entered a crisis of overproduction and surplus of stock in 1927–1928, and, after the beginning of the Great Depression, financial conditions made it even more difficult to sustain the policy. Despite these circumstances, in April 1930 the São Paulo government obtained the only foreign loan issued in London in 1930. This loan totaled 20 million pounds, although the receipts were only 8.5 million pounds. The loan was not enough to maintain the coffee policy, but the Washington Luíz administration maintained the gold standard, and, as a consequence, there was an outflow of capital and an almost total loss of gold reserves in 1931.[54]

Abandonment of the gold standard as a consequence of the Great Depression was a radical rupture with the economic policies of the First Republic and brought with it a period marked by more state intervention in the economy.[55] Monetary policy in 1929 and 1930 was restrictive; reserves fell from 690,000 to 279,000 milreis, and the reserve requirements were increased. In 1930, the Carteira de Emissão e Redescontos (CARED) of the Banco do Brasil was reopened, which affected the monetary base through rediscounting commercial notes and financing coffee stockpiling by the Dirección Nacional de Café.[56]

In 1931 Rothschild proposed that the concession of a new loan required a technical assessment of the economic situation of the country in question and an analysis of measures that must be adopted to ensure the debt payment capacity. In this case, Niemeyer conditionality consisted basically in the stabilization of the exchange rate and the creation of an orthodox central bank.[57] Although this mission was not an isolated case (Montagu and D'Abernon led other missions), Niemeyer's financial mission to Brazil was important for its influence on economic policy-making in Brazil during the 1930s.[58] In any case, Brazil did not create an institution that exercised monetary control until 1945,[59] and an official central bank was not created until 1965. However, the Banco do Brasil had monetary and financial powers, which allowed expansion of the monetary base through rediscount operations and financing of the Dirección Nacional de Café.

In 1931 there was a significant change. The Banco do Brasil was authorized to increase circulation by 300,000 milreis, but only 170,000 were issued; in part, this was used to support the coffee sector. In 1932 there was a regional rebellion whose cost was assumed by the government, by means of an issue of Treasury bonds totaling 400,000 milreis. The Caixa de Mobilização Bancaria (CAMOB), created in 1932, allowed commercial banks to regain liquidity by covering losses due to loans made uncollectable by the depression.[60] In 1933, the Banco do Brasil was granted control of exchange rates, but in 1937 the control disappeared. From 1933 to 1937, the exchange rate control was reflected in the stable evolution of the exchange rate index (Figure 15.1).

Although Brazil, like Argentina, depended on foreign finance, it managed its external debt in a substantially different way. The Brazilian authorities suspended debt service when gold reserves were dramatically reduced in 1931–1932[61] and used the residual reserves to buy depreciated bonds in the international market (reducing Brazil's debt from $1200 to $954 million). In 1933 the authorities declared a unilateral rescheduling and restructuring of the debt. However, the new agreements were not satisfied, and in 1937 a default was declared.

THE INSTITUTIONALIZATION
OF THE REVOLUTIONARY MONETARY SYSTEM

From the colonial epoch to 1905 a bimetallic system operated in Mexico, although in reality the system was a monometallic one based on silver. Flows of gold abroad and the internal accumulation of gold meant that the silver peso dominated as the principal currency. In 1905 the government adopted the gold standard and authorized a system of free banking.[62] The gold standard was suspended after the outbreak of the Revolution in 1910. Between 1911 and 1916, circulation was chaotic, with currencies including gold, silver, "symmetallic" coins (coins made from a mixture of silver and gold), fiduciary notes, and various types of inconvertible bills from the different governments and the private sector.[63] It is clear that the first question about whether Latin American governments strove to return to a prewar parity has little relevance in the case of Mexico since the Revolution made this impossible.

Constitutional debates in 1917 included proposals to create a central bank that would have had a monopoly of issue under the control of the federal government (Article 28).[64] In the same year, Kemmerer visited the country to offer advice on the stabilization of the monetary system and exchange rate and to establish an orthodox central bank; his project for a central bank contrasted sharply with that in Article 28 of the Mexican Constitution. However, given the chaos of the banking system, uncertainty on the part of the public, and the scarce resources available to create the bank, the project foundered.

As the new revolutionary government was undergoing consolidation, the banking system was reorganized. However, at the beginning of the 1920s competition remained among different banks, and financial instability continued into the middle of the decade.[65] During the second half of the 1920s, a more favorable institutional framework was created for monetary policies.[66] The Banco de México started activities with the monopoly of issue. The bank's issue could not exceed double its reserves of precious metals and foreign exchange.[67] However, even though at the time of its creation the money in circulation in the economy was low,[68] the bank did not issue notes because the public still refused to accept paper money.

During the 1920s, the evolution of the gold peso exchange rate was stable (see Figure 15.1), and in February 1927, the Mexican authorities decided to adopt the gold standard. Because money in circulation continued to be both silver and gold, there was the possibility of a flexible exchange rate. Legally, the monetary system was based on the gold standard. However, silver continued to be the most heavily used currency, and the predominant exchange rate was the silver peso with the dollar. Parity between gold and silver corresponded to the international prices of these metals and their internal supply. The government tried to maintain the legal parity by increasing the supply of gold coins while restricting silver coins to take into account changes in the prices of the metals and manage the balance of payments.[69]

Between 1926 and 1931, the current account balance deteriorated due to the effects of orthodox monetary policy, which led to a real appreciation of the peso, and because of exogenous factors, including the fall in oil and mineral export prices, transfers required by agreements on the external debt, and the economic crisis in the United States.[70] Monetary restriction and the appreciation of the peso after 1926 coincided with a decline in exports and GDP that had started before the Great Depression. The restrictive monetary policy was maintained once the Great Depression started, which led to a drain on reserves and a drastic contraction in the money supply; the means of payment were reduced by at least half during 1930 and 1931.

In May 1931 the situation was no longer sustainable. Banks were pressured by their customers in the fear that the government would declare the peso inconvertible to gold. Reform of the monetary system was delayed until July 1931, when the monetary system was virtually exhausted; then, the government had no other alternative than to abandon the gold standard and devalue the exchange rate. In the face of scarce reserves, the exchange rate was floated until June 1932, when it reached a parity of around 3.6 pesos per dollar, where it stabilized until March 1938.[71]

Money supply increased again when silver was coined and notes were issued in 1932. In order that the Banco de México, directed by former president Calles, could increase the circulation of notes and silver coins, various laws were reformed.[72] At the outset, the notes were used to pay overdue salaries of public employees, but later they were used as a normal means of payment. Between 1932 and 1933, coinage of silver rose to 89 million pesos and note issue to 53 million. In 1931, notes constituted only 0.5% of the primary means of payment, but this increased to 10.5% in 1932 and reached 34.8% by 1935. Another significant change was the devaluation of the peso by 60% between the abandonment of the gold standard in 1931 and 1934, when the authorities fixed the exchange rate with respect to the dollar (see Figure 15.1).[73]

When the United States abandoned the gold standard in April 1933, the Banco de México established a fixed exchange rate of 3.6 pesos to the dollar; this allowed the continuity of parity until March 1938. The monetary policy adopted by Roosevelt raised international prices of gold and silver and stimulated Mexican production of these metals.[74] In April 1935, the price of silver in the United States rose to such a level that the metallic value of the Mexican peso was greater than its nominal value. In response, the Mexican authorities decoupled the monetary system from the fluctuations of the price of silver and substituted the silver peso for notes and coins of other metals of lesser quality. This new monetary reform meant that gold and silver coins were abolished as a means of payment, and it was established that the single legal currency would be Banco de México notes. The two major contrasts between Mexico and

Brazil and Argentina were that Mexico did not apply exchange rate controls and that Mexico was less dependent on foreign finance because its debt was under continuous negotiation and default had been declared.

CONCLUSIONS

The shift in exchange rate policies by Latin American policymakers during the interwar period has been cited as one of the main factors that led to the change of growth strategies in the region. In this chapter, we have shown that in the three largest Latin American countries, exchange rate policies were more complex, diverse, and heterodox than has been previously thought.

The first inquiry concerned the commitment of these countries to returning to the prewar gold parities. Argentina was the only country that restored the old parity, but the significance of this was circumstantial, since it was determined by favorable balance of payment conditions. Restoration did not imply that there was a long-term commitment to an equilibrium exchange rate. It is also interesting that, although it restored its prewar parity in the 1920s, it was one of the first to devalue in the 1930s. In the case of Brazil, there was no commitment to restore prewar parity, and the new parity reflected the average value of the volatile trend of the flexible exchange rates during the 1920s. Brazil, however, also belonged to the group that was first to abandon the gold standard. As a consequence of the Mexican Revolution and the ensuing monetary chaos, this government's efforts to return to a prewar parity had little relevance. It is noteworthy that this country adhered for a longer period to the gold standard.

The second question was whether the three largest Latin American countries restored the gold standard and created formal central banks during the 1920s due to the advice of "money doctors" such as Kemmerer.[75] Although Mexico received Kemmerer in 1917 in an attempt to control the postrevolutionary monetary chaos, the contents of the constitutional debate show that the authorities did not follow his recommendations. Brazil and Argentina received the recommendations of Niemeyer in 1931 and 1933, respectively. However, in the former case, the formal central bank was not created until the 1960s; in the latter case, the domestic debate was more influential than Niemeyer's advice when the central bank was finally created in 1935. The central bank in Argentina was actually created as a consequence of the collapse of the gold standard rather than as a means for its restoration. Thus, in these three case studies, foreign missions do not explain why or how the gold standard or central banks were established.

In regard to the third question about the timing and stability of the exchange rates and the extent of depreciation, the statistical analysis of the evolution of the exchange rates has shown the following (see Table 15.1):

1. The Argentine floating index reached a maximum in the restored pre-war gold parity of the 1920s, revealing a real appreciation, whereas the Brazilian average free exchange rate coincided with the new fixed parity.
2. Argentina and Brazil experienced similar fluctuations in both free systems during the 1920s and the early 1930s, although deviations were higher in Brazil.
3. The exchange rate control applied in both countries between 1931 and 1933 had different results. The exchange rate was stabilized more successfully in Argentina than in Brazil.
4. The Mexican exchange rate followed a consistent path before and after the establishment of a new parity. The volatility of the exchange rate

TABLE 15.1

Comparative Analysis of Exchange Rate Regimes:
Argentina, Brazil, and Mexico, 1920–1940

	Exchange Rate Regime	Periods (year, quarter)	Values of the Currencies as Index of Its Gold Parity				
			Average	STD	Range	Trend	Volatility
Argentina	Flexible	1927, 2	88.2	8.0	30.1	1.1	3.7
	Fixed	1929, 3	99.8	0.9	2.1	−0.2	0.4
	Flexible	1931, 2	84.2	7.1	27.9	−4.6	4.1
	Control	1933, 3	60.6	0.5	3.0	−0.2	0.4
	Managed	1936, 4	46.5	1.3	12.9	−1.1	2.7
Brazil	Flexible	1926, 3	103.0	14.0	49.5	−0.4	9.6
	Fixed	1929, 4	99.3	1.5	6.0	−0.0	0.6
	Flexible	1931, 2	81.0	12.8	40.3	−6.3	5.7
	Control	1933, 3	56.1	6.8	31.9	−2.0	7.2
	Managed	1936, 4	42.1	1.4	12.6	−0.2	1.1
Mexico	Flexible	1926, 4	97.6	1.2	6.3	−0.2	1.3
	Fixed	1931, 2	95.7	1.6	7.3	0.3	1.8
	Flexible	1933, 3	59.0	11.5	68.0	−6.7	12.0
	Managed	1936, 4	33.2	0.7	8.7	−0.4	0.9

Source: League of Nations (1925–1938).

was not significantly different during the free and fixed exchange rate sytems of the 1920s. However, the fluctuation in the free system between 1931 and 1933 as a result of the severe depreciation of the peso was more significant than in any other period under consideration in any of the three countries.

5. Finally, the managed floating system applied by the three governments after the U.S. devaluation resulted in the highest levels of stability other than when fixed exchange rates were in operation.

Notes

1. ECLA (1951), Thorp (1984), Fishlow (1990), Cardoso and Helwege (1992).

2. Edwards (1995).

3. Aldcroft (1991), Eichengreen (1992).

4. Marichal (1989).

5. Statistics of the 1920s show that, as is typical of settlement territories, Argentine exports basically consisted of cereals (one-half of exports) and meat and derivatives (one-quarter). Coffee accounted for three-quarters of the Brazilian exports in the same period. Mexican exports included oil, silver, gold, copper, lead, and zinc (Díaz Fuentes 1994).

6. Díaz Alejandro (1984).

7. Thirty percent of Argentine exports went to the United Kingdom, but Argentina's imports from the United States were more important at the end of the 1920s. Brazil maintained a balanced relation with both nations (the United States absorbed 45% of total Brazilian exports and provided 30% of its imports) (Paiva Abreu 1984), whereas the majority of Mexican exports were destined for the United States.

8. This situation has been defined by Fodor and O'Connell (1973) as a "reversed triangular" relation (Argentina–United Kingdom–United States). In contrast, the Brazilian case could be defined as a "virtuous triangular" relation (Brazil–United States–United Kingdom).

9. A discussion on the subject can be found in Friedman and Schwartz (1963), Hamilton (1987), Temin (1989), Romer (1992), and Eichengreen (1992).

10. An analysis of the causes of the crisis shows that there were in addition residual effects other than trade volume (production) and terms of trade (income). In Argentina and Mexico, these residual effects were negative (pro-cyclical), and in

Brazil they were positive (countercyclical) (Díaz Fuentes 1993, pp. 39–40). The different consequences of the residual effects shed some light on the kind of policies undertaken by governments in each country.

11. Díaz Alejandro (1984).
12. Campa (1990).
13. Exchange rate control is effectively a combination of tariff and devaluation policies.
14. Bordo and Eichengreen (1993), Isard (1995).
15. Krugman and Obstfeld (1994).
16. Eichengreen and Sachs (1985).
17. Campa (1990).
18. Bordo and Eichengreen (1993), Eichengreen (1994).
19. Krugman and Obstfeld (1994).
20. Comín (1996).
21. Moggridge (1972).
22. Keynes (1925).
23. Krugman and Obstfeld (1994), pp. 533–534.
24. Bordo and Rockoff (1996, p. 395) have argued that "one of the enforcement mechanisms of the Gold-Standard rule for peripheral countries was presumably access to capital obtainable from the core countries." In this sense, adherence to the gold standard during 1870–1914 served as "a good housekeeping seal of approval." That is, it signaled that a country followed prudent fiscal and monetary policies and this facilitated access by peripheral countries to capital vital to their development from the core countries of western Europe. However, Argentina, Brazil, and Chile broke the rules by intermittently suspending payments and devaluing their currencies.
25. Bordo and Rockoff (1986) show that for England, France, and the United States, policies leading to resumption at the prewar parity were adopted after the major wartime emergency had passed.
26. Eichengreen and Sachs (1985).
27. Drake (1989).
28. Kemmerer (1940).
29. This term was applied to the American Kemmerer mission to the Andean countries: Colombia, 1923–1933; Chile, 1925–1932; Ecuador, 1925–1933; Bolivia, 1927–1932; and Peru, 1930–1933. Guatemala received a Kemmerer mission in 1919 and 1924 and created a central bank in 1925.
30. Triffin (1960), pp. 21–23.
31. The British pound and the French franc were stabilized in April 1925 and December 1926, respectively.
32. Britain was forced to leave the gold standard and floated the pound in September 1931.

33. The United States introduced exchange controls and suspended the gold standard in March 1933, but returned to it in November 1934 (with a depreciation from $20.70 to $35 per ounce). Other governments also used prohibitions, administrative controls, or multiple exchange rates to allocate their scarce foreign exchange reserves to different uses. The period ended in August 1936 when France, the Netherlands, and Switzerland abandoned the system.

34. League of Nations, *Monthly Bulletin of Statistics,* 1925–1938.

35. In each case, these are the values in U.S. cents in New York as a percentage of legal gold parity: Argentina, 96.476 cents per gold peso (August 1927); Brazil, 11.963 cents per milreis (December 1926); and Mexico, 49.85 cents per peso (February 1927).

36. There had been previous, unsuccessful attempts to restore stability to the paper peso. In 1867 a Bureau of Exchange was established as a department of the Banco de la Provincial de Buenos Aires. Seven years later, civil war and the financial crisis in 1874/75 forced it to close down in May 1876. With a few brief exceptions, inconvertibility dominated during the next 23 years. See Williams (1920), della Paolera (1988), and Cortés Conde (1989).

37. However, it had a "national commercial bank," the Banco de la Nación Argentina, which was closely linked to the government. This bank carried out some functions that were typical of a central bank. Argentina also had a Caja de Conversión (Conversion Office) that initially issued notes in exchange for gold in a way similar to an issue department of a central bank, being restricted by rules to maintain the gold standard. However, the Caja de Conversión in some cases exchanged notes for government bonds and commercial notes (Marichal and Díaz Fuentes 1996).

38. In accordance with the terms of the 1899 act, all note issues were to be on a strictly 2.27 basis, but since the redemption fund was limited to approximately one-quarter of the paper currency previously outstanding, it followed that notes and gold stood at something more than a ratio of 2.27 to 1. This resembled the combined gold-backed and fiduciary issues of the Bank of England.

39. On 2 August 1913, the government decreed that all financial operations, including those of the Caja de Conversión and gold exports, would be suspended for eight days. At the same time, two counterbalancing measures were taken. The government decreed that gold deposited at Argentine foreign legations would be treated as if it had been deposited at the Caja de Conversión. At the same time, the Banco de la Nación was authorized to obtain additional notes by rediscounting commercial papers, on the condition that the currency's gold backing should be no less than 40%. See Williams (1920), Peters (1934), Phelps (1938), and Ford (1958). Probably the best definition of the Argentine monetary system is that of

Finance Minister A. Hueyo (March 1932 to July 1933), who defined it as a "sporadic gold standard" (1938).

40. In fact, peso improvement coincided with a heavy dependence on the surge of American foreign lending (Peters 1934, p. 119; Phelps 1938, p. 48).

41. *La Nación* (23 August 1927) and Molina (Finance Minister).

42. Prebisch (1985, pp. 146–147) considered this setback as "the primordial factor contributing to the progressive tension in the local money market."

43. Peters (1934), p. 127.

44. Prebisch (1985).

45. Hueyo (1938), Vilaseca (1988).

46. Pinedo (1961), Niemeyer (1933).

47. Salera (1941).

48. O'Connell (1984).

49. Salera (1941).

50. Fritsch (1988).

51. Villela and Suzigan (1973).

52. This contrasts with the American financial criteria, which did not require these controls in the 1920s (Paiva Abreu 1976, 1984).

53. Brazil had a large "national commercial bank," the Banco do Brasil, which was closely linked to its government. The Banco do Brasil carried out some functions typical of a central bank. For certain periods, a Caixa de Estabilização (exchange rate stabilization office) was in operation (Marichal and Díaz Fuentes 1996).

54. Souza Ries (1934), Cardoso (1979).

55. Villela and Suzigan (1973).

56. Peláez (1969, 1971).

57. Niemeyer (1931).

58. Niemeyer was "voluntarily" invited by the Brazilian government after Rothschild's proposal to condition further credit. He was not a disinterested expert. His prescription was traditional adjustment policy designed to ensure debt payment. The only novel element was the institution of an independent central bank, an idea that was not new in the country.

59. The Superintendencia da Moeada e do Crédito (SUMOC) was created in order to be part of the Bretton Woods System.

60. Neuhaus (1975).

61. Cardoso and Dornbusch (1989).

62. BANAMEX (1934).

63. Cárdenas and Manns (1989).

64. Rodríguez Garza (1995).

65. Manero (1957), p. 129.
66. On 2 January 1925, the National Bank Commission (Comisión Nacional Bancaria) was created. In April of the same year, the government made gold and silver money legal tender with the aim of unifying the account. In September the Banco de México was established (Turrent Díaz 1982). In August 1926 the new law for institutions of credit and banking establishments was set up. The creation of new financial institutions was not limited to those performing central banking functions, since the Banco Nacional de Crédito Agrícola and four regional cooperative banks (*ejidales*) were established. See BANAMEX (1978) and Banco Nacional de Comercio Exterior (1988).
67. Turrent Díaz (1982).
68. Accurate monetary statistics for the period 1910–1924 are not available, but my estimation of the relation M1/GDP shows that this was low: 8.8% in 1925, of which 76% was in coins, 0.3% in notes and 23.7% in demand deposits (Díaz Fuentes 1994, using the methodology developed by Tortella 1974).
69. Torres Gaytán (1980).
70. FitzGerald (1984).
71. On the oil expropriation, see Knight (1990).
72. These profound changes of monetary policies did not imply an open rejection of monetary orthodoxy, since the authorities announced that the benefits of seignorage would be conserved to increase the reserves of note issue, assuming that the country was subject to two fiduciary coins, and they estimated that the circulation could not be constituted exclusively with notes as in other countries (BANAMEX 1978, pp. 100–103; Fernández Hurtado 1976).
73. This devaluation changed the relative prices and encouraged import substitution (Cárdenas 1984, pp. 260–280).
74. BANAMEX (1978).
75. Kemmerer's dogmatism is clear in his recommendation for a return to the rules of the game several years after the collapse of the gold standard.

REFERENCES

Aldcroft, Derek H. "Las consecuencias económicas de la guerra y de la paz (1919–1929)." In *Europa en crisis, 1919–1939*, edited by M. Cabrera, S. Juliá, and P. Martín Acea. Madrid: Pablo Iglesias, 1991.

BANAMEX (Banco Nacional de México). *Quincuagésimo aniversario de su fundación.* Mexico: Cultura, 1934.

BANAMEX (Banco Nacional de México). *Examen de la situación económica de México, 1925–1976*. México: BANAMEX, 1978.

Banco Nacional de Comercio Exterior. *Historia del BANCOMEX*. Mexico: BAN-COMEX, 1988

Bordo, Michael. "The Bretton Woods International Monetary System: A Historical Overview." In *A Retrospective on the Bretton Woods System: Lessons for International Monetary Reform*, edited by Michael Bordo and Barry Eichengreen, 3–98. Chicago: University of Chicago Press, 1993.

Bordo, Michael, and Barry Eichengreen, eds. *A Retrospective on the Bretton Woods System: Lessons for International Monetary Reform*. Chicago: University of Chicago Press, 1993.

Bordo, Michael, and Hugh Rockoff. "The Gold Standard as a 'Good Housekeeping Seal of Approval.'" *Journal of Economic History* 56, no. 2 (1996): 389–428.

Campa, José M. "Exchange Rates and Economic Recovery in the 1930s: An Extension to Latin America." *Journal of Economic History* 50, no. 3 (1990): 677–682.

Cárdenas, Enrique. "The Great Depression and Industrialisation: The Case of Mexico." In *Latin America in the 1930s: The Role of the Periphery in World Crisis*, edited by Rosemary Thorp, 222–243. Oxford: Macmillan-St. Antony's College, 1984.

Cárdenas, Enrique, and Carlos Manns. "Inflación y estabilización monetaria en México durante la Revolución." *El Trimestre Económico* 55, no. 217 (1989): 57–79.

Cardoso, Eliana A. "Celso Furtado revisitado: A década de 30." *Revista Brasileira de Economia* 33, no. 3 (1979): 373–398.

Cardoso, Eliana A., and R. Dornbusch. "Brazilian Debt Crises: Past and Present." In *The International Debt Crisis in Historical Perspective*, edited by Barry Eichengreen and Peter H. Lindert, 106–139. Cambridge: Massachusetts Institute of Technology Press, 1989.

Cardoso, Eliana A., and Ann Helwege. *Latin America's Economy: Diversity, Trends and Conflicts*. Cambridge: Massachusetts Institute of Technology Press, 1992.

Cassel, Gustav. *The Downfall of the Gold Standard*. London: Oxford University Press, 1936.

Comín, Francisco. *Historia de la hacienda pública*. Vol. I, *Europa*. Barcelona: Crítica, 1996.

Cortés Conde, Roberto. *Dinero, deuda y crisis: Evolución fiscal y monetaria en la Argentina 1862–1890*. Buenos Aires: Sudamericana, 1989.

della Paolera, Gerardo. "How the Argentine Economy Performed during the International Gold Standard: A Reexamination." Unpublished Ph.D. dissertation, University of Chicago, 1988.

Díaz Alejandro, Carlos F. "Latin America in the 1930s." In *Latin America in the 1930s: The Role of the Periphery in World Crisis*, edited by Rosemary Thorp, 17–49.

Oxford: Macmillan-St. Antony's College, 1984.

Díaz Fuentes, Daniel. *Las políticas fiscales de Argentina, Brasil y México durante la Gran Depresión.* Madrid: Instituto de Estudios Fiscales, 1993.

Díaz Fuentes, Daniel. *Crisis y cambios estructurales en América Latina: México, Brasil y Argentina durante el período de entreguerras.* México: Fondo de Cultura Económica, 1994.

Drake, Peter W. *The Money Doctor in the Andes: The Kemmerer Missions, 1923–1933.* Durham & London: Duke University Press, 1989.

Drake, Peter W., ed. *Money Doctors, Foreign Debts, and Economic Reforms in Latin America from the 1890s to the Present.* Wilmington: Jaguar Books on Latin America, 1994.

Edwards, Sebastian. *Crisis and Reform in Latin America. From Despair to Hope.* New York: World Bank-Oxford University Press, 1995.

Eichengreen, Barry. "House Calls of the Money Doctor: The Kemmerer Missions to Latin America, 1917–1931." In *Debt, Stabilization and Development: Essays in Memory of Carlos Díaz Alejandro*, edited by G. Calvo et al., 57–77. New York: Oxford University Press, 1989.

Eichengreen, Barry. "The Origins and Nature of the Great Slump Revisited." *Economic History Review* 45, no. 2 (1992): 213–239.

Eichengreen, Barry. *International Monetary Arrangements for the 21st Century.* Washington: The Brookings Institution, 1994.

Eichengreen, Barry, and Jeffrey Sachs. "Exchange Rates and Economic Recovery in the 1930s." *Journal of Economic History* 45, no. 4 (1985): 925–946.

Fernández Hurtado, Ernesto, ed. *Cincuenta años de banca central.* Mexico: Fondo de Cultura Económica, 1976.

Fishlow, Albert. "The Latin American State." *Journal of Economic Perspectives* 4 (1990): 61–74.

FitzGerald, E. V. K. "Restructuring through the Great Depression: The State and Capital Accumulation in Mexico, 1925-40." In *Latin America in the 1930s: The Role of the Periphery in World Crisis*, edited by Rosemary Thorp, 242–265. Oxford: Macmillan-St. Antony's College, 1984.

Fodor, Jorge, and Arturo O'Connell. "La Argentina y la economía atlántica en la primera mitad del siglo XX." *Desarrollo Económico* 13, no. 49 (1973): 1–60.

Ford, Alec G. "Flexible Exchange Rates and Argentina 1885–1900." *Oxford Economic Papers* 10 (1958): 316–338.

Friedman, Milton, and Anna J. Schwartz. *A Monetary History of the United States, 1867–1960.* Princeton: Princeton University Press, 1963.

Fritsch, Winston. *External Constraints on Economic Policy in Brazil, 1889–1930.* Pittsburgh: University of Pittsburgh Press, 1988.

Goodhart, Charles A. E. *The Central Bank and the Financial System.* London: Macmillan, 1995.

Hamilton, James D. "Monetary Factors in the Great Depression." *Journal of Monetary Economics* 19 (1987): 145–169.

Hueyo, Alberto. *Argentina en la depresión mundial, 1932–1933. Discursos y conferencias.* Buenos Aires: El Atenco, 1938.

Instituto Nacional de Estadística, Geografía e Informática (INEGI). *Estadísticas históricas de México.* México: INEGI, 1990.

Isard, Peter. *Exchange Rate Economics.* Cambridge: Cambridge University Press, 1995.

Kemmerer, Edwin W. *Inflation and Revolution: Mexico's Experience of 1912–1917.* London: Oxford University Press, 1940.

Keynes, John M. "The Economic Consequences of Mr. Churchill," reprinted in *Essays in Persuasion.* London: Macmillan-Cambridge University Press, 1925.

Knight, Alan. "México 1930–1946." In *Latin America since 1930. México, Central America and the Carribbean,* Vol. 7 of *The Cambridge History of Latin America,* edited by Leslie Betthell, 3–82. London: Cambridge University Press, 1990.

Krugman, Paul, and Maurice Obstfeld. *International Economics.* New York: HarperCollins, 1994.

League of Nations. *Balances des paiementes et sur les balances du comerce exterieur 1911–1925.* Vol. 2. Geneva: League of Nations, 1926.

League of Nations. *Monthly Bulletin of Statistics.* Geneva: League of Nations, 1925–1938.

League of Nations. *Le cours et les phases de la dépression economique mondiale: Rapport présenté a l'Assemblée de la Société des Nations.* Geneva: League of Nations, 1931.

Maddison, Angus. *Two Crises: Latin America and Asia, 1929–38 and 1973–83.* Paris: OECD, 1985.

Maddison, Angus. "Economic and Social Conditions in Latin America, 1913–1950." In *Long-Term Trends in Latin American Economic Development,* edited by M. Urrutia, 1–22. New York: Inter-American Development Bank, 1991.

Manero, Antonio. *La Revolución Bancaria en México.* México: Talleres Gráficos de la Nación (facsimile Banco Somex-Miguel Angel Porrúa), 1957.

Marichal, Carlos. *A Century of Debt Crises in Latin America: From Independence to the Great Depression, 1820–1930.* Princeton: Princeton University Press, 1989.

Marichal, Carlos, and Daniel Díaz Fuentes. "The Emergence of Central Banks in Latin America: Are Evolutionary Models Applicable?" Paper presented at the Conference on the Emergence of Central Banking: European Association for Banking History, Evora, Portugal, 11 May 1996.

Moggridge, Donald E. *British Monetary Policy 1924–1931: The Norman Conquest of $4.86.* Cambridge: Cambridge University Press, 1972.

Neuhaus, Paulo. *História monetária do Brasil, 1900–1945*. Rio de Janeiro: IBMEC, 1975.

Niemeyer, Otto E. *Report to the Brazilian Government*. London, 1931.

Niemeyer, Otto E. "Report to the Argentinian Government." *Revista Económica* 7, no. 5–6 (1933).

O'Connell, Arturo. "Argentina into the Depression: Problems of an Open Economy." In *Latin America in the 1930s: The Role of the Periphery in World Crisis*, edited by Rosemary Thorp, 188–222. Oxford: Macmillan-St. Antony's College, 1984.

Paiva Abreu, Marcelo de. "The Niemeyer Mission: An Episode of British Financial Imperialism in Brazil." Working Paper for the Centre of Latin American Studies, University of Cambridge, 1976.

Paiva Abreu, Marcelo de. "Argentina and Brazil during the 1930s: The Impact of British and American International Economic Policies." In *Latin America in the 1930s: The Role of the Periphery in World Crisis*, edited by Rosemary Thorp, 144–162. Oxford: Macmillan-St. Antony's College, 1984.

Peláez, Carlos M. "Acêrca da Política Governamental, da Grande Depressão e da industrialização do Brasil." *Revista Brasileira de Economia* 23, no. 3 (1969): 77–88.

Peláez, Carlos M. "Análise Econômica do programa brasileiro de Sustentação do Café, 1906–1945: Teoria, Política e Medição." *Revista Brasileira de Economia* 5, no. 4 (1971): 5–216.

Peters, Harold E. *The Foreign Debt of the Argentine Republic*. Baltimore: Johns Hopkins Press, 1934.

Phelps, Vernon. *The International Economic Position of Argentina*. Philadelphia: University of Pennsylvania Press, 1938.

Pinedo, Federico. *Siglo y medio de economía argentina*. México: Centro de Estudios Monetarios Latinoamericanos, 1961.

Prebisch, Raúl. "Argentine Economic Policies since the 1930's: Recollections." In *The Political Economy of Argentina, 1880–1946*, edited by G. Di Tella and D. Platt, 133–153. Oxford: Macmillan, 1985.

Rodríguez Garza, Francisco. "La nacionalización de la política monetaria durante el período de entreguerras." In *Orígenes del pensamiento económico en México*. Mexico: El Colegio de México, 1995.

Romer, Christina D. "What Ended the Great Depression?" *Journal of Economic History* 52, no. 4 (1992): 757–784.

Salera, Virgil. *Exchange Control and the Argentine Market*. New York: Columbia University Press, 1941.

Souza Reis, F. T. *A Depressão Comercial e o Funding Loan de 1931*. Rio de Janeiro: Lobato e Cia, 1934.

Temin, Peter. *Lessons from the Great Depression: The Lionel Robbins Lectures for 1989.* Cambridge: Massachusetts Institute of Technology Press, 1989.

Thorp, Rosemary, ed. *Latin America in the 1930s: The Role of the Periphery in World Crisis.* Oxford: Macmillan-St. Antony's College, 1984.

Torres Gaytán, Ricardo. *Un siglo de devaluaciones del peso mexicano.* Mexico: Siglo XXI, 1980.

Tortella, Gabriel. "Las magnitudes monetarias y sus determinantes." In *La banca española en la restauración,* edited by G. Tortella. Madrid: Banco de España, 1974.

Triffin, Robert. "Central Banking and Monetary Management in Latin America." In *Economic Problems of Latin America,* edited by S. E. Harris. New York: McGraw & Hill, 1944.

Triffin, Robert. *Gold and the Dollar Crisis: The Future of Convertibility.* New Haven, CT: Yale University Press, 1960.

Turrent Díaz, E. *Historia del Banco de México.* Mexico: Banco de México, 1982.

United Nations Economic Commission for Latin America (ECLA). *Estudio económico de América Latina 1949.* New York: United Nations, 1951.

Vilaseca, Hector, ed. *Banco Central de la República Argentina: sus primeros cincuenta años.* Buenos Aires: BCRA, 1988.

Villela, Annibal V., and Wilson Suzigan. *Política do governo e crescimento da economia brasileira, 1889–1945.* Rio de Janeiro: IPEA-INPES, 1973.

Williams, John H. *Argentine International Trade Under Inconvertible Paper Money, 1880–1900.* Cambridge, MA: Harvard University Press, 1920.

Contributors

Lee J. Alston is Professor of Economics and Director of the Center for International Business Education and Research, University of Illinois; and Research Associate, National Bureau of Economic Research. He received his Ph.D. from the University of Washington. Recent publications include *Titles, Conflict, and Land Use: The Development of Property Rights and Land Reform on the Brazilian Amazon Frontier,* co-authored with Gary D. Libecap and Bernardo Mueller (University of Michigan Press, 1998); *Empirical Studies in Institutional Change,* co-edited with Thrainn Eggertsson and Douglass North (Cambridge University Press, 1996); *Paternalism and the Rise of the American Welfare State: Economics, Politics, and Institutions in the U.S. South, 1865–1965,* co-authored with Joseph P. Ferrie (Cambridge University Press, 1998); and "The Determinants and Impact of Property Rights: Census Data and Survey Results for Land Titles on the Brazilian Frontier," co-authored with Gary Libecap and Robert Schneider (*Journal of Law, Economics, and Organization,* 1996). Lee Alston's research focuses on historical and cross-country comparative issues in the new institutional economics.

John H. Coatsworth is Monroe Gutman Professor of Latin American Affairs at Harvard University, where he also serves as Director of the David Rockefeller Center for Latin American Studies. He was elected President of the American Historical Association for 1995. He taught at the University of Chicago from 1969 until he joined the Harvard faculty in 1992. Professor Coatsworth's research has focused on the comparative economic history of Latin America and the economic and international history of Mexico and Central America. His most recent book, *The United States and Central America: The Clients and the Colossus* (New York: Twayne, 1994), is a history of U.S.–Central American relations.

Gerardo della Paolera (Ph.D. in economics, University of Chicago, 1988) has been Rector of the Universidad Torcuato Di Tella in Buenos Aires since 1991. He has held appointments as a visiting professor at the University of Chicago, Northwestern University, and CEMA (Centro de Estudios Macroeconomicos) and as a visiting scholar at the Research Department of the International Monetary Fund and at the Hoover Institution, Stanford University. He was the Marcos Garfunkel Fellow and a senior associate member in St. Antony's College at Oxford University. He is also a professor of economics at the School of Economics and at the School of Law of the Universidad Torcuato Di Tella.

Alan Dye is Assistant Professor of Economics at Barnard College of Columbia University. He received his Ph.D. from the University of Illinois at Urbana-Champaign in 1991. Author of *Cuban Sugar in the Age of Mass Production: Technology and the Economics of the Cuban Sugar Central, 1899–1929* (Stanford University Press, 1998), his research addresses the roles of transaction costs, contracting, institutions, and technology in the economic history of Latin America.

Daniel Díaz Fuentes is Lecturer in Economics at the University of Cantabria, Spain, where he lectures in economic development and technological policy, and international economics. He obtained his Ph.D. in economics in 1992 from the Universidad Alcalá de Henares, Spain, and since then has held various positions including Lecturer in

Economics at the University Carlos III (1990–93); Visiting Fellow at St. Antony's College, University of Oxford (1993–1995); and Academic Visitor at London School of Economics and Political Science (1995–1996). His research interests include the economic development in Latin America and Spain. His recent publications include *Las políticas fiscales latinoamericanas frente a la Gran Depresión*, Instituto de Estudios Fiscales, Madrid 1994; *Crisis y Cambios Estructurales en América Latina*, Fondo de Cultura Económica, Mexico, 1995; "The Emergence of Central Banks in Latin America: Are Evolutionary Models Applicable?" with Carlos Marichal, in J. Reis (ed.), *The Emerging of Modern Central Banking*, Scholar Press, London, 1998.

Aurora Gómez-Galvarriato is a professor at the Department of Economics of the Centro de Investigación y Docencia Económicas (CIDE) and a Ph.D. candidate in history at Harvard University. She is doing research on the impact of the Mexican Revolution on companies' profits and workers' living standards in the Mexican textile industry. Her most recent publication is "El desempeño de la Fundidora de Hierro y Acero de Monterrey durante el Porfiriato. Acerca de los obstáculos a la industrialización en México," in Carlos Marichal and Mario Cerutti, eds., *Historia de las Grandes Empresas en México, 1905–1930* (Mexico: Fondo de Cultura Económica, 1997).

Stephen Haber is Professor of History, Senior Fellow of the Center for Research on Economic Policy Reform, and Co-Director of the Social Science History Institute at Stanford University. Haber received his Ph.D. from the University of California, Los Angeles in 1985. He is the author of *Industry and Underdevelopment: The Industrialization of Mexico, 1890–1940* (Stanford: Stanford University Press, 1989) and the editor of *How Latin America Fell Behind: Essays on the Economic Histories of Brazil and Mexico, 1800–1914 (Stanford: Stanford University Press, 1997)*. His current research focuses on the impact of the regulation of banks and financial markets on the structure and performance of industry in Brazil, Mexico, and the United States.

Anne Hanley is a lecturer in economics and history at Northwestern University. She earned her doctorate in Latin American history from Stanford in 1995. She is currently writing a book on the participation of domestic capital markets in business development in São Paulo, Brazil, from 1850 to 1920.

André A. Hofman is a researcher at the Economic Development Division of the U.N. Economic Commission for Latin America and the Caribbean (ECLAC) in Santiago. He received his Ph.D. from the University of Groningen, where he also is a member of the Growth and Development Centre. At ECLAC he is a desk officer for Bolivia; his main research interest is in Latin America's quantitative economic history. Recent publications include *Latin American Economic Development: A Causal Analysis in Historical Perspective* (Groningen Growth and Development Centre, Monograph Series no. 3, 1998) and "Standardised Capital Stock Estimates in Latin America: A 1950–1994 Update" (*Cambridge Journal of Economics*, forthcoming).

Gary D. Libecap is Professor of Economics and Law and Director of the Karl Eller Center, University of Arizona, Tucson; Research Associate, National Bureau of Economic Research; and co-editor, *Journal of Economic History*. He received his Ph.D. from the University of Pennsylvania. Recent publications include *Titles, Conflict, and Land Use: The Development of Property Rights and Land Reform on the Brazilian Amazon Frontier*, with Lee Alston and Bernardo Mueller (University of Michigan Press,

1998); *The Federal Civil Service and the Problem of Bureaucracy: The Economics and Politics of Institutional Change,* with Ronald Johnson (University of Chicago Press and NBER, 1994); *The Political Economy of Regulation: An Historical Analysis of Government and the Economy,* with Claudia Goldin (University of Chicago Press and NBER, 1994); and "The Determinants and Impact of Property Rights: Land Titles on the Brazilian Frontier," with Lee Alston and Robert Schneider (*Journal of Law, Economics, and Organization,* 1996). Gary Libecap's research focuses on property rights and regulation in a variety of contexts.

Graciela Márquez is a Ph.D. candidate in History at Harvard University and a full-time researcher at El Colegio de México, Mexico City. Her most recent publication is "La concentracion industrial en México 1930-1950" in M. E. Romero, ed., *Historia de la Industria en México* (Mexico: Facultad de Economia, UNAM, 1997). Her research interests include comparative economic history of Latin America and industrialization and commercial policies in nineteenth- and twentieth-century Mexico.

Bernardo Mueller received his Ph.D. at the University of Illinois at Champaign-Urbana in 1994 and is currently at the Universidade de Brasilia. He has been doing research on property rights in the Amazon and land reform in Brazil. This research has generated a book with co-authors Lee Alston and Gary Libecap, *Titles, Conflict, and Land Use: The Development of Property Rights and Land Reform on the Brazilian Amazon Frontier* (University of Michigan Press, 1998). His research interests include the new institutional economics, property rights, and regulation.

Nanno Mulder received an M.A. from the University of Groningen, Netherlands, in 1991 and is currently finishing a Ph.D. at the same institution. Since October 1996 he has been affiliated with CEPII, a major think tank in international economics in Paris. His research is on the long-term development and productivity performance of services in Brazil, Mexico, and the United States. His current research extends the geographical coverage to OECD countries and links the productivity to the trade performance of countries. His most recent publication, with Bart van Ark and Erik Monnikhof, "Productivity in Services: An International Comparative Perspective," will be seen in *Canadian Journal of Economics,* forthcoming.

Leonard Nakamura is an economic advisor at the Federal Reserve Bank of Philadelphia. He has taught at Rutgers University and lectured at the Wharton School. He has also been an economist for The Conference Board and Citibank. He received his B.A. from Swarthmore College and his M.A. and Ph.D. from Princeton University. His primary area of expertise is banking and credit markets; he has also done work on output and price measurement.

Carlos Newland has studied at the Universidad Católica Argentina, Oxford University, and the University of Leiden. His published work on the history of education in Argentina and Latin America includes his book *Buenos Aires no es Pampa: La educación elemental porteña 1820–1860* (Buenos Aires: Grupo Editor LatinoAmericano, 1992) and articles in a variety of journals. Professor Newland has also published articles on questions in Argentine economic history. He is currently Professor of Economics at the Universidad Di Tella.

William Summerhill is Assistant Professor of History at UCLA. He received his Ph.D. in 1995 from Stanford University. Recent publications include *Order Against Progress: Government, Foreign Investment, and Railroads in Brazil, 1854–1913* (Stanford University Press, forthcoming). His current research focuses on political organization and economic institutions in Imperial Brazil.

Alan M. Taylor (Ph.D. in economics, Harvard University, 1992) has been an assistant professor at Northwestern University since 1993, and a faculty research fellow at the National Bureau of Economic Research since 1994. In 1997–1998 he was a National Fellow at the Hoover Institution, Stanford University. He has served as a visiting professor at the Universidad Torcuato Di Tella in Buenos Aires. He is a recipient of the Alexander Gerschenkron Prize of the Economic History Association.

Gail D. Triner is an assistant professor of history at Rutgers University. Her Ph.D. from Columbia University (1994) is in Latin American history, and her research is focused on the role of Brazilian banking in economic development and state formation during the First Republic (1889–1930).

Michael Twomey (Ph.D., Cornell University, 1974) is currently Professor of Economics at the University of Michigan, Dearborn. He has also taught in Mexico (ITAM, UDLA, COLMEX), Colombia, and Peru (Universidad Católica in Lima). His research has focused on trade and development problems of Latin American countries; his most recent book was *Multinational Corporations and the North American Free Trade Agreement* (Praeger, 1993; Spanish version: FCE, 1996).

Carlos E. J. M. Zarazaga is a senior economist and Executive Director of the Center for Latin American Economies at the Federal Reserve Bank of Dallas. He received a Ph.D. in economics from the University of Minnesota in 1993. A native of Argentina, he has previously served as an economist at the Central Bank of Argentina and at the Federal Reserve Bank of Philadelphia. His latest publication, *Is the Business Cycle of Argentina "Different"?* was co-authored with Finn Kydland. His current research interests include the design of policy rules in imperfect information environments, business cycles of Latin American countries, and international finance and growth.

Index